MICROSOFT® FLIGHT SIMULATOR X FOR PILOTS: REAL-WORLD TRAINING

Jeff Van West and Kevin Lane-Cummings

BICENTENNIAL
1807
WILEY
2007
BICENTENNIAL

Wiley Publishing, Inc.

Microsoft® Flight Simulator X for Pilots: Real-World Training

Published by
Wiley Publishing, Inc.
10475 Crosspoint Boulevard
Indianapolis, IN 46256
www.wiley.com

Copyright © 2007 by Wiley Publishing, Inc., Indianapolis, Indiana

Published by Wiley Publishing, Inc., Indianapolis, Indiana

Published simultaneously in Canada

ISBN: 970-0-764-58822-8

Manufactured in the United States of America

10 9 8 7 6 5 4 3 2

To C., B., one yet to see…and all the other pilots of tomorrow.

ABOUT THE AUTHORS

Jeff Van West (Portland, Maine) is the editor of the professional pilot magazine *IFR* and a contributor to *AOPA Pilot*, *Aviation Consumer*, *Aviation Safety*, and the Internet aviation magazine *AVweb*. He has also written more than a dozen books, CD-ROMs, and training curricula on computers and general aviation, including *Combat Flight Simulator 2: The Inside Moves* for Microsoft Press. He is a Certified Flight Instructor (CFI) in single- and multiengine airplanes and single-engine seaplanes and has developed training programs for glass-panel, technologically advanced aircraft as well as antiques that don't even have electrical systems.

Kevin Lane-Cummings (Seattle, Washington) is the features and columns editor for *AVweb* and does freelance editing for several other aviation magazines. He is also the chief ground instructor at Wings Aloft, a flight club at Boeing Field, Seattle, and—as a CFI there—specializes in technologically advanced aircraft. Kevin has been in science education for years, including managing two planetariums. Kevin also coaches people in giving technical presentations and sings in a jazz choir.

CREDITS

ACQUISITIONS EDITOR
Chris Webb

DEVELOPMENT EDITOR
Kelly Dobbs Henthorne

TECHNICAL EDITOR
Dr. Andrew Herd

PRODUCTION EDITOR
Sarah Groff-Palermo

COPY EDITOR
Kim Wimpsett

EDITORIAL MANAGER
Mary Beth Wakefield

PRODUCTION MANAGER
Tim Tate

VICE PRESIDENT AND EXECUTIVE GROUP PUBLISHER
Richard Swadley

VICE PRESIDENT AND EXECUTIVE PUBLISHER
Joseph B. Wikert

BOOK DESIGNER
Patrick Cunningham

PROOFREADING
Nancy Riddiough

INDEXING
Ted Laux

ANNIVERSARY LOGO DESIGN
Richard Pacifico

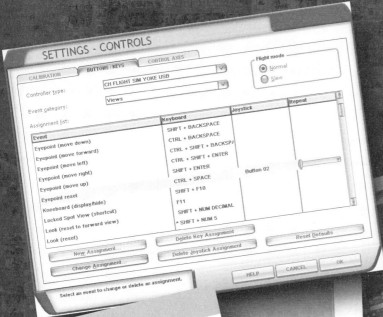

CONTENTS

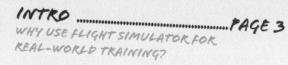

WHY USE FLIGHT SIMULATOR FOR REAL-WORLD TRAINING?

"FLYING IS SO MANY PARTS SKILL, SO MANY PARTS PLAN-NING, SO MANY PARTS MAINTENANCE, AND SO MANY PARTS LUCK. THE TRICK IS TO REDUCE THE LUCK BY INCREASING THE OTHERS."

—DAVID L. BAKER

4

PART I	PART II	PART III	PART IV	PART V	PART VI
PREFLIGHT	SPORT PILOT	PRIVATE PILOT	INSTRUMENT RATING	COMMERCIAL LICENSE	ATP AND BEYOND

WHY WE FLY

If you spend enough time around the airport, or just instructing students, you find that everyone comes to flying with a story. One of the secrets to good flight instruction is to find out what a student's story is, because that's how you find out what motivates them. That's the reason they want to fly.

Some folks love the freedom of being in the air or traveling hundreds of miles in just a couple of hours. Some folks love the technical details and perfecting their technique. Some people even come to aviation to conquer their fear of heights or of flying itself. No matter what your story, however, some underlying drive—some passion—is motivating you and can be satisfied only by learning to fly.

So, what does that have to do with Flight Simulator? Well, flying is expensive, demanding, subject to the whims of weather and maintenance, and sometimes just doesn't fit easily into the realities of our schedules. Flight Simulator lets you feed your passion when, for one reason or another, flying a real airplane is not an option or even desirable.

Even when flying is an option, developing your skills and knowledge using Flight Simulator can make your flying time more efficient and a lot more fun. Whisking your sweetheart away by air for a romantic island getaway sure beats banging out landing after landing trying to get it just right. Judicious use of Flight Simulator can make that island getaway a possibility just a bit faster.

HOW TO USE THIS BOOK

This book mimics the path you might take after you decide to learn to fly, but it does not contain everything you need to know to fly an airplane. Instead, we focus on the items that Flight Simulator teaches well. We also give you the collateral information you would get during real flight training, such as checklists or examples of accidents that illuminate a point. The idea is to use Flight Simulator to give aspiring pilots the best head start possible and help virtual pilots create the most realistic experience.

These items are presented in a chronological order that starts with what a student pilot would learn and ends with a pilot preparing for an airline job. You don't have to read these chapters in order, but at times we will reference something that we explained in an earlier chapter.

⬇ STUDENT OF THE CRAFT

SOME OF OUR FAVORITE AVIATION BOOKS

Too many great aviation texts are out there to list them all, but building a good aviation library is an important part of keeping up your skills as a pilot. Or, at least it's a great excuse to collect a bunch of fun books. Here's a short list to get you going if you need it. In addition, you might want to check out some of the flight manuals for the airplanes you fly in Flight Simulator. Many of them are available through historical aviation merchants and online.

Stick and Rudder, by Wolfgang Langewiesche. A classic since its publication in 1944, this is still arguably the best book on how an airplane flies described from the pilot's point of view.

The Compleat Taildragger Pilot, by Harvey Plourde. This is our favorite book on flying tailwheel airplanes. It's a great reference to help master the Cub.

Weather Flying, by Robert Buck. This is another classic on aviation weather written for the pilot in clear, easy-to-understand terms.

Seaplane Operations, by Dale De Remer and Cesare Baj. This is one of the best general texts on flying floatplanes and flying boats (FSX has both). It contains great graphics and some amazing photos.

Mountain Flying, by Doug Geeting and Steve Woerner. This book is hard to find, but we find it more approachable than Sparky Imeson's classic of the same title. Sparky's text is a great book too, though.

Basic Aerobatics, by Geza Szurovy and Mike Goulian. Read this book, and then strap on the Extra 300 to get a different attitude on flying.

Song of the Sky, by Guy Murchie. This book contains a series of essays from the golden era of aviation that give an interesting perspective on how far we've come in transport-category flying.

Wind, Sand, and Stars, by Antoine de Saint-Exupery. This is arguably one of the most poetic books ever written on the early days of aviation and the people who made it possible.

Fate Is the Hunter, by Ernet Gahn. This is simply a classic and part of any pilot's understanding about life (and death) in the air.

West with the Night, by Beryl Markham. This book contains true tales of early flying in Africa and the first east-to-west transatlantic crossing. It is beautifully written.

Federal Aviation Regulations and Aeronautical Information Manual, by the FAA. Calling this a favorite is a bit disingenuous. Who reads the rules just for fun? But the *FAR-AIM* is the bible of real-world flying in the United States. If you want your sim flying to be as real as it gets, fly according to these rules and procedures.

6

| PART I | PART II | PART III | PART IV | PART V | PART VI |
| PREFLIGHT | SPORT PILOT | PRIVATE PILOT | INSTRUMENT RATING | COMMERCIAL LICENCE | ATP AND BEYOND |

PROCEDURE TRAINING VS. SCENARIO-BASED TRAINING

Flight training has undergone a major shift in the past 10 years. A combination of change in certification standards for airplanes, liability laws, and the availability of cheap electronics has brought a number of complex and capable airplanes onto the general aviation (GA) market. The Garmin G1000 "glass cockpits" in several of the Flight Simulator X (FSX) aircraft are great examples of the kinds of computing power you might find in a GA cockpit.

All that computing power comes at a price. The amount of information a new pilot has to learn, and the amount of information any pilot has to integrate, has gone way, way up. Old-school flight training was based around teaching the procedures for flying an airplane—how the throttle works or how to fly around the traffic pattern in an airport, for example. That was fine when aircraft were fairly simple, but with so many complex systems on modern aircraft, a new system was needed to help pilots integrate thinking skills, technical skills, and physical motions that are needed to work together to use the airplane well.

That's where scenario-based training comes in. Scenarios are kind of like those do-it-yourself stories you might remember from your childhood where you'd read a little bit and then have to make a choice between two actions, each with its own page number. After you chose, you went to that page to find out what happened, read a little more, make another choice, and so on. By the end of the book you could've found the pirate's treasure or ended up stranded on a deserted island.

In scenario-based flight instruction, the instructor guides the student through a scenario where the student has to use all available resources to try to have a successful outcome. For example, while flying from airport A to airport B, the instructor might simulate a partial power loss to the engine. The student would have to fly the airplane in its impaired state, use the GPS to find an alternate airport, and troubleshoot the problem. There are no right or wrong answers, just choices and consequences.

FSX is a great tool for flying scenarios and practicing this integrated approach to flying. Even better than with a real airplane, FSX lets you set up any kind of wind or weather, stop and redo scenarios from any point, and even get the view from outside the airplane. Wherever possible, we'll structure our training around scenarios that you can fly.

WHAT'S ON THE WEBSITE

FSX comes with preinstalled flights that place you in a particular airplane at a particular airport, with some challenge to accomplish. For each of the lessons throughout this book, we have created our own flights and provided them on the website at www.wiley.com. All you have to do is load up the flight and turn to that section in this book to be ready to practice.

Flight instructors regularly demonstrate maneuvers or procedures to their students before asking the student to give it a try. Although we can't sit down next to you at your home computer, we have used FSX's flight recorder feature to record us demonstrating a maneuver so you can play it back and see it for yourself. Several of these flights are on the website.

To get the flights and movies onto your computer, you'll need to move them to the correct FSX folder. Here's what to do under Windows XP:

1. Go to www.wiley.com, and do a search for *Flight Simulator X for Pilots*.

2. Click the link for FSX Flights and Movies. You will be prompted whether you want to open or save the file. Save it somewhere you can find it later.

3. When the download is complete—and it might take a long time if you don't have a broadband Internet connection—double-click the compressed folder you downloaded. It's called `FSX_Files.zip`.

4. This should open the folder and show quite a few files. You can use the "Extract all files" link in the folder tasks on the left, or you can simply select all the files and choose Edit > Copy.

5. Open the My Documents folder on your computer.

6. Open the Flight Simulator X Files inside My Documents.

7. Choose Edit > Paste.

This should copy all the FSX flights and movies referenced in this book into your folder, so they will be available the next time you start FSX.

We've also included several other documents to help with your flight training, such as aviation charts. We'll mention them as they come up in this book, and you can find on the website in a compressed file called `Additional Files.zip`.

Color versions of the black-and-white images in the book are also on the website under the "Book images" link and are organized by chapter.

CHAPTER 1

FLIGHT SCHOOL
SETUP

"[THE AIRPLANE] DOES NOT ISOLATE MAN FROM THE GREAT PROBLEMS OF NATURE BUT PLUNGES HIM MORE DEEPLY INTO THEM."

—ANTOINE DE SAINT-EXUPÉRY

"SPEED IS LIFE."

—ISRAELI AIR-TACTICS MANUAL

10

| PART I | PART II | PART III | PART IV | PART V | PART VI |
| PREFLIGHT | SPORT PILOT | PRIVATE PILOT | INSTRUMENT RATING | COMMERCIAL LICENSE | ATP AND BEYOND |

INSTALLING FSX

Installing Flight Simulator (FSX) is rather pain-less, other than that it takes a long time. It also takes up almost 13GB of disk space. (That's not a typo. It's 13 not 1.3.) When you run FSX for the first time, it will take some additional time to con-figure itself. During this process, FSX will figure out the best display settings to give you a balance between visual performance—how smoothly the airplane appears to fly—and visual quality.

FSX does a pretty good job in striking the right balance, assuming your computer system is fairly high-end. That might be a big assump-tion, but the truth is if you want Flight Simula-tor to accurately represent a real-world airplane, you need to invest in a fairly decent system to run it. FSX will run on older systems, but the frustration of waiting for it to load (Figure 1-1)

Figure 1-1: Even on a ripping-fast computer system, you'll see quite a bit of this progress bar as a flight loads.

each time you want to fly and having a rather cartoonish-looking airplane might take much of the fun out of your virtual flying. We'll talk about customizing your performance settings and why you might want to do this later in this chapter (see "Getting the Right Hardware") and also in Appendix C.

LOOKING AT WHAT'S NEW IN FSX

When FSX finishes all its start-up duties, you'll be at the Learning Center and the Getting Started page. The three huge buttons correspond to three promo movies, which are actually fun to watch if you have some time. One of these movies gives you a rundown of what's new in this version of Flight Simulator. We'll save you the trouble and let you know the key differences right here:

- The video quality of the world overall has increased immensely—if your computer is capable of showing it. FSX has a potential increase in scenery resolution 16 times that of Flight Simulator 2004. Figure 1-2 shows the amazing view from the tower.

Figure 1-2: The view from the tower is new.

- FSX has enhanced the mission concept (common in Combat Flight Simulator and familiar if you know much older versions of Flight Simulator). These are scenarios that you fly for the fun challenge of it and earn rewards, which are stored along with your pilot logbook.

- The number and variety of dynamic objects, such as other airplanes, ground vehicles, and even birds, have increased. The detail is astounding: ferries in Washington's Puget Sound even run on the appropriate schedules (see Figure 1-3).

- The multiplayer function of Flight Simulator has been completely reworked and now not only allows virtual pilots and virtual air traffic controllers to work together but also allows two pilots to share the same cockpit. A shared cockpit has displaced the instructor station, however.

- The air traffic control options have expanded and now include the ability to have air traffic controllers in a tower (see Figure 1-2 earlier).

Figure 1-3: If your computer can handle it, you can see photorealistic clouds, birds, and ferries (which run on real schedules across the sound).

- Several miscellaneous enhancements have also been made, including more camera angles and views and more intuitive user settings.

The increase in potential video quality is also an issue in that, as you use Flight Simulator, sometimes you'll want excellent visuals at the expense of smooth video motion on the screen. Other times, you'll want fluid motion on the screen and have to put up with a fairly rudimentary-looking airplane. To make this compromise as little as possible, we'll now cover what kind of hardware it takes to really run Flight Simulator.

GETTING THE RIGHT HARDWARE

How powerful a computer do you need for FSX? Here's the quick answer: get the fastest processor with the most memory and the best video card you can afford.

We're only half joking. We talked with Hal Byran, whose official title at Microsoft is Flight Simulator Evangelist. Hal told us that FSX was designed to outstrip even the fastest home computers available today. A new version of Fight Simulator releases only once every three years. FSX is designed to still offer something new to the top-end

12

| PART I | PART II | PART III | PART IV | PART V | PART VI |
| PREFLIGHT | SPORT PILOT | PRIVATE PILOT | INSTRUMENT RATING | COMMERCIAL LICENSE | ATP AND BEYOND |

computer released three years after FSX ships. So don't feel bad if your new computer just can't handle FSX running at its ultrahigh simulation level.

Since we're hoping this book will be around three years from now as well, we wanted to develop this text and capture footage that was as high quality as possible. Two companies stepped up to the plate and loaned us some of their top computers. For this book, Jeff used an Area-51 7500 from Alienware computing and Kevin used an IX2 SLI from WidowPC to get the most from FSX and to capture the best visuals possible.

That said, we also have FSX running on our older machines. These are 2GHz systems with 512MB of RAM and video cards that were a year old when Flight Simulator 2004 hit the shelves. The new FSX runs on these systems, but it takes some tweaking to get it just right. We'll give you a quick primer in the following sections of generally what makes FSX sing or croak, but if you want details of maximizing the potential of your personal system, see Appendix C, on the book's website.

PROCESSOR, MEMORY, VIDEO CARDS

Figure 1-4: The Area-51 7500 was one of the fastest available from Alienware when we tested FSX—but FSX performs even better as computers get faster.

Processor speed, RAM, and video card power are the big three for making FSX really sing. Microsoft publishes the minimum requirements, but this is like saying that a Cessna 172 is a four-place airplane. (Putting four people in a Cessna 172 requires some really skinny people and means leaving so much fuel behind you could fly for about only two hours.) Technically, you can run FSX on the minimum system, but it will take so long to load, look so cartoonish, and have motion that appears so jerky that you'll abandon the effort of using it for training. The following are the minimum requirements, according to Microsoft:

- *Processor*: 1.0GHz

- *RAM*: 256MB (512MB for Windows Vista)

- *Video card*: 32MB DirectX 9 compatible

In our opinion, twice as much computer in all categories—2.0GHz, 512MB RAM, and a 64MB video card—is really the minimum for using FSX. Running FSX on our loaner computers absolutely rocks (see Figure 1-4). In fact, to get the frame rate to less than 20 (see "What the Heck Is Frame Rate?" sidebar), we had to go deep into the custom settings and create an ultrareal world.

Here's our setup for the Alienware Area-51 7500:

- *Processor*: Core Duo of 2.93GHz each

- *RAM*: 2GB

- *Video card*: Dual 512MB NVIDIA GeForce 7900 GTX

[handwritten: CQ5231UK-m PC   510 99 inc VAT]

Here's our setup for the WidowPC IX2 SLI:

- *Processor*: Core Duo of 2.4GHz each

- *RAM*: 2GB

- *Video card*: Dual 1GB NVIDIA GeForce 7950 GX2

The other feature both of these computers have is a RAID hard drive that runs at 7200 rpm. This hard drive is actually two fast hard drives working together. This doesn't only have a moderate effect on the actual simulation, but it also makes the program boot up each flight a whole lot faster.

MONITORS

Almost any monitor will work just fine with FSX. The only real catch is that LCD monitors usually look sharp at only one screen resolution. For example, most 19-inch LCD monitors work best at 1280 × 1024 pixels. Your computer might not be powerful enough to drive a screen resolution this high at a respectable frame rate. If you try to drop your resolution to something lower such as 1024 × 768, the motion will be fluid, but the picture will be fuzzy.

To get around this problem, check your display settings. On the Settings tab, you'll usually see an Advanced button that will open the software specific to your video card. Many allow a lower-resolution screen to be displayed centered on the LCD monitor rather than stretched to fill the whole screen. This lets FSX run at a lower resolution—and provide better performance—but lets it still keep a crystal-clear image. CRT monitors don't have this problem.

On the other end of the spectrum, FSX supports multiple monitors. This means you can keep one monitor for flying and one for other items such as your radios or moving map. This isn't essential for training purposes, but it sure is cool. It will cause choppy, unrealistic simulation on less powerful machines, however.

FLIGHT CONTROLS AND HEADSETS

You'll want to invest in a decent yoke and throttle quadrant or joystick. The yoke is more realistic for most of the airplanes in FSX. Yokes also tend to offer more buttons for customization; switches for flaps and gear; and separate throttle, mixture, and propeller controls. Jeff likes his CH Products flight simulator yoke because the controls are rather airplanelike, and it clamps and unclamps easily onto his desk. A joystick might be a better choice if you plan to do a lot of Cub flying or aerobatics in the Extra 300.

14

PART I	PART II	PART III	PART IV	PART V	PART VI
PREFLIGHT	STUDENT PILOT	PRIVATE PILOT	INSTRUMENT RATING	COMMERCIAL LICENSE	FLIP AND BEYOND

We strongly urge getting a separate set of rudder pedals. Even though many joysticks have a twist feature that can be used for rudder control, this is nothing like what we use in real airplanes. Real pedals are almost a must for slips or serious aerobatic maneuvers. They also have brakes, which frees up one more button on your yoke or joystick. CH Products make a great set of rudder pedals as well.

To use a shared cockpit or ATC features, you'll also want a comfortable headset with noise-canceling microphone. We found a perfectly serviceable headset at RadioShack for less than $25. You can also install a second sound card to handle voice communication for the built-in air traffic control (see Chapter 4) and multiplayer (see Chapter 25). You don't need to get top-of-the-line items for any of these—we certainly don't have them—but you'll want to invest a little bit in something comfortable, or you'll just be frustrated trying to make FSX work well.

ADJUSTING PERFORMANCE SETTINGS

Because the realism setting is more a function of actually flying the airplane, we'll talk about that in Chapter 2 when you climb into the virtual Cub. As we said earlier, though, you might want to have different settings for different missions. To see the settings that FSX decided was the best compromise for your computer, click the Settings link on the left side of the home screen. This opens the basic Settings page shown on the left of Figure 1-5.

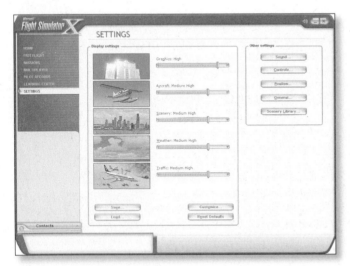

Figure 1-5: The display settings have both a simple mode, allowing you to make an overall adjustment, and a customize mode, allowing you to tweak virtually every setting in the virtual world.

The Settings page controls all FSX settings, but you'll see right away that the lion's share are display settings. This makes sense because the display takes up the bulk of the computer's processing power. You'll see five basic sliders for display settings, as well as a Customize button. If you click the Customize button, you can customize the details for each of these five areas, as shown on the right of Figure 1.5. This is far more detail than you'll ever need to adjust for flight training, but it does allow you to customize FSX's look to your personal tastes.

KEEPING IT REAL

WHAT THE HECK IS FRAME RATE?

Frame rate refers to how fast FSX can draw a completely new picture on your screen. If you think about Flight Simulator as a movie, the faster the frame rate, the smoother the movie appears on your screen. To see the frame rate you're getting at any given time, press Shift+Z twice on your keyboard. The target frame rate for FSX is usually 20 frames per second (fps). The biggest frame rate killers are textures, including both the textures on your aircraft and the texture of the earth below you.

Feel free to play around with display settings to get the best look possible. Just remember that, as far as flight training goes, a consistent frame rate of 20 fps or better is more important than a photorealistic view out the window.

As you can see, you can crank up the display settings to ultrahigh and get beautiful pictures at the expense of smooth flying.

One slick feature of FSX is that you can save and load different display settings so that you can change quickly between them. To save the default settings for your machine, click the Save button on the Settings page. Name this file **default settings**, and click OK. Now take the setting sliders, and move them all one click to the right—that is, if your graphics setting was set to Medium, it'll now be set to Medium High—and click the Save button again. Save this configuration as **prettier**. From this point forward, every time you run FSX, you'll get that higher level of visual display. Now reset the settings to their defaults by clicking the Reset Defaults button on the same page. After you return the settings to their defaults, slide each of the five sliders one notch to the left so they're at a lower quality. Save this configuration as well, calling it **faster**. Click Reset Defaults again to return to the default settings.

16

PART I	PART II	PART III	PART IV	PART V	PART VI
PREFLIGHT	SPORT PILOT	PRIVATE PILOT	INSTRUMENT RATING	COMMERCIAL LICENSE	ATP AND BEYOND

Now you have three display configurations to play with as you get flying in Chapter 2. We'll start you out flying the default settings as set by FSX. If the performance isn't good enough for you, return to this window, click Load, and choose the faster configuration. If your computer seems to handle FSX with aplomb, return to this window, load the prettier settings, and see how it does.

We won't talk much more about adjusting the settings, but you should certainly feel free to experiment with them all you like.

ORGANIZING YOUR COCKPIT

Figure 1-6: Make sure your cockpit is a comfortable space for the controls and for the printed versions of checklists, charts, and any other documents you regularly use.

Cockpit organization is something your flight instructor will talk about, particularly in instrument training. Keeping a well-organized cockpit can mean the difference between having a key chart immediately at hand or having to crane around backward reaching under the seat with one hand while trying to fly through turbulence with the other.

The seat in front of your computer shouldn't be bouncing around in turbulence (unless you live in Southern California), but setting up your cockpit in a realistic way will both improve your training and give you the most realistic flight experience. This includes having real, printed versions of your checklists available and the appropriate physical charts for the flight.

An organized cockpit also means getting all of those flight controls (yoke, rudder pedals, and headset) in a position where they're comfortable for you to use for at least an hour at a time (see Figure 1-6). No sense investing in all that stuff if it's just going to annoy you when you try to use it.

Finally, consider a "Do Not Disturb" sign for the door, turn off your cell phone before flight, and close your email program. It's part of the flight instructor's job to introduce what the FAA calls *realistic distractions*, but having your spouse call you for dinner doesn't count as one of them.

KEY FLIGHT SIM COMMANDS

One of the unavoidable frustrations of the simulator is that it's, well, a simulator. There are plenty of things you would just do in an airplane, such as turn your head to the left to get a good look at the runway or such as reach down with your hand to retract the gear. You have to use the keyboard, mouse, or buttons on your joystick to do this in FSX. The way to make this the least disruptive is to know the key commands for commonly used actions and customize buttons on your joystick or yoke to do exactly what you want them to do.

You can see a complete list of the commands in FSX by viewing your kneeboard—F10 on your keyboard—but we'll get you going with a few you should commit to memory.

ESSENTIAL BASIC COMMANDS

Esc ends your current flight. By default, FSX will verify that this is what you really want to do.

P pauses the simulation. Press P again to resume flying.

Alt reveals all the menus when working in full-screen mode.

Alt+Enter toggles between full-screen mode, where FSX takes up your complete monitor, and window mode, where FSX runs in a window just like any other program. Pressing Alt+Enter twice will get rid of the menus at the top of the screen.

The period key will apply your brakes if you don't have rudder petals with built-in brakes.

ESSENTIAL VIEW COMMANDS

One of the biggest limitations with FSX, or any flight simulator that uses only one screen, is that you have no peripheral vision. Peripheral vision is essential for lining yourself up with the runway and landing the airplane. You get around this in FSX by using different views. To do this efficiently, you need to know how to use the hat switch on your joystick or yoke to look around the cockpit. You'll practice this in the next chapter.

FSX actually has two cockpit views: the normal cockpit view (see the left of Figure 1-7) and the virtual cockpit view (see the right of Figure 1-7). The virtual cockpit view allows you to smoothly look around the cockpit. On a high-end computer like one of our loaners, the effect is amazingly realistic. If you use it, however, you'll need to be able to change the eye point. This sets how high or low in the cockpit your virtual chair sits, as well as how far back from the instrument panel. The farther back from the instrument panel, the more peripheral vision you have—and the more realistic the view—but the more difficult it is to read the instruments.

Ctrl+Enter moves your eye point away from the instrument panel toward the back of the airplane.

Ctrl+Backspace moves your eye point forward toward the instrument panel.

Shift+Backspace moves your eye point down as if you were slouching in your seat.

Shift+Enter moves your eye point up as if you were sitting up straight, just like your mother always told you to do.

Ctrl+spacebar resets the virtual cockpit view both for your eye point and for looking straight ahead. This is an essential command because often you'll use the hat switch to take a look to your right or left and perhaps slightly up or down and then need to swing your virtual head back around to look out front windscreen of the airplane.

18

PART I PREFLIGHT   **PART II** SPORT PILOT   **PART III** PRIVATE PILOT   **PART IV** INSTRUMENT RATING   **PART V** COMMERCIAL LICENSE   **PART VI** ATP AND BEYOND

Figure 1-7: One of the biggest choices in FSX is when you'll use the 2D normal cockpit or the 3D virtual cockpit. It's helpful to toggle quickly between the two by pressing F9 and F10.

The normal cockpit view, also known as the 2D view, is limited to eight views inside the cockpit. The views are broken into 45-degree segments. The default view is straight ahead with an option to look 45° ahead and right, 90° right, 135° rear and right, and so on. The normal cockpit view snaps back to the straight-ahead perspective every time you let go of the hat switch, so you don't need to press Ctrl+spacebar to reset the view. The normal cockpit doesn't let you change your eye point either.

Figure 1-8: When you have a sense of which commands you'll use on a regular basis, make sure they're easy to execute by giving them a simple keyboard shortcut or assigning them to a button on your joystick.

In the normal cockpit view, it can be hard to look over the nose of the aircraft. So, pressing W on the keyboard gets rid of most of the panel, leaving you just a few key instruments. Pressing W again will remove all the instruments, and pressing W a third time will bring back the whole cockpit.

Pressing F10 on your keyboard will give you the normal, 2D cockpit at any time.

Pressing F9 on your keyboard will give you the virtual cockpit.

Knowing the commands is one thing, but hitting them on the keyboard in the heat of battle is something else. We strongly encourage you to customize the buttons on your yoke or joystick so that the commands you want are one simple click away. For example, if you use virtual cockpit regularly, you can customize one of the buttons near the hat switch to be the same as Ctrl+spacebar. That way, you can look around the virtual world yet easily snap back to a forward view.

You customize buttons from the Settings page of FSX. Click the Controls button, and then click the Buttons/ Keys tab. This lists all the key commands in FSX and any joystick buttons that are assigned to those commands (see Figure 1-8). Select the command you want to assign to your joystick, and click Change Assignment. That'll open a new window where you can click the button on your joystick and assign it to the command.

USE OF SLEW FOR PRACTICE

One of the huge advantages of working with the simulator is that you can pick up the airplane and move it anywhere in space and time. You can do this three ways: by starting a simulation at a particular point, by changing position on the World > Map menu, and by using something called *slew*. Slew allows you to fly the airplane to anywhere in the virtual world at hundreds of miles per hour or twisted into any position you like while it hovers motionless in the air. It takes a bit of practice to learn how to use slew well, so much so that has its own appendix in this book. Throughout the book, we might refer to slewing the airplane into a particular position. If you want to learn how to use slew, check out Appendix B.

USING THE FSX BUILT-IN FLIGHT LESSONS

FSX includes many built-in flight lessons hosted by Rod Machado. Rod is practically a living legend as a flight instructor and humorist. We'd love to have the opportunity to fly with him, and we're sure we'd learn a lot. We encourage you to use his lessons as a supplement to the lessons in this book.

But these lessons don't go far enough, in our opinion, if you want to become a real pilot or if you want your virtual pilot training to be as realistic as possible. They also contain a few pitfalls.

One of the issues we've noticed working with students who have a lot of flight simulator time before they transition to a real airplane is that they spent too much time with their heads down in the cockpit looking at the flight instruments. In a flight simulator, this makes a lot of sense because no matter how realistic the view is on the screen, you still lack all of the peripheral vision, as well as tactile cues about what the airplane is doing. Many of the built-in flight lessons rely heavily on the instruments for this reason. But in real airplanes when you're not flying in a cloud, you need to spend most of your time looking outside the airplane.

That's actually why you're starting your training in this book with the Piper J-3 Cub instead of the Cessna 172. The Cub has few instruments, so there's not much to look at. Our goal is to get more of the sight picture in your brain and lay the groundwork for looking outside the airplane, even though that's actually more difficult to do on a computer than just flying on instruments.

Getting to know the Cub could have a secondary benefit if you choose to continue on to real aircraft. The FAA recently approved the Sport Pilot Certificate, giving students the option of learning to fly in a smaller, less expensive, and simpler airplane such as the Cub. The FAA requires only 20 hours of flight time to get a Sport Pilot Certificate, whereas you need 40 hours to get a Private Pilot Certificate. The Cessna 172 is too big and fast to be legally flown by someone who has only a Sport Pilot Certificate.

By contrast, the Instrument Rating lessons in FSX are done in the Cessna 172. This is probably the most common airplane for instrument training in the real world—because it's fairly inexpensive as instrument-capable airplanes go—

but it's not the airplane that a lot of instrument pilots end up flying. Cost is not a factor in flight simulators, so we take you directly to the Mooney Bravo. This is a serious, cross-country airplane and a great trainer for both doing instrument training and working with complex, high-performance aircraft.

SELECTING A REAL-WORLD FLIGHT SCHOOL

If you decide to pursue real-world flight training, you might be surprised by how much information you need in order to make a good decision about a flight school. A bad decision could be costly in money, time, or even safety, so take your time, and check out as many schools as you can to find one that will work for you. In fact, when we meet prospective flight students, we encourage them to go check out several flight schools in the area to find the one that fits them best. (Of course, we hope that after shopping around they come back to us.)

AIRCRAFT TYPES

Find a flight school that has the kind of airplanes you want to fly. FSX and this book give you opportunities to try many kinds of airplanes, and you might decide you want to learn for real in one type. But be open to trying several kinds, because flight simulators cannot show you how it feels to actually sit in an aircraft.

For instance, the real Cessna 172 is only 39 inches wide. If you're a big person and your flight instructor is as well, it can be a tight fit. A Diamond DA20 has a cabin that's a full 5 inches wider. On the other hand, sometimes Flight Simulator does an excellent job of simulating reality. It's hard to see out of the FSX version of the Cub while sitting on the ground. In a real Cub, the student sits in the back, and the view is…just about as bad.

ENVIRONMENT

Some flight schools are set up only to do flight training—they do it well, and they do it thoroughly, but when you're done training, they won't let you rent a plane for fun. Some schools allow you to rent the plane after you're done training, but they don't offer much support for the recreational flyer. If you want to push through your training and become a professional pilot as quickly and cheaply as possible, this might be fine.

Contrast that with a *flying club*, which is much more about recreational flying. Members of the club might actually own shares of the planes or share some other expenses. Some flying clubs are really just private companies. Regardless, a flying club is usually designed to provide events and activities to help pilots keep flying after they get their certificates.

INSTRUCTOR

In our opinion, the number-one determinant for your success as a prospective pilot is your relationship with your flight instructor (usually called a *certified flight instructor*, or CFI, in the United States). When checking out different flight schools, arrange to fly one or two flights with several different CFIs—even at the same flight school—to find out which instructor has the style that lets you learn best.

Try to find a CFI who is at least somewhat familiar with FSX or similar types of flight simulators. It will speed up your training a lot if your CFI can describe what goals and maneuvers will be taught in your next lesson and how you can practice them in FSX before the lesson.

In the end, the most important factor is whether you will be comfortable with the CFI and get along well enough that you can learn (see Figure 1-9). If you don't have to think about any challenges in your relationship with your CFI, you'll be able to concentrate on learning to fly, which is plenty of a challenge in itself!

Some folks will warn you against flying with younger instructors who are just "building time" toward an airline career. Although some young instructors might be bound for the airlines, that doesn't mean they won't do a good job on your training; in fact, they might better remember their aviation knowledge because they just learned it. Use your judgment as to whether someone is working hard to help you or is just along for the ride.

Figure 1-9: Your relationship with your instructor is the single most important factor in your success as a student pilot. Take the time to find the person who is right for you.

COSTS

Why is flying so expensive? Well, it's expensive for a couple reasons. The airplanes are expensive to own and operate. Insurance and maintenance costs are often 10 times as high as comparable prices for your car. Fuel is expensive, costing about $4.50 a gallon in the United States at the time of this writing, and much more in Europe and elsewhere. But even if all that wasn't true, moving a heavy mass through the air takes a lot of energy. And no matter how you slice it, energy costs money to use. The following sections contain some of the details to help you keep the cost from getting out of control.

22

PART I	PART II	PART III	PART IV	PART V	PART VI
PREFLIGHT	SPORT PILOT	PRIVATE PILOT	INSTRUMENT RATING	COMMERCIAL LICENSE	ATP AND BEYOND

AIRCRAFT RENTAL

Most flight schools charge by each 10th of the hour the engine is running, based on a special clock in the airplane called a *Hobbs meter*. If you use the logbook feature in FSX, you'll notice it measures your time in 10ths of hours, too, although it starts counting as soon as you start a flight even if the engine is stopped. Some schools charge a *wet* rate; that is, fuel is included in the rental fee. Others charge a *dry* rate, in which case you pay for the fuel you burn during the flight on top of the rental fee. Be sure to ask which rate the school uses so you can compare this correctly with other schools.

INSTRUCTOR

Just like the airplane, you'll probably pay for your CFI's time teaching in the airplane based on the Hobbs meter.

One big difference between flight schools has to do with how they charge for ground instruction. Before each flight, it's helpful to go over the plan for the flight with your instructor; this gives you a chance to understand the goals and activities for the flight and gives your instructor a chance to make sure you understand the theoretical concepts and procedures the flight will include. Some schools charge for this ground time, and others do not. The latter might seem like a great deal, but it has a hidden pitfall.

If the flight school doesn't pay the instructor for this time, the instructor is likely to shorten or skip this preflight discussion. You'll pay for this when it takes you longer to learn techniques in the air, where both the instructor and the airplane clocks are ticking the dollars away. Airplanes also make lousy classrooms for theoretical concepts or discussions. Your own studying, including FSX and this book, will help prepare you for your lessons so you can be more efficient during your training time, but be sure you and your instructor allow time before the flight as well.

INSURANCE

Airplanes are expensive, and if you bend one during your training, someone is going to have to pay for it. The flight school almost certainly has enough insurance to get the airplane repaired and flying again, but it's possible that the school will ask you to pay the deductible. Deductibles can be substantial on airplanes, sometimes in excess of $10,000.

The sad fact is that we live in a litigious society. When airplane accidents happen, there is often more damage (and more liability and lawsuits) than just repairs to the airplane. It's possible the insurance company that covers the flight school and the airplane doesn't cover you against liability claims resulting from an accident. It's even possible, although rarer, for an insurance policy to allow the insurance company to pay the flight school to repair the airplane but then sue you as the pilot for that amount.

Be sure to find out exactly what kind of insurance the flight school offers, and consider getting some supplementary insurance of your own. Many agencies offer this kind of insurance, which is technically liability insurance, for renter pilots. The Airplane Owners and Pilots Association (AOPA) website has some excellent information about renter's insurance.

INTRODUCTORY FLIGHT

Most flight schools allow you to take an introductory flight for a much lower price than their usual hourly rate, as a way of getting you in the door. Many flight schools participate in the Be a Pilot program (www.beapilot.com), where you can print a coupon for an introductory flight at a reduced price.

The introductory flight can be a real flight lesson, so make it clear you want a lesson and not just a sightseeing flight. Ask to log the time in your logbook so that it will count toward your total, required flying time. However, be aware that in our post-9/11 world, you'll probably need to bring proof of citizenship and a government ID to log the training. If you don't have (or don't want to bring) such proof, you can take the flight, but you can't log the flight time, and it won't count toward total flight time.

We strongly encourage you to take advantage of introductory flights at as many flight schools as you can, even ones that you know you're not interested in (because of distance, cost, or whatever). You'll be able to get an even better idea of what you look for in a school, and you'll spend time with many different instructors and learn what kind of person meets your needs for training.

When you visit a flight school to take an introductory flight, ask for a tour of the facilities. You can learn a lot about a school by seeing the maintenance facility (if it has one), looking at all the types of aircraft available (and their quality), and getting a sense of the culture or environment of the school. Talking to pilots who learned to fly there is an excellent idea too. That said, realize that airplanes, unlike cars, undergo stringent inspections at a minimum of every year. Just because an airplane looks a little rough around the edges doesn't mean that it's unsafe.

WORKING WITH YOUR FLIGHT INSTRUCTOR

A good CFI knows that students need to be prepared for each flight lesson by studying and discussing the procedures and maneuvers they will practice during the flight. Students do not learn as well when they hear about a maneuver for the first time in the air.

Using FSX as part of your real-world training is a great way to prepare for each lesson. At the end of a lesson, ask your CFI what maneuvers or procedures you will be doing in the next lesson. Then grab this book, boot up FSX, and find the lessons that we've set up. After you've practiced several times in the simulator, the real flight will be much easier, and you'll be able to concentrate on controlling the actual airplane, rather than trying to remember what the maneuver was all about. Feel free to change the airplane in our lesson to better match the one you're actually using for flight training.

FSX AS PART OF A LESSON

If you are working with a CFI, let them know you have Flight Simulator and can use it as part of your training. Ask them whether they can give you tasks or scenarios to fly that correspond to your next flight lesson. Heck, give them a copy of this book. At the least, find out what you'll be doing on your next flight lesson, and try it in FSX on your own.

24

PART I	PART II	PART III	PART IV	PART V	PART VI
PREFLIGHT	SPORT PILOT	PRIVATE PILOT	INSTRUMENT RATING	COMMERCIAL LICENSE	ATP AND BEYOND

Figure 1-10: Find an instructor who will work with you on FSX as well.

Consider hiring them for some *ground instruction* time, and have them teach you the lesson in FSX before you go out in the real plane (Figure 1-10). This training method has two advantages: you can practice difficult parts over and over without the extra time (and money) flying the plane out to the practice area and back, and the instructor can set up scenarios that increase your skills in ways that the real world might not allow.

For example, in Chapter 3, you'll learn how to land when there is a crosswind on the runway—that is, the wind is blowing from the side instead of straight down the runway. If your real-world lesson is supposed to be about crosswind landings but the wind is calm that day, you won't learn the necessary skills for adapting to the crosswind. Instead, you or your CFI can use the crosswind lesson from this book (but this time you have a live CFI coaching you), and then in the real flight, you can practice other parts of landings.

SHARED COCKPIT

Flight Simulator used to have something called a *flight instructor station*, which allowed two computers to connect to each other and allowed the instructor to manipulate your Flight Simulator from a different computer. New in FSX is the ability for two pilots running FSX on separate machines to actually *sit* in the same airplane. Originally designed for the two-cockpit crews of virtual airlines, this is a great way to have a flight lesson. Again, connected through the Internet, your CFI can sit in the right seat and can demonstrate maneuvers and procedures for you and then watch your performance as you practice. This will also be detailed in Chapter 25, but you can start thinking about it now and talk to your CFI about incorporating this into your training. For instance, on a day when the weather isn't good enough for a real flight, see whether you can have a flight lesson while you're on your own computer and your CFI is at the airport (or at home) using their FSX, saving you a trip to the airport but still getting in a good lesson.

We wouldn't be surprised if in the not-too-distant future CFIs will start offering their services online to students anywhere in the world.

USING THE PRACTICAL TEST STANDARDS

Real-world pilot training preparing you for a new pilot certificate or rating culminates with a *checkride*, a ground and flight test with an FAA-designated examiner or FAA employee. Pass the checkride, and you're the proud owner of a new pilot's certificate. When you're ready for your checkride, the examiner will use the appropriate Practical Test Standards (PTS) for that pilot certificate as a guide for the checkride. For instance, the first pilot certificate this book will train you for is the Sport Pilot Certificate (see Figure 1-11). If you want to see what a Sport Pilot Practical Test will include and what standards you'll be required to demonstrate to the examiner, check out the Sport Pilot Practical Test Standards PDF file on the accompanying website at www.wiley.com. The FAA updates the PTS regularly, so go to the following FAA website for the latest versions: www.faa .gov/education_research/testing/airmen/test_standards/.

In this book, we will train you using the standards set out in the PTS. For example, on page 1-23 (PDF page 57) of the Sport Pilot PTS, it says that you will be asked to perform steep turns at a 45-degree bank, maintaining the entry altitude ±100 feet, airspeed ±10 knots, bank ±5°, and several other parameters. By studying the PTS and practicing in FSX (and, more important, in the real airplane) to the standards set out in the PTS, your checkride will have few surprises, and you'll be able to tell how you're doing all the way through.

Figure 1-11: You can buy a commercial copy of the PTS, or you can download them in PDF from the FAA.

STUDENT OF THE CRAFT

AVIATION ON THE INTERNET

Whole books have been written about how to get aviation information on the Internet and connect with other pilots. Rather than repeat what you can get elsewhere, here is a brief summary of the websites we've found most useful in our real-world and sim flying:

FAA: www.faa.gov
The FAA has gone seriously digital, with all kinds of documents, training manuals, and more available online. We've included a lot of the pertinent ones on the website that accompanies this book, but the FAA updates its documents frequently, so you'll want to check its website for the latest.

Weather: aviationweather.gov
It's not enough to know it's going to be partly cloudy with a high of 85° today. You need to know how high those clouds are, whether that hot temperature comes with high humidity, and, thus, where the thunderstorms are popping up. Be sure to check out the Java tools on this website as well. They're some of the coolest free tools you'll find on the Web for weather.

Continued

26

PART I	PART II	PART III	PART IV	PART V	PART VI
PREFLIGHT	SPORT PILOT	PRIVATE PILOT	INSTRUMENT RATING	COMMERCIAL LICENSE	ATP AND BEYOND

Live Weather Radar: www.wunderground.com
The weather underground isn't such an amazing site for aviation weather, but it does have the best up-to-the-minute weather radar available for free. You can also get it on your cell phone at `mobile.wunderground.com`.

Visual Flying Charts: skyvector.com
The best maps, or charts, to have for visual flying are usually sectional charts. Free sectional charts for the entire United States, as well as terminal area charts that show busy airspace in greater detail, are available here.

Instrument Approach Plates: naco.faa.gov/index.asp?xml=naco/online/d_tpp
When you get into instrument flying, you'll start using approach plates. All the approach plates for the United States are available online in PDF. This database is updated every 56 days.

Organizations: www.aopa.org
The AOPA maintains an extensive website that's of interest to anyone excited about aviation. The AOPA also does extensive lobbying on behalf of pilots and puts out a great magazine. You might consider joining the organization if all your flying will be online.

Experimental Aircraft Association: www.eaa.org
Known even outside aviation circles for hosting the annual AirVenture pilgrimage to Oshkosh, Wisconsin, the Experimental Aircraft Association (EAA) got its start as a club for people who build their own airplanes. Now it is a home for pilots and wanna-be pilots of all types.

Sim Flying: www.avsim.com and www.flightsim.com
AVSIM Online is one of the best-known flight simulator websites around. FlightSim.com is one of the oldest. Many, many others exist, but if you start with one, you can usually find your way to the rest.

Virtual Air Traffic Simulation: www.vatsim.net
VATSIM is probably the biggest of several systems that flight simmers can connect to in multiplayer mode and fly with other pilots. Unlike the GameSpy Network built into FSX, VATSIM can accommodate thousands of pilots and hundreds of sim air traffic controllers all in the same virtual world.

Flight Aware: flightaware.com
This site includes real-time display of all flights tracked by air traffic control nationwide. It includes both commercial and private aviation.

PLUGGING IN TO PILOT COMMUNITIES

When Microsoft added multiplayer capabilities to Flight Simulator almost a decade ago, the opportunities for connecting with other like-minded sim pilots exploded. Part Six of this book will cover multiplayer opportunities in detail, but here are some examples to show you the capabilities of FSX:

- Sponsor a virtual *fly-in* where sim pilots, connected to one server, all fly to a single airport and watch each other take off and land and even perform an air show. (Virtual $100 hamburgers don't taste as good as the real thing, though.)

- Fly as a two-pilot crew in the cockpit, each with specific duties to perform during the flight.

- Join a virtual airline, using custom paint on FSX airliners, and fly into and out of your airline's hubs.

- Connect to one of several virtual air traffic networks, where both sim pilots and sim air traffic controllers are on duty and with voice communication that sounds just like the real thing. (When your virtual air traffic controller sends your virtual airplane into the virtual mountain killing all 200 virtual passengers, please use only virtual lawyers for your virtual lawsuit.)

New real-world pilots tell us that, besides the skills of flying itself, they are most nervous about using the radio and not sounding silly or ignorant. As the online communities grow and more people learn about flying, the realism of voice communication increases, and students can practice their radio techniques in the safety and anonymity of the virtual world.

The best place to find real pilots is usually at an airport. If you like things that fly, spend a little time hanging out at some of your local airports. You'll meet all sorts of interesting people. Also, quite a few real-world pilot communities meet online, and some online resources can help you find real pilots.

AVSIG (www.avsig.com) started as a computer bulletin board system back in the pre-Internet days and still is a popular aviation message forum. You can post a question or comment and get quick responses from a variety of aviation professionals within hours.

The CFI.com (www.thecfi.com) is technically a website for CFIs, but since the users are also instructors, they're receptive to student questions. It's a great place to lurk and learn stuff as well.

Your local EAA chapter is a great place to meet people enthusiastic about aviation. You can find out more about the EAA at its website, www.eaa.org.

The FAA offers monthly safety seminars in many cities, and all are welcome to come—pilots, sim pilots, and non-pilots alike. Register at www.faasafety.gov.

Pilots Share the Ride (www.pilotsharetheride.com) is a website primarily for pilots, but it's really a way for people to share expenses when traveling in small aircraft. Who knows? You might end up getting a ride with someone heading to a common destination, such as an air show.

Angel Flight is an organization that donates travel in small aircraft for people with medical needs and limited resources (www.angelflight.org). The organization strongly encourages people to sign up to be mission assistants to help both the pilot and the passengers have a smooth and enjoyable trip. These assistants don't have to be pilots, and you don't have to be a real-world pilot to join Angel Flight.

28

PART I
PREFLIGHT

PART II
SPORT PILOT

PART III
PRIVATE PILOT

PART IV
INSTRUMENT RATING

PART V
COMMERCIAL LICENSE

PART VI
ATP AND BEYOND

KEY POINTS FOR REAL FLYING AND FSX BUILT-INS

The following are some key points from this chapter that apply to flight sim flying and real-world flying:

- Take the time to set up your hardware and software to work best for your needs. This might mean investing in some new equipment.

- Take the time to find the best flight school and the instructor who works best for you, for either real-world or virtual training.

- Use your online communities to get help and answer questions. Those forums are full of enthusiasts just like you.

FIRST FLIGHT IN
THE PIPER J-3 CUB

"THE CUB IS THE SAFEST AIRPLANE IN THE WORLD. IT CAN JUST BARELY KILL YOU."

—MAX STANLEY, NORTHRUP TEST PILOT

30

| PART I | PART II | PART III | PART IV | PART V | PART VI |
| PREFLIGHT | SPORT PILOT | PRIVATE PILOT | INSTRUMENT RATING | COMMERCIAL LICENSE | ATP AND BEYOND |

FLIGHT FUNDAMENTALS FOR THE PILOT

Asking what makes an airplane really fly is one of those topics that's bound to get an argument going in almost any group of pilots. If you're thinking that FSX just pretends to simulate the forces acting on an airplane, think again. One of the reasons FSX requires a powerful computer to run is that it's simulating the real forces acting on an aircraft.

Aeronautical engineers and software designers for Microsoft games might need to understand the math behind flight, but we're going to skirt the issue here. Understanding why an airplane can fly is much less important to the pilot than understanding how to control those forces in flight.

That said, a taste of theory is still in order. We'll return to how this theory applies in practice later in this chapter.

We'll keep it simple. Imagine you're standing alone in a wide-open field of tall grass with no trees or buildings anywhere around you. There's no wind, so the air is dead calm. On the horizon, a yellow Cub appears heading toward you. It's flying low, just 10 feet off the ground. You see something interesting underneath and just behind the airplane. The grass is being flattened as the airplane passes. And then as the airplane continues, the grass stands back up. As the Cub passes overhead, you feel a downward blast of air, and then the calm air returns.

An airplane moving through the air displaces a mass of air downward (see Figure 2-1). (It also displaces some air upward, but we'll ignore that for now because there's a lot more total down motion than up.) We can describe how and why this happens in many ways, but in the end, that's what must happen to keep the airplane off the ground. It's analogous to treading water in a swimming pool while holding a bowling ball. If your swirling feet can shove enough water downward, you'll keep yourself and your bowling ball cargo above water.

Can an airplane really displace that much air? It can, and it does. By moving air down, the net reaction is to keep the airplane up and counter the evil effects of gravity. We call that net upward force *lift*.

The airplane can generate enough lift in two ways. It can move through the air quickly and displace a great many air molecules downward but displace each one only a small amount, or it can move through the air slowly, encountering a smaller mass of air but shoving each molecule down with great gusto. How quickly the airplane moves through the air and how much its wings and tail try to redirect that air are the two primary factors you manipulate to control the airplane and make it fly.

Figure 2-1: Every airplane creates a net motion of air downward in order to produce the upward force called lift.

WE ALL HAVE OUR LIMITS

Just think about the wing of the airplane. The faster it moves through the air, the more air molecules—the more air mass—it encounters each second. So, the faster an airplane flies, the greater its potential for lift. But how does the airplane control how aggressively it tries to redirect that air?

To get a feeling for the answer before we describe it, think back to when you were kid with your arm out the window of a moving car. When your hand was flat and parallel to the road, it didn't have a tendency to move up or down. As you twisted your wrist so the thumb side pointed slightly up, your whole arm was forced upward. Your hand was acting like a wing displacing air downward and shoving your arm upward as a result. The more you twisted your thumb upward, the greater the force trying to lift your hand, but only to a point.

Imagine twisting your wrist even further so the thumb side is pointed straight up and your palm is going straight into the wind. Now the wind seems to just push your arm backward, because instead of redirecting air downward, your flat palm is just trying to stop it.

Logic dictates that there must be some point between a slight angle of your hand and a flat palm into the oncoming air where your palm stops effectively redirecting air downward and just causes a big logjam of air and no useful lift. The angle of your palm into the oncoming air is called *angle of attack* (see Figure 2-2). The angle where the air ceases to smoothly follow the top and bottom surfaces of your hand is called the *critical angle of attack*.

Figure 2-2: For a given speed, increasing the angle of attack increases the lift—but only to a point.

When a wing reaches the critical angle of attack, air flowing over the top surface of the wing begins to turn and tumble instead of smoothly following the downward curve. This is called a *stall*. It has nothing to do with an engine stalling such as when your car stalls, but it does mean the airplane begins to shake and sink downward back toward the Earth.

Again, this is a simplified view of lift, but it's enough for us to do what we need to intelligently as pilots. As you pilot the Cub—or any airplane, for that matter—one of your primary jobs is adjusting the balance of how fast air moves over the surfaces of the airplane and how much of an angle of attack those surfaces take into the oncoming wind.

32

PART I	PART II	PART III	PART IV	PART V	PART VI
PREFLIGHT	SPORT PILOT	PRIVATE PILOT	INSTRUMENT RATING	COMMERCIAL LICENSE	ATP AND BEYOND

A GREAT SPIN ON FLYING

One of our favorite websites on how things really fly is John S. Denker's online book *See How It Flies* at www.av8n.com/how/.

The Four Fundamental Gaits of Flight

Different combinations of power and the angle of attack of various parts of the airplane give you the four fundamental configurations for airplane flight: straight and level, turns, climbs, and descents. Early flight author Wolfgang Langewiesche called these the *gaits* of flight. It's sort of like saying a horse has different gaits such as a trot or a gallop.

Master these four fundamentals, and you have essentially mastered flying the airplane because most complex maneuvers are just combinations of these four basic ones. A climbing turn is a combination of climbing flight and level turns. A landing is a combination of descending flight that changes to straight and level flight just above the runway.

Related to gait is an airplane's *attitude*. The orientation of the aircraft compared to the horizon—pitch-high (nose up), pitch-low (nose down), banked left (left wing down, right wing up), banked right (right wing down, left wing up)—is what pilots are talking about when they describe an airplane's attitude. It may seem like this is the same as gait; however, as you'll learn later, you can have a high pitch-attitude but still be descending, you can be banked without turning, and so forth.

Straight and Level Flight

Straight and level flight is just what it sounds. The airplane is flying in a constant direction, meaning it's not turning left or right, and it's holding a constant altitude, meaning it is neither climbing nor descending. To keep a constant altitude, the wings must be producing just enough lift to counteract the pull of gravity. To make this happen, the aircraft must be moving through the air quickly but with its wings at a small angle of attack or moving slowly with its wings at a large angle of attack. This is important to you because you need lots of power and a small angle of attack to go fast, and you need less power but a higher angle of attack to fly slowly.

You'll experiment with straight and level flight at high and low speeds in just a moment.

Climbing Flight

Although an aeronautical engineer might cringe at the statement, a *steady climb* is nothing more than straight and level flight with some energy left over that lets the airplane move farther away from the surface of the Earth. From the pilot's point of view, though, that's really what it is. You'll see this when you fly the Cub.

Descending Flight

We can carry this analogy further and say that *descending flight* is nothing more than straight and level in which at least some of the energy to move the airplane through the air and create lift is coming from gravity. Rather than burning gasoline, you're burning the potential energy of altitude. Again, this concept will be clearer when you try it in flight.

LEVEL TURNS

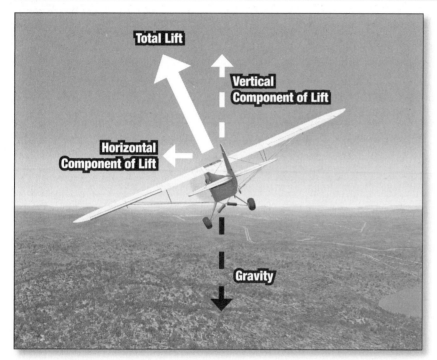

Figure 2-3: Although the full explanation is a bit more complicated, for now just remember that banking the airplane uses some of the lift from the wings to pull the airplane around a turn.

Level turns are a little trickier. When the airplane is in a turn and maintaining a constant altitude, its wings are producing enough lift upward to counteract the effect of gravity downward. But as you know when an airplane turns, its wings are banked. This means instead of the lift being directed only up, it's being directed both up and toward the inside of the turn. The proportion of lift that's pointed upward balances gravity and maintains a constant airplane altitude above the ground.

The proportion of lift that points to the inside of the turn has no force to balance it in the other direction. That unbalanced force changes the airplane's direction, and the airplane turns (see Figure 2-3). The force pulling the airplane toward the inside of the turn continues to change the direction the airplane is pointing—sending the airplane around in circles until the wings are unbanked.

A little math says that the total lift (combined vertical component to counter gravity and horizontal component to create the turn) must be higher than in nonturning flight. That's correct. For anything other than a short turn of a shallow bank, the pilot must pull back on the stick a bit or open the throttle to maintain a constant altitude during the turn.

VISUALIZE YOUR CONTROL SURFACES

One of the great aspects of FSX is that you can simultaneously sit inside the cockpit and move controls while also looking outside the cockpit and seeing those controls in motion. Take a look at the controls for your Cub.

From the FSX home screen, choose Free Flight on the left menu, and then click the Load button. Choose Chapter_02_First_flight, and click Fly Now. This loads your first scenario with a Cub at lovely Post Mills airport in Post Mills, Vermont. This is a small grass runway, far from the hustle and bustle of the world, and a perfect place to learn to fly the Cub.

34

PART I
PREFLIGHT

PART II
SPORT PILOT

PART III
PRIVATE PILOT

PART IV
INSTRUMENT RATING

PART V
COMMERCIAL LICENSE

PART VI
ATP AND BEYOND

This scenario opens with a view from the cockpit, but you actually want two views. Press Alt to show the menus in FSX, and then select View > New View > Outside > Locked Spot. This opens a second window in the upper-left side of the screen. You can make this window smaller if it's taking up too much space on your screen by dragging the lower-right corner up and left.

When FSX has two windows open like this, you can control only one of them at a time. The one that's under your control has a thin white border around the outside. The new, locked spot view should be the one that's under your control right after you open it.

Now you get to have some fun with views. Push the hat switch—the round one with the raised center that looks like the hats Devo used to wear in concert—to the right, and your view should move around the airplane. Stop when you're looking at the airplane from a 45-degree angle from behind, as shown in Figure 2-4.

Figure 2-4: Seeing the same thing from two points of view at once is one of FSX's great strengths. You might need to adjust the view after the window opens to get just the look you want.

You can also zoom in and out on the locked spot view to get a better view of the airplane or to see more of the surrounding terrain. The default zoom is just right for now, but you might want to adjust the view on the virtual cockpit bit. To switch which window you're controlling, click anywhere inside the larger window of the cockpit, or press Ctrl+Tab on your keyboard. The view of your cockpit might not look like the one in Figure 2-4. First make sure you have the virtual cockpit turned on by pressing F9 on your keyboard. Next zoom out a bit by pressing the minus sign two times. (You can reset the zoom to normal view by pressing Backspace at any time.) Finally, use the hat switch to point your view down a bit so you can see the control stick and silver rudder pedals on the floor.

Now move your joystick or yoke forward and back. You see the stick in the cockpit move forward and back and the *elevators* on the Cub in the spot view deflect up and down. You might think this fore-and-aft motion of your yoke is controlling the aircraft's pitch attitude—how high or low the nose is to the horizon—but what it's really controlling is the angle of attack of the wings to the oncoming wind.

LOOKING GOOD IN THE VIRTUAL COCKPIT

If you use the virtual cockpit regularly, you need a way to quickly switch the view back to straight ahead. Pressing Ctrl+spacebar resets the view but also resets any eye point adjustments you made. You have a view command for the look-ahead 3D cockpit. Give this command a keyboard shortcut (it doesn't have one by default), or assign it to a button on your joystick.

Pull back on the yoke, and the tail is sent downward. The nose and leading edge of the wings point upward. The angle of attack increases, and the Cub initially begins to climb. Push the stick forward; the tail rises, the nose sinks, and the Cub descends back toward the Earth. That's where you get the old saying, "Flying is simple. Pull the stick back, the houses get smaller; push the stick forward, the houses get bigger." However, this has limitations. You'll explore those limits further in Chapter 8.

Move your joystick from side to side, or turn your yoke left and right. You see the *ailerons* move on the spot view. You also see the cable crossing the Cub's cabin roof move. This is the way it appears in the real Cub. That cable runs out to each wing and connects to each aileron. Another cable runs back from each aileron, down the wing strut, and into the floor where it connects to the stick.

The key aspect to note on the ailerons is that when you move the stick right, the left aileron goes down, and the right one goes up. Again, this boils down to angle of attack. When the aileron deflects downward, it increases that wing's angle of attack. To understand why, think of the side view of the wing. Now connect the leading edge of the wing with an imaginary line to the trailing edge of the aileron. With the aileron deflected down, that line makes a steeper angle to the oncoming wind than when the aileron is neutral. More angle of attack means more lift. More lift means that the wing rises, as shown in Figure 2-5.

Since the ailerons move in opposite directions, the aileron on the wing toward the inside of the turn will deflect upward. This effectively reduces the angle of attack on this wing, and it sinks.

If you're wondering what stops one wing from rising and one wing from sinking when the plane reaches the correct bank angle, the answer is the pilot. When the plane reaches the bank angle you want, you need to bring the controls back to a neutral position. The plane stays banked and continues to turn. (Actually, for very shallow angles of bank, the plane tends to straighten itself without any help from you. For very steep angles of bank, the airplane tends to continue to roll unless you put in some opposite stick to stop it. Ignore that for the moment.)

Figure 2-5: Deflecting an aileron up or down changes the angle of attack on that wing and gives the wing extra lift or lets it sink.

36 PART I
PREFLIGHT

PART II
SPORT PILOT

PART III
PRIVATE PILOT

PART IV
INSTRUMENT RATING

PART V
COMMERCIAL LICENSE

PART VI
IFR AND GLIDING

If you were to continue to hold your joystick or yoke so the aileron stayed deflected on both wings, the plane would continue to roll right through upside down and, if you didn't hit the ground first, back to right side up. This is great for aerobatics, but it's not ideal for your first flight in the Cub.

Now use your rudder pedals to move the airplanes right or left and right. You see the rudder pedals move in the cockpit, as well as the cables attached to them. This is how it works in the real Cub too. The cables run aft and simply pull on the rudder from one side or the other. If banking the wings is what turns the airplane, then your first thought might be that the rudder is redundant. In some modern aircraft, it is virtually unnecessary. But in the Cub it's essential.

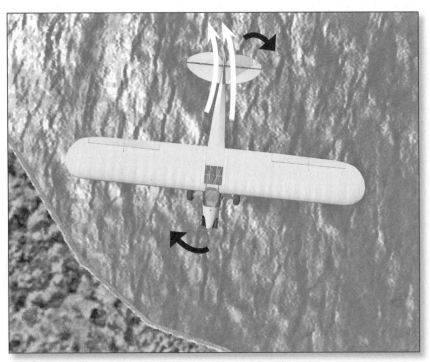

Figure 2-6: The rudder can yaw the nose of the airplane left or right.

Without going into detail, just take it from us that increasing the angle of attack also increases *drag* that slows the wing's motion through the air. So, a left bank tries to turn the airplane to the left, but the right wing simultaneously gets some drag that tries to pull the airplane to the right. Just the right amount of rudder helps move the nose of the airplane smoothly to the left.

The rudder also applies force through angle of attack. Picturing it looking down from the top of the airplane, when you deflect the rudder, airflow follows it, displacing air one way and moving the tail of the airplane the opposite way, as shown in Figure 2-6. This motion of swinging the nose left or right is called *yaw*.

TRIM

Another key skill for expert flying is mastering elevator *trim*. FSX is a great tool for understanding this concept, and you can practice it during your flight in a moment. Right now, though, look down and left in the cockpit view to the crank on the cockpit wall. This controls the trim. Trim sets the *zero point* for your pitch control—that is, if you let go of the joystick or yoke, how high from the horizon does the nose of the airplane point when left to its own devices?

Using the mouse, you can crank the trim in either direction. (If you have a mouse with a scroll wheel, the scroll wheel smoothly cranks the trim.) You can also control the trim with the number pad. Pressing 7 on the number pad cranks the trim wheel forward (nose down), and pressing 1 on the number pad cranks the trim wheel nose back

(nose up). Use the mouse or keyboard now to crank the trim handle so it points forward, as in Figure 2-7. (Note that the keyboard commands work only if Num Lock is *off*.)

What the trim is really doing is controlling the position of the front half of the horizontal part of your tail. This, in turn, controls what angle of attack the wings will maintain as you fly. Since you'll be adjusting this regularly as you fly, we recommend defining two buttons on your joystick for pitch trim, one for up and one for down. Depending on your model of joystick, this might have been set already as a default.

Figure 2-7: The trim handle sets what pitch the airplane maintains when you let go of the joystick or yoke. The black slot at the front of the horizontal part of the tail is really a gap in the fuselage that allows the front of the tail to move up and down. In FSX, the image always shows it in the full-up position. In a real Cub, that would equal an extreme nose-down altitude in flight.

 INSIDE THE GAME

FLYING WITH GREATER REALISM

One of the great features of simulators is that you can let the computer make things easier for you as you learn. FSX can do this through its realism settings. The default realism setting is easy. This is fine to get you going and is a good idea for initially learning most new maneuvers. As you get better with FSX, however, you should crank up the difficultly a bit to something more realistic. This makes the airplane behave in less forgiving ways, especially at low speeds such as during landings.

Don't go overboard, though. The most realistic setting in terms of difficultly is actually the Medium realism setting. It's not that the Hard setting is inaccurate—quite the contrary; it's amazingly precise. The problem is that the lack of peripheral vision and kinesthetic cues (the feeling of your body moving around) gives you less information than with a real airplane.

After you've mastered the Easy setting, putting your realism setting on Medium makes for good habits without too much frustration.

38

| PART I | PART II | PART III | PART IV | PART V | PART VI |
| PREFLIGHT | SPORT PILOT | PRIVATE PILOT | INSTRUMENT RATING | COMMERCIAL LICENSE | ATP AND BEYOND |

FIRST FLIGHT IN THE CUB

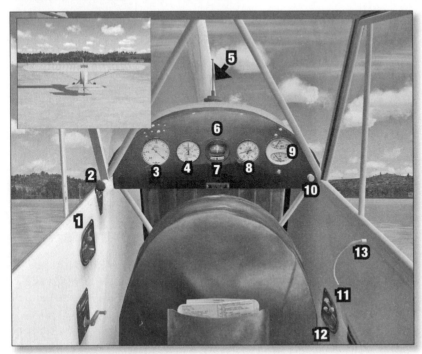

Figure 2-8: Welcome to the Cub cockpit.

We already discussed the trim handle and the stick. Here's what the rest of the Cub cockpit has to offer (the numbers relate to Figure 2-8):

- *Fuel cutoff (1):* Pull this back, and all fuel stops flowing to the engine. You won't be using this control in FSX.

- *The throttle (2):* This is a direct control of your engine power. Push it all the way forward for full power. Pull it all the way back for idle power. Even all the way back, the engine continues to run.

- *Tachometer (3):* The tachometer shows you how fast the engine—and therefore the propeller—is turning. When you open (push forward) the throttle, the tachometer shows an increased value. Note that it shows only the first two digits of the engine speed, so 15 is really 1500 rpm, and note that it moves backward compared to modern tachometers. This is accurate for the Cub.

- *Airspeed indicator (4):* This gauge shows how fast you are moving through the air in miles per hour. It won't show anything until the Cub is moving at about 35 mph.

NOTE!

⬇ MILES PER HOUR VERSUS KNOTS

Early aircraft measured their speed in miles per hour, but modern aircraft use knots, or nautical miles per hour. Weather reporting in aviation also uses knots. We use knots throughout this book except where a particular aircraft— for example, the Cub—uses miles per hour.

- *Fuel gauge (5)*: The metal wire sticking up in front of the windscreen is actually your fuel gauge. Yes, this is accurate to a real Cub. The wire is actually sticking up through the fuel cap on the top of the fuel tank. On the other end of the wire is a cork. The cork floats on top of the gasoline inside the tank. As you burn gas, the cork floats lower and lower, and the wire gets lower and lower. On the real Cub, the wire has some red paint on it. When the red paint gets down to the fuel cap, you're out of gas. By the way, if you're wondering where the fuel tank is, look just underneath the instrument panel, about what the front passenger's knees would be. It's comforting to know that this is only virtual gas in the cockpit with you. More modern airplanes usually put the fuel in the wings partially to reduce the risk of a cabin fire in the event of a crash.

- *Compass (6)*: This is a magnetic compass to help you find your way. As you'll see in Chapter 5, it can be difficult to read accurately while you're flying the airplane.

- *Inclinometer (7)*: Also known as the *ball*, this simple device lets you know whether your turn is *coordinated*. A coordinated turn means you have just the right amount of rudder for your angle of bank. You practice this in flight. The easy way to remember the correction needed is to "step on the ball." If the ball slides to the right side of the inclinometer, apply some pressure on your right rudder pedal. If the ball slides to the left, step on the left pedal—or apply a little less pressure on the right pedal.

- *Altimeter (8)*: When you are more than about 100 feet off the ground, accurately judging your altitude is difficult. This handy device tells you your altitude *above sea level*. That's an important distinction. Right now, the altimeter is showing about 700 feet. That's the altitude of the ground at Post Mills. If you were to climb into the airplane and fly to altitude 1,000 feet above the airport, the altimeter would show 1,700 feet. Altimeters must also be adjusted for the air pressure that particular day, but part of the beauty of the simulator is that you can skip that part for now.

- *Oil temperature and pressure (9)*: These gauges give you some basic information about the health of your engine. Given that the engine in FSX runs flawlessly unless you tell it to fail, these are not a big issue at the moment.

- *Primer (10)*: This is a basic pump that squirts raw fuel into the engine to assist starting. Again, it's not something you have to worry about in FSX.

- *Mixture control (11)*: Early airplane designers figured out quickly that if airplanes climbed high enough, they would get into lower-pressure, thinner air. This meant that the engines would be getting too much fuel for the oxygen available to burn it. The mixture control reduces the amount of fuel entering the engine. This is called *leaning*. Leaning is somewhat accurately depicted in FSX, but since your flights will be a low altitude at first, you won't bother with leaning for a little while. In truth, that's probably what would happen in the real world as well.

- *Carburetor heat (carb heat) (12)*: The purpose of a carburetor is to take the liquid fuel and turn it into a fine vapor that can mix with the incoming air and burn inside the engine. This vaporization cools the fuel substantially (in fact, vaporization is how refrigerators and freezers generate their cold air). This cooling can actually cause ice to form inside the carburetor rendering it useless—and stopping the engine while the plane is still using it for maintaining flight. It's usually not an issue at high power settings; however, at low power when you're descending for the airport or coming in to land, it can be a real problem. Normal procedures for most carbureted airplanes are to turn on the carb heat prior to landing. What this is actually

40

PART I
PREFLIGHT

PART II
SPORT PILOT

PART III
PRIVATE PILOT

PART IV
INSTRUMENT RATING

PART V
COMMERCIAL LICENSE

PART VI
ATP AND BEYOND

doing is sucking air across the exhaust pipes before it enters the engine. That makes it much hotter and drier, and both prevent carb ice from happening as well as melt any ice that has formed. FSX doesn't simulate a substantial drop in engine power when carb heat is turned on, but we'll make a point of using it just to help you build the right habits.

- *Door handle (13)*: Just in case you're wondering, this little wire is actually the handle for the lower door. It flips down and the long window above it flips up and locks to the underside out of the way. Flying with this window and the door open 800 feet above the Earth is one of the true joys of the real Cub.

↓ MORE RESOURCES BUILT IN

Be sure to check out the Learning Center articles on flying the Cub. You'll find lots of great information. We suggest some slightly different procedures than the Learning Center, but you're welcome to try both.

Not depicted in Figure 2-8 but on the upper left of your virtual cockpit is the magneto switch. Virtually all piston aircraft engines have two independent ignition systems. The engine operates on either one but works best when both are used together. The switch lets you turn off both magnetos or either one individually to test the remaining one.

START THE ENGINE

Up until now, you've had the virtual cockpit and the locked spot view open. If you're on a screaming-hot computer, you can keep both open for the actual flights. If not, you'll want to close the second (spot view) window for better performance. On older systems, you'll want to switch to the 2D cockpit view as well for most of your flying to get a smooth simulation. We'll show examples with the 3D cockpit (virtual cockpit or F9 on your keyboard) and a second view throughout most of this book for reference, but you should fly the way that works best for you. Where the visual picture is critical, we'll try to show both the 3D and 2D cockpits, because the picture is quite different.

This scenario starts with the engine stopped, so your first action will be to start the Cub. The real-world procedures for starting a Cub are a bit involved. If you ever fly a real Cub, you'll get really good at them.

To start a real Cub, follow these steps:

1. Conduct a thorough preflight, making sure everything on the airplane is ready to fly, and remove all tiedown ropes except for the one on the tail. Some Cub pilots untie the tail but put wheel chocks in front of both main wheels. You'll see why in a moment.

2. Turn both magnetos off.

3. Set the throttle to idle.

4. Turn the fuel cutoff on.

5. Push the mixture knob to full rich (all the way forward).

6. Use the primer to inject a few squirts of fuel into the engine. The colder it is that day, the more fuel you need. Make sure the primer is locked in the closed position when you're done.

7. Walk around to the front of the airplane, and spin the propeller three or four times to vaporize that fuel inside the engine. Spinning the propeller involves resting your fingertips on one of the prop blades and pulling down and away from the propeller with some vigor. The propeller spins about halfway around and stops again. Some Cub pilots, one of the authors included, prefer to stand behind the propeller on the right side of the airplane just in front of the right wheel. Either way works.

8. Return to the cockpit, and turn the magneto switch to Both, which allows both magnetos to produce the spark that ignites the fuel.

9. Set the throttle open about a quarter of an inch.

10. Return to the front of the airplane, check again to make sure the tail is tied down, check to make sure nobody is nearby, shout "Prop," and spin the propeller again. With any luck, the engine will start.

11. Return to the cockpit, and adjust the throttle to idle.

12. Go untie the tail and remove any wheel chocks.

13. Climb back into the cockpit, and taxi to the runway for takeoff.

Since this procedure is only partially represented in FSX, you'll use the keyboard shortcut to start your virtual airplane. To start an FSX Cub, follow this step:

1. Press Ctrl+E on your keyboard.

As you can see, there's a substantial difference between the two procedures. You're welcome to simulate the full procedure as much as you want when you're working with FSX, but for our money this is a good place to use the power of the simulator and just employ the keyboard shortcut.

After the engine starts, you might need to apply the brakes. If you have rudder pedals with brakes, push forward with your toes to hold the brakes. You can also use the period key on your keyboard or a button defined for the brakes on your joystick. If you have trouble getting your pedals to work, check out Appendix C on troubleshooting.

42

PART I
PREFLIGHT

PART II
SPORT PILOT

PART III
PRIVATE PILOT

PART IV
INSTRUMENT RATING

PART V
COMMERCIAL LICENSE

PART VI
ATP AND BEYOND

Use the throttle control on your joystick or yoke to bring the engine to its idling speed of about 600 rpm, as shown in Figure 2-9. You might need to momentarily move the throttle to full and then back to idle to get accurate control.

Figure 2-9: You might need to momentarily move the throttle on your joystick or yoke to control the throttle in FSX. You should see the throttle in the virtual cockpit moving in tune with your throttle control. You can also use the mouse to move the throttle in the FSX cockpit.

KEEPING IT REAL

DIFFERENTIAL BRAKES

Most modern airplanes allow the pilot to control the braking pressure on the left and right main wheels independently. This helps the pilot steer the airplane by slowing one wheel or the other. In some aircraft, differential breaking is actually the only way to steer at very low speeds. If you have rudder pedals with independent brakes, then you can use differential breaking with FSX.

If you don't, don't worry. You can still use the rudder pedals or rudder control on your joystick to steer and use the button for brakes to stop the airplane when needed.

TAXI

Now that you have the engine running, it's time to move the Cub around on the ground. First, pull the yoke or joystick all the way back. This deflects the elevators up and helps keep the tail of the Cub on the ground. Advance the throttle to about 1500 rpm. This gets the Cub moving. When you're moving, you can reduce the throttle to 1300 rpm. That's enough power to keep the Cub going without going so fast that you lose control.

You need to steer with the rudder. That means using your feet if you have rudder pedals. What you're doing is both turning the rudder, which deflects the airflow on the tail of the airplane and pushes it left or right, and turning the small tailwheel underneath the tail of the airplane, which steers the airplane left or right.

In the 3D cockpit view, you'll have trouble seeing where you're going. This is entirely accurate. In the real Cub you need to make S-turns left and right as you taxi so you can see what's ahead of you (see Figure 2-10). In the FSX Cub, you can use the inset locked spot view to see where you're going or press F10 on your keyboard and then press W to remove the instrument panel that blocks your view.

Figure 2-10: You need to make S-turns—or use an alternate view—to see while you taxi.

The 2D cockpit is also less processor intensive, so if you're getting a poor frame rate while taxiing, the 2D panel cockpit might be the answer. First try closing the inset window. If that doesn't work, switch to the 2D cockpit. If you're getting a poor frame rate while taxiing with the 3D cockpit, you'll get a terrible frame rate while flying, so this is a bit of a test.

When you get to the far end of the runway—the runway is the lighter brown area at Post Mills—steer the Cub to the right side of the runway and then use full left rudder to turn 180° so you're facing in the opposite direction from where you started, lined up as best you can in the center of the runway. After you've turned around, taxi forward for just a bit, and re-center the rudder.

You are now at the east end of the Post Mills airport. Actually, two runways at Post Mills meet at this end. Either one will work, but the more southerly one is a bit longer. If your compass is showing a heading of about 22–220°—then you're lined up with a longer runway.

STUDENT OF THE CRAFT
WHAT'S A TAILWHEEL?

Most antique aircraft have what's known as *conventional landing gear*, otherwise known as *tailwheel airplanes*, which means two main wheels are toward the front of the airplane and one small wheel is underneath the tail. Tailwheel airplanes have the advantage that the propeller is farther away from the ground when the plane is taxing, giving them better clearance on unpaved runways or fields that aren't technically runways at all.

Continued

44

PART I PREFLIGHT

PART II SPORT PILOT

PART III PRIVATE PILOT

PART IV INSTRUMENT RATING

PART V COMMERCIAL LICENSE

PART VI ATP AND BEYOND

They have the disadvantage that they can be difficult to taxi because the center of gravity is behind those main wheels and because the plane has a tendency to try to turn around and taxi tail first if the tail gets too far to the left or the right of the general direction the airplane is moving.

If you want to get a feel for what taxiing a real tailwheel airplane feels like, just go to your local grocery store, throw a couple five-gallon water containers into a shopping cart, and try to push it backward. You'll see that as long as the rear wheels are generally behind the front wheels, it's easy to steer. If you try to make a sharp turn, however, you'll feel how the shopping cart tries to turn around so that the wheels that swivel end up in front of the wheels that don't. That's probably why people usually push shopping carts the right way around the grocery store.

This sudden, uncontrolled reversal of direction is called a *ground loop*. A low-speed ground loop in a real tailwheel airplane results in some embarrassment. A high-speed ground loop results in a call to the insurance company at the least.

Beginning sometime in the late 1940s, most aircraft switched to a tricycle gear configuration with one medium-sized wheel in front of the two main wheels. These planes are much easier to taxi—but they don't look as cool.

TAKEOFF

You can take off in a tailwheel airplane like the Cub in two ways. One is to advance the throttle and just wait. The airplane eventually flies off the ground, and if the trim was set correctly before takeoff, it comfortably climbs. At some point in the process between a standstill and lifting off into the air, the tail of the airplane begins to rise to some degree making it easier to see over the nose.

The other way to take off is to actually lift the tail intentionally after enough airflow is over it to create a lifting force. This is the kind of takeoff we recommend, because we like to see where we're going, and S-turns during a high-power takeoff run are not good for your longevity or your insurance premiums.

 KEEPING IT REAL

WANT A CIGAR?

Just like the extensive start-up procedure for the Cub, the real Cub requires you do several tasks before each takeoff. These tasks just make sure that all the systems are properly set. To get maximum realism, you might want to run through them before each takeoff. You can remember the steps through the mnemonic *CIGAR*.

C: Controls free and correct. Move the stick through its full range of motion to make sure all your controls are working. Move the rudder through its full range left and right.

I: Instruments set. The only instrument here in the Cub that you can set is the altimeter. We'll talk more about this in Chapter 13.

G: Gas. Some aircraft have more than one gas tank. In the Cub, you just want to make sure you have some gas at all.

A: Altitude. This is a reminder to make sure the trim is in the proper position for takeoff.

R: Run-up, or engine ready. For the first flight of the day, real-world pilots bring the engine up to partial power and check both ignition systems (magnetos) as well as make sure that the carb heat and any other systems such as electrical or air-driven systems are working properly.

If you want to do a run-up in the Cub, you need to apply the brakes and hold them, advance the throttle to 1700 rpm, and look up and left with your hat switch to see the red magneto switch. Turn the switch to R, then to L, and then back to Both. The engine should continue to run on any of those settings. Now look down to the right, and use your mouse to pull out the black carb heat knob. The engine should continue to run as well. Push the knob back in before takeoff, and reduce the power to idle.

Figure 2-11: Advance to full power, lift the tail, and when you reach 55 mph, gently pull back on the stick to take flight.

Now advance the throttle to full forward. Keep the yoke full back, and use your feet to steer for about three seconds. Now push the yoke forward, and the tail should rise. You'll suddenly be able to see where you're going. When the tail comes up, however, the airplane seems to try to turn to the left. The higher your realism setting, the greater this left turning tendency is. The left turning tendency is the result of gyroscopic procession of the propeller combined with the lifting force of the tail going up. All that matters to you as a pilot is using your rudder to keep your face pointed down toward the end of the runway.

Since the tail is in the air, the rudder is keeping directional control using only the airflow over the tail, but it is quite effective at this point. The proper height to lift the tail is such that the horizon appears about halfway up the windscreen, as shown in Figure 2-11.

46

PART I
PREFLIGHT

PART II
SPORT PILOT

PART III
PRIVATE PILOT

PART IV
INSTRUMENT RATING

PART V
COMMERCIAL LICENSE

PART VI
ATP AND BEYOND

When the airspeed reaches 55 mph, gently pull back on the stick, and the Cub will lift off. Now let go of the stick. We set the trim on the ground to give us a particular angle of attack as we climbed. The Cub should settle in to climb at about 60 mph. Depending on your realism settings, you might need some right rudder throughout the climb.

Congratulations! You're flying.

PRACTICE THE FIRST THREE GAITS AND TRIM

Let's have some fun with trim while you're climbing. Trim sets the neutral point for the stick. You can override this any time you want by pushing the stick forward or backward. Pull back on the stick until you see 50 mph on the airspeed indicator. Now let go. The airplane might oscillate a bit, but it will return to 60 mph eventually. If it's oscillating a lot, you can manually set it to 60 mph with the stick and then let go, and it should stay there. (That's true for real airplanes, too.)

Now push the stick forward, and let the airspeed grow to 80 miles an hour. Now let go. The airplane zooms back upward and oscillates for a bit, but it eventually settles down on 60 mph.

Now reduce the power to 1900 rpm. The Cub should settle down and fly level. You'll know you're flying level when the altimeter hands stop moving. And, since you have not changed the trim, you will be flying level at 60 mph.

Now reduce the power again to 1500 rpm. The Cub will descend. The airspeed in the descent will be—what a surprise—60 mph.

Bring the power back to 1900 rpm so that the Cub is flying level again.

Although trim maintains a certain angle of attack of the wings, from your point of view as a pilot, trim sets the airspeed the airplane will naturally return to when left to its own devices.

Changing the trim setting changes this airspeed. In the real airplane, you would move the stick forward or backward to change the airplane's angle of attack. When you did this, you would feel pressure on your hand from the stick trying to return to the neutral position established by the trim. If you wanted to keep the new angle of attack, you would adjust the trim handle until all the pressure was off your hand. Then you could let go of the stick, and it would stay put.

In FSX you can't feel the pressure on your hand—even if you invested in one of those force feedback joysticks—so this technique is a bit difficult unless you've done it in a real airplane. In some ways, it's actually more illuminating to just adjust the trim directly and see what happens.

Using joystick buttons for trim up, 1 on the numeric pad, or the mouse, adjust the trimmed nose up one click at a time. The airspeed decreases from 60 mph to 55, then to 50, and then to 47ish. Somewhere shy of 45 mph, you will be at maximum nose-up trim. The Cub will be climbing slowly. Just like on the climbout from Post Mills, you will need some right rudder to keep the Cub flying straight ahead. FSX differs from reality here in that the Cub onscreen tends to turn to the left, but the ball in the inclinometer stays centered. On a real Cub, the left turning tendency would be there, and the ball would be deflected to the right.

If you were to adjust the throttle at any point, the Cub would try to maintain 47 mph but climb more steeply (if you opened the throttle) or descend (if you closed the throttle).

Now adjust the trim down until you see 70 mph. The Cub will descend. Open the throttle to get 2100 rpm. The Cub should fly level at this new airspeed.

DON'T CRASH

If at any time during this exercise you think you're going to fly into a hillside, just go to full power, and climb for little bit at your trimmed airspeed.

BY THE BOOK

TURNING TENDENCIES

Real airplanes manufactured in the United States have a tendency to turn their nose left or right—*yaw*—when you don't want them to do so. If you want a full explanation, you can find it in many aviation texts. Here's a quick rundown of two crucial concepts in case your realism settings are set to Medium or Hard:

Lifting the tail: When the tail goes up on the Cub, that is, when you push forward on the stick, the airplane wants to turn to the left and requires the right rudder to continue moving straight ahead. This is because of the gyroscopic effect of the spinning propeller combined with lifting the tail. Once the tail is up, rudder correction is no longer needed, and the rudder is just used to steer.

P- factor and slipstream effect: When the aircraft is climbing, the descending blade of the propeller actually has a higher angle of attack to the wind than the ascending blade. Since the downward turning blade is on the right side of the engine, as seen from the pilot's point of view, the right side of the propeller is applying more force than the left in the climb. The airplane tends to turn to the left and requires the right rudder to climb straight ahead. The spinning propeller also creates a kind of vortex around the fuselage of the airplane. This applies more pressure on the left side of the vertical stabilizer and rudder, which also tends to turn the airplane to the left.

MAKE TURNS

You've now gotten the airplane to fly straight and level, climb, and descend without having to do much at all. That's one of those secrets about flying: the less work you have to do, the better. Making the Cub turn is only slightly more complicated. If you have your realism settings at Easy and the Autorudder box checked (Aircraft > Realism > Flight Controls), then making turns is easy too. Just push the stick left or right, and the airplane banks and turns in that direction.

That level of realism won't help you be a better pilot, though, so make sure your realism settings have the Autorudder box unchecked. You can try this on Easy first, but practice until you can get it smoothly at Medium or even Hard.

When you have to control the rudder, the Cub's true turning tendencies appear. Note some objects on the horizon directly in front of you when you're flying wings level. Now bank the airplane to the left, and note how the nose of the airplane momentarily swings to the right before tracking to the left. When you roll the wings level with the horizon, the nose of the airplane will overshoot your target slightly and then come back to point in the direction you're going. This is exactly what happens in the real Cub.

48

PART I
PREFLIGHT

PART II
SPORT PILOT

PART III
PRIVATE PILOT

PART IV
INSTRUMENT RATING

PART V
COMMERCIAL LICENSE

PART VI
ATP AND BEYOND

Figure 2-12: While the airplane is rolling into or out of a bank, the point on the horizon in front of the nose should appear to stay put, without moving left or right.

To make a coordinated turn, you need to begin your left bank with the stick and almost immediately add left rudder. The objective is to make the point you see on the horizon, in front of the airplane, stand still while the airplane banks (see Figure 2-12). After the bank is established, you can return the stick to the middle position and maintain just a bit of left rudder, and the airplane smoothly turns. When it's time to roll wings level again, move the stick to the right with just a bit of right rudder. Again, the point on the horizon in front of the nose as you begin to roll out of the turn should seem to be pinned in place and not moving left or right on the windscreen. When the wings are level, the stick and rudder will be neutral, and you should be flying directly toward that new point on the horizon.

This takes some practice and is frankly easier to do in a real Cub than in FSX on the Hard realism setting. Nonetheless, coordination is another key piloting skill and a great one to practice here in the simulator. Post Mills has lots of trees and mountains around it, so just pick some points on the horizon, and practice rolling in and out of different turns until you get it just right.

KEEPING IT REAL

COORDINATION EXERCISES

Here's an extra challenge for those who want it. Pick a point on the horizon, and try banking the airplane left and right while keeping that point exactly the same place on the windscreen. The only way to do this is to use opposing bank and rudder. In other words, when you roll right with the right stick, you'll need to oppose it with left rudder to keep the nose from turning. When you roll back to the left—going completely past wings level and into a left bank—you'll need to apply right rudder. This is quite hard to do, but if you can master it, you've mastered coordination in the Cub.

THE TAIL'S BALANCING ACT

What FSX is showing you is one of the basic maxims of aviation:

Pitch + power = performance

This little equation covers the airplane's performance for three out of four gaits of flight, and the logic behind it comes back to angle of attack.

After the airplane is airborne, you must continually displace air downward to remain aloft. This takes a certain amount of energy. That energy has to come from somewhere. Most of the time that somewhere is the engine. When the airplane is in straight and level flight, the engine is releasing just enough energy to overcome the drag of moving the airplane through the air and displacing enough air downward—and creating the resulting lift—to exactly balance the pull of gravity.

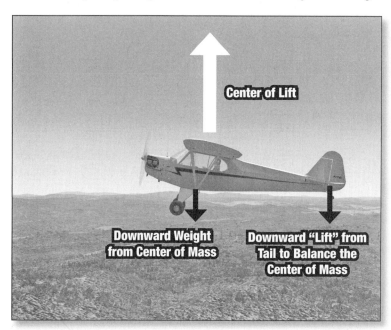

Figure 2-13: The downward force of the tail trying to raise the nose balances the downward force of the center of mass trying to point the nose toward the Earth. These two downward forces combined are balanced by the total lift created by the wings.

You can think of that lift as happening at one point along the wings. We'll call this the *center of lift*, and it's like a string holding the airplane aloft. You can also think about all the airplane's weight as acting from a single point. We'll call this the *center of mass*. In most airplanes, the center of mass sits slightly ahead of the center of lift, which means the airplane has a natural tendency to nose down and point toward the Earth. The tail on the airplane acts as the balance. It also creates a downward force that just perfectly balances the downward force from the center of mass, as shown in Figure 2-13.

When you pull back on the stick, you increase the downward force of the tail and raise the nose. When you ease off on the stick, you decrease the downward force and allow the nose to fall. As you saw during your short flight, when you pull back on the stick and the nose rises, the airplane climbs, but the airspeed decreases. What you've done by pulling back on the stick is change the balance between the energy being used for speed and the energy being used to climb. This is trading airspeed for altitude.

When you pushed forward on the stick, you turned altitude into airspeed. Now energy from the engine was being augmented by energy from gravity pulling you back to Earth. The two combined to allow you to fly faster. If the engine were to stop completely, the aircraft would continue in descending flight, harnessing gravity to maintain airspeed. This is, of course, more commonly referred to as *gliding*.

50

PART I
PREFLIGHT

PART II
SPORT PILOT

PART III
PRIVATE PILOT

PART IV
INSTRUMENT RATING

PART V
COMMERCIAL LICENSE

PART VI
ATP AND BEYOND

The counterintuitive part comes when you add or remove energy from the system using the engine. You might think that by opening the throttle the airplane would simply fly faster. That's not what happens, at least not in the long run. In the first split second after you open the throttle, the airplane accelerates, but as soon as that happens, it starts generating more lift from its wings and begins to rise. At the same time, that downward force of the tail increases slightly, again because of the minutely increased speed, and the nose of the airplane begins to pitch upward.

Because you have set the trim on the tail to try to maintain a specific angle of attack of the wings, the airplane climbs while still trying to maintain the same angle of attack relative to the wind. The result is you climb at the same airspeed you were at a moment ago when you were flying in level flight. Reduce the power, and the aircraft levels off or descends, still at the same airspeed.

Change the trim, and you'll change the balance of how your energy is being spent; 2100 rpm from the engine can be trimmed for level flight at 70 mph, a climb at 60 mph, or descent at 80 mph or more.

Master your combination of power and trim, and you'll have mastered one of the key secrets of flying.

NOTE!

↓ AUTOMATIC TAKEOFF

If you want another demonstration of how an airplane maintains airspeed with trim, position the airplane for takeoff at Post Mills with the trim set as described in your first flight. Now advance the throttle to full, and don't touch any of the controls. The airplane builds up speed until reaching 60 mph and then begins to climb—at 60 mph.

Fly Once Around the Lake

If you put the four fundamentals that you've now learned together, you can take off from the airport, fly around, and return and land. Press Ctrl+; to reset the flight. After some reloading, you'll be back on the ground at Post Mills with the engine stopped. Start the engine again, and taxi to the far end of Post Mills. Turn around, and set the trim for takeoff as described earlier.

When your altimeter shows 1,000 feet, begin a gentle left turn, and continue to climb. Look for a large blue lake on the horizon. (This is Lake Fairlee.) Roll wings level when your nose is pointing toward the middle of that lake. You can wait for the lake to come into your forward view, or you can use your hat switch to look for it out your left window and then slowly bring the view around until the lake is ahead of you. If you're heading to the lake and your compass shows 6, otherwise known as a heading of 060, then you're heading for the right place.

When you reach 2,000 feet on the altimeter, which might happen before your wings are level and you are heading for the lake, reduce the power to 1900 rpm. Since you are trimmed for 60 mph, the Cub should level off and maintain 2,000 feet at 60 mph. Make whatever adjustments to power or trim as necessary if that's not what you see.

Now have some fun, and follow the lakeshore, keeping the water in view just off to your left. You should be able to see it looking straight ahead in the virtual cockpit or with the instrument panel removed in the 2D cockpit.

APPROACH THE AIRPORT

After you round Lake Fairlee's narrow west end, reduce your power to 1500 rpm. Soon, you'll see the Post Mills airport come into view on the horizon. Keep the lake off to your left, and watch the road that borders the lake, as shown in Figure 2-14. The road will fork. Follow the right fork, keeping it off to the left of your airplane.

Figure 2-14: Follow the shoreline of the lake until you're pointed back at the airport. Then take the right fork in the road to set yourself up for landing.

Now comes the tricky part. You need to use your hat switch to keep looking left to keep Post Mills in view and then keep looking straight ahead to see where you're going. When the Post Mills airport is about 45° ahead and to the left, you begin a left turn to line up with the runway (see Figure 2-15). You can then switch to forward view and use it throughout the landing.

Figure 2-15: When the airport is about 45° to the right, begin a left turn to line up with the longer of the two turf runways.

52 | PART I
PREFLIGHT
PART II
PRIVATE PILOT
PART III
PRIVATE PILOT
PART IV
INSTRUMENT RATING
PART V
COMMERCIAL LICENSE
PART VI
AIR AND BEYOND

As you're working your way back to Post Mills, adjust the throttle to lose altitude faster or slower as needed. If you crossed the road in your left turn at exactly 1,300 feet, then a power setting of 1300 rpm should be just about perfect to reach the runway. The view is similar in the virtual cockpit to the 2D cockpit but not quite identical, as shown in Figure 2-16. You are trimmed for 60 mph and shouldn't need to change that.

Figure 2-16: Power to 1300, and watch the arrival end of the runway in either the virtual or 2D cockpit view. It should appear to stay put in the windscreen—moving neither up nor down. Adjust your power to keep it still if need be.

For an extra bit of realism, after you are lined up with Post Mills, look down into the right, and use your mouse to pull the black carb heat knob out. Don't pull the red mixture knob all the way out unless you want to practice gliding into land with a stopped engine!

LAND

Usually, you land an airplane into the wind with the slightest touchdown at the lowest speed possible over the ground. For your first landing in FSX, however, the winds are completely calm, so you don't have to worry. This is another benefit of using a simulator.

Your target now is the near end of the runway; it should appear to remain stationary in the windscreen, not moving higher, which would indicate that you weren't going to make it all the way to the runway, and not slowly disappearing behind the yellow engine cowling, which would indicate you were going to overshoot. If either one of those issues is happening, you can add or remove power to decrease or increase your rate of descent.

When the road just in front of the runway disappears from view, reduce the power to idle, but don't start pulling back on the stick just yet. The airplane continues to descend at 60 mph. When the end of the runway disappears beneath the cowling, begin to pull back on the stick for slowing the airplane to 55 mph, then 50, and then 45. By this point, you are just above the runway in a slightly nose-high attitude. You need to look to the left or right to see the ground at all if you're in the virtual cockpit, but that's similar to the real Cub.

This section of the landing is called the *roundout*. Its purpose is to reduce your airspeed and stop your descent so you're skimming just above the runway. This is a variation on trading airspeed for altitude. In this case, you're giving up airspeed to prevent any more altitude loss.

Pause for just enough time to breathe in and breathe out once. Now pull back gently again on the stick until the yellow cowling is pointing toward the sky just as it was when the Cub was sitting on the ground (Figure 2-17). This section of the landing is called the *flare*. Its purpose is to slow the airplane down to the point where it can no longer fly and let it settle down gently on its wheels.

If your timing is perfect, all three wheels will touch down on the ground at the same time. Don't worry if your timing isn't perfect the first time. The beauty of a simulator is that you can practice all you want.

Figure 2-17: Level off just above the runway, and then continue to pull back gently to touch down. Hold the stick full aft after you're on the ground. In the virtual cockpit, the runway disappears from view, so you need to look to the sides where your peripheral vision is. In 2D view with the panel hidden (W on the keyboard), the transition is much easier.

SEE THE MOVIE

You can load and watch a flight video of this exercise in Ch_02_Around the lake. To do this, load the Post Mills flight—or any flight for that matter—and then choose Options > Flight Video. This shows you all the flight videos from the CD-ROM plus any others you have made or added. Incidentally, this flight features a slightly high and late turn to line up with the runway and other small errors. We decided to leave it as is because it gets the general point across and points out that we're all human.

54

PART I
PREFLIGHT

PART II
SPORT PILOT

PART III
PRIVATE PILOT

PART IV
INSTRUMENT RATING

PART V
COMMERCIAL LICENSE

PART VI
ATP AND BEYOND

ROLLOUT

After all three wheels are on the ground, pull the stick all the way back to help keep the tail down. Now you can apply the brakes and bring the Cub to a stop. If you want to try again, set the trim for takeoff, apply full power, and release the brakes. If you're done for the day, look down to your lower right, and pull the red mixture knob all the way back. Some joysticks or yokes will also have a mixture control you can use. This will give you the satisfaction of watching the wooden propeller stop in front of you and basking in the quiet of your success. For maximum realism, look up and to the left, and set the magneto switch to off.

TAKEOFFS, LANDINGS, AND GO-AROUNDS

Just as you have two ways to take off in the tailwheel airplane, you also have two ways to land. The one we showed you already is called a *three-point landing* because you land on all three wheels at the same time. It's also possible to land on the main two wheels with the tail still in the air. This is called a *wheeled landing*. A wheeled landing usually requires touching down with a bit more speed and sometimes some power.

Figure 2-18: A wheeled landing is when you touch down on the main two wheels first, slow down, and then bring the third wheel under the tail onto the ground. You'll need forward stick right after the main gear touch to keep the tail from swinging down.

If you want to try a wheeled landing at Post Mills, make the same approach, trimmed for 60 mph and at 1300 rpm. Where you would usually reduce the power and begin to lift the nose—the roundout—just bring the nose to what you would usually use for level flight. The Cub begins to slow down but still descends slowly. At this altitude, it flies right onto the runway. When the main wheels touch down, however, you'll need to push forward slightly on the stick to prevent the tail from swinging down and the Cub from lifting off again (see Figure 2-18). Reduce the power to idle the moment the main wheels are on the ground. You can either bring the tail down at this point and hold it there or continue to push forward to hold the tail up for as long as possible. It will eventually drop to the ground no matter what you do as your speed decreases.

Wheeled landings allow you to touch down at a higher speed. This can be handy when trying to deal with strong winds, particularly crosswinds. Since the real world presents at least some level of wind almost every day, let's move on now to handling winds.

⬇ ACCIDENT CHAIN

CARB HEAT AND THE CUB

Vintage airplanes such as the Cub sometimes have interesting locations for their controls. The Cub's carburetor heat control is down low on the right by the mixture control, and it's easy to overlook if you're distracted.

One warm afternoon, one of the authors of this book and a friend took a real Cub into the 2,000-foot grass airfield Wax Orchards (WA69) on Vashon Island in Washington. The wind was blowing strong from the north, and Wax Orchards slopes uphill to the north. This means landing was no problem because it was uphill and into the wind.

Takeoff was another matter. The choice was downhill but downwind or uphill and upwind. The first attempt was made starting at the north end of the field going downhill and downwind. The Cub didn't have nearly enough speed for liftoff by midway down the field, so the attempt was aborted.

Now at the south end an attempt was made to take off uphill and upwind. The Cub lifted off about midfield and started climbing toward the 100-plus-foot-tall Douglas firs at the north end of the runway. The pilot (and author) was sitting in the back with his broad-shouldered friend up front blocking his view of the airspeed indicator and tachometer. The sloping terrain gave the illusion that the Cub was at the right attitude for climb when, in fact, it was too nose high. This cut the climb rate a bit. Although the pilot in back couldn't see the airspeed indicator, he could see the trees...and the Cub was not going to clear them.

The pilot craned his neck around the front-seat passenger and caught a glimpse of the too-low airspeed. With nowhere to turn, there was only one thing to do. Put the nose down, and fly right at the trees to gain airspeed. He did just that, and once he had the critical 55 mph for climbing, he eased the nose up and snuck between two of the taller trees just at 55 mph.

Of course, had he looked at the tachometer or down and to the right, it need not have been so tight. He forgot to turn off the carb heat that had been pulled on during the earlier landing. With it off, he would have had plenty of power and a less "exciting" departure.

Try a takeoff with the airspeed at only 40 mph. You'll see the performance is less than stellar. Now try it with the power set to only 2000 rpm—as would happen with the carb heat full on a summer day.

56

| PART I | PART II | PART III | PART IV | PART V | PART VI |
| PREFLIGHT | SPORT PILOT | PRIVATE PILOT | INSTRUMENT RATING | COMMERCIAL LICENSE | ATP AND BEYOND |

KEY POINTS FOR REAL FLYING AND FSX BUILT-INS

Since our point here is to apply the FSX experience to real-world flying, here's a quick review of the key take-aways for this chapter:

- Understand how to taxi in a tailwheel airplane.

- Practice with use of trim to maintain an airspeed.

- Understand how a given combination of power and pitch results in a specific performance of airspeed and rate of climb (or descent).

- Practice with the four fundamentals of straight and level, climbs, descents, and turns.

- Practice with takeoffs, straight-in approaches to the airport, and landing.

The built-in flight lessons and missions cover much of this material, too, but with some different perspectives and with different techniques. The written background material of the flight lessons can be quite helpful (and, since they're written by Rod Machado, they are fun to read). You'll find the missions on the home screen of FSX. You can find the lessons by clicking the Learning Center of the FSX Home page and then clicking the Lessons tab in the upper-right corner.

Here are the lessons and missions to study after reading this chapter:

- *Lessons*: Student pilot lessons 1–3 and 5–7

- *Missions*: Tutorials 1–5

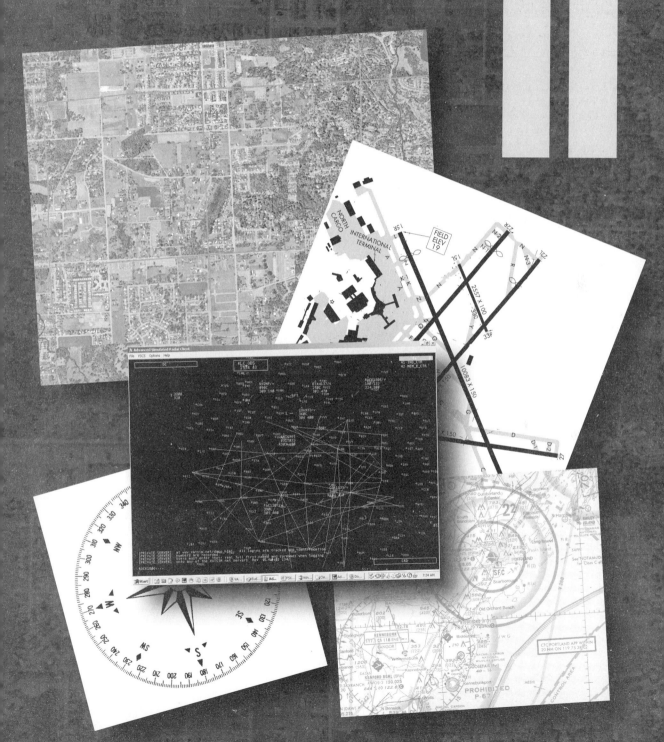

CONTENTS

GROUND REFERENCE MANEUVERS

"ANYONE CAN HOLD THE HELM WHEN THE SEA IS CALM."
—PUBLILIUS SYRUS, FIRST CENTURY B.C.E.

"MIX IGNORANCE WITH ARROGANCE AT LOW ALTITUDE, AND THE RESULTS ARE ALMOST GUARANTEED TO BE SPECTACULAR."
—BRUCE LANDSBERG, AOPA AIR SAFETY FOUNDATION

THE EFFECTS OF WIND

In your training so far, we've set up FSX for you without any wind blowing. But there aren't many real-world days without wind of some kind, and learning to deal with the wind is one of the fundamental skills necessary for being a pilot.

The funny thing is that wind is an issue only when you're trying to go somewhere relative to the ground. If you just want to enjoy the sky, maybe do some aerobatics or a dogfight with another pilot, the wind is irrelevant. But whenever you want to fly from Point A to Point B, or take off and land at a terrestrial-based airport, wind is an issue. Every new pilot goes through learning a series of ground reference maneuvers. These hone your skills at being able to follow a path over the ground in any sort of wind.

Real-world pilots have to wait until strong winds appear in the daily forecast or do their best with whatever winds occur on the day of their flight lesson. FSX lets you set the winds anywhere you want whenever you want, so in this chapter you'll start things blowing and learn how to deal with winds.

A RIVER OF AIR

Figure 3-1: When a boat crosses a river, it has to tack into the current in order to reach the dock straight across in the shortest time and distance.

To help you think about the wind, imagine it as a river of air, flowing along. When you stand on the bottom of a shallow river, you feel the pressure of the water pushing at you, just like you feel a breeze when standing on the ground. But when you're in a boat on the river, you're floating along at the speed of the river, either paddling (or motoring) upstream and making slow progress against the current or cruising downstream and benefiting from the speed of your boat in the water plus the speed of the current.

Now translate that to a plane flying upwind—for example, the wind is coming *from* the south, and you're flying straight into the wind *toward* the south. If the airspeed indicator in your plane says 60 knots and the wind is blowing at 20 knots (that is, the river of air you're in is moving from south to north at 20 knots), you are actually moving only about 40 knots forward *compared to the ground*. But if you turn around and head north, now moving downwind, that 20-knot river of air added to your own 60 knots through the air becomes a total ground speed of about 80 knots.

Things get trickier when the wind comes from the side, but we can simplify it by going back to the river analogy. Let's say you want to cross the river, from shore to shore, in your boat. If you point the boat straight at the dock on the opposite shore and head across, you won't make it to the dock; you'll be swept downstream and land on the other shore quite a ways from the dock. How would you change your navigation so as to get to the dock?

The solution is to point your boat slightly upstream, as shown in Figure 3-1. As you travel, you move both toward the other shore and upriver, but the river pushes you downstream. If you can find the right angle (based on your speed and the speed of the river), you'll arrive right at the dock on the opposite shore.

That's exactly how a real riverboat crosses a river, and it's how airplanes travel in the river of moving air.

STUDENT OF THE CRAFT

A COMPASS PRIMER

If it has been a while since you thought about navigating with a compass, here is a quick refresher.

The compass points north—actually, magnetic north, which is slightly different from the north pole of the Earth. The whole circle is divided into 360°, so north could be called either 0 or 360 (in aviation, it's called 360). South is 180°. East is 90°, and west is 270°. Northeast is 45°, and so on. You learn more about navigation in Chapter 5.

Heading, Course, and Track

This section contains some aviation terminology with which you need to be familiar.

Course is the path along the ground you intend to fly. This could be a straight line from one airport to another; it could be a road, river, or shoreline you intend to follow; or it could be any other planned route.

Heading is the direction the nose of the aircraft is pointing. Usually you measure this direction with a magnetic compass, so technically this is called *magnetic heading*, but almost everyone just says *heading*, and the magnetic part is understood.

Track is the path your plane actually travels over the ground. Think of this like dropping breadcrumbs every few seconds and then looking at the breadcrumbs along the ground. (In fact, many global positioning systems [GPSs] do just that—they indicate a little trail where you've been.)

Let's see how these three terms work together. Say you wanted to follow a highway that goes due west (270°) to a neighboring town. The course you plan is to fly 270°. The heading you choose is 270°. The track the plane actually follows along the ground is 270°, if there isn't any wind.

62

PART I
PREFLIGHT

PART II
SPORT PILOT

PART III
PRIVATE PILOT

PART IV
INSTRUMENT RATING

PART V
COMMERCIAL LICENSE

PART VI
ATP AND BEYOND

Figure 3-2: Flying crabbed to the left, into the wind, means your ground track will follow the road.

Now try it with some wind. With a wind from the south (180°) at about 10 knots and your airspeed about 80 knots, if you ignore the wind and keep flying a heading of 270°—pointed straight down the road—you won't stay above the road; you'll slowly slide off to the north side, because the wind is from your left (from the south), so the river of air you're in is moving to the north. Your desired course is 270°; your heading is still 270°, but your track along the ground is 277°. After flying for 30 minutes, you'll be 5 miles north of the highway! So, to actually stay right above the highway, you need to fly a heading of 263°, as shown in Figure 3-2. (We'll show you how to make these calculations in Chapter 5. For now, notice that even a light wind of 10 knots can really blow you off course.) This is called *crabbing* into the wind, because it makes your airplane look a little bit like a crab moving sideways instead of straight ahead when viewed from above.

KEEPING IT REAL

WIND DIRECTION

The weather reports on the radio or TV usually say something like, "Winds out of the southwest at 15 miles per hour." That direction is not precise enough for aviation. The current (or forecast) weather as reported for pilots would say, "Winds 230 at 13 knots." That means the wind is coming from 230°, roughly southwest. So if you were flying a heading of 090—to the east—would that be mostly a headwind or a tailwind? Well, 230° minus 90° is 140°, so the wind is coming from behind (tailwind) and to your right.

GROUND REFERENCE MANEUVERS WITH WIND

In the following lesson, you'll learn how to fly maneuvers with reference to the ground. For instance, you are asked to fly a rectangular course above some roads laid out in a typical grid pattern. You need to constantly be aware of the wind as you fly the course. When the wind is from your right (a right crosswind), you need to point your heading slightly to the right (crab into the wind) to follow the road. When you turn the corner and the wind is at your tail (you're flying downwind), you can make your heading the same as the course (road) you're following. Then you turn the next corner, and the wind is from your left, so you have to crab your airplane slightly to the left. One more turn, and you're heading into the wind (upwind), so you can again make your heading the same as your course.

Naturally, if the wind is moving diagonally across the grid pattern of the roads, you need to be slightly crabbed on each leg of the rectangular course.

When you're trying to make the track of the plane follow a perfect circle on the ground—as if you were circling over your house to take a picture—the wind becomes your key problem because of its effect on your ground speed. When flying on the downwind side of the circle, your ground speed is faster, and you travel farther. But on the upwind side, your ground speed is slower, so you don't go as far. If you don't correct for this problem, you make a spiral path along the ground, working your way downwind.

To compensate for that, you need to spend more time on the upwind side and less time on the downwind side. How? You do this by banking more steeply on the downwind side (to get around the corner more quickly) and banking more shallowly on the upwind side.

COORDINATED AND UNCOORDINATED FLIGHT

In Chapter 2 you learned about using the ball (inclinometer) in your Cub's panel to help you maintain coordinated flight. Remember to step on the ball when trying to figure out how much to use the rudder during turns.

What we didn't tell you is what happens if you are uncoordinated: it means you're *skidding* or *slipping* through the air, instead of moving straight through it. When you are skidding and slipping, the air is hitting your plane partly on the side, rather than on the front where the plane is more streamlined. This means your plane has much more drag and slows down. Usually, that's a bad thing.

As you'll see later in this chapter, sometimes you actually want more drag for slowing down; therefore, in this lesson, you'll sometimes fly uncoordinated in a slip. For most of the maneuvers, though, you should stay coordinated and keep the ball in the center of the inclinometer. When practicing a maneuver the first few times, you can turn the autorudder on (in the realism settings) so you can concentrate on learning the maneuver with the other controls. But soon you should turn off autorudder so you can practice the way the real Cub flies.

GROUND REFERENCE MANEUVERS FLIGHT

When you load this flight (Chap_03_Wichita_Wind) from the website, www.wiley.com, you should notice that we've moved you away from the Post Mills airport in Vermont where you learned to fly the Cub in Chapter 2.

64

PART I
FREFLIGHT

PART II
SPORT PILOT

PART III
PRIVATE PILOT

PART IV
INSTRUMENT RATING

PART V
COMMERCIAL LICENSE

PART VI
ATP AND BEYOND

We wanted to find a place with a flat landscape and nice rectangular roads, and that's hard to find in the rolling hills of the northeast United States. With a flight simulator, though, you can go anywhere to find the best environment for a particular lesson. So, now you're in Wichita, Kansas, where a lot of roads are at right angles to each other.

The scenario starts at about 700 feet above ground level (2,000 feet mean sea level [MSL] on your altimeter), heading northwest with a wind from the south. Set your throttle for about 2100 rpm to maintain an airspeed of about 70 mph. For the first time through, set your realism to Easy, and activate the autorudder. As you get the knack of adjusting for wind, feel free to increase the challenge by going to Medium realism and the manual rudder. Practicing your coordination always helps, but the point here is learning how bank angles and headings are combined to give you different tracks over the ground.

You need to be able to see the ground in front of you to see how the wind causes you to drift, and the 2D panel blocks the view. Fly this maneuver with the simplified 2D panel showing on the screen. (Press W until you see just the airspeed indicator, compass, and altimeter.) You can do it with the virtual (3D) cockpit turned on if you're really good with switching your views around and you have a fast computer, but it's a bit harder. The other thing that helps is a second view window with a locked spot plane looking down on your Cub (see Figure 3-3). That way, you can really see the effect of the wind, and you can see your position with the roads much more easily.

Figure 3-3: Start of Chap_03_Wichita_Wind flight, 700 feet above a residential area in western Wichita.

BY THE BOOK

THE PRACTICAL TEST STANDARDS

The Sport Pilot Practical Test Standards (see the PDF file on the accompanying website, www.wiley.com) says you must perform the ground reference maneuvers to certain standards when you fly on your checkride with the FAA examiner.

The sport pilot applicant must do the following:

1. Select a suitable reference area and emergency landing area.

2. Plan the maneuver so as to not descend below a minimum altitude of 600 feet above the ground.

3. Apply adequate wind-drift correction during straight and turning flight.

4. Divide attention between the airplane controls and the ground track while maintaining coordinated flight.

5. Maintain altitude at ±100 feet; maintain airspeed at ±10 knots.

RECTANGULAR COURSE

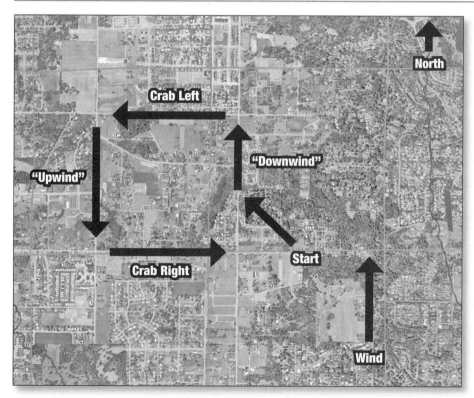

Your first maneuver is to make your ground track follow a rectangular course consisting of roads at right angles to each other (see Figure 3-4).

Figure 3-4: The rectangular course maneuver helps prepare you for flying near airports.

66

PART I
PILE FLIGHT

PART II
SPORT PILOT

PART III
PRIVATE PILOT

PART IV
INSTRUMENT RATING

PART V
COMMERCIAL LICENSE

PART VI
ATP AND BEYOND

THE MANEUVER

As the scenario starts, you're approaching a couple of roads that go off to the right at a 45-degree angle. Pick one, and turn to the right to follow it north, with the wind at your back coming from the south.

Figure 3-5: *This aircraft is on the crosswind leg, with the wind from the left. Note the crab angle needed to maintain the track along the road.*

After a couple of blocks, when a crossroad comes, make a turn to the left (west), and follow it. (You want a major road that goes several blocks.) Of course, here is where the wind comes into play; after you're going west, the wind is coming from your left, so you need to crab to the left to stay above the road, as shown in Figure 3-5. Make sure your wings are level and the rudder is centered; the only part that is different from when you were flying north is that you're not quite flying directly west the way your course (the road) goes.

At the next crossroad, turn left again. Now you're traveling straight upwind, so you won't need to crab at all. But if you look carefully, you can see your ground speed is much slower than when you were heading north.

Continue several times around the rectangle until you can quickly detect the amount of crab needed to stay aligned with the road, and try to roll out right on the road after each turn.

It can be hard to see where the crossroad is if you look only out your front windscreen. You need to switch the view to the left to spot the approaching road and then switch back to center to keep an eye on your instruments. (In real life, it is easier to just look around.) Also use the top-down view to see where the road is—especially if you overshoot it.

When you're comfortable with the left turns, turn around and fly the rectangular pattern with right turns.

NOTE!

⬇ SEE THE MOVIE

Fly the **Chap_03_Rectangular_Course** video to see an example of how this maneuver is flown.

THE CHALLENGES

As you learn the rectangular course maneuver, you want to be careful about the following:

- When flying along the downwind course and getting ready to turn crosswind, your ground speed is higher, so you need to start the turn earlier than the other corners. If you wait too long, your fast ground speed causes you to overshoot past the crosswind road. Also, that turn is more than 90° because you need to roll out in the crab direction, with your heading slightly to the left of the course.

- Conversely, when turning from the upwind leg to the next crosswind leg, you can wait to turn a bit later because your ground speed is slower and because you don't need to turn a full 90°, because of the right crab on that crosswind leg.

- Try to avoid exceeding 30° of bank. The Cub doesn't have an instrument to measure bank, but try to guess based on the angle of the horizon. Excessive bank is dangerous when you're this close to the ground.

- When you're turning, you may slow down a bit; if so, nudge the throttle up a little bit (you probably don't need more than 100 rpm) to maintain the same airspeed and altitude as on the straightaways. Don't forget to bring the power back again when you straighten out.

- When you turn, use your rudder in coordination with your ailerons, just as you learned in Chapter 2. The ball (inclinometer) should be centered at all times.

▼ KEEPING IT REAL

FORMING GOOD HABITS

Possible Emergency Landing Sites

A pilot performs two actions before beginning to practice techniques such as these ground reference maneuvers. First, the pilot *clears the area* to make sure no other airplanes are close; this is usually done by flying one 360-degree turn or two 90-degree turns. Second, the pilot picks an emergency landing spot in case an engine problem occurs or some other reason comes up to get on the ground immediately.

These two actions really aren't necessary when training with FSX.

Continued

68

| PART I | PART II | PART III | PART IV | PART V | PART VI |
| PREFLIGHT | SPORT PILOT | PRIVATE PILOT | INSTRUMENT RATING | COMMERCIAL LICENSE | ATP AND BEYOND |

The Cub's engine is not going to fail unless you intentionally set it to fail in the Aircraft > Failures menu. And, unless you're doing your maneuvers around one of the airports with lots of simulated aircraft traffic, you won't actually have to worry about a midair collision.

But in real life, student pilots do need to develop safe habits that carry them through their flight training and beyond. If you plan to take real-world flight training or if you just want to train as real as it gets, consider clearing the area and finding an emergency landing spot before starting these maneuvers.

TURNS AROUND A POINT

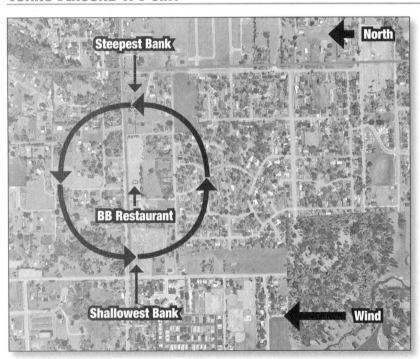

The next maneuver, turns around a point, requires that you find a nice object to circle around (see Figure 3-6). When you restart the Chap_03_Wichita _Wind flight (available on the website, www.wiley.com), look for an easily identifiable intersection of two roads or other obvious landmark. For instance, just as the flight re-starts, there is a store with a yellow and red sign just off to the left of the plane. (It's a BB restaurant, whatever *that* is.) Try to make your ground track a perfect circle (constant radius) around the restaurant—that is, stay the same distance away from it at all times.

The trick, again, is the wind. It's the same wind as before—15 knots from the south—so it's going to keep blowing you north.

Figure 3-6: In the turns-around-a-point maneuver, you're always banked but sometimes more than others.

Start training with the autorudder turned on, and later, when you're comfortable with the maneuver, turn it off.

THE MANEUVER

Approach the restaurant so that it is on your left side, a block or so away. Using your view to the left, roll into a left turn just before it passes right beside you (see Figure 3-7).

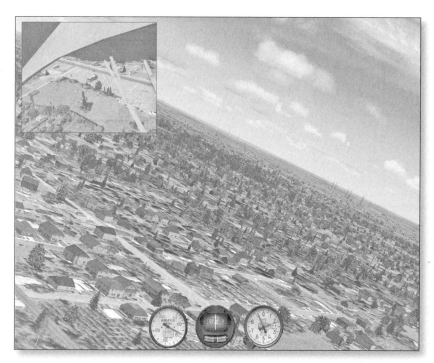

Figure 3-7: The bank angle should be no more than 30° in a turn around a point; in this case, the BB restaurant is your point.

As you turn to the upwind side of the circle, your ground speed decreases, so you need to spend more time on this part of the circle: decrease your bank to slow the turn. At this point, you might be at only 10° or 15° of bank, but that's just fine.

You need to get really good at switching between your forward view (to check your bank angle and make sure your speed and altitude are good) and your side view (to see that you're staying the same distance from the restaurant).

As you come around to the crosswind side of the circle, increase the bank angle slightly, because your ground speed is increasing. Your left wing might not always point right at the restaurant on the ground, but that's OK; the goal is to stay the same distance away from the restaurant.

Continue to the downwind side, where your ground speed is the fastest, so make the bank steeper—but no more than 30°.

As you get to the next crosswind side, your temptation might be to use the same bank as you did on the other crosswind side; however, the wind is blowing you away from the restaurant, so you want a slightly steeper bank here too, remembering to roll back to a more shallow bank as you proceed to the upwind side.

When you get good and comfortable with this turn around a point—or if you just get dizzy—pull away from the restaurant, return, and circle the restaurant to the right.

↓ SEE THE MOVIE

Fly the Chap_03_Turns_Around_A_Point video to see an example of how this maneuver is flown.

THE CHALLENGES

The challenges you deal with when trying to make a turn around a point are almost the same as when flying the rectangular course. These are issues we find all student pilots need to work on, so practice the turns while thinking about the following:

70

PART I	PART II	PART III	PART IV	PART V	PART VI
PREFLIGHT	SPORT PILOT	PRIVATE PILOT	INSTRUMENT RATING	COMMERCIAL LICENSE	ATP AND BEYOND

- It seems like you need to change bank angle continuously during the maneuver, and that's correct! Your ground speed is constantly changing, so stay mentally ahead of the airplane and think about what you need to do on the next part of the circle before you actually get there.

- Avoid exceeding 30° of bank. The steepest bank should come on the downwind side of the circle, so one trick is to *start* on that side and turn 30° of bank; then you know you never have to exceed that anywhere else on the circle.

- Because you're constantly changing your bank, the amount of rudder needed to maintain coordination is constantly changing (if you have the autorudder off). In the real Cub, you can feel that in the seat of your pants, but in FSX all you have is the ball in the control panel. Try to keep it centered at all times.

- End the maneuver when you are back at the point in your circle where you started; roll out, and fly straight ahead.

S-TURNS

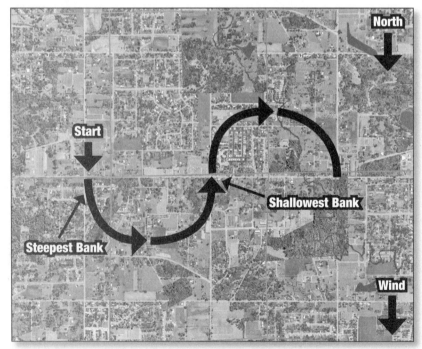

You can think of S-turns as half turns around a point, where the center point shifts after each half turn, as shown in Figure 3-8. In this case, you're going to fly half circles down a road.

Figure 3-8: Practice S-turns along a road to gain skill controlling the Cub.

THE MANEUVER

After restarting the Chap_03_Wichita_Wind flight, add an inset window with a virtual cockpit view out the left side of the plane. Unpause FSX, and get yourself flying north along a road, with the wind behind you from the south. When you get to a long road pointing west, pick a point on the road about a block west—another intersection, a distinctive building, whatever—and start a turn to the left. Your goal is to stay the same distance from that point as you were before you started the turn (a constant-radius circle).

Figure 3-9: Cockpit view of S-turns along a road

As you start the turn, you're heading north—which is downwind—so your ground speed is the highest now. That means your bank should be the highest—30° is good, but no more—when you first roll into the left turn (see Figure 3-9). You slowly decrease your bank angle until you complete the half circle as you cross the road going south.

Roll level as you cross the road. Switch your inset window to show the view out the right side of the plane. Quickly find a new circling point another block west. Start a turn to the right to stay the same distance from this new point. However, you're going upwind, so you won't need much bank at first. Slowly increase the bank angle as needed, checking the view out your right side and then back front to make sure you stay at 2,000 feet.

SEE THE MOVIE

Fly the Chap_03_S-Turns video to see an example of how this maneuver is flown.

THE CHALLENGES

The challenges for S-turns are essentially the same as for turns around a point:

- Your bank angle changes continuously during the maneuver because your ground speed is constantly changing. The only time you hold the wings level is for a few seconds as you cross the road each time.

72

PART I
PREFLIGHT

PART II
SPORT PILOT

PART III
PRIVATE PILOT

PART IV
INSTRUMENT RATING

PART V
COMMERCIAL LICENSE

PART VI
ATP AND BEYOND

- Avoid exceeding 30° of bank. The steepest bank should come on the downwind side of the S-turn, so *start* on that side, and turn 30° of bank; then you know you never have to exceed that anywhere else on the S-turns.

- Because you're constantly changing your bank, the amount of rudder needed to maintain coordination is constantly changing when the autorudder is off. Try to keep it centered at all times.

  ACCIDENT CHAIN

BASE-TO-FINAL SPIN ACCIDENT

It might seem a bit silly to practice something like the rectangular course and S-turns when you probably won't do anything like that after you get your Sport Pilot Certificate.

Or will you?

In Chapter 4, you'll learn about flying the traffic pattern at an airport: you take off, fly a rectangular course, and come back around to land on that same runway. It's the standard way pilots fly around an airport. Read the following real National Transportation Safety Board (NTSB) accident report and see whether you can figure out what went wrong *before* the airplane stalled:

"Witnesses observed the airplane on a tight downwind for landing. The airspeed seemed slower than other airplanes in the traffic pattern. The nose of the airplane was observed to pitch up and down while on the base leg. The airplane overshot the turn to final and started a turn to the left—estimated between 35 ° to 45°. The left wing dropped down 90° as if in a stall, the nose pitched down, and the airplane collided with the terrain.

"The National Transportation Safety Board determines the probable cause(s) of this accident as follows:

"The pilot's failure to maintain airspeed (Vs) while turning on approach from base to final resulting in an inadvertent stall."

In our opinion, the key phrase is, "on a tight downwind for landing." Perhaps there was a crosswind blowing the airplane toward the runway, but the pilot didn't crab properly. Then, when the pilot turned to the base leg and then to final approach, the airplane overshot the final approach. If the airplane was "... slower than other airplanes..." but then pulled a steep turn to get back onto final approach, the wings might have stalled and lost lift, which would have dropped the nose toward the ground. The pilot wouldn't have had time to stop the plane from hitting the ground.

This is why you practice lots of rectangular courses—to get you used to immediately compensating for crosswinds. And this is also why you practice steep turns at a high altitude; if the wings did stall, you would have time (and altitude) to recover the airplane.

STEEP TURNS

So far, we've reminded you to keep safe when near the ground by not exceeding 30° of bank. But the plane—and you—can handle steeper turns, and the time has come to try them. You're going to push the envelope a little and try steep turns—that is, turns of 45°.

THE MANEUVER

Figure 3-10: Start of steep-turns maneuver, heading toward downtown Wichita

As usual, start training this maneuver with the autorudder on, and then practice with it off.

You need to do this at a higher altitude than the other ground reference maneuvers, so after restarting the Chap_03_Wichita_Wind flight, turn west and climb up to 3,500 feet MSL. Eventually, you need to point your plane toward a distinctive but distant landmark. Downtown Wichita, behind you to the east, is good, but it's a bit close. Keep flying west until you get to 3,500 feet, which puts you a good distance away. (You don't need a second, inset view for this maneuver.) Now level off, and turn east toward downtown (see Figure 3-10).

Set power for 2100 rpm, which gives you about 70 mph. (Modern airplanes might have a designated maneuvering speed that is used for maneuvers like this, but a vintage Cub doesn't, so we suggest 70 mph.) Roll to the left until the horizon makes a 45-degree angle. (See Figure 3-11 for a 45-degree angle.) Make sure to coordinate your rudder to keep the ball centered, and pull back slightly on the yoke to prevent the nose from dropping and losing altitude. (Double-check your altimeter every few seconds to stay at 3,500 feet.) Also, this much turning robs some of your speed, so increase the throttle to 2200 rpm to maintain 70 mph.

Your goal is to do a 360-degree turn to the left and roll out back on an easterly heading, pointed toward downtown. But if you wait until you see downtown appear in the left side your windscreen before you start rolling back to level, it'll be too late, because this is a very fast turn (the whole thing takes less than 30 seconds). Instead, you need to look to the left during your turn and spot downtown early and then roll out.

As you roll out, you have to reverse the other controls that you added when you started the turn: push forward on the control stick to keep the nose from going up, and bring the throttle back to 2100 rpm to keep your speed at 70 mph. (And, if the autorudder is off, add rudder as needed to coordinate with the ailerons.)

74

PART I	PART II	PART III	PART IV	PART V	PART VI
PRE-FLIGHT	SPORT PILOT	PRIVATE PILOT	INSTRUMENT RATING	COMMERCIAL LICENSE	AIR AND BEYOND

After maintaining straight and level for just a few seconds to catch your breath, start a 360-degree turn to the right using the same procedure.

And you really might need to catch your breath—or at least you would in a real airplane. At 45° of bank, the g-forces on your body make you feel 20–30 percent heavier than you actually are.

Figure 3-11: Maintain a 45-degree bank like this throughout the maneuver. Start rolling back to level just before you see downtown appear, or you'll turn right past it.

SEE THE MOVIE

Fly the Chap_03_Steep_Turns video to see an example of how this maneuver is flown.

THE CHALLENGES

Common issues student pilots need to work on to perfect steep turns are the following:

- Ensure that you pull back hard enough on the yoke to maintain altitude. To make sure you're keeping the nose from dropping, find a spot straight ahead on the airplane—such as the fuel gauge (that red and white stick on the nose)—and keep it at the same level on the horizon.

- If you accidentally bank more than 45°, the nose also starts to drop as you lose more lift; if you pull back harder on the yoke to raise the nose, you actually start banking *more*. This is the start of a steep spiral that could end in tragedy. Instead, *first* roll back to 45°, and *then* pull the nose up.

- When you roll out of the turn, don't forget to push the yoke forward to get the nose down, or you climb above 3,500 feet.

- Practice leading the roll out so that you always stop right on your landmark (downtown, in this example). If you consistently miss, adjust it and try again.

CROSSWIND TAKEOFFS

Start with the Chap_03_Wichita _Takeoff flight provided on the website at www.wiley.com (see Figure 3-12). This flight has you on the ground at the Maize airport (a few miles north of your rectangular course area), with a 12-knot wind from the west. You want to start this lesson in Easy realism mode but with the autorudder off. As you get better at crosswind takeoffs, feel free to change to Medium realism.

Figure 3-12: The Chap_03_Wichita_Takeoff flight starts on the ground at the Maize airport. Notice the wind sock indicates a good, stiff breeze from the west!

THE MANEUVER

The first challenge is taxiing to the runway. It's not as easy when there's a crosswind—the wind might pick up a wing and tip you over. To counteract that, use the ailerons. The goal is to put the ailerons into a position so that they will hold the wings down if wind blows across them, and you also want to make sure the tail doesn't lift up if a gust comes.

When taxiing with a right headwind (wind coming from the front right of the Cub), turn the yoke to the right, and pull the yoke toward you. The ailerons hold the right wing down in a gust, and the elevator up holds the tail down. If the wind comes from the front left, turn the yoke left, and pull it toward you. If the wind is behind and to your right, you *dive away*—that is, turn the yoke left, and push forward. The ailerons now help hold the right wing down from

76

PART I PREFLIGHT | PART II SPORT PILOT | PART III PRIVATE PILOT | PART IV INSTRUMENT RATING | PART V COMMERCIAL LICENSE | PART VI ATP AND BEYOND

that right quartering tailwind, and the elevator down holds the tail down. And, as you might expect, a left quartering tailwind requires you to dive away by turning the yoke to the right and pushing forward.

Taxi all the way to the south end of the grass runway, turn around, and face north, remembering to change the aileron and elevator positions as you turn. Hold the aileron position even when you're stopped. When you're ready for takeoff, keep holding the left aileron position, push the elevator down to pick up the tail, and apply full throttle for takeoff. Use the rudder to stay on the runway, and slowly decrease aileron input until it's only about ¼ of the full deflection.

When the tail comes up, adjust elevator to keep it in the right spot. When you have takeoff speed (50 mph), quickly pull back on the yoke, and lift off the ground. The slight left aileron control you held in now rolls you to the left; use the rudder to maintain coordination and move quickly into a crabbed climb so that your heading is now slightly to the left (west) of due north. This is just like when you were crabbing around the rectangular course; the only difference is that you're climbing. Climb as usual at 60 mph.

Your goal is to have level wings, the ball in the center (coordinated flight), and a crabbed heading that keeps your ground track on the extended centerline of the runway you just departed. Use the hat switch to check behind you—or check the overhead view—to see whether your ground track goes straightaway from the runway (see the later Figure 3-13). If you drift east, put in a bit more crab correction; if you're west of the centerline, you have too much crab angle, and you need to turn your heading a bit closer to north.

Restart the flight as many times as needed to get the hang of it. You should also take off a few times from the north end, heading south, so that you can practice a crosswind from the right. The principles are the same, but remember to keep your aileron correction to the right this time and crab your heading slightly to the west instead of straight south as you climb away from the airport.

 NOTE! | ⬇ SEE THE MOVIE

Fly the Chap_03_Crosswind Takeoff video to see an example of how this maneuver is flown.

THE CHALLENGES

Most students are pretty successful at crosswind takeoffs after practicing the rectangular course maneuver. But you should remember a few issues:

- Keep at least some aileron input in the yoke as you're accelerating to takeoff speed; otherwise, you start skipping sideways across the runway as the wind blows you just as you lift off.

- As you climb, glance behind at the runway (as best you can in the Cub) to see whether you're maintaining the correct crab angle (see Figure 3-13). Adjust as needed, but stay coordinated.

Figure 3-13: After takeoff, check behind you to make sure your ground track stays aligned with the runway.

FORWARD SLIP

In Chapter 2 you practiced landing after a normal approach. But sometimes you need to make a steeper approach; that is, you need to come down at a steeper angle without just pushing the nose down and speeding up. Maybe some trees are near the end of the runway and you have to pass over them before you can descend to the runway. Or maybe you misjudged the approach and ended up too high. This isn't too bad if you have a long runway—just land farther down—but what if it's a short runway?

If you push the nose down to make a steeper approach, you speed up and actually go farther down the runway than if you stay the same speed.

The solution is the forward slip. You're going to intentionally roll the wings to one side and point the nose with the rudder in the other direction. Yes, this is uncoordinated flight. Usually that is to be avoided, but now you need to do it to perform a forward slip.

78

PART I
PREFLIGHT

PART II
SPORT PILOT

PART III
PRIVATE PILOT

PART IV
INSTRUMENT RATING

PART V
COMMERCIAL LICENSE

PART VI
ATP AND BEYOND

THE MANEUVER

Figure 3-14: Start of the Chap_03_Wichita_Slip flight

Figure 3-15: A normal descent. Notice that the ball is centered, and the plane is tracking in the same direction as the heading, because there is no wind.

Load the Chap_03_Wichita_Slip flight from the website, which starts at 3,500 feet over Wichita without any wind (see Figure 3-14). The realism can be set to anything, but the autorudder needs to be off.

Idle the engine, and descend at 60 mph. Now try the slip: roll the wings to the right—about 30° should do it—and add full left rudder. Hold full rudder, but adjust the bank so that your track along the ground stays lined up with one of the roads below you. Keep the nose down enough to keep your speed at 60 mph. When you get to about 2,500 feet, straighten out, and apply full throttle to climb back up to 3,500 feet. Try it again, but this time roll to the left and hold full right rudder. Practice this a few times, changing the direction you slip each time.

If you keep heading north, you'll soon be near the Maize airport where you practiced crosswind takeoffs. Set up as though you're going to land straight onto the runway heading north, and descend to 2500 feet. When you get close enough that you think it's time to start descending to land (you practiced lots of landings in Chapter 2, right?), wait another 20 seconds, and then chop the throttle to idle and descend at 60 knots. You'll soon realize that you're going to overshoot the runway because of that 20-second delay. Time to slip! Roll right with ailerons, and yaw left with the rudder. Hold full rudder, but adjust the bank angle so that you stay lined up with the runway. (Compare Figure 3-15, a normal descent, to the forward slip shown in Figure 3-16.)

When you get close to the ground—about 1,500 feet on your altimeter—straighten out and hit full throttle to climb back up. Circle around to the south of the airport, and try again a few more times, slipping to both the left and the right. You can land if you want after each slip approach or just go around without touching ground at all.

Figure 3-16: A forward slip descent. The ball is out of the center (uncoordinated flight), and the plane is tracking in a different direction from the heading, because the rudder is fully to the left. Bank (with the ailerons) is used to maintain alignment with the road or runway.

SEE THE MOVIE

Fly the Chap_03_Forward_Slip video to see an example of how this maneuver is flown.

THE CHALLENGES

The following are some of the techniques student pilots need to practice when performing slips:

- Use full rudder to get the steepest descent.

- Adjust your track along the ground with your bank angle to make sure you stay lined up with the runway.

- Don't let your speed get too low—fly a bit faster than usual on the approach. This is because you need some extra lift for safety during a slip.

- As your skills increase, work on making smooth control movements. In the simulated world of FSX, it may not bother you if you jerk the plane around, but in a real Cub, you'll soon grow tired of your self-induced turbulence.

80

| PART I | PART II | PART III | PART IV | PART V | PART VI |
| PREFLIGHT | SPORT PILOT | PRIVATE PILOT | INSTRUMENT RATING | COMMERCIAL LICENSE | ATP AND BEYOND |

SIDESLIP AND CROSSWIND LANDINGS

You've learned how to fly with crosswinds, and you've learned how to land with no crosswinds—time to put them together in crosswind landings!

THE MANEUVER

Figure 3-17: Start of the Chap_03_Wichita_Approach flight

You need a different flight from the website, www.wiley.com, this time: Chap_03_Wichita_Approach (see Figure 3-17). This starts with you heading right for the little grass strip (the Maize airport) where you practiced crosswind takeoffs and forward slips. (Make sure that the autorudder is still off.) And, again, you have a wind from the west at about 8 knots. Set the throttle to 1400 rpm to start a descent.

If you aim your nose straight for the runway as you start descending, you'll notice the wind drifting you to the right (east). Crab to the left to compensate, just like you did when practicing the rectangular course. Keep your wings level, but make your heading slightly to the left of north; however, much is needed for your ground track to stay aligned with the runway. When you're about 50 feet off the ground (1400 MSL), increase power to about 1900 rpm and level off. Fly right above runway in that left crab, adjusting the controls as needed to stay at 1,400 feet with wings level but with your ground track staying over the runway.

⬇ STUDENT OF THE CRAFT
ADVERSE YAW AND THE CROSSWIND

We haven't mentioned it because it's not really simulated in FSX, but aileron control has a secondary function in the crosswind takeoff and landing. The downward-deflected aileron is on the downwind side of the airplane. When the airplane is moving forward, a bit of adverse yaw is working to swing the nose of the airplane away from the wind. This helps counter the tendency of the airplane on the ground to "weather vane" into the wind. On antiques such as the Cub that have a lot of adverse yaw, this effect is important for aircraft control on the ground. In calm winds, you can actually make S-turns using nothing but the adverse yaw of the ailerons and the "wind" of taxiing the airplane.

Figure 3-18: The Cub is in a sideslip, flying just above the runway. Note the track is due north, but the ball is out of center because the wings are banked left and the rudder is turned right.

At the end of the runway, restart the flight back on approach to the airport. As you descend, instead of crabbing to the right, try the approach with a sideslip. A sideslip is different from the forward slip you practiced earlier. In this case, you want the fuselage pointing right down the runway (so that, if you land, your wheels roll straight on), but you want the wings banked slightly to the left to keep you from drifting to the right from the crosswind, as shown in Figure 3-18. This is another time when you won't be coordinated—the ball is out of the center. That's correct, and you shouldn't even look at the ball. The amount of left bank you put the plane into is based only on keeping your plane from drifting to the right in the crosswind, and the amount of rudder you put in is only enough to straighten out your heading and point you down the runway.

FSX doesn't do a great job of showing the Cub doing a proper sideslip. The behavior is accurate if you use the controls correctly—you'll stay properly lined up with the runway—but the visual display will be wrong. (It usually shows the plane with very little bank even if you're putting in quite a bit of aileron control.)

82

PART I	PART II	PART III	PART IV	PART V	PART VI
PREFLIGHT	SPORT PILOT	PRIVATE PILOT	INSTRUMENT RATING	COMMERCIAL LICENSE	ATP AND BEYOND

Again, don't land on the runway yet; increase power and level off just 50 feet above the runway, but stay in that sideslip. Keep adjusting your bank angle and your rudder deflection to stay aligned with the runway. At the end of the runway, reset the flight again.

SIMULATION RATE

If you have a hard time figuring out exactly how much to use the rudders and ailerons during a slipped approach—or any other maneuver—use the power of a flight simulator to slow things down. You can change the simulation rate (Options > Simulation Rate) to half speed so you can practice maneuvers and landings without feeling rushed.

Practice the sideslip many times until you are smooth at adjusting the controls. We teach our own real-world students this way, and we may do five or six passes along the runway without landing before we let the students actually do the crosswind landing.

When you're comfortable, take the sideslip all the way down to a landing. (Crosswind landings really need to be wheeled landings rather than three-point landings—review Chapter 2 if necessary.) As you get close to the ground and level off for landing, keep adjusting the bank (with the ailerons) to avoid sliding sideways off the runway, and keep adjusting the yaw (with the rudder) to point the wheels straight down the runway. In real life, you might even land on the upwind wheel first, and that's good! (FSX doesn't simulate that part.) Hold the right wing up with more and more aileron until it drops down on its own. At that point, maintain full left aileron to taxi, just like you did when taxiing during the crosswind takeoff lesson.

Reset the flight several times to practice your technique. When you're ready, put the simulation rate back to Normal, and practice more landings. If you like, you can fly around to the other side of the airport and land to the south so that the crosswind comes from the right side.

SEE THE MOVIE

Play the Chap_03_Crosswind_Landing video to see an example of how this maneuver is flown.

THE CHALLENGES

Students usually need to work on the following to perfect crosswind landings:

- Constantly adjust the amount of ailerons and rudder you're using to keep the plane lined up properly with the runway.

- Work on keeping the correct final approach speed of 60 mph; it's hard to do when you're making a crosswind landing, especially if there is any turbulence. You need to have more power than normal during the approach, or you land too short; a sideslip landing is still a slip, and the wind is coming at the side of the plane, rather than straight on, so you have more drag, and you descend faster.

- Keep applying control pressure even as you touch down and roll out on the runway. Many students relax the aileron control as they flare because they're afraid to land on one wheel; the problem is they start to drift downwind and then land with too much side force on the wheels, damaging the wheels and the landing gear.

RIDICULOUS WINDS

When you've gotten the hang of taking off, flying, and landing with the winds set up in the predesigned flights, you should modify the winds and make them stronger or from different directions. Or try a different area to fly around, with different landmarks, obstacles, and winds.

↓ INSIDE THE GAME

SPINNING THE WINDS

To customize the winds before you click Fly Now, click the Change button in the current weather section of the FSX home screen. You can change winds during your flight by choosing World > Weather. Both techniques bring you to the same page, where you select User-Defined Weather at the bottom of the window and click Customize. On that page, you select the wind direction on the compass rose and set any wind speed you like.

Alternatively, you can set advanced winds with different speeds, directions, and turbulence at different altitudes with advanced weather. We'll talk about this in Chapter 13, and it's covered in the FSX Learning Center.

MAXIMUM DEMONSTRATED CROSSWIND

Airplanes can land in pretty strong crosswinds, but each plane can handle only so much. Eventually you run out of rudder—that is, when you're landing with a slip, if you have to apply full rudder and you still can't align the aircraft with the runway, the wind exceeds the capabilities of that airplane.

84

| PART I | PART II | PART III | PART IV | PART V | PART VI |
| PREFLIGHT | SPORT PILOT | PRIVATE PILOT | INSTRUMENT RATING | COMMERCIAL LICENSE | ATP AND BEYOND |

The operating handbook of most modern airplanes lists the maximum demonstrated crosswind velocity for that type of plane. (The Cub is too old to have an official number, but you can't land it with more than 20 knots of crosswind unless FSX is in the easiest realism mode, and even then you use a lot of runway and a wheeled landing to do it. The real-life limit is more like 15 knots.) If the amount of crosswind you have to deal with (see "Crosswind Calculation") is more than the maximum demonstrated crosswind, you'd better not take off. And if you're already in the air, don't try to land there; pick a different runway or a different airport entirely. Sure, you might be able to get the plane on the ground, but since the maximum demonstrated crosswind speed was determined by a test pilot, the odds are that you're going to bend some metal.

But because this is a flight simulator and the only thing you'll bend is your ego (or your flight yoke if you get too wild on the controls), see whether you can handle the next scenario.

STUDENT OF THE CRAFT

CROSSWIND CALCULATION

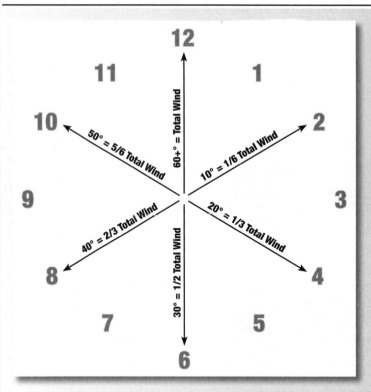

You're getting ready to take off, and you've got a crosswind to contend with. You know the wind is blowing at 20 knots, which exceeds the crosswind capability of your little Cub. But the crosswind isn't a direct crosswind—it's some angle other than 90° to the runway. So, does the actual crosswind exceed the Cub's capabilities?

Here is a quick way to figure it out:

1. Determine the angle difference between your runway and the wind. For instance, if your runway points in the magnetic direction of 60° (roughly northeast) and the wind is from 90° (due east), then the wind is at a 30° angle from your takeoff on the runway.

2. The number of degrees becomes the number of minutes in an hour. In this example, 30° becomes 30 minutes on a clock or your watch; 30 minutes is half an hour.

3. Half an hour means take half the 20 knots total wind to find your actual crosswind—10 knots.

This method works fine for just about any situation. A 20-knot wind 45° off your nose gives about 15 knots of crosswind (45 minutes is ¾ of an hour, and 15 is ¾ of 20). A 10-knot wind at a 20-degree angle is about 7 knots. Ah, but what about a wind 60° or more different from the takeoff direction? Sixty minutes is one full hour, so any wind 60° or more off the nose should be treated as a full crosswind.

If you want to check the accuracy of this wristwatch method, just calculate the sine of various angles. Sin(20) = 0.34. Sin(30) = 0.5. Sin(45) is 0.707, which is just about ¾.

(It isn't a coincidence that the first commercial jetliner Boeing built, the 707, had a 45-degree sweep to its wings!)

WORST CROSSWINDS—KONA, HAWAII

Figure 3-19: Kona, Hawaii, has nasty crosswinds; practice your sideslip, wheeled landings here!

We don't know whether Kona, Hawaii, has the worst crosswinds of anywhere in the world, but it's pretty bad there. The runway goes north-to-south right along the west side of Hawaii. The winds blow either from the east down the mountains or from the west from the ocean, so there's almost always a crosswind and turbulence, and sometimes it's very strong.

The Chap_03_Kona flight from the website puts you in the Cub approaching Kona International Airport on Hawaii, with a wind out of the east at 15 knots gusting to 20 knots (see Figure 3-19). Practice flying along the runway without actually landing—just stay 50 to 100 feet up—with the throttle about

86

| PART I | PART II | PART III | PART IV | PART V | PART VI |
| PREFLIGHT | SPORT PILOT | PRIVATE PILOT | INSTRUMENT RATING | COMMERCIAL LICENSE | ATP AND BEYOND |

1900 rpm. If you can stay on the centerline in a sideslip, with the aircraft pointed straight down the runway—left wing down with ailerons, and right rudder—then try it lower and slower, until you can actually land. The slower you go, the more the crosswind affects you (because it is a higher percentage of your total speed), so it's possible you can do this at 60 knots well above the runway but not at 40 knots when trying to land.

For this reason, a wheeled landing is the usual technique for landing in a crosswind, because you can get the wheels on the ground while still having good airflow over your wings.

We brought you to Kona for the winds, but we didn't tell you that there is actually a control tower here, and technically, you should be talking to them before you get this close and land. That's OK—as far as we know, there isn't a sim-FAA to bust you. But you do need to know how to deal with control towers and complicated airports, so in the next chapter you'll take a look at airport operations.

KEY POINTS FOR REAL FLYING AND FSX BUILT-INS

The following are some key points from this chapter:

- Understand the effects of wind and how to compensate during takeoff, cruise, approach, and landing.

- Practice the use of rudder to maintain coordination or intentionally uncoordinated flight.

- Practice steep turns.

- Practice slips to increase the descent angle without increasing speed.

Here are the lessons and missions to study after reading this chapter:

- *Lessons*: The background information in Private Pilot Lesson 2 may be helpful as a review of steep turns.

- *Missions*: No missions specifically address the maneuvers you practiced in this chapter. A review of tutorials 1–5 could be helpful.

AIRPORT OPERATIONS

"THERE IS NOTHING LIKE AN AIRPORT FOR BRINGING YOU DOWN TO EARTH."

—RICHARD GORDON

88

PART I	PART II	PART III	PART IV	PART V	PART VI
PREFLIGHT	SPORT PILOT	PRIVATE PILOT	INSTRUMENT RATING	COMMERCIAL LICENSE	ATP AND BEYOND

UNCONTROLLED AND CONTROLLED AIRPORT OPERATIONS

During your first lesson in the Cub, you flew around the Post Mills airport in Vermont. Post Mills does not have a control tower, so the FAA calls it an *uncontrolled airport*. However, it is anything but uncontrolled; it is the job of the pilots to keep things from getting out of control. In this chapter, we discuss procedures for finding your way around an airport without a control tower and for talking to other aircraft there. Then you'll fly to an airport that is busy enough to require a control tower, and you'll learn how to talk to the air traffic controllers there.

AIRPORT PROCEDURES

Regardless whether an airport has a control tower, you need to know how to get around safely, both in the air and on the ground.

RUNWAY LAYOUT

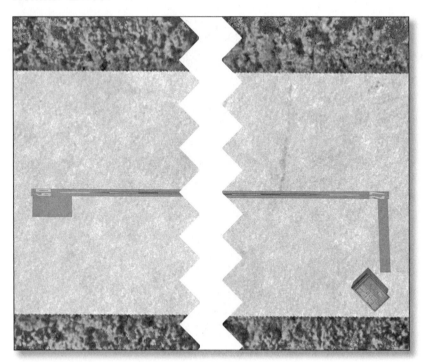

Figure 4-1: The two ends of this runway are numbered 9 and 27, oriented so that you can read them as you approach for landing.

Runways are usually built so that you can take off and land into the prevailing winds. Sometimes, however, local topography requires that a runway be aligned in another direction. You wouldn't want your crosswind-landing skills to go to waste, would you?

Runways are numbered with the magnetic compass direction they are pointing, rounded to the nearest 10°, with the last 0 removed. For instance, if you're about to land on Runway 27, your compass reads about 270°. After landing on Runway 27, if you go all the way to the end of the runway and turn around, you are facing 90° magnetic, and the same piece of pavement (or grass) is called Runway 9 (see Figure 4-1).

AIRPORT INFORMATION

To get information about an airport, choose World > Map from the FSX menu. You will see a map view of the area, including nearby airports and geography. If you click an airport, a Facility Information box pops up with information such as runway lengths, airport elevations, radio frequencies, and so on. Real-world pilots get this information from the Airport/Facility Directory (A/FD).

AIRPORT MARKINGS AND SIGNS

Most airports with only grass runways, like your home base of Post Mills, don't have many airport signs, and even the runway might not have any markings. But larger airports, especially those with paved runways, have signs to help you get around.

Runways are marked with numbers at each end, facing the way you'd see them when landing. Runways also usually have centerline stripes and some other basic markings (see Figure 4-2). Many runway markings are used only by instrument pilots trying to find the runway as they approach the airport in haze and fog.

Figure 4-2: Approaching a runway, you see several markings in addition to the numbers and centerline. The most important one is the threshold, which either is the beginning of the runway or is a white line across the runway with some white chevrons pointing to it; don't land before the threshold even if it looks like good pavement there. For some reason, the airport authorities need you to land farther down the runway, after the white line. The set of vertical zebra stripes is OK to land on, though.

90

PART I	PART II	PART III	PART IV	PART V	PART VI
PREFLIGHT	SPORT PILOT	PRIVATE PILOT	INSTRUMENT RATING	COMMERCIAL LICENSE	ATP AND BEYOND

Figure 4-3: Taxiways are marked with yellow centerlines and yellow signs on the side. In this photo, you're on Taxiway Bravo, because the B symbol is yellow in a black background. Taxiway Charlie is to the left, and Taxiway Bravo turns diagonally to the right here. (Either you or that Cessna will be turning onto Taxiway Charlie, or someone will have to turn around!)

Taxiways have a solid yellow centerline that you follow from the ramp to the runway and back, as shown in Figure 4-3. Instead of numbers, taxiways are identified by letters, or letters and numbers, such as taxiway A, B, B1, TT, and so on. Instead of having the taxiway identification painted on the surface, like runways do, taxiways have signs telling you what taxiway you're on and what taxiway or runway is at the intersection ahead.

Airports can have many other types of signs, such as directions to the terminal or the distance remaining on a runway, but FSX doesn't simulate those.

WIND INDICATORS

The windsock is a classic symbol of an airport, and FSX has at least one at every airport (see Figure 4-4). And it works, too, showing you the direction and speed of the wind. The direction is pretty intuitive: the sock blows downwind. To determine the wind speed, you need to know how the windsock is calibrated. The windsock won't show any wind speed faster than 15 knots, but then again, you probably don't want to take a small plane out in such winds until you're a really skilled pilot!

As mentioned, you usually want to take off into the wind, so when you're ready to pick your departure runway, check the windsock, and pick the runway that puts you heading as close as possible straight into the wind.

And when you're arriving at an airport and you don't know which direction the wind is coming from or how strong it is, fly over the airport and look for the windsock. You want to land into the wind so that your ground speed is as slow as possible, saving wear and tear on the tires and reducing the runway length needed to stop.

Figure 4-4: The windsock is calibrated to show airspeeds from 0 to 15 knots.

FSX WIND CHEAT

Flight Simulator provides a way to check the wind speed and direction without looking for the windsock: press Shift+Z, and you'll see a line of text with your latitude/longitude, altitude, magnetic heading, and the wind.

LIGHTS

Airports that can be used at night are equipped with lights of various kinds. You're probably familiar with the airport beacon, with alternating white and green lights, that can be seen from many miles away. A night-use airport will at least have white lights down the sides of the runway and might also have blue taxiway lights or reflectors. Some airports put two flashing white strobe lights on each end of the runway to help you spot it. Big airports might have

92

| PART I | PART II | PART III | PART IV | PART V | PART VI |
| PRE FLIGHT | SPORT PILOT | PRIVATE PILOT | INSTRUMENT RATING | COMMERCIAL LICENSE | ATP AND BEYOND |

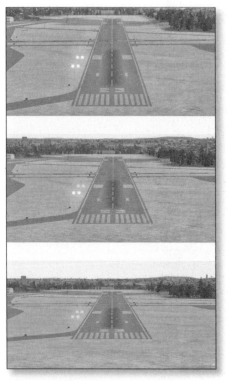

Figure 4-5: The VASI. Red over white, you're all right (approaching the runway on the proper descent path). White over white, you're out of sight (too high). Red over red, you're dead (too low).

white runway centerline lights, green taxiway centerline lights, extra lights off the near end of the runway (to help instrument pilots find the runway in dark, foggy conditions), and even a *rabbit*—a string of sequential strobe lights pointing the way to the runway.

One useful set of lights many airports have is the visual approach slope indicator (VASI), as shown in Figure 4-5. This is used for both day and night operations to help you get the correct angle of descent to the runway. Especially at night, it can be difficult to judge your final approach descent: too steep, and you'll come down too fast; too shallow, and you might hit an unseen tower or hill between you and the runway. When the VASI indicates that you're on the appropriate path—two red lights and two white lights, you can be assured that you won't hit anything on the ground.

TRAFFIC PATTERN

When both taking off and landing at an airport, a pilot usually flies in a traffic pattern, as shown in Figure 4-6. This is a rectangular course (just like in Chapter 3) with several legs: upwind (the leg straight ahead after takeoff), crosswind, downwind, base, and final. Usually the downwind leg is flown at 1,000 feet above the airport elevation, about ¼ to ½ mile from the runway. Faster planes might use a higher pattern altitude and larger pattern. Closer than ¼ mile, and you might not be able to turn the corners properly; farther than ½ mile, and you might not make it to the runway if your engine stops for some reason.

Your goal when flying in the traffic pattern is to make your ground track follow the exact rectangle around the pattern, even if the wind tries to blow you toward or away from the runway: you might need to crab your heading one way or the other, on any of the legs, to fly a proper pattern.

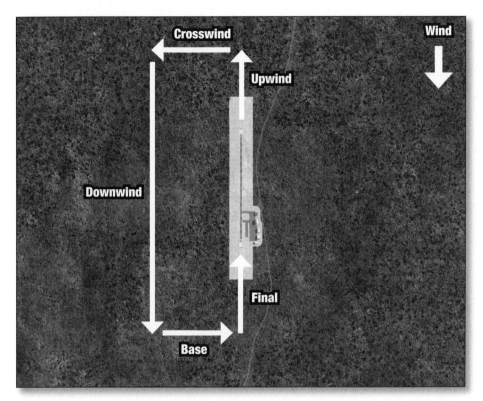

Figure 4-6: The left-hand traffic pattern has all turns to the left, which is helpful when you're sitting on the left side of the plane. Because you're in the middle in the Cub, it doesn't really matter which way the pattern goes!

The standard traffic pattern is flown with left turns; a right-hand traffic pattern is used for runways where geography or other runways make left traffic unsafe. You need to be skilled at flying each.

When you want to practice landing and taking off, you can just *stay in the pattern* and do multiple takeoffs and landings.

DEPARTING AN AIRPORT

When you leave an uncontrolled airport, fly straight out on the upwind leg until you're a half mile or more from the airport before you turn on to your course so that you don't cause a conflict with any other traffic in the traffic pattern.

At a controlled airport, you tell the controller which direction you're going, and then the controller tells you the specific procedure to depart the pattern.

ARRIVING AT AN AIRPORT

When you arrive at an uncontrolled airport, you should smoothly merge into the traffic pattern with enough spacing before and after other airplanes so that you won't cause any conflicts. It is recommended that you enter the traffic pattern on a 45-degree angle to the downwind, usually just called *the 45*, so that you can see other aircraft in the pattern (see Figure 4-7). Of course, all the airplanes will ideally be at the same pattern altitude, making it easier to spot them.

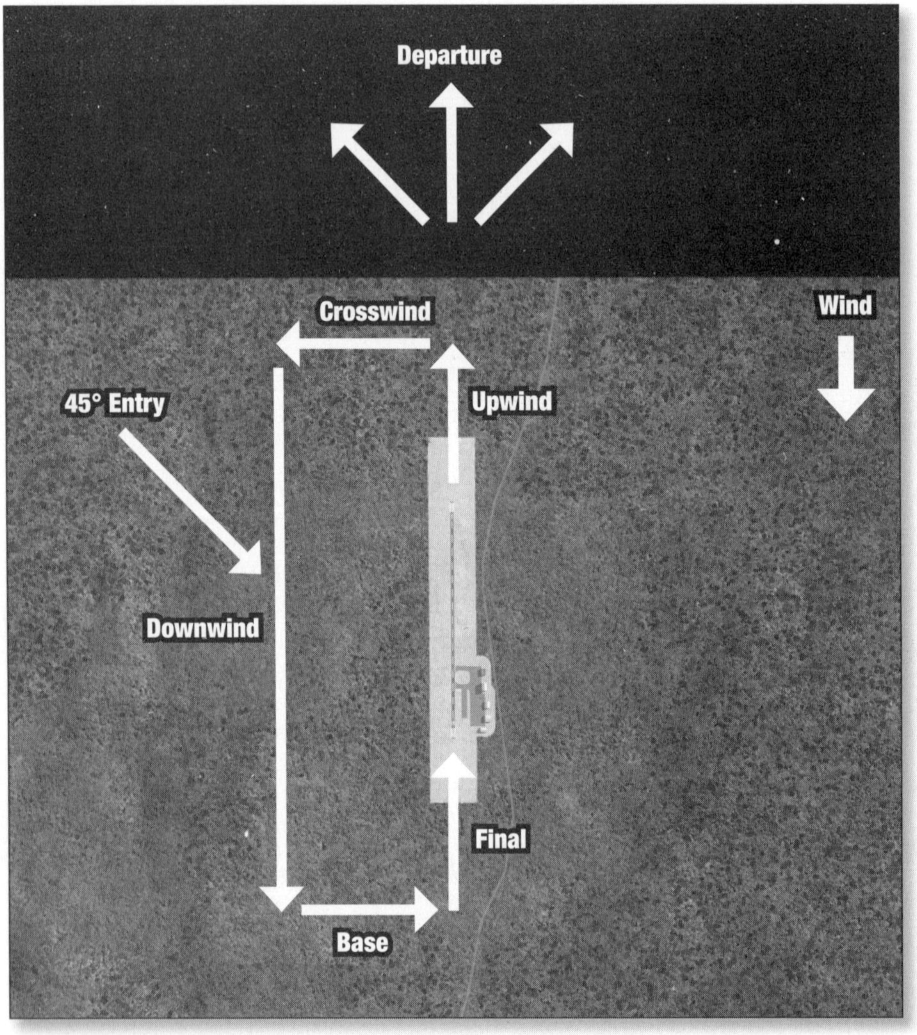

94

PART I
PREFLIGHT

PART II
SPORT PILOT

PART III
PRIVATE PILOT

PART IV
INSTRUMENT RATING

PART V
COMMERCIAL LICENSE

PART VI
ATP AND BEYOND

Figure 4-7: A 45-degree entry and departure from the traffic pattern

If you arrive at an uncontrolled airport from the opposite side of the runway than the traffic pattern, it is safer to overfly the airport 500 to 1,000 feet above the traffic pattern and circle back to enter downwind on the 45-degree entry. It's also safer to do this if you're approaching the airport in such a way that you could just descend straight to the runway without making any traffic pattern turns at all, although legally you make this straight-in approach as long as you safely fit into the other traffic in the pattern.

At a controlled airport, after you call the control tower on the radio announcing your arrival (see "Flight from Post Mills to Lebanon Municipal" later in this chapter), the controller tells you how to enter the pattern; for instance, "Enter left traffic for Runway 12" means you're allowed to maneuver as needed to get into the left-hand traffic pattern for Runway 12. Just follow the controller's instructions.

Depending on the direction from which you arrive, on the winds, and on the configuration of the runways, the tower controller might not have you fly the entire traffic pattern from downwind to base to final. Instead, the controller might tell you to enter the base leg directly from your position; or even, if the landing runway is straight ahead of you, the controller might tell you to proceed straight to the runway. The controller might also have you make a right-hand traffic pattern when the standard pattern for that runway is left traffic (or vice versa); that is the controller's prerogative, and you can assume there's a good reason for doing it.

We discuss more specific information about instructions from air traffic controllers in the next section.

RADIO COMMUNICATIONS

Communicating on the radio can be challenging (well, in the real world it is), but one way to start getting comfortable is to learn the difference between what you say to other aircraft and what you say to a control tower.

UNCONTROLLED AIRPORT

At an uncontrolled field, you're not required to use or even have a radio. In fact, hundreds of deaf pilots legally fly. If you don't have a radio, you need to be extra careful and look for other traffic.

Figure 4-8: The different options in the ATC menu automatically change depending on whether you're in the air or on the ground, whether you're near a runway, and so on. Notice that a plane on the same frequency as you has made an announcement to KDDH (Bennington) Traffic, but you're about to tell traffic at 2B9 (Post Mills) that you're on final approach.

If you do have a radio, you are encouraged to report your position to other airplanes on the common traffic advisory frequency (CTAF). This frequency is published on your charts and can be found in FSX in the map information for the airport. (You can also select the frequency using the FSX ATC menu, which is discussed later in this chapter.) A limited number of frequencies are available for CTAFs, so more than one airport in your area will have the same frequency. FSX simulates this, too. Don't be surprised to hear other simulated pilots on the radio calling out their positions, and they might be at completely different airports, as shown in Figure 4-8. Because of this, pilots say the name of the airport they're at both at the beginning and end of their transmissions.

ALL TRAFFIC, PLEASE ADVISE

CTAFs are used only in the United States, Canada, and Australia. Other countries have different radio procedures when flying near an uncontrolled field.

96

| PART I | PART II | PART III | PART IV | PART V | PART VI |
| PREFLIGHT | SPORT PILOT | PRIVATE PILOT | INSTRUMENT RATING | COMMERCIAL LICENSE | ATP AND BEYOND |

When you depart, you announce to other pilots that you're taxiing to a particular runway, and then you call again when you're ready to take off. You can announce your position as you move around the traffic pattern and then again when you've cleared the runway after landing so other pilots know they can land or take off safely with you out of the way. If you leave the airport completely, announce which direction you're going so that any pilots coming in from that direction will know where to look.

  ACCIDENT CHAIN

COMMUNICATION ERROR ACCIDENT

Want to see why it's so important to correctly use your radio *and* keep a sharp watch outside looking for other airplanes? Take a look at this accident that happened in late 2006.

A Beech P35 and a Beech K35 collided during landing at an uncontrolled airport. No pilots or passengers were injured. Visual meteorological conditions prevailed at the time of the accident.

The first pilot said he was approaching the airport from the north. At a reporting location about 6 miles east of the airport, he reported on the airport's CTAF, 123.00 MHz, his position, his altitude, and his intention to land. The pilot did not receive any transmissions from other aircraft in the area at the time of his approach and landing. The pilot completed his prelanding checks approximately a half mile from the runway threshold and did not note any other aircraft or objects on the runway.

Approximately 10 feet above the runway, the pilot began to initiate his landing flare when he heard a "clunk" sound. The airplane began what the pilot thought was his landing roll; however, his airplane was still 6 to 7 feet above the runway. The pilot then noticed his airplane begin to turn to the right, and he attempted to correct to the left. Subsequently, the pilot observed another airplane underneath his airplane. Both airplanes turned to the right and came to rest on the runway.

The second pilot said he was also approaching the airport from the north. During the approach, he reported his position, altitude, and intentions on frequency 128.00 MHz. The pilot landed the airplane on the runway, and another airplane landed on top of his airplane.

So, what could they have done differently? First, the second pilot was on the wrong frequency, so neither pilot heard the other's transmissions. But that would have been no different than what would happen if one hadn't had a radio; there was no control tower, so radios were not required. Second, and more important, most midair collisions happen near airports because that's where airplanes tend to come close together. Don't assume that just because you don't hear another plane on the radio, there isn't another one near the airport. Therefore, you need to be done navigating and even communicating anything extra when you get close to the airport; you need to be looking everywhere, trying to find that one airplane that is going to get too close to you. Most of the time, at a quiet airport, there won't even be another plane. But then one time...

Conversely, when arriving, you announce your direction and distance from the airport when you're about 5 miles away and announce that you intend to land there (or pass over if you're just flying by that airport on your way somewhere else). Again, you announce your position in the traffic pattern, finishing at the point you leave the runway.

WHAT'S IN A NAME?

The ATC voice in FSX pronounces the phonetic letters of airports when it makes radio calls, so Post Mills traffic would be called "Two Bravo Niner traffic." In the real world, a pilot would say "Post Mills traffic."

CONTROLLED AIRPORT

When you want to fly out of or into an airport with a control tower, you have to establish communication with the air traffic controllers there. Usually that means a radio call—before you start taxiing to the runway for departure or before you get within about 5 nautical miles of the airport when arriving.

When you have the engine running and you're ready to taxi to the runway, you first call the ground controller on a specific frequency. This controller's job is to safely move aircraft around the airport everywhere except on the active runways. After you tell the ground controller your intentions (such as which direction you'll be going after takeoff), the controller gives you taxi directions such as, "Taxi to Runway 36 via Taxiway Bravo." You need to repeat those instructions back to the ground controller to confirm you heard them correctly. Using FSX's ATC menu makes this easy, but you might consider getting into the habit of writing down such taxi instructions and saying them out loud, if you ever want to actually use an airplane's radio.

After you taxi to the active runway, don't get on it yet. Perform your pretakeoff procedures (if you're into total realism), and then switch to the tower controller. Advise that you're ready for takeoff, and when the runway is clear, the tower controller clears you for takeoff. If the runway isn't clear when you first call, the controller says, "Hold short of the runway." That means you shouldn't proceed onto the runway but instead wait on one of the taxiways next to it (see Figure 4-9). After takeoff, the tower controller tells you when to proceed on course to your requested direction.

Figure 4-9: Until you have permission from the tower controller, do not cross the hold-short lines onto the runway.

98

PART I	PART II	PART III	PART IV	PART V	PART VI
PREFLIGHT	SPORT PILOT	PRIVATE PILOT	INSTRUMENT RATING	COMMERCIAL LICENSE	ATP AND BEYOND

When arriving at an airport with a control tower, the process is reversed. You need to call the tower controller before you're within 5 miles of the airport, because you can't enter that area without establishing communication with the tower. Tell the tower controller where you are and what your intentions are (usually you want to land). The controller gives you instructions for entering the traffic pattern. When you're established on the downwind leg, proceed just as you would at an uncontrolled airport, except you don't need to tell the controller or other pilots where you are. The controller is watching you, and when the runway is clear, the controller gives you clearance to land.

It is possible that an air traffic controller gives you an instruction that doesn't make sense or isn't safe. (This isn't likely in FSX, but now is a good time to start thinking about it.) If so, it is your job to ask the controller to repeat or clarify the instructions. "Tower, please confirm you want Cessna Three Four Zulu to land in *front* of that 747?" Sometimes controllers make mistakes, and the simple act of asking them to repeat the information makes them think carefully about what they said and possibly correct it. Other times you just won't be aware of all the information the controller is aware of, and they'll confirm the instruction: "Cessna Three Four Zulu, affirmative, clear to land Runway One Three. You are number one to land. Traffic is a 747 on 7-mile final; you will be off the runway before he lands."

Other Aircraft

As big as the sky is, you're not the only one flying, and that means you have to deal with other aircraft, especially when flying at and near airports. This means you have to obey some rules, and you also have to consider some unwritten rules of aviation etiquette.

Right of Way

When two aircraft are approaching the runway at the same time to land, who has the right of way? What about when you see another aircraft flying at the same altitude and on a collision course—who has to give way?

In FSX, you don't have a lot of traffic to worry about, especially at quiet airports. And at an airport with a control tower, the air traffic controller will tell you who lands first. But at an uncontrolled airport and when flying away from airports, real-world pilots must obey a few rules:

- When two aircraft are approaching for a landing, the lower one gets to land first (although a pilot should not dive lower and cut off another pilot just to take advantage of this rule).

- Aircraft landing have the right of way over aircraft waiting to take off.

- When two aircraft are converging, the one on the right has the right of way, and the other plane should give way and go behind (just like a car at a four-way intersection). Of course, if you have the right of way but you don't think the other pilot has spotted you, be prepared to evade!

- When approaching a slower aircraft from behind, pass on the right (*unlike* passing in a car).

- When two different types of aircraft are involved (such as a plane vs. a balloon), the more maneuverable aircraft should give way to the less maneuverable aircraft.

ETIQUETTE

The freedom to fly means that, even more than in a car, pilots need to remember the Golden Rule: do unto others as you would have them do unto you. With fast, lightweight flying machines, mistakes can be costly, and you can't really play chicken in airplanes. That means you need to follow some rules of etiquette to increase safety and maintain civility, both in how you fly and in what you say on the radio. Most of these rules have no real application to FSX with its computer-controlled simulated air traffic, but if you join an online multiplayer system or you start real-world flying, you'll want to think about how to be a civil pilot.

As you approach an uncontrolled airport, don't try to squeeze in between other airplanes in the traffic pattern or make a diving beeline for the runway and cut off other planes already in the pattern. Fit in with plenty of room in front of you, and announce that you're "Number 2 to land behind the Cessna," or whatever the order in the pattern is. If you are too close to the preceding aircraft, that aircraft won't have time to pull off the runway before you land.

When you land, you should try to get off the runway as soon as possible. Unless you're at a really quiet airport like Post Mills, it is likely another airplane is waiting to take off or land on that runway.

If you're not sure where another aircraft is and you're concerned it is nearby, don't just ignore it and hope for the best. At an uncontrolled airport, it is perfectly acceptable to ask another aircraft to tell you its position, especially if you include your position and some comment like, "Are you on final approach too?" with a bit of concern in your voice. At a controlled airport, proper procedure is not to talk to other pilots directly but instead ask the tower controller, "Did I hear there is another aircraft on final approach too?"

On the radio, whether at an uncontrolled airport or a controlled airport, brevity is next to godliness. Say what you need to say and then stop transmitting. The FSX ATC simulator is pretty realistic; listen to what it has you saying and how it has other pilots and controllers talking, and you'll get a good sense of how to keep it short and sweet for real-world radio communication.

AIRPORT WEATHER AND NOTICES

With a flight simulator, every day can be "clear above, visibility unlimited" if you want it to be. Or you can set the weather to some horribly, windy, rainy day and test your skills. If you don't program the weather yourself in FSX, you can have the software create the weather for you—or you can download real-world weather. No matter how you do it, you will want to know specific information such as the winds, visibility, cloud heights, and more, at the airports from which you're flying.

In the real world, you'd use several different weather reporting systems to get the current weather at airports, and FSX simulates those well.

AWOS AND ASOS

Some uncontrolled airports have an automated weather observation system (AWOS) or automated surface observation system (ASOS). These are computer-controlled weather stations that can monitor, record, and broadcast (on the radio) the latest weather conditions at that airport.

100

PART I
PREFLIGHT

PART II
SPORT PILOT

PART III
PRIVATE PILOT

PART IV
INSTRUMENT RATING

PART V
COMMERCIAL LICENSE

PART VI
ATP AND BEYOND

To hear the weather, you tune in your aircraft radio to the appropriate frequency and listen. (This is a different frequency than the CTAF you use to talk to other airplanes.) The computer transmits a continuous broadcast telling you the winds, visibility, cloud heights, temperature and dew point, and barometric pressure (called the *altimeter setting*). The computer updates the weather information every minute or so, which means it is very current.

STUDENT OF THE CRAFT

ALTIMETER SETTING

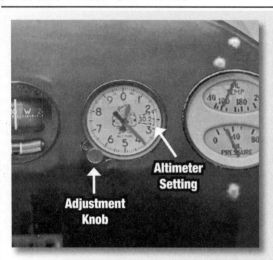

Adjustment Knob

Altimeter Setting

You're probably familiar with the idea of barometric pressure. Weather forecasters sometimes will tell you "The barometer is falling," which sometimes means worse weather, and vice versa when the barometer is rising.

Now consider that the altimeter in your aircraft uses the pressure of the air to indicate your height above mean sea level (MSL). As you go higher, the atmospheric pressure decreases, and the altimeter shows you at a higher altitude. But if the local pressure is dropping because of a storm—your airplane's altimeter will read higher even if the plane is still sitting on the ground!

The solution is that you can set the altimeter for whatever the local pressure is; actually, you set it to the local altimeter setting. After you listen to the airport's weather broadcast and hear the altimeter setting (for example, 30.22), you adjust the altimeter so the little window says 30.22. For quick adjustment, hover your mouse pointer over the dial to the lower left of the altimeter, and then use the scroll wheel on your mouse to adjust the altimeter setting. (If the airport has no weather broadcast, you can just set the altimeter's altitude needles to the airport elevation, and you'll be close enough.)

Here's a Flight Simulator cheat: press B on your keyboard to instantly set your altimeter to the local altimeter setting.

Real-world AWOS/ASOS systems use a voice synthesizer that sounds a lot like the ATC voice system in FSX and is usually quite understandable in the air, as long as you're within 10 or 15 miles from the airport. FSX simulates AWOS/ASOS, and the ATC menu offers you the option of listening to that frequency if the airport has an automated weather system. You also see the text of the weather report across the top of your screen—which is something that real-world small-plane pilots would love to have!

To make sure you're hearing the latest weather, listen to (or read) the beginning of the broadcast loop when the computer says what time the weather was current. "Automated Weather Observation, 2153 Zulu. Wind calm...." If the time is far different from the current Zulu time (see the "Is It Time for Zulu Yet?" sidebar), then the computer must not be getting the latest weather from its sensors.

↓ KEEPING IT REAL

IS IT TIME FOR ZULU YET?

Airplanes can travel so fast that they can easily cross a couple of time zones in a few hours or less. Because of this, pilots throughout the world always use a single "time zone" to plan flights, get weather, and so on. The aviation standard is Zulu time, which is essentially the same as Greenwich mean time (GMT) and Universal Time Coordinated (UTC).

To convert to Zulu time, you need to know how many time zones away from GMT you are. For example, in North America, Central standard time (CST) is six hours earlier than GMT. If it is 10:15 a.m. CST, then it is 4:15 p.m. GMT. Aviation uses the 24-hour clock, so the time is 1615 Zulu. Moscow, on the other hand, is three hours later than GMT, so 1615 Zulu is 1915 (7:15 p.m.) in Moscow.

Daylight saving time adds complexity during those months it is in effect, because Zulu time does not change when you "spring forward" or "fall back." Usually, you subtract one hour: Central daylight time (CDT) is five hours earlier than Zulu time.

The most useful reason to know Zulu time at this stage in your training is because of the weather information you will hear when listening to ASOS/AWOS/ATIS. You will always hear the time of the report in Zulu, so you'll need to convert to your local time to see whether the weather is reasonably current.

ATIS

At a controlled airport, the air traffic controllers could tell you the latest weather information on the radio, but that would clog up the party line with repetitive information, and they need to keep that frequency clear for controlling airplanes. Therefore, most controlled airports have a separate frequency that has a prerecorded weather announcement just like AWOS and ASOS.

This prerecorded announcement is the automatic terminal information service (ATIS), and it is different from AWOS and ASOS in three important ways. First, it is recorded by one of the air traffic controllers rather than a computer voice synthesizer. Second, it is usually recorded only once an hour unless there is a dramatic change in the weather. And third, the controller will also record nonweather information such as which runway is being used, which taxiways are closed, and so on.

ATIS broadcasts in FSX are similar to the real world, except for one element: if the weather changes even just a little bit—the wind gets a bit faster or a few clouds roll in—the FSX ATIS will change, just like AWOS or ASOS.

Also just like AWOS/ASOS, an ATIS broadcast includes the time the information was recorded. But the ATIS also has a phonetic letter assigned to it: "Lebanon airport information *Charlie*, 2153 Zulu, wind 130 at 8…" Every time the ATIS is updated, they assign it the next letter in the alphabet. When you talk to the controllers at that airport, they want to know whether "you have information Charlie?" If you heard information Bravo instead, then you know you have the old ATIS information. You have to switch frequencies and listen to ATIS again to hear Charlie or get the controllers to tell you the new information.

102

PART I	PART II	PART III	PART IV	PART V	PART VI
PREFLIGHT	SPORT PILOT	PRIVATE PILOT	INSTRUMENT RATING	COMMERCIAL LICENSE	ATP AND BEYOND

 BY THE BOOK

AVIATION ALPHABET SOUP

Want to sound cool like a real pilot? Use the phonetic alphabet! Instead of saying "Taxiway T," pilots say, "Taxiway Tango." This system was invented as a way to prevent miscommunication when listening to transmissions on a scratchy, faint radio.

When FSX does the talking for you on the ATC menu, it automatically uses the phonetic alphabet. But for the ultimate in realism, see whether you can say everything correctly before the automated system does. Here's a cheat sheet:

A: Alpha	*N*: November
B: Bravo	*O*: Oscar
C: Charlie	*P*: Papa
D: Delta	*Q*: Quebec
E: Echo	*R*: Romeo
F: Foxtrot	*S*: Sierra
G: Golf	*T*: Tango
H: Hotel	*U*: Uniform
I: India	*V*: Victor
J: Juliette	*W*: Whisky
K: Kilo	*X*: X-ray
L: Lima	*Y*: Yankee
M: Mike	*Z*: Zulu

Most of the numbers are pronounced in their usual way, except *niner* instead of *nine*, *fife* instead of *five*, and *tree* instead of *three*. To be honest, you rarely hear *tree* and *fife*, and sometimes *niner* is forgotten, too.

POST MILLS TO LEBANON MUNICIPAL

To practice flying at both uncontrolled and controlled airports, this flight lesson takes you on a quick flight around the traffic pattern at Post Mills, Vermont, and then on to Lebanon Municipal Airport in New Hampshire, a distance of 16 nautical miles (nm).

The Cub doesn't have a radio installed in it. In fact, it doesn't even have an electrical system! But many Cub pilots carry a battery-powered radio in case they need to talk to other pilots or air traffic controllers, and the FSX Cub does include a handheld radio.

It's good you have it, because you're going to fly to a controlled airport. Lebanon Municipal Airport has a control tower to guide planes to and from the runways, both in the air and on the ground. You'll use your radio to talk to other pilots when you leave Post Mills, and you'll talk to the air traffic controllers when you arrive at Lebanon.

STARTUP

Figure 4-10: Startup of Post Mills departure flight

Load Chap_04_Post_Mills_Departure into FSX (see Figure 4-10). Set the second view on Outside: Top Down view, and zoom out so that you can see the entire airport and half of Lake Fairlee in the view. Notice that you're parked off the runway. Before you leave, let's take a quick look at the information about Post Mills and Lebanon Municipal.

Choose World > Map (see Figure 4-11), zoom in a bit on the chart, and click the 2B9 magenta circle. (You might have to move the black aircraft off to the side.) You should see the facility information about Post Mills, because the unique, three-digit identifier for the airport is 2B9. Note the CTAF frequency (see Figure 4-12). If Post Mills had an ASOS or AWOS weather reporting frequency, you would see that here too, but it doesn't. You can also see runway lengths, elevation of the airport, and so on.

Click Cancel in the Facility Information window, and on the map, zoom out until you can see the blue, dashed ring below (south of) 2B9. Move the map down a bit until the blue ring is in the center and zoom in; you'll see the letters KLEB, which is the identifier for Lebanon Municipal Airport. Click the light blue circle inside the blue, dashed ring, and choose Lebanon Mun (KLEB) from the list.

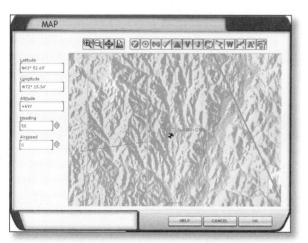

Figure 4-11: Map view of the vicinity of the Post Mills airport

104

PART I
PREFLIGHT

PART II
SPORT PILOT

PART III
PRIVATE PILOT

PART IV
INSTRUMENT RATING

PART V
COMMERCIAL LICENSE

PART VI
ATP AND BEYOND

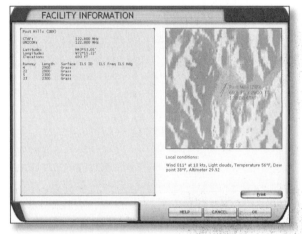

FACILITY INFORMATION

Post Mills (2B9)

CTAF: 122.800 MHz
UNICOM: 122.800 MHz

Latitude: N43°53.05'
Longitude: W72°15.22'
Elevation: 693 FT

Runway Length Surface ILS ID ILS Freq ILS Hdg
4   2900   Grass
22   2900   Grass
5   2300   Grass
23   2300   Grass

Local conditions:

Wind 011° at 10 kts, Light clouds, Temperature 56°F, Dew point 38°F, Altimeter 29.92

Print

HELP   CANCEL   OK

Figure 4-12: Post Mills airport and facility information

The facility information for KLEB is much more extensive than for Post Mills. Write down these key stats: ATIS frequency, CTAF, ground, tower, elevation, and numbers of the runways available. In the real world, you might even carry an airport chart, complete with frequencies, with you in the airplane on a trip like this. We've included such a chart among the files on the accompanying website: `KLEB Airport Diagram.PDF`.

Now click OK to get out of the facility information, and click Cancel to return to the Cub on the field. (If you click OK here, your Cub is moved to wherever you moved it when it was covering up the magenta airport circle.)

TAXI AND TAKEOFF

First you'll take a quick trip around the patch—just a couple of takeoffs and landings here at Post Mills, but this time you're going to use your radio.

Before you pick a runway, you need to know where the wind is coming from. The only way to tell at Post Mills is the windsock—take a look, and you see the wind is from the north at about 10 knots, so you can use either Runway 4 or 5. Runway 4 is longer, so that's the best choice.

Open the ATC menu by pressing the ` (accent) key on your keyboard, select the number for Tune 2B9 Traffic on 122.800, and then select the number for Runway 4 for takeoff. Finally, select the number for Announce Taxi. The automated ATC system announces—as though it were your voice—that you're taxiing to Runway 4. Take a quick look around the airplane to make sure no one is in the way, and taxi to Runway 4. (If the ATC menu is blocking your view, close it by clicking the X box in the upper-right corner of the window or by pressing the accent key on your keyboard.)

NOTE!

⬇ AUTO RADIO

FSX does have a cool function when using the radios: when you make a selection in the ATC menu that changes frequencies, the radios automatically change. You could do it manually, too (press Shift+2 on your keyboard to see the radio), but you have to use the ATC menu anyway to get FSX to make your announcement.

Before you take off, take another quick look around to make sure no one is trying to land (they have the right of way). If you want to be realistic, don't use the spot plane view to do this; instead, spin the Cub in a circle on the ground while you look around for other planes. When you're ready, open the ATC menu, and select Announce Takeoff—Remain in the Pattern. Pull onto the Runway 4, and take off. (You might want to close the second window if you still have it open. It can be distracting and slows the visual performance of FSX on all but the fastest machines.)

Without runway numbers, how can you tell which runway is 4? One runway is 4, and the other is 5; so when you taxi onto the runway, if your heading is 050, then you're on the wrong runway!

After takeoff, climb straight ahead on the upwind leg until you are about 700 feet above the airport elevation (1400 MSL on your altimeter). Then turn 90° to the right (now a heading of 130), and continue climbing another 300 feet on the crosswind leg. Another 90° turn to the left (heading 220), and you're on the downwind leg; level off 1,000 feet above the airport (1700 MSL on your altimeter). This is called the *traffic pattern altitude* (TPA).

APPROACH AND LANDING

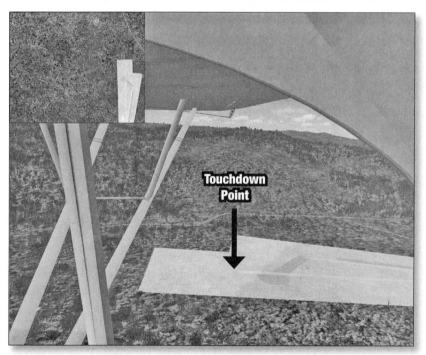

Figure 4-13: On downwind, use your yoke's hat switch to look right to figure out when you're abeam your touchdown point.

With power set at about 2100 rpm, travel parallel to the runway on downwind until the approach end of the runway—where you want to land—is straight out your right side, as shown in Figure 4-13. We say you are "abeam your touchdown point." Switch your views as needed to spot this point. Drop power to about 1500 rpm, and let the nose drop in a descent. When the runway is about 45° behind your right wing, turn 90° to the right onto the base leg. Keep checking the position of the runway using the side view, because you want to start the right turn onto the final approach before you actually line up with the runway, or you'll overshoot the final approach.

Land normally, and pull off the runway to make way for anyone else taking off or landing. Taxi along the grass to the start of Runway 4, and get ready to fly to Lebanon.

SEE THE MOVIE

The website (www.wiley.com) has a video of the trip to Lebanon. You won't be able to hear the specific ATC calls, but you can see what the trip looks like. And if you make your own video of your flight to Lebanon, try this when you're watching your video: as you enter the traffic pattern at Lebanon, switch the view to the tower view. You can pretend you're standing next to the air traffic controllers in the tower, watching your plane land.

106

PART I	PART II	PART III	PART IV	PART V	PART VI
PREFLIGHT	SPORT PILOT	PRIVATE PILOT	INSTRUMENT RATING	COMMERCIAL LICENSE	ATP AND BEYOND

DEPART FOR LEBANON

Figure 4-14: The Connecticut River takes you south to Lebanon, New Hampshire.

Lebanon Municipal is about 16 miles south of Post Mills, but you need to depart to the east toward a river before you head south. So when you're ready for takeoff, use the ATC menu to select Announce Takeoff—Depart East. Take off as before, but continue straight ahead on the runway heading until you're at about 2,000 feet MSL and well clear of the traffic pattern at Post Mills. Make a right turn southeast (to a heading of about 140). Continue climbing, and level off at 2,500 feet MSL with power at about 2100 rpm. When you get to the Connecticut River—it's the big blue line with a divided highway running just west of it—turn right, and follow the river southwest (see Figure 4-14). Your heading will be about 230 as you fly.

APPROACHING LEBANON

The flight takes only about 15 minutes, but you need to start talking to the control tower at Lebanon before you are within 5 nautical miles of the airport, and at cruise speed the Cub is at that point in less than 10 minutes. First, listen to the ATIS information at Lebanon on 118.65. (On the ATC menu, choose the Nearest Airport List, select Lebanon Mun, and then Tune Lebanon ATIS.) When you hear or read the ATIS, write down the ATIS identifier, winds, ceiling, altimeter setting, and runway in use.

Take this moment to check your altimeter setting; make sure it matches what you heard on the ATIS, and change the altimeter if they're different. Next, think about the winds and the runway in use. Will there be a crosswind? A tailwind? (A tailwind would be bad, but the FSX air traffic controller tries to help you land into the wind, or nearly so.) Pause FSX by pressing P on your keyboard, and draw out the winds on your runway chart if it helps you.

MULTITASKING AND DISTRACTIONS

If you stay over the Connecticut River on your way to Lebanon, you make some twists and turns at the same time you're listening to the ATIS, figuring out the winds, setting your altimeter, calling the control tower, and so on. At first, this can be a lot to do in a short period of time while you're also trying to keep the Cub upright and on your (river) course.

Yes, this is multitasking, and pilots were doing it long before it became a buzzword in our modern, cell-phone/iPod/SUV world. But you really can't do many tasks at the same time; you need to prioritize what is important. For decades, flight instructors have been teaching their students a way to remember the priorities: aviate...navigate...communicate.

The first job is to keep the plane safely flying, monitoring the systems, fuel, and so on. Next, check your navigation and keep yourself on course, but don't forget to fly the airplane when you're about to be distracted by keeping on your course. Finally, listen to the ATIS and talk to the tower, but not at the expense of knowing where you are, where you're going, and actually flying the plane.

Figure 4-15: The Lebanon airport is about 7 miles ahead, around the bend in the river. By the time you see the city of Lebanon, you need to call the control tower and tell them you're arriving.

You should be able to see the city of Lebanon on the left side of the river (see Figure 4-15). The airport is around the river bend to the left and barely in view. One of the hardest skills a student pilot has to learn is how to spot an airport, and at a distance of more than 5 miles and only 2,000 feet above the ground, you might not see it yet. But the city of Lebanon is about 5 miles from the airport, so if you're seeing the city, it's time to call the control tower. On the ATC menu, switch to Tune Lebanon Tower, and request a full-stop landing. The tower tells you to enter right downwind for Runway 36.

It's time to plan your arrival; pause FSX if you need time to work this out (if only we could do that in a real airplane). The runway you land on has a

108

PART I
PREFLIGHT

PART II
SPORT PILOT

PART III
PRIVATE PILOT

PART IV
INSTRUMENT RATING

PART V
COMMERCIAL LICENSE

PART VI
ATP AND BEYOND

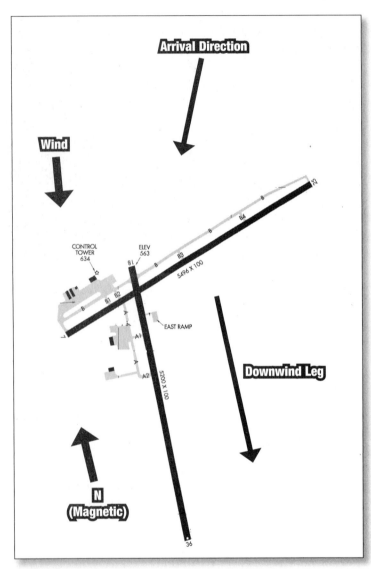

Figure 4-16: *After you find out what runway you're landing on, you can plan how to enter the traffic pattern at your destination. In real life, you probably shouldn't draw it out like this; you should be looking outside to make sure you don't hit anyone (or anything) else out here. But if you can picture this in your head, it will help your arrival.*

heading of 360. The opposite of that is 180, which is the ground track you want when you're on the downwind leg. Your heading as you approach the airport is about 230 or so; therefore, you need to spot the airport early enough to turn to the left (east) side of the airport on a right downwind for Runway 36, as drawn in Figure 4-16.

The Connecticut River is on the west side of the airport, and the control tower wants you on the east side of the airport. If you don't see the airport yet, you're going to have to trust your instructors to guide you. Stay over the river as you pass the city. The river curves more south—you're going at a heading of about 210—and the airport is ahead on your left (see Figure 4-17).

When you spot the airport, you have to quickly decide which runway is 36, so you can fly the right downwind. Your heading now is about 210, and your downwind is 180°, so it's only a quick 30-degree left turn and you're on downwind. That should help you spot your runway. If not, turn to 180°, and see what runway you are parallel to.

Now that you're within a couple of miles of the airport, you need to get down to traffic pattern altitude. Check your notes: what is the altitude of the airport? Add 1,000 feet to that, and you have to get down to 1,600 feet in the next few minutes. Start the descent now so you enter the pattern at the proper altitude (assuming you set your altimeter correctly).

As you enter the right downwind, you should be less than a half mile from the runway, parallel to it, and at 1,600 feet, as shown in Figure 4-18. Run through your prelanding procedures, as you practiced in previous chapters.

Figure 4-17: *Airports can be hard to pick out on a cluttered landscape. Look for a place with few buildings and few trees, sometimes with straight lines cut into the trees. Then you have to pick out your landing runway.*

Figure 4-18: *Entering the right downwind for Runway 36. Stay about ¼ to ½ mile from the runway, at pattern altitude.*

LAND AND TAXI

Continue around the pattern with a right base turn and on to final approach, descending and turning just as you practiced back at Post Mills. At some point, the air traffic controller clears you to land—and you can't actually touch the runway until you hear those words. If you still haven't been cleared to land when you're about 100 feet above the runway, go full throttle, climb back up into the traffic pattern, and try again.

When you land, switch frequencies to ground control (through the ATC menu), and select Taxi to Parking. Now you can either stop or reset the flight back at Post Mills to try it again. Or, if you're really bold, talk to the ground and tower controllers, take off, and fly back to Post Mills yourself, navigating back up the Connecticut River.

TAKE THE CUB TO BEANTOWN

If you're ready for the challenge of a big, busy airport, how about flying to Boston? It's a lot easier to do in FSX than in real life, and it builds on the skills you developed in this chapter.

The elements that make a busy airport like Boston harder than Post Mills or even Lebanon are more airplanes to avoid; more congestion on the radio as the air traffic controllers work with many more airplanes; more complicated runways and taxiways, making it difficult to find the runway you've been instructed to land on or taxi to; and complex airspace that requires special procedures. (We'll cover airspace in Chapter 5; for now, you can ignore some of those procedures and slip into Boston.)

Figure 4-19: Start of Marshfield Departure flight

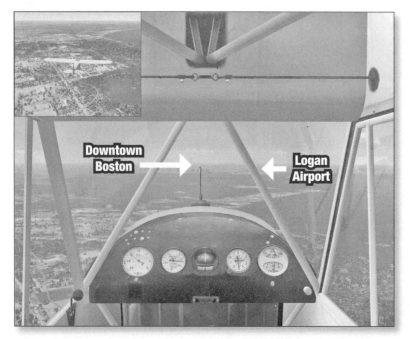

Figure 4-20: When the coastline turns west, look for downtown Boston, and head that direction.

The flight starts at Marshfield, Massachusetts (3B2), about 20 miles south of Boston's Logan International Airport (KBOS). Load the Chap_04_Marshfield_Departure flight, and you're at a parking spot ready to taxi to the runway (see Figure 4-19). Check the windsock to decide whether you want to use Runway 6 or 24. Taxi, announce a northbound departure on the radio, and take off.

After takeoff, make the proper departure from the pattern at Marshfield, and head northeast to the coastline. Turn left, and follow the coast north. Climb to 2,500 feet.

When you're cruising along the coast and level at 2,500 feet, you'll need to get the ATIS at Boston. Use the ATC menu to select the nearest airport list, and look for Logan Intl (KBOS). You might have to select Airports Farther from You to see it. Listen to the ATIS, and write down the key information you'll want handy: winds and runway in use. When you have the weather information, you can select Tune Boston Tower, although it's a bit early to call them.

In the real world, you need to talk to the radar controller at Boston to get permission to enter Boston's airspace when you're still more than 11 miles away. We'll talk in detail about airspace in the next chapter, so for this lesson you can just treat Boston like any other controlled airport.

At this point, you'll probably still be more than 10 miles from Boston, so just continue along the coastline. When the coast turns to the west, look for downtown Boston at

Figure 4-21: Turning onto final approach at Boston's Logan International Airport. Keep your speed up; a big airplane is probably coming in behind you!

a heading of about 320; point the Cub toward downtown (see Figure 4-20), which will take you close to the airport. As you get closer to downtown, look for the airport to the right of downtown on a peninsula.

Call the Boston tower, and request a full-stop landing. Be ready to write down the instructions they tell you for entering the traffic pattern. Pause FSX, and draw a diagram if you need to see how this will work based on your present heading and the instructions they give you.

Enter the traffic pattern as instructed, and when you're cleared to land (see Figure 4-21), bring in your little Cub to the big airport!

At a busy airport like Boston, it's likely you'll need taxi instructions from the ground controller, so don't be shy; ask for what you need. It's better to bother the controller a little than to accidentally pull onto a runway and force a jet to abort its landing…or worse.

Now that you've experienced a couple of short flights from one airport to another, the next chapter shows you how to navigate longer distances.

↓ KEEPING IT REAL

GET UNLOST

When taxiing at an unfamiliar airport, you should have a chart of the airport showing taxiways and runways. We've provided the airport diagram for Lebanon Municipal Airport on the website (www.wiley.com). You can get the latest version of that chart or charts of many other U.S. airports online. But sometimes even having a chart is not enough.

If the airport has a control tower and the ground controller has told you to taxi somewhere that you don't know how to get to, you can ask the controller for *progressive taxi instructions*. Instead of just saying, "Taxi to the terminal" and requiring you figure out how to get there, the controller will say, "Turn left on Taxiway Charlie and right on Taxiway Bravo, and the terminal will be on your left." Be ready to write down the instructions before you call so you don't have to call again!

Continued

This works in FSX, too, but not in the same way. If you select Turn On Progressive Taxi from the ATC menu, FSX displays a line of yellow arrows on the taxiways for you to follow. It's not very realistic, but it's really easy to use!

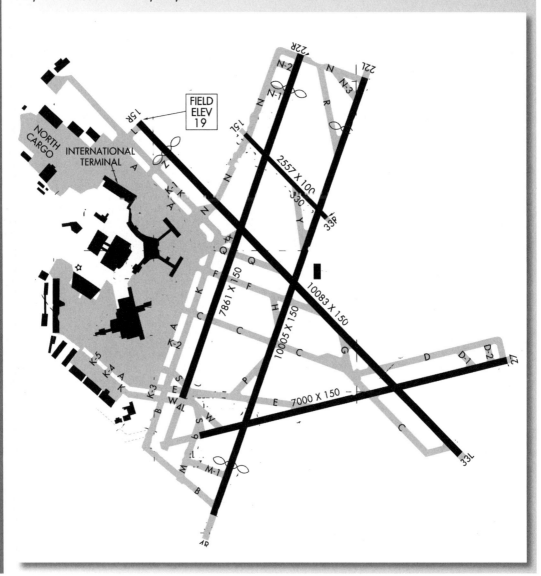

KEY POINTS FOR REAL FLYING AND FSX BUILT-INS

The following are some key points from this chapter:

- Understand airport operations on the ground and in the air around controlled and uncontrolled airports.

- Experience using radios, and practice what to say to air traffic controllers and other aircraft.

- Navigate by following natural and human-made courses such as rivers, roads, and cities.

- Practice getting automated weather and airport information.

- Experience following instructions given by air traffic controllers.

Here are the lessons and missions to study after reading this chapter:

- *Lessons*: Private Pilot Lesson 4 is about the traffic pattern; reading that lesson in FSX might help you understand more about flying around airports. Private Pilot Lesson 5 is about air traffic control and can also be a good review for this chapter.

- *Missions*: The Midwest Fly-In mission is similar to this flight in that you fly from one airport to another. The mission also adds one fun element: flour bombing! (Even in real life you can drop bags of flour, as long as you're careful not to hit anyone or anything on the ground.)

OLD-FASHIONED NAVIGATION

"DURING THIS NIGHT OF UNCERTAINTY, IT WAS A POINT OF REFERENCE AS LONG AS ONE UNDERSTOOD IT WASN'T SOLID GOLD. LOTS OF THINGS IN FLYING ARE THAT WAY, BUT IF THERE ARE ENOUGH PIECES OF INFORMATION, ONE CAN TAKE THE GOOD FROM EACH, USE IT, AND COME CLOSER TO THE TRUTH."
—ROBERT BUCK ON CELESTIAL NAVIGATION

116

PART I	PART II	PART III	PART IV	PART V	PART VI
PREFLIGHT	SPORT PILOT	PRIVATE PILOT	INSTRUMENT RATING	COMMERCIAL LICENSE	ATP AND BEYOND

PLANNING A TRIP

It's funny to think about a lesson on old-fashioned navigation techniques—navigation that doesn't require any kind of computer—and then practice it on a modern flight simulator. But that's exactly what this chapter is going to do. Understanding the old-school way of dealing with navigation is still important in the 21st century for two reasons. All the fancy modern navigation equipment and software works on the foundation of these basic navigation concepts, and when things go seriously wrong and all the pretty displays or computers go dark, old-fashioned techniques might be only techniques that get you home alive.

The purpose of navigation planning is simply to create a plan for getting from airport A to airport B without running out of fuel, getting lost, or hitting anything solid in the process. In addition, planning your trip includes knowing what to expect along the way and upon arrival so you avoid the embarrassment of, say, trying to talk to the tower on the wrong frequency.

Not all trips are the same, so what is appropriate navigation planning for one trip might be completely inadequate for another. In the previous chapter, all the navigation you needed to know to fly from Post Mills, Vermont (2B9), to Lebanon, New Hampshire (KLEB), was to follow the Connecticut River south until reaching the town of Lebanon. You needed to know the appropriate frequencies for the radios and the layout of the runways as well, but FSX provided these via the map.

It's not all that common, however, that you get a trip that just happens to be along the course of a river. So, early in your flight career, you have to a bit more planning so you know which way to turn after takeoff and know about how long it will take you to get there. Then you have to monitor the progress of the plane as you fly. That's what you'll practice in this chapter; you'll look at both how it's done in the real world and how it's emulated in FSX.

⬇ BY THE BOOK
USING THE A/FD

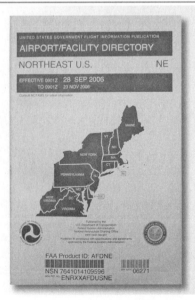

The Airport/Facility Directory (A/FD) is a government publication containing just about everything you might want to know about a public-use airport. The Directory lists radio frequencies, times of operation for part-time control towers, runways layouts, lighting systems, and obstructions. The listing is somewhat cryptic, because it uses a kind of shorthand to cram all that data into something smaller than a Manhattan phone book. But it's not that hard to read once you get the hang of it, and a guide at the beginning can help you decode the shorthand.

The National Aeronautical Charting Office (NACO) that publishes the A/FD also prints runway diagrams for some of the busier airports. The volume is published every 56 days because so much information changes on a regular basis. It's a must-have for your real, or even your virtual, flight bag.

READING CHARTS

One of the coolest parts of aviation is getting to read the maps—usually called *charts* in aviation circles. What makes them so great is how much information is packed into so small a space and in so elegant a format. The charts are also 3D in the sense that they give you information not only about what's happening on the surface but also about how high that surface extends above sea level and what's happening in the air even higher than that.

Figure 5-1 compares FSX's built-in map with a *sectional chart*. The FSX map has the advantage that you can click certain areas and open additional information in a new window. The chart is paper and doesn't have this option, so it encodes all the information directly on the chart.

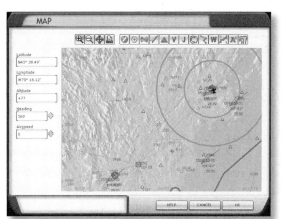
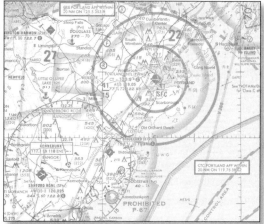

Figure 5-1: The sectional chart is the real-world equivalent to the FSX map.

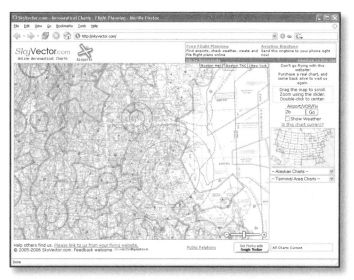

Figure 5-2: Check out SkyVector.com for digital versions of up-to-date sectional and terminal-area charts. The real thing is much more informative, and in many ways easier to use, than FSX's map.

Our purpose here is not to tell you everything you need to know about using a sectional chart (although that would be fun). That's something to do with your flight instructor or on your own. Current charts for the entire United States are available online for free from SkyVector. com. The online charts are interactive and let you zoom in or out on any area. In the United States, you can buy paper sectional charts at almost any small airport for less than $10 apiece. Each chart has an excellent key that explains most of the symbols, but you can download or buy a more extensive guide at `http://naco .faa.gov/index.asp?xml=naco/ online/aero_guide` (see Figure 5-2).

Now you'll plan a flight from Portland, Maine (KPWM), to Sanford, Maine (KSFM), using both the sectional chart and the FSX map. Then you'll fly it.

118

PART I	PART II	PART III	PART IV	PART V	PART VI
PREFLIGHT	SPORT PILOT	PRIVATE PILOT	INSTRUMENT RATING	COMMERCIAL LICENSE	ATP AND BEYOND

A ROUTE FROM A TO B

There's no convenient road or river to follow on a trip from Portland to Sanford. It's also too far for you to simply take off and look for the destination on the horizon without climbing unnecessarily high first. That means you need a plan. The simplest plan is to take off, point the plane in the direction of Sanford, and then fly until you get there. This is known as a *direct route*, and it's the ideal way to travel by air. Let's see how it works.

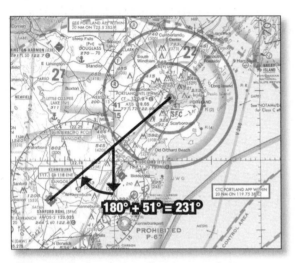

Figure 5-3: You can measure the true course between Portland and Sanford on the chart at 231°.

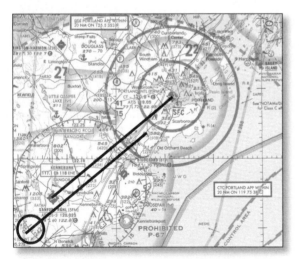

Figure 5-4: Find the true course connecting the two airports (upper line) and mentally slide it over a nearby VOR compass rose (lower line). Read the magnetic course off the compass rose (circled).

The first step is to draw a straight line connecting Portland and Sanford. The second step is to figure out what compass direction this is. The longitudinal lines on the chart represent *true north*. That means if you were to follow one of those lines north, you would end up at the North Pole. Using one of these lines, you can figure out your true course to Sanford. Find where the course between Portland and Sanford crosses one of the longitudinal lines, and measure the angle that makes (see Figure 5-3). In this case, it's 51°, or 051 in aviation parlance. So, the course between Portland and Sanford is the course itself, 180, plus 51 or 231.

Unfortunately, you don't have any instrument in the airplane that measures true course. Instead, you have a compass. If you follow north on your compass, it will take you to the magnetic North Pole of the Earth, which is currently somewhere in Canada (it actually moves a little each year). That means you need to correct for the difference between magnetic north and true north. The amount of difference depends on where you are in the world. In the United States, the two are almost equal right at the Mississippi River, which is kind of convenient. If you're west of the Mississippi River, then north on the magnetic compass points somewhere east of true north.

In southern Maine, east of the Mississippi, the difference between magnetic north and true north is about 17° to the west. This means if you want to use your compass in the Cub to fly directly between Portland and Sanford, you have to add 17° of correction to your 231° true course. The result is that if you follow 248° as shown on your compass, you should fly a straight line between the two airports.

You can quickly estimate this directly from the sectional chart that's shown in Figure 5-4. Just south of your course between the two airports is a compass rose around the Kennebunk VOR. We'll talk about VORs in Chapter 10, but for the time being know that these compass roses show you magnetic north at that spot on the chart. If you mentally slide the course down so that it cuts through the

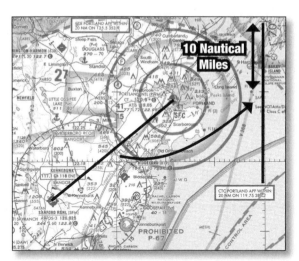

Figure 5-5: You can use any longitudinal line as a scale for measuring distances on a sectional chart.

center of the VOR, you can see where it crosses the compass rose and read the magnetic course right off the chart.

Now that you know which way to go, you have to know how far it is. All charts have a scale printed on them so you can measure the distance on the chart and then compare it to the scale to see how far it is. Rather than measuring in the commonly referred to *statute mile*, aviation uses nautical miles.

You can estimate this quickly as well. Each minute of latitude—each tick mark on the longitudinal line—is one nautical mile (see Figure 5-5). Every 10 minutes, or 10 nautical miles, you'll see a larger tick mark, and every 30 minutes, one half degree of latitude, you'll see a line of latitude running across the chart. This means you can use the same trick of taking the course line and sliding it over to a longitudinal line and measuring how many minutes of latitude the line is. That tells you how many nautical miles long the trip is. It looks like it's just less than 24 nautical miles.

↓ STUDENT OF THE CRAFT

LATITUDE AND LONGITUDE

Here's a quick review if you're not up on your latitude and longitude. *Longitude* and *latitude* are a way of pinpointing a position somewhere on the globe. Longitudinal lines run north to south, and latitudinal lines run east to west. All longitudinal lines meet at the North Pole and the South Pole. Latitudinal lines do not cross. The largest latitudinal line is at the equator, and the rings of latitude get smaller and smaller as you go farther and farther north or south.

Both latitude and longitude are referred to in degrees. Zero degrees of latitude is the equator. Zero degrees of longitude is the line that runs through Greenwich, England. Flying in the northeast puts you north of the equator and west of England, so your latitude and longitude will be read in degrees and minutes (60ths of a degree) north and west. The Portland airport (KPWM) is at a latitude of N 43°38.77' and a longitude of W 70°18.56'. Since pilots have to think in three dimensions, you should also note that Portland is 77 feet above sea level.

DEAD RECKONING

If you know what direction to fly, how far it is, and how fast you travel over the ground, then you can calculate how long it will take you to get there. Your Cub cruises at 70 miles per hour (mph). That equals about 61 knots, or nautical miles per hour. Let's call it 60 knots just to keep the math simple. Sixty knots is one nautical mile per minute. That means if you take off from Portland, turn to a magnetic heading of 248° using your compass, and fly for 24 minutes at 70 mph, you should find yourself directly overhead the Sanford airport.

120

PART I
PREFLIGHT

PART II
SPORT PILOT

PART III
PRIVATE PILOT

PART IV
INSTRUMENT RATING

PART V
COMMERCIAL LICENSE

PART VI
ATP AND BEYOND

This kind of navigation is called *dead reckoning*. It works amazingly well. It's also the math at the heart of all the fancy GPS calculations that keep you on course and say how much longer you have to fly to reach your destination. Unfortunately, it's only this simple if there are no winds. A tailwind will make you fly much faster over the ground and arrive over Sanford in less time than expected. A wind from the side drifts you off course, and the airport passes off one of your wings, possibly unnoticed by you.

You'll play with dead reckoning a little more in the second flight in this chapter. Until then, do what all new students do, which is combine dead reckoning with the view out the window.

PILOTAGE

When you fly from Post Mills, Vermont, to Lebanon, New Hampshire, following the river, what you are doing is called *pilotage*. Pilotage simply means looking out the window and comparing it to a map or what you expected to see out there. When students first start venturing away from the airport, they usually combine a certain amount of dead reckoning with pilotage to verify that they are following the correct course over the ground.

The direct route between Portland and Sanford does not have much in the way of discernible landmarks. To give you a better chance of finding your way, we'll plan a slightly more circuitous route consisting of three short legs that are easy to find and leave you unlikely to get lost.

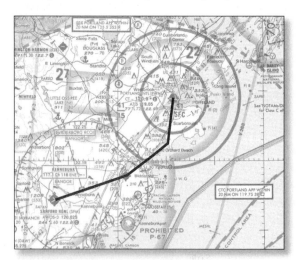

Figure 5-6: Pilotage is the art of flying from one visual landmark to another. In practice, it is usually combined with a certain amount of dead reckoning.

The first leg is from Portland south to a distinctive land formation near Old Orchard Beach. The next leg is from Old Orchard Beach to the Biddeford airport (B19). The last leg is from Biddeford directly to Sanford. See Figure 5-6 for the whole trip plotted on the chart. The plan is to take off from Portland and turn to a heading that should take you between Portland and the north side of Old Orchard Beach. Then look out the front window, and you should be able to see that distinctive spit of land ahead of you. Now you can fly visually to that point. Once you get there, turn to your next calculated heading, and look for the next visual landmark. Each one of these landmarks is commonly referred to as a *visual checkpoint* or a *waypoint*.

A SUDDEN CHANGE OF PLANS

One of the reasons it's important to be able to quickly get an approximate magnetic heading and distance from a sectional chart is that one day you might be en route to a one airport and suddenly have to make a change to land another one. The motivation could be some kind of problem with your airplane, nasty weather ahead that exceeds your capabilities, or perhaps a, uh, pressing biological need that just can't wait another 45 minutes until you land.

Switching to another destination while you're flying along is referred to as a *diversion*. It's almost guaranteed that you will get a few of these sprung on you unexpectedly during your flight training. FSX is a great way to practice them so you're ready.

At any point during your flights, you can decide, "I want to practice a diversion now." The process is to find the course to the nearest suitable airport, head directly there, get the important information about it such as the runway layout and radio frequencies, and then land.

Real-world technology has many ways to help. Even the portable GPS that you can use in the FSX Cub has both a list of nearest airports and a Direct-To button to show you the course to get there. Real-world ATC will always give you a heading and distance to a nearby airport whenever you ask them for help.

For practice, though, try using a sectional chart to find an airport near your position and the quick estimator of heading and distance described in this chapter to get yourself there. Even estimate how many minutes it should be before the airport pops up under the nose. Someday the ability to do this quickly and accurately might seriously save your bacon.

THE FSX FLIGHT PLANNER

Rather than go through the mechanical process of figuring out all of these headings and distances, you'll let FSX do it for you. Few people do flight planning by hand anymore anyway. Many free and low-cost flight planning tools are available on the Internet or for your computer that are much quicker and don't make those annoying math errors.

Click the Load button on the Free Flight page of the FSX home screen, and choose Chap_05_Pilotage. This puts you in the general aviation parking area of the Portland airport. (It's actually called the Portland International Jetport, which makes taking off with a vintage Cub even more fun.)

Choose Flights > Flight Planner. This opens the flight planner window, as shown in Figure 5-7, where you have to select your departure and destination airports. Click the Select button for the departure, and in the By Airport ID field, type **KPWM**. This is the identifier for Portland. Choose a starting point of Parking 1—Ramp GA Small. Click OK. Click the Select button for the destination airport to open the same kind of screen, and enter **KSFM** as the airport identifier for Sanford. Verify that the flight plan type is VFR and that the routing is direct. Click OK.

122

| PART I | PART II | PART III | PART IV | PART V | PART VI |
| PREFLIGHT | SPORT PILOT | PRIVATE PILOT | INSTRUMENT RATING | COMMERCIAL LICENSE | ATP AND BEYOND |

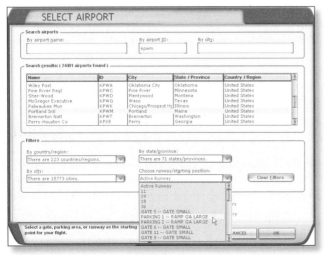

Now click the Find Route button. This lets you see and edit your flight plan (see Figure 5-8). The flight plan you see right now is the same one you calculated when you used the sectional chart to do dead reckoning. Before you edit it, click the NavLog button in the lower right. This shows you FSX's calculations for course and distance between Portland and Sanford. It's good that they're pretty close to what you came up with using the sectional chart. Click the OK button to get back to the flight plan editing page.

Figure 5-7 The built-in flight planner lets you enter your departure and destination airports by airport identifier, name, or city. It also lets you select where at the airport you'll start the flight.

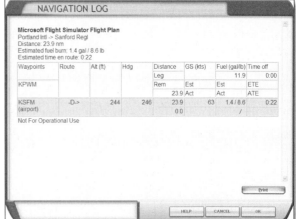

Figure 5-8: The Find Route button reveals the route and lets you edit it.

First, set the altitude to fly to 2,500 feet. This is a fine altitude for a Cub on such a short trip.

To edit your route, all you need to do is drag the red course line to where you want a new waypoint. The line stretches just like a rubber band and adds a waypoint where you let go of the mouse. Before you try to place a new waypoint just north of old Orchard Beach, however, you'll want to declutter the map a little bit. Click the J button and the triangle button at the top of the page. This turns off jet routes, highways in the sky used only by aircraft above 18,000 feet, and named waypoints, which we will talk about when you start flying pressurized aircraft in Chapter 24.

Now grab the red course line anywhere along its length, and place a custom waypoint place just north of the beach; then drag the line between the beach and the Sanford airport to place a second waypoint over the Biddeford airport (see Figure 5-9). When you release the line over a map feature, such as an airport, that feature becomes a waypoint in your flight plan. This is why you turned off jet routes and named waypoints. There was one of each close enough to the north end of Old Orchard Beach to make the course line snap onto them instead of the actual bit of land that you want in your flight plan.

Figure 5-9: Just drag the route to add waypoints, but you might need to turn off a few chart items to place a custom waypoint exactly where you want it.

If you click the NavLog button now, you'll see a three-leg flight plan with separate headings and distances for each leg. Note that taking this seemingly much longer route actually adds only about two miles—and, therefore, about two minutes—to your total flight.

When you click OK to close the navigation log and click OK again to close the flight planner, you will be asked whether you want to save this flight plan. Save it using the default name that FSX provides. You'll also be asked whether you want the aircraft to be placed at the position you specified. You can click OK to this as well.

FSX is ready for you to fly your old-fashioned navigation flight. You still have a few issues to consider when plotting a course between two airports. You'll look at those briefly in the next section before you start flying.

How High to Fly

Because flying is a three-dimensional experience, you not only have to choose which way to go but also how high you want to fly. In the real world, three factors go into this decision: safety, efficiency, and comfort.

The first rule of choosing how high to fly is to make sure you're higher than any solid objects that could bring your flight to a rapid and unfortunate conclusion. Mountains and radio towers figure prominently into flight planning, and you can find their heights on sectional charts.

124

PART I	PART II	PART III	PART IV	PART V	PART VI
PREFLIGHT	SPORT PILOT	PRIVATE PILOT	INSTRUMENT RATING	COMMERCIAL LICENSE	ATP AND BEYOND

One of the interesting features of airplanes is that the higher you fly, the faster you go, with some limitations. As the airplane climbs, it reaches air that is less dense. This means there is less resistance, so the airplane can fly faster for the same amount of power. It also means there is less oxygen for the engine to breathe, so there is less power available. Most single-engine airplanes have a sweet spot where they're most efficient. For the Cub, that's probably in the vicinity of 6,000 feet MSL.

Flying faster has an impact on your flight planning. The extra speed will not register on your airspeed indicator. In fact, as you go higher, you'll start seeing a lower indicated airspeed as well as a lower rpm because the Cub's engine can't produce quite as much power. Your actual speed through the air, called your *true airspeed*, will probably increase, and you'll need to account for this when deciding how long it will take to fly from waypoint to waypoint.

↓ WHAT'S MY TRUE AIRSPEED?

A quick way to figure your true airspeed is to add 2 percent of your indicated airspeed for every 1,000 feet above sea level you're flying. If the indicated airspeed is 60 mph at 5,000 feet, then your true airspeed would be 60 plus 10 percent of 60, or about 66 mph. If you're good at math, you can use 1.8 percent and get a number that's even closer. You can also use a handheld flight computer and get the exact number for your actual altitude and outside air temperature.

You have to balance the added efficiency of flying high with the cost in time and fuel to climb all the way up there. On a short flight like the one to Sanford, it would never be worth it to climb up high. You also have to figure that you'll have a slower airspeed and burn extra fuel while you're climbing and can have a much faster airspeed or burn very little fuel on the way down. In practice, most pilots assume these two will cancel each other out, and usually they pretty much do.

In terms of real-world comfort, the thinner air means less oxygen for your brain. Most people who live at sea level start experiencing reduced reaction time and impaired thinking by 10,000 feet. It's also colder up there, and the change of pressure going up and coming down can be hard on the ears. The sim wins for comfort here, hands down.

Of course, some regulations govern altitude. Federal Aviation Regulation (FAR) 91.159 in the United States says that when flying more than 3,000 feet above the ground, anyone trying to maintain a magnetic course over the ground between 360 and 179 should fly odd altitudes plus 500 feet. These would be 3,500 feet; 5,500 feet; 7,500 feet; and so on. Those maintaining a magnetic course between 180 and 359 should fly even altitudes plus 500 feet, such as 4,500 feet; 6,500 feet; and so on.

In addition, FAR 91.119 says you'll need to be at least 500 feet from any people, structures, or vehicles in most areas and 1,000 above any densely populated areas. You also must always be in a position where an engine failure won't lead to "undue hazard to people or property on the surface."

Fly Left, Look Right

Those convenient headings for each leg of your flight from Portland to Stanford that FSX calculated for you don't take into account any kind of wind. Planning for wind requires some math or some kind of flight computer. The flight computer does not have to be complicated. For decades this kind of planning was done on a circular slide rule commonly called a *whiz wheel*. You'll look at this in the last flight of this chapter when you'll be flying using only dead reckoning. Knowing the wind correction ahead of time could make the difference between a successful flight and landing somewhere in the ocean.

Using just basic pilotage you can still make corrections for the wind even if it's a bit reactive rather than proactive. When you turn onto your course, you should find your waypoint somewhere off the nose. If a crosswind is blowing, you will slowly drift off course, and that visual landmark will move to the right or the left of the nose. You can then correct by turning the nose of the airplane back to and slightly past the waypoint. In doing so, you will work out a heading that allows the airplane to fly in a crab, just as you saw in Chapter 3, yet brings you to the waypoint.

Who Owns This Airspace?

One of the joys of flying out of the real Post Mills airport is that you can just decide to go fly that morning and take off without talking to anybody. (Many of the real airplanes at Post Mills don't even have radios.) That's just not true for many airports, and when you plan a flight, you need to know who owns each chunk of the sky you fly through, as well as how and when to talk to them.

You can, of course, skip this process in FSX, but it's good practice to mentally plan it. Using the ATC window makes much more sense if you understand airspace as well, so the following sections are a quick primer on airspace from the U.S. International standards kept by the International Civil Aviation Organization (ICAO) mean that it's similar for most countries.

Class A Airspace: Above It All

General airspace classification is by letter, and the top dog is Class A. In the United States, this airspace starts at 18,000 feet above sea level and goes up to 60,000 feet. Since the Cub can't get to 18,000 feet without adding a turbo-charger and won't see 60,000 feet without strapping on a rocket pack, you don't have to worry about this airspace yet. You must also be instrument rated to fly there and meet some additional equipment requirements. In general, this is the realm of twin-engine airplanes, jets, and the like.

Class B Airspace: Busy, Busy, Busy

Class B airspace surrounds the busiest airports, and its exact shape varies with each airport. It's often described as an upside-down wedding cake in shape because it's made of cylinders of air that get wider as you go up in altitude (see Figure 5-10). This shape protects the space needed by jets and other high-speed aircraft as they descend and depart the airport at the center.

126

PART I
PREFLIGHT

PART II
SPORT PILOT

PART III
PRIVATE PILOT

PART IV
INSTRUMENT RATING

PART V
COMMERCIAL LICENSE

PART VI
ATP AND BEYOND

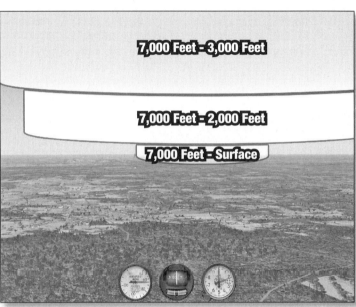

7,000 Feet - 3,000 Feet

7,000 Feet - 2,000 Feet

7,000 Feet - Surface

Figure 5-10: Class B airspace is several cylinders of air stacked atop each other.

Cub pilots must remember two steps. To enter Class B airspace, call the controlling ATC, and get a clearance to enter. This is what you might have done in the second flight in the previous chapter. Once cleared, you can enter, provided you stay in communication with ATC and follow their instructions for where to fly and not to fly. You can also fly under any areas of the inverted wedding cake that don't extend down to the ground without a clearance.

The ATC facility controlling the airspace is named for the primary airport at the center, so if you are near Boston, Massachusetts, the facility is Boston Approach. It's called Approach because you talk to them as you approach Boston's Logan International Airport. Approach guides you in and then hands you off to Boston tower for landing instructions.

The balance you weigh as a pilot is the hassle of getting a clearance and maybe being told to fly a route through the Class B that you don't want vs. the danger of flying low to avoid the Class B or entering it accidentally without clearance.

Class C Airspace: Communicate with Them

Class C airspace is a smaller, two-layer inverted wedding cake over airports with a lot of activity or with radar facilities based at the airport (see Figure 5-11). You don't need a clearance to fly into this space, but you must be communicating with the controlling ATC before you enter. They might give you a discrete squawk code, or they might not. Most Class C has a top of only 4,000 feet above the ground, so you can cross over the top without talking to them, so long as you have a transponder installed in the airplane.

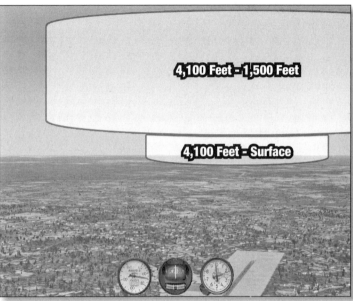

Figure 5-11: Class C airspace usually is two cylinders of air stacked atop each other.

If you were landing at Portland's airport within the Class C airspace, you would contact Portland Approach first, and they would guide you in and hand you off to the Portland tower.

BY THE BOOK

SQUAWK VFR

To fly anywhere inside Class A, within 30 miles of Class B, or inside or over the top of Class C, you need a Mode C transponder in your aircraft. This is a radio device that sees a signal sent from ATC radar and sends a reply message confirming that you are an aircraft.

ATC radar will display a single line for any object it sees in the sky. That could be an airplane or a flock of birds. The transponder signal from your airplane causes a second line to appear beside the first one as well as a number called your *squawk code*. (The transponder got poked by the ATC radar and is squawking a reply, get it?) Mode C transponders also send your current altitude so the controller can see that as well. This is the most common type of transponder. There are also now Mode S transponders that can send and receive data. Garmin G1000–equipped aircraft have this newer type.

The default squawk code for VFR airplanes just flying around is 1200. When you enter Class B airspace, you get a unique code to enter into your transponder for positive identification.

Continued

128

PART I PREFLIGHT | PART II SPORT PILOT | PART III PRIVATE PILOT | PART IV INSTRUMENT RATING | PART V COMMERCIAL LICENSE | PART VI ATP AND BEYOND

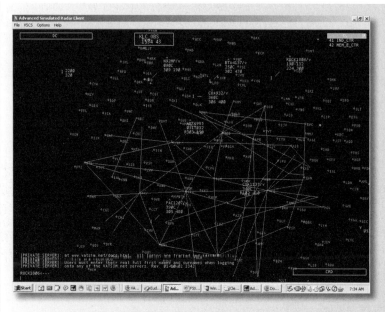

In practice, often the transponder signal is the only thing ATC radar sees, so airplanes that don't have them can be invisible to the controller. That's why transponders are required near and inside busy airspace.

Your Cub doesn't have an electrical system, and it doesn't have a transponder. Ignore that for now, because it lets you do some things that are great for training. In the real world, to fly the Cub near Class B, such as Boston (KBOS), or into Class C, such as Portland (KPWM), you would need a transponder or special permission from ATC beforehand.

CLASS D AIRSPACE: DITTO CLASS C

Class D airspace is a single cylinder of air over any airport with an operating control tower (see Figure 5-12). It's usually 2,500 feet high and has a 5-mile radius around the center of the airport. As with Class C, you don't need a clearance to fly into this space, but you must be communicating with the tower before entering. They will not change your squawk code; they don't have that authority, but sometimes they pass on the instruction to do so from a nearby ATC that does.

If you were landing at an airport with an operating control tower, such as Beverly, Massachusetts, you'd contact that tower by name by calling them Beverly tower.

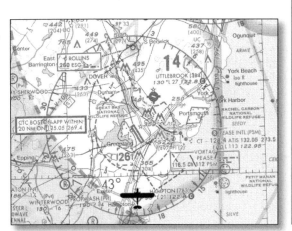

Figure 5-12: Class D airspace is a single, 5-mile radius cylinder around controlled airports.

CLASS E AIRSPACE: EVERYWHERE

Class E airspace is, literally, most of the airspace in the United States. Like classes A–D, it is thought of as *controlled airspace*. That means aircraft under the control of ATC might be operating there, and specific rules apply. How much visibility you need and the minimum distance to clouds are probably the biggest issues.

Despite being controlled airspace, you do not need to talk to anyone to fly in Class E airspace so long as you meet the visibility and cloud clearance requirements for visual flight rules (VFR), which are the rules you've been flying under in the Cub. The controlled aspect is that other airplanes in the area might be talking to ATC, especially if they are flying under instrument flight rules (IFR), which are separate rules for when you're flying through the clouds. We'll train you to do that starting in Chapter 15.

CLASS G AIRSPACE: THE GROUND

Class G airspace is different from A–E in that it is *uncontrolled airspace*. No ATC facility has any authority here. As you might imagine, this airspace is limited in scope. It usually exists only close to the ground or up to various altitudes in sparsely populated or mountainous areas. Some VFR rules are specific to uncontrolled airspace too, but they are more lax than controlled airspace.

WHAT THIS MEANS FOR YOU

For your purposes in flight planning, it's only classes B–D that matter. These are the places where you'll be required to talk to someone at the very least to fly through or land.

130

| PART I | PART II | PART III | PART IV | PART V | PART VI |
| PREFLIGHT | SPORT PILOT | PRIVATE PILOT | INSTRUMENT RATING | COMMERCIAL LICENSE | ATP AND BEYOND |

WHAT HAPPENED TO CLASS F?

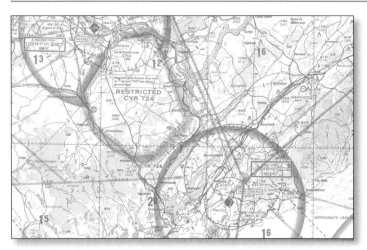

Figure 5-13: Check out charts of different countries' airspace.

The United States doesn't have a Class F. The equivalent is *special-use airspace*. Several of the figures used in this section show a prohibited area, P-67, just south of your proposed flight. Although flying over the Bush family's Kennebunkport mansion in FSX won't get the Secret Service on your case, flying over the mansion in the real world can get you in a lot of trouble. Many kinds of special-use airspace are depicted on sectional charts, and many of them—military operations areas, alert areas, restricted areas, and prohibited areas—present various degrees of restriction to aircraft. Other countries use different symbols for restricted areas, like area CYR in the Canadian chart seen in Figure 5-13.

The real world also has temporary flight restrictions (TFRs) that can appear at a moment's notice and block off larger sections of the sky. In fact, when a sitting president is actually vacationing in Kennebunkport, a much larger area of airspace becomes limited access for general aviation airplanes. That space reaches all the way up to Portland.

TFRs are one of the real downers of flying in the post-9/11 United States. You must check for these before every flight from notification websites or in your preflight weather briefing. Be glad they're not replicated in FSX.

MOVING LOADS, BURNING GAS

An old aviation adage states that the only time an airplane has too much gas is when it's on fire. That's not entirely true, because often the pilot planning for a flight has only so much weight the airplane can carry. That weight must be divided up among the payload, passengers, baggage, and fuel. It is true that you want to err on the side of bringing too much gas rather than too little. You can't just pull over in the air and walk to the nearest fuel pump.

FSX isn't the best place to learn about loading and balancing aircraft. You can take a quick look, however, to get you in the habit of thinking about this before each flight. The Cub is simple. It has only two seats, one small baggage area behind the rear seat, and one 12-gallon fuel tank in front of the front-seat passenger's knees.

The only rules about loading up an airplane like a Cub is that it can't be more than its maximum weight, and the center of that weight, called the *center of gravity* (CG), must be in the right place along the length of the airplane.

Any time during play you can see the load of fuel and people onboard the airplane by selecting Aircraft > Fuel and Payload. This opens the window shown in Figure 5-14. On the left, you see the empty weight of the airplane, which is the weight without consumable fuel or any people aboard. You also see the payload, fuel, and gross weight. The gross weight is the empty weight plus the weight of payload and fuel. Below that you'll see the maximum allowable gross weight and the maximum amount of fuel the airplane can carry.

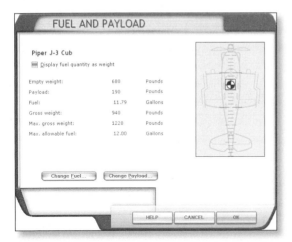

Figure 5-14: FSX lets you adjust the fuel and loading of the airplane at any time.

On the right you'll see a graphic of the airplane and the location of the center of gravity. The Cub is super simple here as well. Adding fuel moves the CG forward. Adding any kind of payload moves the CG aft.

Click Change Payload, and you'll see a small error in the default FSX settings. The human payload is put in station 1 by default in the Cub. This is actually the front seat, and the Cub is flown solo from the rear seat. Go ahead and remove the weight from station 1, and put your own weight in station 2. Twenty pounds in station 3 is probably more than enough for your coat, lunch, and whatever other sundries you decided to take with you on the flight today. Click OK.

You can add fuel in the Cub but only up to 12 gallons. Perhaps this is why many real owners install an auxiliary tank in one of the Cub's wings. So long as the gross weight is less than the maximum gross weight and the center of gravity is between the two large red marks, you're good to go.

VFR rules say you must plan your flight so you land with 30 minutes worth of fuel remaining. Your 65-horsepower Cub will burn on the order of four gallons per hour in cruise flight. You should have plenty of fuel for this 26-minute flight.

  ACCIDENT CHAIN

HE THOUGHT HE HAD ENOUGH GAS

Aircraft: Piper J-3 Cub

Injuries: 2 minor

"The pilot stated that he departed from the airplane's home base airport with about 9 gallons of fuel. The flight to Kent Island took about 45 minutes. He estimated that when he departed Kent Island to return to the home base, the fuel tanks held about 5 gallons of fuel. About 40 minutes after they departed Kent Island and about 5 miles from the destination airport, the engine lost power. The pilot stated that he chose a field to land in, but in order to avoid livestock and power lines, he '...aimed the airplane to a spot just past the middle of the field.' The airplane stuck a small wire fence with the right main landing gear. The pilot stated that the cause of the loss of engine power was fuel exhaustion.

The National Transportation Safety Board determines the probable cause(s) of this accident as 'The pilot's inadequate fuel supply, which resulted in a fuel exhaustion and a loss of engine power. A related factor was the pilot's inadequate fuel consumption calculations.'"

Continued

132

| PART I | PART II | PART III | PART IV | PART V | PART VI |
| PREFLIGHT | SPORT PILOT | PRIVATE PILOT | INSTRUMENT RATING | COMMERCIAL LICENSE | ATP AND BEYOND |

There are two kinds of engine stoppage due to no gas. *Fuel starvation* is when you have gas onboard, but it can't get to the engine. That could be due to a mechanical problem or pilot error, such as accidentally turning the fuel valve to off. *Fuel exhaustion*, however, means running out of gas. This is always pilot error, because it is your responsibility to make sure you have enough fuel when you took off or to change your plans if you determine you don't have enough fuel to get where you planned to go.

A Multileg Flight Using Pilotage

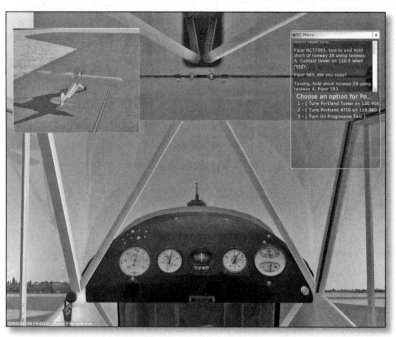

Figure 5-15: The wide spot on the taxiway adjacent to the approach end of the runway is where you do a preflight run-up and any control checks before takeoff.

Picking up where you left off after you used the flight planner to create a multileg flight plan, you are sitting at Portland airport just south of the control tower. For maximum realism, you'll want the ATC window open so you can get the Portland ATIS and get clearance from the ground controller to taxi to the active runway for a south departure. Since winds are calm, that will be Runway 29.

The taxiway has a wide spot just north of the approach end of Runway 29 (see Figure 5-15). This is called a *run-up area*. If you're going to go through a control check before takeoff and do a run-up as described in earlier chapters, then you should pull into this area to do it.

After you're ready to take off, you can pull up to the hold-short line for Runway 29 and contact the Portland tower.

Take Off and Turn South

With your run-up complete and a clearance from the tower for takeoff, you can pull out onto Runway 29, add full power, and depart. Climb straight ahead until reaching 800 feet on your altimeter. This is approximately 700 feet above the ground and the lowest altitude from which you want to make your first turn.

Figure 5-16: Here you are just after takeoff and ready to make your first turn to the southeast.

Here's a spot where the simulator differs from reality and is a real boon. Press P on your keyboard when you reach 800 feet. This pauses the simulation. Now press Shift+F10 to show your kneeboard, and click the Nav Log button, as shown in Figure 5-16. Your first heading is 210. This will be a left turn of about 80°.

Unfortunately, your compass doesn't make this kind of turn easy to do, because it doesn't indicate the correct heading while you turn. If you want to turn to a heading of 210, you'll have to overshoot by about 15°. You need to actually roll out on a heading of 195 by the compass and then see how close you are once the wings are level.

↓ SEEING REAL MAGNETIC HEADING

Remember, you can see the real magnetic heading at the top of your screen by pressing Shift+Z on your keyboard. This will let you see and practice compass errors firsthand. You can also use this tool to get an idea of how early to begin your roll to wings level in order to end up on the correct heading.

↓ STUDENT OF THE CRAFT

MAKING COMPASS TURNS

Correcting for the errors inherent in a compass while turning was one of those skills early aviators took for granted. Now the concept usually isn't even introduced until instrument training where it is an emergency procedure only. Even then, it is often considered less desirable than using a GPS or a stopwatch.

Continued

134

| PART I | PART II | PART III | PART IV | PART V | PART VI |
| PREFLIGHT | SPORT PILOT | PRIVATE PILOT | INSTRUMENT RATING | COMMERCIAL LICENSE | ATP AND BEYOND |

Compass turns don't have to be complicated, and there is huge satisfaction when they work out just right in a real airplane. The beauty of FSX is that the compass reacts exactly like it's supposed to in theory without all the annoying variation that you get in real-world compasses. We won't take the space here to explain why compass turning errors occur, but we will tell you how to account for them so you can make your flight in the Cub.

When you turn the airplane, the compass also begins to swing. If you could watch it closely, you'd see something interesting. Imagine you took off from Runway 29 and leveled off at 1,500 feet pointing due west, or 270. Then you began a 360-degree turn to the south. The compass would swing indicating a turn to the south, but it would seem to be accelerating. By the time the airplane was actually facing magnetic south—180—the compass would read 150. That's a full 30° past the south heading.

As you continue to turn, the compass would seem to start slowing down. By the time the airplane was pointed to magnetic east, the compass would indicate the correct heading of 090. As you continued to turn toward the north, the compass would seem to slow down even more. By the time the airplane was pointed to magnetic north, the compass would have made it only to 030, or 30° shy of the actual heading. If you continued to turn all the way back to west, the compass would seem to accelerate again and correctly indicate west at just about the same time the airplane was actually flying west.

This means if you want to use the compass to make a turn, you need to account for the fact it will overshoot on any south heading and undershoot on any north heading. The worst overshoot or undershoot will be when flying directly south or directly north, and the amount of overshoot or undershoot will be roughly equivalent to your latitude. (In fact, our experience flying around the real Portland, Maine, is that a 40-degree correction for a due southward to north heading works better. FSX seems to like 30, though.) This is easier to explain with a specific example.

If you wanted to turn magnetic south when leaving the Portland airport, you would begin a left turn, go past 180, and roll wings level on the compass indicated 150. While you were flying level, the compass would swing back to indicate 180, or something fairly close, which would be your actual heading. You could then make a small correction to get precisely on course.

To fly southwest on the heading of 225, return until the compass shows a heading of 230, or 15° too far. Here you are overshooting by only 15° because 225 is halfway between west, where there is no compass error, and south, where there is the greatest compass error, so you use only half the 30-degree correction.

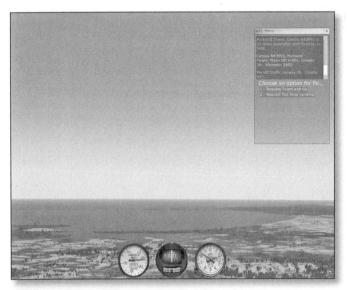

Figure 5-17: After your turn toward your first waypoint, use the best view to find it on the horizon, and head that way.

Figure 5-18: Look for the airport as an open space south of the town.

After you're level, look straight ahead, and try to find that spit of land at the north end of old Orchard Beach. Since you're climbing, it's easiest to switch to 2D cockpit view by pressing F10 and then W on your keyboard to get rid of all but the most essential instruments (see Figure 5-17). When you have your visual checkpoint in sight, head toward it, and continue to climb toward 2,500 feet.

You can see how you're doing on the map at any time by choosing World > Map. You'll notice that by taking off Runway 29, you began the flight slightly off course. This is not a big deal, and you should see the nose of the little airplane symbol pointing toward the first waypoint.

When you get to 2,500 feet, level off and let your speed build to 70 mph. Then adjust the throttle for 2100 rpm, and adjust the trim to keep 70 mph. Fly completely over the checkpoint at the north end of Old Orchard Beach. You might want to put it slightly off to your left or right so you can see it as you fly over. Now turn toward your next checkpoint of Biddeford airport (see Figure 5-18). You'll probably see it in the turn as an open space just across the river and south of the town of Biddeford.

Press P on your keyboard again to pause the simulation. If you don't have your kneeboard visible, press Shift+F10 on your keyboard, and then press the Nav Log button on the kneeboard. You might need to press the button a second time to get the nav log to update. After it's updated, you'll see a comparison between your estimated time of arrival at the checkpoint and your actual time of arrival (see Figure 5-19). You'll also see two entries for this first leg. One time is for the estimated times and speeds, and

136

| PART I | PART II | PART III | PART IV | PART V | PART VI |
| PREFLIGHT | SPORT PILOT | PRIVATE PILOT | INSTRUMENT RATING | COMMERCIAL LICENSE | ATP AND BEYOND |

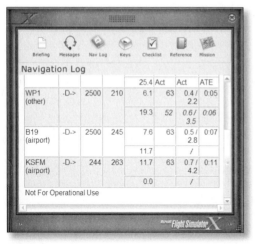

the other is for the actual times and speeds. You'll see that your actual time en route between Portland and the first checkpoint is a little bit longer than the expected one, but that makes sense because you are slower during the climb that you had actually planned for in the flight planner.

Figure 5-19: Press the Nav Log button on your kneeboard to update your navigation log with the actual time en route. In a real airplane, you have to measure the time between each and do all the math.

KEEPING IT REAL

LEANING FOR CRUISE

Checklists in aircraft as simple as the Cub are almost silly. Nonetheless, you still need some way to make sure all the critical tasks get done at the critical times. We recommend something called a *flow check*. Every time you transition from one phase of flight to another, such as switching from a climb to a level altitude cruise or beginning your descent to land, start at the trim wheel, and look over all the instruments in the cockpit to make sure nothing needs adjusting.

The trim wheel is a good place to start because you have probably just adjusted it to level off or begin your descent. Check the flight instruments, and make sure you do not need to enter a new altimeter setting and that the oil instruments are indicating what you expect. Make sure the carb heat does not need to be turned on or off. And make sure the mixture is where you want it.

In the real Cub, you would pull the red mixture knob slightly aft to let less fuel flow to the engine during the cruise portion of your flight. During climb, the Cub burns extra fuel partially to keep its engine cool. This fuel would simply be wasted during cruise. Normal leaning in the Cub means pulling the red knob back until the engine runs rough and then pushing it back forward until the engine smoothes out and then a little bit more.

In FSX, leaning is accomplished by pressing Ctrl+X on your keyboard. If you have flying tips turned on, you might see a flying tip instructing you to do exactly that.

Press P again on your keyboard to resume the simulation, and close the kneeboard if it gets in your way. As you approach Biddeford, the right thing to do would be to monitor the airport's frequency and listen for any other airplanes. You should also announce that you are crossing over the airport at 2,500 feet since this is fairly close to the ground and to any airplanes that might be operating in the traffic pattern at Biddeford.

To emulate this in FSX, you need to tap the Nearest Airport List in the ATC window. You can then tune B19's CTAF. You can't automatically announce that you're five miles northeast and will cross over the field at 2,500 feet, but that's what you would do in the real world.

After you cross Biddeford, turn to a heading of 263 on the compass. Note that this is so close to 270, or west, that no compass correction is needed. You should just see Sanford airport on the horizon.

You'll need to click back in the ATC window to get a list of nearest airports that now includes Sanford. Sanford is uncontrolled, so you'll need to get the weather from the AWOS.

En route to Sanford, check your nav log again to see how things are progressing. The numbers should be pretty close. Note that the longer the legs of your trip, the more likely there will be a difference between your planned time and your actual one because a small difference in speed has time to add up.

Since the winds are calm at Sanford, you can choose any runway for landing. If there is already traffic in the airport pattern, then the protocol is to follow their lead and enter the pattern to land on the same runway they are using. If no one is there, you choose what to do.

Runway 25 is most convenient for you on this heading, so without someone in the pattern, you can head for a spot about 2 miles before the runway and plan to be down to about 1,300 feet—about 1,000 feet above the airport elevation of 244 feet. You can announce your position using the ATC window.

HOW FAR IS THAT?

You can use the ATC window to find out how far you are from the airport by announcing your position. The virtual voice will give a report with your distance to the center of the airport.

We recommend you don't change your throttle setting. Just trim for 75 mph, and the Cub will head down nicely. When you're about 2 miles from the airport, reduce the power to 1,500, and trim for 60 mph. Soon after that you will be in a normal position to reduce the power to 1300, announce that you are on final, and continue for landing.

BY THE BOOK

YOU CAN'T GET THERE FROM HERE

Yet another way to get a bunch of pilots arguing is to ask the best way to enter a traffic pattern at an uncontrolled airport. When you are approaching the airport from the same side as the traffic pattern, it's not that difficult. You can usually enter a 45-degree angle to the downwind leg or the base leg to the runway that's being used. Traffic permitting, you can also land straight in to a runway when it's being used, as you did in this scenario. Etiquette dictates, however, that anyone already in the pattern has right of way, and you'll maneuver to follow behind them rather than cut them off.

Continued

138

PART I
PILOT LIGHT

PART II
SPORT PILOT

PART III
PRIVATE PILOT

PART IV
INSTRUMENT RATING

PART V
COMMERCIAL LICENSE

PART VI
ATP AND BEYOND

The rub comes when you are entering the traffic pattern from the opposite side of the runway. You now must fly over the runway and enter the pattern somehow. Two schools of thought exist. One school says to fly over the airport at least 500 feet, or even 1,000 feet, above the pattern altitude. Then you fly a few miles past the airport, descend to the appropriate altitude, turn around, and come back in from the correct side. This is certainly a safe way to avoid cutting anybody off—or running into them in the air—but it takes a lot of time.

The other school of thought is to cross over the center the airport and pattern at the pattern altitude, and simply make a left or right turn as appropriate to enter the downwind. This position halfway down the downwind is referred to as a *midfield downwind*. It has the advantage of being quicker, and therefore more efficient, but a careless pilot could easily cut off an aircraft that is already on the downwind. It's known as an *overhead join* in Europe.

Both are legal and acceptable in the United States. (The overhead join is the rule in Canada and much of Europe.) Our position is that your primary concern is safety in the busy traffic pattern, and you should approach the pattern from the correct side at the correct altitude. But if, in your opinion as pilot in command of the airplane, a more efficient entry is safe and polite, go ahead and use it.

NOTE!

FLY THERE VIRTUALLY FIRST

An awesome use of FSX for real-world flying is to fly to an unfamiliar airport on the computer before flying there in real life. Although the scenery might not be an exact match, the layout is amazingly similar. The position of the airport relative to surrounding terrain and nearby towns is usually accurate, the layout of the runways is the same, and even the location of buildings around the airfield is usually the same.

SEE THE MOVIE

You can load and watch a flight video of this exercise: Ch_05_Portland_to_Sanford.

SERIOUSLY DEAD RECKONING

Now it's time for some serious dead reckoning. Here's a flight you'd be crazy to do in a real Cub (unless you had a full kit of water survival gear), but it's fun on the sim. You'll be leaving Beverly, Massachusetts (KBVY), and heading for Provincetown on the tip of Cape Cod (KPVC). The catch is that this time there is a strong wind—45 knots from the northeast. This will blow you off course if you don't account for it.

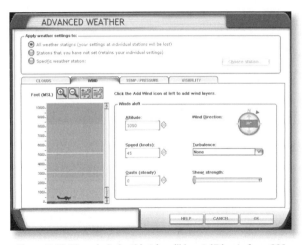

Figure 5-20: The winds for this trip will be at 45 knots from 038.

Load the flight Chap_05_Dead_Reckoning to get yourself on the ground at Beverly and get the winds set. The exact numbers are that they are from 038 blowing at 45 knots at 3,000 feet. If you want to see this in detail, you can choose World > Weather, click the button at the bottom for advanced weather, and then click the Weather tab (see Figure 5-20). Your cruising altitude will be 3,500 feet for this trip.

Now choose Flight > Flight Planner, and enter your departure and destination airports. This time you will fly direct, since there are no visual checkpoints to use. Note that the heading on the navigation log to get to Provincetown is 151. This does not account for the wind.

If you fly this heading, you'll completely miss Provincetown. You'll probably end up in Hyannis. If the winds were blowing you out to sea, you'd end up in deep (blue) trouble.

To find the right heading to fly, you'll need a flight computer. Do a Google search for *online E6B*, and you'll find a bunch. (Figure 5-21 shows one such online E6B.) The flight computer will ask for the wind speed and direction; 45 knots for the speed is easy. You might be tempted to enter 038 for the direction, but not so fast. Winds aloft in FSX and the real world are reporting in degrees true. Your heading is in degrees magnetic. You'll need to add 16° to get the correct magnetic wind direction. (It's 16 rather than 17 in eastern Massachusetts.)

Figure 5-21: The easiest E6B flight computers are available online for free.

140

| PART I | PART II | PART III | PART IV | PART V | PART VI |
| PREFLIGHT | SPORT PILOT | PRIVATE PILOT | INSTRUMENT RATING | COMMERCIAL LICENSE | ATP AND BEYOND |

Now you'll need your true airspeed at 3,000 feet in knots. This is about 63 for the Cub, but you can find online true airspeed calculators too.

The last piece is your course of 151. Enter that, and you should get the correct heading to fly and your estimated ground speed. You'll see that you must point your nose 45° off to the left to get to P-town, and it's going to take a while to get there. Your ground speed is only 50 knots (about 58 mph). It still beats driving, though.

Now fly the scenario. After you're out over the ocean, we recommend you increase the simulation rate to 16 times and look to your right. You'll see Provincetown come into view out the side window! Have fun on the landing. It'll be a crosswind. Just don't forget to reduce the simulation rate to Normal before you land.

▼ STUDENT OF THE CRAFT

FOLLOWING THE MAGENTA ROAD

Having a GPS onboard the aircraft makes all these calculations and concerns a thing of the past. With GPS all you need to do is turn your expected heading—which the GPS can give you once you enter your destination airport—and start flying. The GPS will show both your desired track, which is equivalent to the course you want to fly over the ground, and your actual track, which is the course you are flying over the ground including the effects of any wind. These two numbers appear as magnetic headings beside the symbols DTK and TRK, respectively. If your DTK equals your TRK, you'll go straight to your destination.

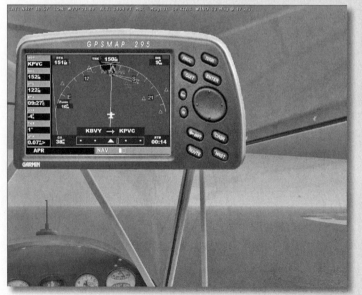

If they differ, then you simply adjust your heading until they are the same. That is the correct heading for wind. You might have drifted off course by the time you figure this out. That's OK, because your course is shown as a magenta line on the screen. Adjust your heading a little bit more so that the symbolic airplane flies back onto the magenta line; then turn to the correct heading to stay on course, and the magenta road will take you where you want to go. What could be easier?

The Cub does have a GPS. It's a portable Garmin 296. To see it, choose View > Instrument Panel > GPS. If you created a flight plan, then the GPS will show you the magenta line without you having to do anything else. On your trip to Provincetown, it would have removed all worry as to whether you could make it to the airport.

GPS makes diversions a snap as well. Most have a Nearest button that will show you a list of your nearest airports and let you select one. The GPS will then give you the course to get there, or DTK, and a magenta line to follow. Many can even show you the airport information, frequencies, and runway layout.

We'll talk more about GPS more in Chapter 11.

KEY POINTS FOR REAL FLYING AND FSX BUILT-INS

The following are some key points from this chapter:

- Conduct flight planning in the real world and in FSX.

- Calculate courses, and select altitudes.

- Make turns using the magnetic compass.

- Fly a multileg trip between two airports.

- Understand headings and wind correction angles.

Here are the lessons and missions to study after reading this chapter:

- *Lessons*: None in this chapter. Check out the Learning Center for more information about changing the weather or your departure and destination airport.

- *Missions*: Game Park Patrol.

CHAPTER 6

EMERGENCIES

"AVIATION IN ITSELF IS NOT INHERENTLY DANGEROUS. BUT TO AN EVEN GREATER DEGREE THAN THE SEA, IT IS TERRIBLY UNFORGIVING OF ANY CARELESSNESS, INCAPACITY, OR NEGLECT."
—ANONYMOUS, DATES BACK TO A WORLD WAR II ADVISORY

"MY DAD ONCE TOLD ME HE LEARNED EVERYTHING HE NEEDED TO KNOW ABOUT EMERGENCIES FROM THE SIDE OF A MAYONNAISE JAR. IT SAID, 'KEEP COOL. DON'T FREEZE.'"
—UNKNOWN

144

PART I	PART II	PART III	PART IV	PART V	PART VI
PREFLIGHT	SPORT PILOT	PRIVATE PILOT	INSTRUMENT RATING	COMMERCIAL LICENSE	ATP AND BEYOND

IN-FLIGHT EMERGENCIES

Figure 6-1: A bad emergency: engine on fire

Learning to control an airplane isn't really that hard, for the most part. But flying is a lot more than just controlling the airplane, and that's one reason there aren't many pilots. Even a poor pilot can usually handle a perfectly working airplane on a clear-sky day with no wind and no other airplanes nearby. The real world is never quite that perfect (see Figure 6-1), so pilots need to have experience dealing with challenging situations and emergencies.

Training can't prepare you for every problem you could ever run into during flight—just too many things could go wrong. Instead, good flight training—and a good flight instructor—will give you the skills to *think* about what is going wrong and come up with ways to deal with a variety of issues. You'll also learn how the various systems work and how they fail. (By *systems*, we mean both human and mechanical systems.) And you'll learn how to get help from others who might know more about your problem.

Using FSX for emergency training has the advantage that you can simulate emergencies that are just too dangerous to do in real life, and you can allow yourself to take a bad situation further than you would in real life to see how the consequences build up.

You can divide emergencies into two groups: *true emergencies*, which require immediate action, and *urgent situations*, which could turn into an immediate-action emergency if you ignore the problem.

WIND THE CLOCK

During military flight training many decades ago, flight instructors told pilots to do one thing first when they had an emergency: wind the clock. Of course, this was before digital clocks. In fact, the clocks then weren't even electric. But why would the instructors say that?

Few emergencies require quick reflex action; for most emergencies, if the pilot did the wrong thing, the problem could get worse. The act of winding a clock took a few seconds, during which the pilot could consider the next actions without actually doing anything. Then, when the clock was wound, the pilot could proceed to complete a checklist, find an emergency landing spot, or do whatever was needed.

IMMEDIATE-ACTION EMERGENCIES

Emergencies that require you to take action quickly—in less than a minute—to avoid damage to the airplane, injury, or death, include the following:

- Smoke, cabin fire, or engine compartment fire

- Flight control malfunction causing immediate loss of control

- Midair collision

- Severe structural icing

- Medical emergency

- Partial or complete power loss

- Loss of oil pressure

We'll discuss some of the ways pilots deal with these emergencies.

TROUBLESHOOTING AND PROBLEM SOLVING

The two likely places for a fire are in the cabin (electrical or other cause) and in the engine compartment. Airplanes are usually equipped with fire extinguishers for a cabin fire, so the danger here becomes incapacitation by smoke inhalation or losing control of the plane while fighting the fire. Engine fires can sometimes be put out by turning off the fuel supply and then diving to a high airspeed to blow out the flames. In either case, you want to get on the ground as quickly as possible using a rapid descent, which you'll practice later in this chapter.

If one of the flight controls—ailerons, elevator, and so on—suddenly locks up or becomes unusable, aircraft control becomes difficult if not impossible. The only real option is to fly the plane the best you can with the controls you have, trying to get on the ground as safely as possible. If flying doesn't take all your concentration, you can spend a little time seeing whether you can fix the problem.

A midair collision—if you survive—becomes a version of the flight control malfunction emergency because usually one or more controls or systems will be damaged.

In a small plane flying away from clouds, it is unlikely that you will get ice on the airplane. (When you work on your Instrument Rating lessons later in this book, you'll learn that ice can get on the plane if you fly in a cloud when the temperature is below freezing.) But ice can accumulate quickly if you fly in freezing rain. Airplanes with ice-covered wings don't fly well—or at all. If this happens, you need to immediately turn around because there wasn't freezing rain where you just were.

Some medical emergencies are so bad that you need to be on the ground immediately—even if that means landing somewhere other than an airport—using the rapid descent.

146

PART I
PREFLIGHT

PART II
SPORT PILOT

PART III
PRIVATE PILOT

PART IV
INSTRUMENT RATING

PART V
COMMERCIAL LICENSE

PART VI
ATP AND BEYOND

Many problems could cause your engine to slow down (drop rpms) or even stop. Your instinct will be to try to fix the problem and get the engine going again, but in the first minute your priority is to head for a landing site—a runway or just an open field—in case you can't fix the engine. For that you should use the power-off descent you'll learn next.

If you notice the oil pressure has dropped below the acceptable range or even gone to zero—and it isn't a failure of the oil pressure gauge—your engine will probably stop very soon. The procedure is the same as a partial or total engine loss: prepare for landing at the nearest spot you can glide to and land.

POWER-OFF DESCENT

When your engine stops, the airplane starts gliding down to the ground. It's not the end of the world, because small planes glide pretty well, and besides, you usually land with the engine idle anyway. You have some time—probably more than a minute for each 1,000 feet you're above the ground—but you need to prioritize your tasks. If you immediately try to restart the engine and can't get it to start, you've wasted precious time (and altitude) that could have been spent heading toward a good landing site. And if you don't pay attention to your airspeed as you glide down, you might not go as far as you need to or you might even stall the wings, which, as you'll learn in Chapter 8, causes you to descend *fast*.

Therefore, you need to memorize the ABC checklist and perform the steps in order:

1. **Airspeed**

2. **Best field**

3. **Checklist**

The airspeed you should fly is the one that gives you the most distance for every foot you descend, which is called *best glide*, or V_g. Each plane has a different V_g depending on the wing design, weight, drag, and so on, so you need to know the V_g of the plane you're flying and the weight it is at the time.

The second step is to find the best field for an emergency landing. Ideally, this would be an airport, so it is important to always keep track of nearby airports when flying so that, if the engine stops, you can head there without delay (especially if the nearest airport is *behind* you). If no airport is within gliding distance, then you need the longest field or area without obstructions you can find. Roads might seem good, but they have two problems: you don't want to endanger anyone on the ground, and usually power lines are crossing or next to roads. Power lines are hard to see and pretty much impossible to avoid if you try to land on roads. After you find the best field to land on, head there, gliding at your V_g.

Only after you've established your best glide speed heading toward an emergency landing site should you try to fix the problem that is causing you to lose power. If you memorized a quick checklist, now is the time to do it, but unless you're just about on the ground, take the time to pull out your written checklists and step through every item on the engine failure checklist. In an emergency situation, you're likely to be nervous, and you won't think clearly or remember everything you need to try.

If the engine doesn't restart and you need to actually land, try to treat it no differently than any other landing, especially if you've practiced landing without power.

TRIM UP FOR GLIDE

In many light airplanes, full nose-up trim is close to best glide airspeed. In a pinch, you can trim full nose-up and head for a field. This keeps the airspeed close to what you need while you troubleshoot.

RAPID DESCENT

For those emergencies where you need to get on the ground as quickly as possible—such as a medical emergency or a fire—the goal is not to glide far but to descend fast. The obvious reaction is to push the nose forward and dive, but your airspeed will be so high that you might break the aircraft, or at the least, you'll have a hard time slowing down after you do get to a lower altitude and get ready to land.

The solution here is to take advantage of the aerodynamics of turns that you learned in Chapter 2. Turning requires energy, and during normal turns, that means you have to pull back slightly on the stick, or you descend. But during an emergency descent, you have too much energy (you're too high), so you *want* to waste it.

You need to get over a place to land, so find it and head that way in a dive of 90 or even 100 mph.

After you're over your landing spot, you must get down as quickly as possible without speeding up. Idle the engine, make a steep turn of 45° or 50°, and hold that bank while letting the nose drop. Using the elevator, maintain a safe airspeed (well above stall speed but nowhere near speeds that would hurt the plane), and maintain the steep turn. For the Cub, 90 mph works well.

If you have the presence of mind to keep your landing spot in sight as you whiz around and around, you can do so, but if not, roll wings level at 1,000 feet above the ground, and look for the spot.

If you can't find the ideal target, you might have to make a rapid descent without a landing spot. This isn't ideal, but it might be the right choice if staying in the air is more dangerous.

STUDENT OF THE CRAFT

CARBURETOR ICE

How can a carburetor on an aircraft engine get ice in it? After all, the engine is hot! Actually, the carburetor is pretty cold. Inside the carburetor, fuel is sprayed into the air going into the engine, and just like spraying mist on your skin, the air cools down a lot. If the air is already cool and moist from humidity, the temperature of the air could drop below freezing, and the moisture would stick inside the carburetor and block air from going in. You would lose power and the engine could eventually stop if you don't turn on the carburetor heat, which pumps warm air into the carburetor.

Modern, fuel-injected car engines don't have a carburetor, so they don't get carb ice. Older cars have carburetors, but they're positioned on top of the engine and kept warm there, so such cars also rarely get carburetor ice. Aircraft engine carburetors are usually on the bottom of the engine and exposed to cold air, and carb ice is a problem. The outside air doesn't have to be really cold either; carb ice can happen at summertime temperatures if there is enough humidity.

148

PART I	PART II	PART III	PART IV	PART V	PART VI
PREFLIGHT	SPORT PILOT	PRIVATE PILOT	INSTRUMENT RATING	COMMERCIAL LICENSE	ATP AND BEYOND

URGENT SITUATIONS

An urgent situation is one that does not cause imminent danger to people or property but, left unchecked, could become dangerous. Some urgent situations include the following:

- Flap malfunction

- Low fuel

- Inoperative trim

- Inadvertent door or window opening

- Electrical malfunction

- Flight instrument malfunctions

- Carburetor or induction system icing (see "Carburetor Ice")

- Engine roughness or overheat

- Feeling ill or other bodily need that can't wait too long

This list is not complete, but it gives you a sense of the issues that can cause problems. Think about each item, and consider why it is not considered an immediate-action emergency. Does it surprise you that none of these items is immediately dangerous? We will not go into the details of solving these problems here, but they are part of real-life flight training, so they are worth considering now.

KEEPING IT REAL

DECLARING AN EMERGENCY

You've got some engine problems, but you think you can make it to a nearby airport rather than just putting the plane down in a field somewhere. You're concerned that there might be other aircraft at your destination, and you'd rather not worry about the control tower telling you to wait your turn to land. Still, the engine is running, and you don't really want to cause a scene.

Should you ask for priority? Do you say "Mayday" on the radio and declare an emergency?

The advantage of declaring an emergency is that you can break just about any FAA regulation to deal with the emergency. You can even declare an emergency in your head; it doesn't have to be on the radio or talking to someone official. But other people—especially air traffic controllers and pilots—can help you a lot if they know that you have an emergency.

If you're talking to other pilots, they will help out any way they can, whether it is helping you try to fix your airplane, circling over your crash-landing site, and everything in between.

Air traffic controllers can do a lot to help you when you declare an emergency. They will clear out traffic from the airport you're heading toward, notify search and rescue, or get the emergency vehicles ready at the airport.

The only disadvantage of declaring an emergency is that you might have to explain it later to an FAA official, but that's not much of a disadvantage unless you were faking the emergency just to get preferential treatment. You'll probably just have to answer some basic questions when the FAA calls, and that will be the end of it.

We've known several pilots who have declared emergencies for real. Only two of them were ever contacted after the fact to answer some questions, and those conversations were friendly and brief.

EMERGENCY TRAINING

Because FSX doesn't include every possible system failure an airplane could have, it is difficult to train for many of them. And many failures that *can* be simulated don't work very well for training if you, the student, know what went wrong because you programmed FSX to make that specific failure. Surprise is one of the causes of a pilot *freezing* and being unable to think through emergencies. That's one reason you need to do your flight training with an instructor, whether on FSX on in a real airplane. We'll discuss multiplayer capabilities in Chapter 25. You can also have FSX create random failures to surprise you; check out the FSX Learning Center for instructions.

But just about all emergencies include one common action: you want to land sooner than you were expecting to land. Getting on the ground (and, sometimes, out of the plane) is usually the best action you can do to protect yourself and others.

Some emergencies, such as an engine failure, require you to descend slowly so that you can get to a safe, emergency landing site that might be far away. Others, such as a fire or medical emergency, call for the fastest descent you can safely attain. This lesson covers both types of descents in the Cub, and then we'll take you through some oddball emergencies to tax your flying and thinking abilities—and have some fun in the process.

150

PART I PREFLIGHT   **PART II** SPORT PILOT   **PART III** PRIVATE PILOT   **PART IV** INSTRUMENT RATING   **PART V** COMMERCIAL LICENSE   **PART VI** ATP AND BEYOND

POWER-OFF DESCENT

Load the flight Chap_06_Barre_Glide. You are near Barre, Vermont, at 4,000 feet (see Figure 6-2). Soon after the flight starts, the engine stops producing power. The propeller probably keeps turning, but that's only because the plane is still moving forward through the air, and the air is spinning the prop.

Figure 6-2: Start of Chap_06_Barre_Glide flight near Barre, Vermont

NOTE!

▼ **"... AND CLEAN THE WINDSHIELD TOO, PLEASE"**

If you have the Flying Tips option turned on, you'll get a message saying that you're low on fuel. FSX's Cub doesn't have an auxiliary fuel tank, so don't cheat on this one!

ABCs

Start with the memorized, engine-out ABCs: airspeed, best field, checklist. With the loss of power, you're already starting to slow down, but your trim is set for 70 mph, so the nose pitches down on its own to maintain 70 mph. Pull the nose back up to a level attitude until you reach the best glide speed of 45 mph, and then pitch down as needed to maintain 45 mph. Set the trim so the elevator stays at 45 mph (you might have to continue to hold back pressure on the stick). As you proceed with the rest of the ABCs, keep glancing at your airspeed indicator to make sure you're at 45 mph.

Look around for the best field to land on—the best would be an airport, but if not, any open field or other decent landing spot is fine at this point. Start by looking ahead of you, and then check to the sides. When you see one that you think is close enough to reach, turn toward it with a gentle turn. (Banking more than 30° either causes the plane to drop rapidly or increases your stalling speed—see Chapter 8 for more information.) As you follow the procedures for trying to restart the engine, keep checking your landing spot to see whether you need to adjust your flight path to set up for landing.

↓ | POWER LINE CUTS

In areas of the country where there are lots of trees—such as in New England where you're flying the Cub—some of the nicest-looking emergency landing spots are the long, straight lines through trees, wide enough to land in and sometimes even with a dirt road down the middle. But unless you're absolutely positive the trees were cut just for the road, don't try to land; there are power lines going right through the cutline.

If you are less than 1,000 feet above the ground (the valleys in this area are between 1,200 and 1,800 feet above MSL on your altimeter), you need to prepare for an immediate landing.

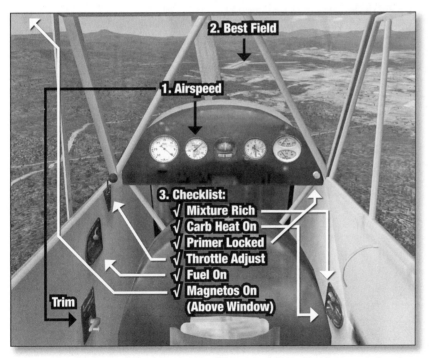

Figure 6-3: Emergency engine-out checklist: airspeed, best field, checklist to restart engine

If you are more than 1,000 feet above the ground, proceed with the engine-out checklist to try to restart the engine. FSX doesn't provide emergency checklists for the Cub, so use the procedure in Figure 6-3 to try to fix what is wrong.

Starting at the lower-right side of the cockpit, ensure the mixture setting is rich, and turn on the carb heat. (It won't help much without the engine running, but it's always a good habit.) In a real Cub, you want to make sure the primer on the front panel is fully locked in place; fuel leaking past it could stop the engine. You can also use it to send extra fuel to the engine. Click the priming switch to see whether that restarts the engine. (We know of at least one pilot who brought a Cessna 152 back to an airport by pumping the primer all the way to keep a fuel-starved engine running.)

Moving to the left side of the cockpit, move the throttle back and forth to see whether you can get any power at all. Check the fuel control switch to make sure it is on. Look up on the left side above the door, and check the magneto switch; even though it normally is on Both, you might get the engine to work on L(eft) or R(ight).

152

PART I	PART II	PART III	PART IV	PART V	PART VI
PREFLIGHT	SPORT PILOT	PRIVATE PILOT	INSTRUMENT RATING	COMMERCIAL LICENSE	ATP AND BEYOND

SECURE THE ENGINE AND LAND

If the engine hasn't restarted (and, in this simulation, it won't), you need to secure the engine and prepare for landing. Put the fuel control switch to off, and set the magneto switch to off. Tighten up your seatbelt (if your chair has seatbelts!), and make sure all cockpit items have been secured and won't fly around if you land poorly. Even though these checklist items aren't simulated in FSX, it is good to mentally step through them and even pretend to tighten up the seatbelt to help you remember them if you're ever in a real plane with a real emergency.

The ATC menu of FSX doesn't have a mayday option, but in real life if you had a radio, you'd be calling "Mayday" at this point on whatever frequency the radio is already tuned to. If you have the presence of mind to think of it, you could tune the radio to 121.500 MHz. Say where you are and what is happening, and hope that someone hears you.

The rest is relatively easy: you need to land. If you're too high to make the beginning of your runway or field, use a forward slip to sink faster, just like you learned in Chapter 3. If you're too low, you'll just have to hit some trees or whatever; don't pull up trying to climb over anything, because you'll just slow down and sink more steeply, possibly stalling (which would be a really bad thing).

NOTE! | ↓ MAYDAY, MAYDAY, MAYDAY

The term *Mayday* comes from the French word *M'aidez* (pronounced the same), which means "Help me."

DO OVER

When this flight lesson began, you probably noticed the airport ahead of you; however, if you tried to land there when your engine quit, you found that you couldn't quite make it there. What you don't know is that the wind is working against you. But if you had actually been flying along for a while—rather than starting in midair like in this simulation scenario—you would have known about the wind. You would also have known that you just passed a small airport a few miles back that is actually closer to you.

Let's do it again, this time remembering the wind and looking for places to land behind you. Press Ctrl+; to reset the flight, unpause, and while waiting for the engine to quit take a look behind you (using the spot plane mode) to find that other airport.

When the engine stops, do the ABC checklist: airspeed, 45 mph; best field, turn right and head for that airport; and checklists, try to restart the engine using the instructions given previously.

If you made that right turn reasonably soon after the engine stopped and if you maintain 45 mph on your gliding descent, you should be able to set up a short approach to the runway at the small airport. You probably won't have enough altitude to fly a proper traffic pattern and go all the way down to the other end of the runway so that you can land into the wind; that's fine. Beggars can't be choosers, and even if the runway is too short for your landing with a tailwind, there is grass after the runway ends. Even if you can't stop before the trees at the end of the clearing, it is better to hit them going only 10 or 20 mph as you're stopping on the ground rather than at 45 mph while in flight.

And if you did a really good job of getting turned around and maintaining the best glide speed of 45 mph, you might actually be a little bit high on final approach. Sideslip to lose altitude; if you overshoot, you can't make a go-around and try again.

RAPID DESCENT

In this scenario, you'll practice a rapid descent. For whatever reason, you need to get on the ground as quickly as possible.

Load the flight Chap_06_Carriers_Descent. When you unpause the simulator, you'll be heading toward that small airport you glided to in the previous section (Carriers Skypark), as shown in Figure 6-4. However, stay at 4,000 feet until you're right over the airport. Idle the engine, roll into a steep-bank turn (45°), and pitch the nose to maintain an airspeed of about 80 mph (see Figure 6-5). Stay coordinated during the turn.

Figure 6-4: Start of Chap_06_Carriers_Descent flight near Washington, Vermont

Figure 6-5: During a rapid descent, maintain a steep bank and an airspeed of about 80 mph. Keep an eye on your emergency landing site so you can roll out with enough altitude to safely land there.

When you're about 500 feet above the ground (about 2200 MSL), roll out to wings level, pitch for normal landing speed (55 mph), and try to land at the airport.

Your engine works fine in this example, so use if it you need to do so. If you had an engine fire, however, you would have shut the fuel off. Try the scenario again, but this time, after you idle the engine, don't use it again, and then try to glide to the airport.

The FSX video Chap_06_Rapid_Descent shows how this maneuver looks when done correctly.

154

PART I
PREFLIGHT

PART II
SPORT PILOT

PART III
PRIVATE PILOT

PART IV
INSTRUMENT RATING

PART V
COMMERCIAL LICENSE

PART VI
ATP AND BEYOND

ACCIDENT CHAIN

DEALING WITH AN EMERGENCY

On February 24, 1989, a Boeing 747 was flying from Honolulu, Hawaii, with a full load of passengers, cargo, and fuel for a long flight to Aukland, New Zealand. As it was climbing past 22,000 feet about 60 miles from Honolulu, the right front cargo door ripped open, taking a chunk of the fuselage and nine passengers with it. One engine on the right wing of the plane immediately shut down because debris got into it. The pilots descended to a breathable altitude and turned back to Hawaii. Meanwhile, a fire started in the second engine on the right wing, and the pilots shut it down. They landed at Honolulu with only the two left-wing engines operating. All the remaining passengers and crew evacuated the airplane safely.

Most of the descriptions of this accident discuss the faulty design of the cargo door and the latching mechanism and some improper maintenance, and the NTSB report discusses those points. But hidden in the investigation are some key actions by the pilots that can teach us a lot about dealing with emergencies.

Pilots of pressurized airplanes are taught that the first step to take if the cabin depressurizes is put on an oxygen mask and start descending. At 22,000 feet without pressurization, you have 5 minutes or less before you go unconscious; unfortunately, you lose the ability to think clearly after even less time. So, the pilots of this airplane immediately started descending to thicker air and put on their oxygen masks. Unfortunately, the oxygen tank for the masks was next to the cargo door—or at least it was until it was ripped out of the plane. They descended and were soon at a breathable altitude, and they also turned toward their chosen "emergency landing site," which was Honolulu. They started dumping their extra fuel overboard to reduce the risk of a fire when they landed and to make the plane lighter because they only had two engines working.

As they approached Honolulu, they used their normal, prelanding checklists. One item said to lower the landing gear. The captain—a senior pilot close to retirement—assessed the situation before he put down the gear: he realized they couldn't maintain altitude on only two engines. Even though they were dumping fuel, the plane was still too heavy, so the plane slowly descended. If they put out the landing gear, the added drag might make them descend too quickly to reach Honolulu. The captain had no way to know for sure, but he didn't want to take a chance. He chose to keep the landing gear retracted until they were just a few miles from the runway.

That decision ended up saving the rest of the passengers and crew. Later experiments in 747 flight simulators showed that the two engines would not have been able to keep the plane from descending into the ocean short of Honolulu if the Captain had allowed the landing gear to be extended the usual distance from the airport.

> Because the Captain didn't rush procedures after the immediate-action emergency (depressurization) was over, he was able to take time to think about each step and make decisions about where he needed to deviate from normal procedures. There was no way for him to know, or catch, that the gear made that much difference. He just had a hunch.
>
> They even had the presence of mind to share an irony on the way back to Honolulu. The first officer said, "What a %$#@! of a thing to happen on your second-to-last month." "No %$#@!" replied the captain.

ODDBALL EMERGENCIES

Many problems could occur during a flight, and we can't cover all of them. Even in real-world flight training, you don't get to experience all the possible issues that could go wrong.

For these final few flights, we've chosen a few situations that are dangerous to do in real-world flight training but that can be realistically represented by FSX. Don't try these in a real Cub, but see how well you can handle these problems in FSX.

AILERON DISABLED

Controlling the airplane when a major flight system like an aileron is broken is a skill that you might never have to use, even in real life, but it gives a good training experience for other similar oddball emergencies. The flight Chap_06_Barre_Aileron_Failure begins near Barre with a broken left aileron, so you have no roll control (see Figure 6-6).

Or do you?

The right aileron works fine, but you might find it isn't strong enough to roll as quickly as you're used to doing. Your rudder will help, though. Use it as needed to turn (you'll be slightly uncoordinated when that happens), and then try to stay coordinated the rest of the time.

Figure 6-6: The left aileron has failed, leaving you with limited roll control. Can you land with just the right aileron and rudder working?

156

PART I
PREFLIGHT

PART II
SPORT PILOT

PART III
PRIVATE PILOT

PART IV
INSTRUMENT RATING

PART V
COMMERCIAL LICENSE

PART VI
ATP AND BEYOND

Make all your movements even more slowly and carefully as you learn how to fly in this new configuration. You want to land as soon as possible, so turn the airplane toward the runway at Barre, and do your best to land safely.

FLIGHT INSTRUMENT FAILURE

Figure 6-7: Your airspeed indicator and altimeter have failed. Use the view out the window and the sound of the wind to estimate your altitude and speed and bring yourself safely to the runway.

The airspeed indicator and the altimeter on the Cub work by taking outside air from little tubes out on the wings. So, what would happen if those tubes got blocked?

The flight Chap_06_Barre_ No_Instruments has just that circumstance: you need to land the plane without knowing your exact airspeed or altitude (see Figure 6-7). But at this point in your training, you can probably make good guesses.

Look outside at the airport, buildings, trees, and so on, and decide how they compare to a normal landing; are you higher than usual or lower? As you turn toward the runway, keep judging your height just by the position of objects and the angle of the runway.

As for airspeed, you have two ways to guess. If you set the power at the right rpm and you pitch the plane to its usual position slightly nose down for descent, you should get the right airspeed. The other way to tell whether you're getting too slow or too fast is to listen to the air whistling past the airplane: if it gets quiet, you're too slow; louder than normal (or higher pitch), and you're probably fast.

By the way, this scenario might seem far-fetched, but we actually practice this with student pilots in real airplanes. No, we don't break the instruments; we just cover up the entire instrument panel with a jacket while on downwind in a traffic pattern, and the student lands the airplane. If you want to try this extreme scenario, on your keyboard press F10 and then press W until you have no instrument panel in front of you. Our students do just fine, and you will too.

KEY POINTS FOR REAL FLYING AND FSX BUILT-INS

The following are some key points from this chapter:

- Discriminate between immediate-action emergencies that need to be dealt with in mere moments and urgent situations that could turn into emergencies if not addressed soon.

- Learn techniques for descending at the best glide speed and maximum safe descent rate.

- Practice finding appropriate landing sites based on the immediacy of the emergency or urgent situation.

Here are the lessons and missions to study after reading this chapter:

- *Lessons*: Commercial Pilot Lesson 3 is about emergency procedures and engine failures. This flight lesson takes place in the twin-engine Beech Baron, which we don't cover in this book until the Commercial License, but the ground lesson on emergency procedures is a good review of this chapter.

- *Missions*: A couple of missions deal with emergencies, but the missions involve airliners. Unless you've already trained on those jets, you'll spend too much time trying to figure out how to fly the planes, and you won't be able to learn from the emergencies themselves.

CHAPTER 7

PERFORMANCE TAKEOFFS AND LANDINGS

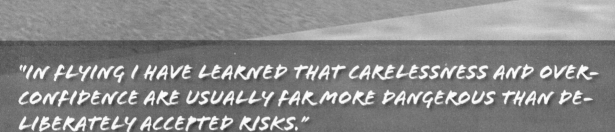

"IN FLYING I HAVE LEARNED THAT CARELESSNESS AND OVER-CONFIDENCE ARE USUALLY FAR MORE DANGEROUS THAN DE-LIBERATELY ACCEPTED RISKS."

—WILBUR WRIGHT

"THERE ARE THREE SIMPLE RULES FOR MAKING A SMOOTH LANDING. UNFORTUNATELY, NO ONE KNOWS WHAT THEY ARE."

—AVIATION CLICHÉ

160

PART I
PREFLIGHT

PART II
SPORT PILOT

PART III
PRIVATE PILOT

PART IV
INSTRUMENT RATING

PART V
COMMERCIAL LICENSE

PART VI
ATP AND BEYOND

Aerodynamics of Performance

The Cub is such a wonderful, light aircraft that it can take off in a short distance from a runway made of asphalt, dirt (as in Figure 7-1), or grass. Other planes you fly in your training and pilot career (sim or real) take more distance and might not be able to use anything but a hard-surface runway. But the skills necessary to really get good performance out of an airplane—such as getting a short takeoff roll or a steep climb—apply to the Cub just as much as they apply to the airplanes you fly in the rest of this training program. Sim or real-world, the procedures are the same.

Figure 7-1: The Cub is designed to go into short, dirt airstrips like this one in Mahoney Creek, Idaho.

Takeoff and Landing Calculations

When you analyze an airport and a runway to see how well your aircraft will perform in takeoff and landing, you need to consider six primary factors:

- Runway surface (asphalt, dirt, grass)

- Runway length

- Obstacles after departure or before landing

- Winds

- Airport elevation

- Air temperature

Other factors, such as the slope of the runway, might be critical at some airports but are not a common concern. (For instance, default FSX runways are flat, but custom scenery might be different.)

As you might guess, a soft runway creates more friction on the tires, making your takeoff roll longer. But the reverse doesn't happen when landing: instead of the grass causing a shorter landing roll, you might actually need more runway when landing on grass because you can't use the brakes as much when you try to stop quickly.

If any obstacles are in your way after takeoff—trees, power lines, whatever—then you have to climb at an angle that clears those obstacles. During landing, if obstacles exist just before the runway, you need to make a steep approach to clear them and still land and stop without running off the far end of the runway.

You've already learned that you can shorten both your takeoff and your landing distance if you fly into the wind and that trying to land or take off with the wind at your tail can really increase the runway you use.

We won't go into detail here about airport elevation and temperature, but it is enough to know that if the airport is at a higher altitude or the temperature is high, or both, you will need more runway to take off and land, and you will not climb as steeply as when flying at a lower-altitude, lower-temperature airport. (This is because your true airspeed will be higher, and your engine won't produce as much power, because of less oxygen in the air.)

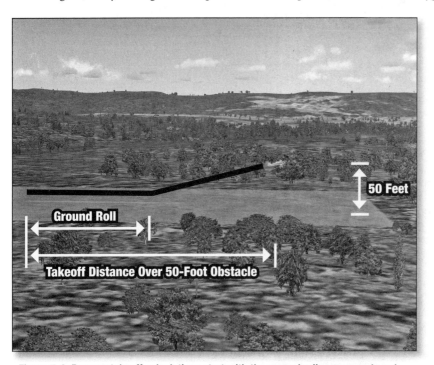

Modern airplanes come with a *Pilot's Operating Handbook* (POH) that you use to calculate the amount of runway needed to take off and land. Those calculations take into account runway surface, winds, elevation, and temperature, and they tell you the total distance needed until you're off the ground (takeoff ground roll), the total distance to the point you're 50 feet above the ground (takeoff over a 50-foot obstacle, as shown in Figure 7-2), the total distance needed to stop on the runway after landing (landing ground roll), and the total distance to land after passing 50-feet above ground (landing over 50-foot obstacle).

Figure 7-2: Runway takeoff calculations start with the ground roll necessary to get airborne and also include the total distance to clear a 50-foot obstacle. The difference is then used for calculating the distance to climb any additional height, in 50-foot increments.

This 50-foot obstacle altitude is not some magic number; runways usually don't have a 50-foot tree or building sitting right at the end. But there might be trees a distance beyond the runway, and knowing how much total length you need to clear them could be important. By knowing how much distance over the ground you need for each additional 50 feet up, you can estimate how much total run you need

162

PART I	PART II	PART III	PART IV	PART V	PART VI
PREFLIGHT	SPORT PILOT	PRIVATE PILOT	INSTRUMENT RATING	COMMERCIAL LICENSE	ATP AND BEYOND

to clear trees that are higher. Most takeoff distance charts list the total distance to clear the 50-foot obstacle including the ground roll, and then separately they list the ground roll distance. You might need to break this up to calculate for taller obstacles.

▣ BY THE BOOK

PERFECT PILOT, PERFECT DAY

The published takeoff and landing distances for aircraft are calculated from several test flights using new aircraft and professional pilots. This means the data you see on those charts is probably as good as that airplane will ever perform. A real airplane with a tired engine or less-than-perfect airframe will have worse performance for takeoff and, possibly, for landing. Poor pilot technique on even a new airplane can mean significantly longer takeoff and landing distances.

The Cub in FSX doesn't come with takeoff and landing data, so you won't be able to do specific performance calculations. (Most real Cubs don't have them either.) But the procedures for getting the best performance out of your Cub can be useful.

RATE AND ANGLE OF CLIMB AND DESCENT

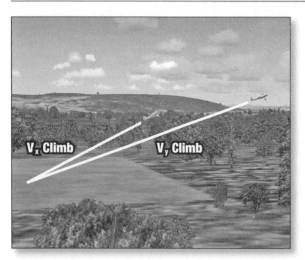

Figure 7-3: The paths an airplane takes when flying at V_x and V_y are very different. The two airplanes have been paused after exactly one minute. Note that the V_y airplane is higher, but the V_x airplane climbed more steeply to clear the trees.

After your wheels lift off the runway during takeoff, the takeoff isn't over yet. If you have obstacles, you need to climb higher than them. If not, you still want to climb up quickly so that you can get to your cruise altitude and pick up speed. You really have two different goals: in the first case, you want the best _angle_ of climb (a condition where you gain the most altitude for the least distance you travel forward); in the second case, you want the best _rate_ of climb (where you gain the most altitude per minute). Figure 7-3 compares the two paths.

A particular airspeed gives you the best angle of climb, and a different airspeed gives you the best rate of climb. For convenience, the best angle of climb speed is shown as V_x (the "V" means velocity), and the best rate of climb speed is shown as V_y. V_x and V_y are different for each type of airplane and also different for a particular airplane depending on weight and altitude.

These two speeds are critical: if you fly slower than V_x, the extra drag will cause you to climb less steeply; and if you climb faster than V_x, again you will climb less steeply because you're moving forward too quickly. This is the same with V_y for the best rate of climb.

But under the pressure of a critical takeoff, maintaining the right speed is easier said than done. Imagine you're taking off from a runway with trees at the far end. You lift off and pitch up the nose of the plane to maintain V_x. As you climb, you see that you're not climbing fast enough to clear the trees. No matter what you do at this point, you cannot clear those trees: if you pull back and slow down, you climb even less; if you push the nose down and speed up, you climb less. What can you do? Well, in FSX, you can crash into those trees and try something different. In the real world, your best hope is to idle the engine, drop down, and land before the trees, hoping you can slow down a bit before you hit them. Really, the problem should have been solved before you even took off, when you calculated how much distance you'd need to clear those trees.

Descending is a little bit different, but some of the concepts apply. No speeds can be figured for the best rate of descent or the best angle of descent because, let's face it, you can just point the nose down and dive at the ground if you want to get down fast! But most airplane manuals do have an airspeed that you should use when making a short-field landing. This speed makes a steeper approach to landing than your normal approach speed.

Short-Field and Soft-Field Procedures

Figure 7-4: Start of Chap_07_Moore flight at Moore Airfield in New Hampshire

The shortest runway you've used for the Cub so far in this book is 2,100 feet long. You probably noticed the Cub got off the ground in much less than 2,000 feet and certainly landed in less. So the question is, can you handle a runway only 600 feet long?

Also, you've been spending a lot of time at airports with grass runways, so technically you've been making soft-field takeoffs and landings. But the FSX grass strips are *perfect* grass—they would put a golf course's putting green to shame. Real grass runways usually have longer grass or it's a bit wet or it's just not as level as a hard surface. So, the lessons in the following sections are about practicing the procedures you would use on a real soft-field runway.

Load the Chap_07_Moore flight, which starts at Moore Airfield (01NH) near Enfield, New Hampshire (see Figure 7-4). You'll use this airport for your short-field practice and then return to Post Mills for soft-field training.

164

PART I
PREFLIGHT

PART II
SPORT PILOT

PART III
PRIVATE PILOT

PART IV
INSTRUMENT RATING

PART V
COMMERCIAL LICENSE

PART VI
ATP AND BEYOND

SHORT RUNWAYS

A runway is short if your normal takeoff procedures won't get you in the air with plenty of room left before running out of runway. Obviously, each airplane has a different length of runway that would be considered short; a fully loaded 747 leaving Denver needs most of its 12,000 foot runway. For the Cub, we suggest that you use a short-field technique on any runway less than 1,000 feet long if there are no obstructions. Tall trees or a hillside might make even a 2,000-foot runway require a short-field technique.

TAKEOFF

The goal of a short-field takeoff is to get in the air before the end of the runway slides under your wheels. When you pull onto the runway to get ready to take off, be sure to use the entire runway, even if it means turning the wrong way and *back taxiing* to the very end; those few extra feet could make a big difference on a really short field. This flight starts with the Cub positioned off to the side of the runway, and if you pull onto the runway there, you lose 10 or 20 feet.

When you turn and line up on the runway, hold the brakes on strongly. (In FSX, you need to set the parking brake with Ctrl+. [period], unless you have a joystick/yoke button that is set for the brakes.) Set the elevator trim to 50 mph (see "A Quick Trim"). Hold the stick full aft so when you apply power with the brakes on, the tail doesn't suddenly rise.

INSIDE THE GAME

A QUICK TRIM

Red Trim
Mark

FSX allows you to set the elevator trim for specific airspeeds if you know the position of the trim handle for each speed, which is exactly what you do in a real Cub. This works only in the 3D cockpit mode. Look at the trim handle on the left on the side of the cockpit. You'll see a red marker there, too, that moves forward and back when you change the trim (either by using the buttons on your joystick/yoke or by clicking and dragging your mouse on the handle).

To get 50 mph, move the trim handle until the red marker is near the back of its range and the handle is pointing toward the rear of the Cub. You'll get a trimmed speed of 55 mph if you put the red marker 3/4 of the way toward the back and the trim handle vertical. Our usual cruise speed of 70 mph has the red marker near the center and the trim handle pointing down. (These are approximate positions; you'll need to set them more precisely based on the weight of the airplane and other conditions.)

Apply full throttle, and once the engine is at 2200 rpm, release the brakes and bring the stick to the neutral position. The Cub jumps forward. (The Cub's brakes really aren't strong enough to hold the plane still, so be ready to start steering with the rudder.) Your goal with the tail is just to pick it up slightly so the tail is low but no longer bouncing along the ground. The Cub lifts off at about 45 mph and starts climbing.

Because this airport has obstructions, you need to climb at the best angle of climb, V_x, which is 50 mph. The trim is set for that, but you should adjust the pitch of the Cub so you get to 50 mph as quickly as possible and hold that speed as you climb, as shown in Figure 7-5. When you're well above the obstructions (100 feet above them is good), lower the pitch for a 60 mph climb to the traffic pattern.

If you had been at an airport with a similarly short runway but no obstructions ahead of you, the takeoff procedure would have been the same, but you would transition to a normal climbing speed of 60 mph after lifting off the ground.

Figure 7-5: Climbing out at 50 mph doesn't give you much visibility over the nose. Perhaps that's better; you won't see the trees you're about to hit!

 FLY HIGH AT V_y

In this book, we suggest climbing at 60 mph because the Cub flies well at that speed, and you can see forward a bit more easily. But the speed for the best rate of climb (V_y) in the Cub is 55. When the plane is heavy with two people and full fuel, you should probably use 55 mph to make sure you climb as quickly as possible.

Proceed around the airport in a left-hand traffic pattern, and set up for a landing. Check out the FSX video called Chap_07_Short-Field_Takeoff to see the technique in action.

166

| PART I | PART II | PART III | PART IV | PART V | PART VI |
| PREFLIGHT | SPORT PILOT | PRIVATE PILOT | INSTRUMENT RATING | COMMERCIAL LICENSE | ATP AND BEYOND |

LANDING

Figure 7-6: To land at Moore Airfield with its 600-foot runway, you need to just clear the trees and then quickly drop down to the runway.

When landing on a short runway, your enemy is speed: the faster you are moving when you touch down on the runway, the longer it takes to stop. Of course, you don't want to go so slowly that the wings stall and lose lift, so a compromise is in order. Also, because the runway here at Moore Airfield has trees in front of it, you need to come in high and descend steeply to the beginning of the runway (see Figure 7-6). Here again speed is the problem; the slower you go, the more steeply you descend.

As you come around the traffic pattern from base to final approach, stay high to simulate going into a runway with trees high in front of it. Try to be about 1,000 feet MSL when you cross the tree line into the clearing and slow to 45 mph. Adjust the throttle so that your descent path is heading right for the end of the runway. You're closer to the stall speed of the wings than usual, so you need to be careful not to go slower than 40 mph; a couple of mph faster than 45 is OK, but don't let it get above 50, or you'll overshoot the runway.

↓ I CAN'T SEE OVER THE NOSE!

When you're flying this slowly, it can be really hard to see where you're going over the nose of the airplane. That's true with the real Cub, too. Of course, with the real Cub you can do a slight forward slip to twist the nose out of the way. You can't do that in FSX because it doesn't show slips properly; but you can take one step the real Cub can't: simplify your panel. Press F10 and then W on your keyboard to display just the airspeed, compass, and altimeter.

When you're over the runway and just a couple feet up, idle the engine, and flare into a three-point landing. As soon as the wheels touch, start braking to a stop. If you've done it right, you stop very quickly, perhaps less than half of the 600-foot runway. Figures 7-7 through 7-9 show the sequence.

The FSX video Chap_07_Short-Field_Landing demonstrates this procedure.

Figure 7-7: Final approach to a short field. Note the plane is at almost level pitch, even though it is descending, because of the slow airspeed (45 mph). This is followed by...

Figure 7-8: ... a slight pitch up to landing flare attitude, which is followed by...

Figure 7-9: ...ground contact and a very short roll to a stop.

SOFT RUNWAYS

Figure 7-10: Start of the Chap_07_Post-Mills flight

Technically, a runway is considered soft if it isn't a hard, human-made surface. Grass might be the first surface that comes to mind, but you can consider dirt, gravel, and mud all to be soft runways. Hard-packed dirt and really short grass could be quite firm. Fresh snow on pavement really is a soft runway. It's up to the pilot to determine whether to use a soft or normal technique.

The runway you were using at Moore Airfield is grass, but it's such a short runway that you can't practice the proper soft-field procedures. Load the flight called Chap_07_Post-Mills to return to your home airport for this lesson. (Or just fly there from Moore; it's only 16 miles north. You can land and taxi to the position shown in Figure 7-10.)

168

PART I	PART II	PART III	PART IV	PART V	PART VI
PREFLIGHT	SPORT PILOT	PRIVATE PILOT	INSTRUMENT RATING	COMMERCIAL LICENSE	ATP AND BEYOND

⬇ STUDENT OF THE CRAFT

GROUND EFFECT

When an aircraft is flying near the ground, a few interesting changes happen that don't happen higher in the air. The drag on the wings is less, which means it is easier to speed up when taking off and it takes longer to slow down when landing. The effect is strongest when you're close to the ground, decreases as you climb, and pretty much goes away by the time you are about one wingspan above the ground.

During operations from a soft field, you can use this to your advantage by getting off the ground a little earlier than usual—at a slower airspeed—and then accelerating in ground effect until you attain climbing speed. During landing, you can use ground effect to help cushion your landing so you don't dig the wheels into the soft surface.

However, ground effect has a downside. If you lift off the ground at a slow airspeed but you don't force the plane to stay in ground effect, you will climb out of ground effect; however, your airspeed is not enough for a climb, and you'll sink back and probably bounce on the runway. And on landing, if you come in too fast, the ground effect again cushions your landing, but this time it actually prevents you from putting the plane on the ground, and you eat up precious runway because the reduced drag of ground effect doesn't slow you down as much as you hoped.

TAKEOFF

The soft-field takeoff procedure is used for any runway that is soft but doesn't have obstructions near the end. The goal is to get the wheels of the airplane out of the soft surface as quickly as possible, even if that means lifting off before the plane has accelerated to a safe flying speed.

If the runway is soft, then it's likely that the taxiways are soft, too. You don't want to get bogged down in the soft surface while you're slowly taxiing, and you don't want the tiny tailwheel to stick either. So, taxi with the elevator neutral, and be ready to pull back quickly if the aircraft starts to nose over or to push forward if the tailwheel gets stuck.

As you arrive at the runway, it is better not to stop because it might be too hard to get started again. Quickly check the area to make sure that no other planes are landing, and roll right onto the runway without stopping.

After you're lined up on the runway, keep holding neutral stick, and give the engine full throttle. Very quickly the tail pops up, but you don't want it to come all the way up to the usual height, where the plane is basically level; instead, keep the tail down slightly and the nose up. Like a short-field takeoff, your goal is to make the plane lift off the runway as soon as possible.

Figure 7-11: Level off just above the runway to stay in ground effect until you're at climbing speed.

When the plane lifts off, gently push forward on the stick to gain the full 55 mph while you're still close to the runway in ground effect, as shown in Figure 7-11 (see "Ground Effect" for more details). Once the Cub starts climbing at 55 mph and you're sure to clear any obstacles, you can transition to a better visibility climb of 60 mph up into the traffic pattern and set up for landing.

If obstructions are off the end of the runway *and* the runway is soft, you have to be sure to climb at V_x speed (50 mph) after you lift out of ground effect.

The FSX video Chap_07_Soft-Field_Takeoff shows the technique of flying in ground effect to gain airspeed.

LANDING

When landing on a soft runway, the biggest danger is landing too hard, causing the tires to dig into the surface and bringing the aircraft to an abrupt halt. In a tailwheel airplane like the Cub, this could mean the nose going down and the propeller striking the ground (the ultimate short-field landing).

The approach is the same as a normal approach—same speed (60 mph), same angle, and so on. Idle the engine as you cross the end of the runway, as usual. The only difference comes when rounding out near the runway: add just a little bit of power (about 200 rpm) as you flare above the runway, which will make the wheels softly kiss the runway. Too much power, and you'll climb up again. Too little, and you'll touch down at the usual descent rate, which might be too hard for the surface. After you touch, you can idle the engine again.

If you made a three-point landing, gently pull back on the stick. Your goal is to keep the tail down as usual without digging the tiny tailwheel into the soft surface. If you landed on the main gear only (wheeled landing), you need to gently let the tail settle so it doesn't dig into the surface. FSX is pretty forgiving on its simulated soft fields, but real mud can be a bear.

Keep moving after you slow down and pull off the runway, using power as needed. If you stop, you might have a hard time getting started, so just taxi right back to the runway for takeoff or over to the ramp and park.

170

PART I	PART II	PART III	PART IV	PART V	PART VI
PREFLIGHT	SPORT PILOT	PRIVATE PILOT	INSTRUMENT RATING	COMMERCIAL LICENSE	ATP AND BEYOND

NOTE!

⬇ SHORT AND SOFT RUNWAYS

Small tailwheel aircraft are great for flying into a runway that is both short and soft, so you'll find real-world Cubs doing all kinds of backcountry flying. But that takes skill, so a new pilot shouldn't go to those places without an experienced instructor. That's a challenge that should be saved for when you're really good at both kinds of landings and takeoffs and sometimes cannot actually be done. In FSX, you can certainly take on that challenge, because the consequences are minor; but in real life, we don't do it unless the runway is a firm soft runway (grass cut short, no rain lately, and so on) and the plane is a really good short-field aircraft such as the Cub.

Off-Airport Operations

In Chapter 6, we discussed how to deal with emergencies, including what to do if the engine stopped and you had to glide to a dead-stick landing. Of course, in a perfect world you'd find a runway to put the plane down. But even FSX isn't that perfect; sometimes you might have an engine failure or other reason you need to land quickly and the only choices are open fields. Unless it's a huge field, you're likely to be landing on a short *and* soft "runway."

⬇ ACCIDENT CHAIN

ACCIDENT REPORT: TOO DARN SHORT

On May 15, 2005, a Cessna Citation 525A (business jet) was substantially damaged during a runway overrun in Atlantic City, New Jersey. The certificated private pilot received minor injuries, and the three passengers received no injuries.

The pilot reported to an FAA inspector that he performed "one circle" around the airport, observed the wind sock, and then performed a landing on Runway 11. During the landing roll, approximately 2/3 down the runway, the pilot "lost the brakes" and was unable to stop on the remaining runway. The airplane then continued off the departure end of the runway and impacted the water.

An employee of the airport saw the jet approach and took a video of the landing and runoff into the water. That video footage is available on the Internet (search for *Atlantic City Citation Overrun*) and provided some key information to the investigators.

The video showed that the wind was actually from the opposite direction so that the jet should have landed on the same pavement but into the wind, which is Runway 29. By landing on Runway 11, he had a tailwind of 10 to 15 knots. But the jet shouldn't have landed there at all. Runway 11/29 is 2,950 feet long, and the airport diagram (found attached to the pilot's control column after the accident) said "Airport closed to jet aircraft."

> According to the aircraft operating handbook, at that weight the jet would take 3,000 feet of runway to land in a no-wind situation. With a tailwind of 10 knots, the jet would take about 3,600 feet.
>
> If you do find that video, you'll see that something very surprising happens about four minutes into the video.

YET ANOTHER RUNWAY SURFACE

Figure 7-12: All FSX water is gently rippled and perfect for landing. Here a Kenmore Air Beaver alights near the San Juan Islands of Washington.

If you want to try takeoffs and landings on a really soft runway, how about water? FSX comes with both a Grumman Goose and a DeHavilland Beaver on floats. We won't be teaching float flying in this book, but both in the real world and on the simulator, it's a whole lot of fun. It's also a great way to work on your overall flying techniques. Slow flight, which we'll cover in the next chapter, is also an important skill for float pilots.

Every normal landing on floats is, to a degree, a soft-field landing because the floats (or hull, in the case of an airplane like the Goose) have no shock absorption. Passengers feel every bump. Since they pay the bills, you want to touch down as gently as practical.

Float-plane pilots have to pick where on the water they want to land, since there usually isn't any defined runway. The advantage is they almost always get to land directly into the wind. The disadvantage is they must assess where that wind is coming from themselves. Most lakes don't have ASOS or even a wind sock! It's common in float flying to make small adjustments in the last moments of flight to get the airplane directly into the wind just by gauging how the airplane is drifting relative to the surface of the water.

That surface poses unique problems, too. A perfect surface for landing is smooth with just enough wave action to clearly define the surface, as shown in Figure 7-12. If the water gets rough with waves, takeoffs and landings require quick work on the yoke to keep the nose from bouncing up or dropping down as it crosses the waves.

172

PART I
PREFLIGHT

PART II
SPORT PILOT

PART III
PRIVATE PILOT

PART IV
INSTRUMENT RATING

PART V
COMMERCIAL LICENSE

PART VI
ATP AND BEYOND

It's also possible for the water to be too smooth—so smooth, in fact, that you can't see the surface as you approach for landing. Landing on so-called glassy water requires getting the airplane into a landing attitude and then adjusting power to descend at 100 feet per minute (fpm) or so. When you feel the floats hit the water, you've landed. (FSX doesn't simulate glassy water, but you can still practice the technique and then try it in the real world on a perfectly calm lake.)

A great place to start is the mission called San Juan Island Run. Be sure to read up on float planes in the Learning Center first. You might also want to check out Chapter 14 of this book because, like the Mooney described there, the Beaver uses flaps on both takeoff and landing and has a constant-speed propeller.

The Beaver also has water rudders that you use only on the water to help you taxi. Don't get caught flying with your water rudders down. If any of the other pilots around Kenmore catch you doing that, you have to buy all the beer and pizza after work!

Key Points for Real Flying and FSX Built-ins

The following are some key points from this chapter:

- Understand the aerodynamic effects of short-field and soft-field performance.

- Practice short-field and soft-field takeoffs.

- Experience maximum performance climb.

- Experience short-field approach techniques.

- Practice short-field and soft-field landings.

Here are the lessons and missions to study after reading this chapter:

- *Lessons*: Commercial Pilot Lesson 2 has additional training in short-field takeoffs and landings.

- *Missions*: The Introduction to Mountain Flying mission is the perfect way to practice your short and soft runway procedures. The Midwest Fly-In also has a short field to fly out of, and you can even do flour bombing at another airport. (Don't try to land on the target, even though it might be tempting; it's a bit too short!) The Africa Relief mission is another challenge with a big tailwheel airplane (the DC-3) and short, soft runways.

SLOW FLIGHT, STALLS, AND SPINS

"DO NOT SPIN THIS AIRCRAFT. IF THE AIRCRAFT DOES ENTER A SPIN, IT WILL RETURN TO THE EARTH WITHOUT FURTHER AT- TENTION ON THE PART OF THE AERONAUT."
—FROM THE FIRST CURTIS-WRIGHT FLYER HANDBOOK

174

| PART I | PART II | PART III | PART IV | PART V | PART VI |
| PREFLIGHT | SPORT PILOT | PRIVATE PILOT | INSTRUMENT RATING | COMMERCIAL LICENSE | UP AND BEYOND! |

TAKING IT SLOWLY

Learning how an airplane handles in slow flight is visceral. Pilots often make corrections and adjustments more by feel and observation than by instruments or procedures. In slow flight and in the early stages of a stall in a light airplane, the stick feels unresponsive to your inputs, your right leg gets tired from holding extensive right rudder, and the whole airplane might vibrate. It's as if the whole airplane is telling you this is not the way you should be flying.

Why is practicing slow flight and stall recovery on FSX valuable when you can't feel any of these responses on the simulator?

Fear.

We have found that many pilots complete their training without ever feeling comfortable with slow flight and stalls. Many times we've met pilots with a few hundred hours of flight time who sheepishly admit they're afraid of stalls and, even more so, accidental spins. Of course, the funny part is we all practice a little slow flight every time we fly in a small airplane. We do it in the last few seconds between the roundout, where you fly level over the runway for a moment, and the flare for landing. When it's only a few inches off the ground, however, it's not so scary.

Getting over this fear usually is just a matter of exploring slow flight in more depth than they did in their private training. The "Aha!" moment for these pilots is when they really understand that the airplane is still controllable when flying slow, stalled, or (if they choose to explore far enough with us) spinning.

Exploring this regime on the simulator first removes the visceral feedback, but it also removes the fear. On FSX, you can practice the procedural part of getting into and out of slow flight, as well as recovering from stalls leisurely, and you can develop a confidence so that it won't be much more dramatic in the real airplane.

We'll now take a moment to discuss what's happening when you fly really slowly.

THE AERODYNAMICS OF SLOW FLIGHT

We want to be clear about what we mean by slow flight. *Slow flight* is flight close to the minimum speed the airplane can maintain without losing altitude. The FAA practical test standards define it as "an airspeed at which any further increase in angle of attack, increase in load factor, or reduction in power would result in an immediate stall." For the Cub, this is about 39 mph.

From the aircraft's perspective, nothing is particularly special about slow flight. It's still moving forward through the air, albeit not very quickly, and the air is still basically following both the top and bottom surfaces of the wings. Because the air is moving over the wings slowly, it must be displaced downward at a steep angle in order to provide enough lift to keep the airplane from losing altitude, as shown in Figure 8-1. This means the wing must have a high angle of attack relative to the oncoming wind. From the pilot's point of view, that usually means the airplane is flying in a nose-up attitude.

It's important that you look at slow flight from the pilot's point of view. Because the airflow over the control surfaces has slowed down, their effectiveness has decreased. The sensation is that the controls feel sloppy. It takes a great deal of stick motion left or right to deflect the aileron enough to raise or lower the wing. It takes back stick to maintain a high angle of attack at any speed, but at low speed it takes even more because there is slower air moving over the tail.

Figure 8-1: Slow flight requires a high angle of attack to produce enough lift to maintain altitude at such low airspeed.

The rudder is noticeably less effective while simultaneously being more important than ever before. At such a high angle of attack, the descending blade of the propeller is creating more thrust than the ascending blade (see Chapter 2). This requires right rudder to keep the plane flying straight ahead just as was required when the aircraft was climbing straight ahead during a normal climb.

Part of the joy of learning slow flight is learning how to turn to a new heading without losing any altitude. As you remember from Chapter 2, turning the airplane requires banking the wings and redirecting some of the lift left or right. This means you have less lift for maintaining aircraft altitude, and you'd usually compensate with a little back stick.

In slow flight, any increase in angle of attack—any further aft motion of the stick—results in the stall. Your only option is to open the throttle. Because you are at such a high angle of attack, a portion of your forward thrust from the propeller is actually pointed upward and adds to your total lift. Opening the throttle gives you just a little bit more lift to balance the lift being used to turn the airplane.

The procedure for turning left or right is often a bit different. Because the plane has such a strong left-turning tendency, you can sometimes accomplish a left turn simply by applying a little *less* right rudder and not moving the stick at all. A right turn usually requires some right stick and a whole heaping load of right rudder.

FSX does a mediocre job of modeling this visually, but it does an excellent job of requiring the correct position on the flight controls. You'll try this in a little bit when you go fly.

THE SEPARATION BEGINS

We mentioned in Chapter 2 that angle of attack can be increased but only to a point. Beyond this point, airflow cannot smoothly follow the top surface of the wing. The airflow over the top of the wing becomes turbulent and no longer contributes to total lift. At this point, the wing has begun to stall.

"Begun to stall? Doesn't the wing just, you know, stall all at once?"

No, it doesn't. This is a common misconception, and partly it probably comes from the word *stall*. Most of us think in the context of an automobile engine when we let the clutch out too fast. The engine suddenly stops, or *stalls*.

176

PART I
PREFLIGHT

PART II
SPORT PILOT

PART III
PRIVATE PILOT

PART IV
INSTRUMENT RATING

PART V
COMMERCIAL LICENSE

PART VI
ATP AND BEYOND

When a wing stalls, it's a process that begins with a slight separation of airflow near the trailing edge of the wing, which creates a small area of turbulent flow. As you slow toward what you think of as the actual stall speed of the airplane, this area widens and spreads toward the front of the wing. The progression looks something like Figure 8-2.

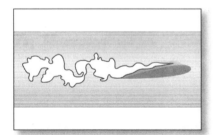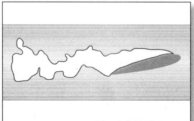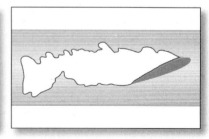

Figure 8-2 The wing doesn't stall all at once. Rather, the stall progresses from the trailing edge of the wing forward (and usually outward) as the angle of attack increases. The design of the wing is the primary determinant in how the stall progresses.

How fast this progression happens depends on the design of the wing. Early aircraft wing designs made for a rapid stall progression. From the pilot's point of view, the wing suddenly stalled, and the plane started losing altitude rapidly and sometimes violently. If you load some of the WWII fighter planes from Combat Flight Simulator or a third-party source and stall them with the realism set to Hard, you can see some pretty stunning stalls (and spins). You can find out more about loading additional aircraft in the FSX Learning Center under Expanding Your Hobby.

Airplanes such as the Cub tend to have benign stalls. Separation begins at the trailing edge of the wing and near the fuselage of the airplane and progresses forward and outward slowly. Rather than a sudden loss of lift creating a sudden drop, the effect is more like a curious sinking sensation. Most pilots refer to this as *mushing*. A vibration often also occurs in the stick and, sometimes, throughout the entire airplane. This is called *buffeting* and is because of the turbulent airflow bouncing around the wings and tail.

The real Cub actually stalls less aggressively than the FSX version, but the procedure to recover from the stall is the same. Because the stall results from an angle of attack greater than the plane's critical angle of attack, the way to unstall the airplane is to reduce the angle of attack. You do this by lowering the nose.

Reducing the angle of attack is the only step you must take to recover from a stall. You do not need to add or reduce power. You don't even need to keep the airplane flying straight ahead. Performing these tasks might reduce the amount of altitude you lose or help you recover with the airplane flying in the direction you want, but reducing the angle of attack is the single and only solution to unstalling an airplane.

STALLS WITH A TWIST: SPINS

Spins are actually a lot of fun—after the fear factor is removed, that is. To spin, the airplane must first be stalled to some degree. In addition to the stall, there must be some rotation. Many things could cause this rotation. One wing might be more deeply stalled than the other, causing asymmetrical lift that makes the airplane bank and begin to turn, as shown in Figure 8-3. The left-turning tendency from the propeller at a high angle of attack could be the source. Or the pilot might have intentionally stalled the airplane and then added a boot full of rudder to start the airplane rotating into an intentional spin because the pilot is seeking some thrills.

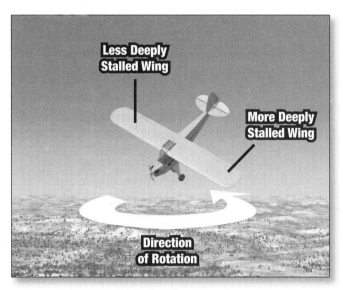

Figure 8-3: *The spin is a combination of a stall plus a rotation.*

Spin recovery requires unstalling the airplane first. At the same time, the pilot usually reduces power to idle and centers both the rudder and the stick. The power reduction is to prevent losing too much altitude, because most airplanes spin in a relatively nose-down attitude. Centering the controls removes any unintentional rotations. The pilot then adds full opposite rudder to stop the rotation of the spin if it's still going. The plane now is in a power-off dive, and smooth back stick can return it to level flight.

Many modern light airplanes are so stable that if they spin, all the pilot really needs to do is completely let go of the controls. The airplanes unstall and stop spinning on their own. More agile airplanes such as military fighters or aerobatic airplanes often require a little more intervention on the part of the pilot to get flying straight again.

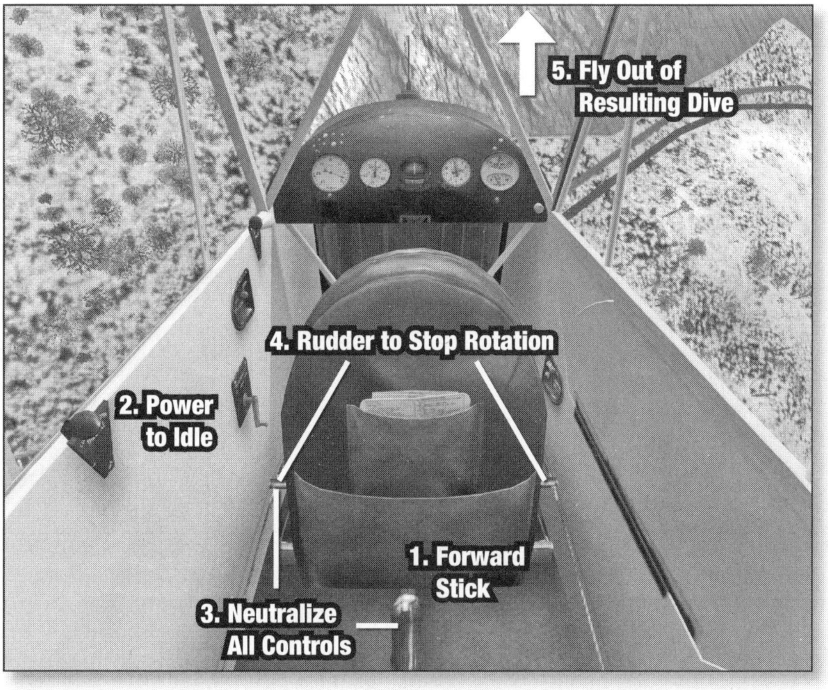

If you ever get the chance to practice spins in a real airplane—and if you're up for the challenge, we strongly recommend you do—you start by making a recovery during the incipient spin, that is, before the airplane has begun to rotate quickly. Recovering during the incipient phase of the spin is what you want to do if you ever accidentally stall the airplane, especially close to the ground.

You later hold full aft stick to keep the airplane stalled and spinning so you can experience a developed spin. At this point, the airplane is rotating rather quickly but is otherwise quite stable and descending a couple hundred feet per minute. You then recover somewhere above a minimum safe altitude or when your stomach has simply had enough (see Figure 8-4).

Figure 8-4: *Recovery from the spin involves unstalling the airplane (reducing the angle of attack), reducing power to prevent unnecessary altitude loss, neutralizing the controls, and stopping the rotation with rudder. You then fly the airplane out of the resulting dive.*

178

PART I	PART II	PART III	PART IV	PART V	PART VI
PREFLIGHT	SPORT PILOT	PRIVATE PILOT	INSTRUMENT RATING	COMMERCIAL LICENSE	ATP AND BEYOND

⬇ STUDENT OF THE CRAFT

STEP ON THE SKY

A growing trend in flight training for both large and small aircraft is "upset recovery training." This training puts pilots in extreme unusual attitudes, such as completely inverted, and has them recover the airplane to normal flight. The mantra of one of these trainers is "Step on the sky," meaning you should apply full rudder on the side of the airplane that is pointing toward the sky as part of the recovery. That's for light airplanes. In big jets, there is a question as to whether that level of control pressure could lead to a structural failure. There was some suspicion that a full-rudder recovery contributed to the rudder separation and subsequent crash of an Airbus off the coast of New York.

This level of unusual attitude recovery isn't part of normal flight training, but it might be part of your flying life if you're in the wrong place at the wrong time. You'll learn to stay out of the wake of large, heavy airplanes in your flight training because they create vortices of air that trail behind the airplane. (Think of a small, horizontal tornado trailing behind the wingtips of a large airplane, and you get the idea.)

We once accidentally passed into one of these vortexes behind a cargo DC-8 while flying a featherweight Cessna 152. The airplane rolled 120° (partially inverted) before we could even react. It stubbornly kept trying to roll itself to the left for the next five seconds until we flew out of the vortex, even though we were holding full right rudder the whole time.

TAKING THE CUB FOR A SPIN

It's time to try some slow flight in your friend, the Cub. Load the flight Chap_08_Slow_flight_and_Stalls. This will put you in the air 3,000 feet over the Connecticut River near Post Mills at 1900 rpm with 65 mph indicated. You're at 3,000 feet, so you have enough altitude to lose some in your stall recoveries and still remain safely above the ground. Of course, in FSX you could try recovering to level flight 5 feet over the river just for fun, but in a real airplane we like to recover from stalls with at least 1,500 feet between us and terra firma.

Press P on your keyboard to pause things, and then choose Aircraft > Realism and set the realism to Hard. If you have trouble with the following exercises, you can reset it to Medium and try again, but settings less than Hard mask some of the behaviors you are trying to study here.

SLOW DOWN

To transition to slow flight, pick a point on the horizon, and keep the nose pointed there. Now reduce power while simultaneously adding nose-up trim. See whether you can maintain your heading and altitude of 3,000 feet as you do this. You need to add right rudder to keep flying straight. You might also need some left stick to keep the wings level.

Figure 8-5: Maximum nose-up trim is still faster than slow flight.

It also might help to reduce the power 100 rpm at a time. Somewhere around 1600 rpm and 47 mph, you are at maximum nose-up trim (see Figure 8-5).

You are in a somewhat nose-high attitude, but you can still see the horizon.

You now want to slow down to 39 mph. Do this by reducing the power further and adding more back stick. You won't need to reduce the power much, though. The Cub is close to its minimum sink speed, which is the speed that requires the least amount of power to stay aloft. It can actually fly slower than this, but it requires more power. In the real Cub, you definitely add a bit of power to keep your altitude as you reduce the final few mph to 39.

When you're down to 39 mph, you still need 1550 rpm, and you are in a very nose-high attitude. The tops of the flight instruments are just below the line for the horizon in either the virtual cockpit or the 2D cockpit with the panel removed (W on your keyboard), as shown in Figure 8-6.

Figure 8-6: By 39 mph, you are nose-high and needing right rudder to keep tracking straight ahead.

180

PART I	PART II	PART III	PART IV	PART V	PART VI
PREFLIGHT	SPORT PILOT	PRIVATE PILOT	INSTRUMENT RATING	COMMERCIAL LICENSE	ATP AND BEYOND

⬇ BY THE BOOK

BEST GLIDE VS. MINIMUM SINK

As you remember from Chapter 6 on emergencies, the purpose of knowing your airplane's best glide speed is to maximize the distance you can travel over the ground without the engine running. Now that you've practiced slow flight, we can talk about minimum sink speed. This is the speed at which the airplane will descend at the slowest rate. You might want to use this speed if you are directly over a landing site and want time to try to restart your engine or call for help.

Unfortunately, such speeds are rarely published for light airplanes. (Gliders have this speed published because pilots use it all the time to maximize their net lift in thermals.) A good estimate, though, is halfway between best glide speed and the power-off stalling speed. The best glide speed is 45 mph for the Cub, and the stall speed is 39. That means your best sink is about 42 mph—pretty slow flight!

⬇ PUT THE STUFF OUT

Slow flight is usually performed in a landing configuration. For airplanes that have flaps and gear, that means the gear is down and the flaps are fully extended.

Now it's time for a bit of fun. Reduce your power to 1200 rpm, and adjust your pitch to hold 39 mph. You are descending, and you are more nose-down than when you were flying level. This makes sense because as you are going down the relative wind is coming more from below. Since you were just below your critical angle of attack in level flight, if you tried to keep the same pitch, you would exceed your critical angle of attack in a descent (see Figure 8-7).

Figure 8-7: You can climb or descend at minimum airspeed by adding or reducing power, but you'll have to adjust your pitch as well.

Bring the power back to 1550, and level off. Now increase the power to 2000 rpm, and maintain 39 mph. This is even more nose-up than level flight at minimum controllable airspeed. Level off again when you're back to 3,000 feet by adjusting both power and pitch.

Release any right rudder you have been holding, and let the airplane drift around to the left. Try to fly a complete, 360-degree turn without losing or gaining any altitude. As soon as you start, the Cub naturally tries to bank left. You need to hold some right stick to keep it from banking too far. You also need to increase power to 1650 or 1700 rpm to maintain your altitude as you turn.

After you go completely around to the left, go to the right. This requires a great deal of right rudder and a little left stick. You might want to press Shift+Z on your keyboard to show your exact heading at the top of the screen.

If at any point during any of these maneuvers the nose suddenly drops, just release some of the back stick, and then gently bring the nose back to the horizon. It's no big deal. You just stalled is all, and that's what you're going to practice next anyway.

⬇ SEE THE MOVIE

The flight video Chap_08_Slow_Flight demonstrates slow flight.

POWER-OFF, OR ARRIVAL, STALLS

You might have lost or gained some altitude in your turns. Get yourself going straight ahead back at 3,000 feet by adding or reducing power as described previously.

Now you'll reduce the power to idle but try to maintain the same pitch you had in level flight. This pitch is the highest possible for level flight, but now with the relative wind from below rather than in front, it is too great an angle, and therefore the Cub's wings stall.

You see the nose sink and then drop. This is the Cub's natural defense against stalls. When the wing stalls, the Cub pitches down. That naturally reduces the angle of attack and unstalls the wing! Figure 8-8 shows the process.

If you continue to hold the stick in about 3/4 aft, the Cub stalls and recovers from the stall, stalls and recovers, stalls and recovers…all the way to the ground. That's exactly what the real Cub will do, too. This is commonly called a *falling-leaf stall* and is a great exercise to both reduce students' fears of stalls and build their skills with the rudder. (You do it with full aft stick in the real Cub, but the FSX Cub tends to make some "overaggressive" recoveries with full aft stick.)

You, too, want to use the rudder to keep the Cub going straight ahead. Don't move the stick left or right to try to turn. It might have the opposite effect of what you think, as you'll see with a spin soon.

Now reset the condition to 3,000 feet by pressing Ctrl+;. Try the stall again, but this time as soon as the nose drops, add full power, and bring the Cub back into a normal climb at about 60 mph. You'll see you lose far less altitude this way. If you ever really stalled the Cub with the power low and needed to recover quickly, that's what you would do. When might this happen? We call these stalls *arrival stalls* because they simulate what might happen if you tried to maintain altitude without enough power as you were coming in to land. You'd be too slow—too high an angle of attack—and stall close the ground. You'd need to recover fast and with minimum loss of altitude.

182

| PART I | PART II | PART III | PART IV | PART V | PART VI |
| PREFLIGHT | SPORT PILOT | PRIVATE PILOT | INSTRUMENT RATING | COMMERCIAL LICENSE | ATP AND BEYOND |

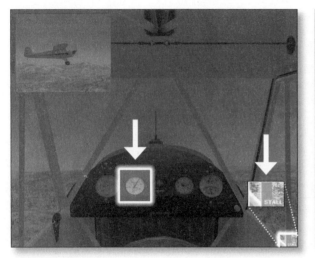

Figure 8-8: The Cub stalls at the pitch attitude for level flight at minimum speed but not enough power to maintain altitude. As it stalls, the nose drops, reducing the angle of attack and recovering from the stall.

 NOTE!

↓ | SEE THE MOVIE

The flight video Chap_08_Arrival_Stall demonstrates an arrival stall.

DEPARTURE, OR POWER-ON, STALLS

Figure 8-9: You can stall with full power, too. You just might be more nose-up when it happens.

It's also possible to stall the airplane with the power on full-blast and climbing. Since you still must exceed the critical angle of attack relative to the oncoming wind, you have to be in quite a nose-high relative to the ground (see Figure 8-9). If you were to climb out too steeply after takeoff, you might end up in this situation.

Press Ctrl+; on your keyboard to reset the simulation again. Start flying, and trim for 60 mph.

Now add full power to climb. If you do nothing, you eventually settle down at a 60 mph climb. Induce a stall, though, by pitching up until the airspeed is dropping steadily, and hold that attitude. If the airspeed stops decreasing, pitch up more. At some point below 39 mph, the Cub stalls.

Again, it naturally recovers, but you can lose less altitude if you simply pitch back to level flight and then back to your climb at 60 mph.

Yeah, it's that simple in the real airplane, too. The catch again is not to use too much left or right stick as you stall and recover. Just use enough stick to keep the wings level, and use your rudder to keep the nose pointed where you want it. In the real Cub, you don't use any stick at all. You simply keep the wings level and the nose directed where you want it with the rudder alone.

You might hear about a *trim stall*, which is a variation on the power-on, or departure, stall. In some airplanes, a sudden application of full power when the trim is set for maximum nose-up zooms the airplane into a nose-high attitude that's high enough for a stall. This doesn't happen in the Cub, but you're welcome to play around with trying to induce a stall hands-off if you want.

 SEE THE MOVIE

The flight video Chap_08_Departure_Stall demonstrates a departure stall.

Now for Some Spin

You'll start looking at spins by seeing what happens in a stall when you do try to steer the Cub with its ailerons. This time, load the flight Chap_08_Spins. The only difference here is that you are at 5,000 feet rather than 3,000 feet.

Slow to 39 mph in level flight with the power at 1700 rpm. (You need a bit more rpm up higher to maintain level flight this high; see "Stalling at the Same Speed or Any Speed.") Now reduce the power to idle and raise the nose so the flight instruments are above the horizon. This definitely results in a stall.

The moment the airplane stalls (look to the lower right of the screen for a clue), apply full left stick. The Cub won't turn left. In fact, it might turn right. The reason is that moving the stick left deflects the left aileron up and the right aileron down. Doing this effectively decreases the angle of attack on the left wing and increases it on the right. Usually this would raise the right wing and lower the left. The Cub would then bank and turn. But when you're flying near the critical angle of attack, that small increase in angle doesn't add lift to the wing. It partially stalls it. Instead of rising, the wing sinks, and the airplane turns the wrong way, as shown in Figure 8-10.

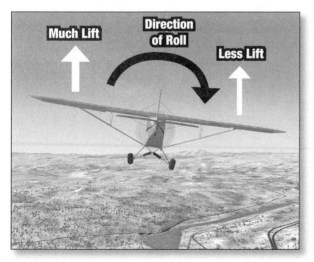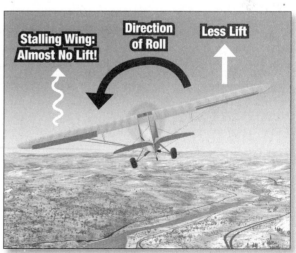

Figure 8-10: Usually, you use ailerons to increase lift on one wing to start a roll. Near the critical angle of attack, your ailerons might work backward as they make one wing stall rather than increase its lift.

184

PART I	PART II	PART III	PART IV	PART V	PART VI
PREFLIGHT	SPORT PILOT	PRIVATE PILOT	INSTRUMENT RATING	COMMERCIAL LICENSE	ATP AND BEYOND

Figure 8-11: Note the near-zero airspeed and stall warning despite the extreme nose-down attitude. This Cub is spinning down with little air actually flowing across its wings.

Now you have a rotation combined with a near stall. Make it a full stall, and you get a spin.

Reset the simulation again, and slow to 39 mph at 1700 rpm. Bring the power to idle. Just as the Cub stalls, add full left stick and full aft stick. Hold it there…and hang on.

You'll see some wild gyrations—none of which happens in the real airplane. Spins are exciting, but not quite as exciting as FSX portrays them (see Figure 8-11). The process for entering the spin and recovering is correct, however, so it's worth doing. The engine might quit as well. This is realistic for some spins.

When you're down to 3,000 feet on the altimeter, neutralize all the controls, and then push forward on the stick. Add full opposite rudder to stop any rotation. You now are diving. Pull out of the dive, and recover to level flight. You might need some serious forward stick too after you come zooming out of the dive. If the engine quits, press Ctrl+E to restart it.

The FSX Cub diverges from reality a bit here in that it tends to spin in an oscillating nose-high/nose-down pattern. The real Cub just spins nose-down with a slight oscillation of more or less nose-down pitch. Imagine getting flushed down a giant toilet with the nose pointed down and toward the center of the bowl, and you get the idea of what the spin actually feels like.

If you want to have more fun with spins, pull into a power-on or power-off stall; then, instead of adding full stick, hold full aft stick, and stomp on a rudder pedal all the way to the floor. Yeehaw!

NOTE! ⬇ SEE THE MOVIE

The flight video Chap_08_spin demonstrates a spin.

⬇ STUDENT OF THE CRAFT

STALLING AT THE SAME SPEED OR ANY SPEED

We talked a bit about true airspeed in Chapter 5. To recap, as you climb, the actual speed you are going through the air is faster than what shows on your airspeed indicator. An interesting twist on this comes when you look at the stalling speed. The wing stalls at a specific angle of attack, but we tend to think about it as a particular airspeed. This works because we're usually thinking about level flight—not climbing, descending, or turning—and in this condition a specific speed plus a specific angle of attack gives you just enough lift to counter the effects of gravity.

When you're flying high, though, your true airspeed is faster than what you see on the airspeed indicator. So when you see 39 mph on the Cub, you're going faster than 39 mph, but as it turns out, the Cub will still stall at 39 mph indicated in level flight.

The reason is that even though you're going faster, the air you're moving through is thinner, and the two factors effectively cancel each other out. The Cub will stall in level flight at 39 mph (or very close to that) at any altitude.

That does *not* mean the Cub will stall only at 39 mph. If the wings are producing more lift than in level flight, such as while the Cub is turning and maintaining altitude at the same time, then the angle of attack is higher for any given airspeed because you must produce more total lift. Bank the Cub 45° and maintain altitude, and the stall speed will be approximately 46 mph. Bank the Cub 60° and maintain altitude, and the stall speed is 55 mph. You will feel the total lift required to turn the airplane and defy gravity as a combined force holding you down in the seat. At 60° of bank, that's two Gs, or twice the pull of gravity.

That's only if you maintain altitude. The Cub can pull just one G at 60° of bank, but it will be descending while making a tight turn. In this case, it would stall at 39 mph because the wings are required to produce only one G of lift.

The point of this is that if you must make a steep turn, you should either lose altitude or accept a higher stall speed. Failing to do so can be tragic. A classic accident scenario is when a pilot overshoots the turn from base to final. The pilot then adds more bank to get back to the runway and pulls back harder on the stick to slow down the resulting sinking feeling. The pilot can make it worse by feeling uncomfortable with the steep bank near the ground.

Now the pilot tries to lift the low wing a bit with the stick while trying to cheat the nose further with some opposite rudder. The airplane stalls near the ground, at a higher-than-expected airspeed, and there is a rotation with the stall.

You can also watch a flight video of this by loading Chap_08_Base-to-true-final.

CATCHING THE BUS

Figure 8-12: Who says aircraft carrier pilots get to have all the fun?

If you want to take this lesson further, we suggest you fly the Loopy Larry mission that comes with FSX. This mission takes you to Oshkosh Airshow (EAA Airventure) where you land a Cub on the top of a moving school bus. It's actually an exercise that is precise slow flight because the bus is moving at 50 mph, and you must fly that slowly while gently descending for the platform on its roof and staying centered on the runway (see Figure 8-12). Oh, and you have to do it before the bus gets to the end of the runway.

Not starting the bus rolling too soon and a wheeled landing help immensely on this mission.

ACCIDENT CHAIN

HEY, WATCH THIS

Aircraft: Aviat A-1B

Injuries: Two fatal

"A single-engine Aviat A-1B airplane was substantially damaged following a loss of control while maneuvering at a low altitude near Edna, Texas. The private pilot and his passenger sustained fatal injuries.

"An eyewitness observed the airplane 'buzzing' the treetops above her location. The witness added that the airplane continued to 'buzz' back and forth above the treetops while someone hollered from the airplane on each pass. The witness recorded the registration number (N-Number) from the airplane with the intention of reporting the low-flying airplane to local authorities. According to the witness, the airplane then flew northeast out over the lake and turned into the wind, as the airplane appeared 'to be almost hovering.'

"The witness continued by stating that the airplane then descended and appeared to dip its main tires into the water several times as it flew in a southerly direction. The airplane then turned around and flew 'very low' back to the north before pulling nearly straight up. The airplane ascended for a short time before the nose dropped and the airplane started descending and spinning in a clockwise direction. The airplane completed about three and a half turns before it impacted the water. The witness further reported that she heard 'no stalling out of the engine' and 'no unusual engine sounds' before the airplane impacted the water.

"The wreckage came to rest about 20 feet below the surface of Lake Texana, approximately 500 feet east of the shoreline."

Mixing slow flight, low altitude, and rapid high-G maneuvers is a recipe for becoming a statistic.

KEY POINTS FOR REAL FLYING AND FSX BUILT-INS

The following are some key points from this chapter:

- Slow flight, stalls, and spins are controllable flight regimes and don't need to be frightening.

- The airplane stalls in degrees, not all at once (well, most airplanes anyway).

- Stalls are the result of exceeding the critical angle of attack. This can happen in any flight attitude.

- Spins are the result of stalls plus some rotational impulse.

Here are the lessons and missions to study after reading this chapter:

- *Lessons*: Practice the Private Pilot lesson called Slow Flight and the Learning Center articles called Stalls and Aerobatics.

- *Missions*: In addition to Loopy Larry, the mission to fly the Extra 300 in the Red Bull time trials is a hoot, but the Extra is not for the squeamish. Let's just say it's a good thing crashes don't hurt in FSX.

PRIVATE PILOT

CONTENTS

FIRST FLIGHT IN THE CESSNA 172SP

"I TAKE THE PARAGLIDER TO THE MOUNTAIN OR I ROLL DAISY [A CESSNA] OUT OF HER HANGAR AND I PICK THE PRETTIEST PART OF THE SKY AND I MELT INTO THE WING AND THEN INTO THE AIR, TILL I'M JUST SOUL ON A SUNBEAM."

—RICHARD BACH

192

PART I — FREE FLIGHT
PART II — SPORT PILOT
PART III — PRIVATE PILOT
PART IV — INSTRUMENT RATING
PART V — COMMERCIAL LICENSE
PART VI — ATP AND BEYOND

Now that you have your virtual Sport Pilot Certificate, you can fly the Cub or other small aircraft around the virtual world of FSX. But you might feel limited by the kinds of planes and operations to which a Sport Pilot Certificate restricts you. For instance, here are some reasons you might want to get your virtual Private Pilot Certificate:

- You want to carry more than one virtual passenger.

- You want to fly faster than 120 knots (138 mph).

- You want to fly higher than 10,000 feet MSL.

- You want to fly an aircraft with retractable landing gear or a controllable-pitch prop.

- You want the challenge of working on a new pilot certificate.

TRANSITION TO THE CESSNA 172SP

For many people who learned how to fly, the Cessna 172 was their first airplane (see Figure 9-1). Originally designed in 1956 and refined nearly every year since, the Skyhawk (as it is also known) has become the most popular airplane in history.

You've spent plenty of time in the Cub, and that knowledge will serve you well. Aircraft are more similar than they are different, and we can build on your Cub training to teach you about the Cessna 172 and about earning your Private Pilot Certificate.

Figure 9-1: The Cessna 172 is an old design, but it's such a good design that it is still produced by the Cessna Aircraft Company.

ACCIDENT CHAIN

BIGGER AIRPLANE, BETTER DOORS

One great reason to step up from a two-seat airplane like the Cub to a four-seater like a Cessna 172 is the extra seats so you can take more than one friend. But sometimes there are other good reasons to take a bigger plane even with only one other person.

One of the authors of this book became a pilot long before he met his wife-to-be but wasn't actively flying when they married. Deciding to get back into flying, he first refreshed himself with a Cessna 152, a two-seat airplane that looks like a smaller sibling of the Cessna 172. But the 152 was slightly older than the Cessna 172 available at the flight school (and cheaper, to be honest). And—most important for this story—the door latches were a little bit flimsier than the ones on the Skyhawk.

And did we mention that the wife was a reluctant passenger? Despite her husband's patient explanations to the contrary, she still was concerned about falling out of the airplane, regardless of the seat belt and shoulder harness. Also, her husband explained, the plane would have to be in a steep sideslip, and the door would be unable to open while the 100-knot induced wind would be blowing it shut. And furthermore, she always checked that door latch before takeoff just to make sure it was secure.

On the day in question, we had nice flight to the coast and some lunch and were returning to the home airport. Steady cruise at 5,500 feet, no turbulence, a beautiful view of the mountains. She might actually grow to like this kind of…CLICK!

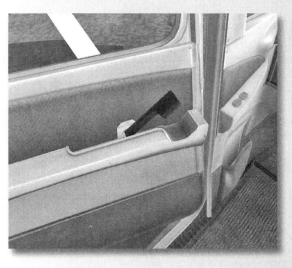

Yes, the door spontaneously unlatched. Sudden roar of wind. Ground visible through open door frame. Panicked look on wife's face. Husband reaches across the (narrow) cabin, pushes the door out as far as he can—which is about 2 inches because of the force of the wind—to get leverage to slam it shut. It seems to have latched. Maybe. Wife snuggles in closer toward husband, but romance is the least of her reasons.

Upon landing, wife insists the airplane be *squawked* (grounded) to fix the broken door latch. Flight instructor dismisses it with a hearty, "Oh, that always happens with those old 152s." Wife insists that, in the future, they will be flying the Cessna 172 with the strong, more secure door latch, and she will be sitting in the backseat—well away from the door.

194

PART I
PREFLIGHT

PART II
SPORT PILOT

PART III
PRIVATE PILOT

PART IV
INSTRUMENT RATING

PART V
COMMERCIAL LICENSE

PART VI
ATP AND BEYOND

This chapter is a transition to the Cessna 172. You'll learn about the systems that are different from the Cub, including instrumentation, engine, flaps, and more. We also teach you some of the procedures and maneuvers that Private Pilot Certificate applicants need to perform for the FAA-approved examiner. But whenever a maneuver or system is similar to the Cub, we'll give you only a brief note about how the Cessna is different. For instance, you perform a steep turn in the Cessna in the same way as in the Cub; the only difference is the airspeed at which you do the turn and the fact that—in the real plane—you're holding a control yoke instead of a control stick.

MODERN AIRCRAFT INSTRUMENTS

The instrumentation in your Cub is basic but reliable. It has to operate without an electrical system and withstand the abuses of a rough-field landing but still give you key information about your engine, airspeed, altitude, and compass direction. The Cessna 172 uses all of those instruments, along with quite a few more, as shown in Figure 9-2. (Older Cessnas are instrumented more like the Cub, so enjoy the fact that the FSX Cessna is a new one.)

Figure 9-2: The Cessna 172 uses the same six primary instruments as most other modern small aircraft.

GYROSCOPIC INSTRUMENTS

You probably noticed when flying the Cub that the magnetic compass is really accurate only when you're flying straight and not accelerating or decelerating. Otherwise, it seems to move around a lot; to fly a particular heading, you have to turn close to that heading, stop turning and wait for the compass to settle down, and then adjust a little bit more. Wouldn't it be great if you had an instrument that wouldn't bounce around like that? Now you do!

The heading indicator (Figure 9-3) looks a bit like a compass, with the cardinal directions (N, E, S, W) and numbers for headings (with the last 0 cut off, so 6 means 60° and 21 means 210°). But behind that instrument—literally

Figure 9-3: The heading indicator is like a compass, only better.

behind it—is a spinning gyroscope about the size of a plum. Any spinning object resists changes to its orientation; this is why you can balance on a bicycle once the wheels start spinning, but you can't when you're stopped—the wheels resist tipping over. A gyroscope in an airplane instrument (like the heading indicator) is a piece of solid, spinning metal. As you turn the airplane, the gyroscope isn't turning, but the plane is, and that shows up as a new heading on the heading indicator.

The heading indicator doesn't have the errors found in the bouncing compass, so you have an easier time turning the airplane to the right heading each time. But the spinning gyroscope does need some form of power to keep spinning, and that comes from a vacuum system. An air pump a bit like a mini–vacuum cleaner is connected to the engine; whenever the engine is running, the vacuum pump pulls air from outside the airplane and in through tubes into the heading indicator (spinning the gyroscope). To make sure the pump is working, the Cessna has a vacuum gauge on the lower left (see Figure 9-4); as long as the needle is in the green arc, the pump is working OK.

The heading indicator has one other helpful device attached to it: the heading bug. It looks like two orange arrows next to each other, and it moves around the heading indicator when you adjust the HDG knob next to the heading indicator. Think of the bug as a memory aid: when you want to fly, say, a heading of 120, move the bug until it's right over the 12, and then it is easier to keep the plane on course because a quick glance shows you whether the bug is right at the top of the heading indicator.

Figure 9-4: The vacuum gauge monitors the health of the vacuum system, which drives two of the gyroscopic instruments: the heading indicator and the attitude indicator.

 KEEPING IT REAL

DRIFTING GYRO

One other issue with gyroscopes in aircraft instruments is that they sometimes *precess*, which means they slowly change and start giving incorrect information. The attitude indicator is subject to temporary, minor errors but has a system inside for self-correcting, and the turn coordinator doesn't have this problem. But the heading indicator slowly drifts and shows the wrong heading compared to the compass. Every 15 minutes, you should reset the heading indicator to match the compass by clicking the PUSH button next to the heading indicator. Of course, you want to do that when you're straight and level, since that's when the compass is accurate.

The realism settings on FSX include the Enable Gyro Drift setting, but even on Hard realism that option is not selected. Select it anyway, because almost all real-world small planes have a precessing heading indicator, and you need to get in the habit of checking it with the compass every 15 minutes.

196

PART I	PART II	PART III	PART IV	PART V	PART VI
PREFLIGHT	SPORT PILOT	PRIVATE PILOT	INSTRUMENT RATING	COMMERCIAL LICENSE	ATP AND BEYOND

Figure 9-5: Watch your attitude! The attitude indicator helps you keep the blue side up and the dirty side down.

The top-center position on your Skyhawk panel is the attitude indicator (see Figure 9-5). The position reflects its importance: if you ever lose sight of the sky or ground, either unintentionally or intentionally (such as when you're an instrument pilot in Part Four of this book), this will become your sky and ground.

But you use the attitude indicator even when you can see just fine out your windows. The little orange lines are your wings, and as you pitch the aircraft up, you'll see the horizon line start to move down and the wings look like they're moving up; you're climbing. The little orange dot in the center represents the airplane's nose. The black lines above the dot in the sky are marked in 5-degree intervals, with the 10-degree lines longer. So if you want to climb at a 10-degree pitch angle, all you have to do is pull back on the yoke until the little orange dot is on the first long black line and adjust the yoke to keep it that way.

Roll is measured in a similar way. The orange triangle at the top points to the white lines marked around the outside of the attitude indicator. The first white line is 10° of bank; then there is a 20-degree line and a 30-degree line, a gap, and then a 60-degree line and a 90-degree line. If you want to roll the airplane to a 45-degree bank (remember steep turns?), you move the yoke to the side until the orange arrow points right between the 30- and 60-degree marks and hold the plane there.

Like the heading indicator, the attitude indicator works because it has a gyroscope spinning inside it, powered by airflow from the vacuum pump. However, unlike the heading indicator, the attitude indicator has its own self-correction system and doesn't need periodic recalibration.

Figure 9-6: Together the turn coordinator and the inclinometer help you perform smooth, coordinated turns.

The third and final instrument that uses a gyroscope is the turn coordinator, as shown in Figure 9-6. This has less importance now than it will when you start your Instrument Rating training, but in a nutshell it tells how rapidly you're turning. If you're in a turn and the little airplane wings line up with one of the lower lines on the side, you will do a complete 360-degree turn in two minutes.

One key difference between the turn coordinator and the other two gyroscopic instruments is that the gyro in the turn coordinator is kept spinning by an electric motor rather than air pulled in by the vacuum pump.

In the face of the turn coordinator is a familiar instrument: the inclinometer, otherwise known as the *ball*. It isn't powered by a gyroscope, and it works just like in the Cub: keep the ball centered ("step on the ball" with the rudder), and you'll be in coordinated flight.

PITOT-STATIC INSTRUMENTS

Figure 9-7: The altimeter indicates your height above mean sea level (MSL) when you put the local altimeter setting in the little window.

Figure 9-8: The airspeed indicator shows more than just how fast you're going; it also shows certain airspeeds such has stall speeds and flap speeds.

Figure 9-9: The VSI measures your speed going up and down.

You learned about the airspeed indicator and altimeter when you trained on the Cub, but we didn't explain how they work. We'll start with a little background.

As you climb higher in the atmosphere, the atmosphere gets thinner, and the air pressure decreases. The amazing fact is that the air pressure drops in predictable amounts: at the surface, the pressure is about 30 inches of mercury (14 pounds per square inch, or 1 bar), and every 1,000 feet you go up, the pressure drops about 1 inch of mercury. An altimeter is a device that can sense small changes in air pressure (it's basically a sensitive barometer) and display those changes as changes in altitude (see Figure 9-7). The outside air that the altimeter uses for measurement comes from the static port. (The air that comes in is called *static* because its pressure isn't affected by the airplane's motion.)

The altimeter has three hands instead of the two in the Cub's altimeter: the hundreds-feet hand, the thousands-feet hand, and a little diamond that represents tens of thousands of feet. Good luck getting a Cessna 172 up above 20,000 feet, but the altimeter could show it if you could get that high. And like the Cub's altimeter, the altimeter in the Cessna can be adjusted to the local barometric pressure (called the *altimeter setting* on ATIS or AWOS radio broadcasts).

The airspeed indicator—shown in Figure 9-8—uses the static air pressure from the static port, just like the altimeter, but it needs to measure the air pressure caused by the forward motion of the airplane, because that's how it indicates your speed through the air. The source of that forward-motion air is called the *pitot tube* (pronounced "pea toe"), and it's out on the left wing. The faster you fly, the more air pressure enters the little hole on the front of the pitot tube, causing the airspeed indicator needle to move and show a higher airspeed.

In the Cessna, the airspeed indicator has colored arcs between various speeds. The green arc is the normal operating range; the bottom of the green arc (48 knots) is the airspeed at which the wings will stall in 1G (unaccelerated) flight, and the top of the green arc (129 knots) is the fastest you should fly in anything except smooth air. The white arc is the flap operating range; the bottom of the white arc is the stall speed in the landing (full flaps) configuration (40 knots), and the top of the white arc is the fastest you should fly with full flaps (85 knots). Only in smooth air should you fly at an airspeed in the yellow arc (above 129 knots), and you should never go above redline speed. By the way, the Cessna's airspeed is measured in knots; the Cub is the only FSX airplane to use mph.

The new instrument in this set is the vertical speed indicator (VSI), seen in Figure 9-9. Like the altimeter, it just measures static air pressure, but instead of displaying altitude, it displays the rate at which you're changing altitude in hundreds of feet per minute. You won't use this much in your Private Pilot Certificate training, but we'll point it out for the few maneuvers where it's useful.

198

PART I
PREFLIGHT

PART II
SPORT PILOT

PART III
PRIVATE PILOT

PART IV
INSTRUMENT RATING

PART V
COMMERCIAL LICENSE

PART VI
ATP AND BEYOND

RADIOS AND OTHER AVIONICS

Figure 9-10: Six radios are in the radio stack, plus a transponder and an autopilot.

Sport pilots can legally fly airplanes with radios, but the Cub doesn't have an electrical system, so you have a radio only if you bring along a handheld, battery-powered one. The Cessna has not one, not two, but seven radios! Two you can talk and listen on, and five are used for navigation (see Figure 9-10).

The radio stack starts at the top with the audio panel, where you select the radios to which you're listening. We'll talk about each of these radios in turn, but remember that you won't hear anything from a radio unless it is lit up here.

The next two boxes under the radio stack are combination communication and navigation radios. COM1/NAV1 is under the audio panel, and COM2/NAV2 is below that. Each radio has four frequencies in view: the one on the far left is the active communication frequency; next to it is the standby communication frequency; next is the active navigation frequency; and finally, on the right side, is the standby navigation frequency. To change frequencies, you can either click the knobs on the front of the radio or click the numbers themselves.

But notice you can change only the standby frequencies. The active frequencies—which are the ones in use—don't change this way. Instead, you click the "flip-flop" double-arrowed button in the middle, and the active and standby frequencies swap places.

We'll discuss the navigation radios in Chapter 10, but you can start using the communication radios now. However, just switching communication frequencies is not enough—you have to talk, too. The ATC menu will continue to be your communication interface, and if you use it, it will automatically switch frequencies for you. But if you dial frequencies on the radio and you choose the right frequency for the next step in your flight (for instance, switching to the tower controller frequency after you're done talking on the ground controller frequency), the ATC menu will update to give you the correct options for what to say. That is the most realistic way you can use the FSX communication radios.

The next radio, below COM2/NAV2, is called an *automatic direction finder* (ADF), and below that is distance-measuring equipment (DME) receiver. We'll explain both in the next chapter and show how to use them in depth when you start doing your instrument work.

Next is a transponder, identified by having four large digits. This device sends a code to the air traffic controller's radar system telling them who you are and what your altitude is. For the most part, you'll leave the transponder on code 1200; we'll tell you if you ever need to change it. (If you do, either click each number or use the numbered keys along the bottom of the transponder.) The Cub didn't have a transponder, but the air traffic controllers in FSX work with you as if you did, so you might not have realized it didn't have one.

Figure 9-11: The Cessna 172SP has a rather sophisticated GPS.

The bottom of the radio stack is an autopilot. This is a pretty nice system, and you'll use it a lot in the next chapter. In this chapter, you'll just use some basic functions such as holding a particular heading and altitude. It won't do much if you're sitting on the ground, though, so we'll talk about that when you're in the air.

The Cessna has a GPS, but it's not part of the panel; instead, it is visible when you press Shift+3 on your keyboard (see Figure 9-11). The Garmin GPS 500 is pretty similar to the Garmin GPSMAP 295 portable GPS in the Cub. We'll show you how to use the GPS in the next chapter, but if you have used GPSs in real life or if you got the hang of the Garmin 295 in the Cub, try this one, too.

THE FLAP ABOUT FLAPS

Figure 9-12: The flaps are retracted for normal takeoff and for cruising flight.

In Chapter 3 you learned how to do a forward slip in the Cub, used when you need to descend steeply but you don't want to accelerate too fast by just pointing the nose at the ground. More sophisticated airplanes like a Cessna 172 use a system of flaps for the same purpose and more (see Figure 9-12).

Flaps do this by increasing the drag against the oncoming air; as they are extended, they stick out even farther into the air and slow down the Cessna even more (see Figure 9-13). This means you rarely have to use a forward slip to descend steeply in the Cessna; fully extending the flaps is almost like having a couple of barn doors hanging off your wings, so you can point the nose down more steeply but stay slow (see Figure 9-14).

200

PART I
PREFLIGHT

PART II
SPORT PILOT

PART III
PRIVATE PILOT

PART IV
INSTRUMENT RATING

PART V
COMMERCIAL LICENSE

PART VI
ATP AND BEYOND

Figure 9-13: The flaps are partly extended (10°) for approach and for short- and soft-field takeoffs.

Figure 9-14: The flaps are fully extended (30°) for landing.

But flaps can also increase lift. In all airplanes, you can influence how much lift the wings create by changing your airspeed or the angle of attack (the angle the wings make with the oncoming, relative wind). By deploying the flaps, you have yet a third way to increase the total lift produced by the wings. Some flaps just increase the angle of attack of the wing, some increase the square footage of the wing (which also increases lift), and most do a combination of both.

Figure 9-15: The flap control is meant to look and feel a little bit like a flap. You'll appreciate that when you start flying airplanes that have retractable landing gear and the gear handle feels a little bit like a tire. On the 2D panel on the left it is easier to see the flap position; on the 3D panel, you can see the actual shape of the flap control.

Having enough lift to hold the plane in the air at slower airspeeds is useful, for instance, during takeoff and landing. If you can get off the ground while going slower, you'll use less runway and wear down your tires less. And on landing, if you can go slower before you actually touch down, again you'll use less runway and cause less tire wear. Without flaps, the wing stalls at about 48 knots. With full flaps, the wing stalls at 40 knots, which means a slower landing speed and shorter ground roll.

The flap control is down and to the right on the instrument panel, mostly hidden by the right-seat control yoke (see Figure 9-15). Like many controls, it's much easier to see in the 2D panel, but you don't even need to see it often. Two keys on your keyboard—F7 and F6—extend and retract the flaps, respectively. For most takeoffs in the Cessna, you don't need any flaps. For short-field and soft-field takeoffs, you use 10° of flaps (one press of F7). For landing, you will extend the flaps in stages, starting with 10°, then 20°, and finally, on final approach, the fully extended 30°.

OTHER SYSTEM DIFFERENCES

The cockpit is not the only place the Cessna is different from a Cub. The engine and fuel tanks are different, the Cessna has a real electrical system, and the third wheel is under the nose rather than under the tail.

ENGINE AND ENGINE INSTRUMENTS

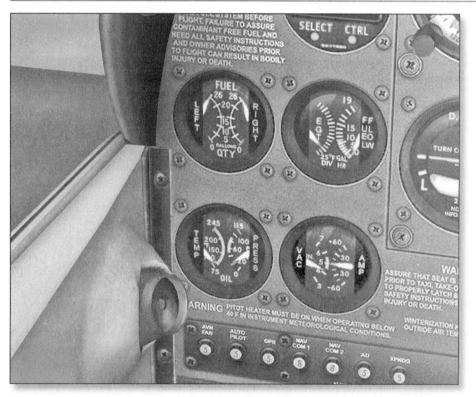

Figure 9-16: The Cessna has more engine instruments than the Cub, but the engine works by the same principles as a car's engine.

The engine on a Cessna 172 has a whopping 180 horsepower, almost three times as much as the Cub. Of course, the Cessna weighs twice as much as the Cub when fully loaded, so a lot of that horsepower is needed just to keep the plane up. But enough is left over that the Cessna can cruise at 124 knots, compared to the 65-knot Cub.

Another difference in the Cessna 172 engine is the lack of a carburetor; like a car, the Cessna has a fuel-injected engine (unless you drive a really old car!). A fuel pump is connected to the engine, but if it ever fails, the Cessna has a backup electric fuel pump available. You have to flip a switch on the panel to get that backup pump running. How would you know the fuel pump has failed? One clue is a new gauge: Fuel Flow. Found on the lower-left side of the instrument panel (see Figure 9-16), it measures how much fuel is going to the engine in gallons per hour. This instrument is most useful for telling how much fuel you're burning in cruise so you can make predictions about how long your fuel will last.

202

| PART I | PART II | PART III | PART IV | PART V | PART VI |
| PREFLIGHT | SPORT PILOT | PRIVATE PILOT | INSTRUMENT RATING | COMMERCIAL LICENSE | ATP AND BEYOND |

STUDENT OF THE CRAFT

MAGNETOS: THE SPARK THAT DRIVES AVIATION

Ever since powered flight began with the Wright brothers, aircraft engines have used magnetos and spark plugs to keep running. This is a different system than in modern cars, so we'll take a moment to explain it.

A gear on the engine turns two small electrical generators called *magnetos*. These magnetos produce a strong spike of electricity almost 100 times a second. The electricity is routed to the spark plugs, and each cylinder (the Cessna engine has four cylinders) has two spark plugs, one driven by each magneto. The system is designed so that both spark plugs in a cylinder fire a spark at the same time to ignite the fuel and oxygen brought into the cylinder.

The system uses two spark plugs per cylinder, instead of the one per cylinder like cars have, for safety and efficiency: if one spark plug fails or if one magneto (connected to four spark plugs, one on each cylinder) fails, the engine will still run, but it won't be as efficient and will waste some fuel.

Because the magnetos turn—and produce electricity—whenever the engine is turning and because the spark plugs are directly connected to the magnetos, the engine can keep running even if the rest of the airplane's electrical system fails.

Just like the Cub, the Cessna engine has a red mixture control knob. In the Cub you really used it only to stop the engine; in the Cessna, it has a bigger role. As you climb, the air gets thinner (less pressure) and contains less oxygen. The engine needs fuel and oxygen for combustion, and if it gets more fuel than oxygen, the combustion is not as good, and you don't get as much power. So as you climb, you need to lean the mixture; that is, you pull the mixture knob out slightly, and the fuel going into the engine is reduced slightly, returning to a balance with the oxygen.

But we won't leave you in suspense about how much to reduce the mixture when you're flying higher: you have a gauge for that, too! Located next to the Fuel Flow gauge is the EGT gauge, which stands for *exhaust gas temperature*. This is a good measurement of how well the combustion is doing in the cylinders. As you lean the mixture, the EGT will rise (as the extra fuel decreases) until, at the point the fuel exactly matches the oxygen and everything gets burned, you get the hottest EGT. If you keep leaning, you will decrease the fuel to the point that there is extra oxygen that doesn't burn and the temperature starts dropping again. (Keep leaning, and you'll take all the fuel away and the engine will...stop.) The point of perfect combustion is called *peak EGT*. We don't usually run the engine long at that temperature, though, because it's harder on the engine. Instead, during climb, we lean until the rpms are the highest. During cruise, we lean to 75° richer than peak EGT if we want the highest power (fastest speed), or we lean to 50° leaner than peak EGT if we want the best economy (miles per gallon, essentially).

No matter what, you need to keep an eye on the health of your engine during flight. Oil cools the engine and lubricates all the moving parts, so you can use the oil temperature gauge and oil pressure gauge to make sure the oil system is doing its thing. Those gauges are located on the lower-left side of the panel also.

FUEL TANKS

The fuel tank in the Cub was right in front of you, below the instrument panel. In the Cessna, fuel is carried in tanks in the wings—one in each wing. Gravity pulls the fuel down from the tanks to the fuel pumps, where it is pumped into the fuel injection system.

You can select whether fuel comes from one tank or the other, or both. Down on the floor, in between the seats, is a selector valve, as shown in Figure 9-17. Usually it is positioned in the BOTH position. But if you notice one tank has less fuel than the other—see, you have *two* fuel gauges on the panel—you can select the fuller tank. Just remember it needs to be on BOTH for takeoff and landing as well as for any maneuvers.

Figure 9-17: The fuel selector valve has three positions, indicating which fuel tank is supplying fuel to the engine: LEFT, BOTH, or RIGHT. Note that there is no OFF setting; you shut off fuel to the engine compartment (for instance, in an emergency) by pulling the FUEL SHUTOFF knob.

KEEPING IT REAL

DON'T TRUST THEM

Fuel gauges in real-world small planes are notoriously inaccurate. In fact, they're required to be accurate at only one point: when the tank is empty. Instead of flying until the tanks get low (which might be too late), pilots set the engine to burn a certain amount of fuel per hour and then plan a fuel stop (based on time) while plenty of fuel is still in the tank.

ELECTRICAL SYSTEM

You've already realized the Cessna has a real electrical system. It works like a car's electrical system. The only major difference between a car system and the one in the Cessna is that the Cessna has a 24-volt battery and a 28-volt electrical system. There is an alternator connected to the engine, and as long as the engine is turning, it generates electricity to run all the electrical equipment. Of course, the problem is getting the engine started in the first place. You probably shouldn't try to start the Cessna by hand-propping the propeller the way you can start the Cub. So, you need an electric starter, and that means you need a battery to power the starter. The battery also provides a little bit of electrical current needed to get the alternator working.

204

PART I
PREFLIGHT

PART II
SPORT PILOT

PART III
PRIVATE PILOT

PART IV
INSTRUMENT RATING

PART V
COMMERCIAL LICENSE

PART VI
ATP AND BEYOND

Figure 9-18: You'll see two MASTER electrical switches, one for the alternator and one for the battery. You can switch on the battery without the alternator going on, but if you switch the alternator on, the battery will come on, just like a real Cessna.

The battery's job is usually over as soon as the engine starts; the alternator recharges the battery and runs the electrical system. But the battery has one more use you might have thought of already: it can keep the electrical system running for a short time if the alternator fails. This doesn't happen often in real life (and happens only in FSX if you tell the program to make it so), but because this training shows you how to deal with as many kinds of emergencies as possible, we'll discuss electrical failures later in this chapter.

To turn on the battery, find the red MASTER switches on the lower-left side of the control panel, next to the magneto switch (see Figure 9-18). This switch actually has two halves—the ALT (alternator) and the BAT (battery).

Next to the vacuum gauge is the AMP gauge, which measures *amperes* (the quantity of electricity) flowing into or out of the battery. If the needle points upward slightly, it means the battery is charging; this happens right after you start the engine, as long as the alternator is working. If the needle points downward, toward the negative numbers, it means the battery is discharging, and the alternator might have failed. You can try resetting the alternator by turning the red ALT switch on and off, but if that doesn't help, you won't have long until your battery is dead.

The Cessna's electrical system has circuit breakers, designed to cut off electricity to any circuit that has a short circuit. (If they didn't cut off electricity, an electrical fire would be more likely to start.) They are the white dots just above the electrical switches, but they don't work in FSX. In the real Cessna, if one pops out and you don't think there is a real short circuit, you can reset the circuit breaker by pushing it back in. If it pops out again, you've got a short circuit, and you need to have that piece of equipment checked by a mechanic.

LIGHTS AND MORE

Figure 9-19: The lights and other electrical devices have switches on the instrument panel. Circuit breakers are right above the switches. It's much easier to see the switches in this 2D cockpit view; in the 3D cockpit view, the control yoke blocks your view of the switches.

Since you have an electrical system, let's take advantage of it and put some lights on this plane. The Cessna 172 has five light switches on the panel (see Figure 9-19), each used for different lights.

BCN turns on the red flashing light on top of the tail. You must have this light on any time the engine is running, day or night.

LAND is the landing light, a bright white light to illuminate the runway as you approach for landing at night. (It's pretty good for takeoff, too.)

TAXI is another white light pointed forward, but it's not as bright as the landing light, and it's pointed in a direction more useful for taxiing. This doesn't work on the FSX Cessna 172.

NAV turns on the navigation lights. Just like a boat, an airplane has to use these lights all night from sunset to sunrise: a green light on the right wing tip, a red light on the left wing tip, and a white light on the tail pointing backward.

STROBE lights are also out on the wing tips—white strobe lights that flash. They're great at night, but they should also be used in the daytime to help other pilots see you.

Right next to the light switches is the PITOT HEAT switch. Remember, the pitot tube is the device on the wing that sends air to the airspeed indicator. If for any reason the pitot tube got ice on it—not likely until you start your instrument training—you would switch on the pitot heat to melt the ice. Otherwise, leave it off.

Just to the right of the light switches is the white AVIONICS MASTER switch, which turns on all the radios.

Oh yeah, you also get a clock (upper left of the panel) with a stopwatch/chronograph, the outside air temperature, and the voltage in the electrical system. Classy, eh?

NOSEWHEEL VS. TAILWHEEL

Figure 9-20: A normal landing attitude in a tricycle-gear airplane, main wheels touching down and nosewheel a foot off the ground

For pilots like you who learned to fly in a tailwheel airplane such as the Cub, transitioning to a nosewheel (tricycle-gear) airplane like the Cessna is much easier than for pilots going the other direction. One big reason airplanes started being built with nosewheels is that they are inherently easier to control on the ground. (In the air there is little difference.) In a taildragger, the center of gravity is behind the main wheels, and it sometimes feels like the plane is constantly trying to bite its own tail.

But some planes are still made with tailwheels instead of nose-wheels for several reasons. (The FSX Maule Orion and Extra 300 are both current-production air-planes that are taildraggers.) On rough surfaces such as gravel, rocks, or glaciers or soft surfaces such as snow or mud, a small nosewheel could catch and "trip" the plane over onto its back. A tailwheel airplane with large, soft, "off-road" main tires can sort of float above the roughness, and the small tailwheel, even if it does catch on the surface, won't trip the plane because it is behind the center of the mass.

206

PART I	PART II	PART III	PART IV	PART V	PART VI
PREFLIGHT	SPORT PILOT	PRIVATE PILOT	INSTRUMENT RATING	COMMERCIAL LICENSE	ATP AND BEYOND

So, what do you need to know to be able to fly a plane with tricycle gear? The only significant changes happen on takeoff and landing. During a regular takeoff, all three wheels stay on the ground until you reach rotation speed and start to climb. Short-field takeoffs are the same. However, soft-field takeoffs are different: you apply full aft force on the yoke right from the start, and the nosewheel pops up (out of the soft surface) quickly, followed shortly by the main wheels. Just like in the Cub, though, you're going too slowly to climb out of ground effect, so you level off 5 or 10 feet above the sod until you attain the appropriate climb speed.

During landing in a tricycle-gear airplane, we almost always land first on the main wheels, as shown in Figure 9-20, holding the nose off in a flare until we get the main wheels solidly on the ground; the pitch attitude of the plane is similar to the three-point landing, but with only the two main wheels touching. Landing with all three wheels at the same time is not a good idea in a tricycle-gear airplane, because you might slam too hard on the nosegear, and it will either collapse or bounce up and possibly put you high above the runway but with little airspeed to keep flying. On a short field, you try to get the nose down quickly so you can start braking. On a soft field, you try to hold the nosewheel off the ground as long as possible so that the wheel doesn't catch in the softness.

Now that you have learned about the differences between the Cub and the Cessna 172, it's time to fly the Skyhawk.

CHECKOUT FLIGHT IN THE CESSNA 172SP

Figure 9-21: The flight Chap_09_C172_Checkout starts with the Cessna shut down at the Anoka County airport near Minneapolis, Minnesota.

Load the flight Chap_09_C172_ Checkout. This checkout flight begins at the Anoka County/Blaine airport (KANE) just north of Minneapolis, Minnesota (see Figure 9-21). Check the map for key information about the airport. Anoka County has a control tower and four runways (two crossing pieces of pavement): Runways 9/27 and 18/36. The airport sits at 912 feet MSL elevation. Make note of the radio frequencies for ATIS, ground, and tower.

The airport has Class D airspace around it. The Minneapolis Class B airspace starts at 4,000 feet MSL above the airport, so you'll need to stay below that (or fly north) unless you want to convince the Minneapolis Approach controller to let you enter the Class B airspace.

We suggest you set the aircraft realism on Medium but also enable gyro drift.

ENGINE START

Figure 9-22: The checklists in FSX are abbreviated from the ones in real Cessnas, but they're actually quite good. Print them and keep them nearby so you don't have to keep pulling them up on the screen.

After preflighting the Cessna (humor us and use the spot plane view to "walk around" the airplane to make sure nothing looks broken), it's time to start the engine. Sure, you can use the Ctrl+E shortcut, but we're trying to be realistic here.

The Flight Checklist in FSX (Shift+F10) is good for this purpose, but we'll expand on a few items shown in Figure 9-22. First, it is important not to turn on the avionics until after the engine is going and the alternator is on, because when you first turn on the alternator, it can send a spike of electricity that could ruin the sensitive radios.

The checklist has you turning on the flashing beacon after engine start, but we think that's too late; if you turn it on when you turn on the battery MASTER switch, folks nearby will know you're about to start the engine.

The checklist says, "Propeller Area: CLEAR," but that means more than just looking around the plane to make sure no one is nearby; we open the window and yell, "Clear prop!" Sure, you might get odd looks from other people near your computer, but you want them to be a safe distance in case the...um...cooling fan suddenly starts dragging your computer around.

RADIOS USE

Figure 9-23: COM1 is set with 120.625 as the active frequency and 121.85 in standby.

Once you've turned on the avionics, you can set up your radios. Using COM1, switch the frequency to the Anoka County ATIS on 120.625 to listen to the current weather and any other information about the airport. (The radio will show the frequency only as 120.62, as you can see in Figure 9-23, but in reality the frequencies go from 120.600 to 120.625 and then from 120.625 to 120.650.) You don't need to use the ATC menu for this, so try it realistically on the radio. Write down the weather report so you have it handy later: the ATIS identifier (letter of the alphabet), wind, visibility, clouds, temperature (it's in Celsius, in case you're wondering), the altimeter setting, and the runway in use.

Set your altimeter to the current altimeter setting; it is correct if the altimeter reads 912 feet, the airport elevation. If there are any winds, picture where they are coming from in relation to the plane and the runways so you can set the proper aileron deflection as you taxi (as you learned in Chapter 4).

Use the top-down view and the airport diagram on the website (www .wiley.com) to figure out where the airplane is located and how you will probably taxi to the active runway.

208

PART I	PART II	PART III	PART IV	PART V	PART VI
PRE FLIGHT	SPORT PILOT	PRIVATE PILOT	INSTRUMENT RATING	COMMERCIAL LICENSE	ATP AND BEYOND

Switch frequencies on COM1 to the Anoka County ground controller on 121.85. When you turn on the ATC menu, you will have all the options for what to say to the ground controller; choose Request Taxi, Depart West, and be ready to write down the taxi directions from the ground controller.

Taxiing and Runup

After acknowledging the ground controller's taxi instructions, follow those directions to the runway, but hold short of the runway (don't taxi onto it yet). Taxi at a jogging pace, and slow down by idling the engine to save wear and tear on the brakes.

Your next task is to perform the Before Takeoff Checklist in FSX. The instruction, "Flight Controls—FREE AND CORRECT" means you should run your control yoke and rudder through their ranges of motions and look outside the plane to make sure the ailerons, elevator, and rudder all move in the proper directions (see "Flight Controls Not Correct" for a reason to do this).

  ACCIDENT CHAIN

FLIGHT CONTROLS NOT CORRECT

Does it seem silly to check the flight controls to make sure the ailerons, elevator, and rudder move the direction they should when you move the controls? Isn't that what mechanics are supposed to do? This accident occurred just a few years ago, as reported by the NTSB:

Aircraft: Cessna 177RG "Cardinal"

Location: Seattle, Washington

"Just after takeoff, the aircraft started rolling to the left. As the pilot applied right roll inputs, the aircraft accelerated its roll to the left. As it reached a bank angle of approximately 80°, it descended into the runway surface. The flight was intended as a post-maintenance test flight after installation of a replacement set of wings.

"A post-accident inspection determined that the ailerons had been misrigged so that they deflected opposite to the inputs of the pilot. Neither the pilot nor the mechanic who accompanied him on the flight detected the aileron reversal during the walk-around inspection or the pretakeoff flight control test."

If you have a control yoke like the real Cessna, there is an easy way to remember which way the ailerons should move: with both hands on the yoke, point your thumbs up and turn the yoke to one side. Your thumbs are now pointing at the aileron that should be deflected up, and the other aileron should point down. Turn the yoke the other way, and your thumbs now point to the other aileron, which should now be pointing up.

When the time comes to set the elevator trim for takeoff, you need to know whether you will be making a V_y (best rate) climb or a V_x (best angle) climb after you take off. The V_y climb is used for most departures, and the V_x climb is for runways that have obstacles off the end. The runways at Anoka County have some trees, but they're not high and they're far from the ends of the runway, so you can do a normal V_y climb after departure.

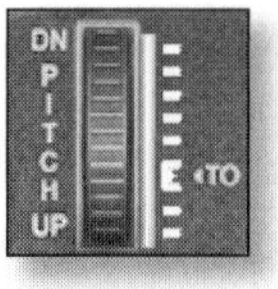

The trim is more easily set from the 2D panel view rather than the 3D panel view. When you move the trim wheel, either with the mouse or with buttons on your yoke/joystick, a little white triangle moves up and down on the trim indicator. When it points to the word TO (meaning "takeoff"), the trim will be set for just about a V_y climb, as shown in Figure 9-24. If you needed a V_x climb, you'd set the trim one full indicator line lower than TO.

Figure 9-24: The elevator trim is set for takeoff and a V_y climb

During the Before Takeoff Checklist, you will be running the engine up to 1800 rpm and performing a couple of checks. You do this to make sure the systems, especially the magnetos and spark plugs, are working properly.

TAKEOFF AND CLIMB

When you're ready to go, switch COM1 to the tower controller frequency of 126.05. Using the ATC menu, tell the controller you're ready for takeoff. (FSX remembers that you asked the ground controller for a west departure, so it has you say that again, which is how you do it in the real world.)

When you're cleared for takeoff, perform one last, memorized checklist that we teach our students: lights, camera, action! Turn on your landing light and your strobe lights so other planes can see you more easily in the daytime. "Camera" is the transponder for ATC to see you on their radar screens; in FSX, it's already turned on, but in the real world (and in online multiplayer worlds), we leave this turned off until we're cleared for takeoff. And "action" means pull on to the runway and go. But be sure to look both ways before entering the runway; there could be another airplane landing or taking off from this or another runway—yes, controllers are human and do, rarely, make mistakes—and so we always check.

NORMAL TAKEOFF (PLENTY OF RUNWAY, NO OBSTRUCTIONS)

- Flaps: Up (0°)
- V_r (rotation speed): 55 knots
- V_y (best rate of climb speed): 74 knots

Taking off in a nosewheel airplane is much easier than in a taildragger like the Cub. After you apply full power, use the rudder to stay straight on the runway as you accelerate, but keep the elevator neutral. Glance at the tachometer to make sure the engine is producing full power (about 2200 rpm), quickly check the oil temperature and pressure (in the green), and then ensure the airspeed indicator is rising. If any of these instruments show something wrong, abort the takeoff immediately: idle the throttle, and maintain runway alignment as you slow down and exit.

210

PART I
PREFLIGHT

PART II
SPORT PILOT

PART III
PRIVATE PILOT

PART IV
INSTRUMENT RATING

PART V
COMMERCIAL LICENCE

PART VI
ATP AND BEYOND

Figure 9-25: This is the view out the front windscreen during a V_y climb at 74 knots.

If all is going well, pull back on the yoke (rotate) at 55 knots, and then pitch the nose for a V_y climb of 74 knots. The pitch attitude for a 74-knot climb will be just about when the horizon is lined up with the top of the instrument panel, as shown in Figure 9-25; on your attitude indicator, it's about 12° pitch up. Your trim should be set pretty close to 74 knots, but if you need to keep holding yoke pressure, adjust trim.

When you get to traffic pattern altitude (1,900 feet), lower the nose slightly so that you can see the horizon over the instrument panel. This is your cruise climb attitude, and you'll probably be going about 80 knots and climbing about 500 fpm (check the VSI). This isn't the best rate of climb, of course; that was when you were flying 74 knots (V_y) and getting about 700 fpm. But it is much safer to fly in a way that lets you see what is ahead of you! Turn west to leave the traffic pattern, and continue the climb up to 3,500 feet.

BASIC MANEUVERS

To help you learn how the Cessna 172 behaves compared to the Cub, you'll now take it through some of the same maneuvers. As always, start with clearing turns to make sure no other airplanes are nearby. You should start these maneuvers at an altitude of at least 3,500 feet MSL (about 2,500 feet above ground level [AGL]), and if any descent is involved, you should never go below 2,500 feet MSL (1,500 feet AGL).

We use a memorized checklist before performing maneuvers and before landing. The acronym is C-GUMPS, pronounced as "see gumps." The letters stand for the following:

- *C*: Carburetor heat on (if installed, such as in the Cub)

- *G*: Gas—fuel tank set to BOTH (for the Cessna) or the fullest tank

- *U*: Undercarriage (landing gear) down (if it is retractable gear)

- *M*: Mixture set (usually rich, unless it's a high-altitude airport)

- *P*: Propeller set to high rpm (on airplanes that have a controllable pitch prop, like the Mooney)

- *S*: Safety check—seatbelts snug, lights on for visibility, and so on

Even though you're not about to land, perform the C-GUMPS checklist now to ensure the plane is ready for whatever you need to do during the maneuvers.

STEEP TURNS

First you'll perform some steep turns. As you might recall, you do these at a 45-degree bank all the way around in a 360-degree turn. Steep turns are usually performed no faster than the maneuvering speed of the plane, which at light weights can be as low as 90 knots. So, slow to 90 knots as you do your clearing turns. Steep turns are supposed to be a "visual" maneuver; that is, you judge your bank angle and maintain your nose level (to maintain altitude) by looking outside at the horizon. But now that you have an attitude indicator, you can cheat a little bit and glance at it to make sure you're getting a 45-degree angle (see Figure 9-26).

Figure 9-26: A steep-banked turn of 45° looks like this in the Cessna.

↓ KEEPING IT REAL
USING REAL WINDOWS BEATS WINDOWS XP

As we've trained people to fly, we've noticed that students who spent a lot of time with flight simulators such as FSX are more likely to watch the instruments instead of using the horizon and outside references for controlling. Besides that the outside world will show attitude changes much more obviously than the instruments, you want your head "on a swivel" looking for other airplanes.

Continued

212

PART I	PART II	PART III	PART IV	PART V	PART VI
PREFLIGHT	SPORT PILOT	PRIVATE PILOT	INSTRUMENT RATING	COMMERCIAL LICENSE	ATP AND BEYOND

That's one reason we started you in the Cub, with its basic instruments. Try to avoid staring at the instruments in the Cessna, and instead continue to control the attitude of the plane with the horizon. If you find yourself spending more than half the time looking at the instruments, change the view to the 2D mode with just the basic instruments along the bottom of the screen.

SLOW FLIGHT

Figure 9-27: To maintain altitude when flying slowly, your pitch attitude needs to be quite high.

As with the Cub, the goal of slow flight is to fly the Cessna as slowly as you can without stalling the wings. Maintain your altitude, heading, and coordination as you fly at about 55 knots with flaps up (0°) and then with flaps fully extended (30°) at 48 knots (see Figure 9-27). Try to make gentle turns without losing altitude and while maintaining the proper airspeed. Stay active with your rudder to make sure the plane remains in coordinated flight.

The real-world Cessna is actually much easier to control in slow flight than the FSX Cessna 172. This is because of the stall warning system. In FSX, the loud buzzer warning of a wing stall happens at about 44 knots with flaps extended, and then the nose drops as the wings lose lift. In the real world, the stall horn comes on at about 45 knots, but the nose doesn't actually drop until the plane slows to about 40 knots. This means a properly performed slow flight procedure in a real Cessna is just flying around with the stall buzzer blaring the whole time but the wing not actually stalling. You can't do that in FSX, so stay at about 48 knots.

STALLS

When practicing recovery from stalls, remember you're trying to lose as little altitude as possible but still fully recover. And the overall goal of stalls is to learn how the airplane behaves during stalls so you can avoid them or at least minimize their hazard. (An uncontrolled stall can easily become a spin.)

Power-off stalls are different in the Cessna than the Cub, because now you have flaps. Because these stalls simulate what might happen if you stall during the approach and landing, we do them with flaps fully extended. Start by slowing down and extending the flaps in stages. Descend at 65 knots with 30° of flaps and the power set at about 1500 rpm. This is the standard configuration you will use on final approach to a landing in the Cessna 172.

NOTE!

⬇ FLAP EXTENSION SPEED

Don't extend the first stage of flaps, 10°, unless you're flying slower than 110 knots. And don't extend the flaps 20° or 30° unless you're flying slower than 85 knots. If you do extend the flaps when flying faster, you could damage them.

When you're descending at 65 knots, idle the engine, and pitch the airplane up to about 5° above level pitch attitude. Without any power, the airplane will slow down, and you'll have to keep pulling back on the yoke to get the pitch to stay there. At about 40 knots or so, the stall horn will buzz, the nose will drop, and the plane will start descending fast (take a look at the vertical speed indicator).

Now you need to perform three tasks simultaneously: apply full throttle, let the nose drop to about 5° below level, and raise the flaps from 30° to 20°. Once the airplane is accelerating and is no longer stalling, start to pull up into a climb and retract the flaps to 10°. Once you're stable in the climb, retract the flaps completely, and climb at about 75 knots back up to 3,500 feet to practice it again.

Your goals are to lose no more than 300 feet of altitude from the time the stall horn goes off and to maintain your heading and keep the wings mostly level. It's also important to maintain coordination with the rudder; an uncoordinated stall is exactly how a spin starts.

You perform power-on stalls (also known as *departure stalls*) just like in the Cub. You'll want to start them lower, at about 2,500 feet MSL, so that when you climb you don't exceed 3,500 feet or so.

Slow to about 70 knots, flying level, with the flaps retracted. Apply full power, and pitch up to a higher than usual attitude (30° seems to work); when the wing stalls, push the nose down to a level attitude until your speed comes back, and then resume a V_y climb at 74 knots. Maintain the heading you started on, keep the wings mostly level, and stay coordinated at all times.

Practice both kinds of stalls until you can detect a stall (based on how the controls respond to your movements) even before the stall horn goes off.

When you're done, if you've been flying for 15 minutes or so, reset the heading indicator to match the compass by clicking the PUSH knob next to the heading indicator.

214

| PART I | PART II | PART III | PART IV | PART V | PART VI |
| PREFLIGHT | SPORT PILOT | PRIVATE PILOT | INSTRUMENT RATING | COMMERCIAL LICENSE | ATP AND BEYOND |

APPROACH AND LANDING

When you're comfortable with steep turns, slow flight, and stalls in the Cessna, head for another airport to practice landings. If you headed west from Anoka County, you should be a few miles north of the Crystal airport (KMIC). The quickest way to find it is to use the Garmin GPS 500. Pressing Shift+3 on your keyboard will bring it into view; look around the map, and see which direction you need to turn. The blue dashed line around it is its Class D airspace; you can't enter that airspace without talking to the Crystal tower controllers, so if you're close, don't turn that way yet.

Listen to Crystal's ATIS information on 125.70, write down what you need to remember, and then switch to the Crystal tower frequency of 120.70. Turn on the ATC menu, and you'll see there isn't an option to talk to the Crystal tower. Select Nearest Airport List, then Crystal, and then Request Full Stop Landing. The tower controller will give you instructions on how to approach the airport, how to enter the traffic pattern, and which runway to use. The traffic pattern altitude is 1,900 feet MSL, so you'll want to descend to that altitude by the time you enter the pattern.

When you're on the downwind for your landing runway, set the power to about 2200 rpm, and perform the C-GUMPS checklist. Your airspeed should settle on about 95 knots or so, if you maintain pattern altitude of 1,900 feet.

Figure 9-28: Final approach in a Cessna gives you quite a good view of the runway.

Abeam your landing point, bring the power back to 1500 rpm, set the flaps to 10°, and pitch for 85 knots. When the end of the runway is about 45° behind you, turn onto the base leg, extend 20° of flaps, and pitch for 75 knots. Look at the runway, and make a judgment whether you're too high, too low, or just right. If you're not just right, use power to adjust it, but keep using the pitch attitude of the plane to maintain 75 knots. When you turn onto final approach, set 30° of flaps and pitch for 65 knots, maintaining the proper approach path with power as needed (see Figure 9-28).

When you're over the end of the runway, idle the engine, but maintain your current pitch attitude. As you descend within 20 feet of the runway, start to roundout and slow your descent, and then flare nose-high a few feet above the runway. If you do it just right, your wings will stall just as your wheels chirp on the runway.

↓ STRAIGHT-IN APPROACH

If the tower controller tells you to fly from your position straight into the runway, without entering the traffic pattern, you need to do your approach and landing steps at different spots. When you're about three miles from the runway, level off at pattern altitude, and do the C-GUMPS checklist. Two miles from the runway, bring the power back to 1500 rpm, set 10° of flaps, and descend at 85 knots. One mile out, set flaps 20° and pitch 75 knots. A half mile away, set flaps 30° and pitch 65 knots.

If at any point during an approach or landing you decide to abort the landing—an airplane or something else is on the runway, or you're just not lined up properly and you can't get back—you need to initiate a go-around. The airplane is slow and the flaps are extended, so it will be hard for the airplane to climb. The trick is to perform three tasks at once (just like recovering from a stall): apply full power, pitch up to a climb attitude, and retract the flaps to 20°. Once you're definitely climbing (check the VSI to make sure), retract the flaps to 10°. When your speed is faster than 70 knots, retract the flaps completely. When everything is settled and you've taken a deep breath from all the excitement, report to the tower controller that you had a go-around. (It's one of the options on the ATC menu.) Proceed around the traffic pattern to try landing again.

When you land, you can taxi back and enter the traffic pattern to practice more landings and takeoffs. If you're comfortable, you can even do a touch-and-go, where you come into a normal landing but instead of stopping on the runway, you retract flaps completely, apply full throttle, and take off again. Be sure to request this, though, so the tower controller isn't surprised when you do it.

ADVANCED MANEUVERS

Figure 9-29: The flight Chap_09_C172_Advanced starts at the Crystal airport, just down the road from Anoka County.

Now that you've flown an introductory flight in the Cessna 172, it's time to practice some advanced maneuvers. You'll be mostly on your own for this: determine how much you need to practice each procedure. If you want an objective reference, check out the Private Pilot Practical Test Standards on the website (www.wiley.com) and on the FAA site (www.faa.gov/education _research/testing/air- men/test_standards/), be- cause that will list the specific skill level for each maneuver.

Load the flight Chap_09_C172_ Advanced. This flight begins at the Crystal airport, this time with some winds (see Figure 9-29). If you want, you can even use the grass strip (Runway 06R/24L) for soft-field takeoffs and landings.

216

PART I | PART II | PART III | PART IV | PART V | PART VI
PRE-FLIGHT | STUDENT PILOT | PRIVATE PILOT | INSTRUMENT RATING | COMMERCIAL LICENSE | ATP AND BEYOND

PERFORMANCE TAKEOFFS AND LANDINGS

Figure 9-30: This is the view out the front windscreen during a V$_x$ climb at 68 knots.

The procedures for short-field and soft-field are as described earlier in this chapter. This section shows the flap settings and speeds. You can practice short-field takeoffs and landings even when the runway is long, and although the Crystal airport has a grass strip, if it is too wet with snow, use the hard runways but follow the soft-field technique (see Figure 9-30).

Here are the flap settings and speeds for a short-field takeoff:

- *Flaps*: 10°

- *V$_r$ (rotation speed)*: 55 knots

- *V$_x$*: 68 knots (if obstructions after takeoff)

- *V$_y$*: 74 knots (if no obstructions)

Here are the flap settings and speeds for a soft-field takeoff:

- *Flaps*: 10°

- *V$_r$ (rotation speed)*: not applicable

- *V$_x$*: 68 knots (if obstructions after takeoff)

- *V$_y$*: 74 knots (if no obstructions)

Here are the flap settings and speeds for a short-field landing:

- *Flaps*: 30°

- *Approach speed*: 57 knots

Here are the flap settings and speeds for a soft-field landing:

- *Flaps*: 30°

- *Approach speed*: 65 knots

In addition, you should practice crosswind takeoffs and landings. The tower controllers at Crystal and Anoka County probably won't let you do it, because the FSX ATC system isn't nearly as flexible as real-world controllers in giving you the runway you want, so you can just turn off ATC and do it anyway. But for more realism, several airports are nearby with runways that aren't pointed into the wind and don't have controllers: Buffalo Municipal (KCFE) is 22 miles west of Crystal. Lake Elmo (21D) is 20 miles east and has two runways, one of which is exactly crosswind to the wind you'll find in this scenario.

EMERGENCY PROCEDURES

With additional systems, the Cessna 172 has more issues that could go wrong than the Cub. Of course, a new airplane is much less likely to have things break, but you do need to know what to do when you get a failure. And, again, FSX won't break any of your systems unless you tell it to do so. But try it to see whether you can handle the following situations.

FLAP FAILURE

Figure 9-31: A no-flap landing approach needs to be faster and shallower than a normal approach.

If your flaps don't extend for landing, what can you do? Do the same as you did with the Cub: land without them. Use an approach speed of 75 knots rather than 65 knots (see Figure 9-31). If you need to approach the runway more steeply, do a forward slip. If the runway is too short for a 75-knot approach speed, go somewhere else; you can't force the plane to land as short as the Cub can.

If you have no flaps for a soft-field or short-field takeoff and you really need them because the runway really is short or soft, you'll have to fix the flaps before you leave.

If you're flying and the flaps get stuck down, you're in a more dangerous situation; 10° of flaps won't affect you a lot, although you'll go slower than you intended. But if the flaps are stuck at 30° for landing and then you have to do a go-around, you won't be able to climb much at all, even with full power. If this happens at a runway with obstructions at the other end and you can't climb over the obstructions, you'll have no choice but to land before you hit them.

218

PART I
PREFLIGHT

PART II
SPORT PILOT

PART III
PRIVATE PILOT

PART IV
INSTRUMENT RATING

PART V
COMMERCIAL LICENSE

PART VI
ATP AND BEYOND

ELECTRICAL SYSTEM FAILURE

Figure 9-32: The annunciator panel warns you of major system problems including low voltage, low vacuum pressure for your instruments, low fuel, and low oil pressure.

Other than a fire, the only real problem you might have with your electrical system is if the alternator stops working. When this happens, you'll see the word *VOLTS* light up on your annunciator panel and the AMP meter will show the battery is discharging, as shown in Figure 9-32. Try turning the ALT MASTER switch off and on again; if this doesn't fix the problem, turn the ALT off and start reducing the electrical load on the battery. In FSX you can't do much other than turn off some lights and maybe skip using the flaps. In the real Cessna 172, you can turn off any radios you're not using, including the GPS. You'll be lucky if you have even 15 to 30 minutes of power in your battery.

You're not in a dire emergency, though, so you can take a few minutes to make a plan. Probably you'll want to land soon but preferably at an airport with a mechanic who can fix the problem. You might not have enough battery power to talk on the radio, but if you're close to an airport with a control tower and you tell them the problem, they can let you come in to the pattern and then signal you with colored spotlights when to land. (There are many instructions they can give using lights, but if nothing else, remember that green means "Cleared to land" and red means "Don't land.") Or just go to an uncontrolled (nontowered) airport, where radios aren't required anyway.

Your flaps might not work when you get ready to land, so don't try to get into a very short or soft runway. And some instruments, such as the fuel gauges and engine instruments—other than the tachometer—run on electricity, so they won't work and you won't know how you're doing on fuel, for instance. So, don't fly too far unless you know you have full fuel tanks.

What about your engine—won't it stop when the battery dies? It would in your car, but the Cub didn't even have a battery, and the engine in the Cessna (or any other small plane, for that matter) doesn't use the battery to stay running. The magnetos (which create the electricity for the spark plugs) are always working as long as the engine is turning.

ENGINE FAILURE AND POWER-OFF DESCENT

If the engine stops during flight, you have a few more items to check than you did in the Cub (see Figure 9-33)—but first, remember your ABCs: airspeed at best glide (65 knots, flaps up in the Cessna); best field for an emergency landing; and checklist, where you look at the following controls:

- *Fuel Selector*: BOTH

- *Fuel Shutoff*: ON (pushed in)

- *Mixture*: RICH (or if it already is rich, try it more lean)

- *Throttle*: ADJUST (sometimes just pumping it in and out helps)

- *Alternate Air Source*: ON

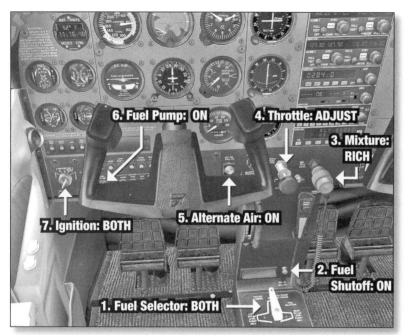

- *Fuel Pump*: ON (or if it is on, turn it off; maybe the engine was flooded with fuel)

- *Ignition/Magnetos*: BOTH (if it already is both, try it on L and R)

If you have no luck restarting the engine, continue your power-off descent without extending the flaps until you're sure you can make it to your emergency landing site. If you will only just make it there, continue without flaps. But if you're high, you can start adding flaps, remembering that they will increase your descent angle. You really want to land as slow as you can if you're not landing on a runway, because you're likely to hit an object on the ground. But you don't want to get so slow that you stall the wings, because you'll sink very fast, so maintain 65 knots right until the landing flare.

Figure 9-33: The engine failure procedure entails a flow around the cockpit to try to restart the engine. However, if you are less than 1,000 feet above the ground, shut off the systems and prepare for an emergency landing.

EMERGENCY DESCENT

If you need to get down fast in a Cessna, you have two choices. You can do the same kind of descent as you did in the Cub, with an idle throttle, a steep bank of 45°, and the nose down until you get up to 130–150 knots. Or you can put out all the flaps, go into a steep bank, and descend no faster than 85 knots. The first method will probably get you down more quickly, but not a lot more quickly, and the disadvantage is that you're now going 150 knots and you need to slow down to land. Therefore, we teach our students to use the procedure of full flaps and 85 knots, as shown in Figure 9-34. But you should be able to perform either type of descent, so the time to practice is now while you don't actually have an emergency to contend with.

Figure 9-34: An emergency descent in the Cessna is usually performed with full flaps, a steep bank, and no more than 85 knots of airspeed.

220

PART I
PREFLIGHT

PART II
SPORT PILOT

PART III
PRIVATE PILOT

PART IV
INSTRUMENT RATING

PART V
COMMERCIAL LICENSE

PART VI
ATP AND BEYOND

KEY POINTS FOR REAL FLYING AND FSX BUILT-INS

The following are some key points from this chapter:

- Understand the aerodynamics of takeoff and landing in a nosewheel aircraft.

- Familiarize yourself with the Cessna 172 systems and procedures.

- Experiment with the instrumentation found in modern, single-engine, piston aircraft.

- Practice basic maneuvers in an aircraft with flaps.

Here are the lessons and missions to study after reading this chapter:

- *Lessons*: The Student Pilot and Private Pilot lessons in FSX all use the Cessna 172. If you haven't already read and flown those lessons, you can do so now. The only lesson that covers material we have not yet covered is Private Pilot Lesson 3, VOR Navigation, which you'll learn in the next chapter.

- *Missions*: FSX tutorial missions 1 through 6 should all be easy for you to do at this point, if you haven't done them yet. In addition, the Sitka Approach and the Swiss Outing missions take you to beautiful parts of the world in the Cessna 172.

RADIO NAVIGATION WITH TRADITIONAL AVIONICS

10

"ELECTRONICS WERE RASCALS, AND THEY LAY AWAKE NIGHTS TRYING TO FIND SOME WAY TO SCREW YOU DURING THE DAY. YOU COULD NOT REASON WITH THEM. THEY HAD A BRAIN AND INTESTINES, BUT NO HEART."

—ERNEST K. GANN

222

PART I	PART II	PART III	PART IV	PART V	PART VI
PREFLIGHT	SPORT PILOT	PRIVATE PILOT	INSTRUMENT RATING	COMMERCIAL LICENSE	ATP AND BEYOND

FOLLOW THE INVISIBLE ROAD

Some concepts in aviation make more sense when you realize they have evolved over time rather than coming into being all at once. This is definitely true of aerial navigation. Early navigation was all done by sight. Pilots followed rivers or roads, headed toward distant mountains, and so on. For long stretches where there were no landmarks, they flew a heading and hacked a stopwatch, which was called *dead reckoning*. It worked, but, like Lindbergh crossing the Atlantic ocean, when they saw the ground again, they weren't necessarily sure where they were.

Some early navigation aids were also visible, such as flashing beacons set on mountaintops, but the breakthrough came when radio was used. This innovation was crucial because at the same time, flight instruments let pilots fly the plane through clouds where they couldn't see anything outside the window. They needed to follow a guidance system that didn't require seeing anything either.

Radio navigation made it possible to know, with varying degrees of certainty, where the airplane was at any time. More important, radio navigation meant the airplane could follow a particular path over the ground. This is essential for instrument flying because it let pilots descend between hills while still in the clouds and line up with a runway that they can't see with their eyes until seconds before actually landing.

In this chapter, you'll look at three main navigation systems still in use for general aviation today: the non-directional beacon (NDB), the very-high-frequency omnidirectional range (VOR), and global positioning system (GPS).

FINDING THE BEACON

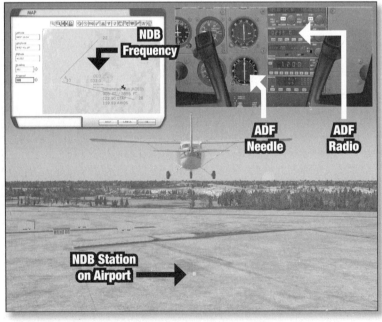

NDB stations are the oldest systems of the three. They are also being steadily decommissioned in the United States because VORs and GPS make them obsolete. Few new light airplanes even have the equipment onboard the airplane to receive them, but the FSX Skyhawk does.

The device in the airplane is called the automatic direction finder (ADF). Tune the NDB frequency, and the ADF needle points to the radio antenna on the ground. It couldn't be much simpler. It's sort of like a lighthouse at the mouth of a harbor at night. If you're out on the ocean, you can see the lighthouse and head that way. You end up at the harbor. Figure 10-1 shows the picture from inside and outside the airplane.

Figure 10-1: With an ADF or a lighthouse, if you keep the beacon off your nose— yellow arrow pointed straight up—you eventually get there.

The catch comes with wind. You might have the beacon directly off your nose at first, but a crosswind causes you to drift. Imagine you turn toward the beacon, and your heading shows due west. You're east of the beacon, and flying due west takes you directly there. However, a strong wind is blowing from the north. On your way to the station, this wind blows you off course, and the needle that was pointing to the nose of the airplane points to the right of the nose.

You could turn to the right and put it off the nose again, drift some more, turn some more, and so on. Eventually, you get to the station, but your course won't exactly be efficient.

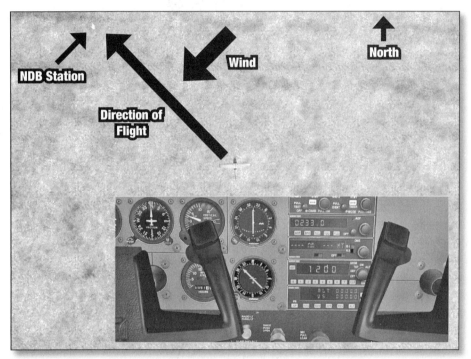

Figure 10-2: With a little mental math, you can fly a specific course to the NDB.

You could also get back on course, but it takes some mental math. Suppose when you drift, your ADF is showing 20° right of the nose. To get back on course, you turn 40° to the right so the needle is now pointing 20° left of the nose. As you head back north, the needle gets more and more off to the left. When it's 40° left, as shown in Figure 10-2, you're on course! Why? Well, if you turn 40° to the left, the needle moves as well, since it always points toward the station. When you stop turning, you are flying west again, and the needle is back on the nose.

Then you turn maybe 20° right and see that the ADF needle is also 20° off to the left. If you hold this heading—and it's the right correction for the wind—the needle stays 20° to the left of the nose, and you stay on course.

Sound confusing? It can be. It's also a dying art, so we don't dwell on it here. (But we'll return to it in instrument work and give you a few techniques to make it easier.) Let's move on past 1940s navigation technology.

224

PART I	PART II	PART III	PART IV	PART V	PART VI
PREFLIGHT	SPORT PILOT	PRIVATE PILOT	INSTRUMENT RATING	COMMERCIAL LICENSE	ATP AND BEYOND

STUDENT OF THE CRAFT

THE A-N RANGE

An even earlier version of the NDB was the A-N radio range. This station broadcast four quadrants that pilots listened to just like a communication radio. Two quadrants broadcast a Morse code letter A (· –), and two broadcast the letter N (– ·). If the pilot was on course, he would hear both letters at once, which made a steady tone. Static, thunderstorms, terrain, and the vagaries of early radio made the system a bear to use, but it worked. Early instrument approaches were even done using the pilot's ears for position…and a bit of faith and luck.

You can download a DC-3 module for FSX that has the equipment to fly these radio ranges from www.dc3airways.com/radio_range_system.html.

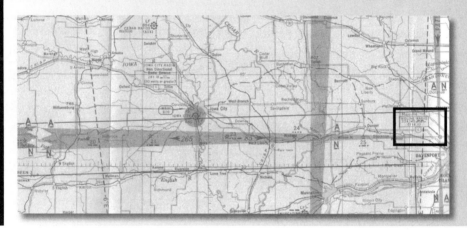

FLYING A RADIAL

We'll now take the lighthouse analogy just a bit further. Say you're tired of drifting off course on your way to the lighthouse and then figuring out corrections with your compass. You get a friend at the lighthouse to put up two colored filters, a blue one on the north side of the lighthouse and a yellow one on the south side. A gap between these colored filters is on the east side of the lighthouse.

Now you can see the lighthouse across the water and look at the color of the light. See yellow light? You're south of your course, and you must sail north. See blue? Sail south. If you see white, you're on course. Just try slight changes of your heading until you find the one that keeps the light white, and you're on course. Even if you never figured out the exact heading to stay on course, you could sloppily zigzag to keep the light white most of the time, and you would basically follow the right course to the lighthouse. By the mid-1950s, you could do this in the air, too.

BEHOLD THE *VOR*

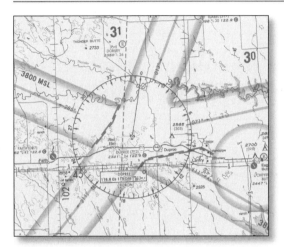

Figure 10-3: The VOR's 360 radials are oriented to the local magnetic north.

The VOR uses an antenna on the ground just like the NDB, but it transmits two signals that are both received by the airplane. By measuring the difference between these two signals, the receiver in the airplane knows what *radial* from the station it's currently on. If the two signals are perfectly in phase, then it's on the 360 radial from the station. That means the airplane is due north of the station, and the station is due south of the airplane. If the signals are exactly out of phase, then the airplane is due south of the station. Flying due north would take you to the station.

Every radial has its own unique signature, and in theory, you could have an infinite number of them radiating out from the station like spokes on a wheel. To keep things simple, think in terms of having 360 radials coming out from the station, one for each degree from 0 to 359. Since pilots think in terms of flying on magnetic headings, these radials are aligned with the local deviation for magnetic north, as shown in Figure 10-3. Radials always come out from the station, too. If you are on the 110 radial, flying a heading of 110 would take you precisely *away* from the station. Flying the opposite heading 290°—110° plus 180°—takes you directly to the station.

KEEPING IT REAL

TUNE AND ID

Right after you tune in either an NDB station or a VOR station, you should identify that you have the correct station. It's possible you read the wrong frequency off the chart and will start navigating toward a station that isn't where you want to go.

Each station has a unique Morse code identifier. Luckily, the actual dots and dashes appear on the chart, so you don't need to know Morse code. To identify the station, you must click the ID button on the radios and listen for the right code. NDB stations and VORs usually have three-letter identification codes. If a station is being repaired, it might still be on the air, but its ID will be T-E-S-T (– · · · · –). You shouldn't use any station broadcasting TEST for navigation.

Some stations also broadcast weather information and say the name of the station in English. In theory, you still must listen to hear that TEST is not being broadcast to use the signal.

Some modern radios, such as the G1000, can identify the station for you, so you don't have to listen. You can stop listening to a VOR once you've identified it because the VOR To/From indicator disappears if the station goes off the air. It's standard procedure to continue listening to an NDB at low volume, though, because the ID is the only way to know the station is still broadcasting a good signal.

Continued

226

PART I
PREFLIGHT

PART II
SPORT PILOT

PART III
PRIVATE PILOT

PART IV
INSTRUMENT RATING

PART V
COMMERCIAL LICENSE

PART VI
ATP AND BEYOND

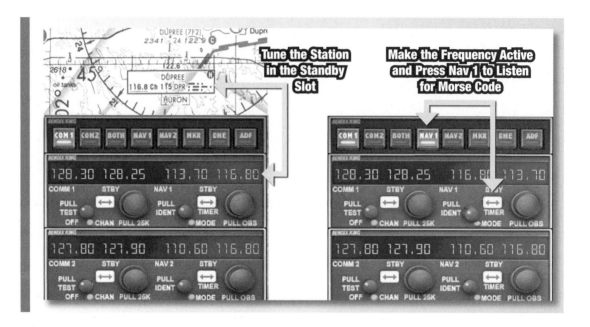

HEADING TO OR FROM THE STATION

Suppose you want to go directly to the station. You tune in the frequency and identify the Morse code to verify that you have correct station (see "Tune and ID"). Then you rotate *omni-bearing selector* (OBS)—can't you just hear the 1950s Tom Swift vernacular at work here?—until the needle in the middle of the OBS centers. The OBS shows courses of 0 to 359°, and if you look at the top of the indicator, you see a course that takes you either directly to or directly away from the station. Remember, the VOR knows only what radial you're on. It has no idea which way the airplane is facing or which way you want to go (see Figure 10-4).

Your salvation is in the *To-From flag*. If it shows a triangle pointing up, then flying the heading at the top of the OBS takes you directly to the station. If it shows a triangle pointing down, then that heading takes you directly away from the station. Some course deviation indicators (CDIs) politely show the words *To* and *From* along with the triangle. If you see a From triangle, but you want a To triangle, twist the OBS another 180°. The needle centers again, but with a To flag.

This is a critical concept with VORs. The needle centers on two (and only two) settings on the OBS: the heading that points directly to the station and the one that points directly away.

It's critical that you get the right one because that needle acts like your blue and yellow lights on the lighthouse. Suppose that you center the needle on 155 and start flying toward the station on a heading of 155. As the wind drifts you off course, the needle in the center starts to move. If you drift right of course, the needle moves left. You must turn left to get back on course. You can see how far off course you are on the CDI, which consists of that needle and the circle and dots behind it. When the needle touches the first dot, you're 2° off course. When it touches the next dot, you're 4° off course. The subsequent dot is 6°, and so forth, all the way to full-scale deflection at 12°.

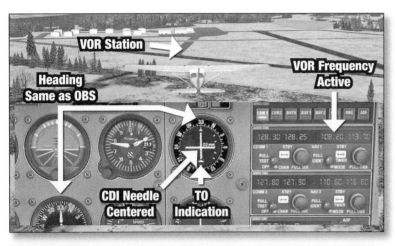

Figure 10-4: The VOR receiver always know what radial you are on, but it doesn't know which way you are pointing or where you want to go.

228

PART I PREFLIGHT

PART II SPORT PILOT

PART III PRIVATE PILOT

PART IV INSTRUMENT RATING

PART V COMMERCIAL LICENSE

PART VI ATP AND BEYOND

As the needle moves left or right, you need to turn toward the needle in order to get back on course. Here's the catch, though: if you are trying to fly *to* the station and the OBS is set for flying away *from* the station, the needle moves the wrong way. Turn toward it, and fly farther off course. This is called *reverse sensing*. The way to avoid it is to make sure that your heading on your heading indicator is the same as or close to the heading on the CDI. Figure 10-5 and Figure 10-6 show both these situations.

Figure 10-5: If your heading roughly matches your CDI, then course corrections using the CDI work correctly.

Figure 10-6: If your heading is roughly 180° from the CDI setting, then the CDI needle shows the opposite of what you really need to do to get back on course.

Just as with using the ADF in the airplane, certain headings keep you on course. The VOR has the advantage that this heading simply keeps the needle frozen in the center of the CDI—no mental math to prove you're on course. The heading that perfectly balances the wind is often called the *freeze heading*.

↓ YOU ARE THE DONUT

> Sometimes students get confused whether a CDI needle to the right means they are to the right of course or they should fly to the right. If you imagine that the airplane is the circle in the center and the needle is the course you want to get back on, you'll instantly know which way to turn.

Riding the Victor Airways

VORs became the backbone of the U.S. airspace system, and regular routes from VOR station to VOR station became codified into something called *Victor airways* (see Figure 10-7). These are essentially highways in the sky. Victor airways can go for hundreds of miles across dozens of VORs. Many routes between VORs are part of multiple Victor airways.

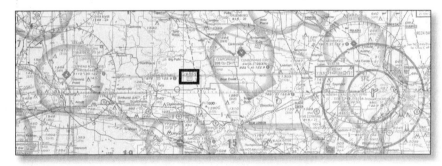

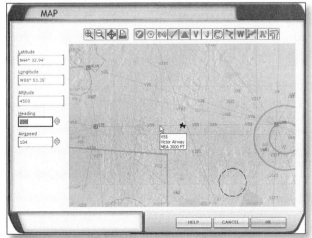

Figure 10-7: Victor airways connect VOR stations into aerial highways.

230

PART I	PART II	PART III	PART IV	PART V	PART VI
PILOT FLIGHT	SPORT PILOT	PRIVATE PILOT	INSTRUMENT RATING	COMMERCIAL LICENSE	ATP AND BEYOND

KNOWING WHERE TO SWITCH

Traveling from VOR to VOR along a Victor airway, you start the trip navigating using the VOR behind you and a From indication on your CDI. At some point you want to switch to the VOR ahead of you and a To indication. When do you switch? Unless you're having trouble receiving one station, you switch halfway between the two. When you start work on your instrument rating, you find charted changeover points on your instrument charts, but that's covered in Chapter 16.

Note that when you pass over a VOR, you don't need to touch the CDI unless you're heading away from the VOR on a new heading. The flag switches from To to From on its own. For a moment, when you're over the VOR, it shows neither To nor From. This is called *flagging*, and it's what happens if your navigation radio can't receive a VOR signal or it can't decide whether to display a To or From flag.

▼ BY THE BOOK

TAKING THE HIGH ROAD

The Victor airway system extends only to 18,000 feet MSL. Above that are the jet routes. These also are connections between VOR stations, but they are stations much farther apart. Given how fast jets fly, this is a good thing.

Don't worry about jet routes for a while, but you should know they exist. They also use only the most powerful VORs. VORs actually come in three sizes, terminal, low, and high, which determine the distance you can be from the VOR and still use it. Jet routes use only high VORs that guarantee the signal will reach 100–300 miles between stations.

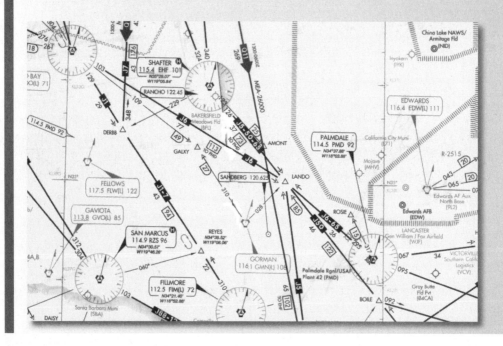

HANG A LEFT AT *CINCI*

Victor airways don't always run just VOR to VOR. In addition, sometimes it's important to denote a specific place along an airway. These intersections are defined by where two VOR radials cross. If you have two VOR receivers, this is easy to find. Intersections have five-letter names to identify them. This is far quicker than saying "the intersection of the 123 radial of ABC VOR and the 345 radial off XYZ VOR."

As a private pilot, you need to know only about intersections to help you fly outbound from one VOR, identify an intersection, and fly inbound to the new VOR on a new course (see Figure 10-8). It's like a changeover point that also has a change of direction. When you become an instrument pilot, intersections take on a whole new dimension.

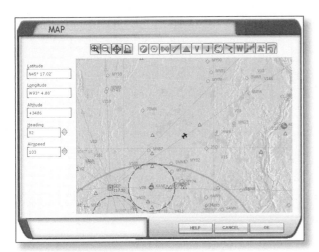

Figure 10-8: Intersections can be anywhere two VOR radials cross.

THIRTY DAYS FOR A VOR

You aren't required to test your CDI needles for accuracy as backup for visual flying, but it's required that you test them every 30 days for instrument flying. The FSX needles are always perfect unless you intentionally fail them.

ONRAMPS TO AERIAL HIGHWAYS

Airports usually aren't right on the Victor airway you might want to join. Now, you could simply go directly to the nearest VOR, but at times you want to intercept a Victor airway somewhere along its length and then proceed along it (see Figure 10-9). The standard procedure is to fly a heading that intercepts the radial at 30° to 45°.

232

PART I	PART II	PART III	PART IV	PART V	PART VI
PRE-FLIGHT	SPORT PILOT	PRIVATE PILOT	INSTRUMENT RATING	COMMERCIAL LICENSE	ATP AND BEYOND

Figure 10-9: You can intercept an airway or VOR radial by flying a heading that crosses it, usually at a 30- or 45-degree angle, and dialing the radial you want to intersect into the OBS. As the needle centers, you turn on course.

For example, if you were leaving Anoka County and wanted to pick up Victor 148 northeast, you probably would fly 020 after you left the traffic pattern and intercept at 30°.

BUT HOW FAR AWAY ARE YOU?

The VOR was a great boon for knowing where you were left or right of course to a VOR, but you still had to play some funny math games and fly a bit intentionally off course to see how far you were from the VOR station. The solution here came as distance-measuring equipment (DME). DME uses a different frequency as the VOR signal, but the DME and VOR frequencies are paired, so if you dial in a VOR and your airplane has DME, it automatically dials the right frequency to show your distance from the VOR station.

DME also shows your ground speed as long as you're flying the radial directly to or from the station. (It shows a speed no matter which way you're flying, but it's accurate only directly to or from the station.)

DME is quite accurate in showing distance, but it shows this distance including your altitude. This is called *slant range*, and it's not a big deal down where the Cessna Skyhawk flies. The deal is that the pilot thinks in terms of his or her distance across the ground between the airplane and the station. But the DME measures the diagonal distance from the station up to the airplane in the air. The difference is insignificant far from the station, but it's noticeable directly over it. If an airplane crosses a VOR at 6,000 feet, the DME still shows the airplane as 1 nautical mile away when the airplane is directly over the station. This is correct because the airplane is 1 mile away—1 mile straight up. Figure 10-10 shows the DME from two positions.

Figure 10-10: As shown here, 12.5 miles on the DME is pretty close to 12.5 miles from the VOR over the ground, and your ground speed is 104 knots. Directly over the VOR, DME still shows 1 mile, ground speed is zero, and the CDI flags.

FLYING WITH GPS

VORs and NDBs work well when you're going directly to or from the transmission station, but pilots often want to fly someplace that doesn't have a station. The ideal navigation system guides a pilot directly between any two points on the globe. This kind of system is called *area navigation* (RNAV). Several systems actually can do this, but the one that was accurate and cheap enough to bring RNAV to the masses is GPS.

GPS uses satellites to calculate your 3D position in space. That means it knows both what spot on the earth you're over and how high you are over it. That's actually all the GPS knows, but it's able to update your position almost immediately, and it keeps a history of where you were previously. It uses this combined information to calculate your position, altitude, ground speed, vertical speed, distance to your destination, estimated time to your destination, and so on. If it has information from the pitot static system and the outside air temperature, then it can calculate the current winds at your altitude. Add data from your fuel system, and it can tell you exactly how far with the current winds your fuel will take you.

To achieve its full accuracy, GPS units need to get good data from 4 of the 24 GPS satellites in orbit around the earth. Most units check this against data from additional satellites to ensure accuracy. Since many GPS receivers can track up to 12 satellites, most units run at full accuracy nearly all the time they can get a view of the sky. When driving a car around a city, GPS signals are often blocked, but unless you're flying low in the mountains, it's rarely an issue for airplanes.

The funny thing about GPS is much of the terminology and functionality comes from the days of VORs and airways. In fact, quite often the GPS is used to navigate along the same airways defined by VOR stations. Of course, GPS has the advantage that at any time you can get guidance to go directly to any airport—be that your destination or the nearest friendly pavement in the event of an emergency.

234

PART I
PREFLIGHT

PART II
SPORT PILOT

PART III
PRIVATE PILOT

PART IV
INSTRUMENT RATING

PART V
COMMERCIAL LICENSE

PART VI
ATP AND BEYOND

Figure 10-11: FSX's Garmin 500-series has almost as many features as the real unit and is a great trainer.

You might have already looked at the direct function on the Garmin 296 on your Cub flight from Beverly, Massachusetts, to Provincetown, Massachusetts, in Chapter 6. The Direct function and the moving map are probably the most often used features of the GPS. FSX's Cessna 172 has a Garmin 500-series GPS as a separate window (see Figure 10-11). This is a more sophisticated unit than the portable 296 in the Cub.

⬇ BY THE BOOK

HOW ACCURATE IS IT?

Years ago two standards of standard GPS existed. The military had the system at maximum accuracy, and civilian traffic had what was called *selective availability*, which intentionally reduced the accuracy. The military turned off the downgraded signal in 2000, and now everyone has a standard GPS accuracy of position to within about 25 feet laterally and 40 vertically at least 95 percent of the time.

The military has an increased accuracy system as well, but you don't get to use that. The civilian equivalent for pilots, though, is here in the Wide Area Augmentation System (WAAS). This is a system of differential GPS where ground stations broadcast a correction signal that lets your airborne GPS fine-tune its location. This pumps up the accuracy better than five times.

WAAS covers most of the United States, but plans exist for a Local Area Augmentation System (LAAS) that would be installed for individual airports. LAAS would have accuracies of 2 feet or less.

Of course, the FSX GPS is exactly correct.

FLYING CROSS-COUNTRY WITH RADIO NAVIGATION

Load the flight Chap10_Radio_Nav, which puts you on the ground at the Crystal airport (KMIC). Your plan is to fly from Crystal directly to the nearest VOR at Gopher (GEP) and then up V13/V505 past the Siren VOR (RZN) and to the Duluth VOR (DLH) and land in Duluth, Minnesota (KDLH). You continue from there via GPS directly to Ashland, Wisconsin, (KASX). Figure 10-12 shows the beginning of this route.

If you want to see this on the map, choose World > Map. Make sure the route button is selected (shaded green) to show the route on the map.

Figure 10-12: When you create a flight plan, it appears on the map. Use the zoom in and out magnifying glass to see the entire route or just one portion of it.

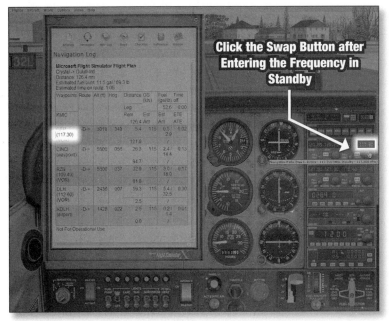

This flight comes preloaded with a flight plan for this trip. To see it, press Shift+F10 to see the kneeboard, and then click the Nav Log button. The nav log conveniently shows the headings you fly for this route, as well as the frequencies for each of the VORs along the way (see Figure 10-13). You also see CINCI. This is an intersection of two VOR radials.

Figure 10-13: After you've moved a frequency from standby to active, that standby slot is ready for another frequency. Use three VORs for this trip: GEP, RZN, and DLH. You can load all three—one each in the active slot of NAV1 and NAV2 and one in the standby of either navigation radio.

236

PART I
PREFLIGHT

PART II
SPORT PILOT

PART III
PRIVATE PILOT

PART IV
INSTRUMENT RATING

PART V
COMMERCIAL LICENSE

PART VI
ATP AND BEYOND

 INSIDE THE GAME

CREATING YOUR OWN FLIGHT PLANS

To make your own flight plan, choose Flights > Flight Plan. You get to select your departure and destination airport first. You can choose the airport by name, city, or airport ID. U.S. airports in the lower 48 start with a K, so Chicago O'Hare is KORD, not ORD. (Note that you are put at the active runway for your departure airport by default. You can change this after you select the airport.)

Right now you're a VFR pilot, but the same planner is used for IFR flights. You can chose Visual Flight Rules for now.

You can then let FSX choose the routing for you or simply connect the two points directly. After the route is calculated, you see a map view where you can add points by dragging the magenta route line like a rubber band. You see a list of waypoints on the right. You can delete any of these waypoints by selecting it with the mouse and pressing the Delete key on your keyboard. When you have the route as you want it, click OK, and off you go.

Whenever you depart on a flight, your first task is to take off and get clear of the airport before turning on course. Since the winds are calm and your first heading takes you north, we've put you ready to go, holding short of Runway 32 Left (32L).

Before you launch, though, get your VORs ready to go. The first step is loading GEP into the active channel of NAV1 (see the earlier Figure 10-13). To do this, look up the frequency on your nav log. It's 117.30. Now bring your cursor over the right tuning knob of the top radio. You see a plus or minus appear at some point over the cursor indicating that you can increase or decrease the selected frequency with a click. Change the frequency to 117.30, and then click the double-headed arrow button to swap the standby frequency you just entered with the active one being used to navigate. Put GEP into the active frequency for NAV1 and RZN in the active frequency for NAV2.

This active/standby setup for radios is common in aviation. It serves the double benefit of letting you set up a new frequency without changing the old one until you're ready, and it makes it tough to accidentally change frequencies.

NOTE!

↓ SCROLLING KNOBS

Whenever you need to twist a knob in any of the aircraft that come with FSX, hover your cursor over the knob, and use the scroll wheel on your mouse. It's much faster than clicking. You can also hover directly over the LED numbers on the radios and scroll to change them. We wish we could do that with a real radio!

Off You Go

Taxi onto 32L, turn left, and take off. As you're climbing out, press NAV1 on your audio panel to listen and identify the Gopher VOR. You can see the IDs on the map, as shown in Figure 10-14. You should also note that there is a To or From triangle rather than the orange and white flag.

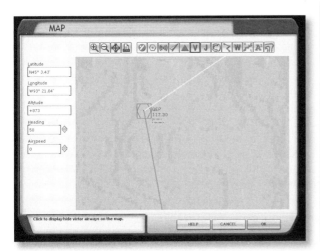

Figure 10-14: The VOR Morse code identifiers are on the map, but you might have to zoom in a bit to see them.

When you're sure that you're receiving the correct station, twist the small knob to the lower left of the NAV1 OBS until the needle centers with a To triangle. If you could immediately turn to that heading, you would be on course directly to the VOR. You can't turn quite that fast, though, so twist it a bit so the needle is one dot to the left of center. Now turn right until your heading is the same as the radial to the VOR. If the needle is centered when you roll wings level, this takes you directly to the VOR, as shown in Figure 10-15. If not, recenter the needle using the OBS knob, and make a slight correction to your heading to match.

Reset the orange heading bug on your heading indicator to your current heading. This helps you stay on the correct heading and on course. Continue your climb toward 5,500 feet.

238

PART I — PREFLIGHT | PART II — SPORT PILOT | **PART III — PRIVATE PILOT** | PART IV — INSTRUMENT RATING | PART V — COMMERCIAL LICENCE | PART VI — ATP AND BEYOND

Figure 10-15: In this case, you're just going directly to the VOR. Exactly what VOR radial to the station you're on doesn't matter.

You're not far from GEP. You can see this on your DME, which is set to RM1, or remote from NAV1. This means it's giving you the distance from whatever VOR is in NAV1. In this case, that's Gopher. Some real VORs don't offer DME, but you won't have to worry about that in FSX.

As you approach GEP, the VOR needle gets quite sensitive. Feel free to turn left or right up to 10° to keep the needle centered, but no more than that. When the DME is less than 1 mile, just stay on your heading until you cross over the VOR and the flag goes from To to From.

THE WIDTH OF THE BUG

If you want to make small corrections to your course, use the heading bug. It's about 10° wide. To turn left 5°, turn until the right side of the bug is at the top of the heading indicator. When you're back on course, recenter the heading bug.

THE FIRST TURN

Now look at your nav log. This time you want to fly the actual Victor airway from GEP to RZN. That's the 056 radial from GEP. Dial 056 into NAV1. Now turn to a heading of 086. (Actually, 085 is fine. We won't quibble.) Turning to this heading puts you on a 30-degree intercept to the airway, as shown in Figure 10-16. Watch for the needle to center. When it's one dot away from centering, begin your turn back to 056. It should center, and you'll be on the airway heading toward RZN.

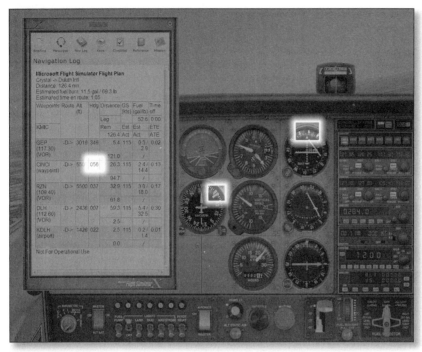

Figure 10-16: Twist the OBS to the new heading, and then twist the heading bug to the intercept heading. You're flying away from GEP, so you'll see the From triangle.

Your next turn is at CINCI, which is an intersection. To set this up, tune and identify RZN on NAV2. Then dial the 037 radial into your NAV2 CDI (the lower one). Note that it shows a To triangle. That makes sense as you're navigating from GEP *to* RZN. You fly using GEP on the upper CDI for guidance—staying centered on the airway—until the lower CDI centers. When it does, turn to 037, and fly using the lower CDI for guidance.

After you're heading up to RZN, you could keep using NAV2 for guidance, but the more common thing to do is put RZN into NAV1 so there's no confusion that this is your primary guidance. Be sure to identify it and to change the CDI of NAV1 to 037 before you start following that NAV1 needle.

NORTH TO DULUTH

You cross RZN just as you did GEP and then intercept the James Bond radial (007) heading up to DLH. If you get bored on the way to RZN, increase the simulation rate. Beware, though: the faster the sim rate, the more sensitive FSX is to small heading errors. Increase the rate enough, and the passive CDI needle gets downright goosey.

Since you moved RZN up to NAV1, you can put DLH in NAV2, identify it, and make it active. The CDI of NAV2 should be set to 007 as well since this airway is a straight shot between RZN and DLH.

It's 60 miles from RZN to DLH, so you need to switch from RZN to DLH at 30 miles. You can use the DME for this or just switch after you've identified DLH and about 20 minutes go by.

GIVING GEORGE THE CONTROLS

Flying the needles from VOR to VOR is a good challenge, but we admit it can get tedious after a while. If you want to let the airplane do the flying, you can use the autopilot—affectionately referred to as George in aviation circles. Combined with an increased sim rate, this essentially zips you to the next exciting part of the flight. (Oh, to do this in real airplanes...)

240

| PART I PREFLIGHT | PART II SPORT PILOT | PART III PRIVATE PILOT | PART IV INSTRUMENT RATING | PART V COMMERCIAL LICENSE | PART VI ATP AND BEYOND |

The FSX Skyhawk autopilot is based on the real KAP 140 autopilot and works almost identically. The first step is to set your heading bug so it's on your current heading. Now push HDG on the autopilot (see Figure 10-17). The airplane now flies wherever you point the heading bug. You control the airplane's altitude, though.

Figure 10-17: Twist the orange bug, and the airplane banks to follow.

NOTE!

⬇ THE AP BUTTON

When you engage the HDG mode, the AP button also lights up. This tells you the autopilot is on. Push AP, and the autopilot turns off.

If you want the autopilot to follow and keep the CDI centered for you, click the NAV button on the autopilot. Now it ignores the heading bug and turns left or right as needed to keep the NAV1 CDI centered (it ignores NAV2). Note that if you are in NAV mode and you change the CDI setting to a different radial, the needle moves and the autopilot follows.

You can let George maintain your altitude, too. First, you need to tell him what altitude to maintain. Move your cursor over the ALT LED numbers on the autopilot, and use the scroll wheel on your mouse to dial them up to 5500. Alternately, you can click the UP button until the autopilot shows 5,500 for an altitude. Now click ALT on the autopilot, as shown in Figure 10-18, and the airplane flies itself.

NOTE!

⬇ FAST ALTITUDE HOLD

If you press Ctrl+Z, the autopilot sets itself to hold your current altitude.

Figure 10-18: If you dial in an altitude that isn't your current altitude and then press ALT, the autopilot will automatically climb or descend at 700 fpm to get to that altitude.

Figure 10-19: The autopilot actually flies the trim system, so expect to see the trim moving on its own as you transition to a climb or descent.

The autopilot can climb or descend as well. Right now you're at 5,500 feet. You want to be about 3,000 feet by DLH so you can easily descend to 2,500 feet for the traffic pattern at Duluth International (KDLH). If you descend 500 feet per minute and average about 120 knots (2 miles per minute) in the descent, you move about 2 miles over the ground for every 500 feet you come down. It takes six minutes to get from 5,500 to 2,500, so you should start that descent when you're about 12 miles from DLH.

To descend using the autopilot, dial 3000 into the Altitude window on the autopilot. The plane immediately starts descending at a VS of –700 (that's a vertical speed of 700 feet per minute down). Using the mouse scroll wheel, dial that number back to –500 (see Figure 10-19). When you reach the target altitude of 3,000, the autopilot automatically levels off.

If you use the autopilot to climb, you see a positive number for VS. Note that the autopilot attempts any descent or climb rate you try, even if it might lead to an overspeed or a near stall, respectively.

With Duluth ahead of you and in sight, you can switch to HDG mode and guide yourself to the runway with the autopilot or disengage the autopilot by clicking the AP button on the panel. Feel free to do a touch-and-go landing at Duluth if you want, but then get back into the air heading southeast at 3,500 feet. Then pause FSX.

242

PART I	PART II	PART III	PART IV	PART V	PART VI
PREFLIGHT	SPORT PILOT	PRIVATE PILOT	INSTRUMENT RATING	COMMERCIAL LICENSE	ATP AND BEYOND

DIRECT WITH GPS

Now it's time to make life easier. Press Shift+3 to see the Garmin GPS 500 (see Figure 10-20). This is a simplified version of a real GPS unit with a great moving map display and the ability to go directly to any point on the globe. You're going to Ashland, Wisconsin (KASX). The FSX GPS is tied to the flight planner, so your previous flight plan to Duluth is still in the GPS as white lines (legs) on the moving map. You could go back to the flight planner and create a new flight plan from KDLH to KASX—and you should do that if you're creating a flight plan with many legs—but since you're just going directly there, use the GPS unit itself.

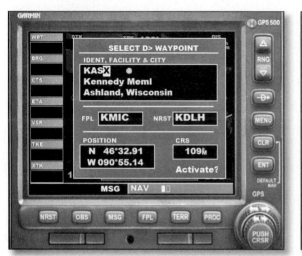

Figure 10-20: You can also show and hide the GPS with the show/hide GPS button (which looks like a radar dish).

NOTE!

↓ MAKE IN SMALLER

The GPS is usually huge when it first opens. You can use your mouse to drag a side and the top to make it look smaller. It looks distorted after the first side you drag but is fixed after you drag the top.

Press the Direct-To button. It's a D with an arrow through it. Now scroll the small, inner knob on the lower right of the unit until you see a *K* as the first letter of the direct-to destination. Scroll the large, outer knob one click to the right to move the cursor to the next position. Now use the inner knob to enter an *A*. Continue until you have the identifier for KASX in there. You see the full name appears below the identifier to verify that you and the GPS are in agreement as to where you want to go. Click the ENT (enter) button three times to accept the destination and activate it.

Now you want to fly in that direction. The heading to get to KASX will be shown on the GPS as your DTK, or desired track. Turn to that heading, and you'll see that your TRK, or track over the ground, changes to match. With GPS, if your DTK is the same as your TRK and you're on the magenta line, you're on course to the destination (see Figure 10-21). If you're not using the autopilot already, engage it and use HDG and ALT modes to get going to Ashland.

Figure 10-21: When you're navigating with a GPS signal to NAV1, the OBS setting is ignored. Although you could ignore the setting, it's good practice to set it for your DTK just as you set the heading bug to your current heading even when the autopilot is following a nav signal.

The GPS has its own CDI right on the screen. It's the box with the triangle and bar right between the GS (ground speed) and ETE (estimated time en route). You can fly this CDI and keep the bar centered over the triangle, but your autopilot can't. To use the autopilot nav function, you must send the GPS signal to the NAV1 CDI. You do this by pressing the NAV/GPS button at the top of the panel. The light shifts from white to green, and George takes his guidance from the GPS.

Your route is clearly depicted on a moving map. Note that this map is showing a lot of blue. This means a cold dip in Lake Superior if you have a power failure now!

One of the hazards of GPS is that direct routes might take you over inhospitable terrain, through restricted airspace, or too close to towers or mountains if you're not high enough. The consequences of this aren't much in FSX, but in the real world, the stakes are much higher. Busting into restricted airspace could result in a suspension of your pilot's license or a close encounter with a military jet on maneuvers. Running into a mountain just because the GPS said to fly that way is never a good idea. Always look at where the direct route takes you before you blithely follow the magenta line.

Enjoy your flight to Ashland. It's a snap with GPS. While you're en route, check out some of the other features of the GPS. We'll be integrating GPS into your training from here on so you can learn the features in context of how you'll actually use them. One of the first exercises is finding your nearest airport.

244

PART I	PART II	PART III	PART IV	PART V	PART VI
PRE FLIGHT	SPORT PILOT	PRIVATE PILOT	INSTRUMENT RATING	COMMERCIAL LICENSE	ATP AND BEYOND

INSIDE THE GAME

THE COMPUTER IN THE PANEL

The GPS 500 is organized into groups and pages. The first group is the Nav group, which shows your moving maps. The first Nav page has a compass rose in a track-up view. This mean the map always shows the world oriented to the direction the airplane is moving. The second nav page shows similar information in a north-up view, like a regular map. To switch between the views, use the small inner knob on the lower right of the GPS.

If you use the outer knob, you'll switch to the next group, which is Waypoint. This shows you all sorts of information about your current or upcoming airport, VOR, NDB, or intersection. You use the inner knob to investigate it across several pages.

The final group is the Nearest group where you can find your nearest airport, VOR, and more.

When you view any page, you can use the same inner and outer knobs to navigate the pages, but you must activate a cursor first. To do this, go to the page you want in the group you want, and then click the bottom center of the knobs in the lower right. You now have a flashing cursor you can move around the screen with the outer knob and select items. Some items, such as runway information, can be selected with the cursor and then changed with the inner knob.

There is too much to learn about the GPS to list it all here. We'll highlight specific features in context, but we strongly encourage you to check out the Learning Center tutorial on GPS.

GETTING UNLOST AND GOING ELSEWHERE

Load the flight Chap10_Lost_and_Found. You start this flight in the air somewhere between RZN and DLH. You're off course, and the world has clouded up beneath you. You have two challenges. First, figure out where you are. You do this by tuning in some nearby VORs and seeing what radial you are on from the VORs. See where these radials cross, and that's your current position.

Figure 10-22: You might want to use the landing view (Shift+5) to help see the airport through the clouds.

Next, you need to get yourself over to the Bong airport (KSUW). This is the only airport nearby reporting clear conditions right now. You need to get there to land. Bong doesn't have a VOR, but if you know your position, you can get a rough course to the airport. Moose Lake is on the 141 radial from Duluth (DLH) at about 8 miles or the 010 radial from Siren (RZN) at 53 miles.

If you need help, you can always use the map view, but see whether you can find yourself and navigate without it and without the GPS. You might find it in a break in the clouds, as shown in Figure 10-22.

Now for fun, restart the flight by reloading it or pressing Ctrl+;. Open the GPS window, and turn the large knob clockwise until you see the list of nearest airports. Click the center of the right small knob to see a cursor, and scroll down with the small inner knob to find KSUW. Now click Direct, and then push Enter twice. You now have a heading to fly and guidance right to Bong. Isn't that easier? You gotta love GPS.

ACCIDENT CHAIN

UNLOST BUT UNDERFUELED

Aircraft: Cessna 152

Location: Klamath Falls, Oregon

Injuries: 1 minor

"In a telephone conversation and subsequent written statement, the pilot reported that during the return leg to Ashland, he become disoriented and requested vectors to the nearest airport because of concerns about the aircraft's total time aloft and '...my fuel situation.'

Continued

246

PART I
PREFLIGHT

PART II
SPORT PILOT

PART III
PRIVATE PILOT

PART IV
INSTRUMENT RATING

PART V
COMMERCIAL LICENSE

PART VI
ATP AND BEYOND

"Seattle Center advised the pilot that Chiloquin, Oregon, was approximately 10 miles north to northwest of his position; however, it was not known if fuel was available at the airport and the ATC specialist asked the pilot if Klamath Falls, approximately 35 miles from his location, would be an option. The pilot believed he had sufficient fuel to complete the flight to Klamath; however, approximately 2 miles from reaching the airport the airplane's engine began to surge and eventually lost power.

"The pilot stated that he was unable to reach the runway and elected to land in an open field. As the airplane touched down in the field, it encountered soft muddy terrain and 'flipped nose-over.' The pilot reported that he believed he had approximately 15 minutes of fuel remaining when the airplane lost engine power; however, he later stated the airplane 'just ran out of fuel.' The airplane was 'topped' prior to departing Ashland. The Hobbs meter indicated that the airplane had flown approximately 3.6 hours since it had been fueled."

The best thing you can do in the real world if you get lost is to get on the radio and get help from air traffic control. They will give you a discrete code for your transponder and find you (you hope) on their radar. Then they can guide you step by step to an airport for landing. Just remember it's better to land and have to bring fuel there in a can than land in a field and have to bring the airplane home on a truck.

KEY POINTS FOR REAL FLYING AND FSX BUILT-INS

The following are some key points from this chapter:

- Tune and identify NDB and VOR stations.

- Navigate directly to or from a VOR.

- Navigate along a Victor airway.

- Get unlost using VOR radials.

- Go direct using GPS.

- Use the GPS Nearest group.

Here are the lessons and missions to study after reading this chapter:

- *Missions*: None for this chapter.

- *Lessons*: Try these lessons: Investigate Private Pilot Lesson on VOR Navigation, Learning Center on GPS, Learning Center on Changing Location, Learning Center on Navigation.

FIRST FLIGHT WITH THE G1000

"COMPUTERS ARE USELESS. THEY CAN ONLY GIVE YOU ANSWERS."

—PABLO PICASSO

248

PART I	PART II	PART III	PART IV	PART V	PART VI
PREFLIGHT	SPORT PILOT	PRIVATE PILOT	INSTRUMENT RATING	COMMERCIAL LICENSE	ATP AND BEYOND

WELCOME TO THE AGE OF GLASS

Powerful, lightweight, and (relatively) inexpensive computers are everywhere. They've changed the way we watch TV, make phone calls, and now how we fly light airplanes. The 3-inch round instruments that were standard fare for cockpit panels have been replaced with LCD monitors and new ways of depicting the same information. These cockpits are fantastic and a joy to fly.

They also come packed with capabilities far beyond your father's airplane, so it takes some effort to learn all the tricks. Like any computer, the mantra of "Garbage in, garbage out" still applies. We show you the basics here and return to the G1000 to point out some specifics in later chapters. Fully explaining the G1000 requires its own book, and FSX doesn't replicate all the real G1000 features. We recommend Max Trescott's *G1000 Glass Cockpit Handbook* or the King Schools' CD-ROM series *Cleared for Flying the Garmin G1000*. Bruce Williams' book *Flight Simulator as a Training Aid* also has a long section on the G1000 as implemented in FSX. In addition, Garmin has a free downloadable manual at www.garmin.com/aviation.

⬇ INSIDE THE GAME

FLYING OTHER GLASS

Three primary competitors exist for glass panels in certified light airplanes. (Dozens exist for experimental aircraft.) The Garmin G1000 comes with FSX. You can download airplanes that feature the other two from third-party vendors. Eaglesoft (www.eaglesoftdg.com) has a module that lets you fly a Cirrus SR20 or SR22 with the Avidyne Entegra glass cockpit. Flight One Software (www.flight1.com) offers a Commander 112 with both traditional gauges and the Chelton glass cockpit (the Commander 112 is currently compatible only with FS2004, however). The Chelton system is especially interesting because it provides a highway-in-the-sky visual road to follow similar to some of the built-in lessons in FSX. The Chelton system does this in real airplanes, though! The Chelton system also creates a synthetic landscape so you can see what the terrain looks like even when you're in the clouds.

A Distributed System

The components that make up the real G1000 are actually scattered throughout the airplane. The LCD screens and audio panel that the pilot controls are equivalent to the keyboard, screen, and video card of your personal computer. They control the system and display information. The radios, GPS, and most of the other system components are actually in a component rack that's usually in the tail of the airplane. They're like your desktop computer without even a DVD drive. They're just boxes that crunch the numbers and send the information to the screens to display.

The G1000 doesn't use traditional gyroscopes. Instead, it uses an *attitude and heading reference system* (AHRS, pronounced "ay-hars"). This is a solid-state system—no moving parts—that provides both the current magnetic heading of the aircraft and its current pitch and roll. The system gets pitch and roll from digital motion sensors that require the airplane to sit still for a few moments after start-up (FSX doesn't simulate this). The heading information comes from a *flux gate*, which directly senses the earth's magnetic field. The payoff for you is that the G1000 is immune to precession errors, and you never have to adjust the display's heading to match the airplane's magnetic compass. In fact, the heading on the G1000 is about as accurate a heading as you can possibly get in a small airplane.

The G1000 also relies on an air data system (ADS) that takes information from the pitot-static system and the outside air temperature. This information is also sent to the screens to display your airspeed and altitude as well as continually calculate your true airspeed and the current winds. Some systems, such as the Avidyne Entegra that is used in the Cirrus aircraft, combine the AHRS and ADS into a single air data, attitude, and heading reference system (ADAHRS, pronounced "add-a-hars").

The Primary Flight Display

Right in front of your face in the G1000 cockpit is the primary flight display (PFD). This display combines all the six-pack instruments and an OBS/CDI needle in one package. Pretty slick, eh? It's actually a little more intuitive to read in some ways and a bit harder in others.

A Big Attitude

The entire 10-inch display provides your artificial horizon, as shown in Figure 11-1. The huge boon here in the real cockpit is that even when you're looking away from the PFD, you can see the horizon in your peripheral vision. If you unintentionally bank, you see it sooner, and it's easier to get back on a level keel.

Your pitch in degrees is also visible by seeing where the inverted yellow triangle sits on something called the *pitch ladder*. This is just like the markings on the old AI but is much larger and easier to see. Your roll in degrees shows up where the lower of two opposing triangles meet the curved white line at the top.

WHEN 2D IS MORE REALISTIC

We suggest you use the 2D cockpit view for the rest of the G1000 discussions and flying. Although the 3D virtual cockpit looks cool, it's actually much harder to control the PFD this way, and it's virtually impossible to control the MFD this way. The 3D view with the G1000 also brings all but the most robust computer systems to their knees in terms of performance.

250

PART I	PART II	PART III	PART IV	PART V	PART VI
PREFLIGHT	SPORT PILOT	PRIVATE PILOT	INSTRUMENT RATING	COMMERCIAL LICENCE	ATP AND BEYOND

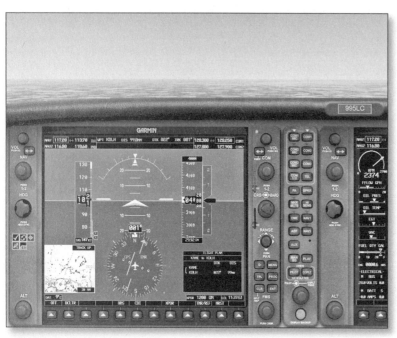

Figure 11-1: Put the inverted yellow triangle on the horizon and the points of the two white triangles together, and you're flying straight and level in cruise flight.

How Fast and How High

To the left of the pitch ladder is the *airspeed tape* (see Figure 11-2). This is equivalent to your airspeed indicator and shows your exact current speed in the center window as well as a scrolling tape of speeds 30 knots faster than the current one to speeds 30 knots slower. The white, green, and yellow arcs are also there, to the right of the numbers.

Figure 11-2: The speed on the airspeed tape is your indicated airspeed. Your true airspeed corrected for altitude and temperature appears below the airspeed tape.

PULL UP TO SLOW DOWN

The G1000 displays a bug for key speeds such as V_y that you might want to fly. The airspeed tape concept can make this confusing. If you're flying faster than V_y, the bug is below your current speed on the airspeed tape. The intuitive reaction is to then pitch down to get to that speed. That's exactly the wrong thing to do, however, since it makes you fly faster, and the bug just drops farther and disappears off the bottom of the tape.

If you think about pulling that bug up to your current speed, you correctly pitch up to get back to the slower speed for V_y. The same would work for pulling down the V_y bug if you were flying too slowly.

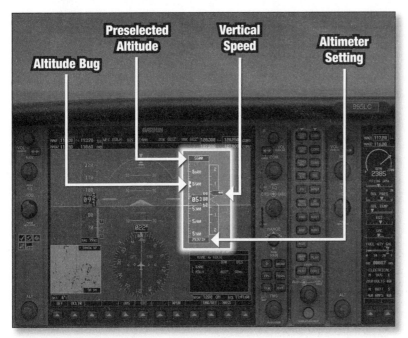

Figure 11-3: As you approach your target altitude, the altitude bug comes into view on tape. When you reach your target altitude, the bug fits perfectly over the end of the altitude readout.

Your altitude is also displayed on a tape with your current altitude in the center of an altitude range from 300 feet higher than you are to 300 feet lower. To the right of your altitude is your vertical speed, shown by a small arrow. The arrow points to your vertical speed from +2000 to –2000 fpm. For any speed greater than 150 fpm, the numeric rate displays inside the arrow.

The G1000 also has an altitude bug set with the ALT knob on either the PFD or the multifunction display (MFD), as shown in Figure 11-3. The bug is just a reminder, like the heading bug on the round heading indicator, where you want to level off. You usually set the bug for your cruising altitude before the flight. Since that altitude probably is more than 300

252

PART I
PREFLIGHT

PART II
SPORT PILOT

PART III
PRIVATE PILOT

PART IV
INSTRUMENT RATING

PART V
COMMERCIAL LICENSE

PART VI
ATP AND BEYOND

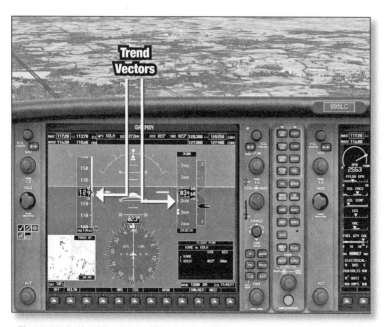

Figure 11-4: Watching the relative position of trend vectors and altitude or heading bugs cues you when to start returning to straight and level.

feet above your current altitude, the bug is off the scale for the altitude tape. In this case, it parks at the end of the scale.

Both the airspeed and altitude tapes have *trend vectors*, as shown in Figure 11-4. These are pink bars that extend up or down from the current airspeed or altitude and show where these values will be in six seconds at the current rate of change. The faster you're changing your speed or altitude, the bigger these vectors get. Eventually, they go off the scale and turn into arrows. Rarely in regular flying would you want to see changes that dramatic. By using the trend vectors for speed or altitude, you can hit the target altitude or speed with ghostly smoothness, especially in a descent.

The G1000 still needs to be corrected to the current altimeter setting. You do this with the outer ring on the CRS/BARO on the PFD. You can see the current setting just below the airspeed tape. Pressing B on your keyboard sets it to the local altimeter setting, just as with other FSX aircraft.

YOUR DIGITAL SITUATION

Figure 11-5: By putting the CDI in the center of your heading indicator, the HSI gives you a top-down view of where you need to fly to intercept and stay on course. Here you are just left of course on a heading that intercepts at a 30° angle.

The G1000 includes a digital version of an instrument that is actually much older. It's a horizontal situation indicator (HSI). The HSI is a combination of a heading indicator and an OBS/CDI (see Figure 11-5). The slick part is that by combining your heading information with the needles to show whether you're on course, the task of intercepting and tracking courses becomes much easier.

The outer ring of the HSI shows the compass rose with your current magnetic heading at the top. There is also a heading bug that you can move with the HDG knob on the PFD. You can also jump the heading bug to your current heading by pushing the HDG knob. This is called *syncing*.

INSIDE THE GAME

BUT I WANTED TO PUSH THE BUTTON

The G1000 requires excellent button control for inner and outer knobs and pushing the knob. Here's a tip: to twist the inner knob, hover your cursor close to the knob, and turn the scroll wheel. To twist the outer knob, hover your cursor both up and slightly to right of the knob. To push the knob, hover your cursor centered and slightly below the middle of the knob, and click. Watch the + and − symbols on the cursor to help you know where FSX thinks you're clicking. The outer knob on the G1000 controls sometimes requires clicking rather than scrolling, such as with the FMS knob.

The inner knob of the CRS/BARO knob controls the CDI. As you rotate it, the arrow points to a particular course. This is the same as dialing that course on the top of the conventional CDI. In the center of the HSI is the same left-right needle that shows whether you are on course or off to one side. The CDI will sync to a direct course to the selected navigation source if you push on the inner knob of CRS/BARO.

Your current heading appears in a window just like airspeed and altitude. If you dial in a course on the CDI, that number will appear off to the side for reference. The color of the CDI also tells you whether you're using GPS for navigation (magenta) or VORs for navigation (green). To cycle between the GPS and either of the two VOR sources controlling the CDI, you use the CDI softkey at the bottom of the PFD.

WHEN GOOD BOXES GO BAD

Any of the computers that empower the G1000 can fail and take out part of the system, but the failures don't look like a normal instrument failure in FSX. If the AHRS fails, the horizon line and heading information disappear. Interestingly, you would need to simulate this in FSX by failing both the attitude and the heading, because there is no checkbox for AHRS (see Figure 11-6). The same is true of the ADS. If it were to really fail, it would take out both the airspeed and the altimeter/VSI. To simulate it in FSX, you need to fail them as individual instruments.

What's cool is that you can't miss the failure. Big red Xs appear, and the numbers are removed. Well, the numbers on the HSI remain, but on a real G1000 they disappear, too. You can still use the CDI even if the heading is no longer valid.

You have backup instruments that let you keep the sunny side of the airplane upright when failures occur. You can see them in 3D virtual cockpit view or by pressing Shift+6 on your keyboard.

254

| PART I | PART II | PART III | PART IV | PART V | PART VI |
| PREFLIGHT | SPORT PILOT | PRIVATE PILOT | INSTRUMENT RATING | COMMERCIAL LICENSE | ATP AND BEYOND |

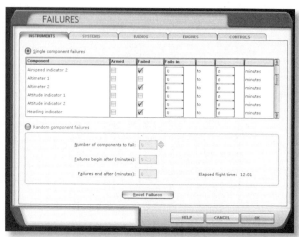

Figure 11-6: To fail the G1000 components, fail the number-two instruments.

OF WAYPOINTS AND FLIGHT PLANS

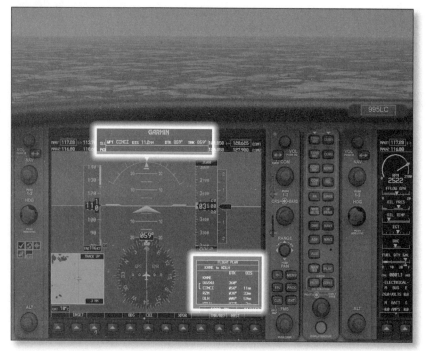

Figure 11-7: Waypoint and flight plan information is available without taking your eyes away from your flight instruments.

Often with the G1000 you don't dial a course into the CDI. It dials the course for you. It does this by referencing your flight plan. We'll talk about flight plans when we talk about the MFD later in this chapter, but you should know that the PFD shows you key information about the next waypoint on your flight plan and can show you a small version of your entire flight plan (see Figure 11-7).

The waypoint information is at the top. It shows the name of the next waypoint, your distance to it, the desired track to get there (the course you entered in the G1000 flight plan), and your current track over the ground. To see the waypoints in your flight plan, press the FLP button on the PFD. A small window opens with your flight plan visible.

A similar small window appears if you click the Nearest softkey (NRST) on the bottom of the PFD. You see a list of the nearest airports with key information such as their bearing, distance, radio frequencies, and instrument approaches.

KEEPING IT REAL

A MORE ROBUST SIMULATOR

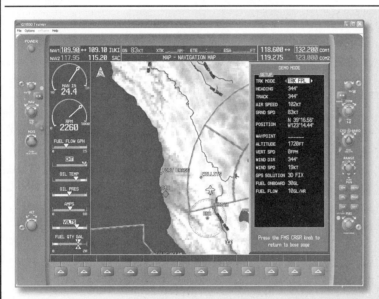

The G1000 implementation in FSX is not complete, and many functions in the real G1000 are not available with FSX, such as display customization and advanced engine instrumentation. If you want to experiment with these, a simulator for the G1000 in specific airframes is available from Garmin (`www.garmin.com/products/g1000/`) for less than $10.

You can see the PFD or MFD only one at a time, but it is exactly like the real airplane. If you want to change the position, altitude, or speed of the simulator—and we're talking about the Garmin simulator, not FSX here—go to the MFD view, and press MENU twice (or M on the keyboard). Here you can change the simulation mode. The help files have all sorts of other great keyboard shortcuts.

USE THE SOFTKEYS, LUKE

On the other side of the PFD from the mini–flight plan is the inset moving map. This is a great feature of the G1000 because it puts a map right next to your flight instruments. You maintain excellent awareness as to your position and where you'll fly next without looking around for it.

You configure this map, and many other PFD functions, from the softkeys at the bottom of the PFD. *Softkeys* are buttons that change their function with context. For example, if you press the XPONDER button at the bottom of the display, the buttons will change to show the numbers 0–7 VFR and IDENT. You can press these numbers to enter a new transponder code or press VFR to quickly reset to the 1200 code for general VFR aircraft. Pressing BACK returns you to the top level of the PFD display.

We'll discuss these softkey functions in context as you use them in flight. Feel free to explore and see what they do on your own, though. That's often the best way to get to know the system.

GETTING YOUR ATTENTION

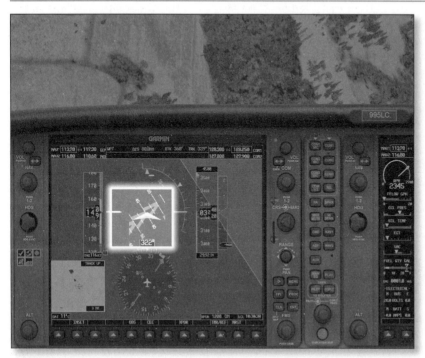

The PFD is great for clearly displaying your attitude in space, but only when you're looking at it. All the other pretty pictures on the G1000 displays can be a bit of a distraction. If your pitch is extremely high or low, red chevrons point you back in the right direction, as shown in Figure 11-8. The real G1000 also automatically removes all the extraneous information so you can focus on getting straight and level.

Figure 11-8: Those chevrons make it pretty clear which way the nose must go to return to level flight.

THE RADIOS

One feature that sets the G1000 apart from many other glass-panel systems is that it's a completely integrated system. This means the PFD and MFD will communicate with each other, and they control the radios. Controlling the radios is often confusing for pilots transitioning to the G1000. The communication radios cause less confusion, so we'll start there.

The COM radios work like a traditional radio with an active and standby frequency. The catch is that there are still two radios (COM1 and COM2), but they're controlled by one set of knobs and buttons.

The first task is determining which of the four frequencies will change when you turn the tuning knob. This is easy; it's the one with the light blue tuning box around it. For COM radios, the tuning box is always on the right and you toggle it between the top frequency, COM1, and the bottom frequency, COM2, by pushing in on the tuning knob. The large, outer knob changes the whole numbers to the left of the decimal point, and the small, inner knob changes the numbers to the right. You can change only the frequencies on the right. These are the ones in standby. The ones on the left are the active frequencies for COM1 and COM2—just as in the conventional radios. Figure 11-9 shows the layout.

Figure 11-9: The COM radios appear in the upper right on both the PFD and the MFD. Both screens show both radios.

Figure 11-10: It might help to remember that the active frequency is always toward the center of the PFD, for both NAV and COM.

The tuning box also determines which of the standby frequencies will trade places with the active frequency. Whichever one is in the tuning box flops to the active position when you press the button with the double-headed arrow. One of the frequencies on the right appears in green. This is the frequency you transmit on. You set that in the audio panel, which we discuss later in this chapter.

Note that the tuning box has no effect on the frequency automatically used when you select frequencies from the ATC window. Frequencies selected from the ATC window go directly to the active slot on whichever COM you have selected for transmission on the audio panel.

Take a look at the NAV radios on the upper left of the PFD. These work identically to the COM radios except that the standby frequency is on the *left* and the active frequency is on the *right*, as shown in Figure 11-10. You can tell this for certain because the tuning box—which toggles only between the two standby frequencies—is on the left.

If you can keep this straight, then you'll have no problem with the radios.

The G1000 NAV radios do two other cool tricks. If you choose to navigate via VORs rather than GPS, you press the CDI softkey on the bottom of the PFD. (Press it once for NAV1, a second time for NAV2, and a third time to return to GPS.) When you're using a navigation frequency on the HSI, that frequency appears in green on the PFD. The NAV radios also automatically ID

258

PART I	PART II	PART III	PART IV	PART V	PART VI
PREFLIGHT	SPORT PILOT	PRIVATE PILOT	INSTRUMENT RATING	COMMERCIAL LICENSE	ATP AND BEYOND

the station and display the three- or four-letter identifier beside the frequency. You can still listen yourself if you want by using the audio panel.

The audio panel sits between the PFD and the MFD in the real airplane, so you can see it in both the virtual cockpit and the 2D cockpit when you're looking at the main panel (PFD).

The audio panel lets you listen to any of the NAV radios by pressing the button for that radio. You can listen to multiple radios at once by pressing more than one of the NAV or COM buttons (but you can ID only one VOR at a time). You can change which COM. you are using to transmit by pressing the appropriate COM/MIC button.

Several other buttons are available for functions that are not simulated in FSX, but if you fly a real G1000, you can pick those up as you go or with Garmin's full-featured PC simulator.

The audio panel is between the PFD and MFD for a good reason (see Figure 11-11). You can control virtually all the functions of both displays from the knobs just to the right and left of the audio panel. When you're viewing the main window in 2D view, this means you have duplicates of some knobs, such as HDG and ALT. Use the ones close to the audio panel for practice.

Figure 11-11: The side-by-side layout of the PFD, audio panel, and MFD puts all the important buttons and knobs in easy reach of the pilot's right hand and just above the throttle quadrant.

THE MULTIFUNCTION FLIGHT DISPLAY

The first challenge in using the MFD in FSX is just seeing it. It's possible to see and use it in 3D virtual cockpit, but it's much more practical to view it using Shift+3 on your keyboard. You can also show and hide the MFD with the show/hide GPS button (which looks like a radar dish) that FSX puts on the PFD just like showing and hiding the GPS in the conventional Skyhawk.

The MFD probably is too small to use well when it first opens. Make it bigger by dragging the top of the window and the side of the window until it's as large as the PFD, as shown in Figure 11-12. It mostly blocks the PFD when you do this, but that's OK. You can still see your airspeed and the edge of the virtual horizon. Even if you were flying on instruments, you could keep the plane straight and level with just these two pieces of information in your peripheral vision. This is what you would be doing in the real airplane, too.

Figure 11-12: A bigger MFD is much easier to use.

The MFD is really two displays on one screen. The left quarter of the display is reserved for engine instruments (see Figure 11-13). Here, you find the tachometer showing how fast the engine (and propeller) are turning. You find the oil temperature and pressure gauges, fuel gauges, vacuum gauges, and so on.

On FSX, the functionality of the G1000 engine gauges is limited. The real G1000 has an ENGINE softkey that accesses additional information and functions such as an engine-leaning assistant. The basic information on FSX is still great for training and shows you what things look like in the real airplane. You also get a sense how sensitive digital gauges really are. We often watch students trying to get exactly 1800 rpm for a run-up. We have to remind them that anything between 1850 and 1750 is just fine—and equal to or better than the accuracy they had on old, mechanical analog gauges.

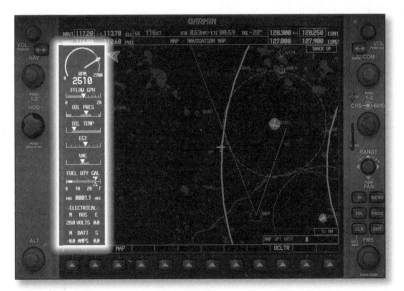

Figure 11-13: The engine gauges stay visible regardless of the other information on the G1000 MFD.

260

| PART I | PART II | PART III | PART IV | PART V | PART VI |
| PREFLIGHT | SPORT PILOT | PRIVATE PILOT | INSTRUMENT RATING | COMMERCIAL LICENSE | ATP AND BEYOND |

ACROSS THE TOP

The top of the MFD is similar to the PFD except that it shows four data fields. It shows your ground speed (GS), which is your true airspeed plus or minus any tailwind or headwind. It shows cross-track error (XTE), which is how many miles you are right or left of course. It shows estimated time en route (ETE) to the next waypoint on your flight plan. Finally, it shows the track angle error, which shows the angular difference between your actual track and your desired track. (Given that your desired track and actual track are also on the PFD, TKE is a contender for the most superfluous data on the G1000.)

On real G1000, these fields are user configurable and can show a wealth of different options. They aren't configurable on FSX, which is a big disappointment. One of our common recommendations for pilots transitioning to the G1000 is to set one of these fields (like TKE) to vertical speed required (VSR). This lets the pilot set a target altitude at a specific waypoint—say pattern altitude four miles from the destination airport—and continuously see the rate of descent needed to get there. This would be a great feature to integrate into FSX training, but it's not supported at all.

THE BIG PICTURE

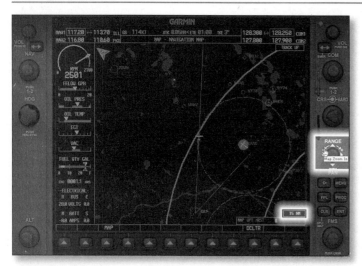

Figure 11-14: The RANGE knob also says PUSH PAN, but that's a function not simulated in FSX.

The main MFD window has four primary functions in FSX: a moving map, information about waypoints, a listing of nearest airports and nav aids, and a place to enter flight plans. Its most common use is as a moving map. The huge display makes it almost impossible to get lost. The FSX map isn't exactly like the real thing, but it's close.

If you're flying on a flight plan, the flight plan appears on the map as a magenta line for the leg you're currently flying and as white lines for subsequent legs. To change the scale of the map and see more of your flight, or to zoom in on your current location, use the RANGE knob on the MFD (see Figure 11-14). The map scale appears in the lower right of the display. This is one of the few times where it matters whether you use the knob on the MFD or the PFD. The PFD RANGE knob controls the inset map scale.

The big MFD map uses symbology similar to the FSX map/flight planner and U.S. VFR sectional charts. We won't go into detail here about what they all mean. Check out some of the books or training programs mentioned earlier in this chapter to find out more. You should know that you can cycle through views with progressively less information using the DCLTR (declutter) softkey at the bottom of the screen.

The MAP softkey lets you change two more features about the map. Press it, and you see a TRAFFIC softkey to show or hide other traffic (see "Traffic, 12 O'Clock"). Press the TOPO softkey to show or hide colored shading for surface elevation. Press BACK to show the default map view. This layered menu of softkeys is common for the G1000. For example, the XPNDR softkey on the PFD displays another list of softkeys for changing your transponder code.

↓ KEEPING IT REAL

TRAFFIC, 12 O'CLOCK

The G1000 is equipped with a Mode S transponder, which gives the G1000 something called *traffic information service* (TIS). TIS displays other aircraft on the moving map; it shows their position above or below your airplane and a trend vector, which looks like a little sword coming off the airplane symbol and shows where the airplane is heading. On the real G1000, airplanes within 500 feet of your altitude appear in yellow to help get your attention.

If you have traffic turned on, see other FSX airplanes on your moving map. If the swords of those other airplanes are yellow and crossing your path, look out!

GROUPS AND PAGES

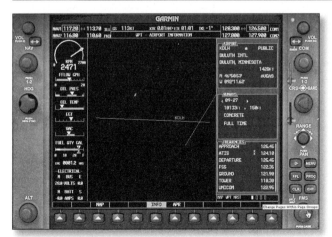

Figure 11-15: The first Waypoint page is for airports, but you can scroll with the inner knob to get information about intersections, NDBs, and VORs as well.

The G1000 MFD is organized into groups and pages like the GNS 500 GPS in the regular Cessna 172. You navigate them the same way, too: the large outer FMS knob changes the chapters, and the small inner knob changes the pages within the group (see Figure 11-15). Only one page is in the Map group, but if you click the outer FMS knob on the MFD—you must click it because the scroll wheel on the mouse works only on the inner knob—you come to the Waypoint group. This should show the next airport on your flight plan on the first page. Here, you can see all sorts of information about that airport including frequencies. If you click the bottom center of the FMS, you get the cursor, and you can scroll down to select a frequency. Pressing Enter puts this frequency in the selected standby

262

PART I
PREFLIGHT

PART II
SPORT PILOT

PART III
PRIVATE PILOT

PART IV
INSTRUMENT RATING

PART V
COMMERCIAL LICENCE

PART VI
ATP AND BEYOND

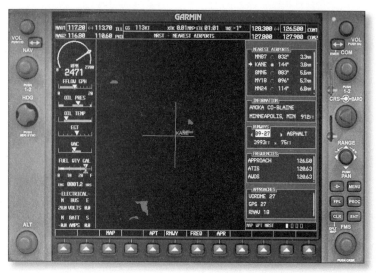

Figure 11-16: Look for green arrows, such as the ones by the runway information here, which mean you can choose from multiple options using the inner knob.

COM on the MFD window. This is less of a benefit with the automatic tuning of the ATC window, but it's a great boon in the real world.

Twist the outer FMS knob once more, and you get to the Nearest group. The first page is a more detailed list of the nearest airports you might need to divert to in an emergency. Selecting any one from the list with the cursor and then clicking the Direct-To key and Enter gets you heading that way in no time.

Sometimes you need to use the soft-keys at the bottom of the display to get the cursor to the frequency or approach area and then use the FMS knobs to select what you want (see Figure 11-16).

 KEEPING IT REAL

TOO MUCH TERRAIN

You can set the big MFD map and the small inset map to different scales and different display options. The FSX G1000 is limited here and doesn't include terrain warnings. The real G1000 does, with yellow for terra firma or towers less than 1,000 feet below you and red for dangers 100 feet below you or less. It's a great idea to turn off the terrain warnings on the big map but leave them on for the inset map as you approach an airport. Passengers get nervous when the entire MFD turns yellow or red as you approach the ground for landing. But they can't see the little map that you have, so you can use that to make sure no red, dangerous terrain appears where you don't expect it.

FLP vs. the Flight Planner

One FSX advantage over the real G1000 is you don't have to enter flight plans using the clunky G1000 interface. You'll enter your flight plans in the flight planner. On a real G1000, you'd use the FPL button to open the flight-planning group and enter the information there. In FSX you create the flight plan by choosing Flights > Flight Planner. Once you've finished creating your flight plan, you return to the G1000 airplane, and, *voila*, it's in as a flight plan. You can see it by pressing FPL. This is true of the GPS 500 in the conventional Skyhawk as well.

Many other G1000 features that you see in a real airplane haven't made it to FSX yet, but they probably will over time. Getting the basics down now, though, will make your future G1000 transition much easier.

G1000 Cross-Country

Load the flight Chap11_G1000_Skyhawk, which puts you on the ground at the Anoka County airport (KANE) just as in Chapter 9. You're going to fly the same flight as in Chapter 10, but you'll depart from KANE and with a G1000 guiding your way.

Get yourself in 2D cockpit if you aren't already, and verify you have the flight plan loaded. Do this by clicking the FPL button on the PFD. You see all the waypoints in the flight plan right there. If the plan is not there, choose Flights > Flight Planner, and load the flight VFR Anoka Co-Blaine to Duluth Intl.PLN.

Taxi to Runway 36 (using the ATC window if you want the practice), or reposition the airplane to the end of Runway 36. If you do taxi there, it's easier to do it with the landing panel visible (press Shift+5 or the short-panel button to the left of the normal-panel PFD).

When you're at a new airport, the MFD map is a great tool for orientation. In the map view, zoom in until the runway diagram fills most of the screen, as shown in Figure 11-17. Now you have a top-down view of the runways to help ensure that you're heading in the right direction.

Normally you'd hold short of the end of the runway and get your G1000 ready to go. Go ahead and position on the runway and stop there. This is a good time to bend the rules of the real world for learning.

Figure 11-17: The runway diagram in map view

Getting Set Up

The first step is ensuring that the flight plan is loaded and ready to go on the G1000. Press the FPL button on the PFD. This brings up the mini–flight plan in the lower right of the screen. The mini–flight plan right in front of you is one of the great features of the G1000.

264

PART I
PREFLIGHT

PART II
SPORT PILOT

PART III
PRIVATE PILOT

PART IV
INSTRUMENT RATING

PART V
COMMERCIAL LICENSE

PART VI
ATP AND BEYOND

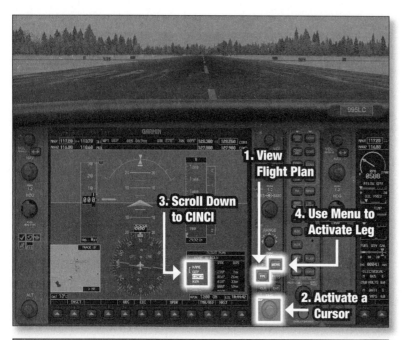

Figure 11-18: The G1000 HSI is a top-down view of your navigation. You can see how it makes more sense to fly straight out and intercept a course to head east rather than depart straight and turn back to intercept a course west.

In addition to making sure you have the correct flight plan loaded, you want to make sure you use the information to plan your climb and first turn on course. Make sure you have the magenta GPS course on your HSI, as shown in Figure 11-18. If not, press the CDI softkey repeatedly until it shows magenta GPS input rather than green VOR input.

You're departing north on Runway 36, which makes sense since your course is to the north. What doesn't really make sense, though, is flying to the GEP first. This would take you west only to turn around and go east soon after. Press Shift+3 to see the MFD and its map if you're having trouble visualizing this. Press Shift+3 again to hide the MFD when you're done. What you want to do is depart north and intercept your course between GEP and the CINCI intersection. (You could also go directly to CINCI and then continue as planned from there because the GPS can go to an intersection as easily as a VOR, but assume ATC asked you to depart north and then fly east.)

Part one is telling the G1000 to skip that first leg to GEP. With the mini-flight plan showing on the PFD, click the center bottom of the FMS knob in the lower right. This gives you a cursor just as with the G500. Click the outer knob to scroll down until CINCI is highlighted. With CINCI highlighted, click the Menu button, and then click Enter to activate the leg from GEP to CINCI. You see the GPS course change to point to the right with the needle showing that the course is to our north. This is perfect. Depart straight out, intercept the course, and then turn to fly directly to CINCI.

You don't have to dial a course into the G1000 CDI with GPS. It dials the course for that leg automatically. You want to set your heading bug to your departure heading of 360 (000) using the HDG knob (it's on the bit of the MFD you can see to the right of the audio panel). You also want to set your target altitude for this trip to 3,500 feet. Do this by dialing the ALT knobs. The outer one changes the setting by thousands of feet, and the inner one changes the setting by hundreds.

AUTOPILOT INTEGRATION

When you set a target altitude on the G1000 in FSX, that becomes the target altitude in the KAP 140 autopilot, too. Don't try that in a real Cessna. The KAP 140 and G1000 altitude bugs are totally separate.

STUDENT OF THE CRAFT

WAYPOINT INFORMATION

The second group on the MFD is the Waypoint group. These pages offer information about the airport, VOR, NDB, or intersection closest to your current position. At the beginning of your flight, this is your departure airport, so it's a great place to get the frequencies for ATIS, ground, tower, and so on. You can also view a basic runway diagram and get runway lengths and headings.

To see the Waypoint group, view the MFD with Shift+3, and then click the outer FMS knob on the MFD. Now you can use the inner knob to scroll between the pages, but the first page is on airports, which is probably what you want.

You can push the center bottom of the FMS knob to get a cursor and use the outer knob to scroll down to any of the frequencies or other items on the airport Waypoint page. On a real G1000, pushing the Enter button for a selected frequency loads it into the selected COM standby slot. On the FSX G1000, this function unfortunately doesn't work. Of course, on FSX you can use the ATC window to load the frequencies for you.

Continued

266

PART I	PART II	PART III	PART IV	PART V	PART VI
PREFLIGHT	SPORT PILOT	PRIVATE PILOT	INSTRUMENT RATING	COMMERCIAL LICENSE	ATP AND BEYOND

One cool use for this feature in both FSX and the real world is to monitor AWOS and ATIS frequencies along your route. As you travel, the Waypoint page will change, and you can look up the closest airport along your route or your destination. You can use the nearest airport page in the Nearest group in the same way.

TAKING OFF

Figure 11-19: The autopilot isn't technically part of the G1000, but the two play well together.

Pour on the coals (open the throttle to full), and depart to the north. Since this flight is all about technology, view the autopilot with Shift+2 and then press AP, press HDG, and press ALT to hold your heading and climb up to 3,500 feet. Now press NAV on the autopilot. For a moment or two, both the HDG and NAV buttons and readout on the autopilot are lit (see Figure 11-19). This means the autopilot continues on the current heading until it intercepts the navigation course—in this case using GPS—and then turns and follows the navigation course. This is referred to as arming the *NAV function* and is analogous to when you preselected an altitude where the autopilot would level off on its own. Once that navigation course is captured, the autopilot follows the GPS flight plan from waypoint to waypoint without you having to do a thing.

The altitude tape is accurate, but it's harder at a glance to notice you're slightly off your altitude compared with a big white altimeter hand that's obviously cocked at a slight angle. When you're flying and not using the autopilot, get in the habit of seeing the whole altimeter tape at a glance. You can develop a feel for when the numbers above and below the current altitude don't look balanced. That will cue you to check the actual altitude in the middle.

STAYING ON TOP OF THINGS

After you're cruising, you don't have much to do but sit back and enjoy watching the G1000 do its stuff. As you cross each waypoint on your flight plan, the CDI automatically changes to show the new course to the next waypoint. This is an important distinction with GPS navigation. Unless you intentionally halt the automatic sequencing of waypoints (which we will discuss when instrument flying in Chapter 17), the GPS always shows navigation to the next waypoint all the way to the end of your flight plan. If you're on autopilot with the NAV function, the airplane follows along.

PUSH TO SYNC

The autopilot ignores the heading bug in nav mode, but it's good form to keep syncing your heading bug with your heading as you fly in case you ever need to take over. You immediately see any corrections for wind here as well. To quickly sync the G1000 heading bug, wait until the turn to a new GPS leg is complete, and then push the bottom center of the HDG knob.

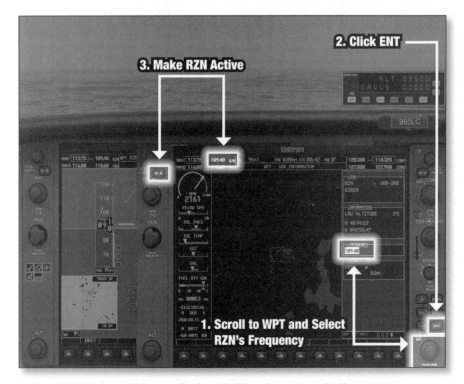

Figure 11-20: You can get frequencies from the Waypoint group or the Nearest group, but FSX supports loading them only with the Enter key from the Waypoint group.

After you pass CINCI but before you cross RZN, scroll the outer FMS knob one click to see the Waypoint group. Now scroll the inner knob three clicks to show the list of nearest VORs. Click the bottom center of the FMS knob to get a cursor, and scroll with the outer knob until 109.40 is selected. Check that the cyan standby box is around the NAV1 standby slot. If it isn't, you can push the lower center of the NAV tuning knob to move it. Now click Enter to put it into the NAV1 standby, and then click the double-arrow button to make 109.40 active. The frequency will ID itself and show you RZN next to 109.40, as shown in Figure 11-20.

268

PART I
PREFLIGHT

PART II
SPORT PILOT

PART III
PRIVATE PILOT

PART IV
INSTRUMENT RATING

PART V
COMMERCIAL LICENSE

PART VI
ATP AND BEYOND

Using VORs

The G1000 can navigate using the VOR signal, too. Since you have RZN selected and you're heading that way, you can switch to VOR navigation easily by clicking the CDI softkey on the PFD, but don't do it just yet! Since you're on autopilot, you immediately turn to get on course with whatever radial is dialed into NAV1.

The smooth way to switch is to make sure your heading bug is on your current heading and then push HDG on the autopilot. This holds your current heading as you get everything squared away.

Push FPL on the MFD to see your fight plan. Push the CDI softkey once to switch to NAV1. Note the RZN frequency at the top of the PFD is green, indicating that you're using that frequency for navigation. Your flight plan shows a course to RZN of 038. This means you want to go inbound on a heading of 038 to the VOR, too (that's inbound on the 218 radial from the VOR on a heading of 038). Use the inner knob of the CRS/BARO knob to change your green navigation course to show 038. As you change the course, you see the exact radial in a temporary window just to the right of your heading. When you're set on the 038 radial to RZN, you can click the NAV button on the autopilot, and you resume flying the navigation source.

Just be aware that you cross the VOR and keep going outbound on the 038 radial from the VOR. Your GPS flight plan continues sequencing, but you must dial the correct outbound radials to keep using VOR navigation, just as you did in Chapter 10. For fun, switch the navigation source back to GPS by clicking the CDI softkey twice. Your CDI guides you to Duluth, but your autopilot might need a little help to follow along.

Note that when you switch between GPS and NAV, the KAP 140 might disconnect and stop flying the airplane for you (see Figure 11-21). This is behavior by design, but you get no warning that it has happened. You might think the airplane is following your flight plan when it's just holding altitude and nothing more.

Figure 11-21: It's always a good plan to temporarily fly using the HDG bug while switching navigation sources.

STUDENT OF THE CRAFT

NEAREST OR DIRECT ON THE PFD

One of the beautiful features of GPS navigation is that it's easy to change your plans quickly. That's especially helpful in a urgent or emergency situation. Pressing the NRST softkey on the PFD opens a mini-window showing the identifiers, names, bearings, and distances to nearby airports. It also shows frequencies and instrument approaches if applicable.

To navigate direct to any of these airports, just scroll with the outer FMS knob on the PFD until the airport name is selected. Then click the Direct-To key, and click Enter twice. You navigate to that airport using GPS.

Why press Enter twice? When you clicked the Direct-To button, you actually changed mini-windows to the direct-to window with the Nearest airport already entered as a destination. The first Enter click was to accept that airport. The second one was to activate direct-to navigation.

You can get to the direct-to mini-window any time by pressing the Direct-To button on the PFD. You can also get a larger version by pressing Direct-To on the MFD. When this window is up, you can enter any airport you want for direct-to navigation, or you can use the outer knob of the FMS control to scroll down to the FPL list. Then press Enter, and you'll see a list of all the waypoints on your flight plan. You can select any one and click Enter twice to navigate directly to that waypoint. This in megahandy under IFR.

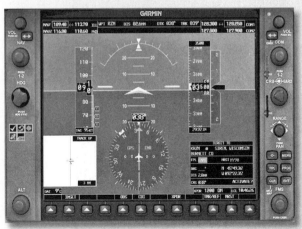

On a real G1000, if you use the Direct-To button on the GPS to go directly to a waypoint on your flight plan, the airplane flies there and then continues the flight plan from that point. On FSX, the direct-to functionality unfortunately erases the current flight plan. This is a drag, but, hey, on FSX you can pause and reload the flight plan to get things back to normal.

270

PART I PRE-LIST

PART II SPORT PILOT

PART III PRIVATE PILOT

PART IV INSTRUMENT RATING

PART V COMMERCIAL LICENSE

PART VI ATP AND BEYOND

TRY IT WITH A CROSSWIND

Figure 11-22: You might not get DTK and TRK exactly the same all the time, but if they stay within a degree, you stay basically on course, no matter what your actual heading is. (Yes, this is an east wind, so as not to give away the correct heading for the sample flight.)

Try that G1000 flight again but this time with some serious westerly winds. You depart KANE and fly north to intercept your course, but you are drifting east as you do. When you're on course, you need to find a heading that keeps you on course. Feel free to use the autopilot, but use only the HDG and ALT functions. The NAV function will find a heading that keeps you on course; the challenge is for you to do it. Load `Chap_11_windy.FLT` to try it.

Don't forget to use your GPS for help, though. One of the handiest pieces of information your GPS shows you is your track over the ground (TRK). The entire point of wind corrections is to get a resulting TRK that equals your desired track (DTK) between two points on your flight plan (see Figure 11-22).

NO WIND VECTOR!?

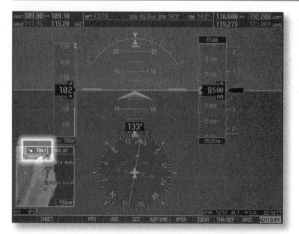

Figure 11-23: The real G1000 shows the wind vector as well as more realistic and useful terrain shading.

The FSX G1000 lacks a great feature from the real G1000: the current winds around the airplane. Since the G1000 knows your speed and altitude in the air and can see your track and speed over the ground, it can calculate the speed and direction of the wind.

The wind vector appears on the moving maps both on the PFD and on the MFD in the real G1000, which is shown in Figure 11-23. Of course, if you want to see the wind speed and direction in FSX, you can always choose World > Weather.

ACCIDENT CHAIN

THE REAL PRIMARY FLIGHT DISPLAY: THE WINDSCREEN

Location: Asheville, NC

Aircraft: Cessna 172S

Injuries: 1 serious, 1 minor

In the "too much attention on the technology" category...

"According to the certified flight instructor, the student pilot was flying the airplane. He stated that, before the departure, they reviewed the weather data on the weather computer for the dark night flight. He stated that they climbed to 7,500 feet and stayed there for about an hour using the moving map display for navigation and the multifunctional display for terrain avoidance. He said the ceiling began to drop, and to stay clear of clouds, they adjusted their altitude to 5500 feet to maintain visual flight. The ceiling dropped some more, and they adjusted their altitude to 4,000 feet. The CFI and the student then descended to 3,500 feet, and according to the CFI, immediately upon reaching 3,500 feet, the airplane began colliding with treetops. He said they collided with trees in a level attitude.

"The National Transportation Safety Board determines the probable cause(s) of this accident as follows: the CFI's inadequate visual lookout and failure to maintain clear of objects during flight. Factors were clouds and dark night."

KEY POINTS FOR REAL FLYING AND FSX BUILT-INS

The following are some key points from this chapter:

- The G1000 PFD and MFD layout and symbology

- Radio use on the G1000

- Navigation on the G1000

- Autopilot integration on the G1000

- Differences between the real G1000 and the FSX G1000

- Tips for using the G1000 in FSX

272

| PART I | PART II | PART III | PART IV | PART V | PART VI |
| PREFLIGHT | SPORT PILOT | PRIVATE PILOT | INSTRUMENT RATING | COMMERCIAL LICENSE | ATP AND BEYOND |

Here are the lessons and missions to study after reading this chapter:

- *Missions*: None for this chapter.

- *Lessons*: Try the Learning Center on GPS and the Learning Center on the G1000.

NIGHT FLIGHT

"I HOPE YOU EITHER TAKE UP PARACHUTE JUMPING OR STAY OUT OF SINGLE-MOTORED AIRPLANES AT NIGHT."
—CHARLES A. LINDBERGH TO WILEY POST, 1931

"IF YOU'RE EVER FACED WITH A FORCED LANDING AT NIGHT, TURN ON THE LANDING LIGHTS TO SEE THE LANDING AREA. IF YOU DON'T LIKE WHAT YOU SEE, TURN 'EM BACK OFF."
—ANONYMOUS

274

PART I	PART II	PART III	PART IV	PART V	PART VI
PRO LIGHT	SPORT PILOT	PRIVATE PILOT	INSTRUMENT RATING	COMMERCIAL LICENSE	ATP AND BEYOND

WHEN DARKNESS FALLS

Figure 12-1: The view from the air at night can be breathtaking.

Night can be one of the best times to fly: winds and turbulence usually decrease, fewer airplanes are flying (so air traffic controllers can get you in and out quickly and can accommodate special requests), and when visibility is good, you can spot the lights from other planes and airports from much farther away (see Figure 12-1). And the view of the lights, the moon, and the stars is often spectacular.

Night can also be one of the worst times to fly, mostly because of what you *can't* see. Clouds don't have lights, and you can accidentally get into one without seeing it coming. Big towers have lights, but small buildings and hills don't, and if you're not well above ground, you could collide with them. If you have an emergency and need to land away from any lit airport, your odds of finding a well-lit place to land are pretty low. Our eyes are not as well adjusted for night vision, so seeing obstacles outside can be even more difficult. In many ways, night flying is a lot like flying on instruments (as though you were in a cloud) even if you're just a private pilot without an instrument rating. And finally, if you're just sleepier at night, you have an increased chance of making a mistake.

But the airplane doesn't know the difference; it flies the same day or night. So, night flight training is mostly about learning to see what you need to see.

VISION AND ILLUSIONS

What you can see at night and how your brain interprets what you see have a serious impact on flight safety, so we'll discuss both issues here. In some ways, flying in FSX is a good way to practice night flying because it can be harder to see things on your computer screen than in real life; on the other hand, you're not as likely to be affected by illusions until you're actually in the air.

Night Vision

Your eyes are designed to see well in the daytime; clear, color, binocular (two eyes) vision is important for a pilot. The center of your field of vision (in your eye's retina) is filled with sensors called *cones* that give good color vision in the daytime, but in low light, those sensors don't work well. Instead, your eyes have *rods* that can pick up faint light but only in shades of gray. That's why you can't see in color very well in the dark. Rods are concentrated in your peripheral vision areas.

Because of this, when it's dark, sometimes you'll see something out of the corner of your eye, but when you look right at it, it's too faint to see. If you look slightly off to the side again, it reappears. That's called *off-center viewing*, and pilots use that technique all the time to see something faint.

The rods in your eye are great for seeing at night, but in the daytime they get overwhelmed with the bright light and, essentially, shut down. When it gets dark, they take a while to adjust and turn back on. *Dark adaptation*, as this is called, can take 30 minutes or more to fully happen, and if you accidentally look at something bright (such as a landing light or flashlight) for more than 8–10 seconds, the clock restarts.

Figure 12-2: Lights in the cockpit are turned down low, and red lights are used whenever possible.

For this reason, pilots take a couple of precautions: lights inside the cockpit are turned down just to the point the instruments can be read, and red lights are used instead of white lights (see Figure 12-2). This is because your eyes can see red much better than other colors, so the light can be dimmer, and you still can see. Pilots use red LED lights or put red filters over flashlights, and interior lights in aircraft are often red.

The disadvantage of red lights comes when looking at writing or markings that are red: red print on a white background lit by red light is nearly invisible. For this reason, pilots usually also carry a weak white light and illuminate only the things they really need to see.

If you're taxiing near other airplanes on the ground at night and you see they're about to shine their taxi or landing lights in your eyes, close one eye so only the other eye loses its dark adaptation. And turn off your own landing and strobe lights when you think it will affect another pilot's vision.

276

PART I	PART II	PART III	PART IV	PART V	PART VI
PREFLIGHT	SPORT PILOT	PRIVATE PILOT	INSTRUMENT RATING	COMMERCIAL LICENSE	ATP AND BEYOND

↓ ACCIDENT CHAIN

ACCIDENT REPORT: NIGHT VFR INTO IMC

Aircraft: Cessna 172 Skyhawk

Location: Knottsville, Kentucky

"The private pilot departed on the 550-mile trip with an unknown quantity of fuel in visual meteorological conditions. He had 125 total hours of flight experience and did not possess an instrument rating. There was no record of the pilot obtaining a weather briefing, nor did he file a flight plan. About four hours into the flight and during the hours of darkness, the pilot reported that the airplane was in instrument meteorological conditions and requested assistance from air traffic control. The conversation between the pilot and the controller continued for several minutes as they discussed weather conditions at various destinations along and around the pilot's intended course. During the conversations, the airplane completed a series of left and right 360° turns and figure-8 maneuvers as the airplane climbed and descended between 7,000 feet and 10,200 feet. As the airplane continued to circle, the controller issued a heading and suggested the pilot check his heading indicator in relation to his magnetic compass. The pilot replied, "…We're trying to keep it under control and get back to the stars here so we got a reference point." Over the next five minutes, the airplane completed three 360° right turns. The final radar plots depicted a descending turn to the right, about 9,800 feet, and then the target disappeared. Examination of the wreckage at the scene revealed no mechanical anomalies.

"Probable cause: the pilot's loss of control in flight due to spatial disorientation. Also causal to the accident was the pilot's inadequate preflight planning, which resulted in his inadvertent flight into night instrument meteorological conditions."

One of the most common causes of fatal accidents in aviation is when a pilot unintentionally flies into clouds or low visibility (instrument meteorological conditions—IMC) when following visual flight rules (VFR) rather than instrument flight rules (IFR). Rules and procedures for IFR are very strict, beginning with the requirement that the pilot have an instrument rating.

It might seem hard to believe that someone would ignore a big, white cloud and blunder right into it, but it doesn't happen that way. It happens when the visibility is already low—hazy, misty, rainy/snowy, or nighttime—and the pilot doesn't see the cloud until it's too late.

The solution, when this happens, is to switch to flying by your instruments, turn around 180°, and go back the way you just came; after all, you weren't in a cloud a minute ago. Even student pilots are required to have three hours of flight training solely by reference to their instruments before they can get their Private Pilot Certificate.

Autopilots are another good way to avoid loss of control because, unless the autopilot has a malfunction, it can't get disoriented. If you put the autopilot on heading mode and altitude hold and then put the heading bug in the opposite direction from where you just were, the plane will turn around on its own and exit the cloud.

ILLUSIONS

Moving in three dimensions with unusual forces on your body can cause you to become confused. Any time your brain gets mixed messages from your eyes, inner ears (the balance sensors), muscles, and so on, you can become disoriented. This can happen day or night in airplanes. However, your brain is so visually oriented that, in the daytime, your visual sense takes over and becomes the primary orienting sense.

At night, though, you can't see as well. The horizon might be invisible, the ground doesn't show the 3D depth perception it usually does, and you can't even see your instruments as well. All these elements conspire to make disorientation in the airplane even more likely at night.

When you're disoriented, you become subject to various illusions, many of which happen at night. Some of the biggest illusions occur when not many lights are on the ground below the aircraft, such as when flying over sparsely populated areas or open water. When a single point of light exists with darkness all around it, the random movement of your eyes can cause the light to appear to be moving; this is called *autokinesis.* If you mistake it for a nearby airplane and take evasive action, you could put yourself in even more danger.

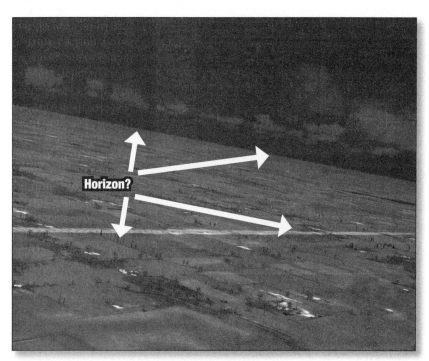

Figure 12-3: Which line is the horizon? One is actually a road.

If the ground is mostly dark but there is a straight road with some lights on it, you might think that is the horizon line and bank the airplane to try to line up with this *false horizon,* as shown in Figure 12-3.

And some pilots have become so disoriented during flight that they actually got turned upside down, thinking the stars were ground lights and the ground lights were stars!

Some other illusions happen during takeoff and landing. During acceleration, your inner ear can trick you into thinking you're tumbling backward. Normally this isn't a problem because your eyes can tell you whether the plane is pitching upward dramatically. But when it is dark and you take off, you see very little out the front windscreen, and therefore that sensation of pitching up could convince your brain it is really happening, so you push forward on the control yoke…and dive right into the ground.

If few lights are near an airport—and that's often true in places where the airports are away from neighborhoods, for example—the darkness makes it difficult to see how high above the ground you are. It's easy during an approach to the airport to get too close to the ground and get trapped by the black hole illusion. (Airports right next to water are prime candidates for this illusion.)

278

PART I	PART II	PART III	PART IV	PART V	PART VI
PREFLIGHT	SPORT PILOT	PRIVATE PILOT	INSTRUMENT RATING	COMMERCIAL LICENSE	ATP AND BEYOND

NIGHT FLYING TECHNIQUES

Pilots have developed a few techniques to keep the aircraft under control and to navigate when it is hard to see outside.

AIRCRAFT CONTROL

Figure 12-4: At night, you'll often use your instruments for aircraft control.

Because it is tough to fly when your outside visual references are hidden in darkness, flying at night can easily become almost the same as flying in clouds: you have to use your instruments to stay upright, on heading, and at altitude, and you have to look outside for other airplanes and for basic navigation (see Figure 12-4).

As mentioned in Chapter 9, when you can't see the ground and sky clearly, your attitude indicator becomes your ground and sky. The attitude indicator doesn't need to move much for a big change to happen in your altitude or heading, so practice holding the attitude in a particular place and waiting for the change to occur.

Obviously, your altimeter and heading indicator are important at night, since it won't be as easy to see how high you are and whether you're headed the right way. And the vertical speed indicator reacts more quickly to any changes in pitch, long before you actually change enough altitude to show much change on the altimeter. But it is easy to "chase the needle" of the VSI by trying to make it stop moving; instead, if you maintain a particular pitch attitude, the VSI stabilizes near what you want.

Glance over at your airspeed indicator once in a while to make sure you're getting the speed you expect. You usually want to pitch the plane for particular airspeeds for a safe climb and not-too-fast descents.

Don't forget to look at your other instruments—especially engine instruments—once in a while to assure yourself the plane is running well.

But don't become completely focused on your instruments to the exclusion of looking outside; you're not flying in the clouds yet, and you still need to look for obstacles and other airplanes and navigate to your destination. Glance inside to check your instruments, and then return to your outside view as much as possible.

NAVIGATION

Figure 12-5: You can sometimes use cities, rivers, and lakes to navigate at night.

In Chapter 6 you learned to navigate with dead reckoning and pilotage; that is, you pick a particular heading and airspeed that, combined with any winds, will move you from one waypoint to the next, and when you spot the waypoint, you adjust your heading as needed to fly over it. That becomes trickier at night; your waypoint options diminish because you can't see much. Lakes and hills disappear; small towns all look the same when you can't see the town's name on the water tower (see Figure 12-5).

Therefore, you need to choose waypoints that you can see at night. Airports are the best, of course, as long as they have lights; you can see airport beacons many miles away. Larger towns and small cities are OK, as long as they are distinctive and not surrounded by lots of other similar-sized towns. The shoreline of a very large lake or ocean can also work, because you'll probably see few lights on the water but some lights on the shore.

You've probably realized by now that the other way to navigate at night is with electronic help. GPS is probably the best thing for day or night navigation, and you should use it if you have it in the plane. For the second flight in this chapter, you get to use the Garmin G1000 system for a cross-country flight at night, and you'll see it's just as easy as in the daytime. But for the first flight in this chapter, you're going to use the slightly old-fashioned radios, the VORs. If you feel the need to brush up on your VOR navigation skills from Chapter 10, do it now while it's still light out.

We should mention what to do if you get lost. This could happen day or night, of course, but at night it is more critical. It's easier to get lost at night, what with the loss of easy-to-see landmarks; and with fewer spots to safely land in an emergency, such as fuel exhaustion, you need to get found soon. We teach the six *C*s to use if you get lost: climb, circle, conserve, communicate, confess, and comply. By *climbing* higher, you can see farther and, perhaps, spot your next waypoint. (Of course, you don't want to fly into clouds, which tend to reduce visibility a lot.) Make gentle *circles* so that you don't get even farther lost and so that you can see all around and perhaps spot something recognizable—even going back to your last waypoint can be enough to get you unlost. After you have climbed a bit and started circling, *conserve* fuel by slowing the engine to a low-cruise setting (2100 rpm on the Skyhawk is good); there's no sense in burning extra fuel when you're not going anywhere. *Call* ATC on any frequency you can find—including 121.50, the emergency frequency—and *confess* that you're lost. They have many ways to try to find you; none of these ways work in FSX, but in the real world they are great. And *comply* with their instructions to get where you're going or, perhaps, to a safe landing spot.

280

| PART I | PART II | PART III | PART IV | PART V | PART VI |
| PREFLIGHT | SPORT PILOT | PRIVATE PILOT | INSTRUMENT RATING | COMMERCIAL LICENSE | ATP AND BEYOND |

LIGHTS

Because of your restricted night vision, you have lights both on the airplane and on the ground.

AIRCRAFT LIGHTING

The goals of aircraft lighting are to see and to be seen. The only lights an airplane is required to have on at night are a beacon and position lights (see Figure 12-6).

The beacon is the red, flashing light on the top of the Cessna's tail. Some airplanes have a white, flashing strobe as their beacon, and some have white strobes *in addition to* their beacon. These lights have the sole purpose of helping other pilots (and tower controllers) spot you from far away and need to be on both day and night. On a clear night, you can spot beacons and strobes more than 10 miles away, much farther than you can see small aircraft in the daytime.

Figure 12-6: Airplanes have many lights to see and be seen.

Position lights, also called *nav* lights, are the running lights just like on boats: red light on the left wing tip, green light on the right wing tip, and white on the tail. Knowing the placement of those lights makes it possible for you to determine the direction of flight of another airplane you see.

For instance, if you see a steady red light on another airplane (in addition to the flashing beacon), then you're looking at the airplane's left wing, and it is passing from right to left of you. Aircraft on your right have the right of way, so you need to make way for this airplane and turn behind it or otherwise avoid it. (Red light means stop—get it?) On the other hand, if you see a green light, then you're looking at its right wing, and you have the right of way. (Green means go.) As always, don't assume the other pilot sees you and is giving you the right of way; be prepared to evade if needed.

If you see just a solid white light, you're behind the other plane, and if you're overtaking, you pass on the right. If you see a red light on the right and a green light on the left, the plane is coming straight for you—break right! (In the real world, the red and green wing tip lights don't shine backward, and the white tail light cannot be seen from the front, making it easier to determine whether a plane is coming toward or away from you; this is not simulated very well in FSX. In fact, in FSX, the white tail light comes on only when the landing light switch is on, unlike the real world where it comes on with the nav light switch.)

Figure 12-7: Panel lights allow you to read your instruments at night. (These are much easier to control from the 2D panel view.)

Some aircraft have landing lights, which are bright, white headlights pointed to illuminate the runway as you get close to landing. These lights usually aren't positioned very well to illuminate the taxiway when you're taxiing, so some planes such as the Cessna also include taxi lights. (There is a taxi light switch in FSX, but it doesn't seem to do anything.)

Inside the aircraft are several kinds of lights, although only the panel lights are simulated in FSX (see Figure 12-7). These lights illuminate the instrument panel, and through their glow, the whole cockpit lights up. In a real Cessna, separate switches exist for the instruments, the panel, and the overhead light (sometimes called a *dome light*). These interior lights are often red lights to prevent your eyes from having to adjust to bright lights and losing their dark adaptation. Pilots also bring along their own lights—flashlights, red LED penlights, and so on—to help read checklists and charts or in case of emergency.

AIRPORT LIGHTING

Airports that can be used at night will have at least a beacon and runway lights (see Figure 12-8). Airport beacons are the lights that alternately flash green and white every five seconds or so—you've probably seen them in real life, too. In FSX, beacons are visible only when you're less than 10 miles away from the airport; in real life, you can see them for dozens of miles if the air is clear.

Figure 12-8: The rotating beacon, flashing green and white, indicates you can use the airport at night.

282

PART I	PART II	PART III	PART IV	PART V	PART VI
PREFLIGHT	SPORT PILOT	PRIVATE PILOT	INSTRUMENT RATING	COMMERCIAL LICENSE	ATP AND BEYOND

Figure 12-9: A large airport such as Minneapolis–St. Paul International (KMSP) has many kinds of runway and taxiway lights.

PAPI

Figure 12-10: The PAPI has four lights to help you adjust your approach path; two red and two white mean you're all right!

Runways are lit with white lights down the sides and sometimes with white centerline lights (see Figure 12-9). Runways used for instrument approaches also have extra lights near the beginning to help pilots spot the runway in low visibility.

A line of green lights perpendicular to a runway indicates the start of the runway (the threshold), and from the other direction those same lights are red, indicating the end of the runway.

Most runways used for night operations also have some sort of lighting system to help pilots stay on the proper descent path to the runway. You learned about VASI in Chapter 4, which sits beside the runway and shows red over white when you're on the correct path. Another kind of approach slope indicator is the precision approach path indicator (PAPI, shown in Figure 12-10). In this case, four lights in a row indicate your approach path; you want to see two white and two red to know you're on the right path. Although it is helpful to have VASI or PAPI at a runway when landing in the daytime, it is vital that you have it at night; they are designed to ensure you don't hit any obstructions on the approach to the runway—obstructions that can be impossible to see at night. In addition, without lots of visual clues, it is easy to get disoriented and not approach the runway correctly. Don't land at an airport at night if none of the runways has approach path lights.

KEEPING IT REAL

THE CLAPPER FOR AIRPORTS

Airports that have night lighting but don't get many aircraft flying in at night would rather turn the lights off and save energy. But if the airport is that small and quiet, they can't pay someone to stay there all night and turn on the lights when a plane arrives or departs. What to do?

Such airports can use the radio equivalent of a Clapper, one of those devices that turns on your room light when you clap your hands. For airports, it is called *pilot-controlled lighting*. The airport beacon stays on all night so pilots can find the airport; however, some or all of the rest of the lights—runway lights, taxiway lights, approach lights, and so on—are turned off but are connected to a radio receiver tuned to the common traffic advisory frequency (CTAF) of the airport. When pilots want to turn on the lights, they tune to CTAF and click the microphone transmit switch three times. The lighting system hears the radio clicks and turns on the lights. Some systems even allow the pilot to turn on the lights brighter with more clicks—five or even seven clicks can get full, blinding lights with all the approach lights and the "rabbit" strobe light running toward the runway.

Because the cost of electricity to run the lights in FSX airports is negligible, the lights at FSX airports are on all night long, so you'll have to fly in the real world to try out pilot-controlled lighting.

By the way, we mentioned in previous chapters that many airports use the same CTAF and that pilots have to say which airport they're using when announcing their position and intentions. Put that together with pilot-controlled lighting, and you'll figure out a little prank that can be performed when flying at night. Not that we've ever done that, of course!

Taxiways, if lit, have blue lights along the sides. Big airports might even have green lights on the centerlines of the taxiways. Airport direction signs might also be lit at night.

And if you're really lucky, even the windsock has a light on it so you can see the wind direction at night.

284

PART I	PART II	PART III	PART IV	PART V	PART VI
PREFLIGHT	SPORT PILOT	PRIVATE PILOT	INSTRUMENT RATING	COMMERCIAL LICENSE	ATP AND BEYOND

OBSTRUCTION LIGHTS

You might spot lights on other buildings and obstacles when flying; these are almost always placed to help pilots avoid the obstacle, whether it's a radio tower, power line, building, or smokestack (see Figure 12-11). The lights could be solid or flashing red or flashing white. Be especially careful of tall towers; the wires that hold them up are usually not lit and extend down at an angle off the sides of the tower. You'll want to fly higher than the tower, not just around it.

Figure 12-11: Towers are easier to see in the daytime in FSX; in the real world, they're actually easier to see at night, because the lights are visible for many miles.

EMERGENCIES

We mentioned in Chapter 9 that the electrical system in the Skyhawk is quite reliable and useful, but it can fail, and if the battery dies, you're out of power. Your engine continues working just fine, but you won't have any lights. Lights are used to see and be seen. No one can see you, but because fewer people fly at night, the danger of a midair collision is less.

More critical for you is seeing—seeing the aircraft instruments as you're flying and seeing the runway without your landing light. You're not legally required to have a landing light unless you're flying as a commercial pilot, so in this chapter's flight lesson you'll practice landing both with and without a landing light.

Seeing the instruments is another matter. Unless the moon is shining right onto your instruments, you'll have a hard time seeing them when the lights are off. In fact, it might be impossible. This is one of those circumstances where FSX does not replicate reality very well; you can easily see your instrument panel even with the battery turned off. The only solution is the flashlight you brought with you. Actually, most pilots carry two or three flashlights for night flights: one big, white light for preflight inspections in the dark and one or two red ones for the cabin if the lights or battery fail.

NIGHT FLIGHT IN THE CESSNA 172SP

Load the flight Chap_12_Night. This night flight takes you from the Anoka County airport (KANE) to the Flying Cloud airport (KFCM) southwest of Minneapolis, a distance of about 22 nautical miles. For this flight, you'll use pilotage and VOR navigation to get to Flying Cloud. Don't use your GPS this time—save that for the next flight so you can develop your nighttime navigation skills.

DEPARTURE

This flight starts with the engine running and the lights on—we don't want you fumbling around in the dark trying to find the battery switch without a flashlight (see Figure 12-12). Your first task is to get from your parking spot to the runway. You're parked in the same spot at Anoka County as in previous chapters, but bring out your airport diagram anyway, before you call the ground controller. Taxi slower than usual because you can't see as far.

At the runway, before you ask for takeoff clearance from Anoka tower, set up your radios for the first leg of the trip. After takeoff,

Figure 12-12: This night flight starts at the Anoka County airport.

you're going to go west a few miles to GEP (Gopher) VOR (see Figure 12-13), so set the NAV1 radio to GEP's frequency of 117.30. You won't know exactly what radial to take to fly straight to the station until you're actually airborne, but it will probably be something like 270, so set your top VOR OBS to 270.

286

PART I
PREFLIGHT

PART II
SPORT PILOT

PART III
PRIVATE PILOT

PART IV
INSTRUMENT RATING

PART V
COMMERCIAL LICENSE

PART VI
ATP AND BEYOND

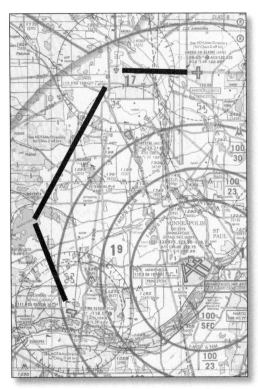

Figure 12-13: The route takes you west from Anoka County to GEP VOR, southwest of Lake Minnetonka and southeast of the Flying Cloud airport.

Figure 12-14: On climbout, use your attitude indicator to set an approximate pitch attitude for a V_y climb, and then fine-tune by adjusting pitch to get the actual V_y airspeed of 74 knots.

After you get clearance for takeoff, start down the runway, rotate, and pitch up to about 12° on the attitude indicator, because it is hard to see the horizon. After you stabilize on climb, pitch as needed to maintain a V_y climb of 74 knots, as shown in Figure 12-14. After you get well above pattern altitude, turn west, balancing your attention between the instruments and the outside world. Soon you start receiving a good navigation signal from NAV1 (double-check by listening to the *ident* of GEP; you should hear "– – · · · – – ."). Turn the OBS dial until the CDI needle centers with a To arrow, read the number at the top of the dial, and fly that heading to GEP. Climb to 4,500 feet.

If you feel comfortable trying the autopilot, set your heading bug (on your heading indicator) to your current heading, set altitude at 4,500, and select the autopilot to maintain heading and altitude. You can then do any turns just by moving the heading bug.

On Course

Figure 12-15: After passing GEP, your instrument panel looks something like this.

When you get to GEP VOR, turn left to a heading of 205. Change the OBS on your VOR to 205. Wait a minute or two, and then maneuver so you can follow the CDI needle to the southwest, as shown in Figure 12-15. Now set your distance-measuring equipment (DME) to R1, and you should see your distance from GEP climbing. If you're ready for a good challenge, set your NAV2 to the next VOR you'll use: Flying Cloud VOR (FCM) on 111.80. Identify NAV2 to make sure you're getting FCM (· · − · − · − · − −). Set the OBS on your second CDI to 155.

Looking ahead, your next way-point is a very large lake—it's a large expanse of black among the city lights, as you can see in Figure 12-16. (You can adjust your view in the 3D mode to see well above the instrument panel, or you can switch to the 2D cockpit view with minimal instruments to help you see the lake.) If you're not sure when you're in the right spot, here are two other ways to tell: you will be exactly 12.5 nm (DME) from GEP, and you'll be on the 335° radial from FCM. (The needle on CDI2 will center, because 335 is the reciprocal of 155.)

Figure 12-16: Lake Minnetonka is the dark splotch among the splotches of city lights.

288

PART I
PREFLIGHT

PART II
SPORT PILOT

PART III
PRIVATE PILOT

PART IV
INSTRUMENT RATING

PART V
COMMERCIAL LICENSE

PART VI
ATP AND BEYOND

ARRIVAL AT FLYING CLOUD

Figure 12-17: The Flying Cloud airport is 7 miles ahead.

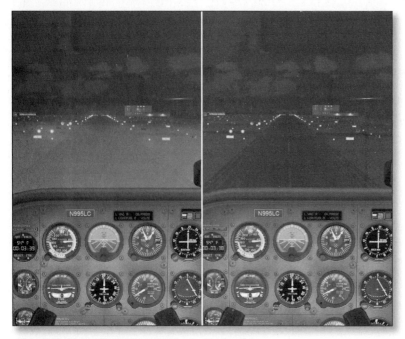

Figure 12-18: Landing with and without a landing light

At the lake, turn left to a heading of 155. You're about 8 miles from the Flying Cloud airport (Figure 12-17), so it's time to descend (traffic pattern altitude is 1,900 feet). If you were using the autopilot to hold altitude, turn altitude hold off (but leave heading hold on for now). Pull the power back to about 2100 rpm to set up a descent. Listen to Flying Cloud's ATIS information on 124.90 to hear the weather and runway in use, pull out the Flying Cloud airport diagram that you printed from the website (www.wiley.com), and call Flying Cloud tower on 125.20 to request a touch-and-go. You've probably spotted the airport by now and can enter the traffic pattern in whatever way the tower requests. (Don't forget to turn off the autopilot entirely.)

Perform a normal approach to the runway, making sure you stay on the correct approach path with the VASI (red over white). Your landing light will illuminate the runway when you're about 100 feet up, which will make it more like a daytime landing. Flaps up, hit full throttle, and take off into the traffic pattern again.

The next time around, turn off your landing light to see whether it makes any difference when you land (see Figure 12-18). You have to use the runway lights to help you decide when to flare—this could be a bit bumpier. You need to be able to land both with and without a landing light in case it burns out when you need it most!

After your last landing, you can taxi to the ramp and park it overnight, or you can head back to the Anoka County airport. Or just reset the FSX flight, and do it again; practice makes perfect!

NIGHT FLIGHT IN THE *G1000*

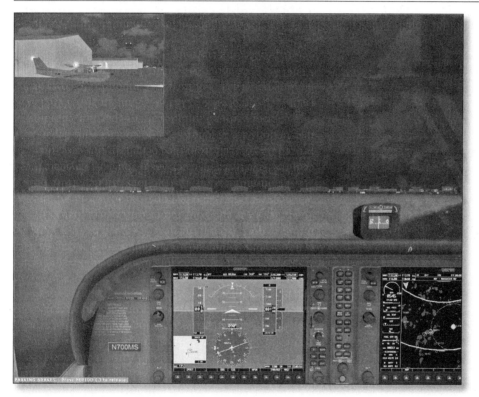

Figure 12-19: The Garmin G1000 cockpit is almost too bright for night flight.

In this book so far, the last flight of each chapter has been an advanced flight, either being more complicated or requiring more skill than the preceding flights. We're changing things this time. For your second night flight, you get to navigate with a GPS, which you'll find is much easier than pilotage and VOR navigation to get from airport to airport at night.

Load the same flight as before, Chap_11_ Night. But this time, change the aircraft to the Cessna 172SP Skyhawk G1000 Glass Cockpit (see Figure 12-19). Using either the Flights > Flight Planner menu or the flight plan (FPL) function on your MFD, create a direct flight from KANE to KFCM.

There's not a lot to say about this flight, because the navigation is so easy. In fact, if you turn on the autopilot, set it on the NAV function (with the Garmin's CDI needle on GPS mode), and hold your altitude, you can practically go to sleep for 10 minutes and wake when it's time to land. Remember, though, that it is still your job to watch for other airplanes, avoid airspace you're not authorized to fly in (or get permission to pass through it), keep track of the nearest airports in case you need to land before you get to Flying Cloud, and so on.

290

PART I
PREFLIGHT

PART II
SPORT PILOT

PART III
PRIVATE PILOT

PART IV
INSTRUMENT RATING

PART V
COMMERCIAL LICENSE

PART VI
ATP AND BEYOND

KEY POINTS FOR REAL FLYING AND *FSX* BUILT-INS

The following are some key points from this chapter:

- Understand how human night vision works and how illusions can affect flight.

- Learn techniques for flying and navigating at night and for dealing with emergencies.

- Become familiar with aircraft and airport lighting systems.

There are no lessons or missions on night flight in FSX.

"I SOMETIMES STILL GO OUT HUNTING FOR BAD WEATHER, FLYING LOW IN SIMPLE AIRPLANES TO EXPLORE THE INNER REACHES OF THE CLOUDS. LESS EXPERIENCED PILOTS OCCASIONALLY JOIN ME, NOT TO LEARN FORMAL LESSONS ABOUT WEATHER FLYING, BUT WITH A MORE ADVANCED PURPOSE IN MIND—TO ACCOMPANY ME IN THE SLOW ACCUMULATION OF EXPERIENCE THROUGH CIRCUMSTANCES THAT NEVER REPEAT, IN A PLACE THAT DEFIES MASTERY."

—WILLIAM LANGEWIESCHE

292

| PART I | PART II | PART III | PART IV | PART V | PART VI |
| PREFLIGHT | SPORT PILOT | PRIVATE PILOT | INSTRUMENT RATING | COMMERCIAL LICENSE | ATP AND BEYOND |

WEATHER THEORY AND DATA

One of FSX's cool advances over previous flight simulator versions is the weather, especially the realistic way FSX shows clouds. Weather has always been an issue for real-world pilots, so in this chapter we discuss some weather challenges and show you how to deal with them.

WEATHER HAZARDS

The most hazardous weather phenomena that a pilot without an instrument rating will face are high winds, turbulence, low visibility, and clouds. Thunderstorms are certainly even more dangerous, but they're really just a nasty combination of all of the preceding. And ice can bring down a plane quickly, but because you can't fly in clouds without an instrument rating, ice can really occur only in freezing rain or flying through wet snowfall, an occurrence that you escape by turning around—immediately.

When planning a flight, then, you have to completely avoid thunderstorms and freezing rain. If freezing rain is predicted in the area, don't even drive to the virtual airport! If thunderstorms are predicted but they will be scattered, you might be able to fly around them. (Stay at least 20 miles from a thunderstorm; even in FSX you can tell where the thunderstorms are—the lightning strikes and thunder give them away.)

On the other hand, if freezing rain is not forecast and thunderstorms are avoidable or nonexistent, you need to look at the forecasts for winds, turbulence, low visibility, and clouds to decide whether the weather will still prevent your flight.

HIGH WINDS AND TURBULENCE

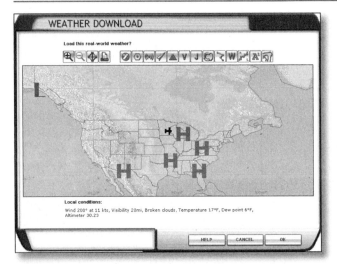

Figure 13-1: High- and low-pressure areas, as well as fronts, are shown on the FSX weather map when you download real-world weather.

You've already had a chance to fly in some windy conditions, so you know a bit about what to expect. Away from the ground, the biggest effect of wind is to change your course (ground track) or speed, and usually both. Near the ground, however, the problem is the transition from ground to air and back. Some winds are so strong—or from the wrong direction—that you can't take off or land at a particular airport.

It's helpful to be able to predict winds so you know whether you can fly at all. As mentioned in earlier chapters, wind is just the movement of large bodies of air, but something has to push or pull them: that something is high- and low-pressure areas (see Figure 13-1). (The air pressure is the *barometric pressure* you hear in a weather report and is why you need to set the altimeter in your plane for the local altimeter setting.) The stronger the pressure difference between the high- and low-pressure areas, the faster the wind.

Air flows from high pressure to low pressure but alas not in a straight line. Due to the earth spinning, an effect called the Coriolis force makes winds move clockwise around a high-pressure area and counterclockwise around a low-pressure area in the northern hemisphere. (It's exactly the opposite for those of you living in the southern hemisphere.) Picture a big hurricane spiral you've seen on satellite photos; hurricanes are areas of very low pressure, and the winds (and clouds and rain and everything!) spiral strongly around the low pressure.

Figure 13-2: Weather reports in FSX include winds, described both in words and with an arrow pointing in the direction the wind is blowing toward.

The FSX weather chart shows high- and low-pressure areas but doesn't show how strong those areas are. Real-world charts do show the strength, and from them, weather forecasters can predict wind speeds. The FSX weather chart does show the winds at various places (see Figure 13-2); it's not a prediction for future winds, but at least it tells you what is going on right now. If you're planning a flight and you check the winds at your departure and destination airports and compare the winds to the available runways, you can decide whether you'll be able to safely take off and land.

Strong winds cause turbulence, which is when the airplane passes from air moving in one direction into air moving in a different direction. Near the ground, even a light wind less than 10 knots can cause a few bumps if it passes over trees or buildings near an airport. Strong winds can make ground turbulence so bad you can't safely fly. When the wind changes direction or speed over a short distance, it's called *wind shear*. That's really what turbulence is, on a small scale.

⬇ ACCIDENT CHAIN

WIND-SHEAR ACCIDENT

Date: August 2, 1985

Location: Dallas, Texas

Aircraft: Lockheed L-1011

"On August 2, 1985, at 1805:52 central daylight time, Delta Air Lines Flight 191, a Lockheed L-1011-385-1, N726DA, crashed while approaching to land on Runway 17L at the Dallas/Fort Worth International Airport, Texas. While passing through the rain shaft beneath a thunderstorm, Flight 191 entered a microburst, which the pilot was unable to traverse successfully. The airplane struck the ground about 6,300 feet north of the approach end of Runway 17L, hit a car on a highway north of the runway killing the driver, struck two water tanks on the airport, and broke apart. Except for a section of the airplane containing the aft fuselage and empennage, the remainder of the airplane disintegrated during the impact sequence, and a severe fire erupted during the impact sequence. Of the 163 persons aboard, 134 passengers and crewmembers were killed; 26 passengers and 3 cabin attendants survived.

Continued

294

PART I
PREFLIGHT

PART II
SPORT PILOT

PART III
PRIVATE PILOT

PART IV
INSTRUMENT RATING

PART V
COMMERCIAL LICENSE

PART VI
ATP AND BEYOND

"The National Transportation Safety Board determines that the probable causes of the accident were the flight crew's decision to initiate and continue the approach into a cumulonimbus cloud which they observed to contain visible lightning; the lack of specific guidelines, procedures, and training for avoiding and escaping from low-altitude wind shear; and the lack of definitive, real-time wind shear hazard information. This resulted in the aircraft's encounter at low altitude with a microburst-induced, severe wind shear from a rapidly developing thunderstorm located on the final approach course."

On a big scale, like near thunderstorms, wind shear can be air moving upward fast, and then, a short distance away, it's moving down fast. You go from climbing so quickly you couldn't descend if you wanted to, to suddenly descending so quickly that even a full-power V_y climb won't stop you from being pushed into the ground.

Wind shear as you're landing or taking off can prevent you from making a good landing. For instance, assume that you're maintaining a nice 65-knot approach speed into a head wind of 15 knots (meaning your ground speed is actually 50 knots). If the wind suddenly shears to a 5-knot tailwind, that's a net change in the wind of 20 knots. Your speed through the air momentarily becomes 45 knots—65 minus 20—and the plane pitches down to get back to your trimmed airspeed of 65 knots. If you're close to the ground, that pitch-down might put you right into the ground.

Low Visibility and Clouds

The term *low visibility* can mean many things. In the western United States, some pilots consider it low visibility when you can't see more than 10 miles, because usually you can see 50 miles or more. On the East Coast, 10 miles is the best visibility you could see all summer, when 5 miles is more common in the haze. Pretty much everyone considers visibility less than 5 miles to be marginal. In fact, aviation meteorologists call this *marginal VFR*. Visibility can drop because of haze, smoke, fog, smog, mist, rain, snow, blowing sand, or even volcanic eruptions.

A pilot must have at least 3 miles of visibility (in most cases) to legally fly under visual flight rules (VFR), as shown in Figure 13-3. Less visibility than that, and you need an instrument rating. But 3 miles isn't much. Imagine you're flying along in your Cessna 172, and you can see all of 3 miles away—and things at that distance are pretty hard to make out. At 90 knots, it's only two minutes between the time you could first see the object—assuming you were lucky enough to be looking in that direction already—and when you would hit it. If another airplane is coming toward you, you have less than one minute to spot it (hard to do), decide exactly which direction it's going (also hard), and then choose an evasive maneuver when you can't see very far in *any* direction.

More dangerous than a midair collision due to low visibility is losing control of your airplane or running into something on the ground—a hill/mountain or building/tower. As you learned in the previous chapter on night flying, when you can't see very well out your windows, you're essentially flying on instruments, even if you're not

Figure 13-3: This is the legal minimum of 3 miles of visibility. Can you spot the smoke stack on the left, the tall buildings on the right, and the aircraft coming right at you straight ahead?

Figure 13-4: A cloud can easily be hidden by low visibility, and you won't see the cloud until you're in it and it's too late.

instrument rated. Low-visibility flight is just like that, only worse. If you can see only 3 to 5 miles, you really can't see the horizon. It's very hard to tell how far you are above the ground, and roads and other *lines* on the ground suddenly distract you into thinking you can tell where the horizon is.

When a pilot hits something on the ground and it wasn't because they lost control of the aircraft, it's called *controlled flight into terrain*. In other words, the pilot was flying normally and just didn't see the obstacle coming.

Low visibility is a sneaky weather hazard for pilots. Airport weather reports state the visibility at that time and place, but visibility can change drastically over a short distance and brief time. That means pilots have to make judgments about visibility as they fly along and decide to turn back when the visibility gets too low for safe flight—even if there is the legal limit of 3 miles of visibility.

One of the more dangerous hazards that could be hiding behind an area of low visibility is an area of *really* low visibility...a cloud (see Figure 13-4). As long as the temperature is well above freezing and there is no ice in the cloud, the airplane doesn't know the difference between flying in good visibility and flying in a cloud. Of course, you know the difference, and many pilots lose control of their airplane when they get into a cloud. The trick, as before, is to double-check your instruments to make sure you stay upright, do a slow turn, and fly back the way you came, out of the cloud.

296

PART I	PART II	PART III	PART IV	PART V	PART VI
PREFLIGHT	SPORT PILOT	PRIVATE PILOT	INSTRUMENT RATING	COMMERCIAL LICENSE	ATP AND BEYOND

As a general weather phenomena, clouds behave a bit differently than areas of low visibility. Most of the time clouds start at a specific altitude above the ground, determined by the amount of moisture in the atmosphere. In aviation the term *ceiling* describes the lowest layer of a cloud deck if the clouds are dense enough that you can't safely fly up through breaks in them.

 STUDENT OF THE CRAFT

CLOUD REPORT

Weather reports for the general public include statements such as "Partly cloudy," but that isn't detailed enough for flying. Aviation weather reports and forecasts use specific terms to describe the amount of sky the clouds cover:

Few: ⅛ to ⅜ of sky is covered by clouds

Scattered: ⅜ to ⅘

Broken: ⅝ to ⅞

Overcast: ⅞ (sky is entirely covered by clouds)

Multiple layers of clouds can be at different altitudes. For instance, you can have scattered clouds at 2,000 feet and broken clouds at 4,000 feet; the altitude listed is the bottom of each layer of cloud. The altitude of the tops of each layer of clouds cannot be easily predicted or seen from the ground and so is not reported.

If the sky is broken or overcast, it is said to be a *ceiling* at the bottom of that layer of clouds.

You can fly under clouds if they are far enough above the ground. For most areas you fly, you must stay at least 500 feet below the bottoms of the clouds. You also need to stay 500 to 1,000 feet (depending on population density) above the surface and any human-made objects on it. The net effect of this is that it is legal to fly in most places with a ceiling of 1,500 feet above ground level. But flying only 1,000 feet above the ground leaves you with few options in case of an emergency, and most pilots prefer to fly 2,000 to 3,000 feet above the ground at a minimum. Lower than that, and you might be accused of *scud running*, that is, flying low under the scud of a low cloud layer. Ah, but why not see how dangerous scud running is for yourself, in a way that is safer than you can do in real life? You'll take the Cub scud running later in this chapter.

ACCIDENT REPORT: SCUD RUNNING

Date: March 16, 1997

Aircraft: Cessna 172

Location: Manchaca, Texas

"A Cessna 172, registered to and operated by a private owner…was destroyed when it collided with a power line during cruise flight near Manchaca, Texas. The non-instrument-rated private pilot, sole occupant of the airplane, was seriously injured. Instrument meteorological conditions prevailed for the personal cross-country flight that departed Austin, Texas, en route to San Marcos, Texas, about 15 minutes prior to the accident. A flight plan was not filed.

"The pilot reported that he 'was scud running and hit [a] power line in clouds.' According to a witness, who was interviewed by an FAA inspector, the airplane's engine was operating normally when the airplane flew over his house, collided with the power line, and then rolled inverted before impacting the ground. The FAA inspector examined the airplane and reported that the outboard section of the right wing was severed and the cabin top had separated from the fuselage.

"The following weather conditions were reported at 1819 for Robert Mueller Municipal Airport in Austin, Texas, located 12 nautical miles north of the accident site: wind 040 at 5 knots, visibility 2 statute miles in light rain and mist, ceiling 300 feet overcast, temperature 10° C, dew point 10° C, altimeter setting 30.17 inches of mercury."

This was not an unusual accident. In fact, more than half of all fatal aviation accidents are caused by a pilot flying under VFR getting into instrument conditions (low visibility, clouds, and so on).

WEATHER CONTROLS AND EFFECTS

In FSX you can really control the weather. You can make it much better than reality (CAVU—clear above, visibility unlimited) or challenge yourself with weather much worse than reality. Or, for a change, how about reality? Yup, with FSX you can download the latest real-time weather and have it simulated in the game. For the flights in this chapter, we control the weather, but we also introduce weather control to you so you can start modifying flights in the future.

298

PART I
PREFLIGHT

PART II
SPORT PILOT

PART III
PRIVATE PILOT

PART IV
INSTRUMENT RATING

PART V
COMMERCIAL LICENSE

PART VI
ATP AND BEYOND

FSX WEATHER CONTROLS

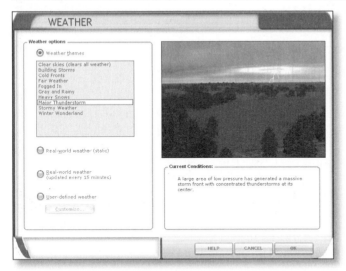

Figure 13-5: The Weather Options settings give you the power of Mother Nature; are you feeling calm or stormy today?

When you choose World > Weather, you have some really basic, intuitive options for controlling the weather (see Figure 13-5). If you don't want to get into the nitty-gritty details of creating weather, use the weather themes, and pick whatever kind of day you want. Be careful, though; some options such as Fogged In and Stormy Weather are not for a VFR pilot like you.

Depending on what is happening out your window, the Real-World Weather option might not be very exciting, if you're used to cranking up the weather challenges. In the real world, there aren't always storms in any one place and certainly not on command. But one feature we really like about using real-world weather is the diversity: you'd never take the time to change the weather at each individual airport in FSX, but by downloading real-world weather—especially with 15-minute updates—you'll see changes in winds, clouds, visibility, and so on, as you move through the FSX world.

WHICH WAY THE WIND?

If you adjust the wind direction in the Weather Options settings and then listen to the wind report on ATIS or ASOS at your airport, you might find a difference in wind direction. This is because meteorologists (and FSX Weather Options) report wind in its *true* direction, but the winds you hear over the aviation radio are reported in *magnetic* direction. In Minnesota, this is only a few degrees difference, so you might not even notice. But on the northwest coast of the United States, where you do your instrument training in the next part of this book, the difference is 20°. So if you intended to set the winds to come from 310° so there would be no crosswind on Runway 31 in Seattle, you might be surprised when there actually is a crosswind.

User-defined weather (the Customize button) is where you can make more specific changes to the weather—either globally or on an airport-by-airport basis (see Figure 13-6). (Actually, those local changes are done on weather stations, because some airports don't have their own weather station, and other places have a weather station but no airport.) Again, you're allowed to set either general conditions (types of clouds, amount of precipitation, and so on), or by clicking Advanced Weather, you can fine-tune the exact heights and thicknesses of clouds, wind speed, and direction to 1 knot and 1°, and so on, as shown in Figure 13-7.

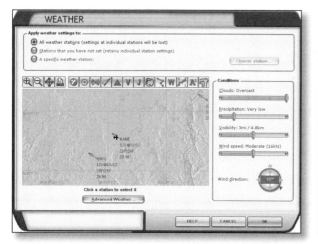

Figure 13-6: You can apply more detailed weather to all stations or just some.

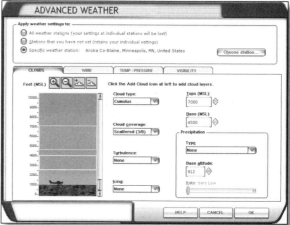

Figure 13-7: You also can make extremely detailed choices about the weather.

WEATHER REPORTS

If you choose to manually create detailed weather scenarios, you'll know what to expect during your flight. But if you choose real-world weather or if you choose one of the broad weather themes, you won't know exactly what the winds are doing, where the cloud bases start, and so forth.

As you learned in Chapter 4, you can listen to the weather report on your aircraft radio. By selecting the AWOS or ATIS frequency at your airport—or one nearby, if the current airport doesn't have one—you can hear all the weather details. This is the most realistic way within FSX to get the weather. But if you're downloading real-world weather, you have more options.

  KEEPING IT REAL

REAL-WORLD AVIATION WEATHER REPORTS

A good aviation weather website for the United States is **www.aviationweather.gov**. It's so extensive that we can't explain everything here, but we'll cover two particular types of weather reports.

Observations > METARs is one piece of weather that is easy for you to understand without a lot of schooling in meteorology; the Meteorological Aviation Report (METAR) is the most recent weather report at an airport. Many airports have METARs, including KANE (Anoka County), and a new METAR comes out every hour or so. Just enter the four-digit code of the airport—the ones in FSX, like KANE, are real—and then click Translated and finally Submit. You need to know the conversion for your time zone into UTC time, but the rest of the weather is translated for you. When FSX downloads the weather from the Internet, it's getting METARs for all the airports in your vicinity.

Continued

300

PART I	PART II	PART III	PART IV	PART V	PART VI
PREFLIGHT	SPORT PILOT	PRIVATE PILOT	INSTRUMENT RATING	COMMERCIAL LICENSE	ATP AND BEYOND

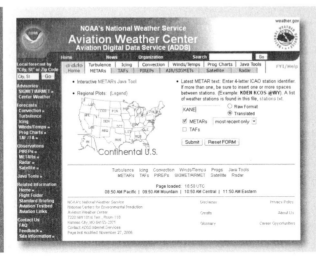

Forecasts > TAF is the place to read about future weather. TAF stands for *terminal area forecast*. Not all airports have TAFs; in fact, you won't find one for Anoka County. But Crystal (KMCI) is nearby, and the forecast there is probably close to what you can expect at Anoka County. TAFs are usually created every six hours and show the forecast weather for 24 hours.

You can look at the rest of the site for more weather, but FSX doesn't model all the details shown there.

On many websites, you can find the current and forecast aviation weather (see "Real-World Aviation Weather Reports"). In fact, it is same weather data that FSX automatically downloads and inserts into the game. The one big advantage that real-world weather reporting gives you is the forecast—an idea of what will happen in the future. For instance, if you're planning a flight from one airport to the next but the forecast shows a line of thunderstorms moving toward your destination, you could choose to fly the other way in FSX. FSX does not model the exact placement of every thunderstorm cell (so don't use those cool Doppler radar charts from the TV station to dodge thunderstorms), but when a real-world storm hits an airport and changes the weather report at that airport, it is reflected in FSX the next time FSX downloads the airport's weather.

PERFORMANCE

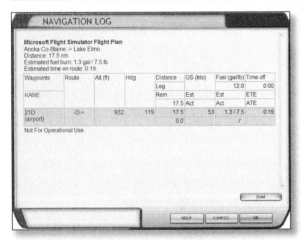

Figure 13-8: The FSX flight planner adjusts your expected ground speed (and flight time) to account for the winds.

As you learned in the chapters on cross-country flying, weather affects your flying in several ways: the winds might try to blow you off course or affect your ground speed, the height and thickness of the clouds affect how high you can fly, and so on.

After you've set up the weather in FSX, whether on your own or by downloading real-world weather, you can start planning your flight based on that weather. The automated flight planner in FSX takes winds aloft into account, so if the wind is anything other than calm at your cruise altitude, the navigation log adjusts for your predicted ground speed (see Figure 13-8). However, the flight planner does not show you what heading to fly at to compensate for any crosswind; the heading listed in the navigation log is really just the ground track (course) you want to follow. You need to adjust the heading yourself to stay on course.

THE JOY OF SCUD RUNNING

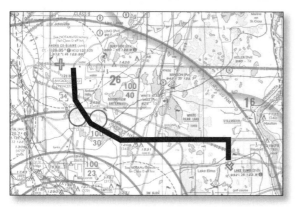

Figure 13-9: On the flight from Anoka County to Lake Elmo, you follow highways to the south and east.

This is your opportunity to try a relatively dangerous flight in the safety of FSX. You're going from the Anoka County airport (KANE) to Lake Elmo (21D), about 20 miles southeast (see Figure 13-9). But it's not a nice day out: the clouds are low, it's a bit bumpy, and it's snowing. In fact, the forecast is for visibility at the bare minimum for VFR flying: 3 miles.

Navigation is a challenge because you can't fly high (due to clouds) and you can't see far (due to snow). And, to make it a real challenge, you're going to take the Cub and *not* use the GPS! Instead, you're going to follow roads and freeways. (Remember IFR—"I Follow Roads"—rather than the official instrument flight rules.)

The advantage of the Cub for something like this is that it is easy to fly it slow, which is good when you can't see far in front of you; also, if you get lost or caught by weather, you can put the plane down in a field somewhere and wait out the weather.

Load the flight Chap_13_Scud_Cub, and check the ATIS weather report at KANE (see Figure 13-10). When you're ready to taxi, tell the controller you'll be making an east departure.

After takeoff, start climbing, but don't go any higher than 500 feet below the ceiling you heard in the ATIS. (For example, if the ceiling is 1,500 feet—which means 1,500 feet above the airport elevation of 912 feet—you can fly no higher than 1,000 feet above the ground, which is 1,900 feet MSL).

Figure 13-10: The flight Chap_13_Scud_Cub puts you back at the Anoka County airport in a snow storm.

302

PART I	PART II	PART III	PART IV	PART V	PART VI
PREFLIGHT	SPORT PILOT	PRIVATE PILOT	INSTRUMENT RATING	COMMERCIAL LICENSE	ATP AND BEYOND

As you leave the airport and go east, you're looking for a divided highway that runs north and south (see Figure 13-11).

Figure 13-11: As you leave Anoka County, follow this highway south.

Follow the highway south until it intersects another divided highway going northwest to southeast; follow it southeast, which is slightly to the left of your current heading (see Figure 13-12).

Figure 13-12: Follow this second highway southeast.

Figure 13-13: Pass by the tall TV towers...but not too close!

After you turn southeast to follow this second highway, you need to spot the TV towers as soon as you can. There is one on the right of your path, and it is more than 600 feet tall. Three towers almost 1,500 feet tall (2400 MSL) are also on your left, which is probably higher than you're flying (see Figure 13-13). (These towers will appear only if you have scenery complexity higher than Very Sparse.)

Turn
East

Figure 13-14: Continue on the highway going due east.

A few miles after you pass the tall towers, you pass a couple of lakes on your left. Then the road splits again, this time going south, and a half mile beyond that, a road heads north. But you continue due east (see Figure 13-14).

304

PART I
PREFLIGHT

PART II
SPORT PILOT

PART III
PRIVATE PILOT

PART IV
INSTRUMENT RATING

PART V
COMMERCIAL LICENSE

PART VI
ATP AND BEYOND

After about 5 miles, this highway you're following turns sharply south, and another divided highway crosses it going straight east; follow this new highway east (see Figure 13-15).

Figure 13-15: When your highway turns south, pick up the new highway going east.

This is where it gets tricky: you're going to go east along this highway about 5 miles, but there isn't an obvious landmark at 5 miles. You're going 70 to 80 mph, so it should take you about 4 minutes. Start a timer if it'll help you remember. When it's about 3 minutes, start looking off to your right; the airport is 2 miles south of the highway. If you still haven't seen it after 4 minutes, you'll need to assume it's there, so turn south anyway (see Figure 13-16).

Figure 13-16: Can you see the airport yet? If it has been 5 miles (4 minutes), turn south anyway.

Figure 13-17: With all the snow, it's hard to see the airport; let's hope you spot the runways before you fly by.

Figure 13-18: Bring it on home, but watch out for snowplows.

Make a radio call to the other traffic at the airport, letting them know you're two miles north. Within just a minute or two, you are right near the airport. Look everywhere, left and right, because you don't know exactly whether you passed it going east. Let's hope there are some flashing lights to help you find the runways (see Figure 13-17).

When you're at the airport, circle to check the wind sock and then set up for a normal landing (see Figure 13-18). Don't brake too hard in case there is snow or ice on the runway.

As you can see, it is a real challenge to navigate in nearly whiteout conditions. FSX doesn't simulate some weather conditions you find in the real world; for example, on a flight like this, it is likely the visibility would go below 3 miles and the clouds would drop below 1000 AGL sometimes, making it both illegal and unsafe. Can you spot the TV tower in time? Can you see the cloud before you're in it? If you do turn back, can you find the airport before it, too, is lost in snow or fog? Sometimes, the safest thing to do is land in a field; it's hard to swallow that ego pill, but it's better than dying.

When you're done with your virtual hot chocolate at Lake Elmo, you can head back to Anoka County or move on to the next flight.

SCUD RUN IN CESSNA 172 WITH G1000

Try the flight to Lake Elmo again, but this time with the Cessna 172 and its Garmin G1000 system. It should be easier, right? Maybe.

You can use the FSX flight planner to draw a direct course from KANE to 21D, and it installs that flight plan right into your GPS system. The problem is that you might not want to fly the direct course; will you pass too close to those TV towers? The way to tell is to use the excerpt of a sectional chart included on the website called Anoka Co. to Lake Elmo Sectional.

Print the chart, and draw a straight line from airport to airport. Check carefully to see whether those towers—or any others—are near the path. Here is where the real Garmin 1000 has a leg up on FSX: a real Garmin 1000 has obstacles such as towers and buildings marked on the MFD map, but the FSX MFD does not. Flying a direct course from airport to airport isn't always the safest way to go, especially when you're down low.

The flight from the website is called Chap_13_Scud_Cessna (see Figure 13-19). Load it, and choose the flight planner to create a flight from KANE to 21D. You can go directly there, or on the Flight Planner > Edit tab, you can drag the course line slightly north to create an intermediate waypoint away from those tall towers—like 7MN5, the White Bear Lake seaplane base. (It's best not to actually land on White Bear Lake this early in the season; the lake hasn't frozen yet.)

When you're in the air, turn on course, and head for Lake Elmo. Remember to stay below the clouds. Just because you have a powerful navigation system and flight instruments doesn't mean you can go in the clouds yet; you need an instrument rating to do that.

Figure 13-19: Chap_13_Scud_Cessna gives you the Garmin 1000 to guide your flight to Lake Elmo.

The danger in using a plane with the capabilities of the Garmin 1000 is that you might spend so much time looking inside the cockpit when instead, given the visibility outside, you need to spend even more of your time trying to spot towers, airplanes, and so on. As before, try to take quick glances at the instruments and return to looking outside.

Flights in low visibility also are a really good time to use the autopilot. Unless there is a malfunction or severe turbulence, the autopilot does not lose control of the airplane in a cloud. By selecting heading or navigation mode and altitude hold, the plane keeps itself upright, and you can concentrate outside to make sure you don't hit anything. Have a safe flight!

KEY POINTS FOR REAL FLYING AND FSX BUILT-INS

The following are some key points from this chapter:

- Understand weather hazards.

- Use weather reports and forecasts to plan aircraft performance.

- Navigate in low visibility using pilotage and GPS.

Here are the lessons and missions to study after reading this chapter:

- *Lessons*: The background section of the Instrument Rating Lessons Overview talks a little bit about weather and about controlling the aircraft using instruments, but you won't find any specific FSX lessons about low-visibility and scud running.

- *Missions*: The Aleutian Cargo Run in the Grumman Goose is a good test of your scud-running skills—with thunderstorms to avoid! And try to spot the "Caspian sea monster."

MAXIMIZING PERFORMANCE

"WHEN IT COMES TO TESTING NEW AIRCRAFT OR DETERMIN-ING MAXIMUM PERFORMANCE, PILOTS LIKE TO TALK ABOUT PUSHING THE ENVELOPE. THEY'RE TALKING ABOUT A TWO-DIMENSIONAL MODEL: THE BOTTOM IS ZERO ALTITUDE, THE GROUND; THE LEFT IS ZERO SPEED; THE TOP IS MAX ALTITUDE; AND THE RIGHT, MAXIMUM VELOCITY, OF COURSE. SO, THE PI-LOTS ARE PUSHING THAT UPPER-RIGHT-HAND CORNER OF THE ENVELOPE. WHAT EVERYBODY TRIES NOT TO DWELL ON IS THAT THAT'S WHERE THE POSTAGE GETS CANCELED, TOO."

—ADMIRAL RICK HUNTER, U.S. NAVY

310

PART I	PART II	PART III	PART IV	PART V	PART VI
PREFLIGHT	SPORT PILOT	PRIVATE PILOT	INSTRUMENT RATING	COMMERCIAL LICENSE	ATP AND BEYOND

QUICK, CLEAN, AND COOL

Like the seven stages of life in Shakespeare's *As You Like It*, pilots move through stages too. You start in slow and simple trainers; you move up to more complex aircraft with more power and somewhat more sophisticated systems. The lowly Cub motors through the air at a pace better than most of the U.S. speed limits. Yet, after a while, even this seems mind-numbingly slow.

Then one day, walking down the ramp, you spy some low-slung, sleek speed machine and just fall in love. You must get some time flying that fast, that high, that…cool. It's time to step up to a high-performance airplane.

Higher performance usually means you have more complex systems to manage, and you have to plan further ahead as you fly. You can practice both of these skills on FSX. We'll now delve a bit into how these systems work.

NO REPLACEMENT FOR DISPLACEMENT

The first step in going faster is just to get some more horsepower (hp) at your disposal. You're going to start flying the Mooney Bravo, which gives you 270 of them. (Actually, the Lycoming TIO-540 engine installed in the Mooney is capable of 350 hp, but Mooney derated the engine so that it would last longer.) Much of the extra horsepower comes from this engine being just plain bigger than any engine you've flown yet. The Skyhawk SP has an IO-360 engine in it.

Figure 14-1: You use the throttle to set the manifold pressure that you want. When the engine is shut down, as it is here, the manifold pressure gauge shows the current barometric pressure of the ambient air.

This means it has a fuel-injected (I), *horizontally opposed*-cylinder (O) engine of 360 cubic inches displacement. That's almost a 6-liter engine, which is what you find in your average muscle car. The Mooney's engine displaces 540 cubic inches. That's almost a 9-liter engine—equal in size to a small truck.

The Mooney is also turbo-charged (that's what the *T* stands for in the engine name). This means the air coming into the engine is pressurized, and the engine can produce all 270 hp until it's more than 20,000 feet above sea level. Turbocharging works by using two fans connected by a common shaft. One of those fans is sitting in a stream of the hot exhaust gas flowing out of the engine. As the gas flows over the fan blades, it spins them at speeds greater than 10,000 rpm.

The other fan on the same shaft sucks extra air into the engine. More air in the cylinders means you can add more fuel, which, in turn, means more power when it's burned. These hot gases leave the engine and spin the exhaust side of the turbocharger even faster. You see where this is going.

If you just let the turbocharging system run unchecked, the engine would pressurize to a dangerous level and probably come apart. You modulate turbocharging through something called a *wastegate*. The wastegate determines how much exhaust air flows through the turbocharger and how much bypasses the turbocharger and just flows out into the air stream. The wastegate in the Mooney is automatic, so you don't have to think about it. What you will do is set the pressure you want on the intake side of the engine. As the Mooney climbs or descends, it automatically adjusts the turbocharger wastegate to maintain this same manifold pressure You read this on the new manifold pressure (MP) gauge, shown in Figure 14-1.

NOT TO COMPLAIN, BUT...

Just for the record, when you adjust the MP in a real airplane, the sound of the engine doesn't change as long as the prop speed doesn't change. The sound does change with the throttle in FSX. We're not sure why they can't correct that, but it has been true for generations of the software.

A New, Blue Control

Figure 14-2: Just behind the shiny prop hub is a governor with weights and springs to direct engine oil under pressure to change the pitch of the propeller blades and maintain a constant RPM. The prop control really sets the balance point for this governor.

You use the black throttle knob to control the MP, but you use a new, blue control to adjust the engine rpm (see Figure 14-2). This knob is called the *propeller control*, or just *prop control*, because that is what is actually being affected by the control.

The propeller in the Cub and the 172 was a solid piece of wood or metal. This meant you could not change the angle of attack of the blades (called the *pitch of the blades*). That's known as a *fixed-pitch propeller*. The situation is sort of like a bicycle with only one gear. When you go uphill, you're working hard, and you move slowly. When you go downhill, the going is easy, and you can pedal fast. Likewise, when the Cub or the 172 was climbing

312

PART I	PART II	PART III	PART IV	PART V	PART VI
PREFLIGHT	LEFT PILOT	PRIVATE PILOT	INSTRUMENT RATING	COMMERCIAL LICENSE	ATP AND BEYOND

and the engine was working hard, it slowed down. If you pointed the nose toward the ground and didn't close the throttle, the engine would speed up.

The propeller blades in the Mooney can change pitch, and it does so to try to maintain a specific rpm. When the plane is climbing, the blades flatten out and displace a smaller amount of air with each revolution. This makes it a bit easier for the engine to turn, and its speed remains constant. When you dive, the blades increase pitch and displace more air. This makes it harder on the engine, and it can't speed up the way it does with a fixed-pitch prop.

Of course, you opened the throttle to climb in the Skyhawk, and you do the same in the Mooney. The difference is that in the Skyhawk, opening the throttle increased the engine rpm. In the Mooney, it increases the MP, but most of the time the rpm remains unchanged.

This just scratches the surface of the theory, but the main concern here is about procedures; you need to know that the blue prop control sets the propeller speed, and the black throttle sets the target MP.

⬇ ONLY SO MUCH TO WORK WITH

The prop control sets rpm at high power. Any reduction of power under about 20 inches MP reduces rpm because the propeller pitch is as flat as it can get. At this point, the throttle controls engine speed much like a fixed-pitch prop.

STUFF HANGING DOWN AND STICKING OUT

One of the fun aspects of a high-performance airplane is that you have lots of items to adjust and tinker with during flight. Many items pop out or into the airframe during different phases of flight.

TAKEOFF FLAPS

The Mooney has only three flap positions: retracted, takeoff/approach, and landing. Remember that the purpose of flaps is primarily to provide more lift at a slower airspeed. Until now, this has applied only to landing, but the Mooney's clean, high-speed wing is going to need some help getting off the ground, too. It's not that it can't take off with the flaps retracted. It just takes a lot less runway if you take off with the flaps in the first notch position.

You also use the flaps to help slow down as you approach an airport. Full flaps are used only for landing.

COWL FLAPS

The Mooney's big engine generates a lot of heat, and it depends on air flowing over the engine to keep it cool. When the airplane is zipping along at nearly 200 knots, this is easily accomplished by air entering the little intakes behind the prop and a small gap where the engine bolts to the rest of the airplane.

On the ground while taxiing around and in a low-speed climb, however, the engine can get quite hot. To get more air flowing over the engine, you can open the Mooney's *cowl flaps*. These are doors below the engine that let more hot air escape. You have them open for taxi, open just enough to help keep things cool during climb, and closed for the rest of the flight.

RETRACTABLE GEAR

Figure 14-3: After you're climbing after takeoff, you retract the gear and the flaps—in that order. When the gear are down, the gear light is green. When they're up, there is no light. When they're anywhere in between, as they are here, the light is red, and a warning light appears.

Dragging things through the wind costs energy in the form of, well, *drag*. Those wheels are useless after you're off the ground, so the Mooney lets you tuck them up behind some drag-reducing gear doors. Nothing is difficult about this. You just switch the gear handle from down to up. The key is remembering to put it back down before you land. FSX is a great place to get this ingrained in your mind. Real-world gear-up landings rarely injure people, but they sure beat up your wallet.

To help with this process and to help you slow down, use the gear as a speed-control tool. You can't put the gear down until your speed is below 140 KIAS, but after it's out, the airplane slows down further.

Figure 14-3 shows flaps, gear, and cowl flaps.

STUDENT OF THE CRAFT

GEAR WHEN YOU'RE CLEAR?

Some folks think you should keep your gear down until there is no longer any chance of landing on the runway ahead of you, just in case you lose the engine. Frankly, we see this as such a rare event vs. the much more likely scenario of wanting to improve your climb performance that we recommend getting the gear up as soon as you're climbing.

SPEED BRAKES

Speed brakes, shown in Figure 14-4, also help control your speed by creating drag, but they temporarily rob the wing of lift. Speed brakes are typically used to let you descend more quickly without gaining more airspeed or to slow down in level flight without gaining any altitude. Of course, you could simply close the throttle to accomplish the

314

PART I
PREFLIGHT

PART II
SPORT PILOT

PART III
PRIVATE PILOT

PART IV
INSTRUMENT RATING

PART V
COMMERCIAL LICENSE

PART VI
ATP AND BEYOND

Figure 14-4: Popping out the speed brakes adds 500–800 feet per minute descent to whatever you were doing before they went out. Retract them, and everything returns to normal.

same effect, but that solution has a real-word problem. Closing the throttle reduces the manifold pressure and the heat being generated by the engine. Cool off this fire-breathing bad boy too quickly, and you could risk damaging the engine though *shock cooling*. Shock cooling occurs when the different metals of the engine cool and contract at different rates, causing engine parts to warp.

There's actually some controversy over the concept of shock cooling. Some mechanics will swear it's a real problem. The bulk of analytical evidence, however, is that it probably isn't an issue or is much less critical than many people think (and, of course, FSX engines are immune). Practicing an engine-friendly descent certainly can't hurt a real-world motor, and it's

a good planning challenge. But if you ever do need to drastically reduce the power to get down fast, it probably won't damage your real-world motor either.

STILL MORE GAUGES AND SWITCHES

As if those weren't enough switches to keep you busy, the Mooney also has an electric fuel pump to turn on and off at various times, electric trim for the rudder to save you some foot work, an electric deice for the propeller in case you get caught flying in a cold cloud, a turbine inlet temperature gauge to guide you in leaning the engine, a fuel system that lets you draw from only one fuel tank at a time, and an addition to the autopilot system called a *flight director*.

That's a lot of things to remember and manage—particularly switching fuel tanks every hour or so of flight. To make life easier, we'll help you formalize and simplify your approach to flying a bit.

INTRODUCING FLIGHT PROFILES

Whenever we start a student on a new airplane or we learn a new one ourselves, we make sure that aircraft flight profiles are part of that first lesson. Flight profiles are baselines for how a particular aircraft flies, and they reduce the endless possible permutations of speeds and configurations to just six. For almost any GA airplane (and, arguably, any airplane), flying one of these six profiles gets everything done except the takeoff and landing. Learning these profiles also serves as the foundation for your instrument flying, which you'll begin in Chapter 15.

ONE UP, THREE LEVEL, AND TWO DOWN

Flying a profile begins after the airplane has left the ground and is clear of any obstacles in the area. At this point, you transition from a full-power climb at V_y to a *cruise climb*. The cruise climb usually is at a lower pitch than V_y to give you better forward visibility and allow for better engine cooling. In the Mooney, it's also at a lower power setting. Every time you need to climb during the flight, you use cruise climb.

After you've reached your cruising altitude, level off and let the plane accelerate to *high-speed cruise*, or just *high cruise*. Use this as your baseline for getting from point A to B as quickly as practical. High cruise is usually the highest normal cruise setting for a given plane.

You might not always want to go that fast, so note two other cruise speeds. *Low-speed cruise (low cruise)* is usually a speed fast enough that the airplane is still easy to control with gear and flaps up but slow enough that you can put the flaps and gear down any time you want (or at least be close to that speed). In the Mooney, you must be slower than 140 to lower the gear and below 110 to lower full flaps. Low cruise should be somewhere between those speeds.

An even slower speed you want is *approach level.* This is the speed you have just before descending on an instrument approach or for flying around the airport traffic pattern. This requires having both flaps and gear down and being slow enough to easily transition for landing.

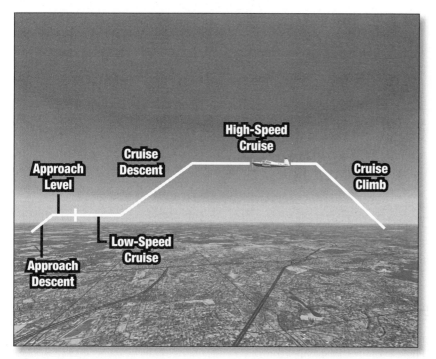

These three level speeds do everything you need for level flight. You can fly other speeds in level flight, but knowing these three actually makes variations easier because any other speed is somewhere along the continuum of high cruise to approach level.

You also need only two descents. One is a descent at high-cruise speed (or better), and the other is a descent at approach speed. These are *cruise descent* and *approach descent*, respectively. These two speeds also mark the ends of a continuum that lets you easily adjust your descent for any speed or rate of descent in between. Figure 14-5 sums up all these profiles.

Figure 14-5: With these six configurations, you can accomplish any flight.

You've actually been using profiles all along; we just haven't pointed it out. When you set the Cub's power to 2100 rpm and pitched for level flight, you got 70 mph, which is high cruise for the Cub. Set power to 1300 rpm with a slight nose-down pitch and you'll get 60 mph and about a 500-foot-per-minute (fpm) descent. This is approach descent for the Cub.

PITCH + POWER = PERFORMANCE

The underlying concept behind flight profiles is that if you have the airplane's flaps and gear in a particular position and have the engine producing a given amount of power, then a particular pitch results in a particular airspeed and rate of climb or descent. You saw this way back in the Cub when you set the power to 1900 rpm and could either fly level and see 60 mph, pitch up and see 50 mph and a climb, or pitch down and see 70 mph and a descent.

You do the same thing in the Mooney, but you use the attitude indicator for your pitch reference. Power is set by a combination of MP and rpm. Here's what to expect for performance numbers:

	MP	RPM	Configuration	Pitch	Indicated Airspeed	Rate of Climb
Cruise Climb	34 inches	2400 rpm	Flaps and gear up	+5°	110	+700 fpm
High Cruise	34 inches	2400 rpm	Flaps and gear up	+0°	160	0 (level flight)
Cruise Descent	32 to 25 inches	2200 rpm	Flaps and gear up	–2°	170 to 155	–500 fpm
Low Cruise	25 inches	2200 rpm	Flaps and gear up	+2°	120	0
Approach Level	25 inches	2200 rpm	Flaps up but gear down	+2°	100	0
Approach Descent	19 inches	Prop control full forward	Approach flaps and gear down	+0°	100	–500 fpm

Would you fly a real Mooney Bravo using numbers just like this? Yes. This is exactly how you fly the real Mooney, as well as the real Cirrus, Columbia, Bonanza, Baron, and so on. When someone talks about flying an airplane "by the numbers," this is exactly what they're talking about.

Profiles let you get "ahead of the airplane" as well. You'll see in your training flight that you'll be humming along in high cruise and then start a cruise descent. During the descent, adjust the power to the low cruise setting. When you level off, the airplane slows on its own to low cruise as if by magic. Watching this happen in a real or simulated airplane is one of those oh-so-sweet moments as a pilot.

STUDENT OF THE CRAFT

SEE THE LITTLE PROBLEMS

One of the side benefits of flying an airplane with baseline flight profiles in mind is that you might see problems before they become emergencies. We can't tell you how many times in the heat of instrument training we've seen students forget something such as raising the landing gear. Students who know their flight profiles pick this up much sooner because they set up for a cruise climb pitch and power but don't see nearly the performance they expect. This sends them searching for the reason, and they find it—the gear is still down, causing performance-robbing drag.

Continued

We've seen pilots catch small problems that would otherwise go undetected because of profiles, such as a bad magneto that was robbing the engine of just a bit of power or a trace of wing icing causing drag but unseen in the dark of night. In each case, the only clue was a high cruise that was 5–10 knots slower than expected.

GET A BASELINE AND THEN ADJUST

Life is simple if you can just use these six profiles. Usually you can, but sometimes you need to adjust them. That's no problem. First you set the closest profile, and then you change pitch and/or power to get what you want. Suppose that you want to do an approach descent at 1000 fpm rather than 500? Set up for the standard approach descent, but then reduce the MP to 15 inches. Watch what happens.

Adding 1 inch MP roughly increases ROC by 100 fpm or airspeed by 5 knots. Removing 1 inch does the reverse. By the same token, keeping your power constant, you can trade 5 knots for 100 fpm ROC.

FLY FAST IN A MOONEY

To get yourself up to speed in the Mooney, load the flight Chap_14_Six-pack Mooney. This flight puts you short of the runway at KANE. Starting a big, fuel-injected engine can be a bit of an art, but each version is different, so you won't bother practicing that here.

Run-up on the Mooney is basically the same as what you're used to on the Skyhawk, except that you check the prop control. This involves pulling the blue control aft until the engine rpm slows from its run-up setting of 2000 rpm down to 1600 rpm or so and then steadily pushing the control full forward again. This guarantees the prop governor is at least doing something and gives you a chance to look for a sheen of oil on the windscreen that might indicate leaking. We've never seen students have real trouble with this, so you won't practice it here.

We have seen students forget to fully configure for takeoff. So, you'll start with that.

GETTING EVERYTHING IN POSITION

Holding short of Runway 36 at KANE, you need to make a quick check of the aircraft to ensure it's ready to go. The first item we have students do is the avionics stack. Why is it so important to get the stack set up *before* you take off? Things happen much faster in a high-performance airplane, and you want to get as much done before getting airborne as possible. If you're using the FSX ATC function, tuning the radios is a snap. Press Shift+3 to call up the Garmin 500 GPS, and push the Direct-To button. Now use the outer (large) FMS knob to scroll to the list of nearest airports. KANE is first on the list for the obvious reason that you're already there. Press Enter twice to select a direct course to KANE. You'll be coming back here to land, and it's one less step if it's already your direct-to destination.

318

PART I
PREFLIGHT

PART II
SPORT PILOT

PART III
PRIVATE PILOT

PART IV
INSTRUMENT RATING

PART V
COMMERCIAL LICENSE

PART VI
ATP AND BEYOND

Figure 14-6: Even if you don't plan to use the autopilot, you need a plan for altitudes and headings before you take off. Altitude and heading bugs help you actually fly that plan.

Figure 14-7: Green LED lights show you the position of the elevator trim, wing flaps, rudder trim, and cowl flaps.

Next set your target heading and altitude for this flight. Do this because the Mooney climbs quickly and you want to be warned about where you will turn and level off. This Mooney has a mechanical HSI similar to the digital one you used in the G1000 Skyhawk. The knob with the orange symbol moves the heading bug, and the knob with the yellow line moves the CDI needle around the compass rose. For now, turn the yellow CDI to north as a visual reference for the runway you'll use for departure, and set the heading bug to 210°. This is the heading you turn to as you fly away from KANE. See Figure 14-6 for how this looks in the airplane.

The Mooney also lets you set your target altitude and vertical speed in two places. You can do it on the KAP 140 autopilot as you did in the six-pack Skyhawk, and you can do it with an alerter on the Mooney panel. Put your cursor over the ALT numbers on the altitude alerter, and use the scroll wheel to scroll up to 6,500 feet. If you press Shift+2 to see your radio stack, you see that the same 6500 is on the KAP 140.

Also make sure that the NAV/GPS switch on the right side of the panel is set to GPS. This switch controls which navigation signal, VOR or GPS, goes to the Mooney's HSI.

The final step is setting the airframe and power configuration for the airplane. The Mooney uses partial flaps for takeoff. This is the norm for high-performance airplanes. Their wings are designed for high-speed flight with low drag, and they don't produce much lift at low speed. The Mooney can take off with zero flaps, but it takes a *lot* of runway to do it. Use the flap switch on the screen or your control yoke to lower the flaps one notch to the takeoff/approach position. Takeoff with full flaps is not approved for the Mooney.

Normally the cowl flaps are already open in the run-up area because you had them open to keep the engine cool for start-up and taxi. On winter mornings in the north, though, we sometimes close the cowl flaps during taxi to keep the engine warm enough for run-up. Just check to make sure they're open for takeoff. Figure 14-7 shows all these indicators.

Finally, make sure the prop control and the mixture are both full forward and the boost pump is turned on.

▼ KEEPING IT REAL

TRIMMING YOUR BEHIND

The Mooney has a setting for rudder trim. This is common in high-performance and multi-engine aircraft. You can use it to do the same task as holding right rudder in a climb. The FSX Mooney doesn't have an overwhelming left-turning tendency, though, so we usually leave it alone. Feel free to experiment with it, though.

POURING ON THE COALS

When you open the throttle to full power, note that the MP reaches its pressurized 40 inches. The Mooney might seem to be accelerating slowly. It isn't. It's just that you need to reach a higher speed for takeoff. FSX says to raise the Mooney's nose at 60 knots, but 70 works a bit better for most people at first. It takes a bigger pull than you used in the 172, and the airplane might not respond for a moment. It lifts off by 75 knots and climbs rapidly while accelerating to 85 knots. Pitch the nose about 8° nose-up, and raise the gear.

CLIMB, CLEAN, COOL, COMMUNICATE

When you're clear of the trees, which ought to take about three seconds, you can start climbing at 105 knots and raise the flaps, as shown in Figure 14-8. After they are up, you can transition to cruise climb. Turn the boost pump off. Reduce the prop speed to 2400 rpm by pulling back slightly on the prop control. It's quite sensitive. Then reduce the MP with the throttle to 34 inches. Pitch for 5° nose-up. The Mooney should settle down into a climb of more than 700 fpm and 110 knots of airspeed.

The engine isn't producing as much power and, therefore, isn't producing as much heat. Close the cowl flaps just halfway (this is often called the *trail position*) to provide some extra cooling during the climb but not too much. You're watching, as far as engine temps are concerned, the cylinder head temperatures (CHTs). The six-pack Mooney shows only one cylinder, but the airplane designers try to connect the gauge to the hottest one. You must keep the temp below its maximum of 500°; below 400° is desirable. CHTs of 400 or less are usually what you like to see.

320

PART I
PREFLIGHT

PART II
SPORT PILOT

PART III
PRIVATE PILOT

PART IV
INSTRUMENT RATING

PART V
COMMERCIAL LICENSE

PART VI
ATP AND BEYOND

Figure 14-8: The Mooney can climb like a rocket at 85 knots. Unfortunately, you can't see anything. After the gear is up, pitch forward to put the glare shield on the horizon and get about 105 knots.

Now that you're in cruise climb, you can turn to your heading of 210 while you climb. Feel free to use the autopilot, as shown in Figure 14-9, if you like. If you had to report something to ATC, you are free to do that now, too. This flight actually takes you into the Minneapolis Class B, but don't worry about that here. If it were a real flight, you would need a clearance to do this.

Whenever you depart an airport or start a climb after abandoning an attempt at landing (a *go-around*), you can remember the four Cs. Start a full-power *climb* at the best angle or rate to clear any obstacles. *Clean up* the airplane by retracting gear and flaps as needed and turning off the boost pump. *Cool* things down by reducing power to climb power and opening the cowl flaps an appropriate amount. *Communicate* with ATC as needed. Start saying this little mantra now, and you'll be thankful when you start instrument training.

Figure 14-9: You can use the autopilot to lighten your workload. Shift+2 shows the stack, but you might want to move it to the upper right to better see everything on the panel. Shift+2 will then toggle it on and off in the new location.

PICKING UP SPEED

Just level off when you reach your cruising altitude of 6,500 feet. Don't change the power. The power setting for high cruise is the same as cruise climb. The only difference is pitch. It will take a while for the airplane to accelerate, but with level pitch, the indicated airspeed should roll right up to 160 knots.

Figure 14-10: You can lean the mixture by finding the peak TIT reading or by finding the fuel flow you know to be correct for that power setting.

Now is a good time for your cruise checklist or flow check. Turn on the boost pump, and then switch fuel tanks to the tank you didn't use for climb. Then turn the boost pump back off. In the real airplane, having the boost on during a tank switch theoretically reduces the chances of an engine hiccup during the switch.

Now you should lean the mixture for cruise. The official procedure is too lean for peak turbine inlet temperature (TIT), with a maximum allowed value of 1725° (see Figure 14-10). TIT is the temperature of the exhaust gases driving the turbocharger. Essentially, TIT is a kind of an exhaust gas temperature (EGT) reading taken where the exhaust gases enter the turbo. Usually you see a TIT of 1650° or so. This is higher than you usually see for EGTs, which rarely get higher than 1500.

STUDENT OF THE CRAFT

FLIGHT DIRECTOR: A HUMAN-POWERED AUTOPILOT

The Mooney Bravo is the first airplane you've flown with a flight director. The same buttons as the autopilot control the flight director, but instead of flying the airplane to meet those demands, the flight director shows you what pitch and bank should be flown. It's then up to you to fly them. This provides you with the guidance to stay on course and altitude but varies from those items as needed.

Continued

The information appears on the attitude indicator as an inverted yellow V. If you tuck the orange attitude triangle so the top of the triangle sits inside the inverted V, you are following the commands of the flight director.

Note in the figure that ALT and NAV are turned on in the autopilot, but the autopilot button (AP) shows it's off. The Flight Director (FD) button is on. You can also have the flight director and the autopilot on at the same time if you want.

Coming Downhill

Let's try a little descent. Pitch down a mere 2° or set the autopilot for a 500 fpm descent to 4500 feet. As you head down reduce the rpm with the prop control to 2200 rpm. The reduction in prop speed is a reduction in total power. Note that the fuel flow decreases. But keeping the MP set for 34 inches helps keep our engine warm and happy on the way down. Speed builds, but that's okay. You strapped on a Mooney because you wanted to go fast, right? In fact, you could have kept the prop at 2400 for the descent if you wanted, as long as the air was smooth. Any travel in the yellow arc of the airspeed indicator is for smooth air only. Your only limit is the 195-knot redline on the airspeed indicator.

Combinations Count

Level off at 4500 but don't change the power setting from 34 inches MP and 2200 rpm. You should see about 150 knots. This makes sense because you have a lower power setting—MP and RPM combined—than you did before. Reset the prop to 2400 but change the MP to 32 inches. The airspeed won't change. So 32 inches MP by 2400 rpm is the same total power as 34 inches by 2200 rpm. How do you choose? It's up to you, but in the real world, lower rpm and higher MPs usually mean less vibration and slightly better fuel economy. Each engine has limits peculiar to that installation though, so each make and model airplane is different.

This example points out two things. One is that your baseline for high cruise would clue you in that you forgot to bring the rpm back up to 2400. The clue was that your indicated airspeed was 10 knots too low. It also shows how you can adjust from the baseline speed for a given situation.

THINKING AHEAD COMING DOWN

The Mooney covers a lot of ground coming down while doing 170 knots. You need to do some planning to get down before you overshoot your destination airports.

GOING DOWN AND SLOWING DOWN

Head back to KANE by pressing Shift+3 on the keyboard to show the GNS 500 and pressing the Direct-To button and Enter twice to get a new course back to KANE. Turn to that heading or use the autopilot NAV function to start flying home.

Now it's time to head down in a cruise descent, so reduce the rpm to 2200 again. This time, however, you slowly reduce the MP, like 1 or 2 inches every minute or so. The idea is to reduce the engine power gradually (to stave off the potential for shock cooling) but still work your way down to the target power settings for low cruise: 25 inches MP and 2200 rpm.

Plan to level off at 2,500 feet. If you reach 2,500 feet before the MP gets down to 25 inches, that's fine; just keep reducing it slowly as you fly level at 2,500 feet (see Figure 14-11).

Figure 14-11: On your way down, your speed stays near your cruise setting, but the reduction in power shows as much cooler CHTs. Try to keep the CHT in the green the whole time.

324

PART I
PREFLIGHT

PART II
SPORT PILOT

PART III
PRIVATE PILOT

PART IV
INSTRUMENT RATING

PART V
COMMERCIAL LICENSE

PART VI
AIR AND BEYOND

ARRIVING AT THE AIRPORT

When you level off at 2,500 feet and get down to 25 inches MP and 2200 rpm, just sit back and watch. This is one of those satisfying moments as a pilot when you set something up to happen and the airplane makes it so. In a few minutes the Mooney slows down and settles in at low cruise of 120 knots (see Figure 14-12). Note that as you slow down, you need to change your pitch to eventually reach about 2° nose-up.

Figure 14-12: Using the GPS distance and VSR can help you plan your descents to reach level flight at low-cruise speed about 8 miles from the airport.

INSIDE THE GAME

TOO MUCH SLOWING

When leveling off after a descent to low cruise, FSX sometimes overshoots and slows down way past 120 knots. If the airspeed is going below 120, increase the MP to just 26 inches for a moment and then back down to 25. This seems to fix this error. This doesn't happen in a real Mooney.

APPROACHING FOR LANDING

In the next section, you start working on your instrument rating, and your approaches to a runway are mostly long, straight-in approaches in which you might not see the pavement until seconds before you actually touch down. The approach level and approach descent profiles are designed for this situation, but they work well in the VFR traffic pattern, too.

Figure 14-13: Another benefit of standard profiles for FSX is knowing where power, flaps, and gear are set even when you can't see them.

Figure 14-14: Use the virtual cockpit, a simplified cockpit view, or multiple views to determine when you're abeam your landing runway threshold. The low-wing Mooney makes it harder to see your landing runway.

If you're alone in the traffic pattern, there is no problem with entering the downwind at 120 knots in low cruise. Since this is your first flight, slow down to your approach-level configuration as you maneuver to enter a left downwind for Runway 36 (see Figure 14-13 and Figure 14-14). All you need to do is confirm that you're below the 140-knot maximum gear extension speed and then lower the gear. The Mooney slows just from the drag of the gear to 100 knots. Do check that you see a green, gear-safe light telling you that all three wheels are down and locked in place.

You'll be coming back to Anoka County in position to enter a base leg or straight-in landing for Runway 36. But one of the things people get in trouble with in faster aircraft is how wide a turn they make. Your radius of turn increases at the square of your airspeed, and you're still doing 120.

Turn left while still on the west side of Interstate 35 (the big, divided highway as you approach Anoka County) to a heading of 360. Go north of the airport to buy yourself some time, and then make a 180-turn back to enter the left downwind for Runway 36. You might want to press W on the keyboard to get rid of the bulk of the Mooney panel to see the airport better. If you want a reference to help you get the right distance to the airport, the downwind happens to be just inside Interstate 35. This is a bit wider downwind than you used for the Cub or the Cessna, but you need a bit more space as you're learning the Mooney because even as you slow down in the pattern, you're still flying faster than you're used to flying.

326

PART I
PREFLIGHT

PART II
SPORT PILOT

PART III
PRIVATE PILOT

PART IV
INSTRUMENT RATING

PART V
COMMERCIAL LICENSE

PART VI
ATP AND BEYOND

A little before the landing threshold is off your left wing, verify that your airspeed is under the 110-knot flap speed limit. Press W twice to see the full panel.

With the full panel in view, turn the boost pump on, reduce the throttle to 17 inches of MP, and push the prop control and the mixture control all the way forward (see Figure 14-15). Your propeller speed won't increase because the MP is so low that the propeller is already at minimum pitch. Pushing the control to the high-rpm setting is getting you ready in case you must abort the landing and climb quickly. Opening the throttle gets you maximum rpm

Figure 14-15: Take one last look at the full panel to make final settings for landing, and then reduce it to basic instruments with W on the keyboard.

now, if you need it. Hold your pitch at the same 2° nose-up you've been using, and the Mooney slows to 90 knots.

If you used 19 inches of MP and pitched down a bit for about 0°, the Mooney would start sinking at 500 fpm and 100 knots. That's what you'll use for approaches in the next section. For an airport traffic pattern, use this variation that works a bit better.

LANDING

Switch back to the reduced view with the W key or virtual cockpit if your computer can handle the graphics demands, and turn to the base leg after you've descended 200 feet from the pattern altitude of 1,900 feet and the runway is about 30–45° behind you. Don't dally rolling into and out of this turn. You're going faster than you're used to and are on base for only a moment. Also consider using a bit more bank angle than you're used to in a slower airplane. The increased angle increases your rate of turn and decreases your radius of turn.

Look forward and left with your hat switch on your control yoke to make sure that the landing threshold is where it should be, and then extend full flaps. The same pitch attitude should give you about 80 knots now. Begin your turn to final. You should be about 500 feet above the runway now.

Figure 14-16: Mooneys have a reputation for floating along just above the ground when the pilot wants to land. Usually, this is the result of landing just a bit too quickly. As the numbers disappear behind the instruments, bring the power to idle, and begin the flare to slow and land.

Lined up on final for Runway 36, you pitch up slightly to slow to 75 knots (see Figure 14-16). Hold this speed all the way down to your landing flare. You can add or remove power as needed to adjust your rate of descent. When you're on very short final, reduce the power to idle. A moment later, you flare the Mooney and settle smoothly onto the runway. If you're using the virtual cockpit view, reduce the power to idle about one second after the numbers disappear beneath the cowling.

The Mooney uses quite a bit more runway on landing than the Cessna or Cub. This is normal. You can challenge yourself by trying to land the Mooney in as short a distance as possible. With precise power control and an approach speed of just over 60 knots, you can actually stop by the first taxiway. Don't try this in a real Mooney, though, or your mechanic will be able to buy a new boat with the money you pay for repairs to your landing gear when it drops hard onto the pavement.

You can see the entire pattern for the Mooney in Figure 14-17.

75 Knots, Gear Down, Full Flaps, MP as Needed

80 Knots, Gear Down, Full Flaps, 17 Inches MP

90 Knots, Gear Down, Approach Flaps, 17 Inches MP

Figure 14-17: Here's the whole traffic pattern for the Mooney Bravo.

328

PART I | PART II | PART III | PART IV | PART V | PART VI
PRESIDENT | SPORT PILOT | PRIVATE PILOT | INSTRUMENT RATING | COMMERCIAL LICENSE | ATP AND BEYOND

⬇ KEEPING IT REAL

TURBO COOL DOWN

Many turbochargers require that you idle the engine for five minutes or so after you land and before you shut down to cool the lubricating oil in the turbocharger. There is some controversy over whether this is really necessary. But if you're planning on flying a real turbocharged airplane, get in the habit of starting a timer in the airplane as you clear the runway.

⬇ SEE THE MOVIE

To visualize entering the traffic pattern in the Mooney, watch the Chap_14_Mooney_pattern flight video on the website at **www.wiley.com**.

MOONEY UNDER GLASS

The FSX Mooney Bravo also comes with the full G1000 glass cockpit. Load the same flight, but change the aircraft to the G1000 Mooney and take it out for a spin. Just be aware that the virtual cockpit version of the G1000 Mooney might bring a lesser computer system to its knees. Be sure to switch to the landing panel, shown in Figure 14-18, when you line up on final.

Figure 14-18: Even the landing panel view for the G1000 obscures quite a bit of the runway. The W key will work with the G1000 Mooney, too, but you'll see steam-gauge instruments.

ACCIDENT CHAIN

ACCIDENT REPORT: COMIN' IN HOT

Location: Burnsville, North Carolina

Aircraft: Mooney M20M

Injuries: 4 uninjured

"The pilot stated that he completed the before-landing checklist, lowered the landing gear, extended the flaps, and activated the speed brakes. The pilot turned on final approach and extended the flaps to the full down position. When the airplane was over the landing threshold, the pilot decreased the throttle. The airplane began to float, touched down on the runway, bounced, and porpoised three times. The airplane was approaching the end of the runway, and the pilot locked the brakes. The airplane went off the end of the runway, through the runway overrun, and down an embankment before it came to a complete stop."

Location: Banner Elk, North Carolina

Aircraft: Mooney M20M

Injuries: 1 minor

"The pilot stated that when he had the airport in sight, he canceled his IFR flight plan and entered the left downwind for Runway 12. He made an unusually steep and fast final approach. The pilot stated that midway down the runway he realized that he was too fast and was afraid to attempt a go-around. The pilot stated that he forced the airplane onto the runway and overran the end of the runway into a ravine."

Location: Gualala, California

Aircraft: Mooney M20M

Injuries: 1 minor, 1 uninjured

"The airplane contacted bushes and rising terrain during an attempted go-around. The pilot said that although he was familiar with his airplane, he had never landed on an actual short-field runway. The airport's Runway 31 is 2,500 feet long, with a 300-foot displaced threshold, and trees are present in the approach path. He followed the specified right-hand traffic pattern and utilized a short-field approach procedure, with the wing flaps fully extended and the approach speed at 65 knots. The airplane drifted over the left side of the runway. Rather than attempting to redirect the airplane's course, the pilot applied full engine power to go around. Seconds thereafter, as the engine power increased, the airplane impacted rising terrain and bushes."

Continued

330

| PART I | PART II | PART III | PART IV | PART V | PART VI |
| PREFLIGHT | SPORT PILOT | PRIVATE PILOT | INSTRUMENT RATING | COMMERCIAL LICENSE | ATP AND BEYOND |

Notice a theme here? Many pilots have gotten themselves into trouble flying high-performance airplanes the same way they flew their low-performance trainers. Successful flights in a Mooney aren't harder; they just require more planning and are less forgiving of inattention or carelessness. We won't even start on the topic of all the incidents of pilots forgetting to lower the gear for landing. In a real-world Mooney or the FSX one, following your standard procedures and profiles as a baseline and then adjusting from there will keep you out of most trouble.

KEY POINTS FOR REAL FLYING AND FSX BUILT-INS

The following are some key points from this chapter:

- Use standard flight profiles for transitioning to a new aircraft and flying high-performance aircraft.

- Understand the increased planning and anticipation needed when flying a faster, more complex airplane.

Here are the lessons and missions to study after reading this chapter:

- *Lessons*: None for this chapter.

- *Missions*: Hawaiian Checkout, Rome–Naples Airline Run, Caribbean Landing. The first mission is actually a Mooney checkout. The other two are basic airline flights, but they reinforce the concept of flying a fast, complex airplane by the numbers.

INSTRUMENT RATING

PART

IV

CONTENTS

CHAPTER 15

BASIC ATTITUDE INSTRUMENT FLYING

"A FIERCE AND MONKISH ART; A CASTIGATION OF THE FLESH. YOU MUST CUT OUT YOUR IMAGINATION AND NOT FLY AN AIRPLANE BUT REGULATE A HALF DOZEN INSTRUMENTS.... AT FIRST, THE CONFLICTS BETWEEN ANIMAL SENSE AND ENGINEERING BRAIN ARE IRRESISTIBLY STRONG."

—WILLIAM LANGEWIESCHE

334

PART I
PREFLIGHT

PART II
SPORT PILOT

PART III
PRIVATE PILOT

PART IV
INSTRUMENT RATING

PART V
COMMERCIAL LICENSE

PART VI
ATP AND BEYOND

FLY IN THE CLOUDS

Figure 15-1: If you want to fly this close to clouds, you have to have an Instrument Rating.

For pure enjoyment of flight, nothing beats a lazy, Sunday-afternoon jaunt over fields and forests, preferably in a Cub with the windows open and the sounds and smells drifting in. But when you really want to take advantage of an airplane's speed and distance-shortening capabilities, you need to be able to fly in less than perfect weather. For that, you need to follow the instrument flight rules (IFR), and that requires an Instrument Rating (see Figure 15-1). Training for an Instrument Rating begins with learning to keep the airplane upright using only your instruments, and that's what's covered in this chapter, using the Mooney Bravo you started flying in Chapter 14.

You're also moving to what might be the IFR capital of the United States—Seattle, Washington, and Boeing Field, (KBFI). Boeing sits just two miles from downtown Seattle on one end and only four miles from Seattle-Tacoma International Airport (KSEA) on the other. It's so close to Sea-Tac airport, as it's called, that the traffic pattern on the west side of the field is only 800 AGL to stay out of the path of landing airliners. Welcome to the big city.

IFR GROUND CHECKS

Before you can venture into the clouds, you need to make sure the plane and, most important, the instruments are ready to go.

When you get the altimeter setting for the airport (by listening to ATIS or ASOS automated weather), set the altimeter as usual with the knob or with B on the keyboard. But now, ensure the altimeter reads airport elevation so you know you can trust it; if it's more than 75 feet off, you can't fly.

You'll be using the vertical speed indicator (VSI) more now in instrument flying, so you want it to be accurate. When you're stopped on the ground, you have no vertical speed at all; if the VSI shows something other than 0, then either get it adjusted or treat whatever number it says as your new 0 fpm.

VOR CHECK

FSX VOR receivers are always accurate (unless you intentionally fail them, in which case they completely fail). Real-world VOR receivers are usually accurate, but over time, they can degrade and become more inaccurate. Unfortunately, you won't know they are inaccurate without a test. To legally fly IFR using VORs for navigation, they have to have been checked (accurate to within 4°) within the last 30 days using one of several possible tests:

- Tune to a VOR test facility (VOT) located at certain airports (not simulated in FSX).

- Taxi the aircraft to a specified spot at an airport, and check the VOR radial from a specified VOR.

- Fly over a specified, easily identified spot on the ground, and check the VOR radial from a specified VOR.

- Use several other, less common test methods.

GPS receivers have their own self-testing systems, so you won't need to worry about them unless they give a warning message saying they are inaccurate.

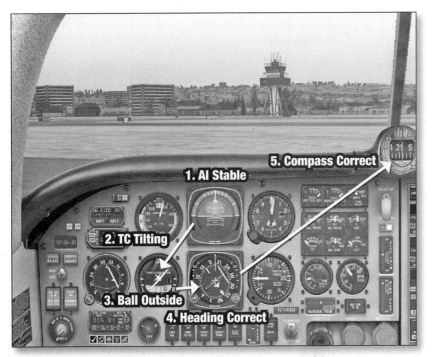

Figure 15-2: Your IFR taxi check is this flow around the instrument panel while turning on the ground.

Before you start to taxi, reset the heading indicator to the same heading as the compass: press D on the keyboard. As you taxi, and especially as you turn corners on the taxiway, glance at the following instruments to ensure they're working as expected (as shown in Figure 15-2):

- *Attitude indicator*: Stable, not tilting more than 5° during taxiing turns

- *Turn coordinator*: Tilting the correct direction with turns

- *Inclinometer (ball)*: Swinging to the outside of turns

336

PART I	PART II	PART III	PART IV	PART V	PART VI
PREFLIGHT	SPORT PILOT	PRIVATE PILOT	INSTRUMENT RATING	COMMERCIAL LICENSE	ATP AND BEYOND

- *Heading indicator*: Also moving with turns and on correct headings

- *Compass*: Swinging freely in turns and, on straightaways, pointing at the correct heading

If any instruments don't operate as expected (and in FSX they should all work fine unless you intentionally set them on fail), have a mechanic take a look before you fly.

When you're cleared for takeoff, memorize and follow this checklist, which uses the acronym LIST-MD:

- *L*: Lights on (as needed)

- *I*: Icing on (if your plane has any anti-icing equipment and you are flying into icing within a few minutes)

- *S*: Squawk (transponder on)

- *T*: Time (record the time)

- *M*: Mixture set for takeoff

- *D*: Directional gyro (now called the *heading indicator*) set (on runway heading, when lined up on the runway)

The IFR Scan: Attitude Is Everything

Figure 15-3: The hub-and-spoke scan system centers on the attitude indicator, with brief glances at the other instruments, always returning to spend the most time on the aircraft's attitude.

When flying under IFR but actually in visual meteorological conditions (VMC), you should fly just about like you always have: look outside the airplane 80 to 90 percent of the time, and use the horizon to control the airplane's attitude, glancing at the instrument panel once in a while to make sure you're on proper heading, altitude, and so on.

When you're about to enter an area of low visibility or clouds—instrument meteorological conditions (IMC)—you need to switch to using your instruments for all your aircraft control information. You can use any of several methods to scan your instruments for information you need, but we find the best scan is called the *hub-and-spoke* system (see Figure 15-3). This is based on the idea that, just like flying in VMC conditions, you can most easily control the airplane if you monitor the plane's attitude. In this case, that means spending most of your time looking at the attitude indicator. (As an FAA safety advisor was fond of saying, "The attitude indicator always has clear skies and unlimited visibility!") Even slight changes in attitude show up on the attitude indicator long before they show up on the altimeter, heading indicator, or other instruments.

However, you should never fixate on any one instrument too long, not even the attitude indicator. The idea is to start at the *hub*—the attitude indicator—and move out a *spoke* to another instrument—like the airspeed indicator—for cross-check before returning to the attitude indicator hub. Try to spend about half of the time looking at the attitude indicator and the other half shared among the other five instruments, with brief looks to engine instruments and radios as needed.

⬇ STUDENT OF THE CRAFT

A SIX-PACK TO GO

The traditional six-pack of primary aircraft instruments makes the hub-and-spoke scan easy to do, with the attitude indicator in the top center position and the other five positions filled with the most important control instruments. Before about 1960, though, instrument panels weren't so well organized. Each manufacturer placed instruments wherever they wanted to fit them. This made it even more important to spend time training on a new aircraft in safe, VMC conditions before venturing into the clouds.

Airspeed is more critical in IFR flight than VFR flight…not because the plane behaves differently but because you're now following specific instructions from air traffic controllers, and they might be expecting you to fly a certain airspeed or, at least, to tell them whether you can't maintain a certain airspeed.

Altitude is also more critical than it was in VFR flight. You need to maintain your ATC-assigned altitude within 100 feet, and controllers are counting on that so they can pass another plane above or below you without causing a midair collision (or at least not passing so close that the controllers have to fill out lots of paperwork). You can't just look around for other aircraft to avoid when you're in the clouds.

Figure 15-4: The turn coordinator and VSI become much more important during instrument flight.

The VSI was merely an interesting device when you were learning to fly, but now it becomes a regular part of your instrument scan (see Figure 15-4). When an air traffic controller advises you to climb or descend to a new altitude, you're expected to go at least 500 feet per minute; if you can't go that fast, you have to tell the controller.

The turn coordinator is also moving from a nice-to-know instrument into an important one. Remember that, during a turn, when the little airplane in the TC is aligned with the lower line, you're in a standard-rate turn of 3° per second, or 360° per 2 minutes. With just a few exceptions, you should make your turns at standard rate when in IMC.

338

| PART I | PART II | PART III | PART IV | PART V | PART VI |
| PREFLIGHT | SPORT PILOT | PRIVATE PILOT | INSTRUMENT RATING | COMMERCIAL LICENSE | ATP AND BEYOND |

And let's not forget the little inclinometer, the ball. Unless you're in a coordinated turn with the ball in the center, you can't expect the plane to behave the way the other instruments seem to be indicating that it should be behaving.

In the previous chapter you were introduced to the idea of control performance as a device for simplifying aircraft control. It becomes even more critical during instrument flight, because you'll be busy with many more things to do.

Here's a review from Chapter 14 of the flight profiles for the Mooney:

	MP	RPM	Config.	Pitch	Indicated Airspeed	Rate of Climb
Cruise Climb	34 inches	2400 rpm	Flaps and gear up	+5°	110	+700 fpm
High Cruise	34 inches	2400 rpm	Flaps and gear up	+0°	160	0 (level flight)
Cruise Descent	32 to 25 inches	2200 rpm	Flaps and gear up	−2°	170 to 155	−500 fpm
Low Cruise	25 inches	2200 rpm	Flaps and gear up	+2°	120	0
Approach Level	25 inches	2200 rpm	Flaps up but gear down	+2°	100	0
Approach Descent	19 inches	Prop control Full Forward	Approach flaps and gear down	+0°	100	−500 fpm

THE AUTOPILOT

The first few times you fly in the clouds, you'll be learning how to control the airplane using only your instruments; it wouldn't exactly be a good training exercise if you used the autopilot to fly the airplane (see Figure 15-5). Later in your instrument training, as you learn about navigating and flying instrument approaches, you can use the autopilot to control the airplane so you can concentrate on learning the technical aspects of IFR flying. Finally, you put them together so you can fly an entire flight by hand. For this chapter, though, leave the autopilot off.

Figure 15-5: The autopilot keeps the shiny side up and the dirty side down if you start to lose control of the airplane.

However, the one thing you don't have in your instrument training that a real-world student would have is an instructor ready to grab the controls if you lose control in the clouds (unless you set up for multiplayer in FSX). Therefore, you need to be ready to use the autopilot if you start to lose control of the airplane. If that happens, just click the HDG and ALT buttons on the autopilot, and it will take control. Even if you've got the heading bug set somewhere completely different from your current heading, the autopilot takes you there slowly and carefully (standard-rate turn, in fact), and you can take the time to breathe and regain control of the airplane yourself. (This is how you do it in real airplanes, too.)

IFR WEATHER

An instrument rating might let you fly in clouds and such, but it doesn't mean you can fly in *any* weather. A small plane can't handle some situations, and there are even some weather conditions that big airliners avoid.

The first issue is ice. To get ice on your airplane during flight requires two things: visible precipitation (rain, clouds, fog, and so on) and freezing temperatures. This is not just a winter circumstance, though; temperature drops at an average rate of 2° C per 1,000 feet of altitude. So, a nice summer day of 30° C (86° F) at sea level in Seattle means it's probably freezing above 15,000 feet MSL, an altitude well within the capabilities of your turbocharged Mooney Bravo. Fly through a nice, wet cloud at that altitude, and you probably get ice. Sure, it melts off as soon as you descend, but meanwhile your pitot tube might get blocked (turn on your pitot heat), and—in the real world—you slow down as you gain weight and the wing becomes less able to produce lift. (FSX doesn't simulate airframe ice, but it does simulate pitot blockage from ice.) On a colder day, of course, it's much more of an issue; there might not be any above-freezing air between you and the ground/hills/towers/buildings.

Don't forget about carburetor ice. You can get carburetor ice when you're in VMC conditions if enough humidity is in the air and it's relatively cool, but now that you're flying in clouds (high humidity), a much greater chance of carburetor ice exists in planes that have a carburetor induction system. (The Mooney has fuel injection, so induction ice isn't much of a problem.)

Most small, real-world airplanes don't have any way to handle ice, beyond pitot heat and carburetor heat. Some aircraft are certified for flight into known icing because they have, in addition to pitot heat, ways to remove ice from the wings, tail, propeller, and at least part of the windshield (so you can see out when you need to land).

Figure 15-6: You can usually avoid isolated thunderstorms, but if they're embedded in layers of clouds, you might not see them until it's too late.

The next issue is thunderstorms. You have to avoid them by a wide margin, whether VFR or IFR, because the turbulence and hail can rip your plane apart (see Figure 15-6). When you're flying in VMC conditions and you see a big, dark cloud ahead of you, you have to go around it. (Ask permission from ATC if you're flying IFR—we talk about that later in this chapter.) But what if you're in clouds already and can't see that thunderstorm ahead? That's called an *embedded thunderstorm*, and it's a serious danger. Some airplanes have onboard weather radar or can upload NEXRAD weather radar like you see on TV, but no FSX planes comes with it. In the real world, the way to avoid a thunderstorm in the air is to give a call to the aviation weather frequency and ask them to check their weather radar; in FSX, you just have to take your chances.

340

| PART I | PART II | PART III | PART IV | PART V | PART VI |
| PREFLIGHT | SPORT PILOT | PRIVATE PILOT | INSTRUMENT RATING | COMMERCIAL LICENSE | ATP AND BEYOND |

The other weather hazards you've learned about, such as microbursts, strong winds, and so on, are more likely in IFR weather, so you have to be even more careful when planning a flight.

As before, if you use the real-world weather option in FSX (which we won't do during training, but you can on your own), you can use real-world aviation weather forecasting to see whether a flight will be safe.

↓ KEEPING IT REAL

VIEW-LIMITING DEVICE

In the real world, we usually accomplish this first instrument flight lesson in VMC conditions and under VFR rules with a device that blocks the student's view out the window. Called a *view-limiting device*, it's designed so the instructor can still see outside for safety.

We have to do this because flying under IFR is restrictive and the controllers are expecting you to behave as a normal IFR flight. They can't deal with a student just learning who can't maintain a heading and altitude.

It's just another advantage of learning to fly in FSX: we can send you into the clouds and ignore ATC for now.

IMC FLIGHT IN MOONEY BRAVO

Training for your Instrument Rating takes place in Seattle, Washington, home of some of the best IMC weather in the country. You won't be flying under real IFR for this chapter, but instead, you take advantage of the virtual reality of FSX and go into clouds so you can practice flying solely by reference to your instruments.

Load the flight Chap_15_ Mooney, which puts you on the ramp at Boeing Field/King County International Airport (KBFI), shown in Figure 15-7. This is probably one of the busiest airports you've been to in the training so far, and the airport is only 3 miles from an even busier airport, Seattle-Tacoma International Airport (KSEA). Don't be surprised to see other planes on the ground or in the air nearby.

Figure 15-7: The Chap_15_Mooney flight starts at Boeing Field in Seattle, Washington. You'll see everything from Cubs heading to Alaska to Boeing 747s returning from test flights.

↓ FRAME RATE IN THE CITY

You might need to decrease the visual quality in your display options when you fly to and from Boeing Field. FSX has very detailed buildings and textures for Seattle, and a lot of ground and air traffic is in the vicinity. Even the authors' customized gaming computers from Alienware and WidowPC don't give a good frame rate (greater than 15 fps) unless Scenery is set to Medium-High or less.

After your preflight and engine start (the FSX checklists for the Mooney are good for these), listen to the ATIS for Boeing Field on 127.75, and set the altimeter; double-check that the altimeter reads 18 feet, Boeing Field's elevation.

Call the ground controller, and ask to depart north. As you taxi to the runway, perform the IFR taxi check to ensure that your instruments are all working well. Call the tower, and when you get your takeoff clearance, perform the LIST-MD memorized checklist. Depart the airport to the northeast (Figure 15-8), and climb to 4,000 feet. (Don't forget to open cowl flaps during taxi, takeoff, and climb and then close them during cruise and descent.)

342

PART I	PART II	PART III	PART IV	PART V	PART VI
PAST FLIGHT	SPORT PILOT	PRIVATE PILOT	INSTRUMENT RATING	COMMERCIAL LICENSE	ATP AND BEYOND

Figure 15-8: After takeoff, turn northeast, and head past Seattle.

At 4,000 feet, set the controls for a low cruise of 120 knots. A solid overcast is about 500 feet above you, and it's time to climb into that overcast and begin your instrument training. To climb to 5,000 feet, transition to a cruise climb—reference your chart if you need a refresher.

When you enter the clouds, remember to spend most of your time looking at the attitude indicator. Level off at 5,000 feet, and accelerate to a high cruise of 160 knots.

Basic IFR Maneuvers

Figure 15-9: To start and end each maneuver, use the attitude indicator to get close to the proper attitude and then fine-tune with the other instruments.

You're now going to practice several simple maneuvers. Because you won't be using the autopilot for these maneuvers, you need to be adept at trimming the airplane. Every time you get the plane into a new configuration and the speed, turn rate, and so on, settle down, trim the plane so you don't have to hold the elevator controls. You're going to need this to be second nature because, in the next few chapters, you'll be doing a lot of other things while flying in the clouds—such as talking on the radio and navigating with complicated charts—so you need all the help with aircraft control that you can get.

One of the best things you can do to help your maneuvers is to start and finish each step by referencing the attitude indicator (see Figure 15-9). For instance,

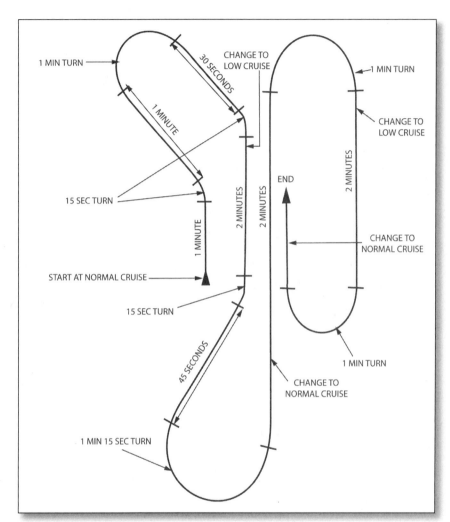

Figure 15-10: Do the basic maneuvers at constant altitude but changing airspeed and heading. (A full-size version of this diagram is available on the website.)

when turning, use the attitude indicator to roll to about a 20° bank (and maintain level pitch). Then look at your turn coordinator to adjust the turn to standard rate. While in the turn, do your normal scan with the attitude indicator at the center of attention. When you're close to your desired heading, stay looking at your attitude indicator to roll level, and then adjust as needed to get the correct heading. It's the same process with a climb or descent.

You do this first set of maneuvers at a constant altitude of 5,000 feet; start at a heading of 360 (north) and 160 knots. You do the turns according to time (for example, "turn for 15 seconds"), so you'll need a clock of some kind— either one of your own or the clock in the Mooney's panel. The speed changes from high cruise (160 knots) to low cruise (120 knots) at various points in the procedure. (Figure 15-10 shows the whole set of maneuvers; print the larger version on the website at www.wiley.com for easy reference.)

Here are the steps:

1. **Fly heading 360 for 1 minute.**

2. **Turn left for 15 seconds (at a standard-rate turn).**

3. **Fly straight for 1 minute.**

4. **Turn right for 1 minute.**

344

| PART I | PART II | PART III | PART IV | PART V | PART VI |
| PREFLIGHT | SPORT PILOT | PRIVATE PILOT | INSTRUMENT RATING | COMMERCIAL LICENSE | ATP AND BEYOND |

5. Fly straight for 30 seconds.

6. Turn right for 15 seconds.

7. Fly straight for 2 minutes while slowing to low cruise of 120 knots.

8. Turn right for 15 seconds

9. Fly straight for 45 seconds.

10. Turn left for 1 minute 15 seconds.

11. Fly straight for 2 minutes while accelerating to high cruise of 160 knots.

12. Turn right for 1 minute.

13. Fly straight for 2 minutes while slowing to low cruise.

14. Turn right for 1 minute.

15. Accelerate to high cruise to finish the procedure.

Briefly turn on the autopilot with a heading of 360 and altitude of 5,000 feet, which should be pretty close to where you are anyway. Let the autopilot fly while you evaluate your performance: Were you able to maintain standard-rate turns? Did you maintain altitude during the turns and when changing speeds? Did you get distracted and not start the next maneuver in time? Did you maintain coordination with the ball? Throughout the maneuvers, did you ever exceed 165 knots or get slower than 115 knots? And, most important, did you spend most of your time looking at the attitude indicator?

One trick that might help you keep on track is to say out loud the time when you glance at your clock. For instance, during a 1-minute turn, you might say, "15 seconds…30 seconds…45 seconds…1 minute, roll out." That trick reminds you when you're getting close to the proper time and you need to stop doing other things and get ready to straighten out (or whatever). And yes, we do say it out loud; for some reason, human brains can multitask better when we actually verbalize. (If you're embarrassed that someone else will think it's silly that you're talking out loud, recruit them to read the steps to you so you don't have to keep looking at this book while you fly. It's hard for them to make fun of you when they're helping you!)

Try the set of maneuvers again, this time talking your way through it. Do it as many times as you need, taking breaks with the autopilot whenever necessary to clear your mind. It's easy to get frustrated with your progress (which might seem like lack of progress sometimes), but flying using just the instruments is as challenging as first learning to fly.

ADVANCED IFR MANEUVERS

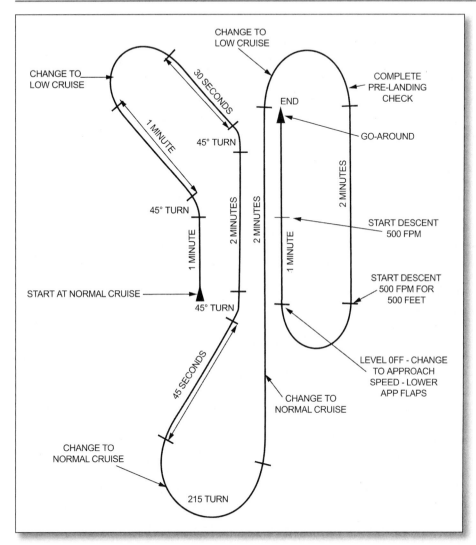

Figure 15-11: The advanced maneuvers are done with altitude changes, airspeed changes, and turns to specific headings. (A full-size version of this diagram is available on the website.)

When you feel comfortable with the first maneuvers, try this next set (see Figure 15-11). This time you are changing airspeed, altitude, and heading, and you're even putting the gear and flaps down and up.

Just like you said the time out loud in the "Basic IFR Maneuvers" section, each time you glance at the heading indicator during your scan of the instruments, say the current heading as well as the heading to which you're turning. For instance, "turning 030 for 120...turning 080 for 120..." and so on. We also use a trick to stop at the right altitude, although we usually say how much we have left to change: "1,000 to go...500 to go...300 to go..." and so on.

Here are the steps:

1. Start the procedure on heading 360 at 6,000 feet and high-speed cruise for one minute.

2. Turn left to heading 315.

346

| PART I | PART II | PART III | **PART IV** | PART V | PART VI |
| FIRST FLIGHT | SPORT PILOT | PRIVATE PILOT | INSTRUMENT RATING | COMMERCIAL LICENSE | ATP AND BEYOND |

3. Fly straight for 1 minute.

4. Turn right to heading 135 while slowing to low cruise.

5. Fly straight for 30 seconds.

6. Turn right to heading 180.

7. Fly straight for 2 minutes.

8. Turn right to heading 225.

9. Fly straight for 45 seconds.

10. Turn left (all the way around) to heading 360 while accelerating to high cruise.

11. Fly straight for 2 minutes.

12. Turn right to heading 180 while slowing to low cruise.

13. Fly straight for 2 minutes.

14. Turn right to heading 360 while descending at 500 fpm to 5,500 feet at low cruise.

15. At 5,500 feet and heading 360, fly straight for one minute while you level off, drop the landing gear, set approach flaps, and slow to 100 knots.

16. Descend at 100 knots and 500 fpm to 5,000 feet.

17. At 5,000 feet, execute a go-around (*missed approach* in IFR terminology): climb at full power, clean up the airplane (gear up, flaps up), and cool the engine (cowl flaps open). Then transition to cruise climb.

18. Level off at 6,000 feet, heading 360, at high cruise. Set autopilot HDG and ALT hold.

How did that go? That was quite a challenge and a bit more realistic. It's actually quite similar to the procedures during an instrument approach you'll do in Chapter 17. If it wasn't as smooth as you eventually want it to be, just practice again.

HEADING HOME

When you're done, descend to 4,000 and turn to a heading of about 170°. When you're out of the clouds, if you know where you are and where Boeing Field is, you can head there now. If you're not sure where you are or if you can't see through the haze yet, use the GPS to go direct to NOLLA intersection. When you're less than 20 miles from NOLLA, it is safe to descend to 2,500 feet.

Figure 15-12: As you fly to Boeing Field from NOLLA intersection, you pass by Seattle's waterfront.

When you're within 10 miles of NOLLA, listen to the Boeing Field ATIS on 127.75, and then call the tower on 118.30.

At NOLLA intersection, turn to heading 130, and head toward the runway at Boeing Field, which is about 7 miles away (see Figure 15-12). You can descend to 1,000 feet until you have the runway in sight. Both Runway 13L and 13R have approach slope lights to help guide you down to the runway.

When you've had a break and you're ready to fly again, try the whole flight from the beginning; you'll find you're a lot better the second time. If you're happy with your performance, jump into the Mooney with the Garmin G1000 flight displays for the next lesson.

IFR FLIGHT WITH GARMIN G1000

Basic attitude instrument flying with the Garmin G1000 has its own benefits and problems. The biggest benefit, as you discovered when flying the Cessna 172 with the G1000, is that huge attitude indicator. It's hard to lose control of an airplane when you can see the attitude even with your peripheral vision.

On the other hand, you need to train yourself to do the scan a bit differently. The concept is the same—spend most of your time monitoring the plane's attitude with brief glances at the other instruments—but the location of those other instruments has changed.

Load the Chap_15_G1000 flight (see Figure 15-13). Do the preflight the same as before, and then fly both the basic and advanced IFR maneuvers you did with the Mooney with regular instruments.

348

| PART I | PART II | PART III | PART IV | PART V | PART VI |
| PREFLIGHT | SPORT PILOT | PRIVATE PILOT | INSTRUMENT RATING | COMMERCIAL LICENSE | ATP AND BEYOND |

Figure 15-13: The Chap_15_G1000 flight begins at the same spot on Boeing Field in Seattle.

One issue you might notice with the G1000 is that you can tell when you're not exactly on the correct heading or altitude. For instance, if you're supposed to be at 5,000 feet but you're at 4990, try to get up those last 10 feet. (When you flew the Mooney with regular instruments, you probably barely noticed when it was 10 or even 20 feet off, because the altimeter needle was only slightly off 5,000.) Yes, you should try to get right on altitude, but remember not to fixate on any one instrument. If you're in the middle of a turn or trying to deal with ATC on the radio, don't distract yourself with perfecting that last 10 feet. Do it when you can concentrate on it. Power settings, however—rpm to be specific—usually require the close enough treatment. They're just too squirrelly.

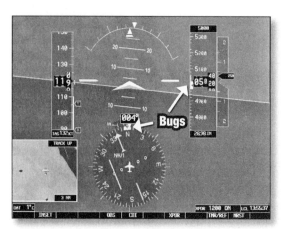

Figure 15-14: Heading and altitude bugs help you spot deviations.

Ironically, if you're not looking right at the altitude on the G1000, you might miss when you're off, because it's just some numbers changing. (The needle on the regular altimeter, when it does get off altitude, catches your attention because it isn't in an obvious position—like straight up when at 5,000.) Setting the heading and altitude bugs—even when you're not using the autopilot—helps you spot when those are off (see Figure 15-14).

When you're good at attitude instrument flying with both regular instruments and the Garmin G1000, you are ready for the next chapter where you start and end the flight in visual conditions. The whole flight itself is in the clouds, and you are talking to air traffic controllers the whole time!

⬇ STUDENT OF THE CRAFT

DUDE, WHERE'S MY RATE OF TURN?

When you first learned to fly with the Garmin G1000 in the Cessna in Chapter 11, you might not have missed the turn coordinator. But as an IFR pilot, you need to know when you're making a standard-rate turn. How can you do it?

You learned that the G1000 has *trend* indicators—the pink lines that show where your airspeed and altitude are in six seconds. Did you notice that the heading indicator also shows a pink arc at the top when you're turning? It's showing where your heading will be in six seconds. Garmin put little white lines above the heading indicator at 9 and 18°, which equals 1.5 and 3° per second or half-standard-rate and standard-rate turns.

Oh, and don't forget that the G1000 also has a ball (the inclinometer)—the split pyramid at the top of the attitude indicator.

KEY POINTS FOR REAL FLYING AND FSX BUILT-INS

The following are some key points from this chapter:

- Conduct necessary preflight checks for airplane and pilot.

- Scan the instruments for attitude and control.

- Understand IFR weather hazards.

- Practice basic and advanced IFR maneuvers.

Here are the lessons and missions to study after reading this chapter:

- *Lessons*: In the Instrument Pilot section, Solo Flight: Scanning the Instruments is similar to this lesson and would be good to fly for variety.

- *Missions*: None.

"ROUTINE INSTRUMENT FLIGHT IS SHROUDED IN A GRAY, UN-KNOWABLE MIST OF ATC PROCEDURES. AND YET IT'S YOUR DUTY TO SLOG THROUGH THIS MIASMA WITH A STEELY EYED GAZE THAT INSTILLS CONFIDENCE IN LOVED ONES STRAPPED TO THE SEATS AROUND YOU."

—PAUL BERGE, IFR MAGAZINE

352

PART I	PART II	PART III	PART IV	PART V	PART VI
PREFLIGHT	SPORT PILOT	PRIVATE PILOT	INSTRUMENT RATING	COMMERCIAL LICENSE	ATP AND BEYOND

FLIGHT PLAN CREATION

The primary goal of an instrument flight—and, therefore, the plan for an instrument flight—is to get you and your plane from the ground into the air and back to the ground without hitting anything or anyone else, all while not seeing more than a few feet in front of you. Sure, on most flights you can see plenty; some IFR flights even take place in completely clear, visual conditions. But the plan has to be able to work even if you go into the clouds soon after takeoff and don't emerge again until you're a few hundred feet above your destination runway.

You have two primary ways to navigate in IFR: radar vectors from air traffic control (ATC) or your own navigation using your instruments and radios. Radar vectors are much easier: just follow the air traffic controller's instructions to "turn left heading 300; climb and maintain 3,000; contact Approach control on 125.90." In the virtual world of FSX, though, radar is available everywhere in the world, and a controller is standing by just waiting for your call.

STUDENT OF THE CRAFT

ATC RADAR

In FSX you're always in radar contact, where the controllers can see you on their radar screens and give you vectors wherever you need to go. In the real world, that isn't always true. Radar antennas are not located everywhere, and if you're not near a big city, it is likely the controller can't see you when you're low either taking off or landing.

So, how can controllers keep you away from other planes if they can't see you on radar? They use the "one in, one out" method. If they give you a clearance to leave an airport, they won't let any other pilots take off or land at that airport until they see you pop up on their radar screen. Pilots nearby who want to land at that same airport might have to go into a holding pattern to wait their turn.

But in the real world, radar doesn't go everywhere; even places that normally have radar might have an equipment malfunction. In fact, a more common situation isn't *radar* failure—it's *radio* failure (this happens more often in the airplane, but sometimes ATC radio failure does happen). If you can't talk to ATC, you can't get vectors. The entire IFR flight-planning system evolved from a nonradar, limited-radio system, so it can get you from one airport to another incommunicado, if necessary.

ATC AND FLIGHT PLANS

As a VFR pilot, you mostly used ATC only for taking off from and landing at airports, but with IFR, you're always dealing with ATC. (In fact, the ATC system was created for IFR flying in the first place!) In IFR, you always need a clearance from ATC. Usually, you get this before you even take off. (This is different from "Cleared for takeoff" from a control tower; an IFR clearance is approval for your whole route from a departure airport to a destination airport.) Often you have a special radio frequency to call the air traffic controllers for your clearance. But rather than clogging up the radio as you tell the controller all the waypoints in your desired route, you should file a flight plan before you even get to the airplane. That's another major difference when flying IFR: you *always* have a flight plan in the ATC computer system when flying IFR (it's optional in VFR flying). In the real world, you can do this by phone or on the Internet; in FSX, you choose the Flights > Flight Planner menu option, which we discuss at the beginning of this chapter's flight.

After you file your flight plan, you get your ATC clearance (see Figure 16-1). A clearance almost always contains the same set of information, so to help you write it down, remember the acronym CRAFT:

- *C*: Clearance limit

- *R*: Route

- *A*: Altitude

- *F*: Frequency

- *T*: Transponder

Figure 16-1 ATC gives you your clearance over the radio; be prepared to write it all down as quickly as you can, or ask the controller, "Say again?"

The clearance limit is almost always your destination airport; in the real world, however, that airport might be so congested with other airplanes that ATC can't be sure what you're going to be asked to do when you get there. In that case, your clearance limit might be a VOR or intersection along the way; if you haven't received an updated clearance by the time you get to your clearance limit, you have to *hold* there for a while. (We discuss holding later in this chapter.)

In the real world, the route and altitude you file on your flight plan might not be what ATC clears you to do. Sometimes—because of other, conflicting traffic or because of standardized procedures in some airspace—ATC needs to put you on a slightly different route or altitude. In fact, this "change to your clearance" (as they put it) could happen right in the middle of your flight, and you need to be ready with a pencil and paper to write down the changes. That won't happen in FSX, thank

354

| PART I | PART II | PART III | PART IV | PART V | PART VI |
| PREFLIGHT | SPORT PILOT | PRIVATE PILOT | INSTRUMENT RATING | COMMERCIAL LICENSE | ATP AND BEYOND |

goodness; FSX gives you the route you ask for, because there's not enough traffic to require a change. However, the FSX ATC takes you off your flight plan route (using vectors) when you get close to your destination.

After takeoff, you switch to the first departure frequency, so ATC gives you that frequency as part of your clearance. From then on, you are told every time you need to contact another air traffic controller and the frequency to call on. And that's yet another major difference between IFR and VFR flying: IFR pilots are *always* talking to an air traffic controller. In fact, if you ever lose contact with ATC and can't raise anyone on any frequency, it's considered an emergency with a host of lost-communication procedures to deal with. (We talk about that in Chapter 19.)

The last element of a clearance is the four-digit transponder code. Virtually all VFR airplane pilots who aren't talking to ATC use 1200 as their transponder code. But every IFR flight has its own, unique transponder code so ATC can tell exactly which plane is which on their radar scopes.

INSTRUMENT CHARTS

Just like when you planned your VFR flights, an IFR flight plan begins with the charts. The difference is that you need charts for four stages in the flight: departure, en route, arrival, and approach. Departure, arrival, and approach charts are specific to an airport; en route charts cover the areas in between airports. (We cover approach charts and procedures in the next chapter.)

⬇ KEEPING IT REAL

REAL-WORLD IFR CHARTS

To fly under IFR, you should have current charts with you in the aircraft. Procedures are updated frequently—sometimes monthly—because obstructions (such as towers) are built, runways are changed, and so on. For flights in U.S. airspace, the National Aeronautical Charting Office (NACO) provides the latest airport, departure, arrival, and approach charts for free online: http://www.naco.faa.gov/index.asp?xml=naco/online/d_tpp.

Click the product that has an effective date when you want to fly. Then enter the airport identifier, or just search by state/airport name. You can download PDFs of all the current charts for that airport.

En route charts are much harder to find online, and you probably won't be able to just download them. You can buy them on DVD from NACO. You can also purchase individual charts at most local airports. We have included a few key charts for this chapter on the website (www.wiley.com).

Of course, the towers, VORs, and so on, in FSX don't change, so for sim flying, you might not want to have the latest real-world charts. In that case, you need charts that match the database in FSX—see "SIMCharts for FSX."

In the next few sections of this chapter, you'll learn IFR procedures for departure, en route, and arrival. It makes more sense if you have the appropriate charts for each procedure. We've included several on the website; if you print them now, you can follow along as we talk about them in this chapter.

Some charts are available for free online or for low cost from the U.S. government. However, many pilots find charts produced by Jeppesen to be more user-friendly, even though they cost a bit more. This private company uses the same data for the charts, but the charts are laid out in an easy-to-use system. Jeppesen has even created a set of charts called SIMCharts for FSX.

  INSIDE THE GAME

SIMCHARTS FOR FSX

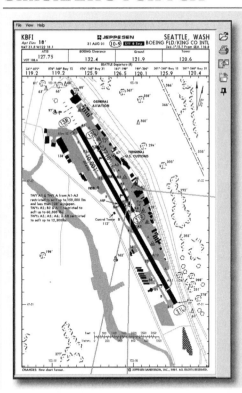

Jeppesen has created software specially designed to show instrument charts with FSX. You get access to Jeppesen's entire library of departure, arrival, and approach charts. Not only that, but the software talks to FSX; as you fly, your position (on some of the charts) is updated with your FSX aircraft's position. With a dual monitor or in windowed mode, you can have both your airplane and your SIM-Chart in view.

If you use SIMCharts for FSX from Jeppesen, you don't have to worry about accuracy, because Jeppesen made the charts accurate for the airport database that ships with FSX. In fact, if you download the latest IFR charts from the U.S. government website at `http://www.naco.faa.gov/index.asp?xml=naco/online/d_tpp`, the charts might contain changes that don't exist in the older FSX database, so technically you won't be using charts current to FSX!

DEPARTURE PROCEDURES

As mentioned earlier, departure procedures are either pilot navigation departures or vectored departures (using ATC radar).

356

PART I	PART II	PART III	PART IV	PART V	PART VI
PREFLIGHT	SPORT PILOT	PRIVATE PILOT	INSTRUMENT RATING	COMMERCIAL LICENSE	ATP AND BEYOND

PILOT NAVIGATION DEPARTURES

A pilot navigation departure could be a simple line of text, such as "After takeoff, proceed on course." Others could be complex and require special procedures to avoid terrain or populated (and noise-sensitive) neighborhoods or to fit between airplanes going to or from other airports.

As an example, look at the ELMAA SEVEN departure procedure at Seattle-Tacoma International Airport (KSEA) available on the website (see Figure 16-2). Examine both the diagram and the following text to figure out how this procedure works:

1. Take off on either Runway 16L or 16C at KSEA.

2. Intercept the Seattle VOR radial 161 until you get to 5 miles (DME) from the VOR (meanwhile climbing to at least 3,000 feet).

3. Turn right to a heading of 250, and fly until you intercept the Seattle VOR radial 230.

4. Follow the SEA R-230 to ELMAA intersection, which is defined as the intersection of the SEA R-230 and the YYJ R-157.

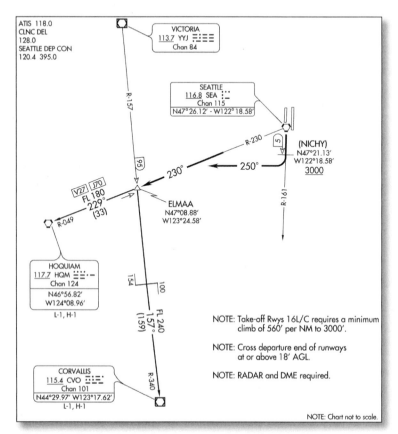

After that, you would follow whatever you planned for your en route section to get to your destination. For instance, if you're going to California, you turn south and follow the YYJ R-157 to Corvallis and beyond—a route that is called "ELMAA SEVEN Departure, Corvallis transition" and is abbreviated ELMAA7.CVO. On the other hand, if you are heading west to Hawaii, you follow the ELMAA7.HQM procedure and go from ELMAA intersection to Hoquiam VOR and across the Pacific Ocean.

Could you navigate this route if the last thing you heard ATC say was "Cleared for takeoff" at Sea-Tac airport? You could, because there are no radar vectors. As long as you made sure the en route portion of your flight plan started at ELMAA, CVO, or another point specified on this chart, you could fly it all by yourself.

Figure 16-2 The ELMAA SEVEN departure procedure from Sea-Tac

OBSTACLE DEPARTURES

A subset of the pilot navigation departures is the obstacle departure. Its only purpose is to help you avoid terrain and obstacles as you climb to the en route portion of your flight.

This kind of departure doesn't have its own chart, so you need to look a little deeper to find the text description of the procedure. For instance, in the online NACO charts, you need to get the *Take-off Minimums and Obstacle Departure Procedures* for the region of the airport from which you're departing. (That PDF for the northwest United States is included on the website.) Dozens of airports are covered in the *Take-Off Minimums* book, listed alphabetically.

> ## WENATCHEE, WA
> ### PANGBORN MEMORIAL
> TAKE-OFF MINIMUMS: **Rwy 7**, NA. **Rwy 12**, 1500-2 or std. with a min. climb of 510' per NM to 2900.
> **Rwys 25, 30**, CAT A,B 1600-2 or std. with a min. climb of 360' per NM to 3100. CAT C,D 5500-3 or std. with a min. climb of 570' per NM to 7200.
> DEPARTURE PROCEDURE: **Rwy 12**, climb runway heading. **Rwys 25, 30**, climbing left turn. **All aircraft** climb via EAT R-113 to 4000 then climbing left turn direct EAT VOR/DME. Aircraft departing EAT R-010 CW R-140 climb on course. All others continue climb in EAT VOR/DME holding pattern (E, right turns, 253° inbound) to cross EAT VOR/DME at or above: R-141 CW R-200 7400; R-201 CW R-009, 8200.

Figure 16-3 The obstacle departure procedure for Wenatchee. Takeoff minimums don't apply to you until you're a commercial pilot, but the departure procedure is important to help you avoid the mountains near Wenatchee.

Let's look at Wenatchee, Washington (KEAT), about 100 nm east of Seattle (see Figure 16-3). The first step is different depending on which runway you launch from: "Rwy 12, climb runway heading. Rwys 25, 30, climbing left turn."

Then you need to get on a radial from the Wenatchee VOR (EAT) until a certain altitude: "All aircraft climb via EAT R-113 to 4000..." Then you go back to the VOR: "...then climbing left, turn direct EAT VOR/DME."

After that, the procedure changes depending on which way you go: "Aircraft departing EAT R-010 CW R-140 climb on course. All others continue climb in EAT VOR/DME holding pattern (E, right turns, 253° inbound) to cross EAT VOR/DME at or above: R-141 CW R-200 7400; R-201 CW R-009, 8200." In this last bit, "CW" means clockwise, so "EAT R-010 CW R140" means all the directions from radial 010 clockwise (increasing radials) to radial 140.

It's unfortunate that no graphic description of this procedure is given, because it would be a lot easier to understand—a picture is worth a thousand words, and all that. Draw a diagram yourself so you can monitor your progress as you follow the procedure.

358

PART I	PART II	PART III	PART IV	PART V	PART VI
PREFLIGHT	SPORT PILOT	PRIVATE PILOT	INSTRUMENT RATING	COMMERCIAL LICENSE	ATP AND BEYOND

 ACCIDENT CHAIN

IGNORING DEPARTURE PROCEDURES

Location: Novato, California

Aircraft: Mooney M20K

Injuries: 1 uninjured

"During the initial climbout, the airplane collided with trees off the departure end of the runway. The pilot had filed an instrument flight rules flight plan but decided to fly according to visual flight rules to his destination airport. He indicated that it was still dark outside for the early morning flight. The pilot said that during the initial climbout he lost visual reference with the ground due to the lack of ground lights and a visible horizon. He activated the autopilot; however, the airplane was not climbing as expected. As he was trying to figure out what the problem was, the stall warning activated; he disengaged the autopilot and attempted to lower the nose. The airplane simultaneously collided with trees. Weather in the accident site at the time of the accident was reported by witnesses to be ⅛-mile visibility with overcast clouds at 100 feet. The pilot stated that there were no mechanical anomalies noted with the airplane. According to the U.S. Naval Observatory, sunrise for the date and location of the accident was at 0541.

"The National Transportation Safety Board determines the probable cause(s) of this accident as follows: the pilot's decision to attempt VFR flight into instrument meteorological conditions during the dark, early-morning takeoff, which resulted in spatial disorientation and led to a collision with trees off the departure end of the runway."

Gnoss Field (KDVO) in Novato has Runways 13 and 31. According to the *Take-off Minimums and Obstacle Departure Procedures*, pilots cannot make an instrument departure from Runway 13. The instructions for an instrument departure from Runway 31 are for a "climbing right turn direct SGD VORTAC before proceeding on course." SGD is approximately heading 060 from KDVO, so it's about a 90-degree right turn.

The NTSB report doesn't say which runway the pilot tried to take off from, but trying to take off VFR when at least one other person said the weather was IMC was the first mistake. It's possible that if the pilot had departed IFR on Runway 31 and remembered to check the IFR departure procedure, he might have seen that right after takeoff he needed to turn, and even though he wasn't climbing quickly, he might have avoided the terrain.

By the way, in the full NTSB report, the pilot states that he figured out why the Mooney wasn't climbing as fast as he expected: he forgot to retract the landing gear. IMC can be a very distracting situation.

VECTOR DEPARTURES

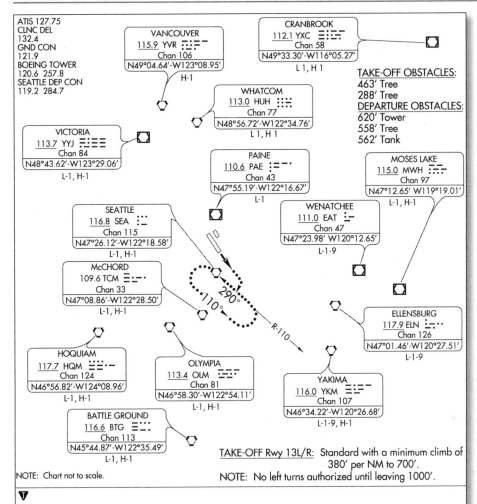

ATIS 127.75
CLNC DEL
132.4
GND CON
121.9
BOEING TOWER
120.6 257.8
SEATTLE DEP CON
119.2 284.7

VANCOUVER
115.9 YVR
Chan 106
N49°04.64'-W123°08.95'
H-1

CRANBROOK
112.1 YXC
Chan 58
N49°33.30'-W116°05.27'
L 1, H 1

WHATCOM
113.0 HUH
Chan 77
N48°56.72'-W122°34.76'
L 1, H 1

TAKE-OFF OBSTACLES:
463' Tree
288' Tree
DEPARTURE OBSTACLES:
620' Tower
558' Tree
562' Tank

VICTORIA
113.7 YYJ
Chan 84
N48°43.62'-W123°29.06'
L-1, H-1

PAINE
110.6 PAE
Chan 43
N47°55.19'-W122°16.67'
L-1

MOSES LAKE
115.0 MWH
Chan 97
N47°12.65' W119°19.01'
L-1, H-1

SEATTLE
116.8 SEA
Chan 115
N47°26.12'-W122°18.58'
L-1, H-1

WENATCHEE
111.0 EAT
Chan 47
N47°23.98' W120°12.65'
L-1-9

290°
110°
R-110

McCHORD
109.6 TCM
Chan 33
N47°08.86'-W122°28.50'
L-1, H-1

ELLENSBURG
117.9 ELN
Chan 126
N47°01.46'-W120°27.51'
L-1-9

HOQUIAM
117.7 HQM
Chan 124
N46°56.82'-W124°08.96'
L-1, H-1

OLYMPIA
113.4 OLM
Chan 81
N46°58.30'-W122°54.11'
L-1, H-1

YAKIMA
116.0 YKM
Chan 107
N46°34.22'-W120°26.68'
L-1-9, H-1

BATTLE GROUND
116.6 BTG
Chan 113
N45°44.87'-W122°35.49'
L-1, H-1

NOTE: Chart not to scale.

TAKE-OFF Rwy 13L/R: Standard with a minimum climb of
380' per NM to 700'.
NOTE: No left turns authorized until leaving 1000'.

DEPARTURE ROUTE DESCRIPTION

TAKE-OFF RUNWAYS 13L/R: Climb runway heading, expect radar vectors to assigned
route/fix. Maintain 2000 or ATC assigned altitude, expect clearance to filed altitude
within 3 minutes after departure.
LOST COMMUNICATIONS: If no contact with departure control within 3 minutes after
departure, climbing right turn direct SEA VORTAC, climb in SEA VORTAC holding pattern
(E, left turn 290° inbound) to cross SEA VORTAC at or above MEA/MCA for direction
of flight before proceeding enroute.

*Figure 16-4 The KENT FOUR departure from Boeing Field is a vectored departure. You can assume
you get vectors from ATC soon after you take off.*

Now compare the pilot navigation departures to vectored departures, such as the KENT FOUR departure procedure at Boeing Field (KBFI), shown in Figure 16-4 and provided on the website:

1. Take off on Runway 13L or 13R.

2. Climb runway heading.

3. Expect radar vectors to assigned route/fix.

4. Maintain 2000 or ATC assigned.

The route on the graphic seems a lot easier, and the text looks simple. ATC does all the thinking for you by giving you vectors: "Turn right heading 230, climb and maintain 9000," and so on. But there are some subtleties to look at in each step after takeoff:

360

PART I PREFLIGHT | **PART II** SPORT PILOT | **PART III** PRIVATE PILOT | **PART IV** INSTRUMENT RATING | **PART V** COMMERCIAL LICENSE | **PART VI** ATP AND BEYOND

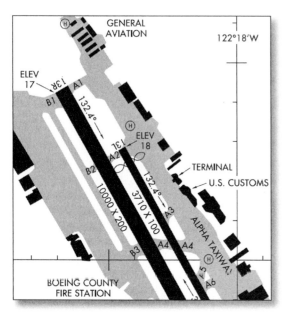

Figure 16-5 The north end of the Boeing Field Airport diagram (full-size version on the website)

- What is the runway heading? You have to look at another chart to find out: the Boeing Field Airport diagram (see Figure 16-5). At the northwest end of each runway you see "132.4°" and an arrow pointing southeast. That's the exact magnetic alignment of the runways. So after takeoff, you fly a heading of 132°.

- It says to "expect radar vectors to assigned fix...," which is fine as long as the radar and radios are working. What if they're not? What if the next "assigned fix" is a VOR 100 miles away and your radios can't detect that VOR when you're only 2,000 feet up? The answer lies in the "Lost Communication" instructions. All departure procedures have these instructions if you can't navigate the procedure yourself from the cockpit. In this case, the instructions are as follows: "If no contact with departure control within 3 minutes after departure, climbing right turn direct SEA VORTAC, climb in SEA VORTAC holding pattern (E, left turn 290° inbound) to cross SEA VORTAC at or above MEA/MCA for direction of flight before proceeding en route."

- Just like the route, the altitude you fly is based on what ATC tells you; or, if you lose communication, you follow the lost communication instructions. In this case, you climb to the MEA/MCA for the direction of flight. (We discuss MEA/MCA in the next section, but you can probably figure MEA out from what the acronym stands for: minimum en route altitude.) The instructions keep you in the holding pattern at SEA VORTAC because that's how they prevent you from hitting the mountains to the east and south until you're safely high enough to cross over them.

When leaving Boeing Field and flying the KENT FOUR departure, you almost always are in radar and radio contact with ATC, in which case it is just like in FSX: you get full vectors on to your course and avoid the climb in the holding pattern. Like everything in IFR flying, though, there are safe procedures to follow if you enter the clouds right after takeoff and don't get any radio contact.

EN ROUTE OPERATIONS

En route operations cover the distances between airports. Usually, you fly along the Victor airways you learned about in previous chapters, but you can also fly direct routes, or—when you fly really high-performance aircraft like jets—you fly along Jet airways at 18,000 feet and up.

ROUTE

The most common way to plan the en route portion of your flight is to find a VOR that is near your departure airport and that also has Victor airways, find out what departure procedure is needed to get from the airport to that first VOR, decide which airways to follow toward your destination, and finally get from the last VOR to the destination airport using arrival procedures (if applicable) and approach procedures.

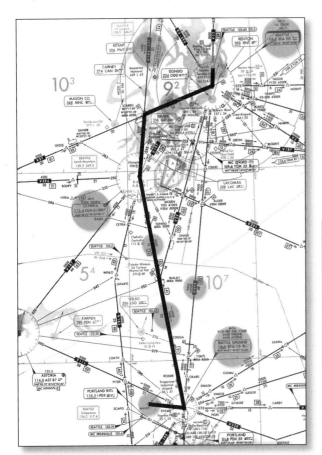

Figure 16-6 En route chart for Boeing Field to Scappoose and the FSX flight plan of the route

As an example, you'll fly from Boeing Field to Scappoose, Oregon (KSPB). The chart sample on the website for this route is called `Chap_16_KBFI-KSPB_Enroute.jpg` (see Figure 16-6). The nearest VOR to Boeing Field (highlighted in pink on the chart) is the Seattle VORTAC (SEA), about three miles south. Many airways start there, including several heading south, so use that VOR to start. (And, as you learned in the previous discussion, the KENT FOUR departure from Boeing Field uses the SEA VORTAC as a "Lost Communication" fix; that's a perfect way to pick your first fix for en route.)

362

PART I	PART II	PART III	PART IV	PART V	PART VI
PREFLIGHT	SPORT PILOT	PRIVATE PILOT	INSTRUMENT RATING	COMMERCIAL LICENSE	ATP AND BEYOND

Now take a look near Scappoose, highlighted in pink at the bottom of the chart. There are a couple of VORs, but the closest is the Battleground VOR (BTG) about 12 miles east of Scappose. Probably some instrument approaches at Scappoose start at BTG, although you don't need to know that until the next chapter.

So, now that you have a place to start (SEA) and end (BTG) the en route section, you need Victor airways to get from SEA to BTG. There happens to be one that goes directly between them: V495. It doesn't get much easier than that! However, that wouldn't be much of a challenge, and the real-world ATC won't give you that route anyway, because of conflicts with heavy iron going in and out of Sea-Tac airport. (FSX ATC doesn't care, because FSX traffic at Sea-Tac isn't nearly as busy as the real airport.) For training purposes, you'll take a slightly different route: SEA to V27 to CARRO intersection and then V287 to Olympia VOR (OLM) and continuing on to BTG.

NOTE!

↓ SHARED AIRWAYS

Notice that V287 from CARRO to OLM is also named V165, and another leg from MALAY intersection to BTG is shared by V287 and V23; that's common in IFR routes. You can pick either one when you plan your route, but you might as well pick the one that takes you the farthest along your route so you can write it in the shortest way: CARRO .. V287 .. BTG is better than CARRO .. V165 .. OLM .. V287 .. TONNO .. V287 .. MALAY .. V23 .. COUGA .. V23 .. ROARK .. V

COURSE

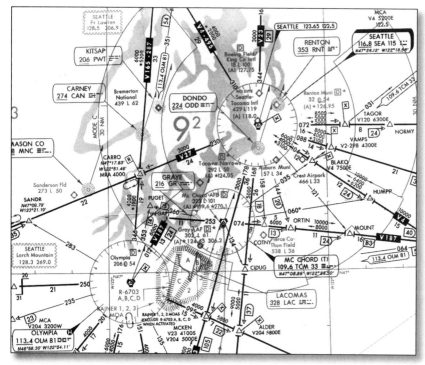

Figure 16-7 En route chart from KBFI to OLM

When you fly this route, it helps if you know the VOR radials that make up each leg so you can properly set up your VORs. For instance, from SEA to CARRO on V27 (see the close-up in Figure 16-7), notice near SEA that V27 comes out at a place that says 230°. That is your course for that leg—R-230 (radial 230°) from Seattle. How long is that leg? It says "24" right below V27, and that's the distance in nautical miles.

The leg from CARRO to OLM on V287 doesn't show a radial number at CARRO, but it does show 346° at OLM. You fly on OLM radial 346 going from CARRO to OLM, but you set your VOR omnibearing selector (OBS) on 166 TO (346°

minus 180°) and fly a heading of about 166° during that leg, adjusting for wind drift as needed. It is 19 nm from CARRO to OLM.

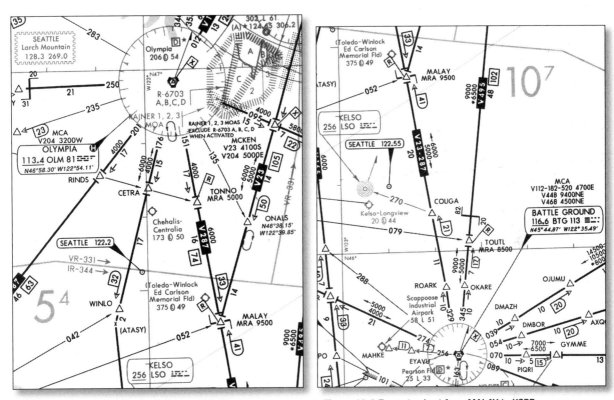

Figure 16-8 En route chart from OLM to MALAY   *Figure 16-9 En route chart from MALAY to KSPB*

Leaving OLM, you fly the OLM R-151 to TONNO (17 nm) and on to MALAY (another 16 miles), as shown in Figure 16-8. Your Mooney has distance-measuring equipment (DME), so you can keep track of your position by checking how far you are from OLM. You get 17 + 16 = 33 nm. But the chart says so, too: Right near MALAY you see a strange arrowed symbol with 33 inside it. That shape is supposed to be like a capital letter *D*, meaning DME. So, your math was correct to say that MALAY is DME 33 nm from OLM.

Normally when flying between two VORs, you'll want to switch to the second VOR when you're about halfway between them. This time, though, they want you to switch over at MALAY intersection, noted with the stick-S shape (⌐). What is the OBS setting when you use BTG? Scan down V287 to BTG (see Figure 16-9), and you'll see it says 329°. The inverse of that is 149°, so you fly course 149 TO BTG VOR.

Another 20 nm takes you from MALAY to COUGA, 11 more to ROARK, and 10 to BTG. Then use whatever instrument approach is necessary to land at Scappoose. (For this chapter's lesson, be clear of clouds before you get to BTG so you can navigate visually to Scappoose.)

364

PART I	PART II	PART III	PART IV	PART V	PART VI
PREFLIGHT	SPORT PILOT	PRIVATE PILOT	INSTRUMENT RATING	COMMERCIAL LICENSE	ATP AND BEYOND

ALTITUDE

After you have a route, you need to check the altitudes. Mountains are all around here, to say nothing of radio towers, buildings, and other obstacles. Stay at least 1,000 feet above everything four miles right and left of your course when flying in nonmountainous regions and 2,000 feet above everything in mountainous regions.

You don't have to figure it out for yourself with a topographic chart; the IFR en route chart shows you. Take a look at V27 from SEA to CARRO in Figure 16-7; 3,000 is the MEA. Because you fly even thousands of feet when your course is between 180° and 360° and because the course from SEA to CARRO is 230°, you need to fly at a minimum of 4,000 feet on this leg. (You probably fly higher for safety or other reasons, but it's good to know the MEA anyway.)

For the leg from CARRO to OLM, you'll see two numbers: 4,000 and *1900. The MEA is 4,000, but because 1,900 has the * in front, it is the minimum obstruction clearance altitude (MOCA). What's the difference between MEA and MOCA? When you're at MEA or higher, your VOR radios can detect the necessary VORs that make up the airway. At the MOCA, you'll still be well above obstructions on the route, but you might be too low for your VOR radios to pick up the VORs signals, unless you're within 25 nm. Because OLM is the VOR and CARRO is 19 miles from OLM, you have no problems receiving the VOR signal. But another good time to use MOCA is when navigating with GPS. You're never too low to pick up the GPS satellite signal—however, in valleys, reception can get limited—so you can use the MOCA as your minimum altitude and program the GPS to fly along the airways. The magnetic course on this leg is 166°, and you fly IFR at odd thousand altitudes when the course is between 0° and 179°. With the MEA of 4,000 (assuming you're using VORs), your lowest usable altitude is 5,000.

Continue with the next leg from OLM to TONNO, and the MEA is 4,000 (see Figure 16-8). Again, the magnetic course requires odd thousand altitudes, meaning 5,000; 7,000; and so on. The next leg has an MEA of 6,000, which requires a cruising altitude of 7,000; 9,000; and so on. The next MEA is 5,000 (MALAY to COUGA) when going southeast (see Figure 16-9). And the 5,000 continues all the way to BTG.

So, the highest MEA you saw on the whole route was 7,000, which is just fine for a jaunt like this. When you file your flight plan with ATC, ask for 7,000.

↓ BY THE BOOK

VFR-ON-TOP

It is certainly possible to fly IFR in visual meteorological conditions (VMC); airliners do all their flying IFR, even if the sky is perfectly clear. But the rules for IFR are strict, and sometimes pilots like a little more flexibility when the weather is good.

During en route flight, ATC gives you a specific altitude to fly in order to separate you from other aircraft that you can't see because of clouds or low visibility. But if it is actually clear and you can see other aircraft, you can ask ATC for "VFR on top." This is a special clearance that is part-VFR and part-IFR. You take all responsibility for spotting conflicting aircraft (as in VFR), and you fly at VFR altitudes (which are at 1,000-foot intervals plus 500 feet, such as 4,500; 5,500; and so on) rather than IFR altitudes (4,000; 5,000; and so on). And ATC usually lets you pick your own altitude, or they say, "Maintain VFR on top between 10,000 and 15,000," or something like that. But IFR rules apply as well: you have to stay above the MEAs for the route, you have to stay in contact with ATC, and so on.

> You can ask for VFR on top only if you can maintain VMC. And, alas, you can do it only in the real world. The air traffic controllers in FSX have never heard of VFR on top, and they get angry if you don't stay at your assigned altitude!

HOLDING

When you're flying along and ATC isn't ready for you to proceed on your route (usually because of heavy traffic ahead of you), the controller puts you in a *hold*. You'll be flying circles just waiting for your turn to proceed to the airport.

Holding is the bane of pilots everywhere. It's boring, it's a waste of time and fuel, and yet it can be tricky to do correctly. Thank goodness the ATC in FSX doesn't simulate a holding procedure. But real-world pilots have to fly holds, and we've even had holds in FSX with multiplayer mode—when a bunch of sim pilots were flying into one airport for a "fly-in."

Holds are not random circles, though. Like the rest of IFR, they are designed to keep you out of terrain and out of the way of other aircraft, all while you're in IMC and can't see more than 10 feet in front of you.

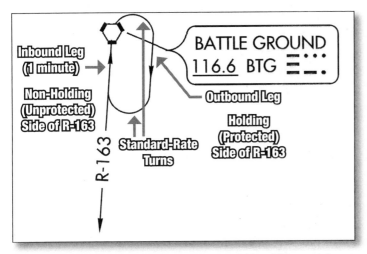

Figure 16-10 A basic holding pattern. The FIX could be a VOR, a certain distance from a VOR (DME) along a radial, or any other navigation spot from which a pilot could identify and hold.

As an example, look at the holding pattern in Figure 16-10. The holding point is the BTG (Battleground) VOR near Portland, Oregon. In this case, you're supposed to make right-hand (clockwise) turns, always flying in toward the VOR on the BTG 163° radial. This means your OBS should be set on 343°, because you are flying *to* the station on R-163.

But there is a lot more to this hold that the chart doesn't show, and you need to know all of it. For instance, how big is this holding pattern? Unless it is marked for a certain distance, the size is actually based on time: you need to spend one minute on the inbound leg (along R-163) to BTG. (You definitely need a stopwatch or the clock in the instrument panel for this.) If you could ignore any wind—and in FSX you can turn the wind off for this practice—you would start at the VOR heading the opposite of 163° (343°), and turn right at standard rate for one minute, which would put you at a heading of 163°. Now fly for one minute on the outbound leg; on this leg, you have no electronic navigation guidance, but that's OK. After one minute, turn right (again at standard rate) for one minute. You should roll out right on 343°. But now you want some electronic guidance to make sure you're on the R-163 of BTG. You probably put BTG VOR in your NAV1 radio so you could fly to BTG in the first place, but what number is your OBS set for now? Not 163, because that's the radial you'd fly away *from* the station. To fly *to* the station along R-163, you need to set 343 in the OBS. Now your course deviation needle (CDI) helps you stay on R-163. Fly for one minute, and you are at the VOR again.

366

| PART I | PART II | PART III | PART IV | PART V | PART VI |
| PREFLIGHT | SPORT PILOT | PRIVATE PILOT | INSTRUMENT RATING | COMMERCIAL LICENSE | ATP AND BEYOND |

GETTING BLOWN AROUND

Now it's even more challenging because of the wind. Imagine if the wind was from the northwest, say from heading 340° or so. Then, when you're flying northwest along R-163 into that wind, going for one minute won't get you to the VOR because your ground speed is lower. Maybe it'll take one minute and 20 seconds to get to the VOR.

But wait, that inbound leg is supposed to be exactly one minute long; how do you fix it? You fix this by shortening the outbound leg to less than one minute. For simplicity, just take 20 seconds off the outbound leg; so when you're flying southeast at a heading of 163°, fly for only 40 seconds before you start the one-minute right turn to 343° and the radial. Then check your time inbound along R-163 again, and if it's not one minute, adjust the outbound a bit again.

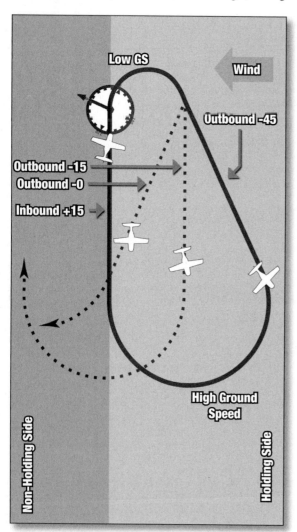

That's fine if the wind is right along the radial on which you're supposed to hold. But it usually isn't. What if the wind is from the east? When you're flying northwest along R-163, the wind is trying to blow you to the west. You'll see that on your CDI needle as a drift to the left of the course, so you compensate by correcting your heading to the right (east). Let's say you find that flying heading 348° (5 degrees east of 343°) keeps you on that R-163.

At the VOR you turn right for a minute, and now you're on the outbound leg; what heading should you fly? You probably guessed that you need to correct for the wind here, too. The wind is from the east, so instead of heading 163°, you'll probably try to fly heading 158°, which is 5 degrees east of 163°. That'll work OK, but wait until you see what happens next. After a minute, you start a one-minute right turn to heading 343° (actually, you remembered to make it 348°); but now that east wind is pushing you toward the west with a higher ground speed. Watch out! You're going to go past R-163 and overshoot onto the west side of the course. That's the unprotected side of the hold; you're not supposed to go there at all.

To fix this next time, you need to change the heading of the outbound leg even more. Instead of doing the same wind correction as the inbound course—5 degrees to the east—you should triple the correction, as shown in Figure 16-11. That means 15 degrees, so your outbound heading is 163° corrected 15° to the east (left), so it's 148°.

And we should remind you that you're supposed to be simultaneously changing that outbound time length to get the inbound leg to one minute!

Figure 16-11 To correct for wind in a hold, it isn't enough to use the same heading correction on the outbound leg as on the inbound leg; you need to triple the inbound correction.

GETTING INTO THE HOLD

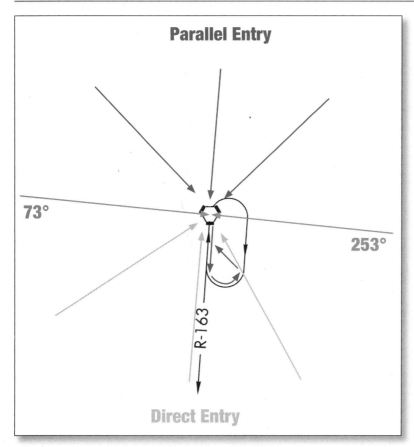

Parallel Entry

73°

253°

R-163

Direct Entry

Figure 16-12 The procedure for entering a hold depends on which way you're coming from.

Now that you know how to fly a hold, we can back up and show you how to get into one in the first place. First, when you're in a hold, you're not going anywhere, so why go nowhere fast? You might as well slow down and save fuel. About three minutes before you get to the hold fix the first time, slow to a low-cruise speed, ensure the mixture is leaned properly to save fuel, and trim the airplane for your new speed.

In the example, if you're flying toward BTG along R-163 already, it's a no-brainer: make note of the wind correction you're using along R-163, wait until BTG, and then start the first right turn to the outbound leg (see Figure 16-12). This is called the *direct entry* into a hold. In fact, you can use a direct entry when you're coming toward the holding fix from anywhere on the inbound side of the fix. That means you use direct entry any time your course is within 90° of the inbound course; in this case, it's from 253° through 343° and on to 073°.

On the other hand, if you're coming from the west, northwest, north, or northeast (course from 073° through 253°), then you fly away from BTG along R-163 for one minute, make a left turn back around to about heading 300, reintercept R-163, and take it to BTG to start the hold; this is called the *parallel entry*.

368

| PART I | PART II | PART III | PART IV | PART V | PART VI |
| PREFLIGHT | SPORT PILOT | PRIVATE PILOT | INSTRUMENT RATING | COMMERCIAL LICENSE | ATP AND BEYOND |

BY THE BOOK

NO TEARS FOR THE LOSS OF A TEARDROP ENTRY

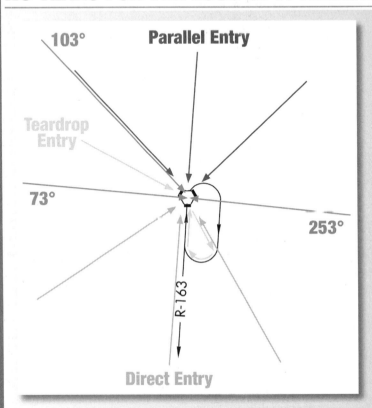

The FAA specifies three ways to enter a hold. In addition to a direct entry and a parallel entry, it has a *teardrop entry.* This is used only for arrivals from a small sector toward the fix.

We're not fans of the teardrop entry, for safety and simplicity reasons. Any entry you could accomplish with a teardrop can be done with a parallel. The FAA says the way you enter a hold is up to you, so we've left it out of this training section. But if you ever become a real-world instrument pilot, you'll probably learn about it, even if you choose never to use it.

As a side note, though, we do tell students about what we call a *reverse teardrop.* It's really a parallel entry where instead of rejoining the inbound radial back to the holding fix, you just turn and go directly back to the holding fix for a direct entry.

One other tip that can help you when doing holds and prepare you for instrument approaches in the next chapter is to learn the five *T*s. This is a memorized checklist of what to do when passing the hold fix and certain fixes during approaches:

1. Time (start your timer)

2. Turn (start turning)

3. Twist (change the OBS course)

4. Throttle (change power and configuration)

5. Talk (to ATC or whoever)

You won't do all five steps every time you pass the fix, but if you recite all five each time you pass the holding fix and just say, for instance, "Throttle—unchanged" for unnecessary items, you'll remember all of them for times, such as on approaches, when you might need to do all of them.

If you don't have an autopilot, you have to do all this while keeping the airplane upright using only your instruments! See why many pilots hate holds? We'll be honest: holding is one of the bigger multitasking challenges of IFR flight, so if you can successfully execute a hold, your skills are strong enough for most other IFR challenges.

ARRIVAL PROCEDURES

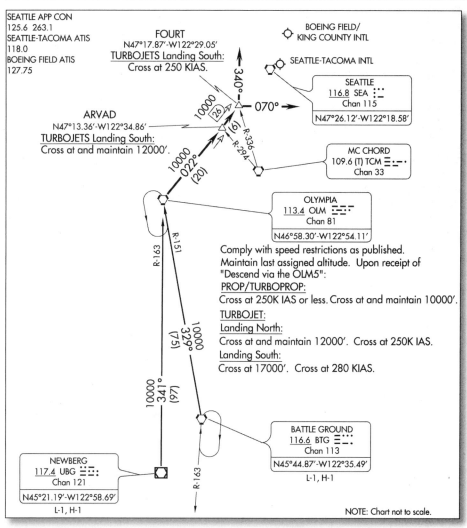

Even in the real world, you're not likely to be asked to use a specific arrival procedure until you're flying airplanes that can get above 18,000 feet and go faster than 250 knots. They're used at busy airports to make the controller's job easier; instead of giving the same complicated set of waypoints to every single airplane, the controller can just tell the pilots to fly a specific arrival procedure.

For example, look at the Olympia Five arrival on the website (KBFI OLM 5 STAR .PDF) and in Figure 16-13. The controller would say, "Airliner 123, at Battleground, cleared to Boeing Field via the Olympia Five arrival," and the pilot takes care of the rest. Aircraft flying into Boeing Field from the south pass over either

Figure 16-13 The Olympia Five arrival into Boeing Field is used by high-altitude, high-speed aircraft arriving from the south.

370

PART I	PART II	PART III	**PART IV**	PART V	PART VI
PREFLIGHT	SPORT PILOT	PRIVATE PILOT	INSTRUMENT RATING	COMMERCIAL LICENSE	ATP AND BEYOND

BTG (Battleground) VOR or UBG (Newberg) VOR in Oregon, proceed to OLM VOR, head northeast toward SEA VOR, and then get vectors to Boeing Field. Like a miniature en route chart, this arrival chart has VORs, intersections, and routes with magnetic courses, altitudes, and distances. It even has a "LOST COMMS" procedure, which is required because there is the section with vectors (after FOURT intersection), and you need to know what to do if you can't get vectors on the radio from Seattle Approach.

▼ KEEPING IT REAL

CRUISE CLEARANCE

A special ATC instruction you might hear in the real world is the *cruise clearance*. Actually, the controller says something like, "Cruise 5,000."

With those two words, the controller is giving you a whole lot of freedom. You can do the following:

- Fly at any IFR altitude between the minimum charted for that leg and 5,000 feet without telling the controller.

- Conduct any instrument approach you want at your destination airport.

Obviously, a cruise clearance is rare; the only way you get one is if no other IFR airplanes are going to or from your destination airport and none is between you and that airport below 5,000. But away from big cities going to small airports, this isn't unheard of. You can always try to request one, even if ATC doesn't offer it.

You'll even see some special instructions, such as the one at OLM: "Prop/turboprop, cross at 250 KT or less. Cross at and maintain 10,000." As you can see from those instructions, they're not really expecting a small plane—even one as fast as a Mooney—to do this arrival procedure. Slower planes get the full vectoring treatment when flying into Boeing Field.

Some instructions are different depending on whether Boeing is *landing south* (that is, on Runways 13L and 13R) or *landing north* (on Runways 31L and 31R). How do you know which way the controllers are landing traffic? You can figure it out by listening to the ATIS at Boeing; they even give you the ATIS frequency at the top of the chart.

The FSX air traffic controllers never assign you an arrival procedure, so practice it on your own in the second flight of this chapter; that way you are prepared to use it in the real world or in FSX multiplayer with ATC.

IFR FLIGHT TO A VISUAL APPROACH

Because we haven't shown you how to fly an instrument approach, this training flight starts and ends in VMC, but the whole en route section of the flight is in the clouds. This is actually quite common in the real world; it isn't often that you have to shoot a real instrument approach all the way to the airport.

Figure 16-14 This flight starts at Boeing Field, ready for a flight to Scappoose, Oregon.

However, this is an IFR flight, so after you load the Chap_16_IFR flight (see Figure 16-14), you need to file a flight plan and get a clearance from ATC. The website has FSX videos of several segments of this flight and the flights in the next section, if you want to see how it looks.

PREFLIGHT

You have to take some extra steps before you can take off on an IFR flight: you have to file a flight plan and get a route clearance, and your before-takeoff checklists include some extra steps, too.

FLIGHT PLAN AND CLEARANCE

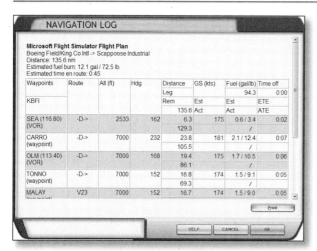

Figure 16-15 The navigation log shows the waypoints for the flight and all the other information you need to track your trip. Scroll down for more waypoints.

For this flight, we've already created a flight plan for you and included it on the website. From the menu, choose Flights > Flight Planner, and then load `IFR KBFI to KSPB.PLN`. This flight takes you from Boeing Field to Scappoose Industrial Airport in Oregon, about 100 nm south.

Click NavLog to see all the waypoints in the route (see Figure 16-15). All the VOR frequencies are there, as well as the headings (actually, courses), distances, fuel burn, and estimated time en route. We've created a similar navigation log for real-world flights as well, both VFR and IFR (see `Flight Plan and Navigation Log (blank).PDF` on the website). If you haven't already printed the en route chart for this flight from the website (`Chap 16 En Route Chart 1.PDF`), do so now so you can see how that route looks on a chart.

372

PART I	PART II	PART III	PART IV	PART V	PART VI
PREFLIGHT	SPORT PILOT	PRIVATE PILOT	INSTRUMENT RATING	COMMERCIAL LICENSE	ATP AND BEYOND

In the real world, if you filed an actual flight plan for this flight, the route would look like this:

```
KBFI .. SEA .. V27 .. CARRO .. V287 .. BTG .. KSPB
```

Print the navigation log from FSX so you can keep track of your progress. When you click OK on the Flight Planner screen, FSX asks you whether you want to "move your aircraft to the departure airport." You don't (you're already there), so click No.

Next, get the latest weather and airport information from the Boeing Field ATIS, and then get your clearance. Use the CRAFT acronym, and practice writing down the clearance as the FSX controller reads it to you:

- *C*: KSPB

- *R*: As filed; fly runway heading

- *A*: 5,000

- *F*: 120.1

- *T*: 4232

When the controller is done reading it to you and you've got it all copied down, read it back to the controller so ATC knows you heard it correctly. If you need to hear it again, ask the controller, "Say again?"

Now check your clearance with the flight plan you filed; are there any differences? The clearance limit is your destination, so that's good. You filed SEA as your first waypoint, but ATC says to fly runway heading. That means you should fly the runway heading after takeoff, and then if you don't establish radio contact to get vectors on to your route, you continue as filed—so you go to SEA and onto your filed route. If the altitude is different from what you filed and they don't say, "Expect 7,000 in 10 minutes," then there was some reason for them to change it. If they don't revise the altitude later, just fly it at the altitude they suggest, unless that is unsafe. The departure frequency is for you to switch to after takeoff, and the squawk code 4232 was automatically set in your transponder when you read back the clearance (see "Squawk This").

If you don't understand any part of the clearance or you can't do something (for instance, if they ask you to fly at 17,000 feet, and you're in a Cessna 172 Skyhawk that can climb only to 12,000 feet on a good day), you need to ask the controller now. (Well, you could do that in real life, anyway.)

INSIDE THE GAME

SQUAWK THIS

 Until now we've mostly ignored the transponder in the various aircraft you've learned to fly. The Cub didn't have one, and during your Private Pilot lessons in the Cessna, the opportunity didn't come up to change your squawk code. VFR aircraft squawk 1200 almost all the time, but IFR aircraft always have their own, unique transponder code.

FSX automatically changes the transponder whenever you read back an ATC clearance that includes a squawk code, so you might not realize that you can change it yourself. In the Mooney with the Bendix/King radios, you click (or use the mouse's wheel scroll) the individual numbers, or you can click the numbered buttons along the bottom, which is how you do it with the real Bendix/King radio. In the second case, if you don't click four numbers within a couple of seconds, the transponder reverts to the squawk code it had before. One more button is on the left side of the transponder—IDT—which stands for "ident." It doesn't work in FSX, but in the real world, if the controller asks you to ident, you press that button, and your transponder sends out a special signal to the controller's radar display. The controller asks that if he isn't sure exactly which aircraft on his display is you (especially if you're squawking 1200 along with every other VFR aircraft he can see).

The Garmin G1000 transponder interface is a bit different. Near the bottom right of the PFD is the word *XPDR* followed by a four-digit number (the current squawk code) and a word, either ALT, ON, or OFF, telling you the current status of the transponder. Using the softkeys along the bottom of the PFD, click XPDR. You then have the option for either VFR (squawk code 1200) or CODE. If you click CODE, eight of the softkeys turn into numbers. As you type the squawk code, you can see the current squawk code flash until you're done with all four numbers. The FSX Garmin G1000 doesn't have an ident feature, but in the real G1000 one of the softkeys along the bottom always is the ident button.

BEFORE TAKEOFF

Now talk to the ground controller, taxi to the runway, do your before-takeoff checklist and anything else you usually do to get ready for takeoff.

Because this is an IFR flight, a few other steps can help you get ready. (Follow along in Figure 16-16.) First, set the radio frequencies you need. You can set the COM1 radio for the tower frequency of 120.6 and then set your COM1 standby frequency for 120.1 so that you can easily switch to the departure controller.

Next, set up your navigation radios. You are navigating with VORs this time, and your first VOR is SEA, so set NAV1 radio on 116.8, as you see on your en route chart. (Don't forget to identify SEA VOR by listening to the Morse code; you might not hear it when you're on the ground, but then again you might.) The next waypoint is CARRO intersection, defined as the intersection of R-230 from SEA VOR and R-346 from OLM VOR and also 24 DME from SEA. Put the OLM VOR in NAV2 (113.4), and set the DME radio on R1 so that it gets its DME reading from whatever VOR is in NAV1 (SEA in this case).

You also need to make sure your HSI gets its course information from the VORs and not your GPS, so find the NAV/GPS switch and set it on NAV. (It's much easier to find this switch on the left side of the 2D cockpit rather than in the 3D cockpit view.)

374

PART I	PART II	PART III	PART IV	PART V	PART VI
PREFLIGHT	SPORT PILOT	PRIVATE PILOT	INSTRUMENT RATING	COMMERCIAL LICENSE	ATP AND BEYOND

Figure 16-16 Set up the radios, autopilot, and so on, before you take off to reduce your workload in the air.

For this flight, it is much easier if you use the autopilot to fly the airplane so you can concentrate on navigating and talking to ATC. The first route instruction in your clearance was to "fly runway heading," so set the heading bug on your HSI to the heading of the departure runway, 132°. Set the autopilot altitude for your first cleared altitude—7,000 feet—but don't turn on the autopilot yet. (Even if you were flying by hand, to help you remember, it is helpful to set the heading bug on your headings and the autopilot altitude selector on your assigned altitude.)

After the aircraft is set up for the start of your flight, you need to organize your cockpit. Instrument flights always involve some charts, and this flight to Scappoose uses several en route charts, so put those in a stack in order. Part of a sectional chart for this flight is included on the website—you'll see why when you get close to Scappoose.

The controllers give you vectors and frequencies at various times, so have a small pad of paper and several pens or pencils nearby. If you have printed checklists for airplane procedures, keep those in their own stack as well. Sure, flight sim pilots don't need to strap all these things down tightly so they don't get lost in turbulence (unless you live in an earthquake zone), but if you start the habit of organizing all your cockpit now, you'll be prepared for real airplanes and the tight cockpit spaces you'll be in then.

As soon as you're ready, ask for takeoff clearance and get going. Remember your final, memorized, takeoff checklist, LIST-MD, from the previous chapter. It's winter in Seattle, and you'll be in the clouds, so you should take the I—meaning icing—seriously; turn on your pitot heat right before you take off, and watch for ice on the wings when you're flying.

FLIGHT

Soon after you take off, the tower controller tells you to contact Seattle Departure. After you acknowledge the handoff, all you need to do is switch the flip-flop button on COM1 and you're on the departure frequency.

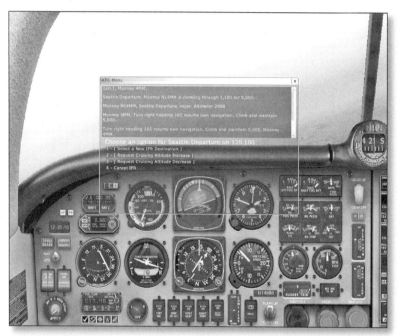

Figure 16-17 Turning to go directly to SEA VOR

Figure 16-18 Vectors for the visual approach to Scappoose. FSX ATC starts vectoring you more than 60 miles from your destination. It's annoying, and not realistic, but they do it nonetheless.

Seattle Departure soon tells you to turn to a particular heading and then "resume own navigation." That means you need to start on that heading, but as soon as you can, head for the first fix on your clearance route. The clearance route was, "as filed," and you filed SEA VOR as your first fix. So you need to proceed directly to SEA VOR. Turn your OBS dial on your HSI until the yellow line is centered and the white to/from arrow points toward the head of the yellow arrow. Then use the heading bug to have the autopilot turn until you're going the same direction as the yellow arrow. That's the easiest way to go directly to a VOR (see Figure 16-17). If you didn't before, listen to the ID (Morse code) of SEA VOR to make sure it is, indeed, SEA VOR.

When you cross over the SEA VOR, you need to proceed as filed, and that means along V27 to CARRO intersection. Set your HSI OBS to 230°, and track R-230 outbound. Now that you're airborne, you can ID the Morse code for OLM to confirm it is the OLM VOR. You need to know when you get to CARRO, so set your NAV2 OBS to 166°, the inbound reciprocal of R-346 from OLM. When the NAV2 CDI centers, you're at CARRO, and you turn toward OLM.

Near OLM, ATC starts vectoring you with headings and altitudes to fly (see Figure 16-18). The real-world ATC probably wouldn't put you on vectors until you're about 20 nm from Scappoose, but FSX seems to treat all aircraft as fast airliners. If the controller says he is vectoring you for the ILS Runway 15, you need to ask for the visual approach to Runway 15, rather than the ILS.

376

PART I
PREFLIGHT

PART II
SPORT PILOT

PART III
PRIVATE PILOT

PART IV
INSTRUMENT RATING

PART V
COMMERCIAL LICENSE

PART VI
ATP AND BEYOND

This is where flying in the clouds gets tricky, because you might not know exactly where you are. When you're doing your own navigating and using charts, you have good *positional awareness*, and you can make sure you're high enough to stay safe. But when you're on vectors, it's easy to relax and let the air traffic controller keep you out of the mud. You shouldn't cede control; you are the pilot in command of the aircraft, and, let's be honest, if you crash, it's your (virtual) self that dies. Controllers are human, too, and sometimes they make mistakes, so you need to know where hills, towers, and buildings are. This is where a sectional chart comes in handy: if you know where you are—even in the clouds—you can check that position on the sectional chart and see how far the obstacles are below you. If you're being vectored off an airway, use your navigation radios to figure out where you are, just as you did in Chapter 10. Tune in BTG VOR on 116.60 (ID the station's Morse code), and then check which radial from BTG you're on, as well as your DME distance.

Needless to say, having a GPS with a moving map makes your positional awareness much easier, but most such moving maps don't show terrain or obstacles, so you still need your sectional chart.

You don't need to second guess the controller every single time, but if heading 250° puts you right toward hills that are higher than you are, feel free to ask, "Ah, Seattle Center, confirm you want me on heading 250?"

⬇ INSIDE THE GAME

NOTHING LASTS FOREVER

When you're being vectored toward Scappoose, you might cross over the Columbia River close to a nuclear power plant cooling tower. This is the Trojan plant, part of the Washington Public Power Supply System (WPPSS, sometimes disdainfully pronounced, "Woops!") The plant produced electricity from 1976 to 1992.

The cooling tower will continue to provide FSX sim pilots with a nice landmark between Seattle and Portland, but real-world pilots can't find it anymore; it was demolished on May 21, 2006.

When you get below the clouds, start looking for the airport. And although Mooney's GPS makes it easier to find, first see whether you can find the airport yourself. Use Figure 16-19 (also on the website) to orient yourself visually. If you don't see the airport right away, the FSX controller helps out by saying the airport is "10 o'clock, 15 miles," or something like that. If you still don't see it, the controller keeps giving you vectors until you're lined up with Runway 15 straight ahead of you (see Figure 16-20). After you do see the runway, tell the controller you have the runway in sight. Then you can switch to the local advisory frequency (there is no control tower at Scappoose), announce your arrival, and make a normal VMC approach and landing at the airport.

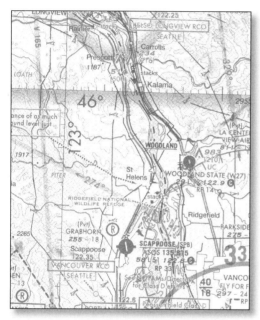

Figure 16-19 Sectional chart showing Scappoose airport and the approach area from the north

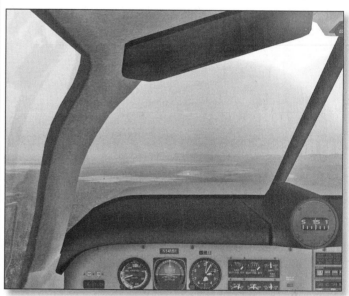

Figure 16-20 The Scappoose airport lies just ahead. A PAPI on the left side will guide your descent.

And that was your first IFR flight! If you had to pause it a few times (and why not take advantage of Flight Simulator for that?), try it again and see whether it's easier. You'll find it helps to be already comfortable flying the Mooney, so if you were a bit rusty, go back to Chapter 14 and practice in VMC. Or practice the IMC flying in Chapter 15. During real-world training, you often move two steps forward and then take one step back, because so much is new and so many things happen fast in IFR that you don't want to forget the basics.

378

PART I
PREFLIGHT

PART II
SPORT PILOT

PART III
PRIVATE PILOT

PART IV
INSTRUMENT RATING

PART V
COMMERCIAL LICENSE

PART VI
ATP AND BEYOND

DEPARTURES, HOLDS, AND ARRIVALS

The FSX air traffic controllers do not authorize three instrument procedures that real controllers expect you to be able to do: departure procedures, holds, and arrival procedures. In this section, you'll practice several examples of these procedures in flights where you won't be talking to ATC, even though you go into the clouds soon after takeoff.

INSIDE THE GAME

NOT QUITE AS REAL AS IT GETS?

Why doesn't FSX simulate departures, holds, and arrivals? The answer lies in understanding why these three IFR procedures were created: to guide you to and from airports where real-world radar can't see you, to delay your flight if there is too much other traffic, and to abbreviate instructions so the controller can spend time helping other traffic. FSX has three things that don't exist in the real world: the air traffic control radar can always see you, there is never too much other traffic, and the controller isn't too busy to give you step-by-step instructions. Plus, let's be honest—most FSX pilots don't take the time to get (and learn to use) departure and arrival charts or learn to fly holds. You'll just be that much more prepared for the real world or for FSX multiplayer with online ATC.

These short flights are pieces of a longer flight from Wenatchee to Spokane, Washington (KGEG), 100 miles east of Wenatchee. You could fly the whole flight at one time, but to save time (and to take advantage of FSX), we break it into three separate flights. First you fly the Wenatchee obstacle departure procedure discussed earlier in this chapter, then you try holding (both without and with wind), and finally you try the ZOOMR ONE arrival into Spokane. You need the following charts from the website:

- TO Mins and ODPs NW US (you just need the page with Wenatchee's departure procedure)

- En route charts for Wenatchee to Spokane

- KGEG ZOOMR 1 ARR

FLIGHT PLAN

Load the flight from the website called Chap_16_KEAT_Departure, and your Mooney appears at the Wenatchee airport (see Figure 16-21).

Figure 16-21 The flight Chap_16_KEAT_Departure puts you in the Cascade Mountains of Washington at the Wenatchee airport.

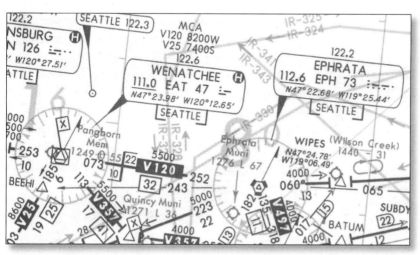

Figure 16-22 This part of the en route chart shows Wenatchee (EAT) VOR/DME and Ephrata (EPH) VORTAC.

In the flight planner, load the flight plan called IFR KEAT to KGEG.PLN. Compare the navigation log to the three charts (departure, en route, and arrival). The flight plan calls for simply going from the airport to EAT VOR—which is right on the airport property—and then on V120 to EPH (Ephrata) VOR (see Figure 16-22). But as discussed, the actual departure procedure is more complicated. After that complicated bit about climbing to 4,000 feet, it says, "Aircraft departing EAT R-010 clockwise R-140 climb on course." Checking the en route chart, you see that V120 between EAT and EPH has an MEA of 5500 and is on R-073. R-073 is between R-101 and R-140, so you can just climb up to your cruising altitude after EAT VOR. You can fly the route at 7,000; 9,000; 11,000; and so on. Therefore, fly at 9,000 this time.

A quick glance at the ZOOMR ONE arrival into Spokane shows how easy this will be. It starts at either EPH VOR or MWH (Moses Lake) VOR. So after EPH, just follow the ZOOMR ONE chart, which takes you to the GANGS intersection. (You actually stop before GANGS and practice holding at ZOOMR.) At GANGS, in real life, you get vectors to Spokane International. Here, in FSX, you just fly visually at that point.

380

PART I
PREFLIGHT

PART II
SPORT PILOT

PART III
PRIVATE PILOT

PART IV
INSTRUMENT RATING

PART V
COMMERCIAL LICENSE

PART VI
ATP AND BEYOND

DEPARTURE

Figure 16-23 Intercepting the EAT R-113 outbound, climbing to 4,000 feet

Perform your normal pretaxi activities, get the latest weather report, and head to the runway that gives you a headwind. (No control tower exists at Wenatchee.) Based on your choice of runway, you need to plan where you're going to turn after takeoff to follow the departure procedure. (If you do need to turn right away and no specific altitude restrictions exist, you're supposed to start your turn 400 feet above the runway.) You know you need to fly the EAT VOR R-113 away from the VOR right after takeoff, so set NAV1 to the EAT VOR, identify the station's Morse code, and set the HSI OBS needle to 113. If you want the autopilot to fly for you, set the heading as specified in the departure procedure to intercept the EAT R-113 after takeoff, and set the altitude setting at 9,000 with 700 fpm climb.

When you're ready for takeoff, review the after-takeoff procedures for the Mooney again. A departure like this, when you're busy turning to a new heading and intercepting a VOR radial all while climbing to avoid terrain, can distract you so much you forget to raise the landing gear, bring up the flaps, set the power properly, and so on. Use this calm moment now to remind yourself what you need to do.

After takeoff, when you're 400 feet off the ground, start turning to intercept the R-113 outbound, as shown in Figure 16-23. When you're at 4,000 feet, turn left until you're headed mostly back the way you came. The instructions say "climbing left turn direct EAT VOR/DME," so you don't have to take R-113 inbound; instead, reset the HSI until the yellow CDI needle centers with the TO indication, and then fly directly to the station. Keep climbing to 9,000 feet.

Figure 16-24 Over EAT VOR/DME, turning to intercept R-073

When you pass over EAT VOR/DME, reset the HSI for R-073, and turn around to intercept that radial and head away from Wenatchee, now on V120 (see Figure 16-24). That's the end of the departure procedure, so you can stop FSX now and load the next flight or just continue along V120 to EPH, follow the ZOOMR ONE arrival chart, and proceed to the next section on holds.

HOLD (NO WIND)

Figure 16-25 The flight Chap_16_Hold_Calm begins in midair along the ZOOMR ONE arrival, about 20 nm from ZOOMR intersection.

Unless you're just continuing the flight from Wenatchee, load the next flight, Chap_16_Hold_Calm, which puts you between EPH VOR and ZOOMR intersection (see Figure 16-25). You're going to hold at ZOOMR. This isn't an official hold on the ZOOMR ONE arrival, but sometimes real-world air traffic controllers ask you to hold at a VOR, an intersection, or some other waypoint. Pretend they gave you the following holding instructions: "November 4MM, hold southwest of ZOOMR intersection, 065-degree radial of Ephrata VOR, expect further clearance at 2030 Zulu, time now 2000 Zulu."

Holding instructions always have the holding fix, cardinal direction, radial/bearing unless the hold is charted, and time to expect further clearance. If

382

PART I	PART II	PART III	PART IV	PART V	PART VI
PREFLIGHT	SPORT PILOT	PRIVATE PILOT	INSTRUMENT RATING	COMMERCIAL LICENSE	ATP AND BEYOND

they want you to make left-hand turns, they tell you; if they don't say, then turn right. You can assume they want you to make the standard one-minute inbound leg unless they tell you a different time or instead to make a certain DME length legs.

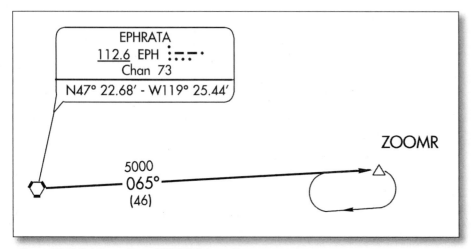

Figure 16-26 Holding pattern at ZOOMR intersection

When the controller gives you an uncharted hold, use a pencil and draw the hold on a chart, as shown in Figure 16-26; that makes it easier to make sure you enter the hold in the best way and execute the hold properly. Southwest of ZOOMR on the 065 radial of EPH is the exact route you're on to ZOOMR, so 065 is your inbound course. The controller didn't say left-hand turns, so draw a quick right-hand racetrack pattern. Finally, decide what kind of entry you do. Coming along the EPH R-065, it's obvious you do a direct entry.

You've got EPH VORTAC in NAV1 radio; to identify ZOOMR intersection, just monitor your DME until you reach 46 nm from EPH. Unpause FSX, and continue toward ZOOMR. About three minutes from ZOOMR (at your speed, that's about 8 nm, which is 38 nm from EPH), slow to your holding speed of 120 knots. As soon as you get to ZOOMR, recite the 5 Ts checklist:

- *Time*: Start the timer (for a one-minute leg).

- *Turn*: Start a standard-rate right turn until you're going the opposite heading from the inbound course of 065°, which is 245°. No wind exists for this flight, so you don't need to compensate during the hold.

- *Twist*: Twist the HSI to the inbound course of 065, which it already is set on.

- *Throttle*: No change—stay in low-cruise configuration.

- *Talk*: If you were actually flying IFR, you'd tell ATC you're entering the hold.

After your right turn to 245°, fly for one minute, then turn right until you reach heading of 065, start the timer again, and adjust your course to get right onto R-065.

You know you're back at ZOOMR when your DME reads 45 again. Do the 5 Ts again, but check your timer before you reset it. Did it take you one minute to go up R-065? Adjust the outbound (245°) leg if needed, but without any wind, you probably won't need to adjust much.

Continue in the hold as many times as you want; if it gets to 2030Z, you'll probably be dizzy anyway, so you can stop now and load the next flight.

HOLD (WIND)

This flight Chap_16_Hold_Wind is tricky for two reasons: First there is—surprise!—wind to contend with. But not just that; ATC has given you a different holding procedure: "Mooney 4MM, hold northeast of ZOOMR intersection, 232 degree radial of Spokane VORTAC, left turns, expect further clearance at 2030 Zulu, time now 2000 Zulu."

Draw it on the chart, as shown in Figure 16-27. Plan your hold entry; does a parallel entry make sense this time? For this flight, open the Garmin GPS 500 map to help you visualize what you're doing.

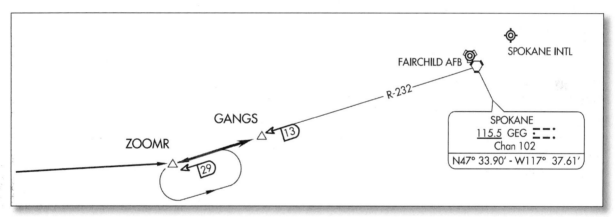

Figure 16-27 Holding pattern southeast of ZOOMR

ZOOMR is defined not only as the EPH R-065 at 46 DME but also as the GEG R-232 at 29 DME, and as you get to ZOOMR, you switch to using GEG as your primary navigation beacon. You've got EPH VORTAC in NAV1 now to get yourself to ZOOMR, so put GEG into NAV2 and also in the standby frequency of NAV1. What about OBS2? Your first move at ZOOMR is to fly along GEG R-232 inbound toward GEG, so set OBS2 for 052°, the inverse of 232°.

Unpause FSX when you think you're ready to continue to ZOOMR. Three minutes before ZOOMR, slow to low cruise. At ZOOMR, do the 5 Ts:

- *Time*: Start your timer for one minute outbound.

- *Turn*: Turn to heading 052 initially, and then follow your CDI2 needle to stay on R-232 (the wind *will* try to push you off course).

- *Twist*: Switch the NAV1 frequency to GEG VOR, and spin the HSI OBS to 232°.

- *Throttle*: No change.

- *Talk*: If you were actually flying IFR, you'd tell ATC you're entering the hold.

384

PART I	PART II	PART III	PART IV	PART V	PART VI
PREFLIGHT	SPORT PILOT	PRIVATE PILOT	INSTRUMENT RATING	COMMERCIAL LICENSE	ATP AND BEYOND

After one minute, start a right turn all the way around to about 270 degrees to intercept the GEG R-232. During your turn, switch your navigation attention back to the HSI. When you're back at ZOOMR, you've finished the hold entry, and you continue as usual in a hold.

Each time around, you need to make sure you check how long the inbound leg to ZOOMR is so you can adjust the outbound leg appropriately and make the inbound leg one minute long. You also need to adjust that outbound leg heading due to the wind; remember, the wind correction should be three times whatever the inbound wind correction is. (You know you've got it right when at the end of the turn from the outbound leg to the inbound leg you roll right out on GEG R-232.)

This one takes a few times practicing, and that's typical. Holds are pretty tricky; visualization is the key, so draw them on your charts whenever you need help figuring out how to do it.

ARRIVAL

After practicing holds with a wind, you can continue the flight from ZOOMR right into this arrival procedure, or you can load the Chap_16_KGEG_Arrival flight and start there.

The ZOOMR arrival is pretty easy after all the tricky work you did on departure and holding. But you should still read it over to make sure you don't miss anything.

When you get to ZOOMR, instead of holding, just fly inbound on the Spokane VORTAC (GEG) R-232 (course 052 TO the station). The segment from ZOOMR to GANGS has an MEA of 5,000, so descend to 5,000 now. (Don't forget to decrease power slowly as you descend so you don't shock-cool the engine.)

After GANGS, the arrival procedure technically ends, because in real life you'd be on vectors from Spokane Approach controllers at that point. Let's pretend you've lost radio contact with them and have to follow the lost communications procedure. It's pretty simple; continue on GEG R-232 to GEG VORTAC. The last assigned altitude was 5,000 feet, but that won't get you out of the clouds.

Figure 16-28 If you fly the procedure correctly, Spokane International will appear just off to your left in the windscreen.

Since you can't shoot an actual instrument approach yet, you have to trust us and descend to 3,500 feet before you get to GEG VORTAC. At that point you (you hope) drop out of the clouds, and the airport is slightly left, about four miles from GEG VORTAC (see Figure 16-28). Welcome to Spokane! (Because you don't want to embarrass yourself when you call the control tower, remember that Spokane is pronounced "spo-KANN"—with the ANN pronounced like the woman's name Ann.)

Now that you're done with these four training flights, you can do the whole flight from Wenatchee to Spokane nonstop, practicing holding wherever you want along the way. For extra challenge, add a bit of wind to the entire area so that you have to compensate during departure, en route, holding, and arrival.

Garmin *G1000*

We also encourage you to do the flights in the Mooney with the Garmin G1000 avionics and GPS navigation. You'll find it's much easier to navigate, but there is a lot more *button pushing* you need to do to keep up with the flight. It's a good challenge!

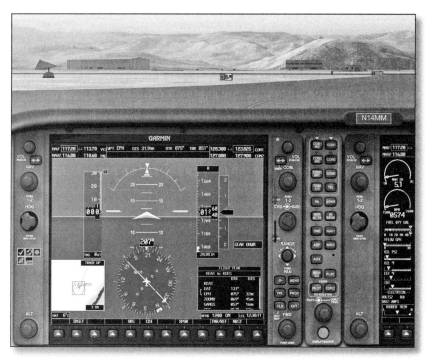

When you load the flight plan IFR KEAT to KGEG. PLN, the Garmin G1000 automatically gets all the waypoints in its flight plan. One cool trick is that you can see the next few flight plan waypoints on the PFD by clicking the FPL button on the PFD (see Figure 16-29).

Even though the leg from EAT to EPH is along V120, the G1000 system doesn't know about Victor airways. When you create a flight plan, you have to make sure you choose the right waypoints to follow the Victor airways.

Figure 16-29 Click the FPL key on the PFD to see the next few waypoints of the flight plan in the lower-right corner of the PFD.

386

PART I
PREFLIGHT

PART II
SPORT PILOT

PART III
PRIVATE PILOT

PART IV
INSTRUMENT RATING

PART V
COMMERCIAL LICENSE

PART VI
ATP AND BEYOND

KEY POINTS FOR REAL FLYING AND FSX BUILT-INS

The following are some key points from this chapter:

- Create flight plans.

- Get and follow ATC clearances.

- Use IFR charts.

- Understand procedures for departures, en route, holds, and arrivals.

Here are the lessons and missions to study after reading this chapter:

- *Lessons*: FSX Instrument Pilot Lesson 3 is a good review of holding patterns.

- *Missions*: Flying Blind Across the Channel is a nice, basic IFR flight in the Cessna 172 with the Garmin G1000 instruments. The skills you learned in this chapter are sufficient to get you to Paris, although there is an instrument landing system (ILS) approach at the end.

INSTRUMENT APPROACHES

CHAPTER 17

"TO THE IFR COGNOSCENTE, IT'S A SERIOUS MISUNDERSTAND-
ING OF INSTRUMENT FLYING TO THINK OF AN APPROACH
PLATE AS A MERE MAP FOR DROPPING OUT OF THE CLOUDS IN
SEARCH OF A RUNWAY. AT THE VERY LEAST, A PLATE IS A WORK
OF ART AND FOR THE TRUE ZEALOT, IT'S A SYMBOL OF MAN'S
CONTINUING STRUGGLE AGAINST THE FORCES OF NATURE."
—PAUL BERTORELLI, IFR MAGAZINE

388

PART I — PRE-FLIGHT PART II — SPORT PILOT PART III — PRIVATE PILOT PART IV — INSTRUMENT RATING PART V — COMMERCIAL LICENSE PART VI — ATP AND BEYOND

THE FINAL MILES BETWEEN HEAVEN AND EARTH

There is an aviation adage that says, "Takeoff stresses the airplane. Landing stresses the pilot." This is certainly true of instrument approaches. Unlike the skill-intensive wrestling match of landing in a gusty crosswind or the adrenaline soak of an expedited landing in an emergency, the instrument approach is a head game. You are unable to see beyond the arc of the propeller, yet you're descending steadily toward the ground, often between obstacles to your left and right.

Sometimes, the descent through the clouds is a bumpy ride, but more often it is an eerie-smooth settling toward the earth. That's why it's a head game. You follow a complicated procedure to get yourself lined up with a runway you can't see and fly toward it on faith that you've done everything correctly. If you have, the runway appears out of the murk, you land, and you get to live and fly another day.

THE INSTRUMENT APPROACH PLATE

Instrument approach procedures (IAPs) are created by the FAA in Oklahoma City. FAA staffers follow an extensive set of procedures called TERPS. (Somehow TERPS is an acronym/abbreviation for U.S. Standard for TERminal Instrument Procedures, although it's not exactly clear how that came about.)

The rules for TERPS are extensive, running hundreds and hundreds of pages. You don't need to worry about that here. As a pilot, you are concerned only with the end product—the instrument approach chart, or *plate*, as it's sometimes called. For all its complexity, the instrument approach plate really tells you only two pieces of information. It tells you who to talk to, and it tells you what headings and altitudes to fly to get from the en route environment down to a position near the runway where you can land.

The most precise of these instrument approach procedures can guide an airplane all the way down to the pavement without the pilot ever being able to see anything. That requires some fairly advanced avionics and a lot of training. The most precise approach in general aviation can guide a plane to within 200 feet of the ground a half mile from the end of the runway.

We cannot go into all the details of approach charts here. In fact, one of the authors edits a magazine for pilots with a monthly clinic looking only at some of the minutia of approach charts. That magazine has been running for more than 22 years and still hasn't run out of topics to discuss.

Instrument approach plates have two uses. The pilot can use them to find an airport and land without any help from ATC. This kind of approach is often called a *full procedure*, because the pilot must start at an en route fix (see Figure 17-1) and execute all the twists and turns of the instrument approach to land safely. In the real world, pilots usually start receiving vectors as they get near their destination airports. Sometimes, the weather is good enough that ATC can vector the aircraft to a position below the clouds where the pilot can see the airport visually and land without further assistance.

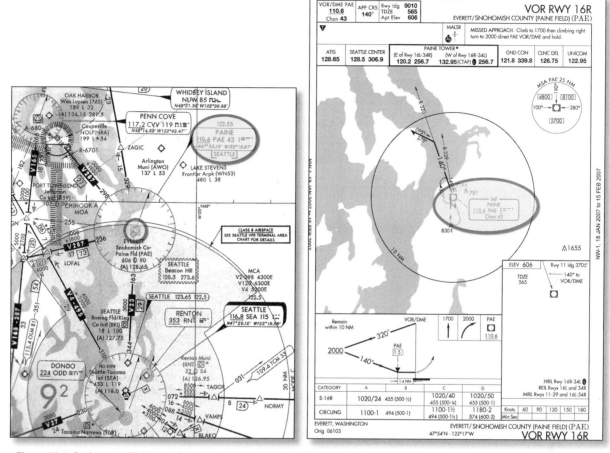

Figure 17-1: During your flight planning, you want to make sure that there is a common fix or nav aid on your route and at least one approach at your destination airport. This common point is where you switch from navigating on the en route chart to navigating on the approach plate.

When the cloud bases are lower, however, the pilot must fly at least part of the charted approach procedure. In this case, ATC vectors the pilot to intercept the final segment of the instrument approach, and the pilot flies the approach from that point forward. This is easier on the pilot, and it allows more airplanes to land at an airport in the same period of time. It requires that the airplane is in radar contact, however, so it can't always be done. FSX allows you to practice both kinds of procedures.

Regardless of which procedure the pilot must fly, instrument approach procedures are intensely unforgiving of sloppy technique or a lack of understanding. Practicing instrument approaches is one of the best uses for a computer simulator, so you'll now look at what these approach procedures encompass.

390

| PART I | PART II | PART III | PART IV | PART V | PART VI |
| PREFLIGHT | SPORT PILOT | PRIVATE PILOT | INSTRUMENT RATING | COMMERCIAL LICENSE | ATP AND BEYOND |

VOR APPROACHES

The first instrument approaches were based on the existing nav aids that pilots had been using during en route flight. Many of these early nav aids no longer exist, but the venerable VOR is still in regular use and is the heart of many instrument approaches.

APPROACH CHART

Take a look at the VOR approach to Runway 16R at Paine Field in Everett, Washington (KPAE), as shown in Figure 17-2. This is the home of one of Boeing's assembly plants, and the Paine VOR (PAE) is actually on top of the hangar right in the middle of the airport.

The top section of the approach plate contains the key frequencies and some other important information for this approach. The upper-left corner shows the frequency for the nav aid used in primary navigation for this approach. The next box on that line shows the final approach course. This is the course over the ground that the aircraft must follow in the last segment of the approach. If winds are totally calm, then the aircraft also flies this heading. If the winds are not calm, then the pilot must enter some kind of heading correction so that the aircraft tracks this course over the ground.

The next section shows any important notes about the approach, the kind of lighting the pilot should expect to see while looking for the runway, and the missed approach procedure to fly if the pilot could not find the runway before time ran out.

That concept of time running out is important. Every instrument approach has a *missed approach point* or *decision altitude*. This is a point over the ground, or an altitude the pilot reaches, at which the pilot either must be able to see the airport with the required visibility and land or must abandon the attempt at landing and reenter the en route environment. You'll learn more about this in a moment.

The center section of the approach chart is called the *plan view*. This shows the entire IAP from above. Each heading the pilot must fly for the entire full procedure appears in this section. The procedure begins at an initial approach fix (IAF). An approach chart might even have more than one IAF. Even with multiple IAFs, though, the chart will show only one final approach course, which is the last heading the pilot will fly in search of the runway. The plan view also shows the path for the missed approach with a dotted line. A hold is usually depicted as well with the dotted line. This is where the pilot can hold after flying the missed approach procedure and figure out what to do now that they've discovered the weather is too bad at the airport to land.

Below the plan view is the *profile view*. This view also shows the headings the pilot will fly, but in addition it shows the altitudes of each segment of the approach up until the last one.

The last altitude the pilot descends to appears in the *minima* section. Here aircraft are divided into four categories, based on how slowly they fly and how much protected airspace they need accordingly. The Mooney is technically a category A aircraft, which means you would use the final altitudes and visibility requirements in the A section. Many category A aircraft would fly the approach at 90 knots; however, you fly instrument approaches in the Mooney at 100, so a safer choice might be to use category B. In practice, the two categories often sport the same numbers, so it matters little. In the case of the VOR Rwy 16R approach at KPAE, the lowest altitude a pilot is allowed to descend to without seeing the runway—called the *minimum descent altitude* (MDA)—is 1,020 feet MSL. At that point the pilot must see some part of the runway environment and have a forward visibility of at least 2,400 feet—essentially half a mile—in order to descend any further and land.

NACO charts also (usually) have an airport diagram on the plate showing the airport layout, lights, and, most important, the course the pilot is arriving from relative to the rest of the airport.

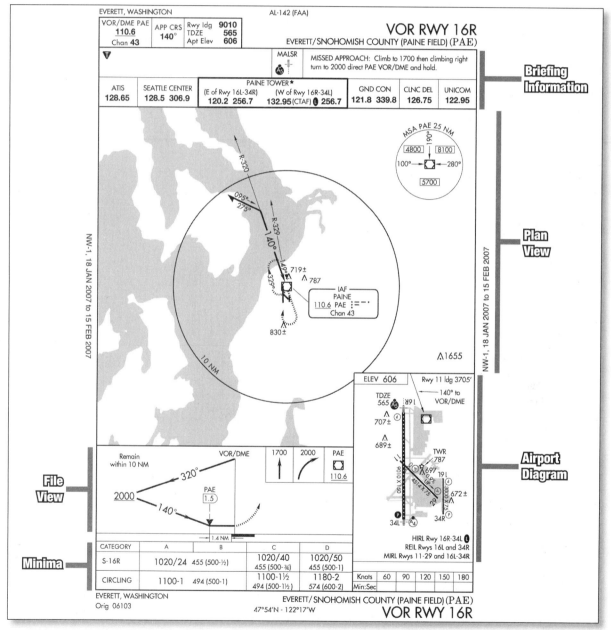

Figure 17-2: Every approach plate is organized in the same layout, which is from the top to the bottom, and is the same order you'll need the information in flight.

392

| PART I | PART II | PART III | PART IV | PART V | PART VI |
| PREFLIGHT | SPORT PILOT | PRIVATE PILOT | INSTRUMENT RATING | COMMERCIAL LICENSE | ATP AND BEYOND |

STUDENT OF THE CRAFT

JEPPESEN APPROACH PLATE ORGANIZATION

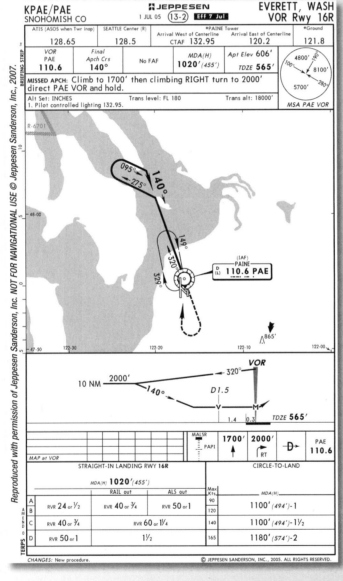

Back when the authors were learning to fly, the difference between Jeppesen approach plates and NACO approach plates was quite significant. They have become more similar because both systems have standardized their organization of frequencies and headings across the top of the plate. Both systems also have a plan view, profile view, and minima section, all in the same places. The differences are mainly in symbology in the plan and profile views, with the Jeppesen plates being somewhat more explicit and generally easier to read. They also depict certain items such as procedure turns differently.

Jeppeson plates do not have the airport diagram on the approach plate. Instead, they have a dedicated plate just for the airport. That airport plate also has the departure procedures and alternate airport restrictions for a specific airport. NACO plates simply show a T or A symbol when there is something unusual about the departure or alternate requirements. Users then have to look up the information in a separate book.

Which plates you use is mostly a matter of preference. Jeppesen plates are more expensive, both in their digital versions for online aviators (SIMCharts) and their paper versions that require no batteries in the cockpit.

PAINT, PAVEMENT, OR LIGHTS

To descend below the lowest allowable altitude on an approach, you must have the runway environment in sight. FAR 91.175 (c) (3) is specific about what this means. It could be any of the following:

- The approach light system, except that the pilot might not descend below 100 feet above the touchdown zone elevation using the approach lights as a reference unless the red terminating bars or the red side row bars are also distinctly visible and identifiable

- The threshold

- The threshold markings

- The threshold lights

- The runway end identifier lights

- The visual approach slope indicator

- The touchdown zone or touchdown zone markings

- The touchdown zone lights

- The runway or runway markings

- The runway lights

That's a lot to remember when you're trying to find a runway through rain and mist. It's a bit easier to remember that you're looking for paint, pavement, or lights.

DO IT WITH VECTORS

ATC gladly helps you set up for this approach by giving you vectors to intercept the 140° course that takes you to PAE. That course is along the 320 radial *from* PAE, but flying it would work just like the VOR navigation you've been doing all along. You would dial 140 into the OBS (on your HSI in the Mooney) and see a To triangle. You would center the needle and keep it centered as you descended and approached the airport.

To get you to that point, ATC sends you in a pattern that resembles an airport traffic pattern, only much wider (see Figure 17-3). Assume that you're approaching the airport from the southwest. There would be a downwind leg where you'll fly on a heading of 320 parallel to the final approach course. Unlike the airport pattern, though, this downwind is about 10 miles away from the airport. The controller then turns the aircraft to a heading of about 050. This is a base leg and is taking the aircraft toward the final approach course. By this point, you want to be in your low cruise configuration.

394

PART I
PREFLIGHT

PART II
SPORT PILOT

PART III
PRIVATE PILOT

PART IV
INSTRUMENT RATING

PART V
COMMERCIAL LICENSE

PART VI
ATP AND BEYOND

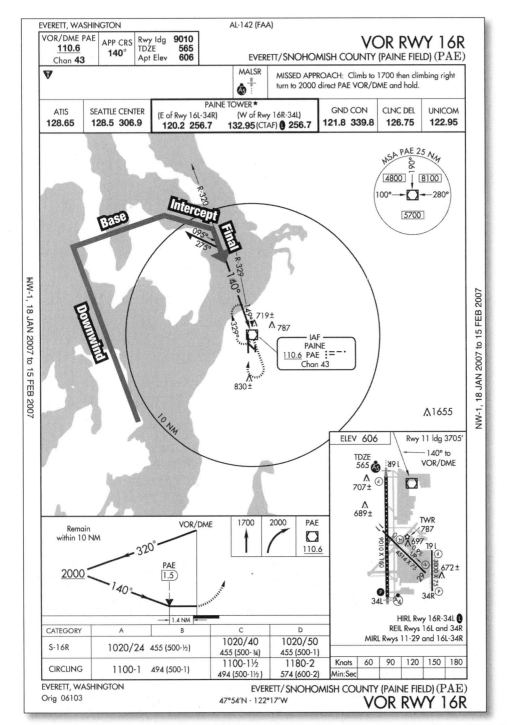

Figure 17-3: The last altitude assigned by ATC is usually also the lowest altitude on the approach plate in the profile view.

The controller gives a least one more turn to a heading of about 110° and at the same time issues what is known as the *approach clearance*. The clearance sounds something like this: "Moony Four Mike Mike is 7 miles from the airport; turn to a heading of 110; maintain 2,000 until established; cleared for the VOR Runway 16 approach. Contact Paine tower on 132.95." You would fly the assigned heading until intercepting the final approach course. This is also when you would slow to your approach level configuration of 100 knots with the gear down. At that point, the pilot will turn to a heading of 140, descend to the MDA, and start looking for the runway. You would also contact Paine tower after you were on the 110 heading, because that was part of your clearance.

If you're approaching the airport from some other direction, say, the north, you would get some part of this procedure, but the last step would always be a heading to intercept the final approach course and a clearance to fly the approach.

PROCEDURE TURNS AND THE FULL MONTY

Perhaps the biggest advantage from a pilot's perspective of vectors for an approach vs. the full procedure is the ability to fly the approach without a *procedure turn* (PT). The purpose of the PT is simply to reverse course, but in instrument flying, this requirement crops up more often than you might think. A look at the approach plate reveals why.

Suppose that you had to fly the VOR Rwy 16 (Figure 17-4) without ATC's help (such as if ATC's radar was out of service or it didn't reach your lower altitude). How would you do it? Let's assume you're at 4,000 feet approaching the VOR from the south. ATC would still issue the approach clearance, but it would sound more like this: "Mooney Four Mike Mike is 3 miles from the Paine VOR; cross the VOR at or above 4,000 feet; cleared for the VOR Runway 16 approach. Report procedure turn inbound."

You would cross the VOR at 4,000, but after that you would fly the altitudes shown in the profile view. In this case, that is 2,000 with a line beneath it. That means you must be at or above 2,000 feet for this section. You would begin a descent from 4,000 to 2,000 while flying away from the VOR on the 320 radial. You would fly away from the VOR for about 5 miles, which might be one or a few minutes depending on your speed. At that point you would begin the procedure turn by turning to a heading of 275 and fly for about another minute and a half. You would make a right turn to 095 and fly until you reintercepted the 320 radial inbound. By this point, you should have gotten down to 2,000 feet and are in the approach-level configuration. After you intercepted the 320 radial, you would turn to 140° and track that radial toward the airport as you descended to the MDA of 1,020 feet. At this point, the approach is identical to the vectored version.

WHEN YOU CAN'T GET VECTORS

The other time you need to do a full procedure is when you've lost radio communication with ATC. If they can't talk to you, they can't give you radar vectors.

If you were coming from the north for this approach, you'd like to intercept the final approach course and proceed inbound, but you can't because you wouldn't know how close to PAE you were. Actually, you could with distance-measuring equipment (DME), and there is a VOR-DME approach for Paine, but we discuss that in the next chapter. Without DME, you might intercept too close to the PAE and not be able to descend, or you might be too far from PAE to safely descend. The safe area at the MDA of 1,020 feet extends only 10 miles from the VOR.

396

PART I
PREFLIGHT

PART II
SPORT PILOT

PART III
PRIVATE PILOT

PART IV
INSTRUMENT RATING

PART V
COMMERCIAL LICENSE

PART VI
ATP AND BEYOND

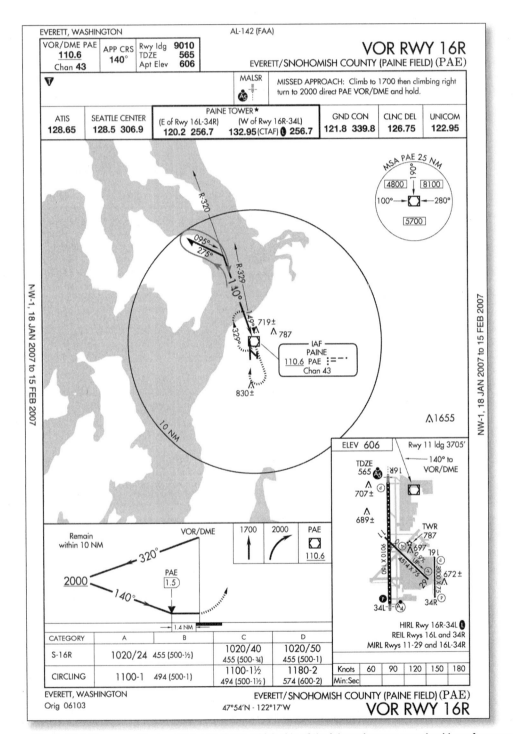

EVERETT, WASHINGTON   AL-142 (FAA)

VOR/DME PAE	APP CRS	Rwy Idg	9010
110.6	140°	TDZE	565
Chan 43		Apt Elev	606

VOR RWY 16R
EVERETT/SNOHOMISH COUNTY (PAINE FIELD) (PAE)

MALSR

MISSED APPROACH: Climb to 1700 then climbing right turn to 2000 direct PAE VOR/DME and hold.

ATIS	SEATTLE CENTER	PAINE TOWER ★		GND CON	CLNC DEL	UNICOM
		(E of Rwy 16L-34R)	(W of Rwy 16R-34L)			
128.65	128.5 306.9	120.2 256.7	132.95 (CTAF) 256.7	121.8 339.8	126.75	122.95

EVERETT, WASHINGTON
Orig 06103

EVERETT/SNOHOMISH COUNTY (PAINE FIELD) (PAE)
47°54'N - 122°17'W
VOR RWY 16R

NW-1, 18 JAN 2007 to 15 FEB 2007

Figure 17-4: The procedure turn barb just shows which side of the inbound course you should use for your course reversal. The actual headings you fly are up to you and often must be adjusted for wind.

> ⬇ BY THE BOOK

ANY TURN YOU LIKE

Procedure turns depicted as a *barb* (NACO) or a *bump* (Jeppesen) are recommended turns, but they can actually be flown any way you like. Some pilots will reverse course by making a 90° turn followed immediately by a 270° turn.

The exception is if the PT is actually depicted on the chart as a holding pattern (racetrack) shape or a teardrop shape. These are drawn when some terrain or airspace feature requires you fly the PT in a specific way, and you must fly them as charted.

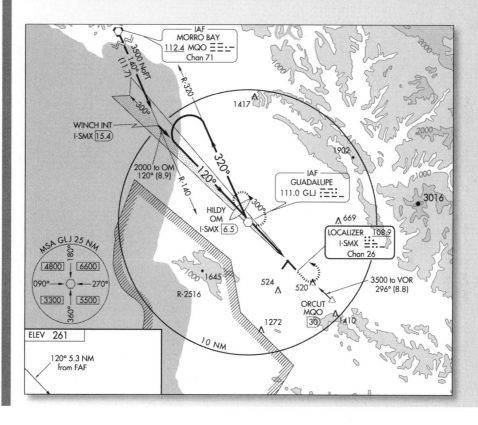

THE FIVE TS ON APPROACH

If you were reading that last clearance carefully, you also noticed that approach didn't tell you to contact Paine tower. They said to report your procedure turn inbound. This means it's up to you to remember to call them on the radio after you've turned back to 095 and are heading southeast to intercept the VOR radial toward the airport. That's something you could easily forget, which is why the 5 Ts you learned in Chapter 16 are a great tool. Every time you cross a fix on an approach or turn to a new heading, you'll want to go through the five Ts. It would go like this.

398

PART I
PRE-FLIGHT

PART II
SPORT PILOT

PART III
PRIVATE PILOT

PART IV
INSTRUMENT RATING

PART V
COMMERCIAL LICENSE

PART VI
ATP AND BEYOND

Crossing PAE heading north:

- *Time*: Start a timer for one to three minutes outbound.

- *Turn*: Turn to a heading of 320.

- *Twist*: Twist the VOR OBS to 320 to track the radial outbound. Correct your heading as needed to get on course.

- *Throttle*: Continue slowing the prop and MP as needed toward the goal of low cruise (25 inches by 2200 rpm/120 knots in level flight). You might need to reduce the MP a couple inches every couple minutes throughout the approach. You can use the speed brakes to help descend without picking up speed if needed. Below 140 knots, you can also extend the gear to help slow down.

- *Talk*: There's nothing to say unless you were asked to report crossing the VOR.

Turning to 275 for procedure turn outbound:

- *Time*: Start a timer for one and a half minutes outbound. If you were flying into the wind, this might be two minutes. If you had a tailwind, one minute would suffice.

- *Turn*: Turn to a heading of 275.

- *Twist*: Twist the VOR OBS to 140 so it's ready when you need to intercept the radial inbound. This is the same 320 radial, but you want to make sure the CDI needle gives you the correct left/right sensing.

- *Throttle*: Continue reducing the MP as needed toward the goal of low cruise (25 inches by 2200 rpm/120 knots in level flight).

- *Talk*: There's nothing to say.

Turning to 095 for procedure turn inbound:

- *Time*: Reset your timer to zero if you like, but there's nothing to time.

- *Turn*: Make a standard-rate, 180° right turn to 095. Note that procedure turns are always made away from the direction you'll be flying the approach. This is just to help ensure you don't end up too close to the airport.

- *Twist*: Verify you didn't forget to set the VOR OBS to 140 a moment ago.

- *Throttle*: Lower your gear, and when you can, lower your flaps to the approach setting. Continue reducing the MP toward a new goal of approach level (25 inches by 2200 rpm/100 knots in level flight).

- *Talk*: Tell Approach that you are "procedure turn inbound."

Intercepting the 320 radial inbound:

- *Time*: There's nothing to time.

- *Turn*: Turn to 140 as the CDI needle centers.

- *Twist*: Note any CDI deflection, and adjust your heading as needed.

- *Throttle*: Reduce MP to at most 19 inches for an approach descent, and use your pitch to maintain 100 knots. Reduce MP further if you want a faster descent rate.

- *Talk*: After your report of the PT, Approach might have asked you to contact the tower in which case you would have already done it. If they didn't, somewhere about now—usually right when you're busy adjusting the heading and throttle—Approach will call and tell you to contact the tower.

THE MISSED APPROACH

So you've gotten down to the MDA, and you're still in the clouds. Bummer. You can continue tooling along at 1,020 feet until you cross the Paine VOR. If you don't see the runway by then, you go full throttle to climb, clean, cool, and communicate, as described in Chapter 14. The climb part has some navigation too. If you look in the profile view, you see three small boxes with arrows and numbers. This is a visual representation of the missed approach.

Climb straight ahead until reaching 1,700 feet, and then continue climbing to 2,000 feet while turning right and heading back to the Paine VOR. Cross the VOR, and make a parallel entry into the hold.

In the real world and in FSX, you actually park in that hold only if you choose to do so. When you report to ATC that you missed the approach, they set you on a vector to shoot the approach again or proceed to another airport. In the real world, they usually ask which you want using the rather ominous sounding, "Mooney Four Mike Mike, say intentions." But if ATC was too busy to chat with you just then or you couldn't raise them on the radio, the hold provides a place to sit and wait while you figure out your next move.

VOR WITH A TWIST

Not all airports have a VOR on the field, and not all VOR approaches end at the VOR. Look at the VOR or GPS-A approach to Yakima, Washington (KYKM), as shown in Figure 17-5. The approach uses the Yakima VOR (YKM), which is about four miles from the airport. The full procedure for this approach would be to fly to YKM at or above 4,000 feet, cross the VOR, and proceed outbound on the 094 radial. After a minute flying outbound, you fly a procedure turn using headings of 139 and then 319 to reintercept the 094 radial inbound. You then fly inbound on the 094 radial (a heading of 274°) at or above 2,800 feet and cross the VOR a second time.

After this second crossing, you turn to the left and intercept the 244 radial outbound from the VOR and descend to the MDA. That's 1,780 feet for the Mooney. You fly away from the VOR toward a MAP that's 3.5 miles from the VOR. By that point, you need to see the airport environment or go missed approach. If you were getting vectors for this approach, you are vectored to intercept the 094 radial inbound to YKM at 2,800 feet, and you fly the rest of the approach from that point forward.

400

PART I
PREFLIGHT

PART II
SPORT PILOT

PART III
PRIVATE PILOT

PART IV
INSTRUMENT RATING

PART V
COMMERCIAL LICENSE

PART VI
ATP AND BEYOND

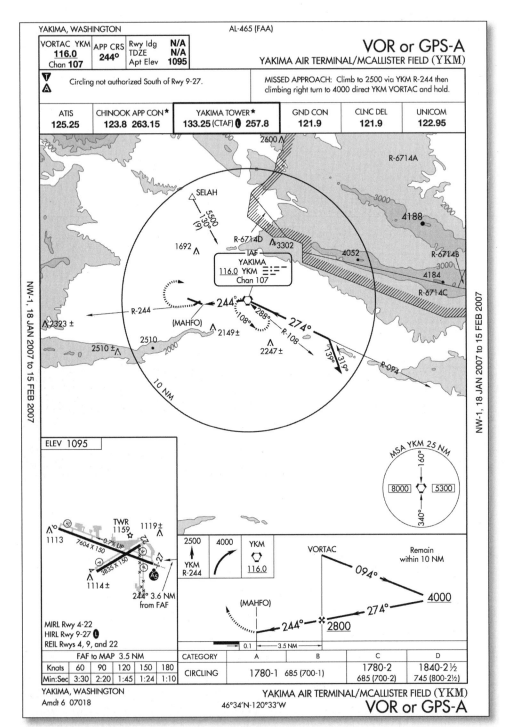

Figure 17-5: When the VOR is not on the field, you have to fly outbound for some distance to the airport. The farther outbound you must go, the less accurate the VOR signal, and the higher the MDA is for the approach.

One sticky point on this kind of approach is how you know whether you've reached the MAP. The approach doesn't require DME, so there must be another way. The way is by time. Just below the airport diagram is a timing chart that shows how long you have to fly to get from YKM to the MAP at various speeds. Your approach speed of 100 knots isn't even on there. Extrapolating between 2:20 at 90 knots and 1:45 at 120 knots, though, says an approach at 100 knots should be about 2:07 (two minutes and seven seconds). But that's a ground speed of 100 knots. If there was a wind, you have to guess at your ground speed and use the time appropriate for that ground speed. In the five *T*s scheme, this would be an all-important "Time: Start a timer counting to 2:07" that you did just as you crossed YKM and just before you turned to 244.

"But I have DME and GPS," you say. "Can't I just use them instead of timing? It would be so much more accurate." The answer is, yes and no. Let's start with DME. Not only does this approach not require DME, it's not approved for DME. Technically, time is the only approved way to determine the MAP. DME would be more accurate than timing (less sensitive to errors or inconsistency in speed during the approach).

You can use GPS to substitute for DME, but if DME isn't legal, then the substitute GPS isn't legal either. This particular approach is a VOR or GPS approach, so you could actually fly the entire thing using GPS, and that would be fine. You'll look at GPS approaches in the next chapter.

Even if you can't use DME or GPS, definitely watch your position on the DME or GPS as you track toward the MAP, but always start your timer and watch it as well. So long as they are in close agreement, you can feel confident that the timing is close. If they disagree significantly, you might not just abandon the timer and use DME or GPS, but you can decide something is amuck and go missed approach to try the whole thing again.

↓ FINAL APPROACH FIX

On the VOR or GPS-A approach to Yakima, YKM is the final approach fix (FAF). The FAF is the last fix you cross before descending to the MDA. The FAF is marked by a Maltese cross in the profile of view of the approach plate. The VOR approach at Paine has no FAF, because you can descend to the MAP as soon as you intercept the VOR radial inbound. In this case, we refer to that intercept as the *final approach point* (FAP).

TRANSITION ROUTES

The approach at Yakima also has a *transition route* (also called a *feeder route*) on the plate. This is a charted transition from some fix in the en route environment to an IAF on the approach plate. In this case, it connects the SELAH intersection to YKM. If you were coming to Yakima from the northwest, you might hear something like, "Mooney Four Mike Mike, proceed direct SELAH; maintain 6,000 until SELAH; cleared for the VOR Alpha approach. Report your procedure turn inbound."

You would then cross SELAH; descend to 5,500 feet; and fly the 310 radial to YKM on a heading of 130. The approach doesn't actually begin until you cross YKM, and you can tell this because YKM is listed as an IAF, but SELAH is not.

Sometimes, these transition routes don't require a procedure turn, in which case *NoPT* appears on the plan view. On the VOR Rwy 5 at Pullman, Washington (KPUW), the route from the Nez Pierce VOR (MQG) is on the 277 radial at 4,500 feet (see Figure 17-6). You'd fly that heading and intercept the 212 radial (032 heading) to the Pullman VOR (PUW). You'd fly inbound to PUW at 4,400 feet just as if you were inbound after a procedure turn. These NoPT routes are often made part of the approach, and MQG is marked as one of the IAFs for this approach.

402

PART I PREFLIGHT PART II SPORT PILOT PART III PRIVATE PILOT **PART IV INSTRUMENT RATING** PART V COMMERCIAL LICENSE PART VI ATP AND BEYOND

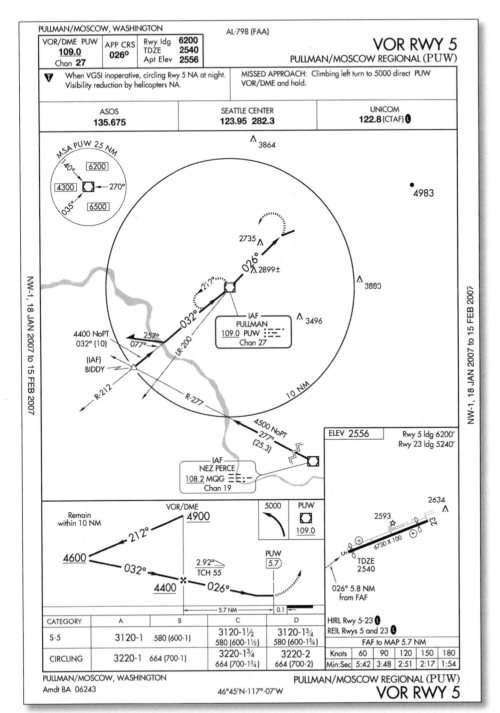

Figure 17-6: Coming from MQG to intercept the radial to PUW, you need to make a pretty big turn. The plate helps you out with a lead radial marked LR-200. When you cross the 200 radial from PUW, that's a good time to start your right-hand turn to actually intercept the 212 radial inbound (with 032 dialed on your OBS).

↓ STUDENT OF THE CRAFT

WHAT'S IN A NAME?

The name of the approach tells you what nav aids are required for the approach and to which runway it leads you. The VOR Rwy 23 approach can be flown using a VOR, and it will lead you within 30° left or right of Runway 23. A VOR-DME or GPS-A approach could be flown using either a combination of VORs and DME or a GPS. Since there is only a letter listed in the name rather than a runway, it will take you to the airport, but you might have to maneuver to line up with a runway and land. The letter helps designate between approaches at the same airport such as GPS-A, GPS-B, and so on.

LOCALIZER APPROACHES

Figure 17-7: Localizer signals can usually be received within 18 miles of the airport and 10° left or right of course. When the aircraft receives both lobes equally, it must be aligned with the runway.

VOR approaches are great in terms of simplicity, but they're wanting for accuracy. The same avionics in the airplane can receive signals from a *localizer* (LOC). The localizer is a transmitter located at the airport and aligned with a specific runway. It transmits two, lobe-shaped signals along the extended center of the runway (see Figure 17-7). (The antennas are small and hard to see, but the buildings housing the transmitting equipment are things you've probably seen at airports. They're located at the end of a runway and painted orange and white.) A receiver in the airplane looks at the relative strength of the two signals and figures out whether the airplane is left of course, right of course, or dead center.

A localizer is about six times as accurate as a VOR. The width of the signal in degrees is tailored so that it is about 700 feet wide at the landing threshold of the runway. The localizer antenna is actually located at the far end of the runway, so the longer the runway, the narrower the localizer.

404

PART I
PREFLIGHT

PART II
SPORT PILOT

PART III
PRIVATE PILOT

PART IV
INSTRUMENT RATING

PART V
COMMERCIAL LICENSE

PART VI
ATP AND BEYOND

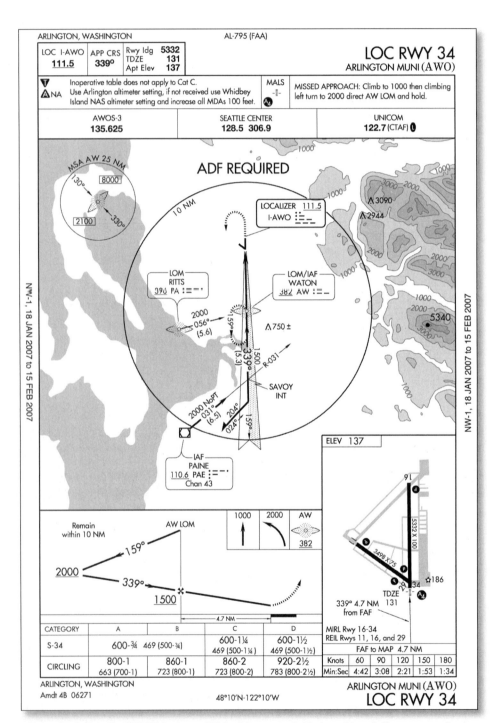

Figure 17-8: *Note that WATON is also an IAF for this approach. That would apply if you were going to proceed direct to WATON and then fly the localizer signal backward, make a procedure turn, and then reintercept inbound to the airport. Flying a localizer signal backward is a bit tricky, so we'll cover that in the next chapter.*

You actually dial in and fly the localizer in almost the same way you do the VOR. The only difference is that you'll find the needle is much more sensitive and the OBS setting has no effect on the CDI needle.

Let's look at the LOC Rwy 34 approach at Arlington, Washington (KAWO), shown in Figure 17-8. To receive the localizer, you enter its frequency of 111.5 into your number-one NAV radio. You could ID it just as you do a VOR, but the ID has four letters in it with the first one being *I*. The CDI needle would show you left or right, of course, and spinning the OBS would have no effect. As a habit, however, it's a good idea to put the inbound heading—in this case 340—on the top of the CDI just for reference.

If you were getting vectors from ATC, you would eventually be vectored on a heading of about 010° to intercept the localizer, and you would be cleared for the approach. You would see the CDI needle start to center just as with the VOR, but it might move a bit more quickly than you're used to because of the increased sensitivity. You would turn inbound on the heading of 340 and then make whatever minor heading corrections were necessary to keep the needle centered. Note that the increased sensitivity of the localizer needle means it is easy to overcorrect when adjusting for wind. As a rule, make heading corrections of no more than 10° at first and no more than 5° when you're close to finding a heading that works.

The missed approach point on the localizer approach is often determined by time after crossing the FAF. The FAF on this approach is something called a *locator outer marker* (LOM). The LOM is actually two radios combined. It's an NDB, like we discussed briefly in Chapter 10, and something called a *marker beacon*. The marker beacon causes a light to flash on the aircraft panel just to the left of the airspeed indicator and a sound to chime just as you cross overhead. Since this is an *outer marker*, the light will be blue, and the sound will be a long tone—Morse code for the letter *O*—repeated. Seeing the light and hearing the sound are your cues to start your timer and descend from 1,500 feet to 600 feet.

A NOTE ON NOTES

The approach at KAWO has a few interesting notes at the top of the plate. One says that if you can't get the altimeter setting for Arlington, you should use the altimeter for the nearby Whidbey Naval Air Station. Doing this raises the MDAs by 100 feet, however. It's up to you to remember to descend to 700 feet instead of 600.

STUDENT OF THE CRAFT

LOW-BUDGET LOCALIZERS: THE LDA AND SDF

Sometimes a localizer antenna cannot be aligned with the runway at the airport because inconvenient objects such as radio towers or mountains block the extended centerline of the runway. You can still use a localizer for accurate guidance to the airport, but because it does not take the pilot to a specific runway, it is referred to as a *localizer directional aid* (LDA).

Another variant on the localizer theme is a simplified directional facility (SDF). This is a localizer-like signal that it is fixed at either 6° or 12° wide. It might or might not be aligned with the runway.

Continued

406

PART I	PART II	PART III	PART IV	PART V	PART VI
PREFLIGHT	SPORT PILOT	PRIVATE PILOT	INSTRUMENT RATING	COMMERCIAL LICENSE	ATP AND BEYOND

Both LDA and SDF approaches are flown just like localizer approaches. The only difference is the accuracy or what you should expect to see when you break out of the clouds.

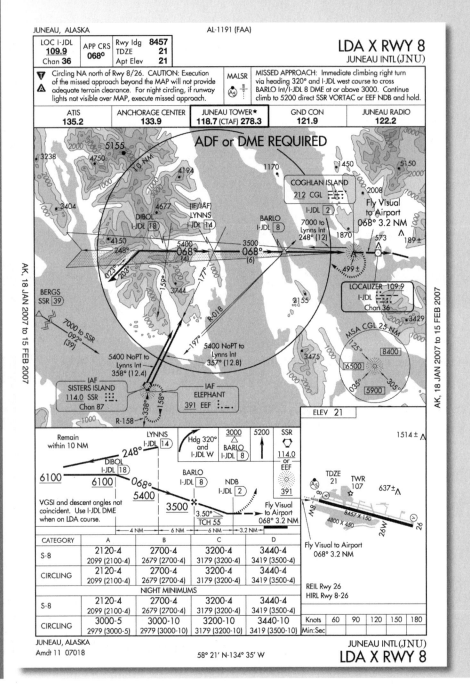

THE BIG KAHUNA: *ILS APPROACHES*

Figure 17-9: With both lateral and vertical guidance, the ILS is the most accurate approach available in FSX and for civilian pilots in the real world. The accuracy is tighter vertically than horizontally and is like flying down an ever-narrowing cone.

The gold standard in instrument approaches is the instrument landing system (ILS), as shown in Figure 17-9. The ILS is the localizer we just talked about combined with the second tool called the *glideslope* (GS). The localizer provides accurate left-right guidance for the airplane. The glideslope does the same in terms of altitude. Much like the visual approach slope indicator (VASI) you saw in earlier chapters, the glideslope guides the airplane on a continuous descent to the spot very close to the end of the runway.

Like the localizer, the glideslope gets more sensitive the closer you get to the runway. By combining the two, you are essentially flying down an ever-narrowing cone. Such precision usually allows you to fly within half a mile of the end of the runway and within 200 feet of terra firma.

The glideslope signal is a completely different frequency from the localizer signal, but you don't have to worry about tuning it. Every localizer frequency has a specific glideslope frequency paired with it. So if you tune in the localizer and that localizer is part of an ILS, the glideslope is also tuned. If you ID the localizer, then you have identified the glideslope as well.

Your position on the glideslope is indicated by two small yellow triangles on either side of the HSI. Just as the yellow needle represents the course in the center of the HSI and your position relative to that course, the yellow triangles represent the glideslope in the center of the HSI and your position relative to that glideslope. ATC vectors you to intercept the localizer far enough from the airport that the glideslope is well over your head. You track inbound on the localizer, maintaining a constant altitude, and see the yellow triangles begin to descend from the top of the HSI.

When they are about halfway between the top of the HSI and the center, you should slow to approach level with the gear extended and the flaps in the approach position. By the time the yellow triangles reach the center of the HSI, you should be down to 100 knots, and a power reduction allows you to descend on the glideslope all the way to the runway.

Because every ILS uses a localizer as part of its navigation system, every ILS approach could theoretically be flown as a localizer approach. Looking at the ILS approach to KPAE (see Figure 17-10), you see in the title that it might be flown as ILS or an LOC to Runway 16R. Obviously, the ILS provides greater guidance and allows you to land in worse weather. It's possible, however, that the glideslope portion of the approach was out of service or the glideslope receiver in your aircraft wasn't working, in which case you fly the localizer version. You'll find different minima for the two approaches in the minima section.

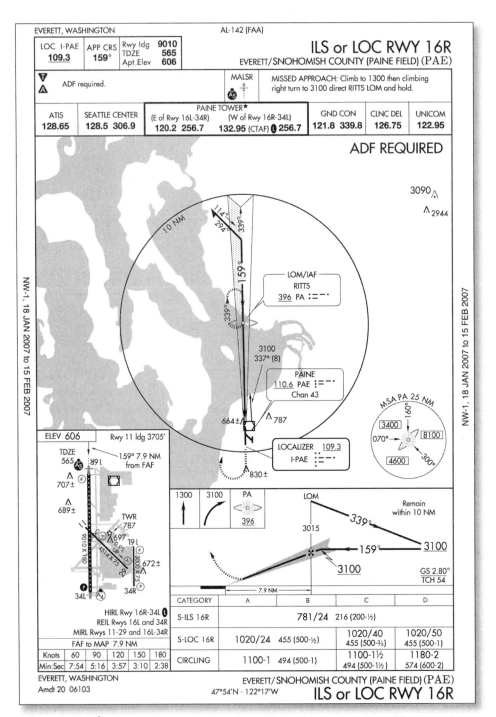

Figure 17-10: The FAF for an ILS is where you intercept the glideslope. Sometimes this occurs at the same point as the FAF for the localizer-only version of the same approach, but usually it occurs a little earlier. Here at KPAE, you intercept the glideslope at 3,100 feet and begin to descend. By the time you cross the outer marker, you are at 3,015 feet.

Because the ILS is so much more precise than any of the other approaches, it earns the title *precision approach*, while the other approaches are called *nonprecision approaches*.

DOWN THROUGH THE MUCK: FLYING APPROACHES

That's a lot of theory on how to fly instrument approaches, and we've just scratched the surface. It's enough to get you flying, however, and that's what we want to do now. Part of the beauty of FSX is that you don't need to go through an entire flight just to get to an instrument approach. You can fly the approach and then immediately back up and try it again.

Don't worry whether you feel you're a bit behind when trying to fly these approaches. This is hard work. We have many friends who fly for commercial airlines and the military and say that single-pilot IFR is harder than anything they do on a regular basis (except when people are shooting at them, that is).

INSIDE THE GAME

STAYING IN THE CLOUDS

Cloud density in FSX is dependent on your display settings. To make sure your IMC experience is full of clouds, do one of two things. On faster systems, be sure the cloud density slider (Options > Settings > Display > Weather) are set to Maximum. On slower systems, choose Simple Clouds rather than Detailed Clouds on the same page. On any system, make sure your visibility in the clouds is set to its lowest value of $\frac{1}{16}$ mile. Even if the clouds are set to overcast, a visibility of 10 miles will punch huge holes in the clouds.

A VOR AT KPAE

Load the flight Chap_17_VOR_at_KPAE. Take a moment to get your bearings before you unpause FSX. You might also want to arrange your radios and GPS, as shown in Figure 17-11, to see everything at once. You're at 4,000 feet, flying at high cruise. You've just been told to expect vectors to the VOR-B approach at Paine Field. This approach was actually replaced with the VOR Rwy 16R approach that you flew earlier in this chapter.

410

PART I	PART II	PART III	PART IV	PART V	PART VI
PREFLIGHT	SPORT PILOT	PRIVATE PILOT	INSTRUMENT RATING	COMMERCIAL LICENSE	ATP AND BEYOND

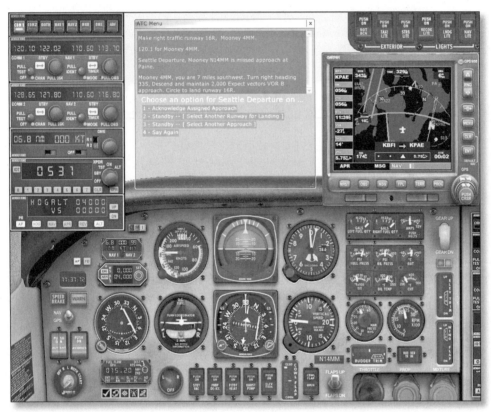

Figure 17-11: When you're in the clouds, there's no point in worrying about what you can see out the window. Feel free to fill that space with your radios and the ATC window.

KEEPING IT REAL

GEORGE DOES MANEUVERS WHILE YOU DO PROCEDURES

Instrument flying encompasses both maneuvers and procedures. Maneuvers are what you learned in Chapter 15 when you learned how to physically fly the airplane without being able to see outside. Procedures are what you've been learning in this chapter and Chapter 16. Procedures are the headings and altitudes you fly at a given moment as well as the radios you use for communication and navigation.

Do yourself a favor and use the autopilot to fly the airplane as you're learning your way around approach plates and instrument approaches. When you've got the approach thing down, then go back and do it again while flying the airplane by hand at the same time.

You should have the GPS visible for all these approaches to keep a bird's-eye view of what's happening. We won't really talk about using the GPS as part of your approaches until the next chapter.

The problem is that the old VOR-B has an inbound heading of 160. You can use the VOR Rwy 16R approach plate if you want, but to better match FSX we've included a VOR-B version of the approach on the website (www.wiley.com). If you're using Jeppesen SimCharts, you have the correct VOR-B approach with a final approach course of 160.

You're on autopilot, and you've just been given a vector and a clearance to descend to 2,000 feet. Your first step is to acknowledge the clearance and start descending. Click the appropriate box in the ATC window to acknowledge the clearance, and then dial 2,000 feet into the autopilot's altitude window, as shown in Figure 17-12. The prop has been slowed to 2200 rpm, but the MP is still in the 30s; reduce the MP by two inches, and note the time. When two minutes go, by reduce the MP by another two inches. Your target is to reach 25 inches and 2200 rpm, so the Mooney slows to a low cruise speed of 120 knots some time after you level off at 2,000.

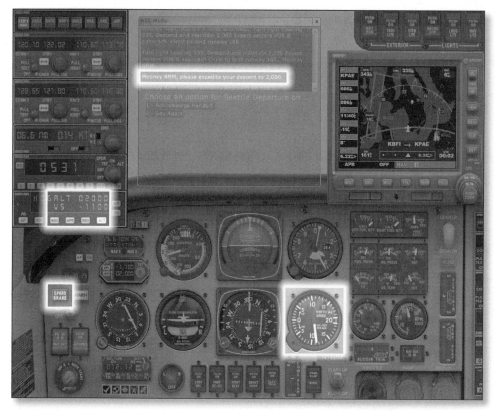

Figure 17-12: If you need to get down faster, you can always use the speed brakes. Just remember to change the vertical speed on the AP if you're using it. (Figure continued on next page.)

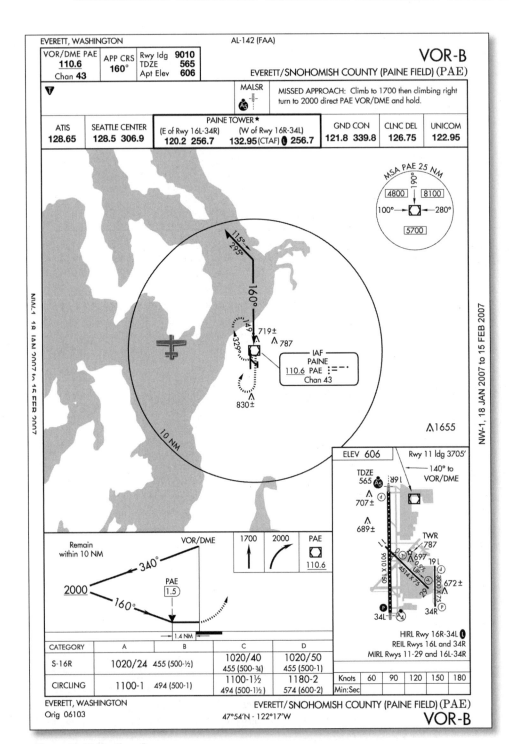

EVERETT, WASHINGTON   AL-142 (FAA)

VOR/DME PAE **110.6** Chan **43**	APP CRS **160°**	Rwy Idg **9010** TDZE **565** Apt Elev **606**

VOR-B

EVERETT/SNOHOMISH COUNTY (PAINE FIELD) (PAE)

MISSED APPROACH: Climb to 1700 then climbing right turn to 2000 direct PAE VOR/DME and hold.

ATIS **128.65**	SEATTLE CENTER **128.5 306.9**	PAINE TOWER ★ (E of Rwy 16L-34R) **120.2 256.7**	(W of Rwy 16R-34L) **132.95**(CTAF) **256.7**	GND CON **121.8 339.8**	CLNC DEL **126.75**	UNICOM **122.95**

MSA PAE 25 NM

Figure 17-12 (Continued)

EVERETT, WASHINGTON
Orig 06103

EVERETT/SNOHOMISH COUNTY (PAINE FIELD) (PAE)
47°54'N - 122°17'W

VOR-B

CATEGORY	A	B	C	D
S-16R	1020/24 455 (500-½)		1020/40 455 (500-¾)	1020/50 455 (500-1)
CIRCLING	1100-1 494 (500-1)		1100-1½ 494 (500-1½)	1180-2 574 (600-2)

Knots	60	90	120	150	180
Min:Sec					

HIRL Rwy 16R-34L
REIL Rwys 16L and 34R
MIRL Rwys 11-29 and 16L-34R

ELEV 606   Rwy 11 ldg 3705'

At some point, you are handed off to Whidbey Approach; they give you vectors for the VOR approach.

As you're on your way down, you can get the KPAE ATIS on 128.65. In the real world, the best way to do this is to ask Approach whether you can leave the frequency for a moment. That way you can listen to the ATIS information without any distractions. You can't do this in FSX, so you need to monitor two frequencies at once. The best way to do this is to put ATIS frequency into COM2 and push both buttons on the audio panel, as shown in Figure 17-13.

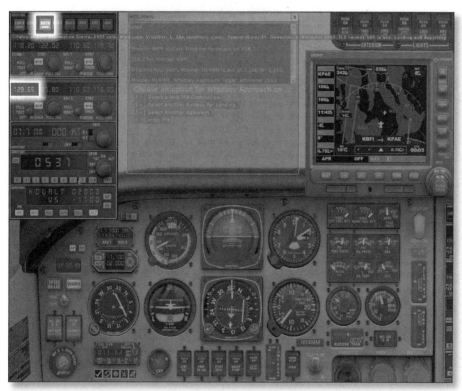

Figure 17-13: Although you can't ask to leave the frequency in FSX, at least you can read the ATIS or AWOS information rather than trying to listen to it while simultaneously listening to radio chatter.

 KEEPING IT REAL

WHY WEATHER MATTERS

Getting the local airport information is always the first step for your approach because that information might change which approach you'll fly. Ideally, you choose an approach that is already lined up into the wind to land straight ahead. Also, you want an approach that has minima lower than the reported ceiling at the airport. Finally, you need the local altimeter setting before you shoot the approach, or you might be at the wrong altitude above the ground as you're skimming through the mist trying to find the airport.

414

PART I	PART II	PART III	PART IV	PART V	PART VI
PREFLIGHT	SPORT PILOT	PRIVATE PILOT	INSTRUMENT RATING	COMMERCIAL LICENSE	ATP AND BEYOND

Make sure you also have PAE dialed in and identified on NAV1. You'll want it on NAV1 because that is the NAV connected to your HSI. The GPS is there for added situational awareness. It shows you your relation to the airport and is a huge help in keeping the big picture in mind. It makes you appreciate the extra apprehension of pilots who trained without moving maps of any kind—a group that includes both authors.

In addition, make sure the OBS arrow on the HSI is pointing to 160. This is your inbound heading to the VOR and means you fly inbound (160) on the 340 radial off the VOR. Any other setting on the OBS has you track the wrong radial to the VOR.

Follow ATC instructions, and use your heading bug to change headings. You are vectored about 90° to the final approach course (Figure 17-14) and then about 25° to the final approach course.

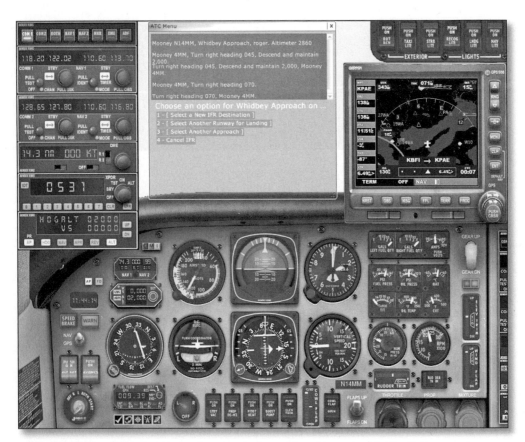

Figure 17-14: You want to be at low cruise when you're on a base leg approaching the final approach course.

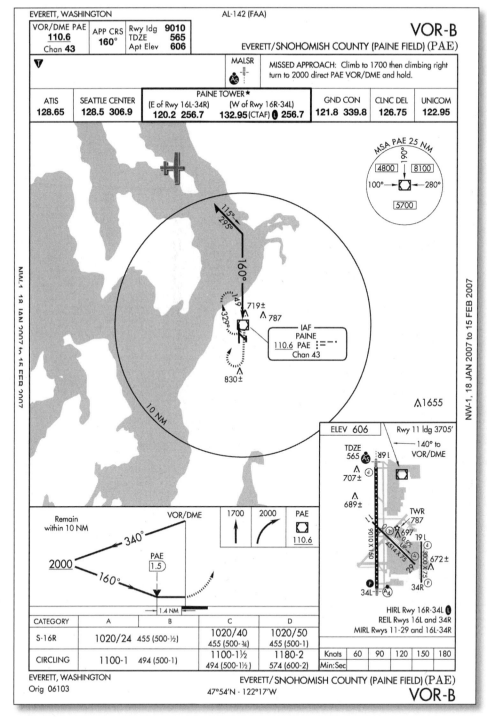

EVERETT, WASHINGTON   AL-142 (FAA)

VOR/DME PAE	APP CRS	Rwy ldg	9010
110.6	**160°**	TDZE	565
Chan **43**		Apt Elev	606

VOR-B

EVERETT/SNOHOMISH COUNTY (PAINE FIELD) (PAE)

MALSR

MISSED APPROACH: Climb to 1700 then climbing right turn to 2000 direct PAE VOR/DME and hold.

ATIS	SEATTLE CENTER	PAINE TOWER ★		GND CON	CLNC DEL	UNICOM
128.65	128.5 306.9	(E of Rwy 16L-34R) 120.2 256.7	(W of Rwy 16R-34L) 132.95 (CTAF) 256.7	121.8 339.8	126.75	122.95

MSA PAE 25 NM

	4800	8100	
100°			280°
	5700		

IAF
PAINE
110.6 PAE
Chan 43

ELEV 606

Rwy 11 ldg 3705'

TDZE 565

140° to VOR/DME

HIRL Rwy 16R-34L
REIL Rwys 16L and 34R
MIRL Rwys 11-29 and 16L-34R

Remain within 10 NM

340°

2000

160°

PAE
1.5

1700	2000	PAE
↑	↱	110.6

1.4 NM

CATEGORY	A	B	C	D
S-16R	1020/24 455 (500-½)		1020/40 455 (500-¾)	1020/50 455 (500-1)
CIRCLING	1100-1 494 (500-1)		1100-1½ 494 (500-1½)	1180-2 574 (600-2)

Knots	60	90	120	150	180
Min:Sec					

EVERETT, WASHINGTON
Orig 06103

EVERETT/SNOHOMISH COUNTY (PAINE FIELD) (PAE)
47°54'N - 122°17'W

VOR-B

NW-1, 18 JAN 2007 to 15 FEB 2007

Figure 17-14 (Continued)

416

PART I
PREFLIGHT

PART II
SPORT PILOT

PART III
PRIVATE PILOT

PART IV
INSTRUMENT RATING

PART V
COMMERCIAL LICENSE

PART VI
ATP AND BEYOND

When you're on the intercept heading, you are cleared for the approach and handed off to Paine Tower. Now is the time to transition to approach level. To do so, drop the gear, and confirm you have a *gear-safe* green light. Contact the tower as your speed decreases.

When the course needle moves toward center on the HSI, make a turn as necessary to center it (see Figure 17-15). You could use the nav function on the autopilot to fly the approach, but stay a bit more involved for training. Continue using the heading bug to control your heading. When you center on course, lower the flaps to the approach position, lower the MP to 19 inches, and set the altitude to 1,100 feet. Turn on the boost pump, and push the prop and mixture controls full forward.

Figure 17-15: Wait until the yellow CDI needle on the HSI is under the white lubber line on the HSI to begin your turn. Turn just enough to keep these two lines connected until you're exactly on course.

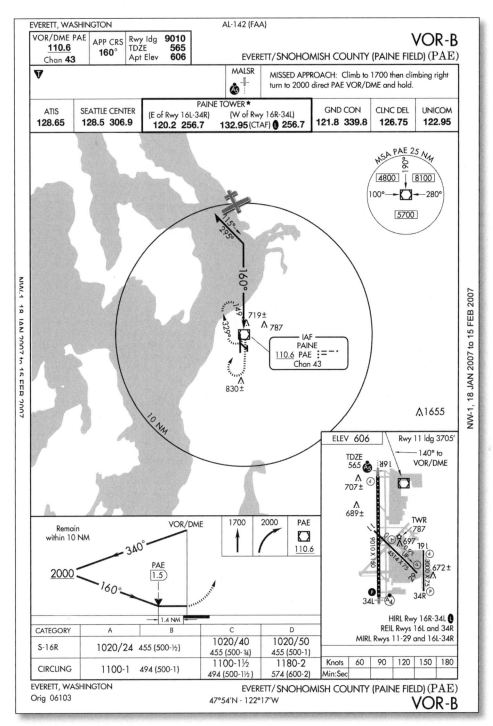

EVERETT, WASHINGTON   AL-142 (FAA)

VOR/DME PAE	APP CRS	Rwy Idg	9010	
110.6	**160°**	TDZE	565	
Chan **43**		Apt Elev	606	

VOR-B

EVERETT/SNOHOMISH COUNTY (PAINE FIELD) (PAE)

MISSED APPROACH: Climb to 1700 then climbing right turn to 2000 direct PAE VOR/DME and hold.

MALSR

ATIS	SEATTLE CENTER	PAINE TOWER *		GND CON	CLNC DEL	UNICOM
		(E of Rwy 16L-34R)	(W of Rwy 16R-34L)			
128.65	**128.5 306.9**	**120.2 256.7**	**132.95**(CTAF) 256.7	**121.8 339.8**	**126.75**	**122.95**

MSA PAE 25 NM

IAF
PAINE
110.6 PAE
Chan 43

Remain within 10 NM

VOR/DME

340°

PAE 1.5

160°

2000

1.4 NM

ELEV 606   Rwy 11 ldg 3705'

TDZE 565   140° to VOR/DME

TWR 787

HIRL Rwy 16R-34L
REIL Rwys 16L and 34R
MIRL Rwys 11-29 and 16L-34R

CATEGORY	A	B	C	D
S-16R	1020/24 455 (500-½)		1020/40 455 (500-¾)	1020/50 455 (500-1)
CIRCLING	1100-1 494 (500-1)		1100-1½ 494 (500-1½)	1180-2 574 (600-2)

Knots	60	90	120	150	180
Min:Sec					

EVERETT, WASHINGTON
Orig 06103

EVERETT/SNOHOMISH COUNTY (PAINE FIELD) (PAE)
47°54'N - 122°17'W

VOR-B

Figure 17-15 (Continued)

418

PART I
FREEFLIGHT

PART II
SPORT PILOT

PART III
PRIVATE PILOT

PART IV
INSTRUMENT RATING

PART V
COMMERCIAL LICENSE

PART VI
ATP AND BEYOND

Now press P on the keyboard to pause the flight. Think about what you're doing here. You're lined up with an airport you can't see descending with faith that it will be there when you break out. Sometimes FSX's ATIS doesn't get the weather quite right, but ceilings for Paine are set to 1,500 feet with less than a mile visibility. This is pretty cool stuff

Before you unpause the flight and continue, press the Alt key to see the menus, and choose Flight > Save. Save the flight under the name "temp." You'll come back to this point in a moment. Unpause the flight, and continue.

Why set 1,100 on the altitude instead of 1,020? Well, you do this because there is no way to set 1,020 on the Mooney. Fly via autopilot to the nearest altitude you can that's above the MDA, and then manually fly the last 80 feet. You never want to go below MDA until you can see the airport and land.

When you get down to 1,100 feet, press Z on your keyboard to disconnect the autopilot, and continue down to 1,020 feet. When you get there, bring the MP back up to 25 inches right away. You need that much power to fly level at 100 knots with both gear and flaps out. Conveniently, the MP is just about the same as approach level where gear was out but flaps were in. Now both gear and flaps are out (more drag), but your prop control is full forward so the RPM is higher (more power).

Press W on your keyboard to see only the critical instruments while you look for the runway (see Figure 17-16). You might want to move the ATC window to the side as well. Do your best to keep 1,020 feet with your pitch. If you need to tweak your MP setting a bit to go faster or slower, do so, but make just a tiny adjustment at a time. When you see the airport, you can head for the runway. When you're sure you can make it to the runway, lower full flaps and land.

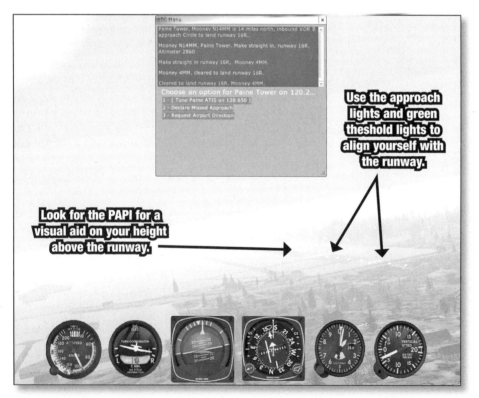

Figure 17-16: The runway is to the right of the VOR, and you might fly past it before you see it. The same visual effect can happen even when the approach is directly to the runway but your heading is to one side or the other to account for the wind.

> ↓ KEEPING IT REAL
>
> # 1,000 TO GO
>
> With instrument students, we strongly recommend they audibly call out altitudes as they descend. For example, the MDA for the VOR approach at Paine is 1,020. Passing 2,520 feet, you would call out "1,500 to go." At 2,020 feet, you'd call out "1,000 to go." At 1,520 feet, the call would be "500 to go," and you'd continue with each 100 feet to the MDA, "400...300...200 and adding power to level...100...level at 1,020."
>
> This helps ensure you do not descend below MDA. It's also easier to do if you've usually pick two spots on the altimeter 180° apart and watch for the hundreds hand as it sweeps past those two places.

THE MISSED AT KPAE

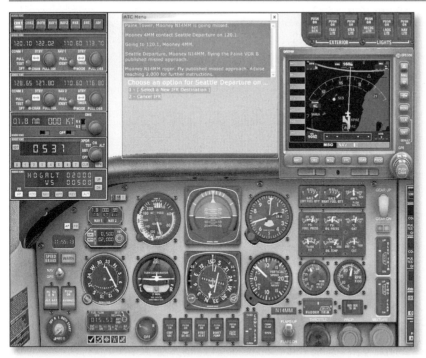

Figure 17-17: Your first segment of the missed approach is to climb straight ahead to 1,700 feet. The next move is back to the VOR. Your OBS and the GPS can help you keep tabs on where that is.

After you've landed at KPAE and congratulated yourself on a job well done, choose Flight > Load and reload "temp." This time let's not find the runway. It'll be easy: just don't press W on your keyboard. Continue until you pass over the VOR, and the To triangle switches into a From triangle.

Now things happen rather fast. *Climb* at full power. *Clean* the airplane by retracting gear and flaps. After a check that you're still climbing, *cool* things off by opening the cowl flaps (partway is fine because this is a short climb) and reducing the rpm to 2400 and the MP to 34 inches. Then *communicate* to ATC that you're on the missed approach by clicking the Declare Missed Approach in the ATC window. You are handed off to Seattle Center, and from them, you should ask for the published missed approach. See Figure 17-17 for what this all looks like in the cockpit.

420

PART I
PREFLIGHT

PART II
SPORT PILOT

PART III
PRIVATE PILOT

PART IV
INSTRUMENT RATING

PART V
COMMERCIAL LICENSE

PART VI
ATP AND BEYOND

This is a lot to do, so feel free to reengage the heading mode on the autopilot and dial in a 500 fpm climb to 2,000 feet, which is your missed approach holding altitude.

▼ REAL VOR-B MISSED MORE COMPLEX

If you're using the Jeppesen SIMCharts, the missed approach shown will be more complex, but for training, you can just fly the missed by turning back to the VOR.

Passing 1,700 feet—and that happens quickly—you need to start a right turn directly back to the VOR. This move often confounds students for a bit because they center the CDI needle and then turn to try to intercept that course back to the VOR. Of course, in the turn, they get way off course and get frustrated. Here's an easier way: You know the VOR is somewhere behind you. Spin the heading bug about 90° west to start the right turn. When N on the OBS is off to the right, spin the heading bug again to line up with north. This gets you going generally in the direction of the VOR.

Now spin the OBS to center the CDI needle with a TO flag. That's the radial you're on, and if you could turn instantly to that heading, you'd go to the VOR. But you can do a bit better. Turn the OBS a bit farther so that you'll intercept that course to the VOR. Usually one-half or even one-quarter scale deflection is enough (see Figure 17-18). You can then intercept and fly back to the VOR for what should be a parallel entry into the hold.

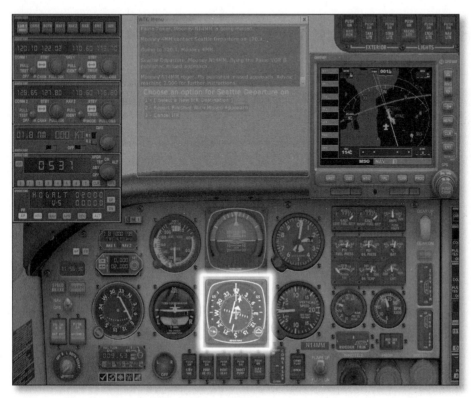

Figure 17-18: The actual course you fly back to the VOR is irrelevant, so long as you get there. Pick a radial you can intercept easily, and track inbound.

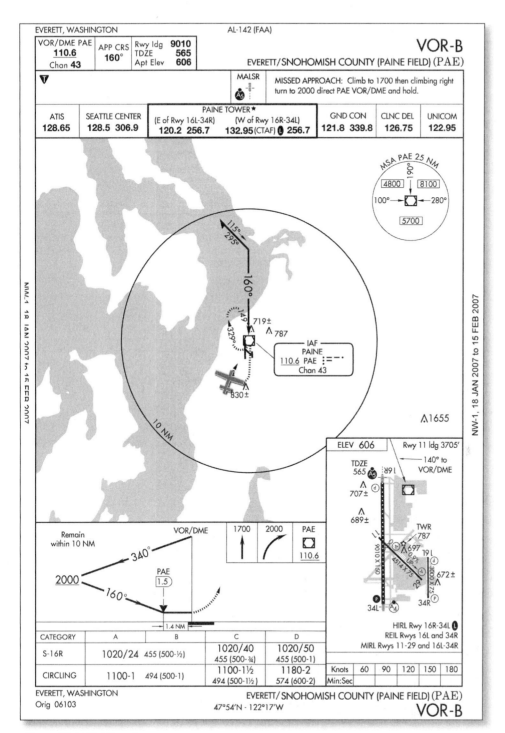

EVERETT, WASHINGTON — AL-142 (FAA)

| VOR/DME PAE 110.6 Chan 43 | APP CRS 160° | Rwy Idg 9010 TDZE 565 Apt Elev 606 | VOR-B EVERETT/SNOHOMISH COUNTY (PAINE FIELD) (PAE) |

MALSR

MISSED APPROACH: Climb to 1700 then climbing right turn to 2000 direct PAE VOR/DME and hold.

| ATIS 128.65 | SEATTLE CENTER 128.5 306.9 | PAINE TOWER ★ (E of Rwy 16L-34R) 120.2 256.7 | (W of Rwy 16R-34L) 132.95 (CTAF) 256.7 | GND CON 121.8 339.8 | CLNC DEL 126.75 | UNICOM 122.95 |

MSA PAE 25 NM

ELEV 606 — Rwy 11 Idg 3705'

CATEGORY | A | B | C | D
S-16R | 1020/24 455 (500-½) | | 1020/40 455 (500-¾) | 1020/50 455 (500-1)
CIRCLING | 1100-1 494 (500-1) | | 1100-1½ 494 (500-1½) | 1180-2 574 (600-2)

| Knots | 60 | 90 | 120 | 150 | 180 |
| Min:Sec | | | | | |

HIRL Rwy 16R-34L
REIL Rwys 16L and 34R
MIRL Rwys 11-29 and 16L-34R

EVERETT, WASHINGTON
Orig 06103

EVERETT/SNOHOMISH COUNTY (PAINE FIELD) (PAE)
47°54'N - 122°17'W
VOR-B

Figure 17-18 (Continued)

422

PART I	PART II	PART III	PART IV	PART V	PART VI
PREFLIGHT	SPORT PILOT	PRIVATE PILOT	INSTRUMENT RATING	COMMERCIAL LICENSE	ATP AND BEYOND

The hold is just for killing time, so you might as well save some virtual gas. Slow to low cruise as you level off at 2,000 feet. Don't forget to close the cowl flaps. When you cross the VOR, do your five *T*s, and fly a parallel entry into the hold as you practiced in the previous chapter.

Take Two: The Full Procedure at KPAE

You can actually fly the approach again from the hold, but let's do it a bit more realistically with some altitude and speed to lose. Load the flight Chap_17_Full_Procedure_KPAE. This is same flight as before except you're a bit farther south. Just for fun and so the procedure turn is easier to do, if you're using the VOR Rwy 16R approach plate from the website, fly it exactly as written and track the 320 radial outbound and the 140 radial inbound. If you're using the Jeppesen SIMCharts, it'll be the 340 radial outbound and the 160 radial inbound.

You've just been cleared to descend to 2,000 feet and expect vectors, but you want to practice the full procedure. You need to request this from the controller. This is how it happens in the real world, too. If ATC can give you vectors, they expect that you want them. It does make life easier, after all.

Figure 17-19: You can change approaches up until you accept the approach. After that, you need to declare a "missed" in order to see the list of approaches again.

In the ATC window, shown in Figure 17-19, you can click the option for selecting another approach. Click that link, choose the VOR-B, and then choose the PAE transition instead of vectors.

You're in basically the same boat as before, and you need to slow down to make this work. Start reducing the power toward low cruise as you did before. You definitely want your speed brakes for this one because you want to be at 2,000 *and* 120 knots by the time you're outbound on the procedure turn.

Proceed directly to the VOR by turning northeast to get yourself in the right direction and then finding a radial directly to the VOR using the OBS on the HSI. After you cross the VOR, your next step is to intercept the 320 radial outbound and track it (see Figure 17-20). Note the time as you cross the VOR. You want to

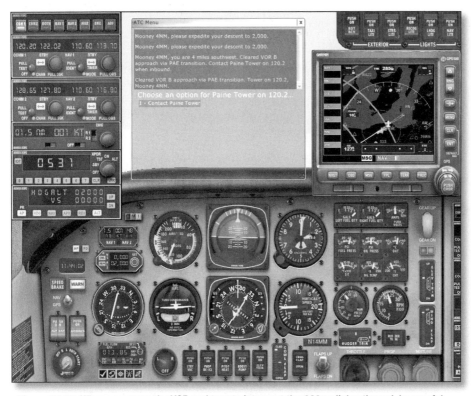

Figure 17-20: When you cross the VOR and turn to intercept the 320 radial outbound, be careful not to intercept on too large an angle, or you'll shoot right through it—as is happening here.

go outbound for about 5 miles. That's about two minutes at 145 knots. You can use DME to keep track of this.

After those two minutes or five miles, go through the five Ts noted when this approach was described earlier in this chapter, with the turn being a turn to a heading of 275. After a minute and a half, make a 180° right turn to 095. While turning, lower your gear to slow to 100 knots in approach level. From this point forward, the approach is identical to the vectored approach you just did. Intercept the 320 radial on a 140 heading inbound, descend, and find the airport.

As before, you're welcome to use the autopilot as you're learning, but use HDG mode for your heading rather than having it track NAV or APR (approach) so you get in the habit of flying a specific heading that results in you staying on course.

A LOC AT KAWO

Load the flight Chap_17_LOC_at_KAWO. This flight has you at 3,000 feet, just south of PAE. You've just been given a clearance to expect vectors for the localizer Runway 34 approach at Arlington (KAWO), shown in Figure 17-21. Read the clearance, and then unpause FSX to acknowledge it and start flying.

Because you're on vectors, you can set up your avionics stack for this approach. Use the approach plate for your briefing. The first step is to get the AWOS for Arlington. Now that you know what ceilings, visibility, and weather to expect, as well as what altimeter setting to use for KAWO, you can dial in the localizer.

The localizer frequency is 111.5 at KAWO (see Figure 17-22). Tune it in NAV1, and identify it. Now turn the OBS a full 360°. Note how the needle always shows deflection on the same side regardless of where it points. You could fly the approach with the OBS pointing anywhere. Make life easier for yourself and dial in 340, which is the inbound course to KAWO.

424

| PART I | PART II | PART III | PART IV | PART V | PART VI |
| PREFLIGHT | SPORT PILOT | PRIVATE PILOT | INSTRUMENT RATING | COMMERCIAL LICENSE | ATP AND BEYOND |

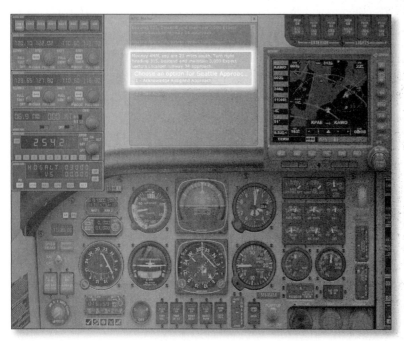

Figure 17-21: You're in high cruise, ready to set up for the approach.

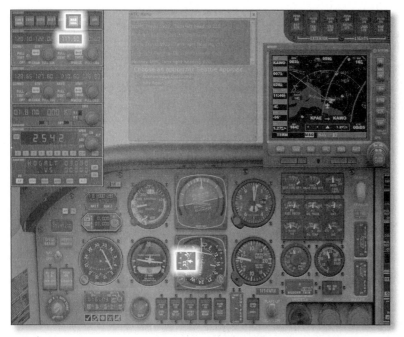

Figure 17-22: After you're on a vector base leg, you'd better start slowing down, get the localizer tuned in, and turn the marker beacons on.

You also want to activate the MKR button on your audio panel. This makes an audible sound as you pass over WATON to remind you to make the final descent from 1,500 to 600 feet. The O light flashes regardless of the MKR button setting.

Soon, you get a turn to 010 and a clearance for the approach. You also descend to 1,500 feet. From here, you fly on the 010 heading until the localizer needle comes alive and begins to center. Remember the localizer is more sensitive than the VOR and centers quickly, even several miles out from the airport.

You might still be going quite fast, too. Your goal is to be in approach level at 100 knots just before you cross WATON. If you intercept the localizer and you're still just going too fast, consider lowering the gear (below 140 knots) to help slow down. You must be at 100 knots at WATON to get an accurate timing from WATON to the MAP.

ATC also tells you to switch to advisory frequency. KAWO is an uncontrolled airport, so you have to report your own position on approach for any VFR aircraft that might be nearby. If the airport is well below VFR minima, then you should be the only airplane there. Unlike airports with control towers, uncontrolled airports can have only one IFR aircraft in the area at one time.

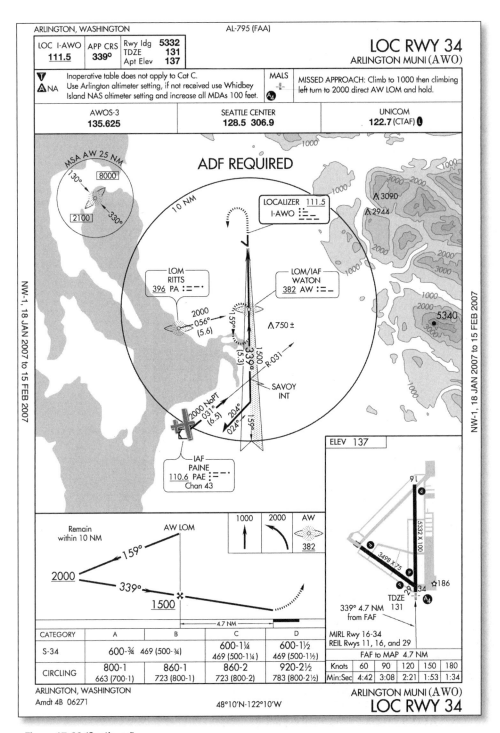

Figure 17-22 (Continued)

426

PART I	PART II	PART III	PART IV	PART V	PART VI
PRE FLIGHT	SPORT PILOT	PRIVATE PILOT	INSTRUMENT RATING	COMMERCIAL LICENSE	ATP AND BEYOND

STUDENT OF THE CRAFT

HOW LONG ON THE CLOCK

When flying approaches at 100 knots, you have to regularly extrapolate time between the 90 and 120 knot values. The easiest way is to look at the difference in minutes between the two speeds. At KAWO it's 47 seconds (3:08 – 2:21). Dividing that by 3 is roughly 16 seconds; 100 knots is one third the way between 90 and 120, so take 16 seconds off the timing for 90 knots. The approximate timing for 100 knots on the LOC Rwy 34 at KAWO is 3:08 – 0:16, or 2:52.

When you cross WATON (Figure 17-23), the marker flashes and sounds. Your five *T*s are as follows: Start a *time* counting to 2:52. *Turn* only if necessary to stay on course. There is nothing more you need to *tune*. Set the *throttle* to 19 inches and the flaps to approach. *Talk* to anybody in the pattern at KAWO to say you're 4.7 miles south at WATON inbound for Runway 34.

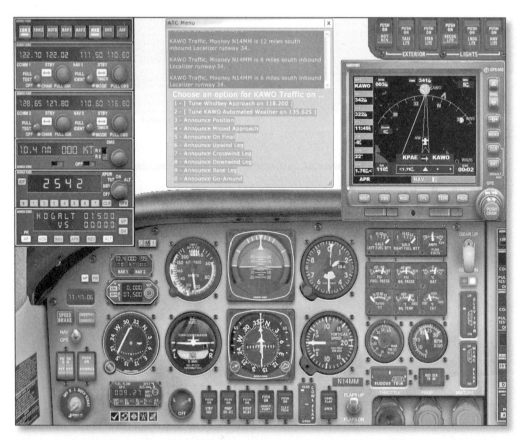

Figure 17-23: When the blue beacon light illuminates and you hear a pulsing tone, switch from approach level to approach descent. Watch the GPS to keep track of AW (WATON) and the direction of the runway.

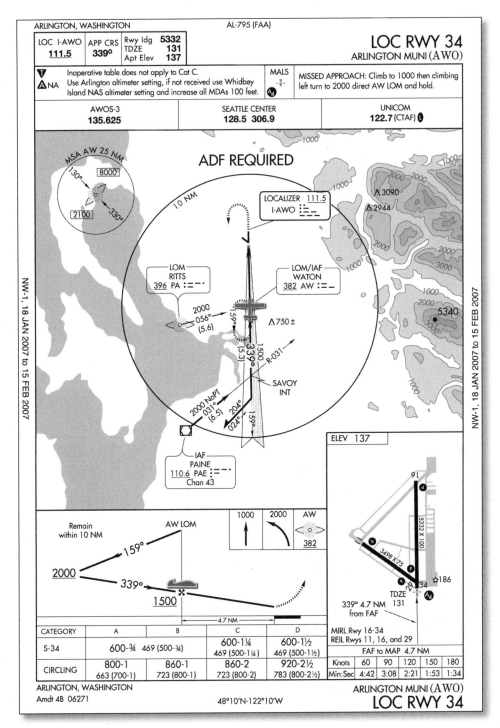

Figure 17-23 (Continued)

428

| PART I | PART II | PART III | PART IV | PART V | PART VI |
| PREFLIGHT | SPORT PILOT | PRIVATE PILOT | INSTRUMENT RATING | COMMERCIAL LICENSE | ATP AND BEYOND |

NOTE!

↓ WHERE IS WATON?

Watch the GPS and your position relative to AW. This is the symbol for WATON. You can also announce your position to any traffic at Arlington and FSX will tell you how far you are from the airport. Since WATON is about 5 miles from the field, subtract 5, and that's how far you are from WATON.

You descend to 600 feet and look for the runway. This time it should appear directly ahead because the localizer lines you up with the centerline of the runway. When you get the approach lights in sight, you can descend below 600 feet but no closer than 100 feet above the ground. When you have the runway environment in sight—and you have the required visibility of ¾ mile at KAWO—then you can land.

↓ STUDENT OF THE CRAFT

HOW DO YOU JUDGE VISIBILITY?

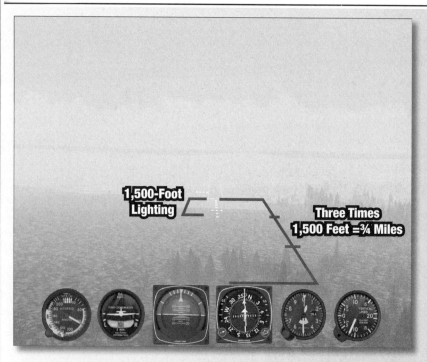

1,500-Foot Lighting

Three Times 1,500 Feet =¾ Miles

You need to have the required visibility for the approach in order to land, but how can you judge distance in such a murky scene? The key is in the approach lights. Approach lights to a nonprecision runway are usually 1,400 to 1,500 feet long, which is about a quarter mile. Mentally triple the length of the approach lights at KAWO, and you have an approximate measure of ¾ of a mile. Precision runways at the end of an ILS approach usually have lighting systems 2,600 feet long, which is about ½ a mile. That happens to be the normal visibility requirement for most ILS approaches, so if you can see the entire lighting system when you break out of the clouds, then you probably have the visibility to land.

You won't fly the missed on this approach because it requires flying to the outer marker using GPS or an ADF, which we haven't covered yet. You also won't fly the full procedure because it requires flying a *backcourse*, which we also haven't covered yet.

If you want a challenge, though, try flying this approach again but using the PAE transition. You have to navigate the route from PAE to the localizer using VOR number two. You have the localizer dialed in on the HSI. As it centers, turn to intercept. Do the whole thing without the autopilot if you can.

An *ILS* at *KPAE*

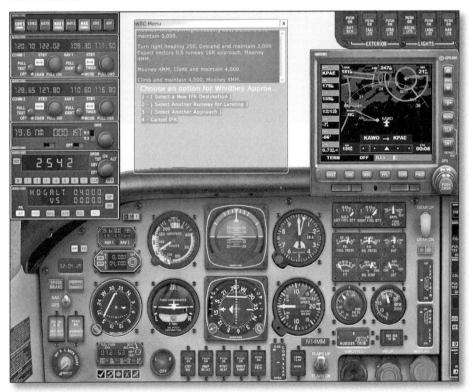

Figure 17-24: It helps to adjust the range on your GPS to see your position relative to the airport while you are setting up for the approach.

Now it's time to put it all together and fly an ILS. You're going back to KPAE and Runway 16R. This time you fly a localizer for left/right guidance and a glideslope to maintain a constant angle of dissent from the final approach fix to the runway.

Load the flight Chap_17_ILS_at_KPAE. This flight starts with you north of KAWO heading southwest toward KPAE at 4,000 feet (see Figure 17-24). You've asked for vectors to the ILS and were told to expect that. The approach is fairly simple in that you intercept the localizer, turn left, and proceed inbound. Let's fly it.

Pretty soon, you get a descent to 3,000 and clearance for the approach. We've started you partially slowed down from high cruise to help. You want to be at low cruise by the time you intercept the localizer and proceed inbound. While you're waiting, get the Paine Field ATIS, and set up NAV1 to the I-PAE localizer frequency of 109.3. Dial your OBS on the HSI to 160, your inbound course.

430

PART I	PART II	PART III	**PART IV**	PART V	PART VI
PREFLIGHT	SPORT PILOT	PRIVATE PILOT	INSTRUMENT RATING	COMMERCIAL LICENSE	ATP AND BEYOND

⬇ LOCS ARE ODD

Just as a tip, localizer frequencies are always odd numbers after the decimal. This helps you avoid the mistake of dialing in the VOR frequency instead of the localizer frequency.

When the CDI needle comes under the HSI lubberline, turn left and proceed inbound (see Figure 17-25). Note that ATC has you at 3,000 feet here, even though the altitude on the approach is 3,100. This can happen in the real world where ATC knows they can vector you lower than the published intercept altitude, but if you're concerned about the discrepancy, you can ask them whether they meant 3,100 feet. Controllers make mistakes too.

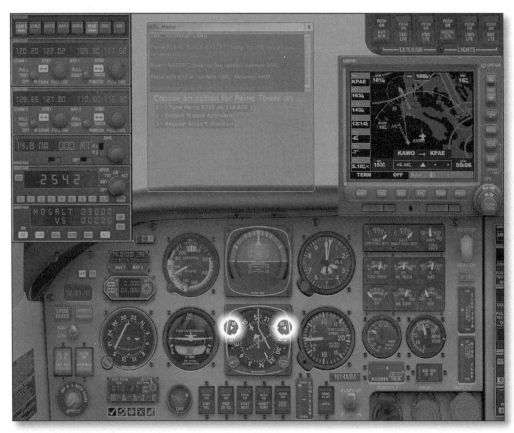

Figure 17-25: The glideslope indicators appear in the HSI as yellow triangles, but they won't start moving down until you get close to the glideslope intercept point.

Watch the glideslope indicators descend as you approach the outer marker at RITTS (PA). When they are at the halfway point as shown in Figure 17-26, lower your gear to slow from low cruise to approach level. Just before they center, disable the autopilot if you're using it, and do your five *Ts*. Note the *time* of intercepting the glideslope. Verify that you're on course and don't need to *turn*. There's nothing to *twist*. Reduce the *throttle* to 19 inches MP, put out approach flaps, set the boost pump on, and the mixture and prop control full forward. *Talk* to the control tower and tell them you just passed RITTS.

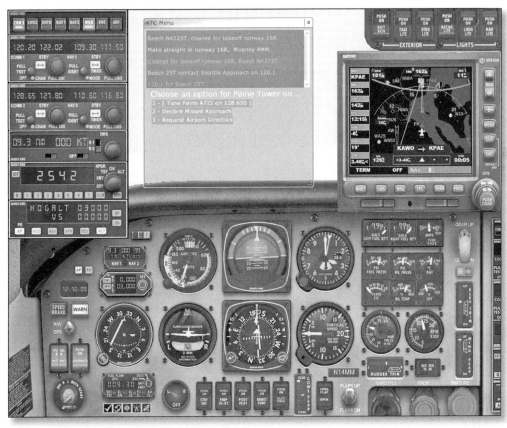

Figure 17-26: You see the glideslope needles descending before you cross RITTS (PA). Here the gear is in transit to continue slowing down to 100 knots. (Figure continued on next page.)

432

PART I PREFLIGHT   PART II SPORT PILOT   PART III PRIVATE PILOT   **PART IV INSTRUMENT RATING**   PART V COMMERCIAL LICENSE   PART VI ATP AND BEYOND

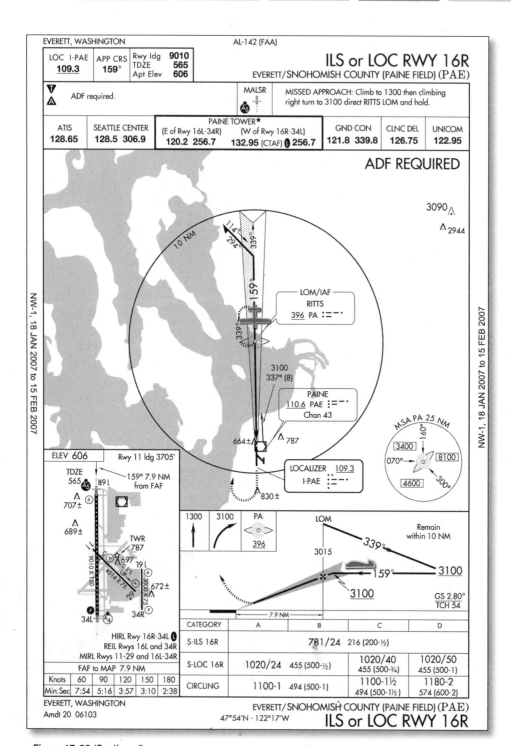

Figure 17-26 (Continued)

Adjust your pitch as needed to stay on the glideslope and your power as needed to keep 100 knots.

A common issue early on is misinterpreting the glideslope indication. Remember that you are the airplane in the middle of the HSI. Just like you would turn left or right to put the center of the HSI back on the yellow CDI needle if it were off center, you pitch up to get the glideslope if it goes up in the HSI window, and you pitch down to get it if the triangles go down (see Figure 17-27).

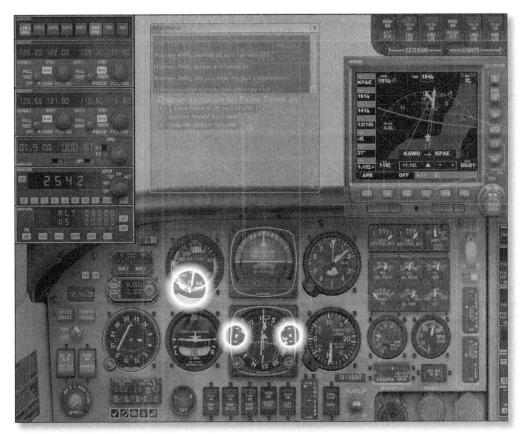

Figure 17-27: Here the airplane is both too fast and too low. Pitch up to recenter the glideslope and let the speed slow on its own to 100 knots. (Figure continued on next page.)

434

PART I · PREFLIGHT · PART II · SPORT PILOT · PART III · PRIVATE PILOT · **PART IV · INSTRUMENT RATING** · PART V · COMMERCIAL LICENSE · PART VI · ATP AND BEYOND

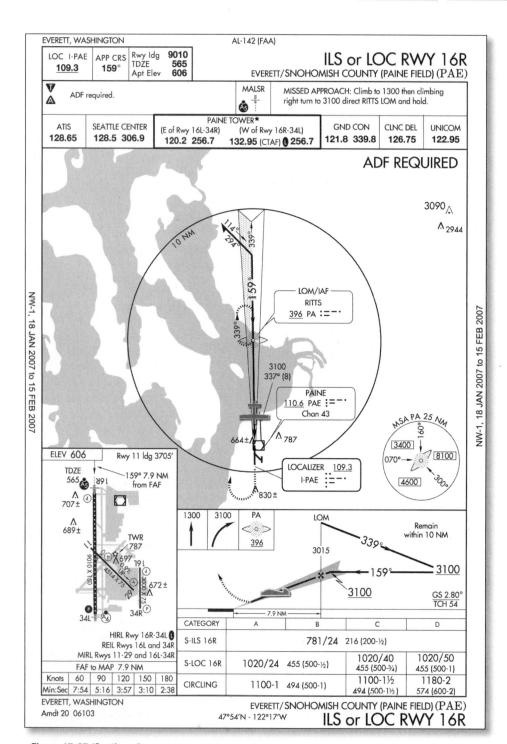

Figure 17-27 (Continued)

Figure 17-28: In both the real world and in FSX, ATC has a way of talking to you at just the wrong time. Your job is to fly the airplane first and talk to them after you're happy with what you're seeing out the window or on the gauges.

Here's where your standard profiles are key: fly a pitch of about 0° initially to have about a 500 fpm descent. Make *small* adjustments to pitch and power as you descend—just 1° at a time in pitch and just 1–2 inches MP. Keep your heading corrections to 5° or less as well. By about 2,000 feet you should have a pitch that keeps you centered on the glideslope and a power setting that keeps about 100 knots. When you do, press W on the keyboard, and start looking for the runway (see Figure 17-28).

Keep the localizer and the glideslope needles centered until you have the runway clearly in sight. In both FSX and the real world, seeing a runway appear out of the murk directly in front of you is one of the best feelings you get in flying.

▼ STUDENT OF THE CRAFT

PITCH VS. POWER, PRECISION VS. NONPRECISION

If you want to get a whole bunch of pilots arguing, just ask them whether aircraft pitch controls airspeed and engine power controls altitude, or vice versa. We've touched on this before, but it's important to bring it up again with instrument approaches. Our feeling is that although pitch and power control both airspeed and rate of descent, it's helpful on approaches to split their duties.

One difference between pitch and power is that pitch usually gives you immediate results, where power often lags a few seconds before you see an effect. We recommend that you use pitch to control whatever factor is the most important on the approach and use power to control a secondary factor.

On an ILS, staying on glideslope is the most sensitive and most important item. Therefore, you should use pitch to stay on the glideslope (which is really a rate of descent issue) and use power to control airspeed.

Continued

436

| PART I | PART II | PART III | PART IV | PART V | PART VI |
| PREFLIGHT | SPORT PILOT | PRIVATE PILOT | INSTRUMENT RATING | COMMERCIAL LICENSE | ATP AND BEYOND |

On a nonprecision approach, it's more important to control your airspeed in order to get accurate timing, and your actual rate of descent is unimportant until you reach MDA where it must become zero. In this case, control your airspeed with pitch, and use power to adjust your rate of descent as necessary.

If you get below MDA, by all means, pitch up while adding power. Let's hope this won't happen to you, though, because instead you anticipated reaching MDA and added power gradually to smoothly bring your rate of descent to zero.

STRING *PAE AWO BFI* TOGETHER

One of the beauties of FSX is you can start these approaches in the air and skip getting from airport to airport. If you want to string these three approaches together, you can by loading their respective flight plans. This section tells you how.

Load the flight plan `IFR Boeing Field King Co Intl to Snohomish Co.PLN`, and choose Yes when asked whether you want the airplane placed at the departure airport. This puts you at Boeing Field ready to take off to Paine Field. Fly the VOR-B at Paine, and commence a missed approach at the end.

Now for the tricky, nonreal part. In the real world, you'd just ask ATC to vector you to Arlington. In FSX, you need to choose the ATC option called Cancel IFR—something you could never really do in the clouds. When it's canceled, you can pause the game and load the fight plan `IFR KPAE to KAWO.PLN`. When asked whether you want to go to the departure airport, this time choose No. You can then request your IFR clearance in the air and continue to Arlington. You can repeat the process after a missed approach at Arlington and load the flight plan `IFR KAWO to KPAE.PLN` to get a clearance in the air from Arlington to Paine. Choose the approach you want in each case.

The other way to do this is to ask for the published missed approach at the first airport. This will give you the option to select a new destination, but if you do, you'll have to save a new flight plan before FSX will let you proceed.

 ACCIDENT CHAIN

THE IMPORTANCE OF THE ID

Back when one of the authors was completing his instrument training, scheduling conflicts and bad weather delayed his instrument checkride for several weeks. The day before the rescheduled checkride, he went up for a refresher flight with his flight instructor. They flew the VOR and ILS approaches at KPAE in that order. The VOR approach went fine. The ILS approach started out fine, but during the last 300 feet of the descent, the CDI needle began to wiggle erratically and then flipped right to left and back again.

The author commenced a missed approach and looked over his instructor wondering why the needle would behave so strangely when an ILS signal is guaranteed to be stable down to 200 feet. His instructor then pointed out that he never flip-flopped the navigation frequency and had just flown the VOR signal as if it were an ILS and misinterpreted the centered glideslope needle as being a perfectly flown ILS when in fact the needle was parked in the center because there was no glideslope signal at all.

Luckily this approach was flown under a view-limiting device on a sunny day so the author got to look up during the climb-out and realized he had flown an ILS that was taking him directly to a Boeing Company hanger instead of a runway. Lucky as well was getting this grievous error out of his system the day before the checkride rather than during the checkride.

Do It with Wind

All four of the saved flights in the previous section have an additional version with the suffix *windy*. These are identical flights, but the wind is blowing from either the east or the west. You have to adjust your heading to correct for this in order to stay on course throughout the approach (see Figure 17-29). To get a clue of where the wind is coming from, listen to the ATIS or AWOS for that airport. The winds will be stronger at altitude, but they will be blowing from approximately the same direction.

As you descend, you should know how to make adjustments in your heading for the changing wind speed and direction. And that's exactly what happens

Figure 17-29: When shooting an approach with a strong wind, you need to fly a heading that is slightly different from the course you're trying to maintain.

in the real world. A great help in figuring this out is to use your GPS TRK information. It's at the top center of the GPS screen. TRK is your track over the ground. That track must match the inbound course you're trying to fly if you're going to stay on course. The key is to find a heading that results in the desired track and keeps the CDI needle centered. Then you fly that heading precisely using your heading bug.

438

PART I — PREFLIGHT
PART II — SPORT PILOT
PART III — PRIVATE PILOT
PART IV — INSTRUMENT RATING
PART V — COMMERCIAL LICENSE
PART VI — ATP AND BEYOND

KEEPING IT REAL

COUPLED APPROACHES

You can have the autopilot fly the approaches for you. This is called a *coupled approach.* When you are on a vector toward the final approach course, use the heading mode on the autopilot, and then push the APR button on the autopilot. APR stands for *approach mode* and is similar to the NAV function except that it is more aggressive in staying on course.

If the CDI needle is fully deflected, the approach mode arms, but the heading bug still controls the direction of the aircraft. When the aircraft begins to intercept the approach course, the HDG indicator disappears on the autopilot leaving only APR. Now the airplane banks as needed to stay on course and ignores the heading bug. Just for situational awareness, however, it's still a good idea to keep the heading bug matched to the inbound course.

You can still use the altitude mode to step the airplane down in altitude all the way to the MDA on nonprecision approaches. On precision approaches, the autopilot has an extra trick up its sleeve. When the glideslope centers, the autopilot pitches down and keeps the aircraft centered on the glideslope as well as the localizer. All you need to do is adjust power to maintain the airspeed you want and extend the appropriate flaps and gear. Disconnect the autopilot when landing is assured, extend full flaps, reduce the power, and land.

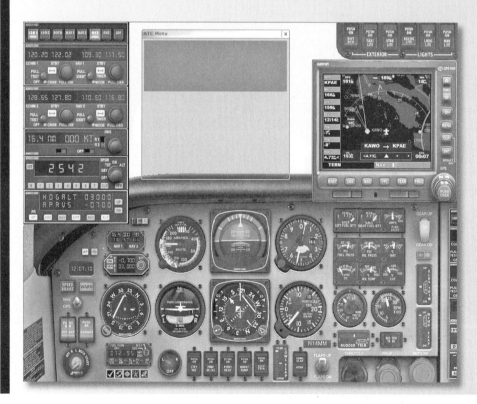

KEY POINTS FOR REAL FLYING AND FSX BUILT-INS

The following are some key points from this chapter:

- Read an instrument approach plate.

- Understand how VOR, LOC, and ILS approaches work.

- Integrate flight profiles and phases of the approach.

- Understand flying missed approach procedures.

- Adjust your heading to get correct track/courses on approach.

Here are the lessons and missions to study after reading this chapter:

- *Lessons*: The VOR Approach, The ILS Approach.

- *Missions*: Flying Blind Across the Channel.

"THERE ARE MANY WAYS TO FLY INSTRUMENTS. TO BE FAIR, I'D SAY THAT MOST TECHNIQUES ARE SATISFACTORY AS LONG AS THEY DON'T REQUIRE YOU TO USE THE WORD DEDUCTIBLE."

—ROD MACHADO

442

PART I
PREFLIGHT

PART II
SPORT PILOT

PART III
PRIVATE PILOT

PART IV
INSTRUMENT RATING

PART V
COMMERCIAL LICENSE

PART VI
ATP AND BEYOND

No Ground Station Needed

All the approaches you saw in the previous chapter used a signal from a ground-based transmitter. You've already seen how GPS provides for greater accuracy than most VORs, so why not use it for approaches? You can use a GPS for approaches, but the process is a little more complicated because you must load the approaches into the active flight plan of the GPS. Lucky for you, the approaches are kept in the GPS database, so it's pretty easy to get and use them after you know how the system works.

You can worry about how to load and activate GPS approaches while flying the airplane a little bit later in this chapter, but you need to review a couple quirks of the GPS approach plate first.

A Basic GPS Approach

The GPS Rwy 23 at Shelton, Washington (KSHN), is about as simple a GPS approach as you can get (see Figure 18-1). The IAF is OYRED. There is no frequency to tune because the location of OYRED is determined entirely by GPS. OYRED is referred to as a *waypoint* and is the IAF for this approach. The FAF is also a waypoint. In this case, it's PORSY. If you were receiving vectors this approach, you would be vectored to intercept the line between OYRED and PORSY at 2,000 feet and be cleared for the approach. After crossing PORSY, you would descend to 860 feet and look for the runway.

The MAP on a GPS approach is also a waypoint. Usually, the waypoint is at the threshold of the runway and is named for the runway. In this case, that's RW23. So, there is no timing of the GPS approach. Either you see the runway and land before reaching the missed approach waypoint, or you fly the missed approach.

The GPS provides guidance through the missed approach as well. In this case, it takes you to a waypoint called CARRO. That waypoint happens to be over an NDB with the same name, but you can use your GPS to get you there rather than relying on the less accurate ADF.

You see a big holding pattern at OYRED. This holding pattern is for course reversal if you are not getting radar vectors for the approach. Note that it is not a procedure turn and, therefore, must be flown as a holding pattern. The procedure would be to cross OYRED and fly either a direct entry or a parallel entry as needed. When you returned to OYRED, you would be lined up with the final approach course and could continue on to PORSY and fly the approach. These holding patterns in lieu of procedure turns (HILPT) are standard fare for GPS approaches.

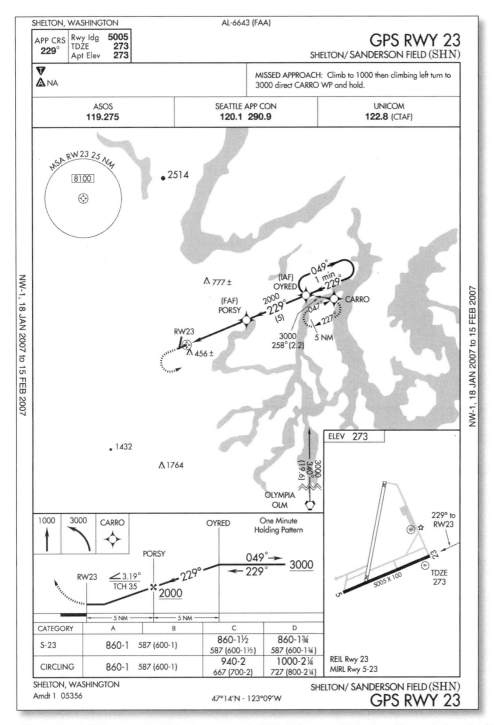

Figure 18-1: A GPS approach might reference nearby VOR stations as with the transition route from the Olympia VOR.

444

| PART I | PART II | PART III | PART IV | PART V | PART VI |
| PREFLIGHT | SPORT PILOT | PRIVATE PILOT | INSTRUMENT RATING | COMMERCIAL LICENSE | ATP AND BEYOND |

OVERLAY APPROACHES

As you saw in Chapter 11, you can enter VOR stations into your GPS, and the GPS treats them like waypoints. You can't use a GPS for VOR approaches willy-nilly, however. The approach must say "GPS" somewhere in the title for you to have the privilege of using it. You must also be able to retrieve the approach from the GPS database. The VOR approaches at KPAE and KPUW must be flown with a VOR as your primary navigation source. That doesn't mean you can't use your GPS to help verify that you're in the right place and give you a bird's-eye view on a moving map. But you can't fly the approach using the GPS.

  BY THE BOOK

GPS FOR DME AND ADF

In almost all cases, you can use an approach-certified GPS receiver with a current aeronautical database to substitute for a chartered requirement for DME or an ADF. Few light airplanes sold in the United States these days leave the factory with either the DME or an ADF installed.

So, what does *approach-certified* mean? You can't use just any GPS to fly GPS approaches. The GPS must meet the standards of FAA Technical Service Order C-129, which is a fancy way of saying it must be an approach-certified GPS. FSX's Garmin GNS 500 is approach-certified, so you can use it.

Other approaches give you the option, such as the VOR or GPS Rwy 6 at Hoquiam, Washington (KHQM), shown in Figure 18-2. Note that because this approach is really a VOR approach that has simply been approved to fly with GPS, it does not show the traditional waypoints you expect for a GPS approach. It shows the VOR and DME information instead.

There is still an advantage of flying this approach with GPS. The approach has two sets of minima. The lower one of 620 feet requires that you can identify four DME from HQM. Without DME on board the aircraft, the lowest you could go is 740 feet. GPS can substitute for DME, however, and D 4.0 should appear as a waypoint when you fly the approach using GPS. The VOR approach requires timing or DME to identify the MAP. The GPS version shows RW06 just like any other GPS approach.

  WATCH THE NOTES

The notes for the VOR or GPS Rwy 6 state that the approach is not authorized without a local altimeter setting. It's possible you could get all the way to KHQM and have ATC tell you the ASOS transmitter on the field is busted. Neither you nor they can get the local altimeter, so you can't shoot the approach. Reading notes should be an important step in your preapproach review.

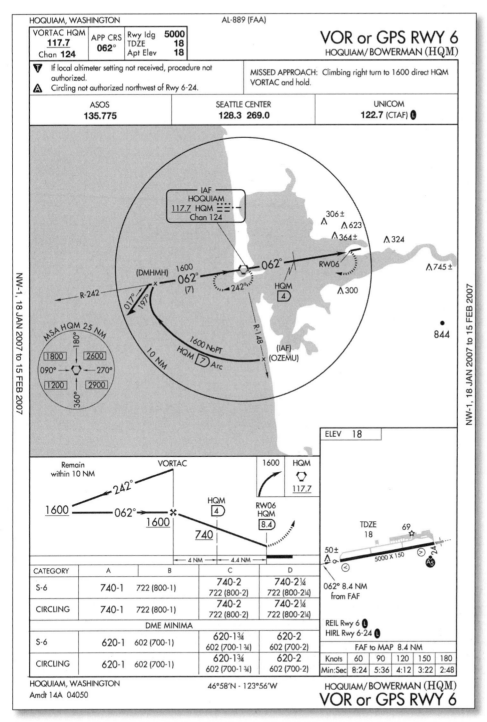

Figure 18-2: When you're flying a VOR or GPS approach using GPS, you don't need to have the VOR tuned, but you are required to have a VOR in the aircraft for all but the most modern GPS receivers.

446

PART I	PART II	PART III	PART IV	PART V	PART VI
PREFLIGHT	SPORT PILOT	PRIVATE PILOT	INSTRUMENT RATING	COMMERCIAL LICENSE	ATP AND BEYOND

RNAV APPROACHES

Although GPS is one way of determining your position without using any ground-based transmitters, several others exist (although they are mostly used by the military or airlines). The FAA has begun renaming GPS approaches as *area-navigation* (RNAV) approaches. Anyone who has equipment that meets the required RNAV accuracy can fly the approach, regardless of how that equipment gets its position. If it says RNAV in the title, then you can fly it with your GPS—assuming the approach is in the database, that is.

Take a look at the RNAV Rwy 7 approach to Oak Harbor, Washington (76S), shown in Figure 18-3. Three possible IAFs are charted for this approach: one at ICILA, one at ORCUS, and one at LUCRI. Notice, too, that LUCRI is marked (IAF/IF). IF stands for *intermediate fix.* This is because an approach starting at ICILA or ORCUS will still cross LUCRI.

Note as well that WATTR is not labeled as an IAF and doesn't say NoPT. If you are arriving via WATTR, you must cross LUCRI and then fly once around the holding pattern before crossing LUCRI a second time and proceeding inbound. That makes the transition from WATTR a true transition route, which you can see by the thinner arrow used to depict it on the approach plate.

This is also the place to note the difference between the waypoint stars without circles around them and the waypoint stars with circles around them. Ones without circles are *fly-by waypoints.* This means you might begin your turn before you actually cross the waypoint. The only one with a circle is VUCUS, the MAP. VUCUS is a *fly-over waypoint.* You must completely cross the waypoint before beginning any turn. MAP waypoints are always fly-over.

EASY AIRSPACE

The approach plate for Oak Harbor shows three kinds of airspace you like to stay out of: MOAs, alert areas, and restricted airspace. A side benefit of IFR is that ATC takes care of keeping you out of this airspace if it's hot when you're on vectors. During an approach, however, it's up to you to stay on course and away from places you're not supposed to be.

The ability to turn early is important on this approach. Imagine you are arriving from ICILA. You have a 90° turn to make when you cross LUCRI, and you'll considerably overshoot the segment from LUCRI to JEKPO. A better choice is to begin your turn a bit before LUCRI and roll out on course to JEKPO. Part of the beauty of flying with GPS is that it looks at your ground speed, anticipates how much room you need to make this turn, and then tells you to start your turn at just the right moment.

These approaches where IAFs are arranged in a T-shape are common for GPS/RNAV approaches. (See "More GPS Fun: TAAS and APVS.")

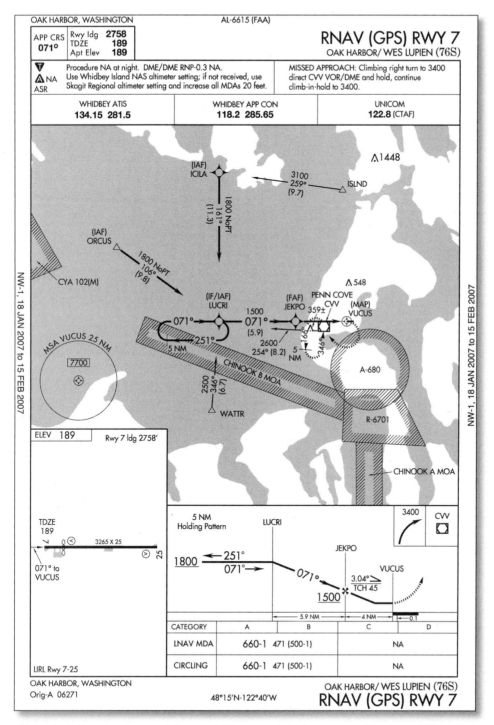

Figure 18-3: The missed approach has you holding over a VOR, but you can still use your GPS to do this.

448

| PART I | PART II | PART III | PART IV | PART V | PART VI |
| PREFLIGHT | SPORT PILOT | PRIVATE PILOT | INSTRUMENT RATING | COMMERCIAL LICENSE | ATP AND BEYOND |

↓ STUDENT OF THE CRAFT

MORE GPS FUN: TAAS AND APVS

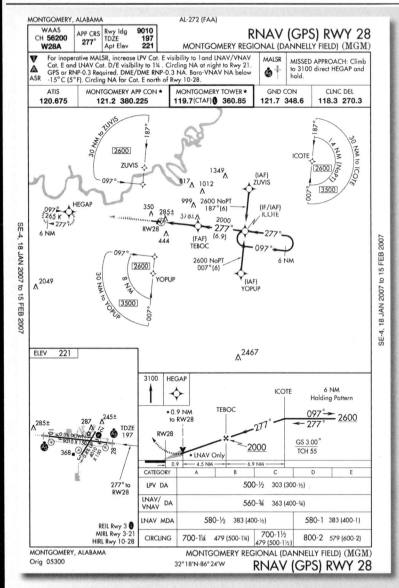

GPS has been changing all aspects of instrument approaches. Two important new advances for light aircraft are terminal arrival areas (TAAs) and approaches with vertical guidance (APVs).

You can see both on the RNAV Rwy 28 approach to Montgomery, Alabama (KMGM). Rather than specifying individual transition routes, the entire area is divided into quadrants. These quadrants are arranged around a T-shape, where the stem of the T becomes the final approach course. Anyone arriving from the top of the T—in this case, the east between 007° and 187°—will fly straight in to ICOTE and then proceed inbound to the FAF at TEBOC. Within 14 miles of ICOTE, they can

descend to 2,600 if they have been cleared for the approach. Someone arriving from the northwest could fly to ICOTE, but then they would have to fly the holding pattern course reversal. Instead, ATC should send them to ZUVIS. From there, they fly a NoPT route to ICOTE, turn right, and continue. The fix at YOPUP does the same for people arriving from the southwest.

> If the pilots just have a TSO-129c approach-certified GPS, then they can descend to 580 feet. This is the minima for people who have only lateral navigation (LNAV). The latest GPS units are certified to TSO-146a and take advantage of the wide area augmentation system (WAAS). These GPS units are even more accurate and can provide vertical guidance much like an ILS. For the time being, however, the FAA is not convinced the approaches are as accurate as ILS, so they are not calling them precision approaches. They are called *approaches with vertical guidance* (APVs) instead. You'll see two types of vertical-guidance approaches on this plate, LNAV/VNAV and LPV, with LPV being the more accurate of the two.
>
> You fly APVs just like ILSs, using the same centered CDI needle and glideslope indication. Unfortunately, you can't practice these in FSX just yet.

GPS Sensitivity

Ground-based navigational aids radiate a signal from an antenna. This means the closer you are to the antenna, the more accurate the signal becomes. For example, if you intercept a VOR signal 40 miles from the station, you see the CDI needle center slowly. Intercept that same VOR signal 5 miles from the station, and the needle centers quickly. Intercept a localizer 5 miles from the source, and by the time you start your turn to intercept, you're already crossing over to the other side of the course.

GPS is different. The sensitivity of the CDI needle is completely arbitrary. A single needle sensitivity won't work for all situations, though. You want sensitivity that isn't too great as you travel the long distances between airports. A super-sensitive CDI needle would just be annoying. For a GPS approach, you want much greater sensitivity because it's more critical that you're exactly on course.

Approach-certified GPS units handle this problem by offering three levels of sensitivity and switching between them automatically. During long stretches between airports, the GPS unit is using *en route sensitivity*. This means that a full-scale deflection of the CDI needle is 5 miles. If you see half-scale deflection and the GPS is using en route sensitivity, then you're 2.5 miles off course.

When the GPS unit senses that the aircraft is within 30 miles of its destination, it smoothly transitions to *terminal sensitivity* with a full-scale deflection of 1 mile. The transition must happen smoothly because if it suddenly switched to 1 mile, one moment it would look like you are on course, and the next moment a needle could be half deflected or further.

As the GPS comes within 2 miles of the final approach fix on a GPS approach, it ramps down even further to *approach sensitivity*. At this maximum sensitivity, full-scale CDI deflection is only 0.3 miles, or about 1,800 feet left or right of course.

The FSX GPS does simulate en route and terminal sensitively realistically (see Figure 18-4), but it switches to approach sensitivity the moment you load an approach rather than as you fly the approach. It also cranks up the sensitivity only on the CDI shown on the GPS map (see "Not Sensitive on the CDI" on page 480) and not on your HSI needle. We think this is a bug, and we hope it's fixed in a patch.

450

PART I	PART II	PART III	PART IV	PART V	PART VI
PREFLIGHT	SPORT PILOT	PRIVATE PILOT	INSTRUMENT RATING	COMMERCIAL LICENSE	ATP AND BEYOND

Figure 18-4: The GPS sensitivity appears in the lower left: ENR for en route, TERM for terminal, and APR for approach sensitivity.

USING THE GPS

We simply can't describe all the features of the GNS 500 here. The GPS article in the FSX Learning Center is a must-read. Note that some of the techniques of the FSX GPS are not quite the same as a real GNS 500. You'll look at the key features in context as you use them on approaches. Here's a quick orientation, though, to get you started.

THE PRIMARY NAV PAGE

You'll have this screen up most of the time you fly the GPS. You've been looking at it already if you used the GPS for a moving map in the previous chapter. Figure 18-5 notes the key items on the GPS screen. In addition, you should note that the primary Nav page is also a track-up page with the track of the airplane—your path over the ground—always oriented to the top of the page.

Figure 18-5: Pressing the CLR (Clear) key declutters this page removing information from the display. Each time you press CLR, more items disappear until you reach the maximum level of declutter (three button pushes). Push CLR again, and all the information comes back.

Key items on the primary Nav page are the name of and bearing to your next waypoint. Note that the bearing also appears in the map view as a green chevron along the compass rose. That compass rose is also a distance marker. The distance from your airplane to the edge of the rose appears in the left of the map. You control this distance with the range buttons on the upper right of the GPS.

Five fields are shown on the map itself, all of which have a use. Starting in the upper left is Desired Track (DTK). This is the direct route between waypoints when you pressed the Direct-To button or the desired routes between waypoints on an instrument approach. The latter is more important because the purpose of the approach is to have you follow certain routes over the ground at certain altitudes. The DTK is also shown on the map as white or magenta lines. The magenta line is the segment you are currently navigating. Hence, the mantra of GPS flying: "Just put the airplane on the magenta line."

Track (TRK) is the actual path your airplane is flying over the ground, including any drift in the wind. Wind might mean that your TRK is different from your heading on the HSI. As an instrument pilot, the actual heading is irrelevant. What you care about is TRK. If your TRK is the same as the course you're supposed to fly for that segment of the approach, you stay on course (presuming the CDI needle is centered, that is). Since your DTK is, by definition, the course you want to fly for that segment of the approach, your DTK should equal your TRK any time you're not intentionally turning.

This makes wind correction quite easy. Find a heading that makes your TRK what you want, and then keep flying that heading. What could be simpler?

The final three items going clockwise around the display are distance to the next waypoint (DIS), estimated time en route (ETE) to the next waypoint, and ground speed (GS). The latter two are most important to you in IFR flying. ETE gives you a sense of how much time you have to slow down or reconfigure if need be before crossing the next waypoint, and ground speed gives you a good sense of the winds. Ground speed is also handy when · shooting an approach that requires timing. You might be flying the approach at 100 knots, but if your ground speed is 90 knots, you use the time for the 90-knot approach. GPS approaches don't use timing, so that's not an issue there.

You access the secondary Nav page by clicking the inner FMS knob one click to the right. It's similar to the primary page but is north-up rather than track-up and without the extra information. It has little practical use in flight training on FSX.

452

PART I	PART II	PART III	PART IV	PART V	PART VI
PREFLIGHT	SPORT PILOT	PRIVATE PILOT	INSTRUMENT RATING	COMMERCIAL LICENSE	ATP AND BEYOND

↓ INSIDE THE GAME

GPS TABLE OF CONTENTS

Sometimes it helps to have the master view of the GPS organization. Here's what it looks like. Remember that there are submenu and inset screens such as Direct-To in addition to these pages.

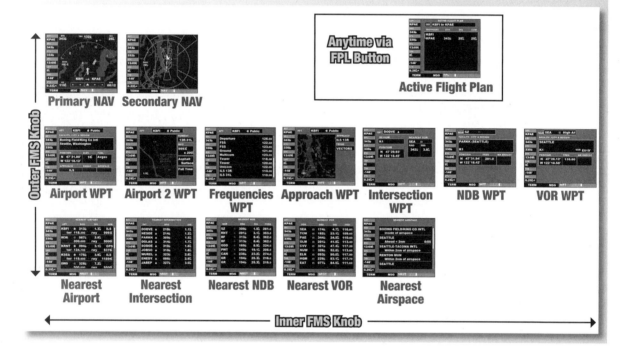

THE WAYPOINT PAGES

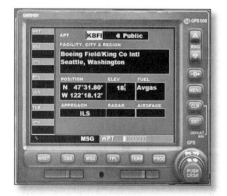

Click the outer knob one click to the right, and you get to the Waypoint pages (see Figure 18-6). There are quite a few, and you scroll through them with the inner knob. These offer lots of information about specific airports, frequencies, and so on. Since FSX dials frequencies for you automatically, these pages have less use than in a real airplane. The approach page, though, can be handy because it lets you see all the instruments approaches for the airport.

Figure 18-6: Pushing the lower center of the FMS knob to get the cursor is a key skill with the GNS 500. You can also choose a different waypoint by scrolling the cursor up to the airport name and entering a different airport.

To select a different approach to see, press the center of the FMS knob to activate the flashing cursor. Use the outer knob to scroll to the approach in question. Now click the inner knob to get a pop-up menu of all the approaches, and scroll between them. Click Enter to see one in more detail. You can use a similar technique on the airport pages in the Waypoint group to view details for different runways at a single airport.

⬇ KEEPING IT REAL

DIALING IN A NAME

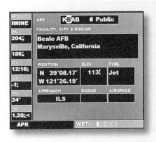

When you want to enter an airport or fix name in the Waypoint pages, Direct-To page, or flight plan page, you twist the inner knob to choose the first letter and the outer knob to move to the next letter. You click ENT when done. As you enter letters, the GPS uses an autocomplete feature to guess at what you want and save you some dialing. This is really handy in the airplane, but in FSX you can just use your keyboard and type it in once you have the single, flashing cursor.

THE NEAREST PAGES

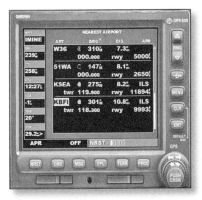

Turn the outer knob (without a cursor showing) one more time, and you see the Nearest pages. The most important page in this group is the Nearest Airport page (see Figure 18-7). In an emergency, this list gives you the bearing and distance to nearby airports and tells you their runway lengths and most accurate approach. You can select any one of these airports, push the Direct-To button, and then hit Enter to get guidance directly to the airport.

In the real world, we occasionally use the Nearest VOR page when making a pilot report on weather or the Nearest ATC pages when transitioning from VFR to IFR, but these uses really have no corollary in FSX.

Figure 18-7: Just like most other GNS 500 pages, push the center of the FMS knobs to get a cursor, and then use the outer knob to scroll through the list.

⬇ BACK TO THE MAP

Any time you want to get back to the map page, just hold down the CLR button. You can also just click CLR to undo your last button push in many GPS functions.

454

PART I	PART II	PART III	PART IV	PART V	PART VI
PREFLIGHT	SPORT PILOT	PRIVATE PILOT	INSTRUMENT RATING	COMMERCIAL LICENSE	ATP AND BEYOND

THE FLIGHT PLAN PAGE

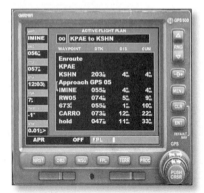

Figure 18-8: The FPL page shows the distance to waypoints along the approach, but you'll find that ETE information on the map page is really more useful.

Pushing FPL on the GPS opens the flight plan page (see Figure 18-8). Pushing FPL again toggles it off. In the real world, there are often many waypoints here you can edit as you go. In FSX, it shows whatever you entered in the flight planner. This might be direct between two airports, or it might be a long string of VORs and other fixes between your departure airport and your destination.

The FPL page shows your DTK and DIS to all these waypoints, as well as the cumulative distance remaining (CUM).

Unfortunately, you can't edit your flight plans on this page as you do in the real airplane. You also can't select a waypoint along an instrument approach and head there with the Direct-To button. This makes the FPL page most useful for seeing the waypoints along an approach, but that's about it.

THE DIRECT-TO PAGE

Click the Direct-To button, and you can enter any waypoint and proceed directly to that point (see Figure 18-9). You can also select any airport or nav aid from the Waypoint or Nearest page and press Direct-To to see that waypoint come up as the selected destination. Unlike the real GNS 500, going directly to a waypoint replaces the current flight plan with a new flight plan containing only the direct-to waypoint.

There are other buttons, such as PROC, but you'll look at these in context as you fly some approaches.

Figure 18-9: An underutilized feature of the Direct-To page is that you can scroll down with the outer knob to see a list of waypoints on your flight plan or nearest airports. Select any one with the inner knob to go directly to it.

TOO MANY MESSAGES

If you're getting too many messages, such as "airspace ahead," click the MSG button three times. OFF should appear at the bottom of the GPS screen; this tells you the message feature is off. We're not quite sure how to get the messages to come back on, though.

FLY SOME *GPS* WITH A *SIX-PACK*

GPS approaches have quite a bit more "buttonology" than traditional approaches. The sequence of events makes a lot more sense when you're actually flying the approaches, so let's zip through a few of them in the Mooney.

KSHN GPS RWY 23

Load the flight Chap_18_GPS_at_KSHN.PLN. This flight has you in the air at 4,000 feet west of Boeing Field. You're en route to Shelton via radar vectors and have been told to expect the GPS Rwy 23 approach (see Figure 18-10). Winds are light, but they do exist in this flight. Hey, with GPS wind correction is a snap, and you've been getting off easy so far on winds.

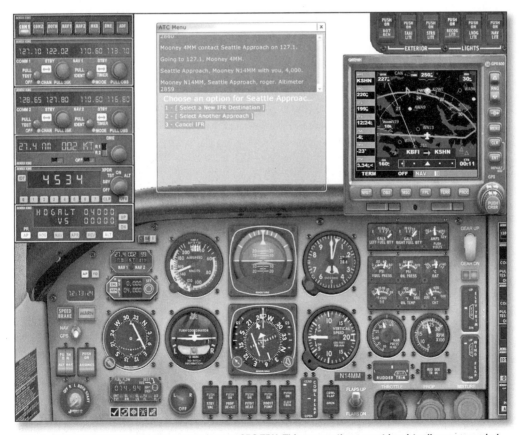

Figure 18-10: Your heading is 250 and so is your GPS TRK. This means there must be virtually no crosswind. Watch the relationship between heading and TRK as you fly. The slower you fly, the more effect crosswinds will have.

456

PART I	PART II	PART III	PART IV	PART V	PART VI
PREFLIGHT	SPORT PILOT	PRIVATE PILOT	INSTRUMENT RATING	COMMERCIAL LICENSE	ATP AND BEYOND

 INSIDE THE GAME

FLYING THE BOEING LOC

If you want to fly the entire flight from takeoff, you can load `Chap_18_GPS_at_KSHN_Full.PLN` to start on the ground at KBFI. You'll have to get your own clearance and head toward KSHN.

If you ever are departing an airport that's low IFR, it's a good idea to preload the best instrument approach to get back into that airport or into another nearby airport. That way if you have an emergency soon after takeoff, you're all ready to shoot the nearest approach to get back to safety.

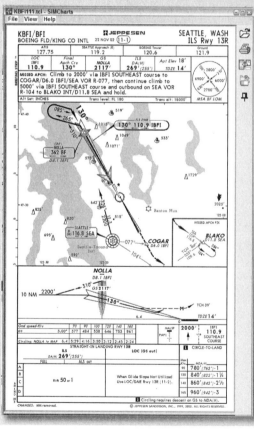

SETTING UP THE GPS

Your first task is to load the approach at your destination. Because you already have a flight plan of a direct route from KBFI to KSHN, the GPS knows you probably want to shoot an approach at KSHN. To load the approach into the GPS, press the PROC (Procedure) button on the GNS 500. Select Approach should be highlighted. (If it isn't, you can use the outer FMS knob to scroll to it.) Next click Enter. Figure 18-11 shows the whole process.

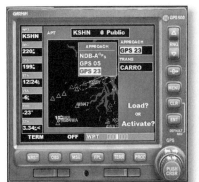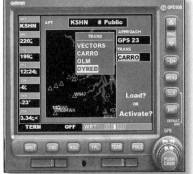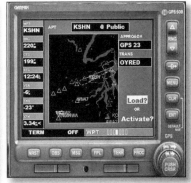

Figure 18-11: Loading approaches use the same logic of a cursor and inner and outer FMS knobs as any other GPS function.

Now you need to choose the approach. If the GPS 23 is not highlighted, use the inner knob to scroll to it, and click Enter. The GPS now asks you for the transition. This means it needs to know which way you're arriving to the airport so it can give you the correct guidance. Since you're on a vector, you can simply choose Vectors. This loads only the final approach fix and draws an extended magenta line leading to that fix for you to see as a situational awareness tool.

In the real world, we recommend loading the approach from a fix until you get close to the airport. We find this gives better situational awareness by having more fixes visible on the map. You're also better prepared in the real world for when you get hit with a change of plans and have to fly the full approach. It's not quite the same in FSX, but you can look at this as you fly.

When the approach is loaded, you see the flight plan page with a whole bunch more fixes on it. These are the fixes in the GPS approach. You're not flying the approach yet, though. You're still navigating directly to KSHN as far as the GPS is concerned, and that's why the Nav page shows the magenta line from KBFI to KSHN.

Clean up the Nav page a bit before moving on. Press the CLR button twice to eliminate most of the unnecessary information from the GPS map page. Two levels of declutter removes most of the distractions. You can click once more to remove all but the destination airport. Also, take this opportunity to make sure that the CDI on your HSI is set to get its info from the GPS, as shown in Figure 18-12.

STOP THIS TRAIN

In FSX, you can pause the simulation and still program the GPS. This is handy if you need more time or brain power while learning.

458

PART I PREFLIGHT   PART II SPORT PILOT   PART III PRIVATE PILOT   **PART IV INSTRUMENT RATING**   PART V COMMERCIAL LICENSE   PART VI ATP AND BEYOND

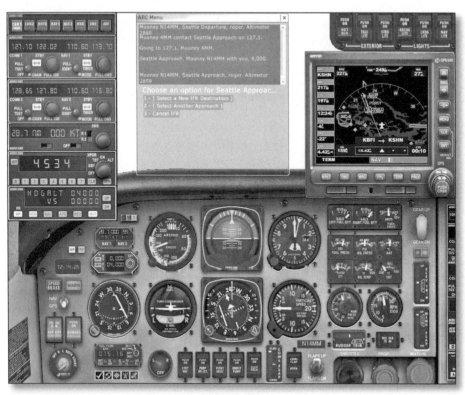

Figure 18-12: You might need to periodically adjust the range to see the whole approach or just the next waypoint with greater clarity on the moving map.

The GPS won't actually let you fly the approach until you activate it. At that point, it assumes you want guidance to the first fix in the approach. That's OYRED in this case. Press the PROC button again, and you'll see the highlighted option is Activate Approach. Click Enter to activate the approach. You'll get a course line from your present position to OYRED. You'll also see all the waypoints on the approach beyond OYRED. If you toggle between FPL and the Nav page, you can see the waypoints in your flight plan and on the moving map (see Figure 18-13).

 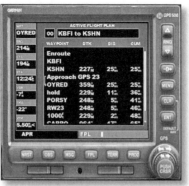

Figure 18-13: On the FPL page you can see which section, or leg, you're navigating with the magenta arrow. On the map, the leg appears at the bottom of the screen.

If you tried to fly the approach now, the GPS could guide you, but it's thinking you need to do a course reversal—fly the racetrack pattern—at OYRED. You also won't get a good CDI needle to use for intercepting the inbound course.

You need to activate vectors to final. To do this, press PROC again, and use the outer FMS knob to scroll up to Activate Vectors to Final. You'll see the moving map view and the FPL page change, as shown in Figure 18-14. The GPS creates an extended magenta line coming off the FAF at

PORSY. This is the course you intercept and fly inbound to the MAP at the threshold of Runway 23.

With vectors to final active, you can fly the approach. You want to make sure you have the CDI set to the inbound course of 229. Like an ILS, it works no matter where it's pointing, but it's a lot less confusing if it's pointing straight up. Start slowing for low cruise, and get ready for a descent to 2,000 feet.

Figure 18-14: Note the VTF on the map page showing PORSY as the final approach fix.

INSIDE THE GAME

DON'T SIM TOO FAST

If you crank up the simulation rate for en route stretches, keep it at 4× or less. Faster than that, and you get an instruction from ATC; and before you can drop the simulation rate, you get three "Did you hear me?" calls, and then they cancel your IFR clearance. If you sim faster than 4× during long stretches, press Pause the moment you hear a clearance for you, and then drop the sim rate to normal.

If 2,000 feet seems too low, take a close look at the GPS approach plate from the website (www.wiley.com); 3,000 feet is the altitude for the holding pattern at OYRED. You're going to be vectored onto the leg from OYRED to PORSY. This has an altitude of 2,000 feet.

At some point, ATC turns you to an intercept heading and clears you for the approach. You need to watch the CDI and turn to the inbound heading to PORSY of 229 as it centers (see Figure 18-15). While you're intercepting, tune the KSHN AWOS, and get the current weather including the KSHN altimeter.

Figure 18-15: VTF gives you course guidance on the CDI to intercept the route inbound to PORSY. (Figure continued on next page.)

460

PART I
PREFLIGHT

PART II
SPORT PILOT

PART III
PRIVATE PILOT

**PART IV
INSTRUMENT RATING**

PART V
COMMERCIAL LICENSE

PART VI
ATP AND BEYOND

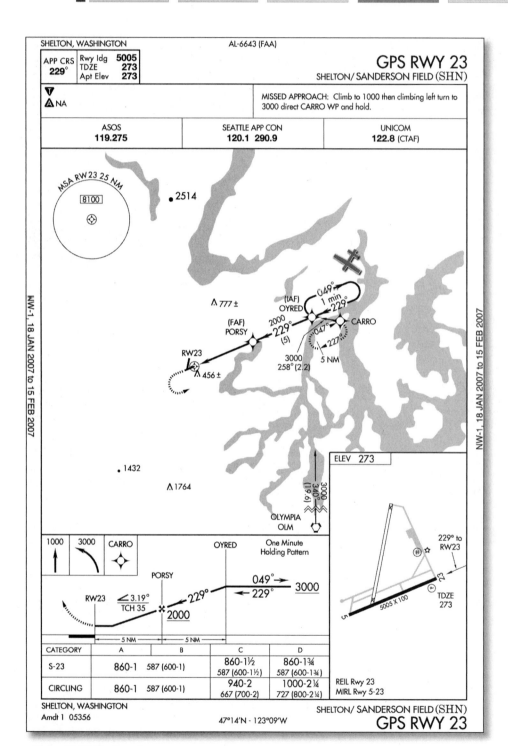

Figure 18-15 (Continued)

NOTE!

⬇ WATCH THE ALTIMETER SETTING

You've had kind of a free lunch so far with the altimeter setting in that it has been the same wherever you go. This time, we're changing it subtly from airport to airport, so when ATC gives you a new setting or you get one from the ATIS/ASOS, be sure to put it into your altimeter.

⬇ KEEPING IT REAL

A GREAT INSIDER TIP: FLY LEG

If you like seeing the extra waypoints and the holding pattern but want to fly vectors, you have another option for getting correct guidance. Load and activate the approach starting at OYRED. Now press FPL to view the flight plan. Push the center of the cursor button to activate the cursor, and scroll down with the outer knob to PORSY.

Now push the Menu button. You'll get a Fly Leg? option. Push Enter, and the GPS will give you guidance on the course from OYRED to PORSY just as with VTF, but all the visible waypoints remain.

This option is a great tool on the real GPS as well and is available in more places.

Now watch the GPS to see how far you are from PORSY. The FSX GPS is a bit unrealistic here because it shows the ETE without seconds, so it reads 00:00 for a minute before crossing PORSY. The real GPS switches to seconds and counts down for you.

Slow to approach level with the gear out. When you cross PORSY, it's the five Ts, but some don't matter:

- *Time*: There's nothing to time, but it's good to note your ETE to RWY23, which is your missed approach point.

- *Turn*: Continue on the inbound course. Few GPS approaches change course after the FAF.

- *Twist:* There's nothing to twist.

462

PART I
PREFLIGHT

PART II
SPORT PILOT

PART III
PRIVATE PILOT

PART IV
INSTRUMENT RATING

PART V
COMMERCIAL LICENSE

PART VI
ATP AND BEYOND

- *Throttle:* Power to 19 inches and flaps to the approach setting. Descend for 860 feet. If you're using the autopilot, set it for 900 feet, and then descend the last 40 feet by hand.

- *Talk:* Announce your position to KSHN traffic over PORSY, 5 miles from the runway.

As you track inbound from PORSY to RWY23 (Figure 18-16), watch the TRK on the top of the screen. Adjust your heading as needed to show a TRK of 229, the inbound course. Having TRK available means you can find a heading immediately that provides all the wind correction you need. Does this work in a real airplane? You bet! We teach this to all our instrument students who have GPS available. In fact, if we had to choose between just a moving map or just TRK, it would be a tough call.

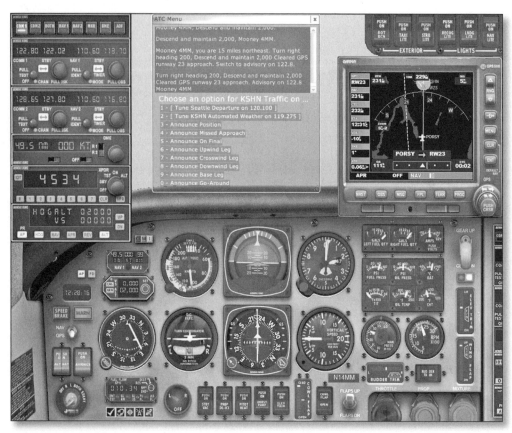

Figure 18-16: The GPS is your cue that you've crossed PORSY, but you're still flying the CDI needle on the HSI to stay on course.

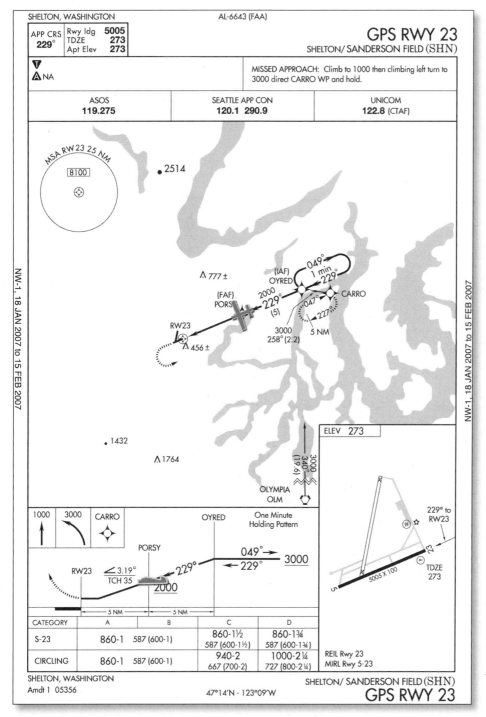

SHELTON, WASHINGTON   AL-6643 (FAA)

APP CRS	Rwy ldg	5005
229°	TDZE	273
	Apt Elev	273

GPS RWY 23
SHELTON/ SANDERSON FIELD (SHN)

MISSED APPROACH: Climb to 1000 then climbing left turn to 3000 direct CARRO WP and hold.

ASOS	SEATTLE APP CON	UNICOM
119.275	**120.1 290.9**	**122.8** (CTAF)

MSA RW 23 25 NM
8100

• 2514

Λ 777 ±

(IAF)
OYRED
049°
1 min
229°

CARRO

(FAF)
PORSY
2000
229°
(5)

RW23
Λ 456 ±

047°
227°

3000
258° (2.2)
5 NM

• 1432

Λ 1764

3000
340°
(19.6)

OLYMPIA
OLM

ELEV 273

229° to RW23

H

23
TDZE
273

5005 X 100

5

1000 ↑	3000 ↱	CARRO ◆	OYRED	One Minute Holding Pattern

PORSY
049° → 3000
229°
← 229°

RW23
≤ 3.19°
TCH 35
2000

5 NM   5 NM

CATEGORY	A	B	C	D
S-23	860-1	587 (600-1)	860-1½ 587 (600-1½)	860-1¾ 587 (600-1¾)
CIRCLING	860-1	587 (600-1)	940-2 667 (700-2)	1000-2¼ 727 (800-2¼)

REIL Rwy 23
MIRL Rwy 5-23

SHELTON, WASHINGTON
Amdt 1 05356

47°14'N - 123°09'W

SHELTON/ SANDERSON FIELD (SHN)
GPS RWY 23

Figure 18-16 (Continued)

464

| PART I | PART II | PART III | PART IV | PART V | PART VI |
| PREFLIGHT | SPORT PILOT | PRIVATE PILOT | INSTRUMENT RATING | COMMERCIAL LICENSE | ATP AND BEYOND |

As you descend to MDA, press W on the keyboard to show only the key instruments, but then press Shift+3 to see the GPS as well (see Figure 18-17). Look for the runway to appear out of the haze. If you see it, fine, but don't land just yet. You need to take a look at the missed approach with a GPS.

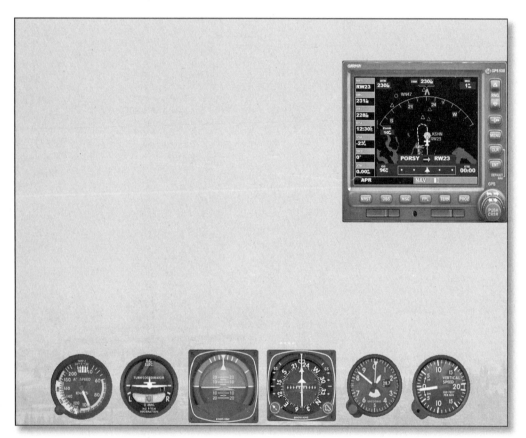

Figure 18-17: The missed approach point on the GPS approach is usually right over the runway threshold. Note that here you're already high for landing, and you're not at the MAP yet, as shown on the GPS.

INSIDE THE GAME

WATCH THE ALTITUDE

Feel free to fly the GPS approaches with the autopilot. Again, use HDG mode to keep your head in the game. If you fly the approach with the autopilot in APR (approach) mode, note that the FSX autopilot has a bad habit of disengaging altitude mode when you switch from HDG mode to APR mode. Presumably, this is because you would want to descend for the approach, but usually you want to maintain altitude for a while. Watch out for this.

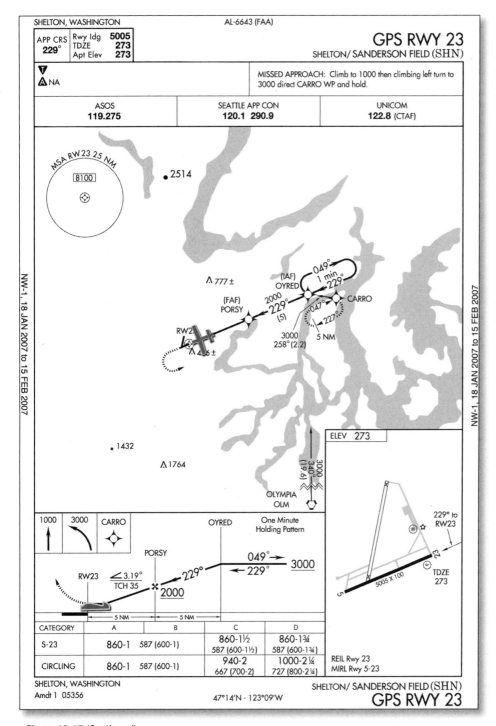

SHELTON, WASHINGTON   AL-6643 (FAA)

APP CRS 229°	Rwy ldg 5005 TDZE 273 Apt Elev 273

GPS RWY 23
SHELTON/ SANDERSON FIELD (SHN)

▼
△ NA

MISSED APPROACH: Climb to 1000 then climbing left turn to 3000 direct CARRO WP and hold.

ASOS 119.275	SEATTLE APP CON 120.1 290.9	UNICOM 122.8 (CTAF)

MSA RW 23 25 NM
8100

• 2514

△ 777 ±

(IAF)
OYRED
049°
1 min
229°

CARRO

(FAF)
PORSY
2000
229°
(5)

047°
227°

RW23

△ 456 ±

3000
258° (2.2)
5 NM

ELEV 273

• 1432

△ 1764

3000
340°
(19.6)

OLYMPIA
OLM

229° to
RW23

TDZE
273

5005 X 100

NW-1, 18 JAN 2007 to 15 FEB 2007

1000	3000	CARRO		OYRED	One Minute Holding Pattern

PORSY
049° →
← 229°
3000

RW23
3.19°
TCH 35
229°
2000

5 NM — 5 NM

CATEGORY	A	B	C	D
S-23	860-1	587 (600-1)	860-1½ 587 (600-1½)	860-1¾ 587 (600-1¾)
CIRCLING	860-1	587 (600-1)	940-2 667 (700-2)	1000-2¼ 727 (800-2¼)

REIL Rwy 23
MIRL Rwy 5-23

SHELTON, WASHINGTON
Amdt 1 05356

47°14'N - 123°09'W

SHELTON/ SANDERSON FIELD (SHN)
GPS RWY 23

Figure 18-17 (Continued)

466

PART I
PREFLIGHT

PART II
SPORT PILOT

PART III
PRIVATE PILOT

PART IV
INSTRUMENT RATING

PART V
COMMERCIAL LICENSE

PART VI
ATP AND BEYOND

FLYING THE GPS MISSED

When you break out close to the runway threshold on a GPS approach, you might be too high to land. We'll talk about circling around to land in the next chapter, but for now if you can't land, you'll have to fly the missed approach.

This is a bit different with a GPS, and FSX diverges from the real world in one key way.

You might not have noticed, but when you're navigating along a flight plan using GPS, the TO-FROM arrow always shows TO. This is because you're always flying to the next waypoint. (In the real world, GPS navigators actually show FROM for just a moment as you pass over the waypoint just to let you know it happened.)

When you cross the MAP with a real IFR GPS, it goes into SUSPEND mode. That means it stops automatically sequencing you—and guiding you—from one waypoint to the next. The GPS actually acts more like a VOR when this happens, and it shows you navigating from the waypoint RWY23. In the real world, you must manually press the OBS button to restart sequencing for the missed approach. In addition, the first part of the missed, which is climbing straight ahead to 1,000 feet, you must do on your own and *before* you press OBS to start GPS sequencing again.

The reason the real IFR GPS is set up this way is that as soon as you press OBS, the GPS draws a straight line from your current position to the missed approach holding fix, which is CARRO in this case. Real-world GPS units are not capable of giving you guidance for that climb and turn.

Not so, the FSX GPS. It will happily give you guidance through the entire missed approach. Here's how it works.

↓ KEEPING IT REAL

LIMITED SUSPENSE

On the real-world GP, the OBS button is a key tool in using the GPS. In FSX, it does stop automatic sequencing, but it doesn't behave anything like the real GPS. About the only use for it in FSX is if you need to lose altitude in a hold before starting an approach and don't want the GPS to keep sequencing you along until you're ready. Other than that, don't bother with the button.

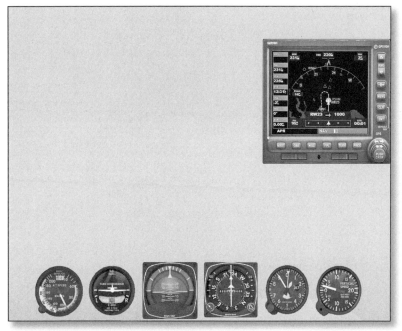

When you fly over the missed approach waypoint, the GPS will sequence to the next leg of RWY23 -> 1000. It even provides a tiny magenta line for this leg (see Figure 18-18). Again, we can't stress enough that a real-world IFR GPS will *not* do this.

Figure 18-18: The GNS 500 in FSX (unrealistically) guides you through every step of the missed approach exactly as it appears on the plate.

When you start the missed approach, it's the four Cs again: *climb* attitude and full power, *clean* up the gear and flaps, *cool* the engine with your climb power setting and cowl flaps, and *communicate* to KSHN traffic and then to Seattle Departure that you're flying the missed approach. When you do, click the option in the ATC window to tell Seattle Departure that you're flying the published missed approach (see Figure 18-19).

Figure 18-19: In FSX, the autopilot can fly you through the entire missed approach if you want. Don't bother setting an altitude of 1,000, though. Go straight to 3,000, even if you turn well after passing 1,000 feet. (Figure continued on next page.)

468

PART I PREFLIGHT · PART II SPORT PILOT · PART III PRIVATE PILOT · **PART IV INSTRUMENT RATING** · PART V COMMERCIAL LICENSE · PART VI ATP AND BEYOND

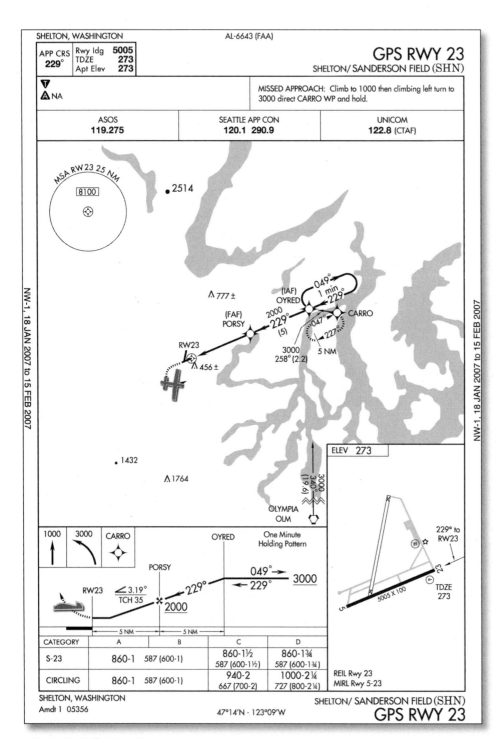

SHELTON, WASHINGTON   AL-6643 (FAA)

APP CRS **229°**	Rwy Idg **5005** TDZE **273** Apt Elev **273**

GPS RWY 23
SHELTON/ SANDERSON FIELD (SHN)

MISSED APPROACH: Climb to 1000 then climbing left turn to 3000 direct CARRO WP and hold.

ASOS **119.275**	SEATTLE APP CON **120.1 290.9**	UNICOM **122.8** (CTAF)

NW-1, 18 JAN 2007 to 15 FEB 2007

MSA RW 23 25 NM
8100

•2514

(IAF)
OYRED

049°
1 min
229°

CARRO

(FAF)
PORSY

2000
229°
(5)

047°

227°

3000
258°(2.2)

5 NM

RW23

∧ 456 ±

∧ 777 ±

•1432

∧1764

ELEV 273

OLYMPIA
OLM

3000
340°
(19.6)

229° to
RW23

5005 X 100

TDZE
273

ELEV 273

1000 ↑	3000	CARRO		OYRED	One Minute Holding Pattern

049° →
← 229°   3000

RW23   PORSY
≤ 3.19°   229°
TCH 35
2000

5 NM   5 NM

CATEGORY	A	B	C	D
S-23	860-1	587 (600-1)	860-1½ 587 (600-1½)	860-1¾ 587 (600-1¾)
CIRCLING	860-1	587 (600-1)	940-2 667 (700-2)	1000-2¼ 727 (800-2¼)

REIL Rwy 23
MIRL Rwy 5-23

SHELTON, WASHINGTON
Amdt 1 05356

47°14'N - 123°09'W

SHELTON/ SANDERSON FIELD (SHN)
GPS RWY 23

Figure 18-19 (Continued)

As you fly the missed approach, it doesn't matter which way your CDI is set because you'll get the correct left/right guidance, but take a guess at your route back to CARRO—probably about 050—and set it on the CDI for reference.

When you get to 3,000 feet, you'll want to reduce power right away and let the Mooney accelerate only to low cruise. The hold is just a place to kill time until you figure out your next move. There's no reason to burn a bunch of gas. The entry to the hold is almost always a direct entry on a GPS approach that isn't an overlay of an older kind of approach. In the real world, the GPS would go into suspend mode again, and you'd have to work your way around the hold with the holding waypoint acting like a VOR. FSX depicts the hold without suspending the GPS sequencing (see Figure 18-20).

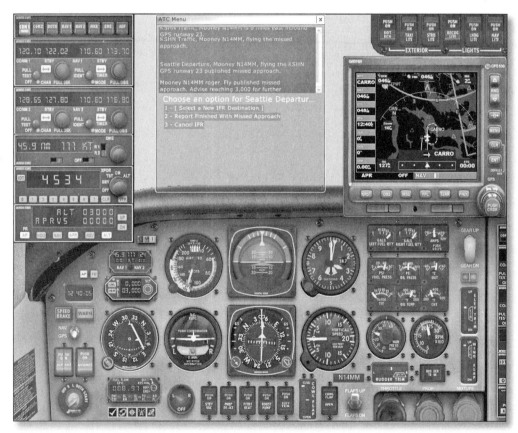

Figure 18-20: The FSX autopilot can fly you around the hold all on its own. Few real-world autopilots in light aircraft will do this for you. (Figure continued on next page.)

470

PART I	PART II	PART III	PART IV	PART V	PART VI
PREFLIGHT	SPORT PILOT	PRIVATE PILOT	INSTRUMENT RATING	COMMERCIAL LICENSE	ATP AND BEYOND

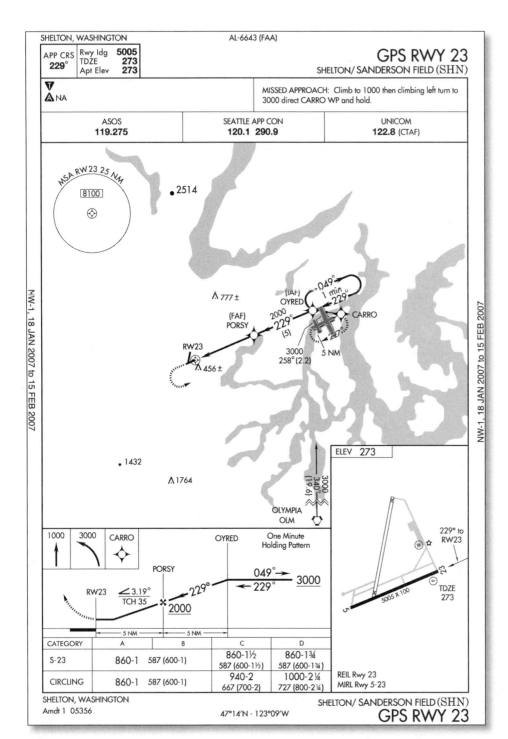

SHELTON, WASHINGTON   AL-6643 (FAA)

GPS RWY 23
SHELTON/ SANDERSON FIELD (SHN)

APP CRS	Rwy ldg	5005
229°	TDZE	273
	Apt Elev	273

MISSED APPROACH: Climb to 1000 then climbing left turn to 3000 direct CARRO WP and hold.

ASOS	SEATTLE APP CON	UNICOM
119.275	**120.1 290.9**	**122.8** (CTAF)

MSA RW 23 25 NM   8100

• 2514

• 777 ±

(IAF) OYRED   049° 1 min   229°

(FAF) PORSY   2000 229° (5)

CARRO

RW23   Λ 456 ±

3000 258° (2.2)   5 NM

• 1432

Λ1764

3000 340° (19.6)

OLYMPIA OLM

ELEV 273

229° to RW23

5005 X 100   TDZE 273

Profile

| 1000 | 3000 | CARRO | | OYRED | One Minute Holding Pattern |

PORSY   049° → 229° ← 3000

RW23   3.19° TCH 35   229°   2000

5 NM   5 NM

CATEGORY	A	B	C	D
S-23	860-1	587 (600-1)	860-1½ 587 (600-1½)	860-1¾ 587 (600-1¾)
CIRCLING	860-1	587 (600-1)	940-2 667 (700-2)	1000-2¼ 727 (800-2¼)

REIL Rwy 23
MIRL Rwy 5-23

SHELTON, WASHINGTON
Amdt 1 05356

47°14'N - 123°09'W

SHELTON/ SANDERSON FIELD (SHN)
GPS RWY 23

NW-1, 18 JAN 2007 to 15 FEB 2007

NW-1, 18 JAN 2007 to 15 FEB 2007

Figure 18-20 (Continued)

RAIM

Receiver autonomous integrity monitoring (RAIM) is a safety feature that verifies GPS accuracy for the approach. If the GPS cannot maintain the RAIM standards, it will warn you, and you must discontinue the approach. The receiver is allowed to wait five minutes to give the RAIM warning, however. During this period, it's still accurate enough for you to fly the remainder of an approach if you've already started it.

*RNAV R*wy *34 A*pproach *at KFHR*

The approach at Oak Harbor you looked at earlier is interesting, but it's not in the FSX GPS database. To fly a GPS approach, the approach must be in the GPS. You can't just cobble the waypoints together on your own.

You'll fly from Bellingham, Washington (KBLI), to Friday Harbor, Washington (KFHR), instead. The route will take you to the ISLND intersection and then to the HILPT at UGTAW. This approach is interesting in that it has a turn at the final approach fix DFUCA. That's unusual for an RNAV or GPS approach that isn't an overlay. (By the way, DFUCA would be pronounced "De FEW Ka." Sometimes the hardest part of working with GPS waypoints is knowing how to pronounce them on the radio. In this case, the waypoint was named for the Straight of Juan de Fuca, where the waypoint is located.)

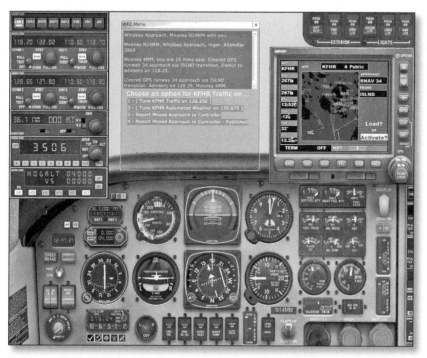

Figure 18-21: With your approach active, you can navigate to ISLND.

Load the flight Chap18_KBLI_to_KFHR, and you find yourself at 4,000 feet heading for the ISLND intersection for the approach. (Load Chap18_KBLI_to_KFHR_full if you want to fly the entire thing from takeoff to touchdown.)

Your first step is acknowledging the clearance for the approach. Do so with Whidbey Approach in the ATC window. Your next step is loading the approach. It works just like before. Because your flight plan is to KFHR, pushing the PROC button lets you select an approach. Choose the RNAV 34 approach and the ISLND transition. Activate the approach; you can push the FLP key to see things on the moving map and twist the CDI as needed to give you good sense of the way to ISLND (see Figure 18-21).

472

PART I	PART II	PART III	PART IV	PART V	PART VI
PREFLIGHT	SPORT PILOT	PRIVATE PILOT	INSTRUMENT RATING	COMMERCIAL LICENSE	ATP AND BEYOND

STUDENT OF THE CRAFT

LOONY WAYPOINT NAMES

Who says the FAA doesn't have a sense of humor? One of the most famous oddball set of waypoints is the RNAV Rwy 16 into Portsmouth, New Hampshire (KPSM). Portsmouth was the birthplace of Mel Blanc who did the voices for all the Looney Tunes characters. Flying the complete approach with the missed will cause you to fly over ITAWT, ITAWA, PUDYE, TTATT, and IDEED.

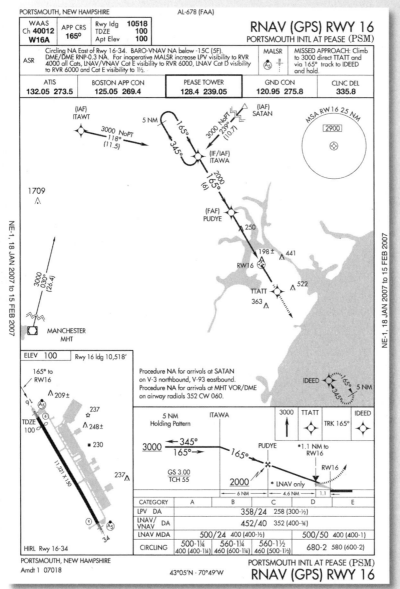

Oddly enough, you'll also find the waypoint SATAN on the same plate.

Since you're cleared for the approach, the restriction on your altitude at 4,000 goes away once you're on a published route. After you cross ISLND, start your descent to 2200 as published on the plate (see Figure 18-22). Also start working your power back toward the low cruise setting. It might seem like you're late in bringing back the power at this point, but you've got a fair amount of ground to cover to use for slowing down. Don't expect to hear anything from ATC for the rest of this approach. You're on your own for this one.

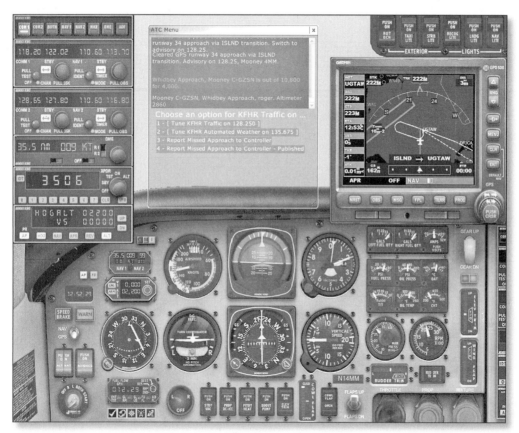

Figure 18-22: You'll have to make a parallel entry at UGTAW for the hold/course reversal. (Figure continued on next page.)

474

PART I
PREFLIGHT

PART II
SPORT PILOT

PART III
PRIVATE PILOT

PART IV
INSTRUMENT RATING

PART V
COMMERCIAL LICENSE

PART VI
ATP AND BEYOND

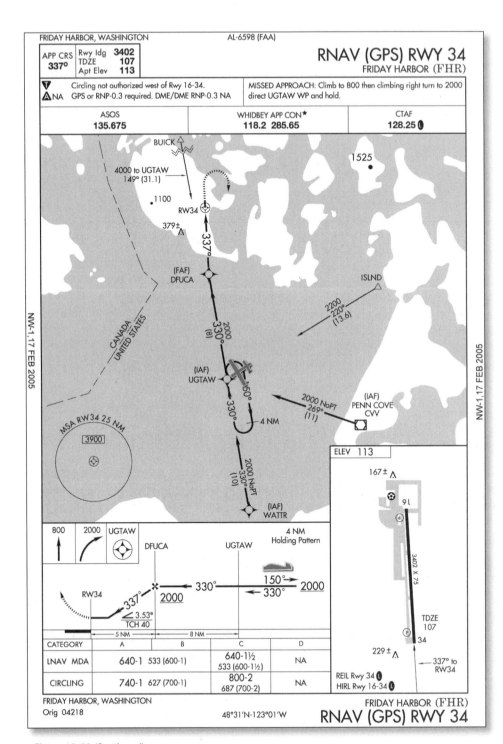

Figure 18-22 (Continued)

WATCH THE DTK

If you wonder where to set the CDI for each leg of the approach, watch the DTK at the top of the moving map. That DTK is the course you want to fly and what the CDI should be set to. You can see all the DTKs from the FPL page or from the approach chart itself.

When you cross UGTAW, you can descend another 200 feet to 2,000 and reverse course. Your five *T*s are a handy tool here to make sure you don't miss anything you're supposed to do. You don't need to fly a complete holding pattern here. You need only turn outbound to a heading of 150 and fly a minute away from UGTAW. Next you start a left turn to reintercept the 330 course inbound to UGTAW (see Figure 18-23). If you need more time to slow down, you might use the hold to do it, but realize that you have 8 miles from UGTAW to DFUCA to slow the rest of the way to 100 knots in approach level with the gear down. Since you can drop the gear at any speed under 140 knots, you can use them to help slow down too.

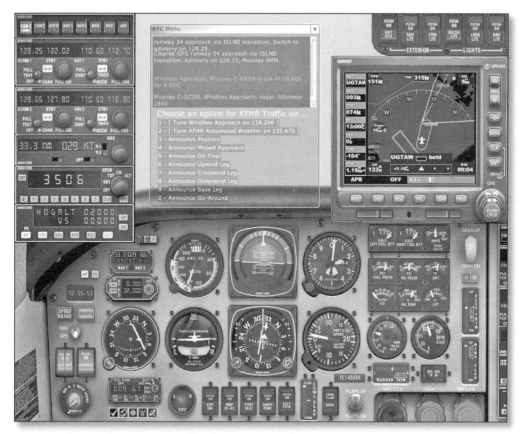

Figure 18-23: The autopilot will not fly the parallel entry correctly. You must do it manually or with HDG mode. (Figure continued on next page.)

476

PART I
PREFLIGHT

PART II
SPORT PILOT

PART III
PRIVATE PILOT

PART IV
INSTRUMENT RATING

PART V
COMMERCIAL LICENSE

PART VI
ATP AND BEYOND

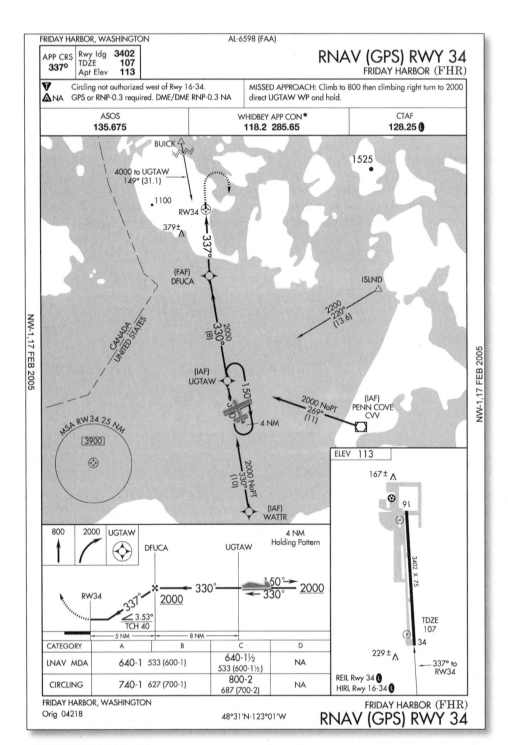

Figure 18-23 (Continued)

BY THE BOOK

CAN'T I JUST GO STRAIGHT?

A regular argument among instrument pilots is when you must do the PT and when you can skip it. The regulations say one thing, and the real world behaves differently.

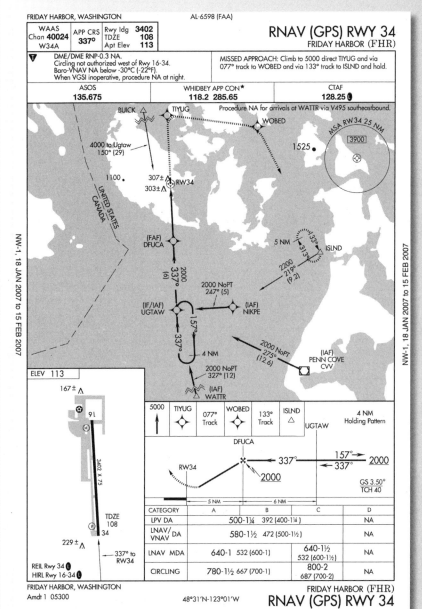

The regulations say that unless you are on a transition route that specifically says "NoPT," then you must fly the procedure turn as charted—even if you could easily fly straight on to the final approach course. For example, on the KFHR approach, arrivals from Penn Cove (CVV) or the WATER intersection can cross UGTAW and proceed straight in. Arrivals heading directly to UGTAW from a position between CVV and WATTR, however, would technically need to fly the PT. This is, of course, ridiculous, but that's how the rules read.

In the real world, controllers often shortcut the whole thing by giving a clearance

Continued

478

PART I
PREFLIGHT

PART II
SPORT PILOT

PART III
PRIVATE PILOT

PART IV
INSTRUMENT RATING

PART V
COMMERCIAL LICENSE

PART VI
ATP AND BEYOND

direct to UGTAW even though the aircraft is on neither transition but they expect the pilot to fly straight in. There is a clause in the controller's handbook that allows this if the aircraft is within 4 miles laterally of a published route and the turn when they reach the fix is no more than 120°.

Technically, the controller should say, "Proceed direct UGTAW; cleared straight-in RNAV Rwy 34 approach." If you're ever uncertain, you can ask ATC whether you are cleared straight in.

You can also shortcut the process by looking at the approach and asking for a route via a NoPT waypoint. People must have complained about this at KFHR because the newest approach (which is not the one used in FSX) has an extra waypoint called NIKPE near UGTAW that appears to serve exactly this purpose.

Perhaps it's called NIKPE because the people who worried about this were "nit-picking." You'd be surprised how many waypoints have names with ironic meanings.

You should be at 100 knots by DFUCA and ready for final approach. Cross DFUCA (Figure 18-24) and do your five *T*s:

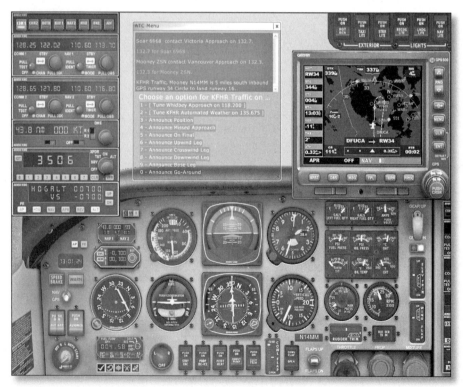

- *Time:* There's nothing to time, but it's about two minutes to the MAP according to the GPS.

- *Turn:* Turn to a heading of 337, and watch for a TRK of 337 on the GPS.

- *Twist:* Twist your OBS to 337.

- *Throttle:* Throttle to 19 inches, prop forward, approach flaps.

- *Talk:* Give a position report on KFHR CTAF.

Figure 18-24: Crossing DFUCA is a good time to make a position report to other aircraft at KFHR. Since this is the fifth T*, you should have no trouble remembering to do it.*

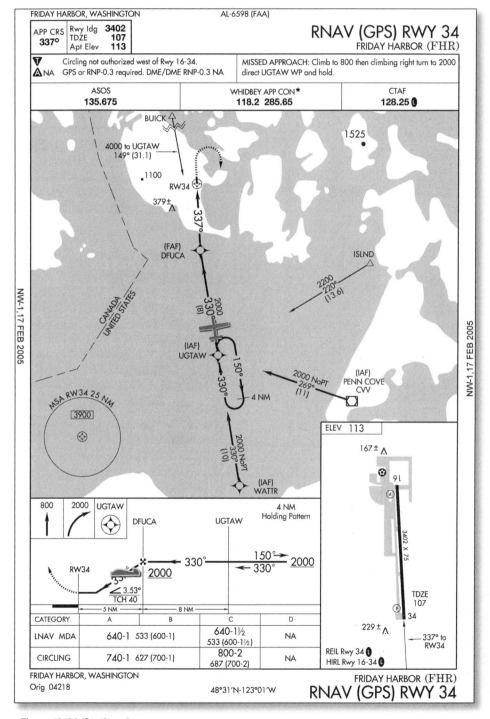

FRIDAY HARBOR, WASHINGTON AL-6598 (FAA)

APP CRS	Rwy ldg	**3402**
337°	TDZE	**107**
	Apt Elev	**113**

RNAV (GPS) RWY 34
FRIDAY HARBOR (FHR)

▽ Circling not authorized west of Rwy 16-34.
△NA GPS or RNP-0.3 required. DME/DME RNP-0.3 NA

MISSED APPROACH: Climb to 800 then climbing right turn to 2000 direct UGTAW WP and hold.

| ASOS | WHIDBEY APP CON★ | CTAF |
| **135.675** | **118.2 285.65** | **128.25** |

ELEV 113

CATEGORY	A	B	C	D
LNAV MDA	640-1 533 (600-1)		640-1½ 533 (600-1½)	NA
CIRCLING	740-1 627 (700-1)		800-2 687 (700-2)	NA

FRIDAY HARBOR, WASHINGTON
Orig 04218

48°31'N-123°01'W

FRIDAY HARBOR (FHR)
RNAV (GPS) RWY 34

Figure 18-24 (Continued)

480

| PART I | PART II | PART III | PART IV | PART V | PART VI |
| PREFLIGHT | SPORT PILOT | PRIVATE PILOT | INSTRUMENT RATING | COMMERCIAL LICENSE | ATP AND BEYOND |

When you get to the straight-in minimums of 640 feet, look for the runway. If you see it, land. If not, go missed approach.

▼ INSIDE THE GAME

NOT SENSITIVE ON THE CDI

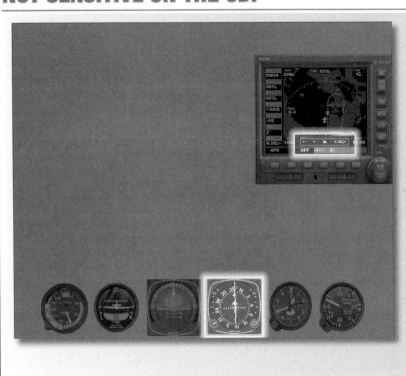

One place where FSX gets it very wrong is with the CDI sensitivity on GPS approaches. The CDI on the HSI should be as sensitive as the CDI on the GPS. That is, it should be .3 miles to full-scale deflection. It isn't. That means it might look like you're on course with the HSI, but you're not nearly close enough to see the airport on a nasty day. Watch the CDI on the GPS too, and make sure it's centered as well.

THE VOR OR GPS RWY 6 AT KHQM

Last up is an approach designed as a VOR approach but flown with the GPS. Load the flight Chap18_KBFI_to_KHQM to start the flight in the air here on V205 heading for HQM. Load the "_full" version if you want to take off from KBFI yourself. Remember you need to ask for the VOR Rwy 6 approach with the HQM transition.

You're in an interesting situation here (see Figure 18-25). It's one that's common in IFR flying. You're at 4,000 feet only five minutes from the VOR at your current speed. Crossing the VOR you're going way down to 1,600 feet while doing a procedure turn. That turn will take about two minutes out from the VOR, one and a half minutes on heading 197, and about two minutes back on 017 and then inbound on 062. That's five and a half minutes to lose 2,400 feet *and* slow down to 100 knots before crossing the VOR inbound.

This would be a good time to ask ATC for a lower altitude, but FSX won't let you, and in the real world on this route, you're unlikely to get it because of the proximity of some low mountains. Plan B is to slow down now to low cruise and then come down fast without gaining airspeed. Let's see how it works out.

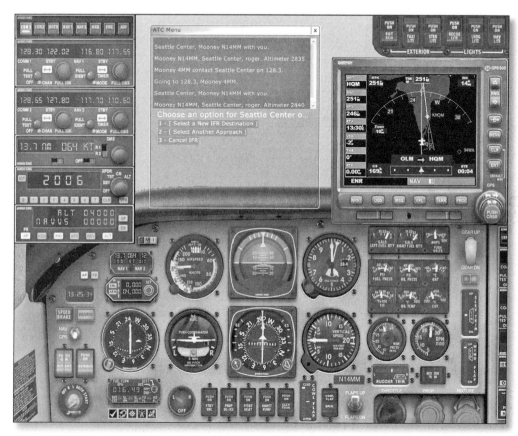

Figure 18-25: As you get close to the airport, set your map range to see the VOR and the destination field. Get yourself switched to your fullest fuel tank and the approach loaded now, before you get too busy.

SOMETHING TO DO WITH NAV2

Since this is a VOR approach, you can monitor your progress with the VOR too. You can't do it on the HSI—that's being used for the GPS—but you can put HQM on NAV2 and set your DME to read from NAV2 as well.

482

PART I	PART II	PART III	PART IV	PART V	PART VI
PREFLIGHT	SPORT PILOT	PRIVATE PILOT	INSTRUMENT RATING	COMMERCIAL LICENSE	ATP AND BEYOND

Start slowing down, and then press the PROC button on the GPS. Select the VOR 06 approach. You'll see the little letters "GPS" beside the approach, which means you can fly this approach using the GPS rather than the VORs. Select the HQM transition, and activate the approach. Since you're already flying to HQM, your CDI won't budge, but when you cross HQM, the GPS will sequence you through the approach.

You want to get the weather for KHQM because it has an impact on how you fly this approach. A south wind at the airport means you want to fly outbound on the PT longer or at an angle greater than 45°. If you don't, you'll overshoot the inbound course back to the VOR when you turn around. A north wind might mean a shorter outbound on the PT or, at the least, being ready for the inbound course to come in slowly.

You get the clearance to start down just before the VOR (see Figure 18-26).

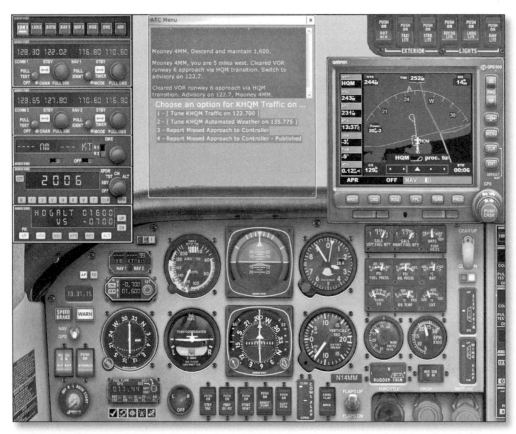

Figure 18-26: If you're still screaming along by the VOR, do whatever you need to do to slow down in airspeed but still come down at 700 fpm or more.

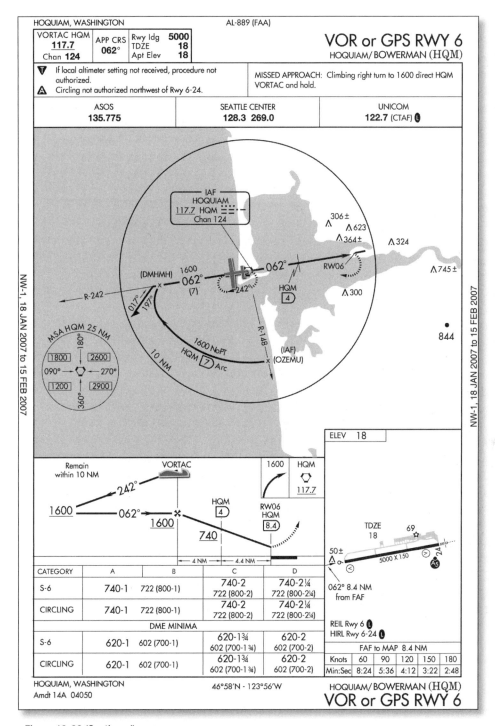

Figure 18-26 (Continued)

484

| PART I | PART II | PART III | PART IV | PART V | PART VI |
| PREFLIGHT | SPORT PILOT | PRIVATE PILOT | INSTRUMENT RATING | COMMERCIAL LICENSE | ATP AND BEYOND |

Crossing the VOR, fly outbound for two minutes on 062. Turn to a heading of about 197, depending on how much wind correction you want to add, and fly outbound for about 1.5 minutes. Turn right to 017, and intercept the 062 heading back to the VOR.

The GPS should show you your progress as you go around the PT (Figure 18-27), but because FSX tries to actually guide you around the PT, there is a problem. If you manually fly the PT or fly it with the HDG function of the GPS, the GPS does not sequence you along the approach. (If you use the APR mode on the autopilot, it works fine.) You can hand fly the PT, but then you'll have to go to the flight plan page on the GPS, push the FMS knob in the center to get a cursor, scroll down to the HQM that comes after the PT, and click Menu. Then you can click Enter to fly the leg back to the VOR, and the GPS will work correctly. This is not an issue on the real Garmin GNS 500.

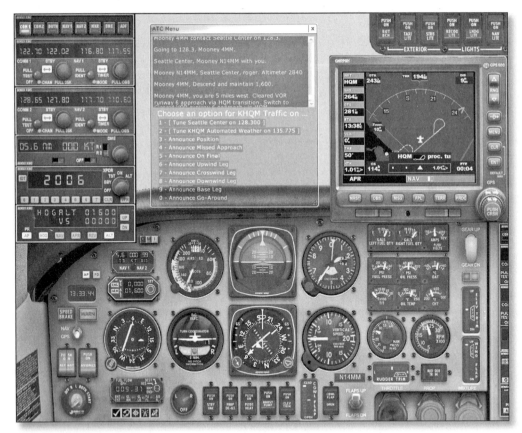

Figure 18-27: You don't have to fly the PT where the GPS shows it. It's totally up to you. You must stay within 10 miles of HQM, however.

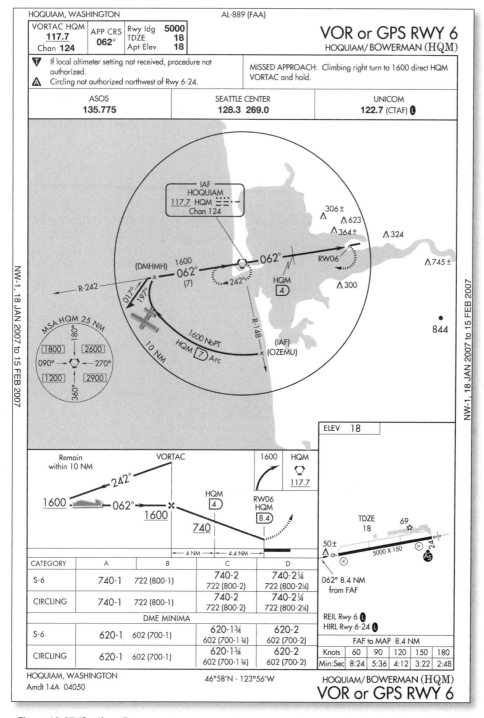

Figure 18-27 (Continued)

486

PART I
PREFLIGHT

PART II
SPORT PILOT

PART III
PRIVATE PILOT

PART IV
INSTRUMENT RATING

PART V
COMMERCIAL LICENSE

PART VI
ATP AND BEYOND

It's your five *T*s crossing the HQM VOR and down you go to 740 feet (see Figure 18-28). You might need to watch the NAV2 DME to see your distance from HQM to descend further to 640 at DME 4 from HQM. Alternately, you can descend when you're four miles from RWY06. That's inside the 4.4 mile distance shown on the approach plate, so it's legit. On a real IFR GPS, this point would be a waypoint on the approach called D4.0, so you'd know exactly when you passed it.

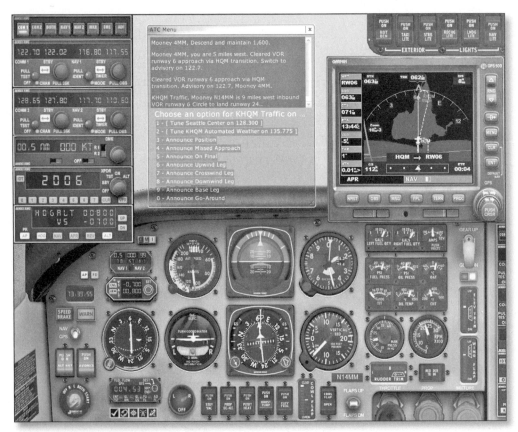

Figure 18-28: Watch the GPS TRK to help stay on course. You might not want to be in too much of a hurry to get down. The GPS map shows an awful lot of water below you and not much land.

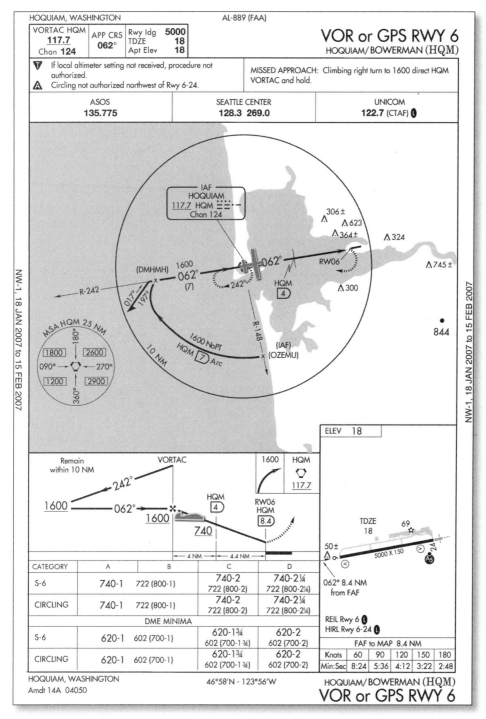

Figure 18-28 (Continued)

488

PART I	PART II	PART III	PART IV	PART V	PART VI
PREFLIGHT	SPORT PILOT	PRIVATE PILOT	INSTRUMENT RATING	COMMERCIAL LICENSE	ATP AND BEYOND

The winds are such that you might have a challenging landing at KHQM, but when you get it in sight, go ahead and land. The airport used to have a great café. Perhaps it's still there for a virtual lunch!

 ⬇ KEEPING IT REAL

GPS ON NON-GPS APPROACHES?

You can load many approaches into the GPS that you can't fly using the GPS as your primary navigation. Here, the airplane is on the ILS Rwy 13R into Boeing Field. There's a strong cross-wind from the right, but it's easy to stay on course because the track is there on the GPS and there is the magenta line from the FAF to the runway, right along the path of the localizer.

The ILS approach is in the database with the GPS approaches, and you load and activate it the same way as any other approach. The only difference is it's for situational awareness only. Note that the HSI is driven off NAV1, however, where the localizer frequency of 110.9 is dialed in.

INSTRUMENT APPROACHES ON THE *G1000*

The G1000 implementation in FSX is strong in some ways but weak in others. It's a great place to practice your instrument scan for the PFD—not that the scan is that different than with a traditional six-pack with a *huge* attitude indicator that's visible behind all the other instruments. Certain aspects, such as reading altitudes—and noticing when you're off your assigned altitude—take some practice on the G1000.

Some of the buttonology details, though, are different enough on the real G1000 vs. the FSX version that the training utility is limited, or perhaps even what we call *negative transfer*. That is, it's done differently enough in the real world that you're better just learning the real G1000. Managing your frequencies for COM and NAV radios are like this.

It's still worth flying some approaches on the G1000 system, though, so let's look at two examples: a GPS approach with the G1000 and an ILS.

INSIDE THE GAME

JUGGLING G1000 SCREENS

Using the keyboard to show different items on the screen is even more important with the G1000 Mooney.

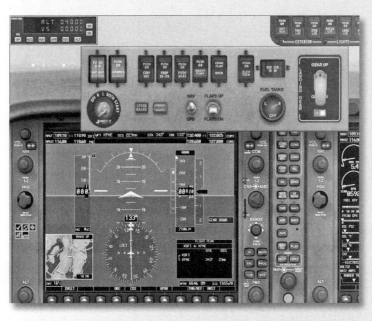

Shift+1 shows the full PFD and engine instruments of the MFD. This is good for en route IFR flying.

Shift+2 shows the KAP 140 autopilot. We recommend just turning this on and dragging it to the upper left of the screen.

Shift+3 shows the MFD. By default it's small—too small to use as far as we're concerned. Make it appear, and drag the top and left side to make it as big as the PFD. Then toggle it on and off when you need to see it.

Shift+4 shows the PFD separately, but since you already have that, you never need to use this command.

Continued

490

PART I · PREFLIGHT   PART II · SPORT PILOT   PART III · PRIVATE PILOT   PART IV · INSTRUMENT RATING   PART V · COMMERCIAL LICENSE   PART VI · ATP AND BEYOND

Shift+5 shows the PFD landing panel. It's good for taking off, landing, and VFR flying. You can toggle between Shift+1 and Shift+5 easily, or you can use the FSX buttons on the lower-left panel to get the same result.

Shift+6 shows your backup instruments in case of AHRS or air data failure.

Shift+7 shows your throttle quadrant, but this is moot if you have a joystick with power controls.

Shift+8 is critical because it shows a number of switches and settings, including your speed brakes and fuel selector. You'll want to be able to toggle this on and off.

Shift+9 is the overhead panel of switches that you just view and leave visible.

GPS Rwy 1 at KPWT

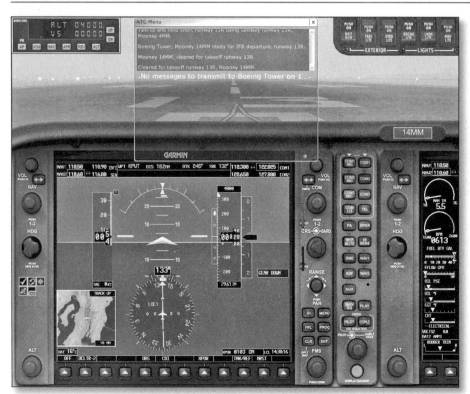

Load the flight Chap 18_KBFI_to_KRNT. This puts you on the ground at Boeing Field, getting ready to fly to nearby Bremerton airport (KPWT). You start on the ground for this one, as shown in Figure 18-29.

You're at the end of Runway 13R, and you have the Boeing localizer loaded into NAV1. You also have the CDI on the PFD set to show the localizer. This is a difference with the G1000 because you ignore the NAV/GPS switch on the Shift+8 panel and use the CDI softkey to switch between GPS navigation and VOR/localizer navigation.

Figure 18-29: Note that the G1000 automatically identifies the active NAV frequencies, IBFI and SEA in this case. IBFI is green because you're using it for navigation on the PFD.

Also, you'll want to set your heading bug for the runway and your altitude bug for 4,000, your clearance altitude. Remember that the heading bug is on the PFD, and the altitude bug is on the MFD section you can see next to the PFD. The outer altitude knob is thousands of feet, and the inner one is hundreds. Setting the altitude bug on the G1000 also sets it on the KAP 140. If only that were true in real life too. You can set your altimeter by just pressing B on the keyboard or entering it using the Baro knob on the PFD.

TRANSPONDER ON THE PFD

Remember that you'll need to use the softkeys on the PFD to enter a transponder code.

Get your clearance, and take off. You need the Shift+8 panel (or the MFD) to see the position of your flaps. You also need the Shift+8 panel to turn off the boost pump. Once the gear are in the wheel wells, the flaps are up, and you're in cruise climb (Figure 18-30), you can press the CDI button on the PFD to switch to GPS navigation.

Figure 18-30: Don't sweat getting exactly 2400 rpm or 34 inches of MP. The target is more 33.5–34.5 inches and 2350–2450 rpm. That's close enough.

492

PART I	PART II	PART III	PART IV	PART V	PART VI
PREFLIGHT	SPORT PILOT	PRIVATE PILOT	INSTRUMENT RATING	COMMERCIAL LICENSE	ATP AND BEYOND

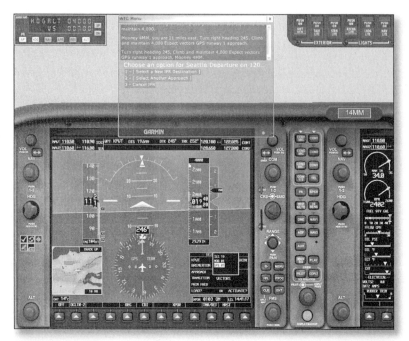

If you just play along with FSX ATC, you'll get vectors for the GPS Rwy 1 Approach, but to see how the G1000 really works, use the ATC window to request a different approach. Ask for the GPS Rwy 1 but with the CARRO transition. Once approved, you'll get cleared direct to CARRO, so you'd better load the approach.

Load the approach for KPWT. You can do it from either the PFD or the MFD. On the PFD, press the PROC button. An inset window appears in the lower right, as shown in Figure 18-31. This window is similar to the GNS500 Proc window and uses the same logic. Choose Select approach. Then choose the GPS 01 and the CARRO transition using the outer and inner FMS knobs on the PFD just as you did on the GNS500 GPS. Press Enter each time you want to make a choice. If you activate the approach, the G1000 will give you guidance direct to CARRO, which is exactly what you want. When you activate the approach, the PROC mini-window will be replaced by a flight plan mini-window on the PFD (see Figure 18-32). This shows the same information as the flight plan window on the GNS 500.

Figure 18-31: The advantage of loading the approaches on the PFD is simplicity and seeing your flight instruments. The advantage of using the MFD is seeing more information about the airport.

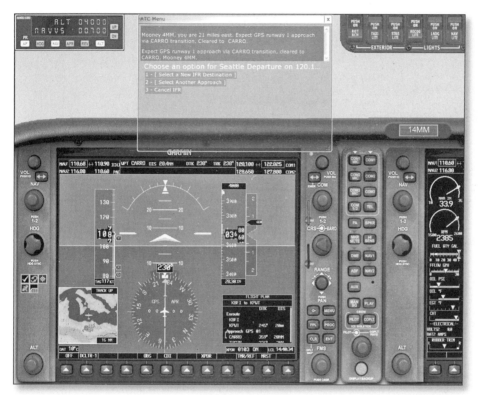

Figure 18-32: Make sure you have the mini–flight plan visible on the PFD to see all your upcoming waypoints (unless you need the timer, which takes up the same space and is opened using the softkey on the PFD).

To do the same thing on the MFD, first view the MFD with Shift+3. Next press the PROC button on the MFD. This fills the MFD screen with information about KPWT. Use the outer FMS knob on the MFD to scroll down to approaches. Use the inner knob to select the GPS 01. Press Enter on the MFD. Select the CARRO transition and press Enter again, and then select Activate and press Enter.

After selecting and activating the approach using either method, turn to the DTK shown at the top of the PFD window. Now that you're flying IFR, these four bits of information at the top of the waypoint window—WPT, DIS, DTK, and TRK—are your friends. You always know where the G1000 is taking you, how far away it is, the course you should be covering to get there, and your actual track over the ground. Watch your TRK, and make sure it matches your DTK throughout the approach. If you want to see your ground speed (GS), cross-track error (XTE), or estimated time to the next fix (ETE), then you'll need to use Shift+3 to glance at the MFD.

STUDENT OF THE CRAFT

WHICH G1000 MAP?

The G1000 offers two moving maps, one on the PFD as an inset in the lower left and one on the MFD. You'll see that even at the same zoom level, the MFD is much easier to see. The PFD map also always has the topographic colors, while the MFD can toggle this on and off. We recommend you declutter the PFD inset map and keep the range at 10 miles or less. More than that is just too hard to read on the small map.

Continued

494

PART I
PREFLIGHT

PART II
SPORT PILOT

PART III
PRIVATE PILOT

PART IV
INSTRUMENT RATING

PART V
COMMERCIAL LICENSE

PART VI
ATP AND BEYOND

On the MFD map, you can have no declutter and turn on traffic warnings to see other aircraft and still have it easy to read. Set the range on this map to see at least your next waypoint and everything that lies between you and it.

Note that you can toggle a detailed flight plan on and off with the FPL button on the MFD.

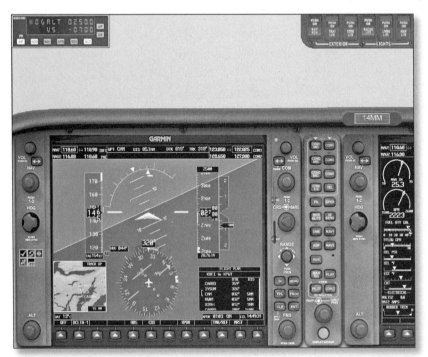

After you get your clearance for the approach, tune in the KPWT ASOS to get a current altimeter as well as a sense of the winds and ceilings. Crossing CARRO, you can descend to 3,000 feet, and crossing IYSUM, it's down to 2,500 (see Figure 18-33). By the time you reach CAN, you should be slowed to 100 knots with the gear down in the approach-level configuration.

Figure 18-33: The real G1000 advances the mini–flight plan so you can always see the current waypoints. In FSX you have to push the FMS knob to get a cursor and scroll down to show the rest of the waypoints on the approach.

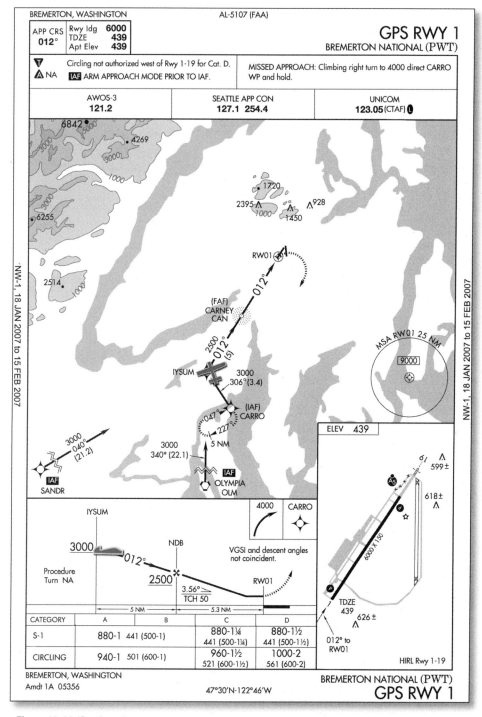

BREMERTON, WASHINGTON   AL-5107 (FAA)

GPS RWY 1
BREMERTON NATIONAL (PWT)

APP CRS	Rwy Idg	6000
012°	TDZE	439
	Apt Elev	439

Circling not authorized west of Rwy 1-19 for Cat. D.
NA   IAF ARM APPROACH MODE PRIOR TO IAF.

MISSED APPROACH: Climbing right turn to 4000 direct CARRO WP and hold.

| AWOS-3 | SEATTLE APP CON | UNICOM |
| 121.2 | 127.1 254.4 | 123.05 (CTAF) |

MSA RW01 25 NM
9000

ELEV 439

TDZE 439

012° to RW01

HIRL Rwy 1-19

IYSUM
3000
012°
NDB
2500
3.56°
TCH 50
RW01
VGSI and descent angles not coincident.
Procedure Turn NA
5 NM
5.3 NM
4000   CARRO

CATEGORY	A	B	C	D
S-1	880-1 441 (500-1)		880-1¼ 441 (500-1¼)	880-1½ 441 (500-1½)
CIRCLING	940-1 501 (600-1)		960-1½ 521 (600-1½)	1000-2 561 (600-2)

BREMERTON, WASHINGTON
Amdt 1A 05356   47°30'N-122°46'W

BREMERTON NATIONAL (PWT)
GPS RWY 1

Figure 18-33 (Continued)

496

| PART I | PART II | PART III | **PART IV** | PART V | PART VI |
| PREFLIGHT | SPORT PILOT | PRIVATE PILOT | INSTRUMENT RATING | COMMERCIAL LICENSE | ATP AND BEYOND |

As you fly toward CAN, you might need to lead your turns at each fly-by waypoint more than the G1000 indicates. Depending on how fast you're going and how steeply you're willing to bank in the clouds, you may overshoot the course for the next leg.

Also, the real G1000 warns you of each approaching waypoint in the top center of the PFD under the box showing Distance, and so on. The FSX version doesn't offer this nicety.

> **↓ NO PT AT KPWT**
>
> **A curiosity of the GPS Rwy 1 at KPWT is there is no charted procedure turn. For this reason, none of the transitions says "NoPT," even though you wouldn't do a PT from any of them.**

The drop from CAN to the MAP is unusually steep, as noted by the 3.56° descent angle shown on the approach plate profile view. You need to adjust the approach descent pitch and power settings accordingly to come down at 1000 fpm or better and still keep 100 knots. The landing panel still blocks much of your view unless you're coming down fast in a nose-low attitude, which you are in this case, but as soon as you level off a bit, you lose sight of the runway, as shown in Figure 18-34. We recommend toggling between the full panel and no panel at all using Shift+1. If you pick up the runway, you can do a low pass over the pavement for fun. Watch for the winds on the windsock. It'll be a challenging landing. But don't stay on the ground. Launch again, announce the missed approach, and start your climb up to 880—the final altitude for the approach—before making a right climbing turn back to CARRO.

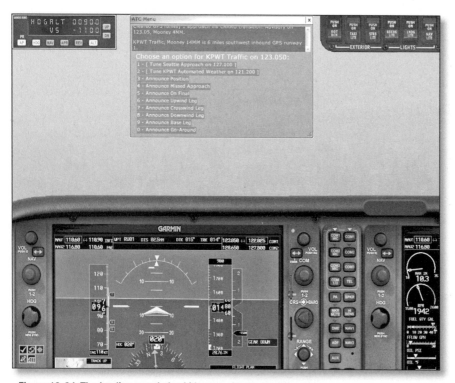

Figure 18-34: The landing panel also hides your handy moving map.

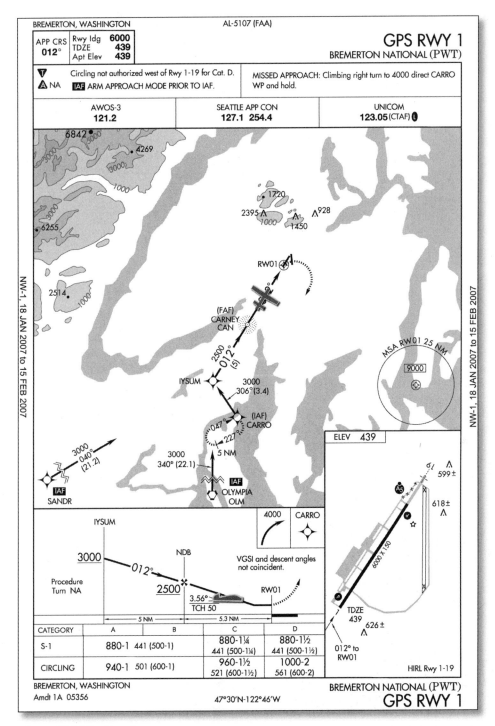

BREMERTON, WASHINGTON   AL-5107 (FAA)

GPS RWY 1
BREMERTON NATIONAL (PWT)

APP CRS	Rwy Idg	6000
012°	TDZE	439
	Apt Elev	439

Circling not authorized west of Rwy 1-19 for Cat. D.
NA   **IAF** ARM APPROACH MODE PRIOR TO IAF.

MISSED APPROACH: Climbing right turn to 4000 direct CARRO WP and hold.

AWOS-3	SEATTLE APP CON	UNICOM
121.2	**127.1 254.4**	**123.05** (CTAF)

MSA RW01 25 NM
9000

ELEV **439**

NW-1, 18 JAN 2007 to 15 FEB 2007

VGSI and descent angles not coincident.

	IYSUM	NDB			CARRO

	3000				
	012°				4000

Procedure Turn NA   2500   RW01
3.56°
TCH 50

	5 NM		5.3 NM	

CATEGORY	A	B	C	D
S-1	880-1 441 (500-1)		880-1¼ 441 (500-1¼)	880-1½ 441 (500-1½)
CIRCLING	940-1 501 (600-1)		960-1½ 521 (600-1½)	1000-2 561 (600-2)

TDZE 439
012° to RW01
HIRL Rwy 1-19

BREMERTON, WASHINGTON
Amdt 1A 05356   47°30'N-122°46'W

BREMERTON NATIONAL (PWT)
GPS RWY 1

Figure 18-34 (Continued)

498

PART I
PREFLIGHT

PART II
SPORT PILOT

PART III
PRIVATE PILOT

PART IV
INSTRUMENT RATING

PART V
COMMERCIAL LICENSE

PART VI
ATP AND BEYOND

To see it in action, fly the missed approach. When you talk to ATC, you can ask for the published missed approach. What you'll see is that it's even easier on the G1000, especially with the huge MFD moving map. Be careful not to forget your cowl flaps as you climb back up toward CARRO. They're easy to forget, and you have only one small CHT indicator on the engine section of the MFD to warn you. FSX seemed to forget to give you a cowl flap position indicator on the G1000 Mooney.

Enter the hold at CARRO so you can have the pleasure of doing it with the G1000. Then use the ATC window to select a new IFR destination. This opens the flight planner window. Choose Tacoma Narrows (KTIW) for your destination, and then click Find Route. Click OK. Save this route with the default name for now. When asked whether you want to have your airplane put at the departure airport, click No. You'll go back to the airspace above CAN where you can ask for your clearance over to KTIW. You may need to ask for vectors to the ILS Rwy 17 approach.

ILS 17 AT KTIW

You get some quick vectors as the FSX ATC tries to decide what to do with you, but pretty soon you'll be on a down-wind for the ILS 17. Slow toward low cruise to buy some time, and then use PROC (on either the PFD or MFD) to select and activate the approach with vectors.

You'll need to load the ILS frequency into your active NAV. Now on the real G1000, you have a few options. First, you can load it into NAV1 or NAV2. Either can drive the HSI for you. We'll show how to use NAV1 for simplicity. Second, you can load the frequency two ways.

You can manually enter the frequency as described earlier in this book. Use the NAV frequency knobs on either the PFD or the MFD to dial 109.1 in the standby box (cyan box) and then switch the frequency to active. This is what you must do on FSX.

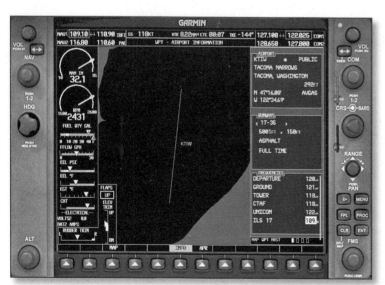

If you didn't have the approach plate, you could get the frequency by viewing the MFD with Shift+3 and use the outer FMS knob to go to the Waypoint WPT pages. On the airport page you should see KTIW. If not, push the lower center of the FMS knob on the MFD to get a cursor, and then click the inner knob to start entering KTIW. You can just type **KTIW** after this process is started. Click Enter.

Now you'll see the waypoint page for KTIW (see Figure 18-35). On the soft-keys at the bottom of the MFD screen, choose Info. Now press the lower center of the FMS knob to get a cursor, and scroll down. You'll see all the frequencies for KTIW. On the real G1000, pressing Enter for any of these frequencies, COM

Figure 18-35: All sorts of airport information can come from the Waypoint page, but you must load frequencies manually.

or NAV would load it into the selected standby. This is a great feature once you master it, and it's sadly not emulated on FSX. But at least you know it's there.

When ITIW is dialed in, you'll want to navigate with it using the CDI softkey on the PFD. Unlike with a GPS course, you need to set the OBS for VORs and the localizer (see Figure 18-36). Granted, you don't have to set the inbound course on the CDI for a localizer, but it's a lot less confusing if you do. The OBS is set with the CRS knob on the PFD. As you adjust the course, the exact number appears in a pop-up window so you know what you're dialing in down to the degree. You might or might not have noticed that the same thing happens when you dial in a new heading on the heading bug.

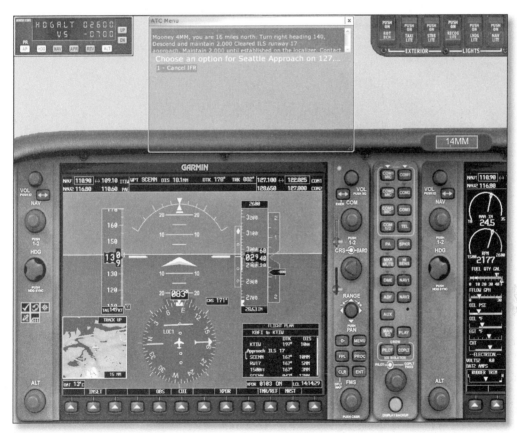

Figure 18-36: Be careful adjusting your course not to accidentally adjust your altimeter setting instead. The two knobs are on the same shaft. The inner one is the course. (Figure continued on next page.)

500

PART I PREFLIGHT · PART II SPORT PILOT · PART III PRIVATE PILOT · **PART IV INSTRUMENT RATING** · PART V COMMERCIAL LICENSE · PART VI ATP AND BEYOND

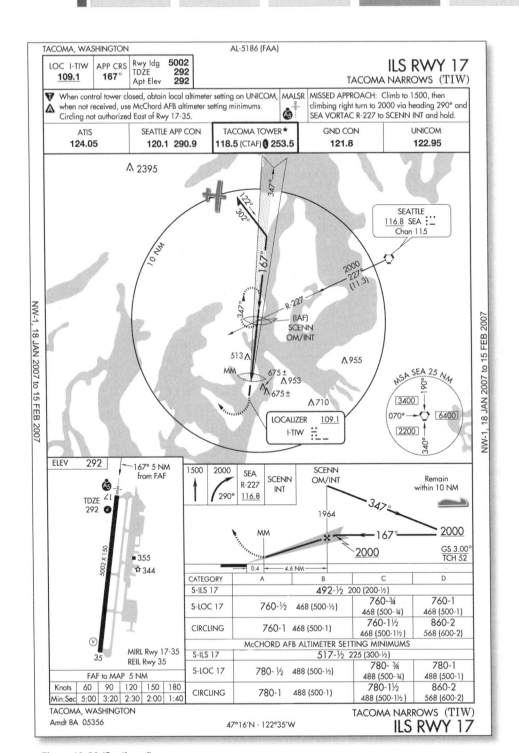

TACOMA, WASHINGTON
AL-5186 (FAA)

LOC I-TIW	APP CRS	Rwy Idg	5002
109.1	167°	TDZE	292
		Apt Elev	292

ILS RWY 17
TACOMA NARROWS (TIW)

When control tower closed, obtain local altimeter setting on UNICOM, when not received, use McChord AFB altimeter setting minimums. Circling not authorized East of Rwy 17-35.

MALSR

MISSED APPROACH: Climb to 1500, then climbing right turn to 2000 via heading 290° and SEA VORTAC R-227 to SCENN INT and hold.

| ATIS | SEATTLE APP CON | TACOMA TOWER ★ | GND CON | UNICOM |
| 124.05 | 120.1 290.9 | 118.5 (CTAF) ⓒ 253.5 | 121.8 | 122.95 |

TACOMA, WASHINGTON
Amdt 8A 05356

47°16'N - 122°35'W

TACOMA NARROWS (TIW)
ILS RWY 17

Figure 18-36 (Continued)

Intercept the localizer, slow to approach level, and watch for the glideslope to center. The glideslope indicator is a small green diamond on in a box to the left of the altitude (see Figure 18-37). When it centers on its scale, add approach flaps, reduce power, and head on down.

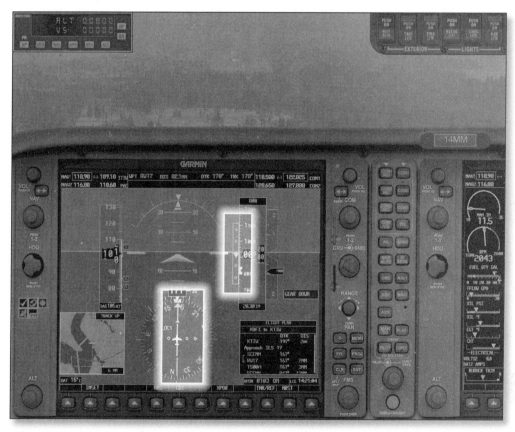

Figure 18-37: It can be confusing looking up by the altitude for the glideslope and down on the HSI for the localizer, but it comes easier with practice. (Figure continued on next page.)

502

PART I
PREFLIGHT

PART II
SPORT PILOT

PART III
PRIVATE PILOT

PART IV
INSTRUMENT RATING

PART V
COMMERCIAL LICENSE

PART VI
ATP AND BEYOND

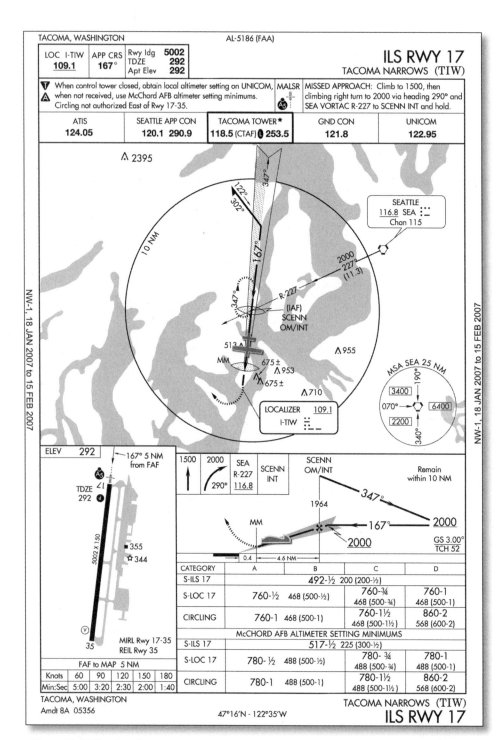

Figure 18-37 (Continued)

FLYING OFF THE MAP ON A GPS APPROACH

Accident Location: Ferguson, Kentucky

Aircraft: Cessna 421

Injuries: Three fatal, four serious

"The airplane joined the inbound course for the GPS instrument approach between the intermediate approach fix and the final approach fix and maintained an altitude about 200 feet below the sector minimum. The last radar return revealed the airplane to be about ¾ nautical miles beyond the final approach fix, approximately 1,000 feet left of course centerline. An initial tree strike was found about 1 nautical mile before the missed approach point, about 700 feet left of course centerline, at an elevation about 480 feet below the minimum descent altitude. Witnesses reported seeing the airplane flying at a 'very low altitude' just prior to its impact with hilly terrain and also described the sound of the airplane's engines as 'really loud' and 'a constant roar.' Night instrument meteorological conditions prevailed at the time of the accident. There was no evidence of mechanical malfunction."

The NTSB said the probable cause was "The pilot's failure to follow the instrument approach procedure, which resulted in an early descent into trees and terrain. Factors included the low ceiling and the night lighting conditions."

GPS is a great tool, and GPS approaches with a moving map have been a great boon to aviation utility and safety. But you've still got to fly the procedure as published—and resist the temptation to let all that extra information allow you to cheat even a little bit.

KEY POINTS FOR REAL FLYING AND FSX BUILT-INS

The following are some key points from this chapter:

- Read GPS/RNAV approach plates.

- Use the GNS 500 in FSX for approaches.

- Use the G1000 in FSX for approaches.

There are no specific lessons and missions to study after reading this chapter.

ADDITIONAL INSTRUMENT APPROACHES

"CLOUD-FLYING REQUIRES PRACTICE, EVEN IF YOU HAVE EVERY MODERN INSTRUMENT, AND UNLESS YOU KEEP CALM AND COLLECTED, YOU WILL GET INTO TROUBLE AFTER YOU HAVE BEEN INSIDE A REALLY THICK ONE FOR A FEW MINUTES. IN THE VERY EARLY DAYS OF AVIATION, 1912 TO BE CORRECT, I EMERGED FROM A CLOUD UPSIDE DOWN, MUCH TO MY DISCOMFORT, AS I DIDN'T KNOW HOW TO GET RIGHT WAY UP AGAIN. I FOUND OUT SOMEHOW, OR I WOULDN'T BE WRITING THIS."
—CHARLES RUMNEY SAMSON, 1931

506

PART I PILOT LIGHT
PART II SPORT PILOT
PART III PRIVATE PILOT
PART IV INSTRUMENT RATING
PART V COMMERCIAL LICENSE
PART VI ATP AND BEYOND

MORE WAYS TO GET AROUND AND DOWN

Now that you can fly the most common types of instrument approaches (ILS, VOR, and GPS), you probably could get into most of the airports in the world with instrument approaches. But a few more approach types exist—especially in places with less money to spend on aviation—such as non-directional beacon (NDB) approaches and localizer back-course approaches. In addition, one more type of instrument approach is actually flown more often in real life than all the other approaches combined: the visual approach.

NDB APPROACHES

As you learned in Chapter 10, NDBs are the grandparents of modern instrument navigation. But they're very cheap to build and maintain (they're really just an AM radio station without an annoying DJ). And the ADF receiver in your airplane that is used to navigate to NDBs is also much cheaper than an instrument-approved GPS unit, although they are getting harder to find. Thus, NDB approaches still exist and are likely to exist for a long time, especially in parts of the world where money to certify even GPS approaches is hard to come by. Knowing how to fly one, therefore, is a necessary skill for flight-sim pilots as well as real-world pilots.

Few airplanes built today even have an ADF receiver because they have GPS, but most IFR planes more than about 15 years old have one; the FSX Mooney Bravo has it, but you can see it only if you select the 3D panel. The Mooney with the Garmin G1000 system doesn't have an ADF at all.

NDB NAVIGATION BASICS

It can be confusing to navigate with NDBs, so one way to calculate the magnetic bearing (MB) to an NDB is with the following formula:

MH + RB = MB

THE VEGETARIAN APPROACH

To help pilots remember MH + RB = MB, someone came up with the following catch phrase: Mary Had Roast Beef; Mary Barfed. It's not the most pleasant imagery, but it's definitely memorable.

MH is your current magnetic heading. RB is the relative bearing to the NDB; you read this right off your ADF needle. If the NDB is at your 3:00 position (abeam to the right), the needle points to 90°, and, thus, the RB is 90°. If the NDB is off to your left but still in front of you, the needle (and the RB) might be something like 350°.

As an example, if you were flying a heading of 030° and the NDB was at a relative bearing of 100°, as shown in Figure 19-1, the magnetic bearing to the NDB would be 130. This is the heading you would fly if you wanted to go directly to the station (unless there is some wind, in which case you'd need to crab a little bit into the wind). The formula can be confusing when the numbers get big: what do you do with a magnetic heading of 300° and a relative bearing of 270°? Add them, and you get 570°, which isn't a heading you can fly. But 0° is the same as 360°, so if you subtract 360 from

Figure 19-1: To find the magnetic bearing to the NDB, add the magnetic heading to the relative bearing. In this case, 030° + 100° = 130°. If you wanted to fly to the NDB, you'd fly a heading of about 130°.

570, you get 210°, which is the magnetic bearing to the NDB.

For instrument flying, some procedures require you to fly a particular magnetic bearing to the NDB. For example, let's say the magnetic bearing to the station is 210°, but you need to move over to the course that has a bearing of 180° to the station, as shown in Figure 19-2. First *parallel the course* by turning to a heading of 180°. Now you can check the ADF needle to see you need to move to the right to get onto the 180 bearing to the station. Turn right 45° (to 225°) or so to intercept that course. When your ADF needle points exactly 45° to the left (RB of 315°) and your heading is still 225°, the NDB is a magnetic bearing of 180° from you, and you're on course. Turn left to follow the course to the NDB.

On the other hand, sometimes you need to fly away from an NDB. In that case, use the tail of the ADF needle for your information. If you're somewhere southwest of the NDB but you intended to fly outbound on the 270° bearing *from* the NDB (due west), as shown in Figure 19-3, you'd again parallel the course (turn to heading 270°) and see that the NDB is behind and to your right, at about a relative bearing of 130°. Since 270 + 130 = 400 and 400 – 360 = 40, the mag-

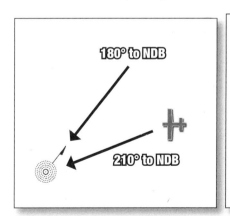

Figure 19-2: Intercepting the 180° bearing to an NDB. (The half-pointed arrow out from the NDB points to 0° magnetic.)

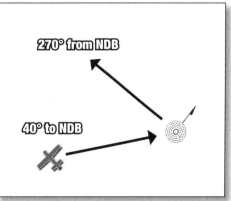

Figure 19-3: Intercepting the 270° bearing from an NDB

netic bearing *to* the station is 40°. But you just need to intercept the 270 bearing from the station, so you turn 45° to the right (heading 315°) and wait until the tail of the ADF needle points 45° left of straight ahead (315°), and then you're on course.

And we haven't even talked about correcting for wind, but we'll save that for later.

508

| PART I | PART II | PART III | PART IV | PART V | PART VI |
| PREFLIGHT | SPORT PILOT | PRIVATE PILOT | INSTRUMENT RATING | COMMERCIAL LICENSE | ATP AND BEYOND |

To the Beacon

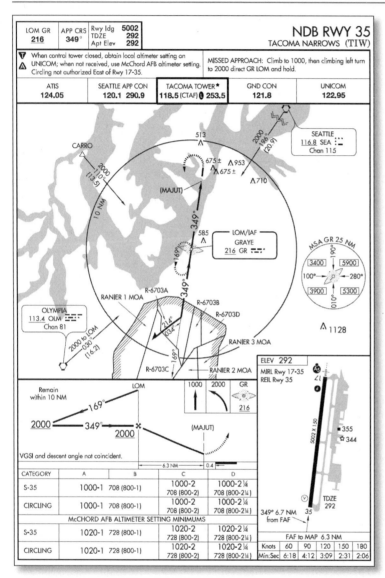

Figure 19-4: The NDB RWY 35 Approach at KTIW

The NDB approach you fly later in this chapter is the NDB RWY 35 at Tacoma Narrows Airport, Washington (KTIW), shown in Figure 19-4. Starting at the top of the chart, you can see right away that this approach cannot be conducted if you have a GPS instead of an ADF; if you could, it would be called the NDB or GPS RWY 35. (Actually, there is a separate GPS RWY 35 approach to KTIW, but ignore that for now.)

The approach starts at GRAYE NDB, which is the initial approach fix (IAF) and final approach fix (FAF) for this approach. GRAYE is a locator/outer marker (LOM), which means that, in addition to the outer marker beacon you learned about in Chapter 17, a compass locator is here. That's a fancy name for an NDB used for an instrument approach. Just like when you were learning to navigate with NDBs during private pilot training, tune the frequency on the ADF receiver, listen to the Morse code ID to make sure that you've got GRAYE, and confirm your ADF needle points right to the station. By the way, if you want to navigate with an NDB, you have to keep listening to the Morse code all the time, because there is no warning if it goes off the air or if the signal is too weak to use.

The approach procedure says that, after arriving at GRAYE (on one of the three transition routes from SEA, CARRO, and OLM), you proceed outbound on the 169° bearing *from* the NDB for 4 or 5 miles (just a couple of minutes) until the procedure turn. During that leg, you can descend to 2,000 feet. Coming back north after the procedure turn, you have to intercept the 349° bearing *to* the NDB and hold that course to the NDB. After passing the NDB, you now fly the 349° bearing *from* the station (which is straight ahead anyway) while you descend to the MDA of 1,000 feet (or 1,020 feet if you can't get any KTIW weather and have to use the weather at McChord AFB, about 8 miles away). The only way to know when you get to your missed approach point is to time yourself from GRAYE and, based on your ground speed, when time is up, go missed approach. That's a climbing left turn to 2,000 feet and then direct back to GRAYE. But on what bearing to the NDB? It doesn't matter—just turn until the NDB is straight ahead (RB 0°), and fly toward the station. Then try to stay on that course by adjusting for any wind blowing you off course, which we'll describe later in this chapter. (This is the great aspect of NDBs: you always know where the NDB is because the needle always points right to it.)

And just to make your life even more difficult, if you need to wait before ATC can give you more instructions, you have to enter the holding pattern at GRAYE. The procedure is the same as holding using a VOR, but it's really tough at an NDB. It's a good thing you can practice in the safety of FSX before you try it in a real airplane.

When you see the diagrams like we've given you, NDB procedures and approaches start to make sense. In fact, it makes sense to draw on your charts when you're approaching an NDB from an uncharted direction so you can prevent yourself from getting lost. But don't be surprised when you do get lost; NDB approaches take a lot of practice. After you get them, you can be very proud of your accomplishment because, without a GPS moving map, they are tough.

DME Arcs

As you have seen, distance-measuring equipment (DME) is sometimes used as part of other kinds of approaches, but it also can be used for a very creative way to get from the en route environment to the final approach course. Before GPS was available, if you were arriving at an airport and the final approach course you wanted went the opposite way from your arrival direction, you'd have to do a *course reversal* like a procedure turn to get turned around. A DME gives a different option.

Take a look at the VOR-DME or GPS RWY 35 at Olympia, Washington (KOLM), shown in Figure 19-5. Three initial approach fixes (IAF) are WINLO (at the bottom of the plan view), OZEYO (left of center), and MCKEN (on the right side). WINLO is right on the final approach course (Olympia VORTAC [OLM] R-176), and it's also on V165 from the south; that's an easy way to get from the en route environment to the approach.

But what if you're coming from the north? You'll probably be flying to the OLM VORTAC, but this approach does not have a procedure turn or any other course reversal to get from OLM out to the south and back on the final approach course.

Instead, you would proceed from OLM to the MCKEN intersection, which is an IAF. The transition to MCKEN isn't charted on this approach chart, but it is actually V204 on the en route chart: OLM R-095, 4000 MEA, for 15 nm. At MCKEN, you fly the procedure called a DME arc: you're going to follow a curving path to the southwest that arcs around OLM at 15 nm DME. Without GPS and a moving map, this can be a challenge, but there are tricks to doing it safely and successfully.

It's helpful to have the primary VOR (OLM, in this case) in both of your NAV radios. Set the DME radio to get its readout from NAV1. As you fly to MCKEN, you are on R-095 from OLM, so your OBS1 (the HSI) should be on 095 FROM. Set OBS2 on 346° (10° less than the inbound final-approach course at the end of the arc 356°)…you'll see why in a minute.

When you're about 30 seconds (1 nm) from MCKEN (in other words, 14 DME from OLM), do your five *Ts* and turn right onto the arc. During the arc, you do not have lateral guidance from your HSI needle; instead, you have to keep checking your DME readout to stay near 15 nm. If you turn slightly more than 90°—say, 100° and

510

PART I	PART II	PART III	PART IV	PART V	PART VI
FREE FLIGHT	SPORT PILOT	PRIVATE PILOT	INSTRUMENT RATING	COMMERCIAL LICENSE	ATP AND BEYOND

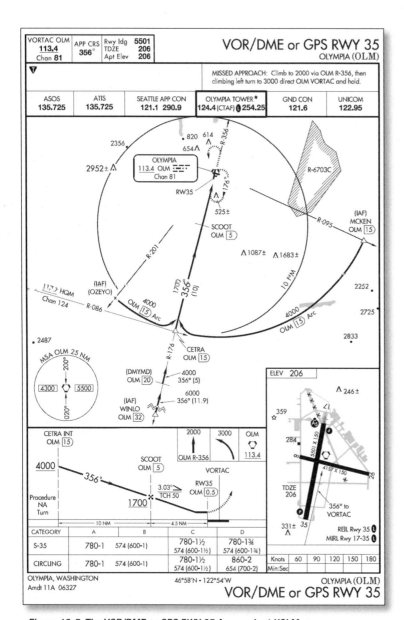

round up to the nearest 10° (to heading 200°)—then you start coming slightly toward OLM; therefore, your DME starts to drop. If it gets below 14.5 nm and keeps dropping, then you're turned too far to the right (perhaps a wind is blowing you from left to right). Correct 5° left to 195°, and wait. Eventually, the DME climbs; when it gets up past 15 nm, turn right another 20°. Work your way around the arc this way; fly a particular heading (use the heading bug to remind you), and then when the DME climbs above 15, reset the heading bug another 20° to the right and fly the new heading.

Figure 19-5: The VOR/DME or GPS RWY 35 Approach at KOLM

PLENTY OF ROOM ON THE ARC

When you're flying an approach and you're past the IAF, you need to stay close to your prescribed course, and the people who created the chart are counting on it. They've made sure that the minimum altitude on each segment gives you at least 500 feet of clearance above any obstacle within 3 miles of your course. It gets even smaller when you get to the final approach fix, although the width is different depending on what kind of navigation device you're using; as you can imagine, they expect you might be a bit further off when you're using an NDB.

Surprisingly, when you're flying a DME arc, you're safe up to 4 miles on either side of the arc. That means on a DME-15 arc you could get out to 19 nm and still be protected. Like everything, though, pilots don't like to push the limits when a mistake could be catastrophic, so if you stay legal at ±1 nm, you are really safe. In fact, you should be more concerned about staying on altitude, because an incorrect altimeter setting combined with a moment's inattention could easily put you 500 feet low.

Figure 19-6: When you're on the arc, DME is your primary course guidance as you stay 15±1 nm from OLM.

As long as you're within 1 nm of the arc, you're legal and safe. (In fact, you're safe if you go more than 1 nm off DME 15—see "Plenty of Room on the Arc"—but sloppiness won't help you.) If you forget and let it get as much as 0.5 nm off (15.5 DME), you may need to correct more than 20°; 30° to the right may be required (see Figure 19-6).

If there is any wind, your wind correction has to change slightly as you go around the arc. For instance, if the wind is from the east and was blowing you toward OLM VORTAC at the beginning of the arc, it is just a tailwind when you're getting close to CETRA intersection. But it really isn't hard, because you keep watching your DME and make little adjustments as needed along the way.

Meanwhile, set your HSI to 356°, the inbound final approach course. If for any reason you need to know when you're on a particular radial (like for an altitude step-down—this approach doesn't have any) or you need to check your position on the arc, just change the HSI as needed, and then return it to 356°. Your OBS2 was set for 346° because that will be your early warning device; when the CDI2 needle starts to move, you know it's time to start paying attention to your final approach course; and when CDI2 centers, you know you're 10° from your final approach course of 356°. From here on, it's a VOR intercept just like you've done in VOR approaches (see Figure 19-7). As you intercept the VOR inbound course at CETRA, do the five Ts, descend to 1,700 feet for the transition segment to SCOOT, and continue the approach.

512

PART I	PART II	PART III	PART IV	PART V	PART VI
PREFLIGHT	SPORT PILOT	PRIVATE PILOT	INSTRUMENT RATING	COMMERCIAL LICENSE	ATP AND BEYOND

DME arcs are used for more than just VOR approaches. You could arc to an ILS approach or a LOC approach as well. The trick for these is to use your NAV2 radio and OBS2 to tune in the localizer, track the localizer inbound when you come around the arc and intercept it, and then switch NAV1 to the ILS or LOC frequency and continue navigating on NAV1/OBS1.

Figure 19-7: Getting close to R-176, you start a turn to intercept the radial inbound. It's just a regular VOR approach from here on.

▽ BY THE BOOK

GPS EASY

Because the approach is titled "VOR-DME or GPS Rwy 35," you can fly it with an approach-certified GPS as your primary navigation device (or with the Garmin G1000 in GPS approach mode). In this case, following the arc is a no-brainer, because the HSI needle follows the GPS course, which is right on the 15-nm arc all the way around. Just turn in little increments as needed to stay on the course. It's good to know how to do it without a GPS in case your GPS (or the GPS system) fails, but when you've got it, use it.

LOCALIZER BACK-COURSE APPROACHES

An ILS costs a little more than a million dollars to install and more to maintain, so it's impossible to put them on every runway. But one unique and fortuitous fact is that the localizer signal doesn't go only one direction: it also points backward. You will discover this if you fly inbound on an ILS or LOC approach, fly right down the runway without landing, and continue on past the other end of the runway; your CDI needle will continue to show you the correct left/right deviations even after you pass the transmitting antenna near the departure end of the runway. Of course, the needle is ludicrously sensitive when you fly right over the antenna, but then the *cone* of the localizer signal starts spreading out again as you fly away from the airport. In fact, some ILS and LOC approaches have a missed approach procedure that sends you straight out from the airport, continuing on the back side of that localizer signal you used to get to the runway in the first place.

▼ INSIDE THE GAME
DUAL ILS

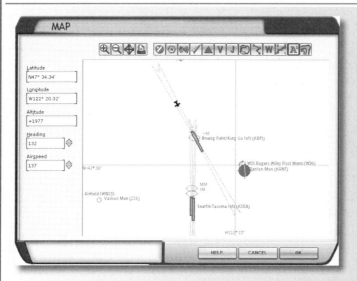

Some airports have ILS systems going both directions from one piece of runway pavement so that inbound aircraft can have a full ILS for either runway. And at some airports, those two ILS systems use the same frequency; but they are never turned on at the same time. (For instance, Boeing Field has ILS Rwy 13R and ILS Rwy 31L, both on 110.90 MHz.) This requires control tower personnel to switch one off and the other on when the winds change direction. The Morse code is different for each direction (I-BFI and I-CHJ) so you know which one is turned on when you identify the station.

That's not a problem in the real world. But in FSX, the controllers don't switch the ILS systems on and off; both ILS directions are on all the time. This causes some unusual behavior; for instance, if you fly the ILS Rwy 13R, the missed approach procedure is to follow the localizer's back course for a few miles past the runway. But that's the area covered by the ILS Rwy 31L localizer, and it's turned on all the time, too. So, your course needle shows reverse sensing in that area if you're flying away from the airport. (The Morse code is correct on each side, and you hear the code appropriate for whichever side you're on at the time.) Fortunately, that doesn't happen in FSX at an airport that has different frequencies for each ILS, and it doesn't happen in the real world at all.

Someone eventually had the bright idea to use the localizer's back side (called the *back course*) as its own instrument approach for times when the wind is coming from the wrong direction to use the front-course ILS or LOC; however, some hidden problems exist.

First, not all airports are able to handle approaches from the back course. Terrain would be the most likely culprit, or it could be another airport nearby.

514

PART I	PART II	PART III	PART IV	PART V	PART VI
PREFLIGHT	SPORT PILOT	PRIVATE PILOT	INSTRUMENT RATING	COMMERCIAL LICENSE	ATP AND BEYOND

Second, the ILS glideslope for the front course doesn't work on the back course. So, this is a nonprecision approach, just like a localizer-only approach, and you'll use some other method (such as intersections, DME, or marker beacons) to step down to the minimum descent altitude (MDA) and to determine (perhaps by timing) when you're at the missed approach point.

It's All Backward

If the terrain allows a back course and if an approach has been created, then you have to deal with the third problem with a back-course approach: the back course shows reverse sensing on your CDI. This is just like when you are navigating with VORs and you have the wrong setting on your OBS, such as if you were tracking toward a VOR but you didn't notice you had the wrong OBS number and a FROM arrow on your CDI needle. A back-course needle drifts to the left when you're actually moving to the left of the course. You try to correct by following the needle on the left, but you get only farther and farther off course. So, when flying a back course, you have to be the needle and move the airplane (needle) to the right.

This reverse-sensing issue is enough of a safety problem that back courses are slowly disappearing, especially with the advent of GPS approaches and (someday) GPS precision approaches. But for now, you need to be able to fly localizer back-course approaches, and at times you'll fly along a back course when you're shooting an ILS approach, which is discussed later in this chapter.

Fortunately, the Mooney has a piece of equipment that can make the reverse-sensing problem go away on a localizer back course: when you use an HSI instead of just a plain OBS/CDI (like your NAV2 setup), you can make it show the proper left-right needle.

Step by Step

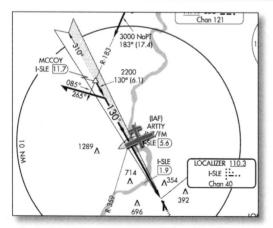

Figure 19-8: The LOC BC RWY 13 approach into Salem takes advantage of the ILS going the other way; without adding any equipment, the airport gets two approaches for the price of one.

Let's see how this works. Take a look at the Salem, Oregon (KSLE), LOC BC Rwy 13 approach chart in Figure 19-8. This is a classic back-course approach based on the ILS set up for Rwy 31.

If you were arriving from the north, near Portland, you'd be on the UBG R-183 heading toward MCCOY intersection. You'd know you were at MCCOY when you're at 17.4 DME from UBG, but MCCOY is also the intersection of the UBG R-183 and the localizer back course. You put UBG in NAV2 and use your OBS2/CDI2 to follow R-183, and then you set NAV1 on the localizer frequency of 110.3. Then set your HSI to the *front* course of 310°, even though you are flying a ground track of about 130° after you're on the localizer back course. That's the key to flying a back course with an HSI. If you don't have an HSI, then set the OBS1 to 130°, just to remind you of your inbound course; it has no effect on the needle, and you need to fly the course with reverse sensing.

As the chart shows, the segment from UBG to MCCOY is at 3,000 feet, and you don't have to do the procedure turn. As you approach MCCOY, the yellow HSI needle then starts on the right side and moves toward the center as you approach the localizer back course (and, therefore, MCCOY). Intercept the back course, and you can descend to 2,200 for the 6.1 nm leg to the FAF, ARTTY BCM (back course marker).

You know you're at the FAF when you're DME 5.6 on ISLE (see Figure 19-9). (In the real world, there is another way to identify the FAF: your marker beacon starts flashing, and a tone plays in your headphones. FSX shows the back-course marker beacon on the World > Map screen, but no light or tone indicates it in the cockpit.) After the FAF, you can go down to 800 feet. If you don't have DME, that's as low as you can go (see the minimums table at the bottom of the chart). If you do have DME, when you're at 1.9 nm, you can descend to the MDA of 600 feet.

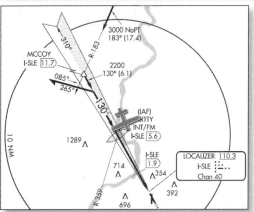

Figure 19-9: When you're at 5.6 DME, you're at the FAF. The aircraft is slightly left of the localizer back course; the HSI shows this correctly, but the CDI2 shows reverse sensing.

516

| PART I | PART II | PART III | **PART IV** | PART V | PART VI |
| PREFLIGHT | SPORT PILOT | PRIVATE PILOT | **INSTRUMENT RATING** | COMMERCIAL LICENSE | ATP AND BEYOND |

The missed approach point is DME 0.6 or, without DME, is a certain time (depending on ground speed) from the FAF. The missed approach procedure involves flying straight ahead, along the *front course* of the localizer to TURNO, which has a marker beacon and a locator (NDB) on 266 KHz (tuned on your ADF) and is DME 5.0 on I-SLE.

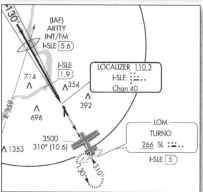

Figure 19-10: Arriving from the south, fly the front course of the localizer starting at TURNO just to get to ARTTY.

FRONT COURSE TO THE BACK COURSE

A couple of other tricks to this approach have to do with it being a back course. TURNO is an intersection on V23 between the Eugene (EUG) and Battleground (BTG) VORs and a transition route from TURNO to ARTTY (MEA 3,500 feet; 310°; 10.6 nm). The course guidance for this transition is the localizer front course, so set NAV1 on the localizer frequency, and set the HSI on 310°. After passing the IAF at ARTTY, wait one minute, execute the procedure turn (you can do it at 3,000 feet), and continue with the back-course approach as before.

If you arrive from Corvallis (CVO) VOR to the southwest, you proceed direct to ARTTY, turn left (outbound) on the back course (Figure 19-10), and continue on to the procedure turn.

▼ STUDENT OF THE CRAFT

NO FAF AT ARTTY?

Observant pilots spot the note at the top of the chart that says ARTTY intersection is not authorized for final approach fix. But ARTTY sure looks like the FAF—the profile view has the Maltese cross at ARTTY. Actually, ARTYY intersection is defined as the place the localizer back course intersects the R-359 from CVO. When arriving at the approach from CVO, you are at 4,000 feet, and you can find ARTTY as your IAF. After you turn around in the procedure turn, however, you are at 2,200 feet, which might be too low to receive the signal from CVO. The FAF, therefore, is really DME 5.6 on I-SLE and, in the real world, the point where the marker beacon alerts you.

BACK COURSE TO THE FRONT COURSE

There is one other time you have to fly with reverse sensing on your CDI needle (or make sure that your HSI shows correct sensing): on a full-procedure ILS approach. Because there are fewer and fewer actual localizer back course approaches anymore, the ILS full procedure is a back course you're more likely to run into.

Since you're already at Salem, look at the KSLE ILS Rwy 31 chart. If you're getting vectors to the ILS localizer or if you're coming from the southeast from JAIME intersection (a NoPT transition), it's an easy ILS. But from any other transition, you are doing

Figure 19-11: If you fly the full procedure to the ILS 31 at KSLE, you actually fly backward on the localizer, which is a form of the back-course navigation. (Figure continued on next page.)

518

PART I	PART II	PART III	PART IV	PART V	PART VI
PREFLIGHT	SPORT PILOT	PRIVATE PILOT	INSTRUMENT RATING	COMMERCIAL LICENSE	ATP AND BEYOND

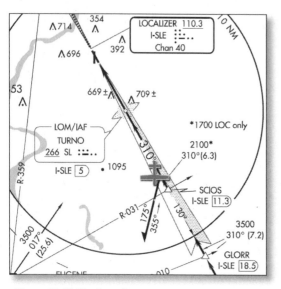

Figure 19-11 (Continued)

a full approach procedure with the procedure-turn course reversal. The transitions get you to TURNO LOM (locator outer marker) as your IAF, and then you have to fly outbound (southeast) on the localizer (see Figure 19-11). That leg is a back-course situation; with an HSI, you're fine as long as your OBS is set for 310°. If you don't have an HSI, navigating that route causes reverse sensing on your CDI.

VISUAL AND CONTACT APPROACHES

Even in rainy Seattle, it's a rare day when a pilot has to fly an instrument approach and doesn't see anything more than the inside of a cloud until the missed approach point. Ceilings of 1,000 to 2,000 feet above the ground are more common in winter, to say nothing of cold, CAVU days. Two types of instrument approaches are used for days when the weather isn't so bad: the visual approach and the contact approach. Note that these are not VFR procedures; you're still under IFR rules and protections when flying these approaches.

VISUAL APPROACH

On those days when the weather is actually VMC, you'll probably fly a visual approach. Add all the times an aircraft shoots each kind of instrument approach in a year, and you'll count more visual approaches than all the rest.

In fact, you already flew a visual approach: during your first IFR cross-country flight in Chapter 16, you flew a visual approach to Scappoose, Oregon, because the clouds were high enough to see the airport from a distance.

Most visual approaches are easy: if you can see the destination airport and can maintain visual contact with the airport the entire time (as in Figure 19-12), you can ask ATC for a visual approach. In fact, if the weather is good enough that ATC is pretty sure you'll be able to see the airport long before you get there, they will announce on the ATIS that visual approaches are in use, and they'll start giving you vectors for the visual approach. Officially, the weather report at the airport must show a ceiling of at least 1,000 feet and a visibility at least 3 miles for a visual approach to even be considered.

Figure 19-12: If you spot the airport and can make it there without entering a cloud, ask for a visual approach.

In one circumstance you can ask for a visual approach when you can't see the airport yet, and that's when you can see airplane in front of you that you're following to that airport. ATC will ask whether you can maintain visual separation from that aircraft, and if you can, they will clear you for the visual approach following that aircraft. (FSX ATC doesn't give this kind of visual approach, but they do vector for visual approaches, and like you discovered in the Scappoose trip, they'll keep vectoring you until you report the airport in sight.)

Some visual approaches are actually charted; in this case, ATC wants you to follow a particular route. Boeing Field has one such approach: the Harbor Visual Rwy 13R (see Figure 19-13). The procedures for this approach are quite specific on the chart, including altitudes, routes for noise abatement, and even weather. (The approach is not authorized unless the ceiling is at least 3,100 feet and the visibility at least 4 statute miles.) There is even information for using the localizer for 13R as a guide, although that's just to help you stay on course for the airport; you're not actually flying the localizer approach. The ATC in FSX doesn't offer or accept a charted visual approach, but you can definitely get them in multiplayer mode with a sim controller, as discussed in Chapter 27.

520

PART I PREFLIGHT   PART II SPORT PILOT   PART III PRIVATE PILOT   **PART IV INSTRUMENT RATING**   PART V COMMERCIAL LICENSE   PART VI ATP AND BEYOND

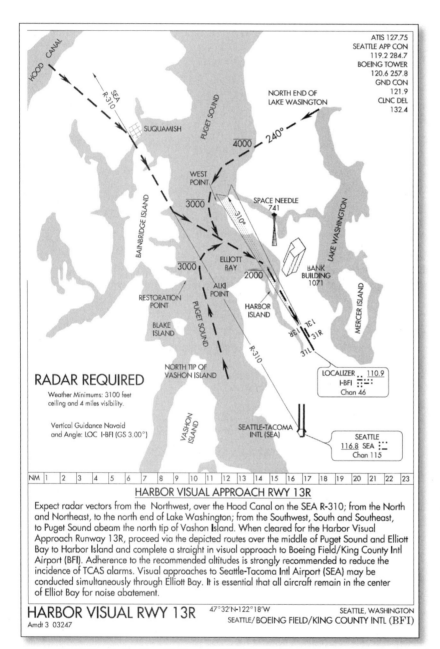

HARBOR VISUAL APPROACH RWY 13R

Expect radar vectors from the Northwest, over the Hood Canal on the SEA R-310; from the North and Northeast, to the north end of Lake Washington; from the Southwest, South and Southeast, to Puget Sound abeam the north tip of Vashon Island. When cleared for the Harbor Visual Approach Runway 13R, proceed via the depicted routes over the middle of Puget Sound and Elliott Bay to Harbor Island and complete a straight in visual approach to Boeing Field/King County Intl Airport (BFI). Adherence to the recommended altitudes is strongly recommended to reduce the incidence of TCAS alarms. Visual approaches to Seattle-Tacoma Intl Airport (SEA) may be conducted simultaneously through Elliott Bay. It is essential that all aircraft remain in the center of Elliot Bay for noise abatement.

HARBOR VISUAL RWY 13R   47°32'N-122°18'W   SEATTLE, WASHINGTON
Amdt 3 03247   SEATTLE/BOEING FIELD/KING COUNTY INTL (BFI)

Figure 19-13: The Harbor Visual to Runway 13R at Boeing Field can get you to the airport faster than a full instrument procedure, but it has rules of its own.

CONTACT APPROACH

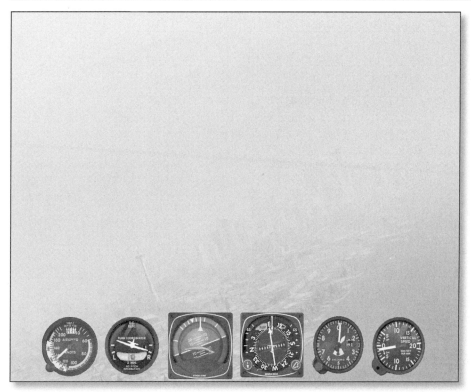

Figure 19-14: You have to find the airport yourself on a contact approach. But first you have to avoid buildings and other airplanes.

A contact approach is definitely rarer than a visual approach. In it, you fly visually, using landmarks you recognize, to get to the airport, even if you can't see the airport when you first get clearance for the contact approach.

The rule says that you must have at least 1 mile of visibility and be able to stay clear of clouds and that those weather conditions are expected all the way to the airport. There must be an instrument approach charted for that airport (although you won't be using it), and ATC has to keep you separated from all other aircraft (usually by not letting anyone else in or out of that airport). One interesting rule about contact approaches is that ATC cannot offer them to you; you have to ask for one.

The reason only the pilot can ask for a contact approach is because of what happens during the approach: you are responsible for your own obstruction clearance. With only 1 mile of visibility, you have little time to avoid anything popping out of the gloom (see Figure 19-14). Therefore, the only safe way to perform a contact approach (and we're being pretty liberal with the word *safe* here) happens when you're intimately familiar with the area and know all the hills, towers, power lines, and so on. The controller has no clue whether you know this area like the back of your hand or whether it's your first time, so they don't mention it.

You might wonder what all the bother is about a contact approach; why not just take the instrument approach into that airport? It's a shortcut; if the instrument approach requires you to fly 20 miles out of your way to approach from the other side of the airport and you're familiar with how to get to the airport from this side, you'll be on the ground in 5 minutes rather than 25.

(FSX controllers have never heard of contact approaches, but there is a trick: when you're arriving at an airport you know well, just ask the controller for a visual approach and say that you have the airport in sight. It might not be true, but the effect is the same as a contact approach.)

522

PART I
PREFLIGHT

PART II
SPORT PILOT

PART III
PRIVATE PILOT

PART IV
INSTRUMENT RATING

PART V
COMMERCIAL LICENSE

PART VI
ATP AND BEYOND

ACCIDENT CHAIN

CIRCLING IN THE FOG

Location: Los Angeles, California

Aircraft: Mooney M20K

Injuries: 2 fatal

"During an attempted missed approach in instrument meteorological conditions (IMC), the airplane descended into a residence. The pilot had successfully completed a flight review ten days before the accident flight. During the review, the pilot flew his airplane about two minutes under simulated instrument flight conditions. No other evidence of instrument flying was found during the preceding six months.

"The accident occurred while the pilot was returning home following a vacation. As the pilot approached the airport, a fog bank moved in, and the local weather conditions deteriorated. The VOR/GPS circling instrument approach procedure for the airport lists a minimum descent altitude of 680 feet MSL, with a 1-mile minimum visibility requirement. The overcast ceiling was 400 feet above ground level (597 feet MSL), and the visibility was 1 mile as the flight entered the terminal area. Near the time that the pilot received his instrument approach clearance, the visibility decreased to ½-mile, and the ceiling lowered to 200 feet AGL (397 feet MSL); however, that information was not disseminated to the pilot by either the tower or approach controller, contrary to Federal Aviation Administration (FAA) internal directives. The pilot's approach was monitored by both the radar approach controller and by the local tower controller on the tower's digital bright radar indicator (DBrite).

"Radar data showed that the airplane was consistently left of course, and the local tower controller advised the pilot of that fact and asked him if he was correcting back. About 0.4 miles from the runway's end, the pilot advised the controller that he was going around. The pilot failed to adhere to the published missed approach procedure. During the next one to two minutes, the radar data showed the airplane making 360° turns about 0.5 miles from the runway until descending with what ground witnesses described as increasingly steep angles of bank into a house. The airplane was certificated and equipped for flight into IMC. Examination of the wreckage found no evidence of any mechanical malfunction.

"The National Transportation Safety Board determines the probable cause(s) of this accident as follows: the pilot's loss of airplane control while maneuvering due to spatial disorientation. Contributing factors were the low ceiling, reduced visibility (fog), and the pilot's lack of instrument flying currency. An additional factor was the failure of air traffic control personnel to follow established Federal Aviation Administration directives to disseminate updated weather information."

This accident raises several safety issues. First is the pilot's inexperience: two minutes of instrument time in the last six months is not legal and is way beyond safe maintenance of skills and judgment. Second, weather can change quickly: even though the controller's were supposed to give the pilot an update, the best weather report comes from the pilot at the moment of decision. You see the runway, and you can land. Finally, once the pilot decided to "go around" (which probably meant a missed approach), he should have stuck with it and started climbing. He might have glimpsed the runway during his go-around and thought he could circle and land (those 360° turns), but the clouds were there and uncertain. Circling to land in low clouds is definitely a hazard.

CIRCLE TO LAND

When you're arriving at an airport on an instrument approach and you actually need to land on a runway other than one straight ahead of you (because of wind, runway length, convenient access to the bathroom—whatever), you will execute the circle-to-land procedure. Like the visual and contact approaches, this maneuver requires you to see things outside the aircraft; in this case, you have to be able to see the runway on which you want to land.

Consider the situation in the ILS Rwy 16R at Everett, Washington (KPAE), that you flew in Chapter 17. It's a precision approach, which is usually preferable to other approaches. But what if the wind is from the north? KPAE has a GPS Rwy 34L, but if you didn't have a GPS or if you were arriving from the north anyway, you can fly the ILS Rwy 16R; then, if you break out of the clouds in time, you can circle around the airport and land on Runway 34L so that you land into the wind (see Figure 19-15).

Figure 19-15: If you want to fly the ILS 16R at KPAE but land on 34L, circle at low altitude. (Figure continued on next page.)

524

PART I	PART II	PART III	PART IV	PART V	PART VI
PREFLIGHT	SPORT PILOT	PRIVATE PILOT	INSTRUMENT RATING	COMMERCIAL LICENSE	ATP AND BEYOND

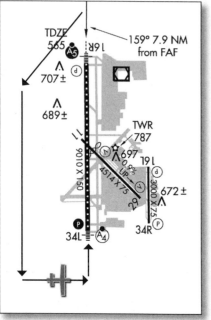

Figure 19-15 (Continued)

The first challenge is "if you break out of the clouds in time..." Take a look again at the chart. On the bottom—in the minimums list showing decision heights (DH), minimum descent altitudes (MDA), and visibility limits—is the row titled "CIRCLING." For approach category B, which is the Mooney, the MDA for circling is 1,100 feet, and the minimum visibility is 1 statute mile. So as you fly down the ILS glideslope, instead of continuing to the DH of 781 feet, you'd level off at 1,000 feet (like on a precision approach). But if you don't see the runway yet, you have to go missed approach. If you do see the runway, however, and you have at least one mile of visibility, you will circle around the runway (probably on the right side of the runway—a standard left-hand traffic pattern—unless ATC says otherwise), staying exactly at 1,100 feet until you're ready to make a final descent to the runway.

  KEEPING IT REAL

CIRCLE STRAIGHT IN?

Some approach charts don't publish straight-in MDAs and visibility minimums but instead have only circling minimums. You saw this in Chapter 17 with the Yakima VOR-A approach. The fact that the approach doesn't have a runway in the title is the clue that there will be only circling minimums. But as you saw there, you can still fly practically straight in to Runway 27.

There are complicated reasons why they don't publish straight-in minimums. All you need to know is that if you see the runway and you can make a proper descent to it, regardless of how much turning you have to do, go right ahead and land on that runway or any other.

Although we said it's like a left-hand traffic pattern, it isn't quite the same. Normal VFR traffic patterns are usually about 1,000 feet AGL, but 1,100 feet MSL is only about 500 feet AGL at Everett. This is a very low, potentially dangerous maneuver. You're probably right under the clouds, so you can't climb much, but you don't want to descend and hit any trees or buildings. You want to stay close enough to the runway to keep it in sight but far enough away to safely make those turns from downwind to base to final.

There are also limits on how far from the runway you're allowed to fly. Figure 19-16 is how the FAA shows it: for approach category B, you can fly no more than 1.5 miles from any part of the runway environment. This is because, if you go farther away, there might be obstacles that are higher than 1,100 MSL.

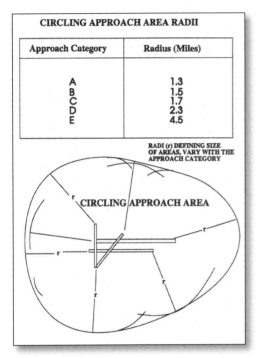

CIRCLING APPROACH AREA RADII

Approach Category	Radius (Miles)
A	1.3
B	1.5
C	1.7
D	2.3
E	4.5

RADII (r) DEFINING SIZE OF AREAS, VARY WITH THE APPROACH CATEGORY

r CIRCLING APPROACH AREA

Figure 19-16: The speed you're flying limits how far away from the airport you're protected from colliding with stuff on the ground.

So far this actually sounds fun. You don't often get to fly so low, and there is certainly an element of skill to pull off the tight turns needed to stay close. But you do need to keep the runway in sight at all time, stay the right distance, and get set up to land. If visibility is low, it is easy to get disoriented. You have to use your instruments for reference—to stay at the right altitude and remain level—but you need to keep the runway in sight too, even if it's on the other side of the plane (like when circling to the right).

You're no longer navigating by radios, you're navigating visually; what do you do if you enter a cloud after you start circling? The wrong move now could be deadly. The answer is to turn toward the airport, or where it was when you last saw it. Start climbing, and try to get over the airport (by guessing how long you should go that way). Then fly the charted missed approach, whichever direction that is.

Circling approaches *are* fun, actually, and they're really good to practice in FSX, because the weather can be set just right, with low visibilities, clouds scudding in and out, and winds pushing you toward or away from the airport. It seems like half the time you fly into Everett in the real world, it's either clear skies (in which case circling is too easy), or the clouds go down to 100 feet above the ground, in which case you can't circle at all.

 STUDENT OF THE CRAFT

CIRCLE WITH GPS

Circling approaches can be so dangerous that some commercial operators forbid them. The issue is losing sight of the airport while circling. GPS can help immensely here. Before you cross the MAP, press OBS to suspend waypoint sequencing. Then use the moving map and the cross-track error (XTE) to keep perspective on where the runway is.

In this example, you just flew the approach to Runway 01 but clearly have a tailwind (check out that ground speed at your 100-knot approach speed) and want to circle to Runway 19. Because you pressed OBS, the GPS won't start guiding you down the missed approach when you want it to just keep showing your latter distance to the runway. That distance is the XTE from the final approach course to Runway 01, which is just less than 1 mile right now. So, the runway is a mile off your left wing. The moving map will help keep you oriented as you fly downwind to base and let the runway get behind you.

In the real world, you can do the same thing and don't have to press OBS. The GPS automatically suspends waypoint sequencing when you cross the MAP.

Continued

526

PART I	PART II	PART III	PART IV	PART V	PART VI
PREFLIGHT	SPORT PILOT	PRIVATE PILOT	INSTRUMENT RATING	COMMERCIAL LICENSE	ATP AND BEYOND

MULTIPLE APPROACHES—CALM WIND

The first set of flights in this chapter are all conducted with no wind; they are plenty tough enough to fly that way, and we'll save the windy weather for the advanced flights later in this chapter. You won't fly every kind of approach either; there's no need to fly a calm-wind visual approach because that's really what you've been doing all along before you started instrument training. But the rest are worth training.

As before, we encourage you to use the autopilot to fly the approaches while you learn the procedures. We prefer HDG mode in addition to ALT hold, because of all the procedure turns and so on. When you're comfortable, though, try flying by hand. Also, start by not using the GPS map for reference, because it's too easy to cheat. See whether you can do it just with the other radios. After training is done and you're flying instrument approaches for real, of course, safety comes first, so use the GPS for your position awareness.

Most of these flights are just too easy if you use the Mooney with the Garmin G1000. After you're done flying them with the regular six-pack Mooney, you can try the approaches again with the G1000 to make sure you know how to properly program the system. But we won't coach you through the steps, because by now you're probably able to figure them out yourself.

An NDB at KTIW

Figure 19-17: There's not much to see out the window, but you're on SEA R-196, headed toward GRAYE NDB.

This flight, Chap_19_NDB_Calm, starts just southwest of SEA on R-196, heading toward GRAYE NDB and the NDB RWY 35 approach at KTIW (see Figure 19-17). You're using NAV1 and the HSI to navigate along at 2,000 feet. Although the real Seattle Approach wouldn't have told you to change frequencies so soon, the FSX controller has already told you to contact Tacoma tower when you're inbound from the NDB to the airport, so you won't have to deal with ATC for a while. Take a moment to listen to the weather on KTIW's ATIS frequency. (The full-size approach chart is on the website at www.wiley.com.)

Tune in GRAYE NDB, and check the Morse code. Remember that you need to listen to the Morse code the entire time you're using the NDB for an approach; just turn the volume down to a tolerable level.

3D ADF

You have to use the Mooney's 3D panel to see the ADF radio and needle; if that puts too much strain on your graphics system and your frame rate drops below about 15 fps, adjust the Display: Scenery setting. This approach is tough enough without slow visual response!

Start bringing the power back, because you want to be at low cruise by the time you start the approach at GRAYE. The ADF has no way of telling distance from the NDB, but your DME off SEA is 20.9 at GRAYE. Also, as you get close to the NDB, your ADF needle starts to move more quickly to one side or the other; don't chase it but just hold your heading until you're sure it's passing by (as shown in Figure 19-18), and then use your five *Ts* procedure:

528

PART I
PREFLIGHT

PART II
SPORT PILOT

PART III
PRIVATE PILOT

PART IV
INSTRUMENT RATING

PART V
COMMERCIAL LICENSE

PART VI
ATP AND BEYOND

- *Time*: Start your timer (for two minutes of outbound).

- *Turn*: Turn to heading about 169°, and then adjust as needed to maintain 169° bearing from the NDB.

- *Twist*: There's nothing to twist on an NDB approach.

- *Throttle*: Your speed should be at low cruise already, and altitude stays at 2,000 feet.

- *Talk*: This is not needed yet.

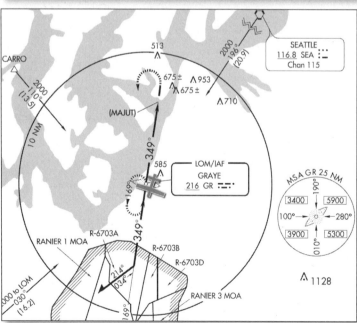

Figure 19-18: You're passing GRAYE, turning outbound.

Two minutes later, turn to heading 214 for one minute, and then continue through the procedure turn. Now comes the tricky part: when are you back on the course of 349° bearing to the NDB? If your heading is 034° on the last leg of the procedure turn, 349° is 45° to your left, which is a relative bearing of 315 (see Figure 19-19). (Remember MH + RB = MB? 034 + 315 = 349.) If you wait until the ADF needle is on 315, you'll blow past it; start turning to heading 349° when the relative bearing is about 320°, which is about 5 or 10 seconds earlier.

As you fly back north toward GRAYE, do your approach checklist and configure for approach-level speed. At GRAYE, do the five *T*s again:

- *Time*: Start your timer (to identify the missed approach point).

- *Turn*: There's no change.

- *Twist*: There's nothing to twist.

- *Throttle*: Drop power, and descend to the MDA of 1,000 feet MSL, maintaining your approach airspeed so your timing will be consistent.

- *Talk*: Tell Tacoma tower you're inbound on the NDB approach.

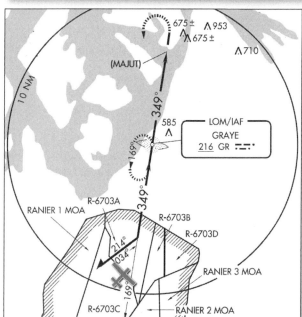

Figure 19-19: Now that you've done the procedure turn, intercept the 349° bearing to the NDB.

530

| PART I | PART II | PART III | **PART IV** | PART V | PART VI |
| PREFLIGHT | SPORT PILOT | PRIVATE PILOT | INSTRUMENT RATING | COMMERCIAL LICENSE | ATP AND BEYOND |

Figure 19-20: Look hard for the runway, but watch out for the bridge off to the right.

Figure 19-21: Your turn from downwind to base to final will be tight because you'll be low and close to the airport.

The Tacoma tower controller tells you to fly left traffic for Runway 17 when you arrive; yes, you get to do a circle to land, too. But, first, you have to spot the runway. It'll take about three and a half minutes to get from GRAYE to the airport, so after about two minutes, when you've leveled off at 1,000 feet and brought your power back up to hold approach-level speed, start looking for the runway lights (see Figure 19-20).

Here, you have another unreal aspect of FSX: in a real plane, you'd be moving your head all around trying to spot the runway; the way the FSX 3D panel is designed, it blocks your view of the runway after you get close enough to see through the fog. You need to press the Shift+Enter keys on your keyboard, which represents you sitting up higher in your seat or even raising the seat. Also, look everywhere in front of you for the runway; NDB navigation isn't perfect, and the airport might not be straight ahead.

After you spot the airport, follow the controller's instructions and circle on the right (east) side of the airport (see Figure 19-21). Be careful; you're only 600 feet AGL, and the Tacoma Narrows Bridge is over here somewhere, too, with towers that rise to 700 feet MSL. (The real-world Tacoma tower controller would have you fly a right-hand traffic pattern on the west side, because circling is prohibited on the east side, as shown on the approach chart.)

A DME Arc at KOLM

Figure 19-22: The flight Chap_19_Arc_Calm starts with the plane approaching OLM.

Next, you fly the DME arc that is part of the VOR-DME or GPS RWY 35 approach at KOLM. Load the flight called Chap_19_Arc_Calm, which puts you on V165 heading toward OLM from the north (see Figure 19-22). Before you get to OLM, check the ATIS weather at KOLM, and get your radios set up for this approach. (You want OLM VORTAC in both NAV radios, and it is helpful to put 095° in OBS2, because that is your course outbound from OLM. (Figure 19-5 earlier in this chapter is a small version of the approach chart; the full-size approach chart is on the website at www.wiley.com.)

When you arrive at MCKEN, do the five *Ts* to start the approach:

- *Time*: (This is not needed).

- *Turn*: Turn right to a heading of about 100° from the radial you're on, rounding up to the nearest 10°. In this case, R-095 plus 100° is 195°, rounded up to 200°.

- *Twist*: Change the OBS1 (HSI) to the next OLM radial you need to know about. The only one is the R-176 you fly inbound for the final approach, but you'll be flying TO the VORTAC, so set the HSI to 356°.

- *Throttle*: Slow to low cruise now that you're past the initial approach fix. If you're above 4,000 (the MEA for the arc section of the approach) and you're cleared for the approach, you can descend.

- *Talk*: (This is not needed unless ATC told you to report MCKEN.)

532

PART I
PREFLIGHT

PART II
SPORT PILOT

PART III
PRIVATE PILOT

PART IV
INSTRUMENT RATING

PART V
COMMERCIAL LICENSE

PART VI
ATP AND BEYOND

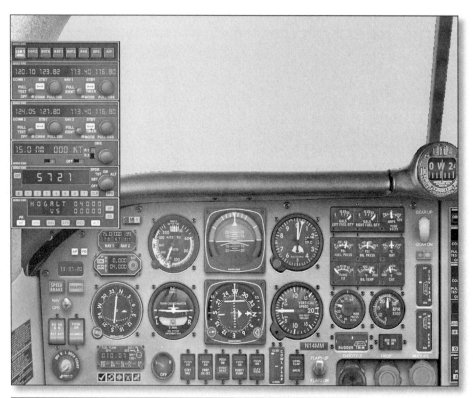

Proceed around the arc as discussed previously, making 10° to 20° changes every few minutes as needed to maintain DME 15±1 nm (±0.5 nm ideally). If you need to check your progress around the arc, use the HSI and center the needle: you're on that radial. When you get close to the final approach course of 356° to OLM (Figure 19-23), configure for approach level, and intercept the course. Descend as published to 1,700 feet, and perform your final approach checklist. Do the five *T*s again at SCOOT, the FAF, and drop down to the MDA of 780 feet MSL. The missed approach point is the VOR, so you don't need to time the approach.

Figure 19-23: You're on the DME arc, about 10° from the inbound course.

A BACK COURSE AT *KSLE*

Head down to Oregon for a back-course approach. Load Chap_19_BC_Calm, which starts between the Corvallis VOR-DME and ART-TY as you get ready to fly the LOC BC RWY 13 approach into KSLE (see Figure 19-24). As always, start at the top of the chart (available on the website) to read and set the frequencies, check the notes, and talk yourself through the missed approach. If Salem was your original destination, then you would have looked over the chart before you took off to make sure that you had the necessary equipment on board, and so on, but now you need to formally brief the approach.

Figure 19-24: When Chap_19_BC_Calm starts, you're approaching ARTTY intersection from the south.

Listen to KSLE's ATIS weather information. You're already cleared for the approach, so you need to make sure you can tell when you get to ARTTY. Your NAV1 and HSI is on CVO, but now would be a good time to put CVO in NAV2 and navigate on R-359 with your OBS2/CDI2 so that you can get NAV1 set up for the localizer. Remember the key to avoiding reverse sensing with an HSI is to put the OBS on the front course direction, which is 310°. When the HSI starts to center, you're approaching the localizer; it happens quickly (remember, localizers are a lot more sensitive than VORs), so start turning to 310° now (see Figure 19-25).

534

PART I
PREFLIGHT

PART II
SPORT PILOT

PART III
PRIVATE PILOT

PART IV
INSTRUMENT RATING

PART V
COMMERCIAL LICENSE

PART VI
ATP AND BEYOND

Then do the five *T*s:

- *Time*: Start the timer for the two-minute outbound toward the procedure turn.

- *Turn*: You're already turning to 310°.

- *Twist*: There's no need to change anything.

- *Throttle*: You can descend from 4,000 to the procedure turn altitude of 3,000.

- *Talk*: Not yet— call them when you're procedure turn inbound.

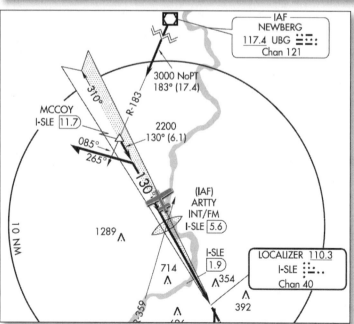

Figure 19-25: Flying outbound toward the procedure turn, navigating on the localizer back course and descending to 3000.

After the procedure turn, you'll be on a heading of about 130°. After that, it's really a basic approach, because the HSI gives you normal left-right guidance. You have a couple of altitude changes to make at various DME distances, and you want to start your timer at ARTTY inbound in case the DME flakes out on you. If you see the runway (Figure 19-26), land and pull off to the right; there's a great restaurant overlooking the runways, and the food is actually pretty good!

Figure 19-26: There's nothing quite like spotting the runway after a tough approach.

A CONTACT APPROACH AT **KBFI**

Although a contact approach is an IFR procedure, the ATC in FSX doesn't know about it. So do the procedure outside of ATC's control, which you wouldn't do in the real world. As you start the flight, Chap_19_Contact, you're just entering Elliot Bay, with the neighborhood of Magnolia on your left, flying at 1,000 feet MSL. (See Figure 19-27 and the website for a bit of a terminal area chart showing Elliot Bay.) Just fly it VFR, because FSX ATC won't let you ask for a contact approach.

Figure 19-27: The terminal area chart for the area north of Boeing Field; the flight starts where the airplane figure sits. A contact approach is an IFR procedure, but you need this VFR chart to make it safely.

536

PART I	PART II	PART III	PART IV	PART V	PART VI
PREFLIGHT	SPORT PILOT	PRIVATE PILOT	INSTRUMENT RATING	COMMERCIAL LICENSE	ATP AND BEYOND

A contact approach requires good familiarity with your destination airport, and although you've flown into quite a few, we've tried to get you back to Boeing Field once in a while. Let's hope the area is familiar, especially the area north of the airport. You're returning from somewhere northwest, perhaps up in the San Juan Islands. The winds today are from the northwest (yeah, this flight has winds), favoring Runways 31L and 31R. But if you're flying IFR, ATC takes you 10 miles southeast of the airport to put you on the ILS Rwy 31L. That'll take at least 30 minutes, and you can see more than 1 mile (but not much more). This is the perfect time for a contact approach.

The faster you go, the harder it is to see anything. At 120 knots, buildings that appear in the haze 1 mile away will be a collision in 30 seconds. If you turn away at the standard rate, 30 seconds puts you only at right angles to the building, not going away from it. And that's assuming you actually spot the building—or tower, or bridge, or airplane—when it's a mile away. This is a good situation to go slower—maybe 100 or even 90 knots with flaps at approach setting. Don't go too slowly, though—you don't want to lose control in the haze.

You also need to see as much as you can outside, so press the W on your keyboard to switch to the minimal instrument view.

If you keep the shoreline just off to your left, you avoid the Space Needle and all the big buildings in downtown Seattle. Don't even bother calling Boeing tower to get cleared to land; they'll just tell you the airport is IFR (because the visibility is less than 3 miles).

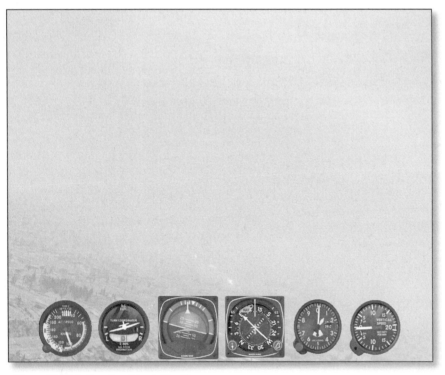

Figure 19-28: Is the airport in sight yet?

After you pass the sports stadiums south of downtown, you need to work your way southeast until you see the runway lights (see Figure 19-28). A heading of about 140 should work if you can't figure out where the hills are. You might even spot the cars on Interstate 5 and follow them. (I-5 goes just along the east side of the airport.) Don't descend below 1,000 feet until you're sure you have the runway lights (or the PAPI/VASI) in sight. And don't forget that the wind is actually from the north, so you probably want to do a tight traffic pattern and land the other way. Traffic pattern altitude on the east side is 1,000 feet MSL, and on the west side it is 800 feet MSL.

Multiple Approaches—with Wind

You're getting so good at this that we can be brief in our explanations of most of the advanced flights in this chapter. You'll fly most of the same approaches, but this time with wind. We won't tell you where the wind is coming from or how strong it is; don't cheat by having the FSX data readout show you. Listen to the ATIS at the airports to get an idea, although the winds are different (usually stronger and more westerly) in the air.

Use the Garmin G1000 Mooney for any of these approaches if you want to, and if you don't, feel free to use the GPS in the regular Mooney. We sure would!

The last flight is a real challenge: it's a DME arc that leads into a localizer back-course approach while you deal with intermediate altitudes stepping down six times as you avoid the Cascade Mountains near Yakima, Washington.

NDB Approach with Wind

Figure 19-29: The heading is 175°, and the needle shows the NDB is 6° to the right of straight behind; therefore, the plane is on the 169° bearing from the station.

To fly the NDB approach at KTIW with wind, load the flight Chap_19_NDB_Wind. The most difficult part of flying an NDB approach with wind is keeping track of your crab while staying on course.

Let's say you've figured out that the wind is from the west. When you're outbound on the 169° bearing from the station, you know you need to correct into the wind, so you fly a heading of 175° (see Figure 19-29). But that means your tail is no longer pointed right back at the NDB; in fact, the NDB should be 6° to the right of straight behind you. In other words, the NDB has a relative bearing of 174° on your ADF needle. If you hold a heading of 175° and the RB starts to move lower (like toward 170°), then you must be drifting farther left (east) than you want.

So you have to correct more—try another 5° right, to heading 180°. But when you do that, the RB moves another 5° to 165°. Hold steady and wait. If the ADF needle starts moving back toward 170°, you're correcting properly. You'll know you're on course when the RB correction (11° to the right of exactly behind you) matches your heading correction (11° to the right of 169°).

538

PART I	PART II	PART III	PART IV	PART V	PART VI
PREFLIGHT	SPORT PILOT	PRIVATE PILOT	INSTRUMENT RATING	COMMERCIAL LICENSE	ATP AND BEYOND

Figure 19-30: During an approach with a crosswind, the airport does not appear dead ahead. You'll have to look side to side, too.

Tricky, eh? It's also tricky when you're on the procedure turn; the wind from the west will probably cut down on the distance you go toward the southwest and then speed you back across the inbound 349° bearing to the NDB. It would be a good idea to have that first procedure turn leg last for two minutes rather than the usual 90 seconds.

When you're on your final approach segment heading and looking for KTIW, remember to look slightly right of straight ahead, because you'll be correcting (crabbing) to the left for wind (see Figure 19-30). Many pilots make a certain mistake during instrument approaches with wind: they've got a great wind correction going when navigating on instruments, but when they spot the runway, they turn the airplane straight toward the runway. They forget that they need to maintain the crab until the wind decreases or they switch to a slipped landing. It's something about that transition from instruments to visual flight that throws them off.

DME Arc with Wind

The flight Chap_19_Arc_Wind starts in the same place as the calm wind flight, approaching OLM on V165 (see Figure 19-31). Remember that your wind correction changes because the wind comes from a different relative direction as you work your way around the arc.

Figure 19-31: Flying a DME arc is so much easier with GPS. Here the HSI is getting information from the GPS, so it's easy to stay on course. Note that the heading (225°) is quite different from the TRK (208°) because of wind.

LOC BC Approach *with* Wind

The LOC BC approach in wind (Chap_19_BC_Wind) is not as tough as the NDB approach and DME arcs were (see Figure 19-32). You're used to correcting for wind with a localizer because of your LOC and ILS approaches in Chapter 17. If you want a real challenge for this approach, fly it with the Cessna 172; it doesn't have an HSI, so the CDI1 needle shows reverse sensing as you fly inbound on the localizer.

Figure 19-32: A localizer back course is tough when you've got wind and you don't have an HSI. Sounds like a challenge, eh?

Combo with a Side *of* Wind

Yakima, Washington, has the KYKM LOC DME BC-B approach, which is a complicated approach combining a DME arc with a localizer back course and six different altitudes to descend to and level off (see Figure 19-33). As you can see on the chart, the approach exists because there is an ILS available on Runway 27 at KYKM. But this localizer back-course approach takes you in from the west, and if you are able to land straight in, it will be on Runway 9.

The flight is Chap_19_DME_BC_Wind, and it starts on V298, northwest of YKM VORTAC about 30 miles from YKM and coming in fast. You've got about five minutes to do the following:

1. Slow down to low cruise.

2. Get the ATIS weather from KYKM.

3. Call Seattle Center to open your IFR clearance (the flight plan from KBFI is on file already).

4. Ignore Seattle Center's vectors to the ILS 27; change your IFR approach request to the localizer back-course B starting at YKM 310 radial, 16 DME.

540

PART I	PART II	PART III	PART IV	PART V	PART VI
PREFLIGHT	SPORT PILOT	PRIVATE PILOT	INSTRUMENT RATING	COMMERCIAL LICENSE	ATP AND BEYOND

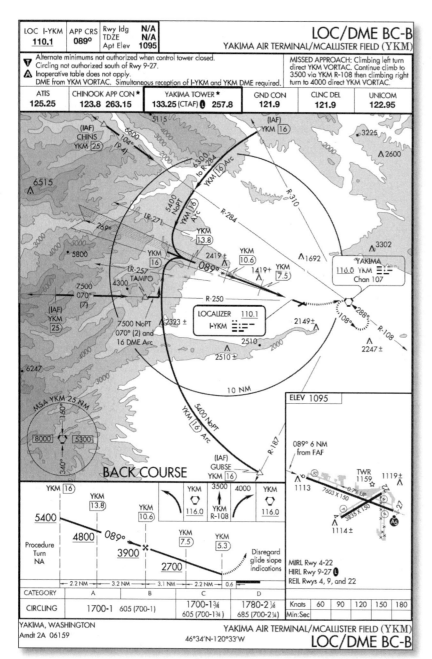

Figure 19-33: The LOC DME BC-B at Yakima is one of the most challenging approaches in the area.

5. Get your radios ready.

6. Brief the approach.

One thing that helps is the following: leave NAV1 on YKM, but have the localizer frequency in the standby for NAV1. Set NAV2 on the YKM frequency in the standby, with 271° in OBS2 (you'll see why in a minute). Set the DME radio to get data from NAV2 (R2).

The IAF is at DME 16 on the YKM R-310. When you get to DME 17 nm from YKM, turn right and get on the 16 DME arc (heading 220° will work). That segment has an MEA of 6300, and you've been cleared for the approach so you can descend to 6300. Follow the previous procedure for flying a DME arc, staying 16 nm ± 1 nm from YKM. Set your HSI to 284°, which is the next step-down altitude; when you get there, you can descend to 5,400 feet.

Now change NAV1 to the localizer frequency that was in standby and ID the station, and then set the HSI for the front-course of 269°. YKM R-271 is marked on the chart, not because you can change altitude there but because it's a lead radial (LR)—that's why you set it in NAV2/OBS2—to tell you to start turning to a heading to intercept the localizer back course.

After you're on the localizer, you can step down to 4,800 feet MSL. The next step down is at DME 13.8. But is that 13.8 nm from the localizer? Nope. See how it says "YKM" above the 13.8 DME notation? That's the YKM VORTAC, not IYKM for the localizer; the localizer doesn't have DME. That's why you have the DME on NAV2. You have to ignore that OBS2 needle entirely during the localizer approach, well, right up until you fly the missed approach, in which case you fly directly to the YKM VORTAC. You know, this approach is sounding more and more complicated all the time. But wait, there's more.

The second-to-last altitude on the approach is 2,700 feet, and then at DME 7.5 you can drop to the MDA of 1,700. But you have to get down to 1,700 within 2 miles because DME 5.3 is the missed approach point. And that MAP is only ½ mile from the end of the runway, but you're still 600 feet above the runway. (A normal approach would have you at 200 feet at that point.) That's why this is the LOC DME BC-B approach and not the LOC DME BC RWY 9 approach; they know you might have to do serious maneuvering to manage to land on Runway 9. You can do it, but it takes good flying skills.

Now imagine doing this approach in a twin-engine airplane with one engine out (see "This Is a Test"). All the approaches we've done in IFR have been with everything functioning, but the next chapter will challenge you with emergencies and system failures.

KEEPING IT REAL

THIS IS A TEST

If you can successfully fly the KYKM LOC/DME BC-B in IMC, you're as good as a professional pilot. Several cargo airlines in the northwest United States use this approach to test pilots who want to fly for them. In a "real" flight simulator, the pilot launches out of Yakima. (The departure procedures are tricky, too.)

But of course this is an interview test, so nothing goes as planned. During the departure, one of the two engines quits (yes, they do it in a twin-engine simulator), and they have to return to Yakima on the DME arc to the localizer back course. Single engine. IMC. With icing. Probably without an HSI. Probably tired and cranky after long, grueling interviews, with a job on the line. Just about how you'd feel at the end of a real late-night cargo run over the mountains in bad weather, where it's just you, the airplane, and your adrenaline to get you safely on the ground.

KEY POINTS FOR REAL FLYING AND FSX BUILT-INS

The following are some key points from this chapter:

- Learn and practice procedures for executing NDB approaches, DME arcs, localizer back-course approaches, visual and contact approaches, and circling maneuvers.

- Compensate for wind when on an NDB approach and a DME arc.

- Understand the challenges of flying when monitoring the instruments and looking for the airport in low-visibility conditions.

542

| PART I | PART II | PART III | PART IV | PART V | PART VI |
| PREFLIGHT | SPORT PILOT | PRIVATE PILOT | INSTRUMENT RATING | COMMERCIAL LICENSE | ATP AND BEYOND |

Here are the lessons and missions to study after reading this chapter:

- *Lessons*: None of the built-in lessons apply to this chapter.

- *Missions*: The Dutch Harbor Approach is an NDB approach in a King Air; it'll be faster than the Mooney, so it's a fun challenge.

IFR EMERGENCIES

"IN THOSE DAYS THE MOTOR WAS NOT WHAT IT IS TODAY. IT WOULD DROP OUT, FOR EXAMPLE, WITHOUT WARNING AND WITH A GREAT RATTLE LIKE THE CRASH OF CROCKERY. AND ONE WOULD SIMPLY THROW IN ONE'S HAND: THERE WAS NO HOPE OF REFUGE ON THE ROCKY CRUST OF SPAIN. 'HERE,' WE USED TO SAY, 'WHEN YOUR MOTOR GOES, YOUR SHIP GOES, TOO.' THE NIGHT CAME WHEN IT WAS MY TURN TO BE CALLED TO THE FIELD MANAGER'S ROOM. HE SAID, 'NAVIGATING BY THE COMPASS IN A SEA OF CLOUDS OVER SPAIN IS ALL VERY WELL, IT IS VERY DASHING, BUT,'—AND I WAS STRUCK BY THE GRAPHIC IMAGE—'BUT YOU WANT TO REMEMBER THAT BELOW THE SEA OF CLOUDS LIES ETERNITY.'"

—ANTOINE DE SAINT-EXUPERY

IFR EMERGENCIES IN THEORY

When you have an emergency when flying under IFR but you're in visual meteorological conditions (VMC), then the solutions are no different from when you were flying under VFR. The challenges come when you're in the clouds and something goes wrong.

This chapter addresses three general types of IFR emergencies: those that happen when one or more of your primary control instruments fail, other emergencies in the clouds, and what to do if you lose radio contact with ATC.

One tip is worth mentioning right up front: for nearly all the emergencies in this chapter, you want to tell ATC about it right away. The controller assumes you can do everything all the other IFR aircraft can do, and there might be limitations on your capabilities because of the emergency. (Obviously, you can't tell the controllers when you have a communication failure, but they'll figure it out soon enough. And there is no way to tell the FSX controllers when you have any of these emergencies anyway, but perhaps in the next version of Flight Simulator...)

PARTIAL-PANEL FLYING

If one or more of your primary control instruments (the *six-pack*) fails, then you are said to have a *partial-panel* situation. Depending which instrument(s) failed, you might have a much harder time keeping control of the aircraft. First you have to notice an instrument failed, and then you have to figure out how to fly without it.

DETECTING A PARTIAL-PANEL SITUATION

You might think it would be obvious when a flight instrument fails, but sometimes it isn't. Let's use the example of the attitude indicator and HSI in the FSX Mooney Bravo. If your vacuum system fails, you might notice the HI/LO VAC warning light come on. But if you miss it, there is no indication on the AI and HSI that the gyroscopes inside them are winding down. The AI slowly starts to show a nonexistent climbing left turn, and the HSI just stops moving and shows one heading all the time. (This is so insidious that some AIs and HSIs are built with warning flags that come down in front of the instrument when the gyroscope fails. The FSX Mooney does not have this feature.) So, if there isn't an obvious signal something is wrong, how can you tell?

The way to detect a partial-panel situation is by cross-checking one instrument with others (see Figure 20-1). For instance, you know you're in a climb when the AI points up, the altimeter is rising, the VSI is indicating a climb, and the airspeed is going down (unless you added power for the climb). So if your AI says you're climbing but the altimeter, VSI, and airspeed indicator say nothing has changed, you would know something is wrong. But what is wrong?

To be able to debug the error, you need to know what happens when each instrument fails. You also need to know what can cause a failure so you know whether there is any collateral damage in other instruments.

As mentioned, the AI fails by showing a climbing turn and then just sitting there. You'd know it was wrong if you cross-checked with the pitot-static instruments (airspeed, altimeter, and VSI). But perhaps the pitot-static system was what failed and those three are not correct—what then? The compass and turn coordinator would show a turn when you were really turning, so if they don't show a turn but the AI does, suspect the AI. Once you determine that the AI has failed, you want to know whether it is just the AI or whether anything else has failed. The AI and HSI on the FSX Mooney are both powered by the vacuum pump, so check your annunciator panel for a vacuum failure and cross-check the HSI.

Figure 20-1: If the instruments don't make sense with each other, suspect one or more has failed. For instance, why is the AI showing a left turn but the turn coordinator is showing a right turn?

Figure 20-2: Here, the HSI isn't moving even though you're in a turn (check the compass).

The HSI fails by just stopping on the current heading and not changing anymore (see Figure 20-2). If you cross-check with the turn coordinator and the compass and they both say you're turning, the problem is either the HSI or *both* the turn coordinator and compass. The odds of both of those two failing are lower than the HSI failing alone, and you can easily test it by turning the aircraft the other direction. If the HSI still doesn't move, you've isolated the problem.

The turn coordinator has an electric gyroscope, so it won't fail if the vacuum system fails. But if you lose electrical power, then that gyro slows down and stops, and the turn coordinator just sticks on a turn, one way or the other. At that point, you'll probably be a lot more concerned about the loss of radios, and so on, because of no electrical power; but the turn coordinator could fail by itself. Cross-check instruments? That'd be the AI, the HSI, and the compass. (The ball in the bottom of the turn coordinator uses no power at all, so it almost never fails, unless you get frustrated with your broken turn coordinator and smash the glass trying to get it to work.)

The pitot-static instruments are simple, reliable machines, and they don't often break. But the pitot tube could be clogged with ice, bugs, or dirt, and the static port could also be plugged with ice or water. So let's step through the failures here:

546

PART I PREFLIGHT PART II SPORT PILOT PART III PRIVATE PILOT **PART IV INSTRUMENT RATING** PART V COMMERCIAL LICENSE PART VI ATP AND BEYOND

1. If the pitot tube gets blocked, your airspeed indicator reads 0 knots. (A blocked pitot tube has no effect on the altimeter and VSI.) Usually this happens slowly—the blockage taking several minutes to occur as the airspeed goes down. Cross-check with your other instruments: Are you climbing? Power decreasing? Flaps or landing gear suddenly got extended? If none of these has caused you to actually slow down, then it's probably your pitot tube.

2. If the static port gets blocked (again, it probably happens slowly), then all three pitot-static instruments are affected. Your altimeter will stop moving even when you're pretty sure you're climbing or descending. Your VSI will sit on 0 fpm (see Figure 20-3). And your airspeed indicator will be inaccurate. (This one is subtle: as you descend at a constant airspeed, the airspeed indicator will show slightly faster and faster speeds.) So if you are pitched down (AI) and you can hear the wind whistling faster past the airplane but your altimeter and VSI are locked in place, suspect the static port.

Figure 20-3: According to the AI, you're in a dive. Why does the VSI show 0 fpm?

USING WHAT YOU'VE GOT LEFT

What do you do after you determine that an instrument (or two or three) has failed? Now that you know about how the systems work, you can try to fix the problem; at the same time, your understanding of cross-checking helps you use other instruments to compensate.

Attitude indicator failure: First double-check to see whether it's a vacuum system failure and whether you'll also lose your HSI. If your aircraft has a backup vacuum system, turn it on now (the FSX Mooney does). For continuing flight without the AI, use all the other available instruments, especially the altimeter and VSI for pitch and the turn coordinator for turning. As you can tell, however, those other instruments don't do a very good job of telling you your attitude. In fact, losing your AI is one of the most dangerous system failures (apart from an engine failure, of course) and, if it occurs in IMC, often leads to an uncontrollable airplane and a crash.

Heading indicator failure: Again, if your HSI is powered by the vacuum pump, double-check the vacuum system and the AI. If it's just the HSI, use your compass for determining heading. Unfortunately, it bounces around a lot and has other errors that we've talked about in previous chapters. The best solution we've found is called *timed turns*. This is based on the idea that a standard-rate turn on your turn coordinator causes a heading change of 3° per second. So, if you're flying steady on a heading of 030° and you need to turn to heading 070°, that's 40°, or about 13 seconds, at a standard rate. Start a standard-rate turn, count 13 seconds (or use a clock/timer), roll out, and then check the compass after it settles down on the new heading.

NOTE!

↓ GPS

If you have a GPS—even just a handheld one—you can use that to show your track (course) along the ground if your HSI fails. It doesn't update instantly, so you want to roll out turns a few seconds before the GPS says you're on the desired track. But at least it doesn't show strange errors like the compass does when you're turning.

Figure 20-4: When the turn coordinator fails, use your AI, and make a guess for the bank angle needed for a standard rate turn.

Turn coordinator failure: If you can't tell when you're doing a standard-rate turn, where's the harm? Actually, ATC counts on it, and it's also a good way to keep yourself from getting in a steep turn that could cause disorientation. But there's a trick available: as you learn to fly on instruments, you'll realize that a standard-rate turn happens at a particular bank angle depending on your airspeed. The faster you are going, the steeper you need to turn to get a standard-rate turn. So if you know that at high-cruise, your plane requires a 28° bank for standard rate; then when your turn coordi-

nator fails, you just have to make a 28° bank, and you'll get pretty close to a standard-rate turn (see Figure 20-4).

548

PART I	PART II	PART III	PART IV	PART V	PART VI
PREFLIGHT	SPORT PILOT	PRIVATE PILOT	INSTRUMENT RATING	COMMERCIAL LICENSE	ATP AND BEYOND

Altimeter and VSI failure: If your static system fails, you're kind of stuck. No other instruments give the same information. (Some GPS units do show altitude, but it can be several hundred feet off. The GPS 500 in the Mooney doesn't have altitude reporting at all.) Most airplanes have a backup static source that can be turned on. This opens a small tube so the altimeter and VSI can get static air from inside the cockpit. The air in the cabin is at a slightly lower pressure than the outside air, so the altimeter reads slightly higher than you actually are, and the VSI responds more slowly to altitude changes. The FSX Mooney does have an alternate static source, but you can see it only in the 3D panel mode; it's right below the throttle and is marked "ALT AIR PULL ON." That's a bit of a misnomer, because *alternate air* is usually used to mean an alternate source of air for the engine if the main intake is blocked.

Figure 20-5: If you were really going 0 knots, you probably wouldn't maintain altitude; the GPS ground speed readout is usually close, especially if you know the wind's speed and direction and can mentally compensate for it.

Airspeed indicator failure: Your ears become attuned to the sound of the wind at various speeds, so that can be a gross check of speed; you probably won't get too close to stall speed without knowing in advance by the sound. But at normal speeds, the best thing to do is use the flight profiles introduced when you started flying the Mooney. If you know that a +2° pitch with 25 inches MP and 2200 rpm while maintaining altitude gives you a low cruise setting of 120 knots, you don't need the airspeed indicator to tell you; you'll be close enough. One other trick is a GPS, if you have one in the airplane (see Figure 20-5). It shows ground speed, which won't be quite the same as your airspeed, but again it'll be close enough.

NOTE!

↓ ATC IS YOUR COPILOT

In the real world, you have one other great source of information: the air traffic controller to whom you're talking. If the controller can see you on radar, you can ask for your current heading (actually, it's your track along the ground), your ground speed, and your altitude. You'll already have told the controller that you have a problem, so the controller should be able to give you any help you need.

FLYING A PARTIAL-PANEL APPROACH

As mentioned earlier, losing some of your primary control instruments can be quite dangerous, especially as you get close to the ground during an instrument approach. Therefore, we want to reiterate that if at any point you break out of the clouds and can proceed visually to your airport (or another nearby airport), you should do that rather than try to press on; too many people have lost control during the tricky maneuvering of an approach when they didn't have all their instruments available.

But if you don't have a choice and have to shoot an instrument approach, pick an airport with the kind of approach that is easiest to perform given your failed instruments (see Figure 20-6). Usually, that is an ILS approach because you can almost fly that with only the localizer and glideslope needles, the altimeter, the VSI, and the compass. If the best nearby airport doesn't have an ILS, then a localizer approach is probably second best, and a GPS approach would be third best, assuming you have an IFR GPS available.

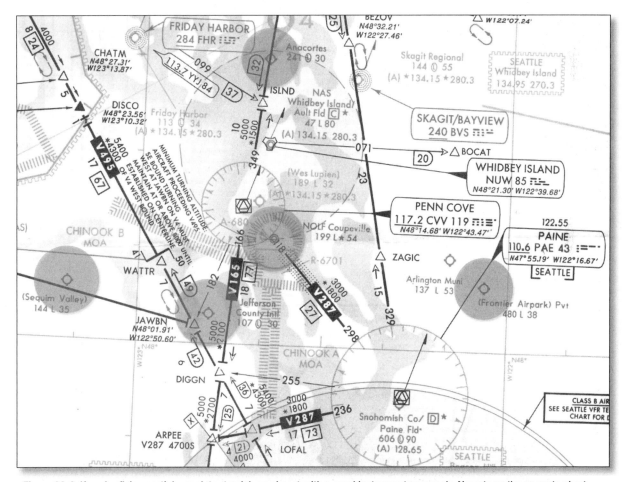

Figure 20-6: If you're flying partial-panel, try to pick an airport with a good instrument approach. Airports on the en route chart labeled in brown text (highlighted in this figure with shaded circles) don't have any instrument approach at all.

550

PART I	PART II	PART III	PART IV	PART V	PART VI
PREFLIGHT	SPORT PILOT	PRIVATE PILOT	INSTRUMENT RATING	COMMERCIAL LICENSE	ATP AND BEYOND

Figure 20-7: This handheld GPS unit from Garmin has what looks like a partial six-pack instrument panel, missing only the AI. But information on these instruments really comes from the GPS system and, therefore, could be inaccurate.

Your choice of airports should also be influenced by finding one where a controller can see you on radar. This is not just because the controller can tell you your course and ground speed; you can also ask for a *no-gyro* approach. That's the term you use to tell the controller you can't use one or more instruments that have gyroscopes. Most controllers are not pilots, and they don't really know what "losing a gyroscope" means—so don't explain it over the radio. But they will change how they give you heading changes. Instead of saying, "Turn right heading 030," they will say, "Start right turn…," and when you're close to heading 030, they will say, "stop turn." In the complex environment of an approach, it's a lot easier to use no-gyro instructions from a controller than it is to do timed compass turns. (FSX controllers cannot give a no-gyro approach, but it might be fun with a real instructor in multiplayer mode.)

Most of the instructions in the previous section (about using other instruments to replace the information you lost when one instrument fails) still apply. For instance, a GPS really helps during an approach, even if you're not making a GPS approach. Some GPSs even have a screen with a sort of simulated instrument panel, with altimeter, VSI, turn coordinator, heading indicator, and airspeed (see Figure 20-7). Technically, it's not showing heading—it's showing ground track—and it's not showing airspeed but instead ground speed. And, as mentioned before, the altitude readout could be off a lot. But when you've lost some instruments, the GPS can really help.

USING THE GARMIN G1000 SYSTEM

Those spinning gyroscopes in the AI, HSI, and turn coordinator are reliable, but nothing spinning at thousands of rpm lasts forever. And vacuum pumps have a poor reliability record. Stepping up to the all-electric Garmin G1000 system, which uses solid-state gyros for all that position and attitude data, means that the odds of having a partial-panel situation are tiny. (You still could get the pitot tube or static ports blocked, of course.)

Nonetheless, systems do fail, and it's nice to have a backup system (see Figure 20-8). In the FSX Mooney with the G1000, you have backup instruments available by pressing Shift+6 on your keyboard. (Real-world airplanes with a G1000 also have these instruments.) The backup

Figure 20-8: When the AHRS system fails, parts of the G1000 PFD get big red X symbols, but the other information stays on. Switch to using the backup AI on the right side (or by pressing Shift+6).

AI uses an electrically driven gyroscope, so if the AHRS system of the G1000 fails, you can still keep your attitude. The backup airspeed indicator and altimeter are tapped into the same pitot-static system as the G1000 system, so if there is a blockage somewhere, it affects everything.

INSIDE THE GAME

FAILING G1000 INSTRUMENTS

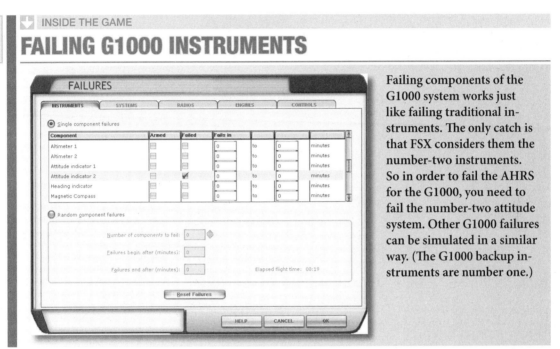

Failing components of the G1000 system works just like failing traditional instruments. The only catch is that FSX considers them the number-two instruments. So in order to fail the AHRS for the G1000, you need to fail the number-two attitude system. Other G1000 failures can be simulated in a similar way. (The G1000 backup instruments are number one.)

The real-world G1000 is even better, though. If your PFD fails, you press the red DISPLAY BACKUP button, and the MFD becomes your PFD, with the engine instruments along the left side. If the MFD fails, when you press the red DISPLAY BACKUP button, then the PFD gets the engine instrumentation on the left side. Either way, you no longer have a moving map, but you can still navigate with all your instruments, including GPS.

OTHER *IMC* EMERGENCIES

Even if you still have all your primary control instruments, some emergencies can arise during IFR flight.

*I*CE

To get ice on the airplane during flight, you need visible moisture and near- to below-freezing temperatures. Visible moisture could be rain, snow, or even just clouds. Yes, flying through a nice, soft cloud on a winter day is a good way to pick up ice.

Figure 20-9: The throttle is full, and the propeller is set on high rpm, but the engine is practically idling; this is FSX's simulation of severe icing. The only way to maintain airspeed is to descend at 1000 fpm.

Ice will affect an airplane in several ways. FSX simulates two: the pitot tube gets blocked with ice, and the engine slows down (see Figure 20-9). You can fix the iced pitot tube by turning on the pitot heat before you enter a below-freezing cloud, but there doesn't seem to be a solution to the engine power problem.

Loss of your air-speed indicator is bad but even worse is losing actual airspeed, which is what happens when you get ice on your airplane. The ice usually accumulates on the leading edges of your wings and tail surfaces, as well as your propeller. Ice is heavy, so your plane weighs more and more, which slows you down. Also, ice is usually not smooth, so the wonderful streamlined shape is now jagged and rough, and drag slows you down. The ice changes the shape of the wing into a form that doesn't provide as much lift, so you have to pitch up a little more to get enough lift, which increases the drag further. And all these changes increase the stall speed of the airplane, so your speed slows down, but the stall speed comes up, and at some point, they meet, the wings stall, and you fall.

In a real airplane, you can often see the ice accumulating on the wings, but you can't see it on the tail, and it is actually going to accumulate faster there. You also won't see it on the propeller, but the prop is an airfoil, and it starts getting more drag and more weight while providing less and less *lift* (called *thrust*) and—guess what?—slowing you down even more.

And if all that weren't enough, you probably will get ice on the windshield. This doesn't matter in the clouds, because you can't see outside anyway. But the defrosters on small airplanes are not very strong, so you might not have a clear windshield when you pop out of the bottom of the cloud and have to land that airplane.

APPROVED FOR ICING

Most small planes like the ones you've flown so far have almost no equipment to deal with ice. Most have pitot heat, and those with carbureted engines have a carburetor heat system, but it's expensive to design, test, and then build an airplane that can get rid of ice.

Planes used for commercial purposes—from big airliners down to small cargo planes—usually have good financial reasons for getting through the icing conditions to the destination, so it is worth putting on systems to remove ice from those airplanes.

Wings and propellers can be deiced with rubber boots that inflate and break off the ice or with heating elements to melt it. Windshields have some kind of heating element. And the plane must have a light that shines on the leading edge of the wing so the pilot can see whether ice accumulates at night.

Have we convinced you that getting ice on your airplane is an emergency? You have a couple of choices for solutions. If you think you're near the top of the clouds, you can try to climb up out of them. But you have to be sure you can top the clouds within just a few minutes, or it will actually be worse for your plane. The better response is to go down—the temperature will rise as you descend, and you might be able to get into air that is above freezing. Of course, when you're flying IFR, the minimum altitudes might be still too high to melt the ice. The surest solution is to turn around; after all, there wasn't ice back where you were. If there *was* ice back there, why did you keep going?

SYSTEM FAILURES

We've touched on a few system failures that affect IFR flight, such as the vacuum system. A few others to note include the electrical system, navigation equipment, and engine.

If your alternator fails, you will be on battery power only (see Figure 20-10). With all your radios (both communication and navigation) vital to IFR flight, plus your turn coordinator requiring power, you're in a world of hurt in IMC without electricity, so you need to save what you have in the battery. Immediately notify ATC that you need to get on the ground (or into VMC) within 15 to 20 minutes. Turn off anything you don't need: second communication and navigation radios, ADF, DME, lights, and so on. Tell the controller you'll be talking less (transmitting takes a lot of power). Be prepared to lose radio contact with ATC at any point as your power drops too low for the transmitter. Ideally, you should land in VMC, so if your navigation radios fail, you can get down; ATC has access to weather reports at many airports, so they can help find a close airport.

Navigation radios can also fail for reasons other than loss of power. The Mooney comes with a total of four kinds of radios, so use whatever is available. NAV1 gone up in smoke? Use NAV2, combined with DME to figure out your position. GPS on the blink? Let's hope you know how to use that ADF to figure out where you are!

Probably the worst possible failure that could happen in IMC, other than a midair collision, is to have the engine stop in a single-engine airplane. You'll be gliding down with no idea whether you'll break out of the clouds

554

PART I
PREFLIGHT

PART II
SPORT PILOT

PART III
PRIVATE PILOT

PART IV
INSTRUMENT RATING

PART V
COMMERCIAL LICENSE

PART VI
ATP AND BEYOND

Figure 20-10: The alternator has failed, and the battery is discharging; turn off anything you don't absolutely need.

Figure 20-11: If your engine fails in IMC, your best choice is to use your GPS to circle over an airport and hope you break out of the clouds in time.

with enough time to spot a field and land on it. And even though we practice such emergencies with student pilots in VMC conditions, we would never practice it in IMC with instruments. Well, we wouldn't in real life, anyway. But with a flight simulator, we can.

So what piece of equipment would become not just convenient but absolutely necessary to safely glide to, ideally, an airport when in IMC? The GPS and its moving map (see Figure 20-11). The best thing you can do is point the airplane toward the airport, and if you still have altitude to lose once you get there, just make a nice spiral, using your GPS to keep yourself over the airport. Some GPSs even will draw a line showing final approach for a runway; if you're 1,000 feet from the ground and you still haven't broken out of clouds, set yourself up for a short approach along that line. Keep the landing gear, flaps, and speed brakes retracted until you know you're high on final approach; then put out the landing gear first, flaps if you need to descend more quickly (if it looks like you will overshoot), and speed brakes if all that isn't enough.

RECOVERY FROM UNUSUAL ATTITUDES

In previous chapters we mentioned the possibility of getting into an "unusual attitude." This seemingly innocuous label belies a significant problem, especially in IMC.

In its simplest form, the definition of an unusual attitude is a pitch or bank angle that exceeds the angle required for any part of normal flight. That's a subjective definition, though, so for now use the following: if you exceed 60° of bank or 20° of pitch, you're in an unusual attitude.

▼ STUDENT OF THE CRAFT

SO YOU LIKE TO GO UPSIDE DOWN?

Unusual attitudes are a problem because of an airplane's design. If you have a bank of 60° and try to maintain altitude, you will put 2 Gs of force on the airplane (and yourself and everything in the airplane, too). Even the most basic small plane is designed to handle 3.8 Gs, but you're now closer to that limit. You've also increased the stall speed a lot, so if you slow down the wings might stall.

As for pitch, an exceedingly high pitch up will cause such a quick climb—and simultaneously slowing down—that it's likely the wings will stall, probably with one wing dropping and possibly in a spin. And if you point the nose down too much, the airspeed will increase very fast, possibly beyond V_{ne} (never exceed speed) causing parts of your plane to fall off. If you recognize the problem and start to pull out of the dive before you exceed V_{ne}, you might pull so many Gs that, again, you break the airplane.

If you want to see what it's like to spend lots of time in unusual attitudes—inverted, anyone?—you need a plane that is designed for much more stress. An aerobatic aircraft is especially strong, so strap on the FSX Extra 300 and have some fun!

When you're flying in clouds or low visibility, it's easy to get disoriented (just like you learned in night flying in Chapter 12). Without the visible horizon, you're left with your instruments. When you're disoriented, you might not read the instruments correctly, especially if they don't match what your body (sense of balance, and so on) says is going on. And if one of your instruments has actually failed—a partial-panel situation—the odds of getting into an unusual attitude skyrocket.

Therefore, you have to practice getting out of unusual attitudes while using only your instruments for reference. You can use two procedures: one for when you are climbing too steeply and the other if you're descending too steeply.

If you find yourself in a high-pitch, slow-airspeed situation (turning or not), your biggest concern is your airspeed (see Figure 20-12). You need to speed up, or the wings will stall. Simultaneously push the control wheel forward, roll level if you're turned, and increase the throttle. The goal is to get level, get your bearings again, and then get back on course and proper altitude.

556

PART I	PART II	PART III	PART IV	PART V	PART VI
PREFLIGHT	SPORT PILOT	PRIVATE PILOT	INSTRUMENT RATING	COMMERCIAL LICENSE	ATP AND BEYOND

Figure 20-12: Recovery procedure from a high-pitch situation is to simultaneously pitch down, roll level, and throttle up.

Figure 20-13: The recovery procedure from a pitch-down situation is to roll level, throttle down, and then pitch up.

On the other hand, if you're pointed down and descending fast, the procedure is a bit different (see Figure 20-13). First, if you're turning, you need to roll wings level, while you decrease the throttle. Then, start pulling up to level pitch, but don't pull so hard that you increase more than 2 or 3 Gs. (Your instructor can tell you roughly how many Gs you're pulling; in FSX, press Shift+Z a couple of times until you see the G reading in red at the top of your screen.) The reason you roll level first is that you don't want to start pulling up while you're still banked in a turn; because of aerodynamics, a hard pitch up while banked will actually increase the angle of bank. Once you level off and slow down, bring the power back to normal, and resume your desired course and altitude.

For most students, training on recovering from unusual attitudes is exciting and not too scary. We even teach it to students who are becoming private pilots, because one of the biggest killers of pilots is flying VFR into IMC and losing control. But in IFR training, you will have the added bonus of learning to recover from unusual attitudes with your attitude indicator failed. Think about the recovery techniques we discussed earlier: how would you know when the pitch was level without the attitude indicator? You'll find that it happens when the VSI changes direction and then the altimeter stops moving. What about a bank? Use the turn coordinator; as long as the ball is centered (with the rudders), the turn coordinator will pretty accurately show level (no-turn) flight.

In the real world, you don't train for unusual attitude recovery in actual IMC conditions for two reasons. First, your instructor could get disoriented and might not be able to recover the airplane if you cannot. And second, if you're in IMC, you are talking to ATC, and they don't like when you get so far off altitude and heading. Using FSX for this training, though, is almost perfect because neither of those reasons is a problem here. But FSX isn't a perfect training environment for one important reason: you won't feel any of the G forces on your body. One of the biggest parts of IFR training is learning to ignore what your body is telling you and believe the instruments. You'll have to get in a real airplane—preferably an aerobatic airplane—to really train unusual attitude recovery.

⬇ ACCIDENT CHAIN

ACCIDENT REPORT: PARTIAL PANEL

Location: Englewood, Colorado

Aircraft: Mooney M20K

Injuries: 1 uninjured

"According to the pilot, he was in instrument meteorological conditions (IMC) and climbing to his cruise altitude when the horizontal situation indicator (HSI) failed. He became disoriented, the airplane got into an unusual attitude, and he lost control of the airplane. When the airplane broke out of the clouds, it was descending rapidly, and he pulled back hard on the control yoke to arrest the descent. During the recovery, the airplane's structural limitations were exceeded, and the airplane was overstressed. According to a telephone interview with a mechanic who replaced the HSI at...a repair shop located at APA, a plastic gear in the HSI was 'stripped,' and the heading bug caused the compass card to 'hang up.' According to an FAA airworthiness safety inspector, the wing was wrinkled, and the accompanying rivets were 'popped.' Damage to the wing was such that the insurance company wrote off the airplane as a total loss.

"The National Transportation Safety Board determines the probable cause(s) of this accident as follows: the pilot's failure to maintain control of the airplane and the pilot's improper use of unusual attitude recovery procedure. Contributing factors were the failure of the HSI and the clouds."

LOST COMMUNICATION

First a quick definition: you are said to have *lost communication* (or *lost comm*) when you have absolutely no way to communicate with ATC. So if you can figure out some way to talk to them—for instance, by relaying information through another aircraft or another FAA facility (such as a flight service station) or by using your cell phone—then you haven't really lost communication, and the rules and procedures for lost comm don't apply.

558

PART I	PART II	PART III	PART IV	PART V	PART VI
PREFLIGHT	SPORT PILOT	PRIVATE PILOT	INSTRUMENT RATING	COMMERCIAL LICENSE	ATP AND BEYOND

▼ INSIDE THE GAME

LOST COMM IN FSX

If you think lost comm can't happen in FSX because ATC and their radar always works, think again. If you (or your sim instructor) intentionally fail your communication radios, then you'll be lost comm. The ATC menu will keep popping up on your screen, and you can select some of the options, but you won't actually say or hear anything on the radios. For the total lost comm experience, you can then close the ATC window. This is another place FSX is better for training: you would never intentionally go lost comm in real-world IFR, although some audio panels allow the instructor to talk to ATC without the student hearing the radios, even though the instructor and student can still talk together on their intercom.

Figure 20-14: When your communication radios fail, you won't have ATC yakking in your ear, but then again you won't have ATC's help in your ear, either.

As we've said before, IFR is all about working with ATC, so if you can't talk to them, it's a big deal (see Figure 20-14). And if you're in the clouds or in low visibility (IMC), it's a *really* big deal. So the first rule of lost communication goes something like this: if you're in VMC or if you get into VMC, stay in VMC, and land as soon as practicable.

If it's a nice day and you were flying IFR for other (nonweather) reasons, then "as soon as practicable" might be all the way to your destination. Or, if you're above a layer of clouds that you think goes all the way to your destination, you might look for a hole or another area where you can drop down below the clouds and proceed to an airport.

But if you're in the clouds and you can't get out of them or there is no way to get down to land without going through clouds, then you need to follow specific procedures. ATC will be expecting you to follow these procedures as they clear other aircraft out of the area so you can safely proceed.

ROUTE

You should choose the route you take from your current position to your destination according to the following list. Use the acronym AVEF ("Avenue F") to remember it:

- *Assigned*: This is the last route on which ATC cleared (assigned) you.

- *Vectored*: If you were being vectored, proceed directly to the fix, route, or airway to which you were being vectored; then proceed on the assigned route.

- *Expected*: If you were not assigned a route but told to expect one soon, follow that.

- *Flight plan*: If you were not assigned a route or told to expect one, follow your flight plan as you filed it.

Let's put this into practice. Say you filed the following route (see Figure 20-15):

KBFI .. SEA .. V4 .. YKM .. KYKM

Your clearance was, "Cleared to Yakima via radar vectors, Victor 4, then as filed." So if you lose communication soon after takeoff, you'd get yourself to V4 (probably by flying directly to SEA if you hadn't gotten there yet) and then continue on your assigned route.

If you were approaching your destination and you hadn't been told to expect a specific instrument approach, then proceed to the initial approach fix of whichever instrument approach you think is best (based on the last weather report you heard from that airport), and shoot that approach to the airport.

If the last thing you heard the controller say was, "Fly heading 180, vectors for ILS Runway 27 at Yakima," then once you realized you were lost comm, you'd try to intercept the ILS Runway 27 on your own, or if you are unable to safely navigate to it, you'd return to the initial approach fix or some other place from which you can get to the ILS without radar vectors.

560

PART I	PART II	PART III	PART IV	PART V	PART VI
PREFLIGHT	SPORT PILOT	PRIVATE PILOT	INSTRUMENT RATING	COMMERCIAL LICENSE	ATP AND BEYOND

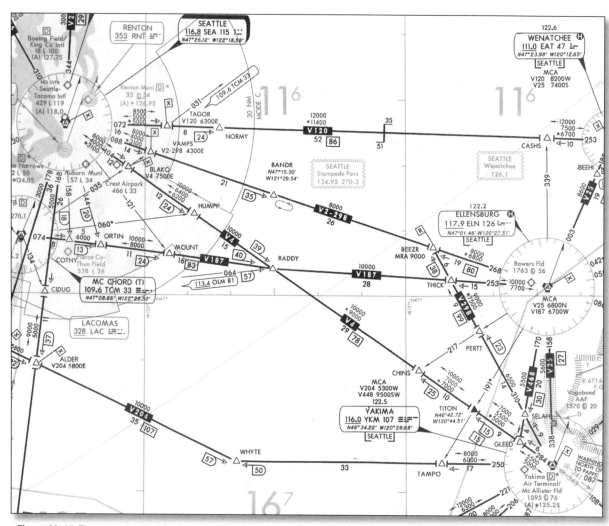

Figure 20-15: The en route chart for Seattle to Yakima.

↓ BY THE BOOK

BETTER LATE THAN EARLY, BUT DON'T WAIT

There is one other lost comm rule that we should mention here for completeness: if you arrive at the clearance limit before your flight plan said you would arrive at that point, then you have to wait until that flight plan time is up. ATC's expectation of your arrival time is based on your filed true airspeed and what time you took off.

Every air traffic controller we've talked to says that—unless you're more than about 30 minutes early—you should ignore this rule, because they have to spend a lot of effort to get everyone out of your way when they lose contact with you. The sooner you land and call them (on a telephone), the sooner they can open the airspace up again to other planes. So, don't dilly-dally at the clearance limit just to wait out the clock.

Also, if you're in an approach environment near a major airport (as opposed to out in the sticks), they often can see your transponder, or at least a basic radar return for your aircraft, and have been updating your progress even without talking to you.

ALTITUDE

The altitude you fly after losing communication also follows specific rules. In this case, you need to fly the highest altitude from the following list, which you can remember with the acronym MEA:

- *Minimum*: The minimum altitude for IFR operations (such as minimum en route altitude, and so on) along that particular segment of your route

- *Expected*: The altitude ATC told you to expect

- *Assigned*: The altitude ATC assigned you

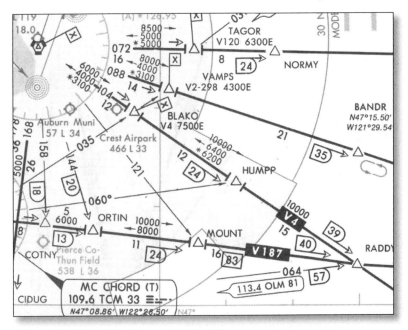

Figure 20-16: The MEA changes a lot along V4.

Because the minimum altitude changes as you fly along, you will probably end up changing altitudes several times during your flight, as shown in Figure 20-16.

As an example, let's say your clearance included, "Climb and maintain 2,000; expect 8,000 three minutes after departure." If you lost radio contact right after takeoff, then three minutes after you take off, go to 8,000 right away, unless the minimum for that area is higher (it isn't). Once you're on a route (let's use V4 from the previous example), the minimum en route altitude (MEA) for that leg is 8,000 but you're going east on V4, so you need to be at 9,000. About 40 miles from SEA, the MEA on V4 goes to 10,000, so you need to bump up to

562

PART I	PART II	PART III	PART IV	PART V	PART VI
FIRST FLIGHT	SPORT PILOT	PRIVATE PILOT	INSTRUMENT RATING	COMMERCIAL LICENSE	ATP AND BEYOND

11,000. When you're 25 miles from YKM, the MEA drops to 7,000, but that isn't as high as the altitude of 8,000 you were told to expect, so now the expected altitude is higher, and you need to be there—but at 9,000 because of the direction of flight. As you get close to YKM, the MEAs drop even further, but the "expected" altitude trumps, so you stay at 9,000. When can you drop down then? You can drop down when you get to the initial approach fix for the instrument approach you want to conduct; you might need to spiral down in a holding pattern to properly execute the approach.

IFR EMERGENCIES IN PRACTICE

For these first few flights, you'll have a chance to practice several of the failures you read about earlier in this chapter.

PARTIAL PANEL

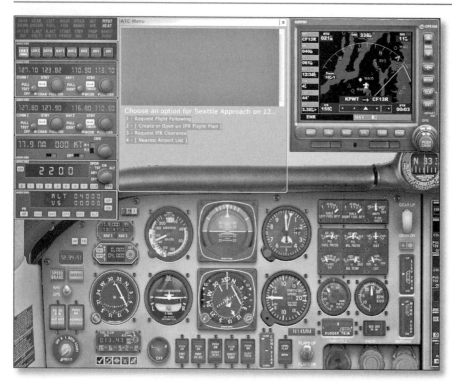

Figure 20-17: The Chap_20_Partial_Panel flights start in the clouds with a full panel...but not for long.

Load the Chap_20_Partial_Panel_AI flight (see Figure 20-17). You're flying near Seattle, about to get vectors to the Boeing Field ILS Runway 13R. When you unpause the flight, use the ATC menu to ask ATC for your IFR clearance to Boeing Field. (The flight plan is already on file; if it doesn't load properly, reload the flight plan called IFR KPWT to KBFI, but don't allow FSX to move the plane to the starting airport.)

ATC will give you your clearance and will soon start vectoring you for the ILS Runway 13R at Boeing Field. Set up all the radios, and so on, that you can, and take a look at the chart for the approach on the website at www.wiley.com.

In a few minutes, your attitude indicator will fail. Use your other instruments to determine your attitude and heading. Your autopilot is unusable in this situation, so you'll have to fly by hand.

Follow the vectors ATC gives you (in real life you'd ask for a no-gyro approach, which is not an option in FSX), and intercept the ILS to get yourself home to Boeing Field.

When you're satisfied with your performance after losing your AI, load the Chap_20_Partial_Panel_Vacuum flight. This flight starts in the same place as the previous flight (so get your IFR clearance to Boeing and set up the radios), but this time your whole vacuum system will fail a few minutes after you start. Your first solution will be to turn on your standby vacuum pump to restore your AI and HSI. But—sadly—that won't fix it (apparently this was a serious vacuum system failure). So use all the other instruments (especially the GPS and compass) to guide yourself to the ILS. By the way, even though your HSI stops turning, the yellow CDI needle on it will still show the ILS properly, so you can use it for course guidance; just turn the OBS dial until the needle points up.

ICING SIMULATION

At any time during this training, you might get ice in the clouds. After all, you're flying in Seattle in the winter and the western side of Washington's Cascade Mountains isn't called the "Ice Machine" for nothing. However, because FSX doesn't simulate ice on the wings, it is hard to detect (other than your pitot tube blocking and your airspeed indicator showing 0). Instead, icing will just appear at random during other emergency training flights. Deal with it as you read about previously in this chapter.

The final partial-panel flight, Chap_20_Partial_Panel_Airspeed, is one where your airspeed indicator fails. When it fails, it might not just go to 0 knots; it might stick on some other speed. Let's hope you'll notice that. Turn on the pitot heat, because ice is the usual suspect. (It won't help, but it's a good habit anyway.) The flight starts in the same place as the previous ones, ready for vectors to Boeing Field. Use your GPS ground speed to get an approximation of your airspeed, and remember to fly using the Mooney performance profiles from Chapter 14.

ELECTRICAL FAILURE

To practice what to do if you lose your alternator, load the Chap_20_Electrical flight (see Figure 20-18). In this case you're VFR over a solid cloud layer somewhere west of Seattle. About one minute into the flight, the alternator will fail, and you'll be on battery power. You've got less than 20 minutes to get on the ground, and there's nothing but clouds below you.

564

PART I	PART II	PART III	PART IV	PART V	PART VI
PREFLIGHT	SPORT PILOT	PRIVATE PILOT	INSTRUMENT RATING	COMMERCIAL LICENSE	ATP AND BEYOND

Use the ATC menu to open an IFR flight plan (create your own, or use IFR KBFI to KPWT on the website at www.wiley.com), call ATC, and get an IFR clearance to Bremerton (KPWT). You'll get vectors for the ILS Runway 1 at KPWT. (See the chart on the website; the procedure is slightly different between the chart and the one in your GPS, but it works fine.) Meanwhile, follow your procedures for saving power: turn off every piece of electrical equipment you don't really need. Let's hope you'll break out of the clouds before your battery runs out of juice and you can't navigate at all.

Figure 20-18: You're above the clouds now, but you've got to get down through them, and your battery is losing power.

Unusual Attitude Recovery

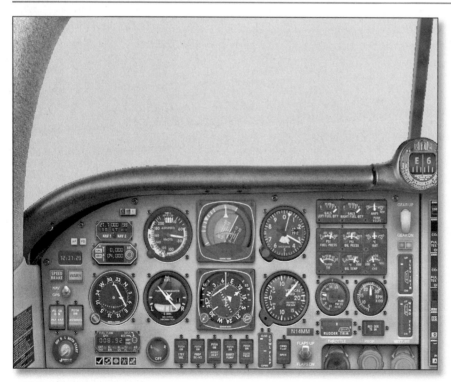

If you totally lose control of your airplane, you'll need to be able to recover from an unusual attitude. This training will begin in VMC conditions so you can practice while using outside references, but the second part of the training will take place in clouds.

Before you load the flight, get yourself and your "cockpit" ready, because this flight does *not* start paused. When the flight comes on, the airplane will already be in an unusual attitude, and it will be getting worse. If you don't respond quickly, the plane might not be recoverable. See earlier in this chapter to remind yourself how to

Figure 20-19: It's all out of control now; let's hope you can fix it!

recover from an unusual attitude. When you're ready, load the flight Chap_20_Unusual_Attitude_VMC flight (see Figure 20-19). Good luck!

The second unusual attitude flight follows a similar situation: it starts out bad and gets worse fast. This time, though, you're in the clouds. Load Chap_20_Unusual_Attitude_IMC when you're ready to tackle it.

NOTE!

↓ LOST COMMUNICATION TRAINING

Because of the way the ATC system works in FSX, there isn't much training value in having a specific flight where you lose communication with ATC. In fact, you've already done quite a few IFR flights where you ignored ATC. You might lose radio contact in one of the following unexpected emergencies, however!

UNEXPECTED EMERGENCIES

Figure 20-20: Everything seems OK now, but in a few minutes something bad is going to happen. And we're not going to give it away in the photo!

For the advanced flight challenges of this chapter, you're going to really make use of the flight simulator and do things you absolutely cannot do in real life. For one thing, we won't tell you in advance what will happen during each flight. You'll just have to pay attention to the airplane and figure it out and then get safely on the ground (see Figure 20-20). That's certainly the most realistic way to train.

Yes, you could cheat and check the Aircraft > Failures menu to see which instruments will fail and when, but the reason you're reading this book is because you want more realism in your flight sim. Just play along, try each one, go back and try them again to see whether you can improve your reactions, and have fun.

566

| PART I | PART II | PART III | PART IV | PART V | PART VI |
| PREFLIGHT | SPORT PILOT | PRIVATE PILOT | INSTRUMENT RATING | COMMERCIAL LICENSE | ATP AND BEYOND |

The other things to watch for are compound and system problems. For instance, don't be surprised to have both the pitot tube *and* the static port get blocked or to have the entire electrical system go belly-up. (Sorry about that lightning strike, Ace!)

The first thing you should do, during the few minutes you have at the beginning of each flight before something goes wrong, is to get situational awareness: where are you, where are you headed, how high are you, and where is the nearest (or best) airport when you're ready to land? We've included a few more charts on the website, including some sectional charts and approach charts for the Seattle area, in case they help. (And remember, ATC and ASOS/AWOS can be a great help, too.) Then just sit back, relax, and enjoy the...umm...why is it doing that?

The advanced training flights for this chapter are on the website and are titled as follows:

Chap_20_Advanced_Emergency_1

Chap_20_Advanced_Emergency_2

Chap_20_Advanced_Emergency_3

Chap_20_Advanced_Emergency_4

Chap_20_Advanced_Emergency_5

Chap_20_Advanced_Emergency_6

When you can comfortably deal with these advanced emergencies, you'll be more than ready to be an instrument pilot. On the website is the Instrument Pilot Practical Test Standards (PTS), so you can read how skilled you need to be able to fly on instruments. You can take the FSX built-in checkride, and then you'll be an instrument pilot—congratulations! (You might want to practice flying IFR in the Cessna 172 a bit first, because that's what you fly in the checkride lesson. Everything happens a bit slower than in the Mooney.)

Next you'll get to learn to fly the twin-engine Beech Baron as a commercial pilot.

KEY POINTS FOR REAL FLYING AND FSX BUILT-INS

The following are some key points from this chapter:

- Detect and deal with instrument and system failures.

- Fly partial panel en route and approaches.

- Recover from unusual attitudes.

- Execute lost communication procedures.

Here are the lessons and missions to study after reading this chapter:

- *Lessons*: You are capable of flying any of the Instrument Pilot lessons as well as the Instrument Rating Checkride lesson.

- *Missions*: You can fly any of the instrument flights unless they are in an unfamiliar airplane. Note that several of the airline missions involve unexpected twists that are, or could turn into, serious emergencies.

COMMERCIAL LICENSE

CONTENTS

MULTIENGINE FLYING IN THE BEECHCRAFT BARON

"WHEN YOU HAVE TWO ENGINES, YOU HAVE TWO ENGINES THAT CAN FALL TO BITS. WHEN YOU HAVE FOUR, YOU HAVE FOUR THAT CAN FALL TO BITS. THE LESS ENGINES YOU HAVE, THE SAFER YOU ARE."

—FRANK FICKEISEN, CHIEF ENGINEER FOR BOEING, REPLYING TO A COMPLAINT ABOUT THE DANGERS OF FLYING TWO-ENGINE AIRPLANES ACROSS THE PACIFIC

572

| PART I | PART II | PART III | PART IV | PART V | PART VI |
| PREFLIGHT | SPORT PILOT | PRIVATE PILOT | INSTRUMENT RATING | COMMERCIAL LICENSE | ATP AND BEYOND |

FLYING MULTIENGINE AIRPLANES

Why put a second engine on the airplane? Sure, it looks cool and gives you that "real pilot" feel. But it also burns a lot more gas and adds complexity. The aircraft doesn't fly much faster even though you have potentially twice the power available. That's because the power required goes up at roughly the cube of desired speed. Doubling your speed by just adding power would require a power increase of eight times ($2^3 = 8$)!

It's really about weight and rate of climb. Stepping into a twin, these two items are the big changes. The Baron can carry more than the *entire* J-3 Cub weighs. It can also climb at well over 1000 fpm near sea level while carrying all that weight.

Actually, flying the twin isn't that different from flying a single, as long as both engines are running. You generally move both throttle controls as if they were a single lever. The main differences pilots usually notice transitioning to normal operations in the twin are that it's bigger, heavier, and faster than their previous mounts.

You'll find, though, that even normal procedures on the twin are grounded in a preparation for losing one engine and immediately deciding what to do.

⬇ KEEPING IT REAL

ACCELERATE-STOP AND ACCELERATE-GO

Light multiengine aircraft usually have two charts in their flight manuals that are new to single-engine pilots. These are the accelerate-stop and accelerate-go charts. Accelerate-stop gives the distance required to bring the airplane up to rotation speed with both engines running and then abort the takeoff and come to a complete stop. Accelerate-go gives the distance required to get to a critical speed, have complete failure of an engine, continue to accelerate and take off on the remaining engine, and clear a small obstacle (usually 50 feet high or less).

We'll talk about engine failures in Chapter 23, but you'll see that the thinking about losing an engine affects even normal, multiengine operations.

REDLINE AND BLUELINE

As you transition to more sophisticated aircraft, you'll hear about two new V speeds. These are V_1, which you can think of as the "committed to takeoff speed," and V_2, which is the takeoff safety speed.

V_1 is both the maximum speed that the pilot could still abort the takeoff and stop the airplane within the accelerate-stop distance (see "Accelerate-Stop and Accelerate-Go") and the minimum speed that the pilot could continue the takeoff with a failed engine and still clear the required obstacles. Is this always the same speed? Well, technically, no. Especially if you were taking off from a super-short runway. In light twins, we rarely calculate both figures for V_1. Instead, we look at what our single-engine rate of climb would be after takeoff and make sure we can still climb well enough to get up to the pattern and swing around to come back and land.

V_1 in a light twin is often replaced with V_r, the speed we rotate. This speed varies with each model airplane, but for most light twins it's about 5 knots higher than the minimum controllable airspeed, or V_{mc}. If we're off the ground below this airspeed, the loss of one engine while the other is churning at full power could put us in a roll that is physically impossible to stop, because there isn't enough air flowing over the rudder. We won't ever leave the ground at a speed less than V_{mc}.

Figure 21-1: The Baron panel is a bit more of what you're used to seeing. There are two sets of engine instruments, and the airspeed indicator has two extra marks, redline at 84 knots and blueline at 101.

What's convenient about this is that V_{mc} is marked on the airspeed indicator with a red line (see Figure 21-1). So, we make our decision to abort or continue as the Baron passes 90 knots, and we begin our rotation.

Just as an aside, look how far you've come from the beginning of training. The Cub you started in can barely do 90 knots in a dive. Now you need that speed just to take off!

There is a second speed marked on the multiengine airplane airspeed indicator that's even more critical than V_{mc}, and that's the blueline or best single-engine climb speed (V_{yse}). Your takeoff procedure will be to rotate at redline plus five and let the airplane accelerate to blueline before you start to climb. Some aircraft have a redline and a blueline close enough together that standard procedure is to rotate 5 knots before blueline.

You'll remember that V_y is your best rate of climb speed and is the best speed to hold after takeoff. Twin-engine airplanes have a V_y as well, but pilots often uses V_{yse} close to the ground. The reason is that losing an engine will kill not half your climb rate, but most or all of it. In fact, many light twins operating well above sea level can't even hold altitude with just one engine running when they are near gross weight. You want to already be at whatever speed will give you the best climb—or at least minimum sink—in the event of an engine failure right after takeoff.

This huge loss of climb often doesn't make sense until you look at the math behind it. Here it is in a nutshell: a certain amount of horsepower is required to maintain level flight at a given airspeed. Let's say that's 200 horsepower for a moderately loaded Baron at Vyse. With both engines producing full power at sea level, you have 600 horsepower at your disposal. That means you have 400 horsepower in *excess power* to use for climb.

Now kill one engine. You have only 300 horsepower to use, and 200 is required just for level flight. That's only 100 horsepower in excess power for climb. So, you went from 400 horsepower for climb to 100 horsepower for climb, a

574

PART I	PART II	PART III	PART IV	PART V	PART VI
PREFLIGHT	SPORT PILOT	PRIVATE PILOT	INSTRUMENT RATING	COMMERCIAL LICENSE	ATP AND BEYOND

reduction of 75 percent. You will lose at least 75 percent of your climb performance with one engine out. The realities of having only one engine turning creates some other issues such that the real-world loss is even greater.

It gets worse at altitude too, because the Baron's nonturbocharged engines put out less power as you climb.

We'll get into this more in Chapter 23, but you should know why multiengine pilots are so sensitive about their speeds even when both engines are working fine.

SOME OTHER BARON POINTS

Before you take to the air, we'll make sure you're familiar with a couple other items on the Baron.

THREE TRIMS

Figure 21-2: The danger of all these trims is that you can trim the airplane into flying along hands-off but totally uncoordinated. Watch that you're flying straight when trimmed out.

The Baron offers you elevator, rudder, and aileron trim (see Figure 21-2). You've been working with elevator trim since the first flights in the Cub, so you know all about that. You had rudder trim in the Mooney, but we didn't talk about it much because the Mooney didn't need much rudder pressure in the climb.

The Baron has a left-turning tendency in the climb too, because both engines turn in the same direction, so it will need rudder on the climb. You can use the rudder trim for this if you want—it's nice if you're settling in for a long climb—but it's not required. (Some light twins have propellers that turn in opposite directions, and these have no turning tendency on climb.)

The aileron trim is something that gets handy on a larger airplane where there might be more weight on one side of the airplane than the other. This will make the airplane tend to roll toward the heavy side, and you must compensate by holding a bit of opposite aileron. You can use the aileron trim to hold it there. Sometimes the trim control on the FSX panel is hard to click just right. Ctrl+Num 4 and Num 6 will add trim left or right. Remember, the Num Lock key must be *off* for this to work. If you get the trim all messed up, F11 and F12 on the keyboard will recenter the aileron trim and rudder trim, respectively.

TWO ALTERNATORS

Figure 21-3: Here the right engine is shut down so the right alternator is offline. In a real Baron, you'd see the right vacuum/pressure pump was offline too.

The Baron has two engines so it has two alternators from which to draw. Most of the time this doesn't matter to the pilot because the two alternators act together to handle the total electrical load. You can have some fun turning one off, though, and seeing all the electrical gauges move around and the annunciator light appear on the panel in FSX (see Figure 21-3). In the real airplane, losing one alternator might require turning off some of the electrical components so as not to demand more power than the remaining alternator can produce. This is usually a problem only if you're using something that draws a lot of power such as the prop and windshield deicer.

INSTRUMENT AIR

The Baron has a gyro pressure system instead of a vacuum system. The principle is the same except air is blown through the instruments rather than sucked through them. In fact, it's usually the same kind of pump used for vacuum or pressure systems. The difference is in how it's connected. There is an instrument air gauge rather than a vacuum gauge in the upper left of the panel. FSX doesn't simulate it, but in the real Baron and most multiengine airplanes, the loss of one of the two vacuum/pressure pumps will show up on the instrument air gauge as a bright red dot.

DEICE BOOTS

The Baron also uses pressure for inflating pneumatic boots on the leading edge of its wings and tail. These bust off accumulated ice, which gives the pilot more time to fly in icing conditions before it becomes a problem. The switch is there in FSX, but ice accumulation on the wing and tail is not accurately simulated, so it's not a real training bonus.

576

| PART I | PART II | PART III | PART IV | PART V | PART VI |
| PREFLIGHT | SPORT PILOT | PRIVATE PILOT | INSTRUMENT RATING | COMMERCIAL LICENSE | ATP AND BEYOND |

PROP SYNC

Any real-world multiengine pilot loves a propeller synchronizer system that works. Whenever the two propellers are turning at different speeds, even slightly different speeds, there is an audible harmonic in the cockpit. It sounds like a "waa-waa-waa," with the speed of the oscillating sound depending on the difference in the speed of the two props. It will drive you nuts.

FSX doesn't simulate the sound, but it will show you whether the props are in sync with the little fan-shaped indicator between and below the MP gauges. If it's spinning, the props are not synchronized. You can see this only if you manually move the prop controls independently or shut down one engine. FSX will immediately resync the props when you move the prop controls together or restart the dead engine. The position of the prop sync switch on the panel makes no difference.

  KEEPING IT REAL

HIGH FLIER

Part of flying a high-performance aircraft such as the Baron is going up high, but sometimes you'll find yourself landing high. We picked Colorado for your training for several reasons, but one is just to practice landing at an airport where the altimeter says 5,400 feet when you're on the ground! You'll also see in Chapter 23 how the high-altitude airport makes an engine failure on takeoff an even more critical event to manage correctly.

Your indicated airspeed and your true airspeed differ significantly at this altitude, however. It's critical that you have your realism settings such that FSX displays the indicated airspeed rather than the true airspeed. Indicated airspeed is the default, so unless you changed this, it should be fine.

  BY THE BOOK

CATEGORY AND CLASS

We haven't dwelled too much on how pilot certificates are structured, but it makes sense to talk about them now, even if just as an aside. When you started flying in the Cub, you were going through training toward your Sport Pilot Certificate, but that certificate had limitations on it. It allowed you to fly only single-engine land airplanes. If you wanted to fly anything else, such as a seaplane or a gyrocopter, you had to get additional training and a logbook endorsement.

When you got your Private Pilot Certificate, you got additional privileges, such as being able to fly at night, but you were also limited single-engine land airplanes. If you wanted to fly seaplanes or gyroplanes as a private pilot, you needed additional training and had to pass an additional checkride.

Private pilots can fly multiengine land airplanes such as the Baron, but we're assuming you want to raise the bar higher and get a Commercial Pilot Certificate with both multiengine land and single-engine land privileges. There are two ways to do this. You can get your initial Commercial Certificate in a single-engine airplane and then add multiengine privileges, or you can get your Commercial Certificate in a multiengine airplane and add single-engine privileges.

It's rare to start your commercial pilot training in a twin-engine airplane because it's more expensive. FSX lets you use any airplane you want for the same cost, though, so let's get going in the Baron right from the start. You'll see in the next chapter that you'll fly a few additional maneuvers in your old pal the Mooney to cover the additional training for that single-engine land add-on.

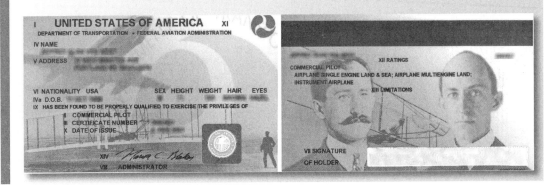

GETTING UP TO SPEED IN THE BARON

Since this is a new airplane to you, you'll start on the ground with the engines off. Load the flight Chap_21_Baron_First_flight. You're at the Jefferson County (Jeffco) airport (KBJC) just outside of Denver, Colorado. The winds are calm, and the day is fair. This is perfect for an aircraft checkout.

Before you even start the engines, you need to get your windows arranged. During the next few chapters, you'll want to be able to juggle the different Baron windows smoothly, particularly the throttle quadrant. Make sure you're in 2D cockpit to start. The 3D, virtual cockpit is stunning and fun to fly if your computer has the processing horsepower to make it work, but it's easier to learn your way around in the 2D view first.

Press Shift+2, Shift+3, and Shift+4 to show the avionics stack, GPS, and throttle quadrant. You might want to resize them smaller and shuffle them around to your liking. We like the configuration in Figure 21-4 because it puts the throttle quadrant in the more intuitive lower right and lets you view it without blocking the picture out the windscreen. You might need to resize the floating windows smaller by dragging their edges to better fit items on your screen. We did this with the throttle quadrant so it doesn't block the engine instruments.

578

PART I	PART II	PART III	PART IV	PART V	PART VI
PREFLIGHT	SPORT PILOT	PRIVATE PILOT	INSTRUMENT RATING	COMMERCIAL LICENSE	ATP AND BEYOND

Figure 21-4: Get the extra floating windows where you want them, and memorize the keys that turn them on and off.

 STUDENT OF THE CRAFT

ALTIMETER SETTINGS UP HIGH

Before you start the Baron, look at the MP gauge, and look at the altimeter. The MP gauge shows the air pressure at the intake manifold of the engine. When the engine is not running, that's the same as the outside air pressure. Down at sea level, the outside air pressure is the same as the altimeter setting. In fact, that's rather the definition of the altimeter setting.

Up here in Colorado, it's a bit different. The outside air pressure will be about 5 inches different from the altimeter setting. Remember, you're more than 5,000 feet above sea level. The altimeter setting near Denver is what the outside air pressure would be corrected for the altitude. Essentially, it's what the air pressure would be today if Denver were at sea level.

Figure 21-5: You can toggle floating windows on and off in the 2D or 3D cockpit using the same keyboard commands.

If you'd like to go through the entire official checklist for start-up and run-up, press Shift+F10 and go right ahead. To jump right into things, though, press Ctrl+. to hold the brakes, reduce the throttle to idle, and then press Ctrl+E to start the engines. They'll fire up one after the other. Press Shift+4 to see the throttle quadrant and open the cowl flaps on each engine, and pull the mixture control about halfway back to cut off. You're at more than a mile above sea level here, and you don't need nearly so much fuel running into the engine with this thinner air.

With both engines running, press ` (accent) on the keyboard to see the ATC window. Get the current ATIS, set your barometer, and get a clearance to taxi for a north departure. Choose the 2D or 3D cockpit view as you like and your computer allows. We find zooming out to about .50 zoom in the virtual cockpit gives a more realistic look (see Figure 21-5). Just make sure you can see out the windscreen for taxi and takeoff!

TAXI THE TWIN

There is no real difference from other aircraft in taxiing the Baron except that you have an additional tool to turn if you need it: differential power. Try it on your taxi by advancing the throttle on only right engine for a left turn and the left engine for a right turn. Although the plane will turn with just differential power—a handy trick on an icy ramp—the best technique is to use the rudder pedals first and add differential power to tighten the turn as needed.

580

PART I	PART II	PART III	PART IV	PART V	PART VI
PRE-FLIGHT	SPORT PILOT	PRIVATE PILOT	INSTRUMENT RATING	COMMERCIAL LICENSE	ATP AND BEYOND

INSIDE THE GAME

ONE CONTROL, TWO ENGINES

If you have a single throttle, prop, and mixture control on your joystick or yoke, moving it will move both the right- and left-engine levels. If you press E on your keyboard and then 1, you'll get control of the left engine only. Press E and then 2, and you'll control only the right. Press E and then move the lever on your joystick before touching any other key, and the two controls will resynchronize and move together.

Another option is customizing the controls of your a three-lever yoke for twin-engine training. You can set lever 1 for the left throttle only, lever 2 for the right throttle (it's normally the prop control), and lever 3 for prop control for both engines. You have no level for mixture control, so you'd need to check the box for automixture in the realism settings or use the mouse to move the onscreen lever.

A LEAN MACHINE

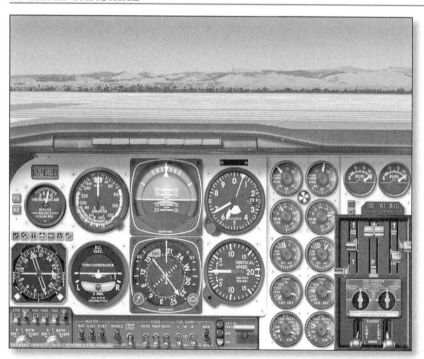

Figure 21-6: In the real world, you'll want to set the mixture on both engines individually. In FSX, you can do the run-up on one and then just set the mixture on the other to match.

Before you take off in the Baron, you need to adjust your mixtures for the current altitude. This step is not explained in the FSX checklist, although it is mentioned. Since it's simulated in FSX—and because forgetting to do it has killed real people when their over-rich engines couldn't produce climb power—we'll run through it here.

Press Ctrl+. to hold the brakes, and then set the right-engine mixture to full rich. Bring the right engine up to 2000 rpm. Now pull back the mixture, and watch the engine rpm, fuel flow, or EGT. You'll see the engine rpm rise to about 2200 rpm, the fuel flow rise to about 7 gph, and the EGT rise. If you continue to lean, all three values will begin to fall. What's happening here is you're finding the best mixture for the current temperature and pressure at 5,700 feet. You want to set the mixture on the richest setting that still gives you the highest rpm, or fuel flow. It's also where the EGT begins to decrease as you go from peak EGT to a richer setting (see Figure 21-6). Just as an aside, the fuel flows won't go up and then down when ground leaning in real Baron. They just go down. This procedure does not apply to turbocharged engines such as on the Mooney. In fact, every engine handles this a bit differently, so be sure you get the right procedure before doing this in a real-world airplane.

Once you have the right engine set, leave the mixture where it is, and retard the throttle to idle. Now do the left engine.

The Takeoff Briefing

It's common in twins and larger airplanes to brief the takeoff. On very large planes, this is partially because the V_1 and V_2 speeds vary with each set of takeoff conditions. On smaller planes, it's more to preload your brain to take the right action without delay. It might sound like this:

"We're holding short of 29 right. We'll position and bring both engines to full power. If I note an immediate engine or instrument problem, I'll close both throttles and stop on the remaining runway. If an engine fails before I reach 90 knots (V_{mc} + 5), I'll close both throttles and stop on the remaining runway. If an engine fails after 90 knots, I'll accelerate to 101 while climbing, retract the gear, and follow with the engine-out procedure.

With normal indications, our first turn is to the right for a north departure."

Glider pilots often do a similar briefing as to what they'll do in case of a tow-rope break. It's odd that we don't do a similar (albeit simpler) briefing for single-engine airplanes. Some folks recommend you do, and we can't argue with the logic.

Patience, Patience

The first thing most pilots notice about taking off in a twin is that it seems to take a long time. When you get your clearance from the tower, position on Runway 29R, and advance both throttles. Verify you're getting 2700 rpm from both engines and that all other parameters are equal between them. Then sit back and wait for 90 knots.

Here near Denver, it will take even longer than it would at sea level because the engines have less than their sea-level 300 horsepower available and because you rotate at 90 knots indicated airspeed. At 5,700 feet MSL, that's about 100 knots true airspeed. You'll feel like you're really booking down the runway by the time you rotate—and you are. You'll enjoy the same experience on landing soon.

You also have the Baron loaded to within 100 pounds of its maximum gross weight. A lighter load would improve performance.

Rotate at 90 knots, and let the airplane pass blueline of 101 before you start climbing. With a positive rate of climb, you can raise your landing gear. You'll climb at whichever is higher of V_{yse} or V_y. They are 101 and 105, respectively, so you'll climb at the V_y of 105. You have lots of excess thrust, so the pitch is about 10° nose up to see 105 knots.

It's not uncommon in an airplane like the Baron to climb at a faster airspeed just to get some forward visibility. If you drop the nose to about 5° nose up, you'll see about 130 knots. Figure 21-7 shows the view with both the steep and shallow climbs.

582

PART I	PART II	PART III	PART IV	PART V	PART VI
PREFLIGHT	SPORT PILOT	PRIVATE PILOT	INSTRUMENT RATING	COMMERCIAL LICENSE	ATP AND BEYOND

Figure 21-7: The initial rotation is slow and is a shallow pitch to reach blueline. After that, the pitch is steep to maintain 105 knots in the climb or shallow for 130 knots.

As you pass 6,400 feet (700 feet above the ground), begin a right turn to the north. Passing through 1,000 feet AGL, you can transition to cruise climb, as shown in the flight profiles table below.

⬇ WHAT? NO FLAPS?

The Baron can take off with approach flaps or flaps retracted. Net performance is about equal either way, so you'll leave them up for your Baron takeoffs.

FLIGHT PROFILES FOR THE BARON

Your goal on this flight is to get acquainted with the airplane and learn the same standard profiles as you did for the Mooney. The following table shows what the numbers will look like for the Baron. Note that unlike the turbocharged Mooney, the MP setting is a number or "max." As you climb, the maximum MP you can see decreases. Past a certain altitude, you just leave the throttle full open. Note that as you climb or descend in the Baron, if you don't adjust the throttle, the MP will go up or down as you descend or climb.

A note on this chart: the two rates of climb are what you'd expect at sea level and what you see in Colorado. Note that the same power and pitch will yield quite different indicated airspeeds at different altitudes.

	MP	RPM	Config.	Pitch	Indicated Airspeed	Rate of Climb
Cruise Climb	25 inches or max	2500 rpm	Flaps and gear up	+5°	150/130	+1500/+700 fpm
High Cruise	25 inches or max	2300 rpm	Flaps and gear up	+0°	175/155	0 (level flight)
Cruise Descent	25 to 18 inches	2300 rpm	Flaps and gear up	–2°	175	–700 fpm
Low Cruise	18 inches	2300 rpm	Flaps and gear up	+2°	150/135	0
Approach Level	18 inches	2300 rpm	Approach flaps and gear down	+2°	110	0
Approach Descent	15 inches	Prop control full forward	Approach flaps and gear down	–2°	110	–500 fpm

Climb on a heading of 355, and get established in the cruise climb configuration. Reaching 8,500 feet, transition to level flight, and let the Baron accelerate. There is no adjustment on throttle or prop here, but do close the cowl flaps. You might want to engage the autopilot in heading mode to take care of flying the airplane while you experiment with power and speed.

You should see about 155 knots indicated, which is about 176 knots true in high cruise over Boulder, Colorado. Now reduce the power to the low-cruise settings, but maintain altitude. The Baron will laze along at 135 knots.

  STUDENT OF THE CRAFT

MOVE THIS LEVER, NO THAT LEVER

Rod Machado makes a big deal about the order you move the propeller and throttle during his Baron flight lessons. Ironically, it's the opposite of what he recommends in the FSX written lessons.

Frankly, we don't care which lever you move first in the FSX Baron or the real one. Some misinformed phobias have arisen around this issue that date back to some real issues with big, radial engines on World War II–vintage aircraft. The issue doesn't apply to modern engines like the ones on the Baron.

We like to always set the rpm first because it's less total fiddling. If you set the MP first, when you subsequently reduce the rpm, the MP will rise. That's because the Baron engines aren't turbocharged. The slower-turning engine (after you reduce the rpm) gives the ambient air more time to flow into the cylinder and gives a higher MP. Setting the rpm first has no such issue because the propeller governor will maintain that rpm as you adjust the throttle.

Note that without a turbocharger, you will need to open the throttle as you climb just to maintain the same MP setting. That's because the air is getting less dense as you climb.

The opposite is true in a descent. You must manually close throttle in small amounts to keep constant MP while descending. You must close it even further to *reduce* the MP in descent, as you would need to do if you started the descent at high cruise but wanted to level off and slow to low cruise.

584

PART I	PART II	PART III	PART IV	PART V	PART VI
PREFLIGHT	SPORT PILOT	PRIVATE PILOT	INSTRUMENT RATING	COMMERCIAL LICENSE	ATP AND BEYOND

Figure 21-8: Don't be afraid of speed; 170 knots is a leisurely speed for descent in the Baron. In smooth air, you should feel comfortable seeing more than 200 knots.

Figure 21-9: Whatever view you use to see the airport, plan to fly a larger airport pattern than you're used to flying.

Now go back to high cruise. When you're back at 155 knots indicated, turn back to a heading of 150, and point the nose down about –2°. Leave the throttles wide open and the rpm at 2300. You'll see about 175 knots (see Figure 21-8). If you want to have more fun, pitch the nose down to –5°. You'll be coming down well over 1000 fpm and see around 200 knots.

As you come down in the Baron, you'll need to reduce the throttle to keep the MPs at 25 inches (you'd reduce them more aggressively to level off with an MP of only 18 inches for low cruise). Level off at 7,000 feet, and let the Baron slow to high cruise.

Now call up your GPS (Shift+3) and find KBJC (you might need to do a direct-to). Head that way. If you like to use the ATC window, open it now to view the nearest airports. Select KBJC, and ask for a full-stop landing (you might need to click through several lists before Jeffco is an option). You'll probably get approved for a right base for Runway 29R. Plan for and target to be at pattern altitude of 6,700 feet and slowed down to low cruise by the time you're 5 miles from KBJC. The Baron doesn't have speed brakes, so it's easy to come in with too much airspeed. Make a 360° turn if you must to help slow down. You'll want to be on an extended base in the approach-level configuration (see Figure 21-9).

A TOUCH OF FLAPS

If you want to slow down to a lower low cruise in the Baron, put out the flaps to the approach configuration, but leave the gear up. You'll see about 120 knots for the same power setting. This is handy to share an airport pattern with slower aircraft or buy time getting ready for an instrument approach. You can extend approach flaps any time below 152 knots indicated, just like the landing gear. Full flaps require 110 knots or less.

Figure 21-10: Overshooting final, as is happening here, is a common error transitioning to a faster airplane like a twin.

Now that you're on a wide base, reduce the power to 15 inches of MP, and ensure you're configured for landing. Don't move the mixtures full rich because you'll want them set for maximum power in case you need to go around.

You're going faster for a traffic pattern than you're used to, and you won't slow down much. That means you'll need more room to turn, so watch the landing runway and turn final earlier than you think you'll need to do (see Figure 21-10).

As you roll out on final, line up with the centerline, and put out full flaps. This should slow you to 105 knots (see Figure 21-11). This is your approach speed all the way until you cross over the approach end of the runway. You might need to add power to keep from getting too low. That's fine. Crossing the end of the runway, slowly reduce the power to idle as you continue to descend, and try to touch down at about 85 knots (see Figure 21-12).

586

| PART I | PART II | PART III | PART IV | PART V | PART VI |
| PREFLIGHT | SPORT PILOT | PRIVATE PILOT | INSTRUMENT RATING | COMMERCIAL LICENSE | ATP AND BEYOND |

Figure 21-11: You'll feel like you're coming in too fast and flat, but trust in the numbers. Don't idle the engines too soon, or you'll slow down too much and/or drop like a stone.

If you're having trouble getting the landing right, use the Slew command (Y) and drag the airplane straight back from the runway and up to altitude so you can do a long, straight-in approach. Once you've mastered coming straight in, an airport traffic pattern is easier.

Figure 21-12: This is the slowest landing you'd want to see in the Baron. The wheels should be on the ground by the time you cross under redline. Up to 5 knots faster is fine.

⬇ INSIDE THE GAME

G1000 AND VIRTUAL COCKPIT IN THE BARON

We didn't set up any flights in the G1000 Baron (dubbed the G58 Baron by Raytheon, which owned Beech at the time the new Baron came out). The only real difference between what you've flown on the Mooney is the engine instrument strip on the MFD. You have two engines to monitor, so the system for displaying the information is a bit different. It's highly intuitive, though, so just use Aircraft > Select Aircraft to switch to the G1000 Baron if you want to try it. It's fun to fail items on individual engines and watch the G1000 bring it to your attention.

G1000 or not, the 3D virtual cockpit is outstanding for the Baron. If you have the system resources to display it, we highly recommend doing takeoffs and pattern work in the 3D cockpit. You might still want to show the instruments only for landing, though.

NOTE!

⬇ EASY DOES IT

The real Baron is heavier on the controls than any airplane you've flown so far. This control feel helps avoid overcontrolling the real airplane. Unless you have a great force-feedback system, FSX won't give you this feel, and it's easy to overcontrol the Baron. Make smooth, small corrections as you fly, and you'll be rewarded with a compliant airplane.

BARON ON THE GAUGES

Part of your multiengine training is instrument approaches. They get really interesting when you have one of your two engines failed, but that's for Chapter 23. For now, load Chap_21_ILS_to_KFTG, and you'll fly an ILS with everything working. There is a little turbulence in these clouds, though. It's not much, but it's just enough to keep it fun. (If it's too much, you can choose World > Weather > User-Defined Weather, and click Advanced Weather. Now change the cloud type from Cumulus to Stratus for all stations.)

588

PART I
FIRST FLIGHT

PART II
FIRST PILOT

PART III
PRIVATE PILOT

PART IV
INSTRUMENT RATING

PART V
COMMERCIAL LICENSE

PART VI
ATP AND BEYOND

This approach is the ILS Rwy 26 into the Front Range airport (KFTG), and the plate is on the website at www .wiley.com. The flight starts you at 9,000 feet approaching Denver International Airport. You'll pass by Denver on your way to Front Range. You're on a vector so you can set up for the approach. Just for fun, find out what you should expect at KFTG. Put the ATIS frequency of 119.02 in your COM2, and listen in.

When you've gotten the weather—sounds fun doesn't it?—go ahead and press Direct-To button on your GPS, and select KFTG by typing it in or choosing it from your flight plan. Now you'll have a distance and time estimate to the airport just for reference. Put the ILS frequency of 109.3 in NAV1, and set your OBS on the HSI to the inbound course of 260. Now put the Falcon VOR (FQF) in your NAV2 and the SKIPI locator outer marker (LOM) on your ADF. The ADF is in the avionics stack and is on the frequency of 321. Both signals will show up on a new instrument called a *radio magnetic indicator* (RMI), found on the lower-left corner of the panel.

The RMI has two needles. The green, hollow one shows the bearing to the VOR. The yellow, solid one shows the bearing to the NDB or LOM. Note that the RMI has a compass rose that, like your HSI, turns with your heading. This means you can always see what course you'd have to fly to get to either of these stations. In Figure 21-13, flying a course of 165 would take you to FQF, and flying a course of 126 would take you to SKIPI.

Figure 21-13: Getting yourself set up for the approach in the Baron is similar to the Mooney, except for the RMI.

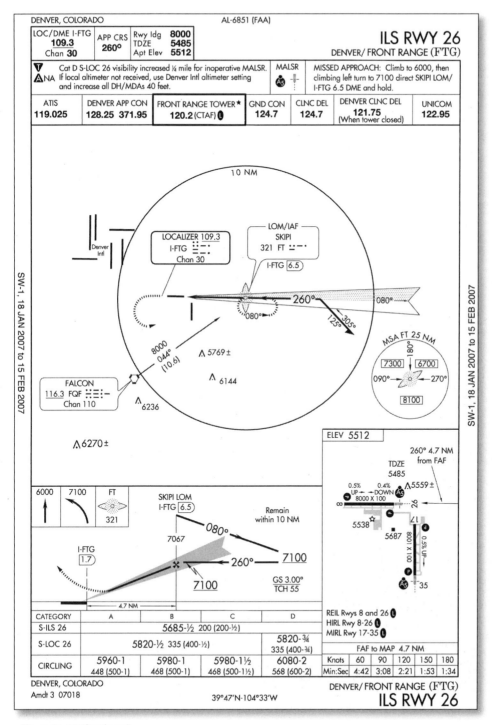

Figure 21-13 (Continued)

590

PART I
PREFLIGHT

PART II
SPORT PILOT

PART III
PRIVATE PILOT

PART IV
INSTRUMENT RATING

PART V
COMMERCIAL LICENSE

PART VI
ATP AND BEYOND

Fly the vectors as you are given them, remaining at high cruise until you are on a base leg to the localizer. Then slow to low cruise. You can also now select and activate your approach on the GPS. You'll still fly the approach using the localizer signal, but the GPS is useful for situational awareness. This is also a good time to verify the HSI is being driven by NAV1 and not the GPS.

After you intercept the localizer and start tracking inbound, watch your speed. If you're going faster than 120 knots, you can extend approach flaps below 152 knots to help slow down. When the glideslope indication is at one quarter scale deflection, as shown in Figure 21-14, drop the gear, extend the flaps to approach setting if you haven't already, and reduce the power to 15 inches as the glideslope centers and you head down for Front Range.

Watch the RMI as you pass over SKIPI. We forgot to tell you to turn on your marker beacons here (although you might have remembered on your own), but since the RMI shows the bearing to both SKIPI and FQF, you can identify crossing SKIPI by being on the 044 bearing from (224 bearing to) FQF or by watching the yellow ADF needle swing from pointing at your nose to your tail.

Figure 21-14: Like the Mooney, speed and power management are key. Once you're on glideslope, you adjust power as necessary to keep 110 knots and pitch to stay on glideslope.

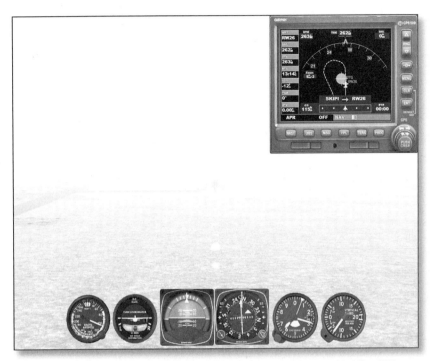

Just like the Mooney, you'll want to press W on the keyboard and then Shift+3 to see your GPS moving map for the end of the approach and landing (see Figure 21-15). If you were flying a nonprecision approach and wanted to level off while looking for the runway, you add power and fly the approach level profile we discussed earlier in this chapter.

Figure 21-15: The key upon breaking out is just extending full flaps and holding 105 until you cross the runway threshold.

STUDENT OF THE CRAFT

START WITH THE DIFFERENCE

If you're carrying more power than you expected, such as 20 inches instead of the expected 18 inches for approach level, transition to approach descent by reducing power by the same difference as you expect. If you expected to go from 18 inches to 15 inches, that's 3 inches. If you actually needed 20 inches in approach level, reduce power from 20 to 17, which is 3 inches. Then adjust further as needed.

DOING PERFORMANCE TAKEOFFS AND LANDINGS

Now that you have a feel for the Baron, it's time to push the envelope a bit. Part of your commercial checkride and your commercial career will require taking the Baron into shorter runways and handling nasty crosswinds. Let's start with the short runways.

592

PART I PREFLIGHT PART II SPORT PILOT PART III PRIVATE PILOT PART IV INSTRUMENT RATING PART V COMMERCIAL LICENSE PART VI ATP AND BEYOND

WHAT MAKES THE FIELD SHORT?

Load the flight Chap_21_Short_1. This puts you at the end of Runway 26 at Boulder Municipal Airport (1V5). There are a few interesting tidbits to note before you take off. First is that this field is 4,100 feet long. OK, we can hear you saying now, "4,100 feet? That's not short." Maybe it's not short for the Cub, but you're in a fully loaded Baron at an elevation of 5,400 feet MSL. There are quite a few buildings at the departure end of this runway, not to mention those mountains in the distance. Suddenly, 4,100 feet seems kind of scant.

Let's see how you do. The procedure will be to hold the brakes and run each engine up to 2000 rpm. Lean the mixture to get peak power (peak rpm, fuel flow, or EGT). Then go full power, and release the brakes.

The short-field rotation is at 87 knots with a climb of 92 knots (V_x) until clearing the obstacles (see Figure 21-16). That's almost a 15° pitch up even at this altitude. (It's more like 18° near sea level.)

Note that 92 knots is well under blueline of 101. If you lose an engine at V_x in the Baron, you will have to put the nose down to gain speed. Why? Because the V_{xse} or V_{yse} is faster than V_x and you won't climb with a single engine at 92 knots. This might cost you altitude that you don't have to spare. What happens then? You crash, that's what. Sorry, sometimes failures are unrecoverable. The odds of the failure happening right then are slim, but if the risk is unacceptable to you, then don't fly your Baron out of Boulder.

Figure 21-16: That would count as using all the runway for takeoff. And this was with a slight headwind.

Get your gear up as soon as you're climbing. You want to climb over obstacles as quickly as possible so you can pitch down a bit and accelerate to a V_y of 105. Climb up to the pattern altitude of 6,300 and fly right traffic for Runway 26 (the pattern is to the right to keep airplanes from flying over town). When you reach 6,300, power back to 2300 rpm and 18 inches, and extend approach flaps. When you're abeam the numbers for Runway 26, drop your gear, reduce the power to 15 inches, and start back down for a landing at Boulder.

Boulder's 4,100 feet might have been tight for takeoff, but landing is easy. A normal landing would do, but you'll practice a short-field landing here. The approach is the same until final, where instead of 105 until crossing the threshold, you maintain 97 knots. Pick a target spot near the runway threshold, and try to hit that spot with your main landing gear. Bring the Baron to a stop as soon as you can. If flown expertly, you can be down and stopped just past the VASI lights, in the first half of the runway.

Figure 21-17: This is not the view you want at rotation speed. Planning for short-field takeoffs is a must, and you should know how late you can abort and still stop when it's clear you won't make it.

Figure 21-18: It's a steep approach to clear the trees, but you can still be stopped by the last taxiway turn.

Now load the flight Chap_21_Short_2. Here you're on the ramp at Glenwood Springs, Colorado (KGWS). The field elevation is just shy of 6,000 feet, and the runway is a mere 3,300 feet long. The winds are calm, so you can take off using either runway. Runway 14 has some trees right off the end, and Runway 32 sends you flying up a canyon in which you'll need to turn around. Pick your poison, and give it a go. Don't forget to lean for peak power. You'll need it. Even so, we expect you'll see a view something like Figure 21-17.

So, that probably didn't go so well. The life-enhancing point here is that *short* is a relative term that varies with the aircraft you're flying, the conditions that day (such as a head-wind), and the load crammed into the airplane.

Can you take off from here in the Baron? You can but not fully loaded. Load the flight Chap_21_Short_3. Here you are at the end of Runway 14 with calm winds again. This time, however, you are the only person aboard, and the fuel tanks are only half full. This should go better, but don't forget to lean for max power and don't dally in getting up the landing gear.

After you're clear of the trees, fol-low the valley southward and climb to 7,000 feet and low cruise. When the valley widens, turn around and head back to KGWS. Slow to ap-proach level, and when appropriate, slow to a final approach speed of 97 knots with full flaps. Land on Run-way 32, but be careful of any trees on the end (see Figure 21-18).

594

PART I	PART II	PART III	PART IV	PART V	PART VI
PRE FLIGHT	SPORT PILOT	PRIVATE PILOT	INSTRUMENT RATING	COMMERCIAL LICENSE	ATP AND BEYOND

STUDENT OF THE CRAFT

THE TEARDROP PATTERN

It's rather an aside for this chapter, but landings at mountain airports often require nonstandard traffic patterns. It's also common for you to take off in one direction and land the other way regardless of wind. It happens when the runway has a significant slope—you take off downhill and land uphill—or some inconvenient object such as a mountain blocks one end of the runway.

Here at KGWS, you might not want to deal with the trees at the end of the Runway 32, but the canyon is too narrow to fly a downwind for 14, especially in a fast aircraft like the Baron. What you would do is fly over the runway and past the airport. Then you'd make a teardrop turn in the canyon and return to land on 14.

Welcome to life in the mountains.

CROSSWIND APPROACHES

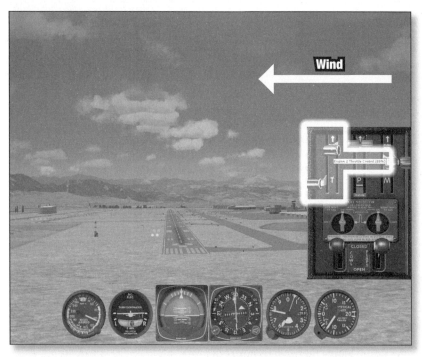

Figure 21-19: When you carry split power, expect to have the upwind engine working at high power because it's providing most of your thrust and lift.

Crosswind approaches in the Baron, or any multiengine airplane, require the same skills you practiced in the single-engine airplanes. You're going faster, which actually helps because you often have greater control authority. Load the flight Chap_21_x-wind. You're on an extended final for Runway 29R at KBJC again, and you're cleared to land. There is an 18-knot direct crosswind from the north (your right side). The Runway 29R ILS is also dialed into your HSI to help you tell you're centered on the final approach path. (You asked to land Runway 2, but it seems they're repainting it today. Too bad.)

First fly the approach using the technique you know: crab into the wind until short final, and then put your upwind wing down and hold opposite rudder. As we noted earlier in this book, the visual picture in FSX isn't quite right for this, but the net effect on the aircraft is close to accurate.

After landing, press Ctrl+; to reset the flight. Make the approach again, but this time, instead of using rudder to balance the turning tendency of your lowered right wing, open just the right throttle some more and close the left throttle some, as shown in Figure 21-19. You'll probably want the power quadrant available to do this. It's Shift+4 for the Baron.

The uneven power of the two engines is doing the same thing as your rudder deflection was, but in the real world, this can be more stable and more comfortable for the pilot. It also tends to make the airplane want to roll toward the high wing, which feels more stable as well.

As you flare for landing, reduce power on the both engines maintaining the power differential until the downwind engine is idle, and then continue reducing power on the upwind engine. Use your rudder to iron out any wiggles of the nose as you do.

This landing with uneven engine power is just a taste of what's coming in Chapter 23. There you'll land with one engine working hard…and the other not working at all.

▼ ACCIDENT CHAIN

ACCIDENT REPORT: DRIVEN TO DISTRACTION

Location: Minden, Nevada

Aircraft: Beech Baron

Injuries: 1 uninjured

"During the approach, the pilot failed to extend the landing gear, and the airplane touched down on the runway with retracted landing gear. The pilot was an airplane mechanic, and he was in the process of preparing the airplane for export. The accident occurred during the first flight following his replacement of both engines' propeller assemblies. On departure, while concentrating on synchronizing the engine's speed, the pilot detected 'a slight smell of electrical burning' in the cockpit. The odor increased on the downwind leg, and the pilot 'expedited' the base leg and believed that he had extended the landing gear. During the landing flare, the stall warning horn sounded, and the propeller blades contacted the runway.

"Subsequently, the Federal Aviation Administration coordinator conducted an examination of the airplane. The airplane was placed on jacks, and the landing gear system was tested. The landing gear was completely cycled three times with positive indications of the gear being up and then in the down position. This was noted by the gear up and down indicator lights and also by the gear mechanical indicator. The starter vibrator was found discolored and charred, indicating the presence of an overheated condition.

"The National Transportation Safety Board determines the probable cause(s) of this accident as follows: the pilot's failure to lower the landing gear during landing approach, which resulted in his inadvertent gear up landing. A factor was his distraction due to a component malfunction."

Continued

596

PART I	PART II	PART III	PART IV	PART V	PART VI
PREFLIGHT	SPORT PILOT	PRIVATE PILOT	INSTRUMENT RATING	COMMERCIAL LICENSE	ATP AND BEYOND

The Baron is a complex aircraft that demands many skills and tasks of a single pilot. This pilot was distracted from task A (synchronizing the engines) by task B (dealing with a suspected fire) and missed task C (extending the landing gear). The result harmed only egos and metal parts. Although it was correct to prioritize the fire over most any other task, the Baron, or any complex aircraft, is unforgiving of fixation or oversight.

KEY POINTS FOR REAL FLYING AND FSX BUILT-INS

The following are some key points from this chapter:

- Practice basic principles of flying multiengine airplanes

- Understand flight profiles for the Beechcraft Baron.

- Practice instrument flight in the Baron.

- Get some exposure to high-altitude and mountain operations.

Here are the lessons and missions to study after reading this chapter:

- *Lessons*: Commercial Pilot Lessons 1 and 2. Note that Rod indicates you can't put in approach flaps until the white arc. This is misleading. Approach flaps at 152 knots is fine. Note that the short-field lesson seems to have a bug where FSX thinks the runway is about 50 feet north (left) of where it appears onscreen.

- *Missions*: Amazon Trek and Aleutian Cargo Run in a seaplane, and Africa Relief in the DC-3 are all good multiengine missions. As with any mission, be prepared for the unexpected to test your skills. To hone your Baron skills further, take a look at some precision flying in the next chapter.

COMMERCIAL FLIGHT MANEUVERS

"DESIGNING AN AIRPLANE IS SCIENCE; FLYING ONE IS AN ART. DON'T LET ANYONE TELL YOU OTHERWISE. ART IS NEVER WRONG; IT JUST SOMETIMES LOOKS FUNNY."

—DAVID DIAMOND

"THE LENGTH OF DEBATE ABOUT A FLIGHT MANEUVER IS ALWAYS INVERSELY PROPORTIONAL TO THE COMPLEXITY OF THE MANEUVER. THUS, IF THE FLIGHT MANEUVER IS SIMPLE ENOUGH, DEBATE APPROACHES INFINITY."

—ROBERT LIVINGSTON

598

PART I	PART II	PART III	PART IV	PART V	PART VI
PREFLIGHT	SPORT PILOT	PRIVATE PILOT	INSTRUMENT RATING	COMMERCIAL LICENSE	ATP AND BEYOND

LOADING AND PERFORMANCE

A commercial pilot needs to know a lot more about an airplane so that paying passengers don't have to worry about safety. In this chapter, you'll learn even more about how to control an aircraft smoothly and safely, but first you'll look at how loading the airplane matters and how it affects performance. Welcome to the world of weight and balance.

WEIGHT

Figure 22-1: In a level, 60° bank, the entire airplane weighs twice as much as when on the ground, so the wings have to provide twice as much lift if you want to maintain altitude.

The weight and balance of an aircraft are actually things real-world private pilots and even sport pilots need to understand, but we've saved them for the "Commercial Certificate" part of this book because they take on more significance and have a much bigger effect when you're flying larger airplanes such as the Beechcraft Baron.

The total weight of an airplane (gross weight) has a significant effect on its performance. A heavy airplane takes longer to get up to rotation speed, and that rotation speed needs to be faster to provide enough lift for the climb. During the climb, a lightweight airplane can go faster or, at the same airspeed, gain altitude faster. During cruise, a heavy airplane requires more lift to maintain altitude; usually that means the wings are at a higher angle of attack, which increases drag as well, keeping the heavy airplane slower than a light airplane.

Those are the obvious issues of weight, but there are more subtle ones. You've learned about G forces and how—in a level turn, for instance—you feel heavier; in fact, at a 60° bank (as shown in Figure 22-1), you'll feel twice as heavy as normal (2 G). So does the airplane. The wings have to provide enough lift to hold up that "twice as heavy" airplane. The aircraft is designed to handle at least 3.8 positive Gs (more for aerobatic airplanes), but that assumes the aircraft is at its maximum certified weight. If you overload your airplane, you're a test pilot.

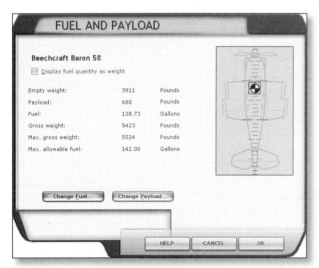

Figure 22-2: The Fuel and Payload page automatically calcu-
lates your aircraft's weight and balance.

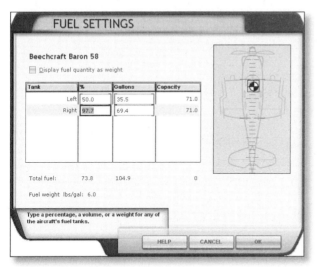

Figure 22-3: Adjust the quantity of fuel in each tank; just remember to keep enough on board to get where you're going!

And don't assume that you could avoid the problem by never doing a steep turn or intentionally
pulling high Gs; turbulence can easily bump you at 3
or 4 Gs for an instant—that's not enough to hurt you
(unless you bang into some part of the cockpit), but
it's enough to hurt the airplane if it is overloaded.

Real-world pilots always have to calculate the
weight and balance of their aircraft before a flight.
Formulas and spreadsheets are available to speed it
up, but you do eventually need to know how it works,
and we can't get deep enough into this subject here
to help you with a real airplane. You can cheat because FSX does a lot of the load calculation work
for you. All you have to do is choose the amount
of fuel you're carrying and how much each passenger weighs, and FSX will tell you whether you're
overweight.

On the Aircraft > Fuel and Payload page, you'll
see the elements that make up the total weight of
the aircraft (see Figure 22-2). Starting with the
empty weight, you add payload (which includes
those passengers plus baggage) and fuel to get the
gross weight. If your (automatically calculated) gross
weight exceeds the maximum gross weight, you get a
warning about how overweight the aircraft is.

The final calculation is the maximum allowable
fuel; if the plane is overweight, this is a suggestion
for how much fuel the airplane can hold without going over the maximum gross weight. You just change
the actual fuel level to match the maximum allowable fuel level: click the Change Fuel button, and you
can adjust the fuel levels either by percentage or by
gallons (see Figure 22-3).

600

PART I
FIRST FLIGHT

PART II
SPORT PILOT

PART III
PRIVATE PILOT

PART IV
INSTRUMENT RATING

PART V
COMMERCIAL LICENSE

PART VI
ATP AND BEYOND

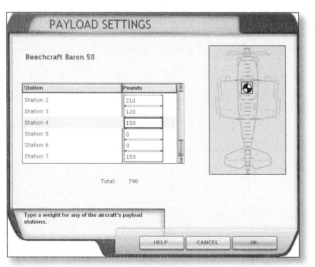

Figure 22-4: As you change the weight at each station (passenger seat and baggage compartment), the total weight changes, but FSX won't tell you that you're overweight until you click OK and return to the Fuel and Payload page.

Back at the Fuel and Payload page, click Change Payload (see Figure 22-4). The payload settings are where you include the weight of the people and baggage on board. The word *station* is used in aviation to mean the distance from the front of the plane to the location of the passenger seat or baggage area. It doesn't show in FSX, but real-world aircraft manuals have a chart showing that, for instance, the pilot seat is at Station 65, which is 65 inches from the front of the airplane. In FSX, Stations 1 and 2 are the two front seats, Stations 3 and 4 are the next seats, and so on. The last station (Station 5 in the Mooney or Station 7 in the Baron, for instance) is the rear baggage area behind the last seats.

CG and Aircraft Performance

In addition to weight, a pilot has to be concerned about balance—specifically, where the airplane's center of gravity (CG) is located. What is CG? It's a mathematical convenience, really. You can think of all the cumulative effects of the empty airplane, humans, cargo, and fuel weights at all those different stations as one lump-sum weight sitting somewhere near the middle of the airplane.

You can picture this if you think about how you might load an airplane: if you're the only one in the plane, the CG is more toward the front. If you put some big people in the back seats and load heavy suitcases into the baggage compartment, then the CG is more toward the rear.

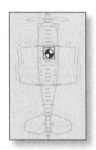

The diagram on the right side of the Fuel and Payload page (Figure 22-5) shows the airplane's CG superimposed on a diagram of the airplane. As you make changes to the weight at each station, you'll see the CG move around. It doesn't cause many problems if the CG is to the left or right of center. It is a very big issue if the CG is far forward or far toward the back (see Figure 22-6).

Figure 22-5: The CG diagram on the right side of the Fuel and Payload page shows the CG symbol moving back and forward as you load or unload the stations.

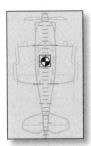

Figure 22-6: Here the CG seems to be about in the middle of the overall range from front to back; actually, the CG is too far back, and the plane cannot even get off the ground.

INSIDE THE GAME
WHERE IS THE BEST CG?

FSX tells you whether you've overloaded the airplane, but it doesn't give you any guidance about whether you've loaded it too far forward, too far back, or just right. That CG diagram is nice, but similar real-world diagrams actually tell you when you're in the legal (and safe) CG range and when you're out of range. The FSX diagram appears to show the proper CG range between the red brackets, but in fact it isn't true. You can load the aircraft so tail heavy that it plunks down on its tail, even though the CG is still within the allowable range shown on the diagram.

That's unfortunate, because it gives you the wrong idea about how important CG is. In the real world, if you fly a slightly overloaded airplane, you'll cause extra stress and wear in the long run, but it probably won't kill you right away. But if you fly a real airplane that is out of CG, you may very well crash on that flight.

There's one more CG problem to deal with: changes in CG during flight. In some airplanes, as fuel is burned, the CG shifts forward or back. In other planes, there is a big weight change when you drop your payload in midair (such as when carrying skydivers or bombs). Therefore, you should calculate your CG for both the takeoff and landing loadings.

602

PART I	PART II	PART III	PART IV	PART V	PART VI
PREFLIGHT	SHORT PILOT	PRIVATE PILOT	INSTRUMENT RATING	COMMERCIAL LICENSE	ATP AND BEYOND

CG has a complement called *center of lift* (CL). You can think of CL as the total lifting force exerted by the wing lumped into a single station along the body of the airplane. The pilot can't change CL. (Well, flap deployment and such affects it, but we'll skip that here.)

CG must stay forward of CL so that the airplane has a natural tendency to nose down, but it can't get too far forward. With a forward CG, the airplane will be "nose heavy." You'll have to pull up harder on the yoke to get it to rotate for climb, and you'll have trouble flaring during landing. Conversely, if the CG is far back, the control force needed for rotation on takeoff (and flare on landing) may be so little that you will pull too hard, the aircraft will pitch up too high, and you'll stall. If you can't pitch the nose forward when the aircraft stalls, it is possible to get the aircraft into a flat spin that cannot be stopped. If CG is ever behind CL, the airplane will nose up all on its own, and you won't have any power to stop it. So, like Goldilocks, you want the CG to be just right—or at least somewhere within the allowable range. That is hard in FSX (see "Where is the Best CG?").

One other interesting effect of CG is that the farther back you move the CG, the faster the plane will go at cruise. You don't want to go too far back, of course, but as long as the CG is near the rear of the allowable range, the drag caused by the lift from the wings will be lower, so your cruise speed will be higher.

⬇ ACCIDENT CHAIN

OVERLOADED AND OUT OF BALANCE

Location: Morganton, North Carolina

Aircraft: Beech 95-B55 Baron

Injuries: 2 fatal, 1 serious, 3 minor

"During the landing, the airplane touched down (bounced) nosewheel first and began to porpoise. Following the second bounce, the airplane pitched nose up, and the pilot initiated a go-around; however, the airplane bounced a third time. After the third bounce, the airplane remained airborne about 6 to 15 feet until it collided with trees beyond the departure end of the runway; then it came to rest inverted.

"Examination of the engines, propellers, and flight controls revealed no evidence of pre-impact failure or malfunction. Calculations showed that at the time of the accident, the gross weight was 192 pounds over the maximum limit, and the center of gravity (CG) was 1.56 inches behind the aft limit.

"The National Transportation Safety Board determines the probable cause(s) of this accident as follows: the pilot's delay in initiating a go-around (aborted landing). Factors relating to the accident were the pilot's failure to ensure proper weight and balance of the airplane and his improper flare and improper recovery from a bounced landing."

Overloading an aircraft is easy to do, because most light planes cannot handle full fuel tanks and passenger seats without exceeding the maximum allowable gross weight. But overloading isn't the only concern—CG is the other. If the CG is outside the allowable range and something happens that requires unexpected maneuvering (such as the bounced landing), the plane may be uncontrollable.

⬇ BY THE BOOK

COMMERCIAL PILOT PTS

During your commercial pilot checkride, the maneuvers you'll be tested on are the same ones you were tested on to become a private pilot. (You'll practice the maneuvers that are new during this chapter's flight.) But the standards are higher; if you want to be paid to fly, you need to be a better pilot.

For instance, when performing a short-field landing, you have to touch down within 100 feet of the specified spot on the runway, rather than the 200-foot allowance you were given for your private pilot checkride. When at cruise, you have to maintain the specified altitude within 100 feet, not 200 feet, and maintain heading within 10°, not 15°.

The rest of the standards you will have to maintain are found in the Commercial Pilot Practical Test Standards (PTS) on the website at `www.wiley.com` and on the Internet from the FAA.

FLIGHT MANEUVERS—EIGHTS ON PYLONS

Commercial pilots need to be able to perform several new maneuvers that demonstrate mastery of an aircraft and the ability to get it to perform safely and competently. The maneuvers don't necessarily replicate typical missions a commercial pilot would have to do but instead are skill and precision maneuvers. They are as follows:

- Steep turns (at least 50° of bank)

- Emergency approach and landing

- Steep spiral

- Chandelle

- Lazy eights

- Eights on pylons

The only maneuver that requires a thorough explanation of aerodynamics before you head to the plane is eights on pylons. We'll explain the rest during the flights.

The eights on pylons maneuver is another ground-reference maneuver like the turns around a point you did in the Cub over Wichita, Kansas, in Chapter 3. You have a wind to deal with, and you're trying to fly around some reference points on the ground, but there is a trick: this time, instead of staying the same distance from the point as you curve around it, you have to keep your wing tip pointed right at it (see Figure 22-7).

604

PART I
PREFLIGHT

PART II
SPORT PILOT

PART III
PRIVATE PILOT

PART IV
INSTRUMENT RATING

PART V
COMMERCIAL LICENSE

PART VI
ATP AND BEYOND

Figure 22-7: Pivotal altitude is the altitude that keeps the ground object right in your line of sight along the wing.

Figure 22-8: Your ground speed is going up (tailwind), so the pivot point is moving behind you.

This maneuver is based on the idea of "pivotal altitude." If you want the airplane to pivot around a particular object on the ground, you want the line from your eyes to the end of the wing tip to point straight at the ground object. For each airspeed, a particular altitude will accomplish the perfect pivot. For example, let's say you wanted to pivot around the end of a runway at 120 knots. The pivotal altitude may be something like 800 feet AGL.

As long as you maintain a constant ground speed, this would be easy. But—and you could see this coming, couldn't you?—there's that pesky wind. When you're flying downwind, your ground speed goes up, and the runway numbers appear to drift behind you, as you can see in Figure 22-8. When you're flying upwind, the runway numbers seem to get ahead of you. The only way to adjust for this is to change your airspeed so that your ground speed stays the same all the way around. If you remember from our discussions of pitch and power in the Cub and in the Mooney, both affect airspeed and rate of climb, but pitch is immediate, while power takes a moment to have an effect. Instead of changing the throttle, which takes time to affect airspeed, you'll use the quicker method of climbing and descending.

The title of this maneuver, *eights on pylons*, comes because you don't just circle around one ground object; you have two of them about a mile apart (see Figure 22-9). As you're finishing a loop around one, cut a diagonal path across the line between the objects, and then roll the other direction and pivot around the other end of the runway.

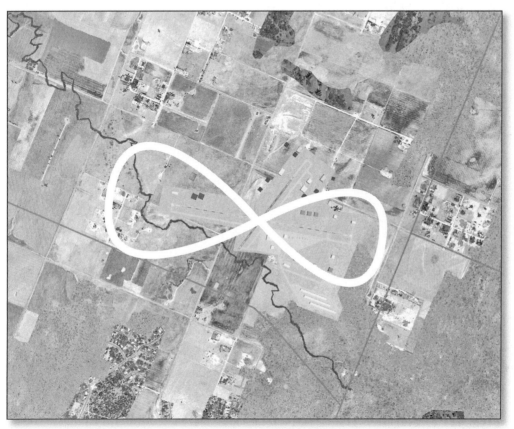

Figure 22-9: The path of eights on pylons is roughly the shape of a figure eight over the ground, stretched out because of wind.

COMMERCIAL FLIGHT MANEUVERS

Pilots training for the Commercial Pilot Certificate have to perform several of the same maneuvers as on the private pilot checkride, but with a few twists. You'll do steep turns and stalls in the Beech Baron. We've also added some interesting weight-and-balance experiments that you would never do in real life (unless you become a test pilot) but are a good challenge in FSX.

But there is also a set of maneuvers that you have to perform only if you're getting a Commercial Pilot Certificate in a single-engine airplane. So, we'll give you back your Mooney Bravo for a couple of flights.

606

| PART I | PART II | PART III | PART IV | PART V | PART VI |
| PREFLIGHT | SPORT PILOT | PRIVATE PILOT | INSTRUMENT RATING | COMMERCIAL LICENSE | ATP AND BEYOND |

SEE THE MOVIES

The website at www.wiley.com has videos of some of these maneuvers so you can see a demonstration before you have to do it yourself.

STEEP TURNS

Figure 22-10: A steep-banked turn of 50° looks like this in the Baron.

You last practiced steep turns during your private pilot training in the Cessna 172. They're part of every aircraft checkout, because each model of airplane behaves slightly differently when pulled into a steep turn, and the Baron is no exception. Load the flight Chap_22_ME_Maneuvers, which begins at 7,500 feet northeast of KBJC (Jeffco) near Denver, Colorado.

As you may recall from your sport pilot and private pilot training, steep turns are done at a 45° bank all the way around in a 360° turn. However, commercial pilots are held to a higher standard: you have to maintain at least a 50° bank all the way around (see Figure 22-10).

Steep turns are performed no faster than the maneuvering speed of the plane, which in the Baron is 156 knots. You want to stay below that, so configure for low-speed cruise as you do your clearing turns. During the steep turn, judge your 50° bank angle, maintain your nose level (to maintain altitude) by looking outside at the horizon, and glance at your attitude indicator to make sure you're getting a 50° angle. Don't forget to add some power to maintain airspeed—it could take as much as 5 inches of MP on such a steep turn.

Once you get around to your original heading, roll immediately into a turn the other direction. Practice until you can meet the Commercial Pilot PTS: maintain at least a 50° bank, hold altitude within 100 feet, hold airspeed within 10 knots, and end each turn within 10° of the heading on which you started.

Slow Flight and Stalls

The procedures for slow flight and stalls in a twin are the same as in a single-engine airplane. We practice them to learn how each airplane behaves near the stall so that we can avoid a stall (and its much more dangerous child, the spin) during nontraining flights.

The aerodynamics of slow flight and stalls on a wing are complex, and FSX (like most such simulators) has a tough time modeling them. Twin-engine aerodynamics are even more complicated, because the propellers blow air right over each wing and can greatly affect the lift when power is changed. Nonetheless, it is worth practicing in FSX so that in a real twin-engine airplane you are better prepared (see Figure 22-11).

Figure 22-11: In slow flight, it's really hard to see over the instrument panel in any airplane; use the minimal panel for the Baron.

You can use the flight Chap_22_ME_Maneuvers to practice slow flight and stalls, but 7,500 feet is pretty close to the ground for stalls. Climb up to 8,500 or so while slowing down. For slow flight, a good airspeed to maintain in the Baron is 90 knots with flaps full and landing gear down. (Don't ever go below V_{mc} of 84 knots.)

Weight and Balance Flight Testing

Because you're training to be a commercial pilot, we'll put you to work testing your aircraft. You're going to see how the Baron behaves in two configurations: with a forward CG and with a rearward CG.

Load the flight Chap_22_CG_Test, which starts with the Baron at the hold-short position on the runway, as shown in Figure 22-12. (Test pilots don't have time to waste sitting on the ramp!) Your first flight is with a forward CG, so choose Aircraft > Fuel and Payload, and set the following conditions:

608

| PART I | PART II | PART III | PART IV | PART V | PART VI |
| PREFLIGHT | SPORT PILOT | PRIVATE PILOT | INSTRUMENT RATING | COMMERCIAL LICENSE | ATP AND BEYOND |

- *Fuel*: 25 gallons each tank (50 gallons total—300 pounds)

- *Station 1*: Your personal weight, plus 10 pounds of flight equipment such as charts, headset, and so on

- *Stations 2–7*: Nothing

Figure 22-12: The Baron is ready for some test flights. On the left is the view with a forward CG; on the right, the Baron is loaded with a rearward CG. The Baron tilts up with weight in back.

Test pilots are also scientists, so here are the parameters you need to notice as you're flying:

- Elevator force/movement needed for rotation

- Runway distance needed for takeoff

- Ease of maintaining climb attitude

- Pitch attitude needed to maintain cruise climb airspeed

- Elevator Trim Tab position needed to maintain cruise climb airspeed

- Climb rate during cruise climb

- Cruise airspeed when cruising at 9,500 feet MSL at high-cruise configuration

- Elevator force/movement needed for rotation

The flight is relatively simple: normal takeoff, cruise climb to 9,500 feet, accelerate and maintain high-cruise speed, return to the airport, and perform a normal landing.

Try the procedure again, this time with a rear CG:

- *Fuel*: 25 gallons each tank (50 gallons total—300 pounds)

- *Station 1*: Your personal weight, plus 10 pounds of flight equipment

- *Stations 2–4*: Nothing

- *Stations 5 and 6*: 300 pounds of sandbags in each seat

- *Station 7*: 300 pounds of sandbags in the baggage compartment

Now perform the same flight profile, and record the key parameters listed earlier. Any differences? Besides the numbers, did it feel any different to control the Baron? We've discovered that many pilots who train with just themselves and their CFI in the cockpit (low weight and forward CC) are surprised by the aircraft's behavior when they go out with their friends on board (maximum gross weight and rear CG). It's good to practice both ways when training on a new aircraft.

SINGLE ENGINE–ONLY MANEUVERS

Five of the maneuvers in the commercial pilot checkride are necessary only if you're taking your checkride in a single-engine aircraft. Let's pull the Mooney Bravo out of the hangar and work on these maneuvers.

STEEP SPIRAL

Combine a constant-radius turn around a point (as you did in Chapter 3) with the engine-idle emergency descent (from Chapter 6), and what do you get? The steep spiral.

This flight, Chap_22_SE_Maneuvers, begins high over the Jeffco airport (see Figure 22-13). Your task will be to circle over the Runway 20 numbers so that your ground track maintains a perfect circle with the same radius around the numbers, as you descend from 9,500 to 6,000 feet.

As usual on this kind of maneuver, there is a wind blowing you one way, so you'll have to adjust your bank angle to maintain a constant horizontal distance from the runway numbers, but don't exceed 60° of bank (see Figure 22-14).

As you descend, adjust your pitch to prevent the plane from going faster than the maneuvering speed of 156 knots.

If you want to add a little more challenge at the end, try to leave the engine idling and do a power-off landing on Runway 20.

610

| PART I | PART II | PART III | PART IV | PART V | PART VI |
| PREFLIGHT | SPORT PILOT | PRIVATE PILOT | INSTRUMENT RATING | COMMERCIAL LICENSE | ATP AND BEYOND |

Figure 22-13: The flight Chap_22_SE_Maneuvers is the start for several maneuvers you need to practice for your commercial checkride.

Figure 22-14: As you descend, try to stay a constant horizontal distance from the runway numbers.

EMERGENCY APPROACH AND LANDING

Figure 22-15: Chap_22_Power_Off puts you in the uncomfortable position of having the engine stopped, and you have to land safely on the runway.

The emergency approach and landing is just like the power-off descent you practiced for your Sport Pilot Certificate, except that time you just headed for any open field and then broke off the approach and climbed again once you proved you could land if you had to land. This time, you have to land.

Start the flight Chap_22_Power_Off (see Figure 22-15). Take a quick look around to get your bearings, and then unpause FSX. The engine has stopped, and you need to get the Mooney on a runway. In fact, you need to get the Baron on a specific spot on the runway: on the aiming-point markers (see Figure 22-16). These lines are about 100 feet long, and you actually have to land within 200 feet of your target, so if you miss them by a little bit, you will still pass the checkride.

Figure 22-16: To successfully complete the power-off landing, you must land on the aiming-point markers.

As with all power-off situations, use the ABCs: *airspeed* on best glide speed (115 knots), *best* field (that'd be Jeffco), and *checklist*. You won't try to restart the engines because you don't have time. Your landing gear is down, but the flaps are retracted right now. The trick will be deciding when to put the flaps down.

Don't try to make a normal traffic pattern, because you can fly that pattern only with engine power. This will be a much tighter pattern; in fact, you might decide to turn your base leg soon after you get the plane descending at best glide speed.

You need to fly the base leg in such as way that, when you get to final approach, you're much higher than normal; without power, you'll be losing altitude fast. At the same time, you can't overshoot the landing spot; you'll need to start adding flaps when the time comes to steeply drop to the runway and land. Sure, there's plenty of runway, and if this were a real emergency, you'd land wherever you could on the runway—even running off the end if you couldn't stop. But for training purposes, you need to land on the touchdown zone markers (shown in Figure 22-16).

As always, practice this maneuver until you can safely land within the proper area on the runway. If you're having trouble, perhaps we forgot to mention you have to contend with some wind!

CHANDELLES

A *chandelle* is a maneuver where you reverse course 180° while at the same time making a maximum performance climb. Load Chap_22_SE_Maneuvers again to begin the chandelle in the Mooney.

It's actually easier to explain how to do it than it is to explain what it looks like:

1. Turn to a heading of 030° at 9,500 feet in low cruise configuration (but with prop at 2400 rpm).

2. Roll briskly to the left to a 30° bank.

612

PART I	PART II	PART III	PART IV	PART V	PART VI
PREFLIGHT	SPORT PILOT	PRIVATE PILOT	INSTRUMENT RATING	COMMERCIAL LICENSE	ATP AND BEYOND

3. As soon as you're banked, start smoothly pulling back on the yoke to pitch up, and at the same time increase throttle to 35 inches; throughout this part of the turn, your bank needs to stay at 30°, but your pitch must be constantly increasing.

4. By the time you get turned 90° from your starting point (heading 300), your pitch angle should be about 10°. Maintain that 10° pitch through the rest of the maneuver; however, start smoothly and slowly decreasing your bank angle.

5. Your goal is to reach the 180° point (heading 210) exactly when your wings roll level and at the same time your speed slows just to the clean stall speed (just before the stall horn starts to sound), as shown in Figure 22-17. Whatever altitude you are at that point, maintain it by slowly lowering the nose and accelerating back to low-cruise speed. Bring the power back to low cruise once you get up to speed.

Figure 22-17: By the time you get completely turned around in the chandelle, you should be slowed almost to the stall speed.

STUDENT OF THE CRAFT

DEAD-END CANYON TURN

The chandelle is similar to an important emergency maneuver called a *canyon turn* but is different in a couple of significant ways. The canyon turn is used if you're flying up a valley or canyon that turns out to be a dead-end and you can't get enough altitude in time to climb over the ridge.

In such a case, you need to turn around; the problem is that the sides of the canyon are closing in and you might not have room to turn.

> The trick to the canyon turn is based on two principles: first, the slower you go, the smaller the turn radius when turning; and second, if you unload the wings (by briskly pushing the yoke forward), your stall speed goes down, and you can avoid a stall.
>
> So the first thing you do is slow down so your turn will be tighter: the quickest way to do that is to pull up and start a steep, high G, climbing turn. But you don't want to stall, so as soon as your speed starts decreasing, you need to push forward on the yoke to reduce the Gs and let the nose pitch down as you continue to turn. Let's hope at this point you will be enough around the turn that you're going downhill and out of danger as you roll back to wings level.
>
> This is one of those challenges that is part of mountain-flying training and is much safer in a flight simulator than real life. Unfortunately, the aerodynamics of such turns are so tricky that flight simulators cannot perfectly replicate an aircraft's behavior. But it's still a lot of fun to try in FSX!

Sounds easy, right? It isn't. As you slow down, the elevator becomes less and less able to hold your the airplane at the pitch you set, so you'll have to pull the yoke a little bit more. It's the same with the bank angle: you need to hold 30° for the first half of the turn and then slowly decrease bank; however, the slower you go, the less effective the ailerons are, so you have to adjust as you go.

In addition, the 10° pitch is a general guideline; you'll have to experiment a bit to find the pitch that makes the maneuver work. If it's too steep, you'll stall before you get to the 180° heading; if it's too shallow, you won't slow down by that time. (As before, you can't actually get so slow the stall horn starts beeping; FSX airplanes immediately drop altitude when that happens, unlike real airplanes that give you a couple of knots of safety margin.)

And don't forget the cardinal rule of maneuvers like this: you have to stay in coordinated flight, with the inclinometer ball centered at all times so that you stay away from spins.

You need to be able to chandelle to the left and to the right, so practice both ways.

LAZY EIGHTS

Commercial pilots are very comfortable with their airplanes; they understand much more than lesser-skilled pilots what it takes to get the airplane to do what they want. A *lazy eight* is a precision maneuver that can really show how well you know your airplane. (Or it will show, in very obvious ways, when you don't know how to fly the airplane well.)

The term *lazy eight* comes from the sideways-eight shape the airplane's nose makes in the sky during this maneuver. (Really, it's the infinity symbol ∞, but for some reason early pilots didn't want to call this the "infinite maneuver.") But it's hard to show even in a photo like Figure 22-18, because the aircraft nose points over a huge expanse of sky. Figure 22-19 shows the maneuver from outside the airplane, which might help you visualize it.

614

PART I	PART II	PART III	PART IV	PART V	PART VI
PREFLIGHT	SPORT PILOT	PRIVATE PILOT	INSTRUMENT RATING	COMMERCIAL LICENSE	ATP AND BEYOND

Figure 22-18: The nose of the airplane moves around the sky in a pattern like a sideways eight—thus the name of the maneuver.

Figure 22-19: This 3D view of the lazy-eight flight path is the best representation we can give in a photo; you really have to just try it to see how it works.

As before, start with the flight Chap_22_SE_Maneuvers, level at 9,500 feet, at heading 030, and at low-cruise speed in the Mooney. Find an obvious landmark off your left wing. Then follow these steps:

1. Slowly increase pitch attitude, and even more slowly start banking to the left.

2. When you're 45° of heading from where you started (345° heading), your bank angle should be about 15°, but your pitch attitude should be about 20° (the maximum it will get during the maneuver). Your airspeed will be very low at this point—just above stall. Start letting the pitch drop slowly, but keep increasing the bank.

3. When you're 90° from where you started (300° heading), with your landmark dead ahead, your pitch should be level, and your bank should be 30°—the maximum it will ever get. Keep lowering the pitch (below level), but start reversing the bank.

4. When you're 135° from where you started (255° heading), your pitch should be the lowest it ever gets—about 10° low; start pitching up. However, the left bank should be back to only about 15°—keep lowering the bank bit by bit.

5. When you're 180° from where you started (210° heading), your pitch should be level, and your bank should be 0 also. Your airspeed and altitude should have returned to where they were when you started, although you're facing the opposite direction.

6. Without stopping, reverse the entire process: slowly pitch up, followed by an even slower roll to the right.

7. At the 45° point (maximum pitch up), start lowering the nose, but continue rolling right.

8. At the 90° point (maximum bank, level pitch), let the nose slide down, and start decreasing the bank.

9. At the 135° point (maximum pitch down), start raising the pitch, and continue decreasing the right bank.

10. Roll out and level out exactly on your original heading of 030° at the starting altitude of 9,500 and starting airspeed.

As usual, this maneuver is done in coordinated flight at all times. More important, though, the pitch and bank should *never* stop changing. Even when you're getting close to level pitch or roll, they should still be changing a little bit. To do this well, you need to really take your time; it should be done smoothly and almost lazily (perhaps *that's* why it's called the lazy eight!), although you'll be actually working hard all the way through.

If you noticed, the only controls you needed to adjust throughout the maneuver were the yoke and rudder pedals; everything else stays the same. But the amount of force on the controls needed to make the plane do what you want is constantly changing, so you'll be constantly moving the yoke and the rudders.

This maneuver is so unexpectedly tough that many pilots don't like to practice it, but once you can successfully fly a lazy eight, you have a much better feel for your aircraft and will be a safer, smoother pilot. And your paying passengers will appreciate that even more!

EIGHTS ON PYLONS

You're going to use a runway at nearby Erie Municipal Airport (48V) for this maneuver. Usually you wouldn't do ground-reference maneuvers so close to an airport because it would interfere with other airplanes. But FSX traffic is light enough that you probably won't see any other planes, and this way you'll have good reference points even if you have to set your graphics display set on low quality scenery.

Load Chap_22_Eights, which begins at the start of the long runway (Runway 33) at 48V. Take off, and climb to 6,000 feet MSL, which is about 850 feet AGL. Circle left back toward the airport, with the goal of lining up with the short runway (about heading 090). Configure for low cruise.

After you cross over the big runway, roll to the right so that you can see the numbers for Runway 33 over your right wing (see Figure 22-20). Adjust your airspeed (by varying your altitude) to maintain the numbers in the same spot over the wing: pitch down (which causes you to speed up) if the numbers start moving forward of the wing; pitch up to slow down if they drift behind the wing.

616

PART I
PREFLIGHT

PART II
SPORT PILOT

PART III
PRIVATE PILOT

PART IV
INSTRUMENT RATING

PART V
COMMERCIAL LICENSE

PART VI
ATP AND BEYOND

When you come back around almost 90° to the big runway, roll level, and look left: as soon as the other end of the runway (numbered 15) is just about lined up with your left wing, roll left, and keep the numbers just above your left wing.

Now that you have a good feel for the Mooney and the Baron, it's time to fly the Baron like the Mooney—with only one engine!

Figure 22-20: This would be a great way to keep an eye on the pivot point—and in FSX you can do it this way. But also try looking from the cockpit, because that's more realistic.

KEY POINTS FOR REAL FLYING AND FSX BUILT-INS

The following are some key points from this chapter:

- Understand the performance issues caused by aircraft weight and balance.

- Gain experience with commercial pilot maneuvers.

Here are the lessons and missions to study after reading this chapter:

- *Lessons*: Commercial Pilot Lesson 3 is all about a double-engine failure (most of which you learned in Chapter 6), and the Solo Flight—Engine Failure lesson is a double-engine failure in the Baron, which is a good review for the flights in this chapter.

- *Missions*: None of the missions directly relates to this chapter.

FLYING WITH ONE FEATHERED

> "WHEN ONE [ENGINE] FAILS, THERE IS ALWAYS A THIN LINE BETWEEN POSSIBLE AND IMPOSSIBLE, BETWEEN SUCCESS AND FAILURE. THAT'S WHY TWINS HAVE A FATAL-ACCIDENT RATE BECAUSE OF ENGINE FAILURE THAT IS TWICE AS HIGH AS THE RATE FOR SINGLES."
>
> —RICHARD COLLINS

618

| PART I | PART II | PART III | PART IV | PART V | PART VI |
| PREFLIGHT | SPORT PILOT | PRIVATE PILOT | INSTRUMENT RATING | COMMERCIAL LICENSE | ATP AND BEYOND |

ONE ENGINE DOWN

There's a cliché in multiengine flying that says the purpose of the remaining engine is to carry the airplane to the crash site. That's only half in jest. Losing an engine in the cruise section of flight is usually not that big a deal—well, OK, it's always a big deal, but it's usually not dangerous. Losing an engine while climbing away from the ground is often deadly.

The Beechcraft Baron is one of the few light twins that will climb reasonably well on one engine. You've got this in your favor. The real Baron, especially the older, straight-tail Baron, has a small vertical fin and rudder for its power. As you'll see in this chapter, a small vertical surface makes it more susceptible to loss of control when an engine unexpectedly quits.

SINGLE-ENGINE AERODYNAMICS

When an engine fails in a twin, everything gets worse. There is a 50 percent reduction in power that, as we discussed in Chapter 21, will result in a 70–90 percent reduction of climb rate. What we have not looked at as much is that this power is also asymmetrically distributed. This causes a host of problems.

WHAT A DRAG

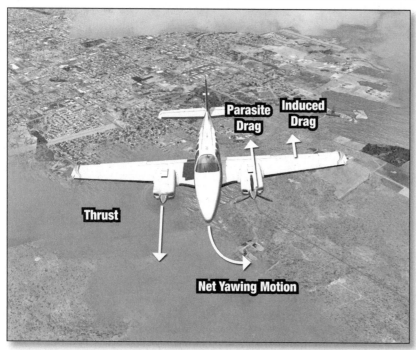

Let's assume the engine on the left wing quits. The propeller that was being spun by the motor will keep spinning, but now it's the airflow passing over the propeller blades that is spinning the propeller. This creates significant drag on the left side of the airplane (see Figure 23-1). The drag will exacerbate the problem of lost lift. Not only do you have less lift to use for climbing, but you also have more drag to overcome, which means you need even more lift than normal to keep climbing.

The drag is also off-center in that it's acting only on the left wing. This means the airplane will try to yaw to the left; that is, the nose will swing toward the dead engine. The thrust coming

Figure 23-1: The total yaw is a combination of the lost lift, the added drag, and any increase in adverse yaw as you try to raise that wing.

from the good engine makes this worse. Rather than pulling along the centerline of the airplane, the good engine is pulling from out on one wing. It will also try to yaw the airplane toward the dead engine.

What's your reaction? You stomp some right rudder, of course. This is a good plan and will stop the nose from swinging, but that heavily deflected rudder is even more drag. Now you're sinking faster…see how this is starting to add up?

ROLL ME OVER

If all that yawing wasn't bad enough, the airplane will also try to roll toward the dead engine. Part of the roll is just a factor of the yaw. You already saw, when you first started your training, that just deflecting the rudder will start the airplane skidding in a yaw but will also start a roll in the direction of the turn.

The failed-engine scenario is a bit worse, though, because the wing area directly behind a running engine actually produces extra lift from the accelerated air flowing through the propeller. Kill the engine, and this bonus lift becomes inhibited lift because the windmilling propeller actually disrupts the airflow over the wing. Now you have significantly different amounts of lift on the two wings, which causes a rolling moment toward the dead engine (see Figure 23-2).

You're ready for this too, so you turn the yoke to counter the roll. That's fine except the increased lift from the aileron creates some adverse yaw, which adds to the yaw toward the dead engine.

Now you're sinking and yawing and rolling. You need more power to at least stem the altitude loss. The only way to do this is to bring the good engine up to full power if it wasn't there already. Of course, adding power to the running engine just makes all the discrepancies we just discussed even worse.

Figure 23-2: Although the yaw is what you notice first, it's the roll that's really dangerous.

620

PART I	PART II	PART III	PART IV	PART V	PART VI
PREFLIGHT	SPORT PILOT	PRIVATE PILOT	INSTRUMENT RATING	COMMERCIAL LICENSE	ATP AND BEYOND

⬇ STUDENT OF THE CRAFT

CENTERLINE THRUST

Designers have tried to reap the added safety of having two engines without the dangers of asymmetrical thrust. Usually this means mounting the two engines along the centerline of the airplane with one in the nose (like a single-engine airplane) that pulls and one in the tail that pushes. Usually this means a creative tail configuration to accommodate a spinning propeller.

The Cessna 337 was one of the most successful airplanes of this type, but even it was plagued by overheating problems with the rear engine and noise in the cabin.

The latest attempt at this design is the Adam Aircraft A500. It's too early to tell whether the A500 design will truly deliver on twin redundancy at single-engine simplicity, but so far the outlook is good.

It's interesting to note that the demands of flying a traditional twin with wing-mounted engines are so different from a centerline thrust design that pilots getting their multiengine rating in a centerline-thrust airplane will have a restriction on their license saying "limited to centerline-thrust airplanes only."

YOUR CRITICAL ENGINE

On the majority of propeller-driven, twin-engine airplanes, losing the left engine is more dangerous than losing the right engine. This is for the same reason that single-engine airplanes turn left when they're climbing: because the engine rotates clockwise from the pilot's point of view. You'll remember that this is called "p-factor," where the descending blade, which is on the right side of the airplane, has a greater angle of attack, and therefore a greater thrust, than the ascending blade on the left side of the airplane.

On a twin, both engines have some asymmetrical thrust in a climb—and, yes, the twin will wander left in the climb with both engines running—but it's worse for the right engine.

Picture the Baron from above (see Figure 23-3). The descending blade of the right propeller is farther from the center of the airplane and has more of a lever arm to apply its yawing force. So if the left engine fails and leaves you with only the right engine for the climb, you'll need more rudder force to keep flying straight ahead than if the right engine had failed and you were climbing using only the left engine. Because the failure of the left engine creates a more hazardous situation, the left engine is thought of as the critical engine.

Figure 23-3: The more power and nose-up pitch, the greater the impact of p-factor and the more critical the difference between losing a right or left engine.

Some aircraft have counter-rotating propellers. With very few exceptions, counter-rotating propellers both rotate toward the fuselage, so the yawing effect of the engine loss is at least minimized. On these airplanes each engine is equally "critical." They also have no turning tendency in a climb with both engines running.

↓ WHEN YOU WANT ASYMMETRICAL THRUST

An oddball twin-engine airplane in many ways is the P-38 WWII fighter. Its two engines both rotate away from the fuselage, making an engine-out worse. This design was an attempt to correct some aeronautical problems with the P-38, but pilots discovered that they could use it to help the fighter turn tighter. The P-38 was fast, but not particularly maneuverable.

V_{mc} AND THE UNCONTROLLED ROLL

As we said in Chapter 21, V_{mc} is defined as the minimum controllable airspeed with the critical engine inoperative and is important enough to be shown as a big red line on the airspeed indicator. Below V_{mc} there isn't enough rudder authority to prevent the yaw—and, much more important, roll—toward the dead engine. An airplane flying below V_{mc} with full power on only one engine might roll toward its dead engine and crash without being able to prevent it (see Figure 23-4).

622

PART I
PREFLIGHT

PART II
SPORT PILOT

PART III
PRIVATE PILOT

PART IV
INSTRUMENT RATING

PART V
COMMERCIAL LICENSE

PART VI
ATP AND BEYOND

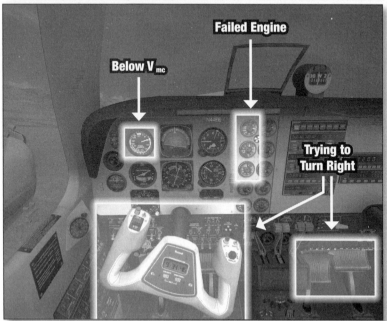

Figure 23-4: Don't go here. You're better off reducing the good engine to idle and putting the airplane into the trees ahead of you than experiencing a V_{mc} roll.

That definition glosses over some details, though. Many factors affect V_{mc}. The farther aft the center of gravity, the higher the V_{mc} becomes because the rudder has less of a leverage arm to counter the yawing motion. Having landing gear extended would lower V_{mc} because the gear would act like a vertical fin helping to stabilize the airplane. You can read the "The Full Scoop on V_{mc}" for the full list of what goes into V_{mc}, but for our purposes, we'll say that the published redline is the highest V_{mc} the Baron will see. Actual V_{mc} might occur at a lower airspeed, but by never being airborne below V_{mc} (in a real Baron anyway), we won't risk the V_{mc} roll.

So, you might wonder why you can't just reduce the power on the good engine if the aircraft starts to roll. Wouldn't that stop the roll and let you level the wings? Sure it would. It would also stop you from climbing, which could be a serious problem with an engine failure near the ground. It would still be preferable to crash land with the wings level and some control than to hit inverted with one engine screaming at full throttle.

There is a dangerous misconception, though, that develops in flight training with V_{mc} on this very question. Most of the light trainers that people use for flight training have low-power engines and big rudders. The V_{mc} roll is slow, and a power reduction combined with a healthy dose of rudder will easily stop the excursion. These trainers also have low stall speeds, so V_{mc} is well above the stalling speed of the airplane.

Higher-performance airplanes, including the Baron, have higher stall speeds and a snappier V_{mc} roll. They are also more likely to be under their gross weight just because they can carry bigger payloads but often fly without all those seats filled. They might be close to the stall speed when the V_{mc} yaw and roll hits, and the yawing motion could stall the wing on the inside of the turn. This is the setup for a spin. Spins in many light twins are difficult or impossible to recover from.

The moral to the story is to respect that redline on all real-world airplanes!

↓ BY THE BOOK

FULL SCOOP ON V_{MC}

Here's the actual text from FAR 23.149, *Minimum control speed*. As you can see, the details vary depending on the airplane. Overall, though, these criteria create a worst-case scenario and yield the highest V_{mc} the airplane will see. That's the number designated as redline and put on the airspeed indicator. There is also a V_{mcg}, which is the minimum controllable airspeed when the aircraft is still on the ground. This is more an issue with large, transport-category aircraft with their huge jet engines.

(a) V_{mc} is the calibrated airspeed at which, when the critical engine is suddenly made inoperative, it is possible to maintain control of the airplane with that engine still inoperative and thereafter maintain straight flight at the same speed with an angle of bank of not more than 5°. The method used to simulate critical engine failure must represent the most critical mode of power plant failure expected in service with respect to controllability.

(b) V_{mc} for takeoff must not exceed 1.2 VS1, where VS1 is determined at the maximum takeoff weight. V_{mc} must be determined with the most unfavorable weight and center of gravity position and with the airplane airborne and the ground effect negligible, for the takeoff configuration(s) with

(1) Maximum available takeoff power initially on each engine;

(2) The airplane trimmed for takeoff;

(3) Flaps in the takeoff position(s);

(4) Landing gear retracted; and

(5) All propeller controls in the recommended takeoff position throughout.

(c) For all airplanes except reciprocating engine-powered airplanes of 6,000 pounds or less maximum weight, the conditions of paragraph (a) of this section must also be met for the landing configuration with

(1) Maximum available takeoff power initially on each engine;

(2) The airplane trimmed for an approach, with all engines operating, at VREF, at an approach gradient equal to the steepest used in the landing distance demonstration of Sec. 23.75;

Continued

624

PART I	PART II	PART III	PART IV	PART V	PART VI
PREFLIGHT	SPORT PILOT	PRIVATE PILOT	INSTRUMENT RATING	COMMERCIAL LICENSE	ATP AND BEYOND

(3) Flaps in the landing position;

(4) Landing gear extended; and

(5) All propeller controls in the position recommended for approach with all engines operating.

(d) A minimum speed to intentionally render the critical engine inoperative must be established and designated as the safe, intentional, one-engine-inoperative speed, V_{SSE}.

(e) At V_{mc}, the rudder pedal force required to maintain control must not exceed 150 pounds, and it must not be necessary to reduce power of the operative engine(s). During the maneuver, the airplane must not assume any dangerous attitude, and it must be possible to prevent a heading change of more than 20°.

ENGINE-OUT PROCEDURES

Exact engine-out procedures vary from aircraft to aircraft, but right thing to do is generally the same in most light twin-engine airplanes. This is the procedure you'll use in the Baron.

ALL FORWARD

When an engine fails in flight, the nose will drop, and the aircraft will yaw and roll. You'll instinctively do the first correct step: maintain control with pitch, rudder, and roll.

More specifically, you'll pitch as necessary to maintain altitude (or your current climb or descent as appropriate), but you won't fly slower than a blueline of V_{yse}. If the airplane reaches V_{yse}, you'll pitch to maintain that speed and accept whatever rate of descent you get. You'll also use your rudder to keep the nose pointing straight ahead and whatever aileron input you need to keep the wings level for the moment.

You just lost half your power, and you might not even be sure which engine it was. You'd be surprised how intuitive correcting your heading with rudder and roll can be. You don't think about it; you just do it. Since you're not certain which engine it is, you'll push both throttles to full power, followed by both prop controls to full power. This should give maximum power on the good engine and have no effect on the windmilling one.

Next you'll move both mixture controls to max power. This might be full forward, but it might mean leaving them put. It's often not a bad idea to move them a bit forward no matter what just in case you had them too lean and that caused the engine stoppage.

If you have gear and flaps extended, raise them now to reduce your total drag.

RAISE THE DEAD

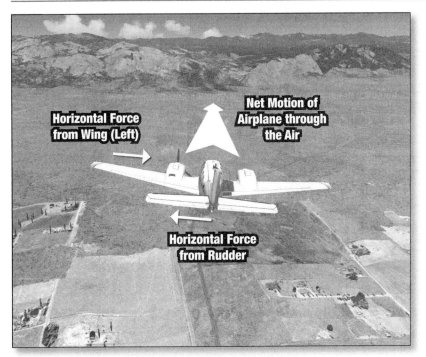

Figure 23-5: It's only a slight bank. The small horizontal component of lift balances the rudder's horizontal force, and the net result is the airplane actually flies straight through the air with less drag.

After checking to see that you're still flying straight and aren't about to hit anything, you can better your situation by banking the airplane slightly toward the good engine. Some folks will tell you to bank exactly 5°. This is hogwash. You want to bank enough to eliminate the sideslip through the air caused by the deflected rudder. Although it's hard to tell where this point is without a yaw-sensing device on the airplane, you get a feel for it in the real plane. It's often just a couple degrees of bank, as shown in Figure 23-5.

If you bank the right way, you'll feel the rudder pressure decrease, and the airplane will track straighter through the air. The ball in the inclinometer under the turn coordinator will be about ½ a ball width off center, but that's just fine.

If you bank the wrong way, you'll feel that more rudder is needed. In fact, as you bank toward the dead engine, you're increasing V_{mc} at the rate of about 3 knots per degree of bank.

SECURE THE ENGINE

Now it's time to identify which engine is down, verify that you have it right, and then attempt to either restart the engine or secure it.

Retard the throttle on the engine you think has failed. If you retard the wrong throttle, it will be immediately clear because you'll rapidly have no engine power at all. If the throttle has no effect, you can assume you have the dead engine identified.

Now you must take a look around and decide whether you have time to troubleshoot the problem. If you do, you'd attempt a restart just as you did in previous chapters. Let's assume you don't have that luxury. You're near an airport, barely holding altitude, and need to land. Pull the prop control for the dead engine *halfway* back, and verify you are moving the correct prop control both by looking at the throttle quadrant and by feeling that the available power didn't diminish. Now pull the prop control the rest of the way back to the feather position (see Figure 23-6). This will stop the propeller and turn it so it presents minimum drag. Your V_{mc} will decrease when this happens, and the airplane should climb better and need even less rudder and bank.

626

PART I
PREFLIGHT

PART II
SPORT PILOT

PART III
PRIVATE PILOT

PART IV
INSTRUMENT RATING

PART V
COMMERCIAL LICENSE

PART VI
ATP AND BEYOND

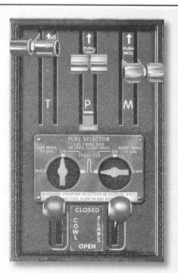

Now verify which mixture control is for the dead engine, pull it to idle cutoff, and turn the fuel for the dead engine to off.

Take a moment now to look after your *good* engine. Open the cowl flaps as needed. Adjust the power, prop, and mixture as needed. Prepare for a single-engine approach and landing.

Figure 23-6: FSX doesn't visually simulate the feathered propeller on the Baron (which is too bad because it looks cool), but the airplane flies as if the propeller were feathered.

STUDENT OF THE CRAFT

CROSS FEEDING THE FUEL

In the Baron, the fuel in the right wing feeds the right engine, and the fuel in the left wing feeds the left. When you lose an engine, though, you'll need to pull fuel from both wings at different times to keep the two wings balanced and have enough fuel available to complete your trip on one engine.

The Baron fuel selectors have three positions: on, off, and crossfeed. On selects fuel from the same side as the engine, so the left fuel selector sends fuel from the left wing to the left engine when it's set to on. Off shuts off fuel to that engine, so when the left fuel selector is off, the left engine won't get any gas from either wing.

Crossfeed will draw fuel from the opposite wing. So if the left fuel selector is on crossfeed, it gets fuel from the right wing and no fuel from the left.

Note that you can run both engines off one wing. Imagine you had a fuel leak in your right wing. You didn't notice it until the right engine quit in flight. Since there's nothing wrong with the engine other than it ran out of fuel, you could run both engines off the left wing tank. The left fuel selector would be on, and the right fuel selector would be set for crossfeed. Of course, you'd want to land soon because you'd be burning through your fuel twice as fast.

SINGLE-ENGINE APPROACHES AND LANDINGS

You'll start your flights with the most benign of engine failures: failure during cruise flight. You're in a lightly loaded Baron and at 8,500 feet en route from Cheyenne, Wyoming (KCYS), back to your base at Jeffco (KBJC). About a minute into the flight, your left engine will fail. Your job is to land at Jeffco safely.

WHAT'S HAPPENING HERE?

The first step is realizing you even have a failure (see Figure 23-7). Since you're cruising with the autopilot on, you'll see the heading wiggle, but the autopilot will try to compensate. Start looking to find the problem. The prop-sync pinwheel spinning is a tip that something is up with the engines. You'll see from the left-side engine gauges that you have a serious issue.

Figure 23-7: In addition to the engine gauges, you can see there's a problem in your slightly-off heading and the coordination of flight.

628

PART I
PREFLIGHT

PART II
S POST PILOT

PART III
PRIVATE PILOT

PART IV
INSTRUMENT RATING

PART V
COMMERCIAL LICENSE

PART VI
ATP AND BEYOND

ALL FORWARD

Sophisticated autopilots can handle an engine failure well. This autopilot doesn't qualify, so disconnect it. You'll immediately need some right rudder. Watch your speed now. It's above blueline, so you're fine for the moment, but it will rapidly drop. When it hits 101, pitch to keep 101, and accept the slow descent. Push the throttle and prop controls full forward to get maximum power. Set your mixtures for max power, which probably means leaving them alone if you already set them for altitude.

RAISE THE DEAD

Bank toward your right (good) engine about 3–5°. Use enough rudder to keep the black inclinometer ball about ½ off center (see Figure 23-8). In the real world, this will reduce drag and reduce V_{mc}. It doesn't seem to have quite the right effect in FSX, but it's close enough to practice the correct procedure.

Figure 23-8: The balance of slight bank and rudder is tough to feel on FSX, but the flight behavior is fairly close to the real thing.

SECURE THE ENGINE

Since you've got a little altitude and time, you can troubleshoot this engine. This is an urgent situation but not an emergency. Before you go any further, though, keep your good engine happy by opening the cowl flaps and periodically checking on it. Also keep heading for KBJC. As you can see in Figure 23-9, you've got a situation and will need to land sometime soon.

Figure 23-9: As you're troubleshooting, watch your altitude and descent rate. Troubleshooting is a luxury afforded only to those with altitude to spare.

Figure 23-10: Switch off everything having to do with the left engine, but verify you have the correct engine control before you act on each step.

We failed this engine with the Aircraft > Failures option, so there's no way it will restart. But engines stop for want of at least one of three things: fuel, air, or spark. Check those systems now by doing the following:

- Enrich the mixture a bit more for start.

- Try the crossfeed fuel selector for the dead engine.

- Try the boost pump in case the fuel pump failed or there is vapor lock in a fuel-injected engine.

- Try any alternate air intake for the engine (the FSX Baron doesn't model this, and some engines have automatic-only systems for this).

- Try each magneto individually. The ignition switch might have a short that is causing the problem.

Note that you do not need to cycle the ignition switch to Start. The propeller is spinning in the wind. If you get the right conditions in the engine for combustion, the engine will start on its own.

OK, it won't start. You'll cut your losses and secure it, as shown in Figure 23-10. Step one is to make sure you have the correct engine by pulling the throttle to half throttle and then to idle. When that doesn't have any effect, do the same to the prop control. When you pull the prop control fully aft, you'll be in the feather mode, and the propeller on the wing will stop. Remember you can press E and then 1 on your keyboard to

630

| PART I | PART II | PART III | PART IV | PART V | PART VI |
| PREFLIGHT | SPORT PILOT | PRIVATE PILOT | INSTRUMENT RATING | COMMERCIAL LICENSE | ATP AND BEYOND |

make your joystick control the right engine controls. You will need to move the actual feather control onscreen or press Ctrl+F1 to pull the prop to minimum rpm and then press Ctrl+F2 to pull it further to feather.

With the prop stopped, you'll turn off all the fuel to that motor: mixture to idle cutoff, fuel selector to off, any boost pumps off, and magnetos off.

THE SINGLE-ENGINE APPROACH

The last step is to fly the visual approach with only one engine. It's not hard to do, but the key factor is managing drag. Right now, the Baron has its gear and flaps up. Put those gear down, and you'll be descending about 500 fpm without changing anything. The flaps will net about 400 fpm. Flaps *and* gear could be as much as 1000 fpm down when coming into this high-altitude airport. You'll have to plan this approach carefully.

Oh, and not to add any pressure, but your single engine won't supply enough power to go around if you botch the approach. You have one shot to get it right.

For that reason, pick a long runway for the approach so you can aim partway down the runway and have some cushion to overshoot or undershoot. If you have the option, your best bet is usually a long, straight-in approach. That way you can get a steady descent rate established and take it to the runway with few changes. If you have to fly a traffic pattern, fly with the good engine on the same side as the runway. That way you'll make all your turns into the good engine and maintain maximum control.

If the airport has a tower, let them know you're a single-engine approach, and tell them what you want to do. They'll work with you and let you fly right traffic or a long straight in and get other airplanes out of your way.

You should be over the airport or nearby by now. Since FSX ATC can't handle special requests, you'll fly this one yourself.

You'll try both a straight in and a pattern. So you can get back to this point quickly, choose Flights > Save, and save this flight right now as "temp." Now turn eastbound, and use your GPS to get about 5 miles from the airport and turned back inbound to Runway 29R. If you do this efficiently, you should still be higher than 7,000 feet MSL.

Now get lined up with the runway, and lower your landing gear. See what this does to your rate of descent while maintaining 101 knots. If you're still looking good for getting to the runway, reduce the power by a few inches and see how well that works. Your aiming point shouldn't be the runway threshold but rather the thick, white 1,000-foot marks down the runway. If you're still looking good, lower approach flaps, and see what that does.

Figure 23-11: Right now you're gear down and approach flaps with almost full power on the good engine. Add full flaps, and you might not make the runway.

Figure 23-12: Your GPS can be a great tool in keeping your position relative to the airport clear as you maneuver.

The goal here is a configuration with the gear down and whatever degree of flaps you can manage that gives you about 500 fpm down while still going 101 knots (see Figure 23-11). Ideally, you'll be at a few inches less than full throttle, too. That way you have some power to add if it looks like you're going to come up short.

Each condition will be different. A lightly loaded Baron at sea level might be able to make a final approach with gear down and full flaps with less than full power on one engine. A heavy Baron at altitude may need to make the approach with gear and flaps up and full power on one engine until short final. The gear would come down only 20–30 seconds before touchdown. This is one of those places where flying becomes an art.

Press Ctrl+; on your keyboard to reset the flight. You're back in the air with a feathered engine. Now you'll need to maneuver to enter a *right* downwind for Runway 29R. This is a bit trickier. You know when you put the gear down that you'll start coming down at 500 fpm. So where do you start? Maneuver to enter a wide downwind at pattern elevation of 6,700 feet (see Figure 23-12). You may need to overfly the airport and turn to lose a bit of altitude before you enter the pattern.

632

PART I
PRE-FLIGHT

PART II
SPORT PILOT

PART III
PRIVATE PILOT

PART IV
INSTRUMENT RATING

PART V
COMMERCIAL LICENSE

PART VI
ATP AND BEYOND

Figure 23-13: It's hard to see where you are over that right wing and engine. Your GPS can help, or you can give it your best guess.

Figure 23-14: You're high for landing on Runway 29R, but the visual glide path for Runway 29L behind it says you're not excessively high.

Fly the downwind in level flight with the gear up. When you get abeam your landing target of 1,000 feet down the runway, lower the gear, and let the Baron descend, ideally about 500 fpm (see Figure 23-13). After you've come down 200 feet to 6500 feet, turn right for the base.

As you roll out on base, make your judgment as to how high or low you are, and add flaps accordingly (see Figure 23-14). You're better off too high than too low. Remember as well that your aim point is not the threshold, but 1,000 feet down the runway. Turn final when you're ready. Only lower flaps to approach or full if you're certain you have the runway made. At this altitude, it's unlikely you'll want full flaps, and landing with only partial flaps is fine.

If you don't make it, well, be glad it's a simulator. Reset the flight, and try again.

Single-Engine ILS

Load the flight Chap_23_IMC_failure. You're at 10,000 feet flying from Cheyenne to Jeffco again, but the weather isn't so hot this time; there's rain and low ceilings all around. It's a good thing you have two engines…oops, there goes one of them. We'll let you figure out which one. It might, or might not, be the same one we use in the following figures.

Once you've figured out it won't restart, feather and secure it. Your first issue is that you won't be able to maintain 10,000 feet and stay above blueline (see Figure 23-15). In the real world, you'd tell ATC about your problem and get cleared to a lower altitude immediately. You can't do that in FSX, so just acknowledge when they tell you to climb, and ignore the requests to expedite.

Soon you'll get a descent to 7,200. You're going pretty slow, so if you want to keep the power up and just point the nose down, be our guest. Be sure you have full power on the good engine when you level off. You should be able to maintain altitude here at 7,200. Once you're at 7,200, choose Flights > Save, and save this flight as "temp." You'll be asked whether you want to replace the old temp. Click Yes.

Follow ATC's vectors. When you intercept the localizer, adjust your throttle setting to get 110 knots. This is your normal approach speed, and in an abnormal situation like this, you want to keep as much normalized as possible. Load and activate the ILS Rwy 29R approach in your GPS for extra situational awareness too.

Figure 23-15: You can still use your autopilot, but you'll have to disable the altitude hold and trim for your target airspeed.

634

| PART I | PART II | PART III | PART IV | PART V | PART VI |
| FIRST FLIGHT | SPORT PILOT | PRIVATE PILOT | INSTRUMENT RATING | COMMERCIAL LICENSE | ATP AND BEYOND |

When you see the glide-slope needle fully center, start down the ILS, *and then lower your gear*. If this seems backward, it is, but we find getting that small boost in speed pointing down the ILS and then adding the drag of the gear helps avoid getting too slow on the approach (at least on the FSX Baron). You might not need to adjust the power at all, but if you do, adjust it just enough to maintain 110 knots. Keep the flaps up for this high-altitude approach until you have the runway made. In fact, you're probably best off not bothering with them at all (see Figure 23-16).

Figure 23-16: Gear down and flaps up with nearly full power on the good engine

SINGLE-ENGINE GPS APPROACH

Flying an ILS like this is the preferable approach for the same reason as with the long straight-in visual approach. You have more time to gently adjust your parameters to get a stable descent to the runway. Alas, an ILS isn't always available, so you'll need to know how to fly a nonprecision approach sans engine as well.

Press Ctrl+; or load the flight temp. Now you're back in the air en route to KBJC. Use the ATC window to request another approach, and get the GPS Rwy 29R for KBJC. The approach is essentially the same except for one scary tidbit. Once you drop the gear, you will not have enough power to maintain altitude up here. You'll fly the approach at 110 knots *with the gear and flaps up* (see Figure 23-17). This will allow you to level off at intermediate altitudes and the final MDA of 5,900 feet. When you see the runway and have at least red over white on the VASI, you can lower the gear and slow to 101 for a final approach. If and when to extend approach flaps is up to you.

All the engine failures you did in flight earlier were at a light weight. If you want some additional insight into how weight matters, take off in this fully loaded Baron and then fail an engine at altitude. You'll see how much more difficult it is to get back to pavement safely. For the opposite effect, try any of the engine-failure flights at sea level. You'll find it much easier.

Figure 23-17: Gear up? Well, you gotta do what you gotta do. If you hear a beeping when you reduce the good throttle, that's the Baron reminding you to lower that landing gear just before landing.

KEEPING IT REAL

MOUNTAIN IMC

Instrument flight over the Rockies requires the power of turbocharging or two engines. That works fine until one of the engines (or the turbocharger) fails. For an added challenge, fly IFR from Grand Junction, Colorado (KGJT), to Jeffco and have an engine fail about halfway there. Make sure the ceilings are high enough to maneuver between the hills. You might need it.

SINGLE-ENGINE CROSSWIND LANDINGS

There isn't much to this one beyond the planning. The key is remembering that you want to maneuver to land with the good engine on the upwind side. This might mean crossing over an airport and coming back to land the other way. You already did a crosswind landing with much more power on the upwind engine compared to the downwind engine. Now all the power is on the upwind engine.

636

PART I
PREFLIGHT

PART II
SPORT PILOT

PART III
PRIVATE PILOT

PART IV
INSTRUMENT RATING

PART V
COMMERCIAL LICENSE

PART VI
ATP AND BEYOND

Load the flight Chap_23_X-wind_failure. The initial placement and wind is identical to the crosswind landing you did in Chapter 21. This time, one of your engines will fail (we're not telling which one), and you'll have to make it to the airport and land. As with any single-engine landing, carefully manage your power and drag to make sure you can arrive at the airport.

ADDITIONAL SINGLE-ENGINE WORK

There are some aspects of multiengine flying that occur only in training and some that we hope only occur in training. You'll start with one we never simulate in real-world training but that you can actually try in the simulator. It's the worst-case scenario: a total engine failure just as you rotate for takeoff.

ENGINE FAILURE ON TAKEOFF

Now for the big time. You've gotten a feel for how engine failures affect your flight, but you've always had altitude to spare when it happened. This time you'll fail an engine right after takeoff and try to make it back to the airport in one piece. The odds are a bit against you by working from an airport that's already a mile above sea level, but it's better you see a tough scenario on the sim than in the real world.

We'll stack the deck a bit in your favor the first time by using the lightly loaded Baron. Load the flight Chap_23_Bad_luck_1. You're on the end of Runway 29R, and the winds are light. Get yourself ready for takeoff.

Press Shift+4 to open the throttle quadrant and place it where you can see it. You can't set the timing of an engine failure to simulate the worst-case scenario of a failure right at rotation. Instead, position your cursor on the OFF position in the left fuel selector. Advance both throttles with your joystick control, and roll for takeoff.

When you hit V_r of 90 knots, rotate for takeoff, and then click your mouse button to cut off fuel to the left engine (see Figure 23-18).

Figure 23-18: Start your rotation, and then cut off the fuel.

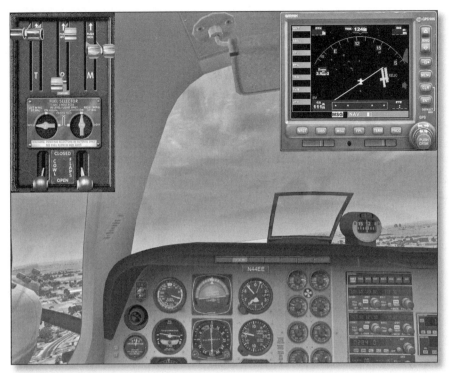

Figure 23-19: Here you are at 200 feet AGL on the downwind. Let's hope no wisecracking tower controller will start giving you low-altitude alerts.

The next few seconds will determine whether you succeed or crash. Success requires four things: getting the gear up, maintaining blueline, feathering that left propeller, and getting turned away from the rising terrain ahead of you. You'll do these things quickly and in that order. Gear up and pitching for 101 can happen at once, really. Pull the left throttle back (or quickly pump it back and then full forward just in case you grabbed the wrong one) to make sure you've got the correct engine. Then pull the left prop control halfway back, pause for a heartbeat, and then pull it to feather. Turn right into the good engine, and get back to lower terrain and an airport (see Figure 23-19).

If you're having trouble, don't fret. It's hard. You can practice a bit at a lower altitude by resetting the flight and changing the airport to KPAE, which is Paine Field in Everett, Washington. There you're only 600 feet MSL. This makes the right-turning tendency worse when the engine fails, but you'll have more power to play with on the good motor. Power is everything with a failure on takeoff. You did remember to lean before takeoff in Colorado, didn't you?

Not all takeoffs with a failure are even possible. Load the flight Chap_23_Bad_luck_2. This Baron is at gross weight. Try the same engine failure. Did you make it? What happens if you rotate at 101 instead of 90 and fail the engine then? It's actually possible to fly this flight and land at an airport without crashing, but it's not easy…and the airport might not be Jeffco.

638

| PART I | PART II | PART III | PART IV | PART V | PART VI |
| PREFLIGHT | SPORT PILOT | PRIVATE PILOT | INSTRUMENT RATING | COMMERCIAL LICENSE | ATP AND BEYOND |

⬇ STUDENT OF THE CRAFT

THE TELLURIDE CHALLENGE

Telluride, Colorado (KTEX), is a challenging airport in many ways; it's at more than 9,000 feet above sea level and up a box canyon for starters. Load the flight Chap_23_Telluride_challenge. You're at the end of Runway 27, which takes you straight out and down the canyon. Take off in this gross-weight Baron—you'll use almost all the 9,000-foot runway—and lift off. Fail the left engine with the fuel selector just after takeoff. Now you'll need to weave down the valley as you slowly sink and find a place to land. Use your GPS, and stay out of the trees. There is an airport out there. You just have to find it.

V_mc Demo

The commercial PTS for the multiengine rating includes a demonstration of V_{mc}. The real-world demo involves just bringing an engine to idle, not actually shutting it down. Recovery is also at the first loss of control. You'll shut the engine down and run right into a V_{mc} stall for fun. Hey, it's a simulator, right?

Load the flight Chap_23_multi_demos. You're back near Seattle, just 3,000 feet MSL. You'll want some power to do these well, so you'll leave Colorado for a bit. You're level at 3,000 feet on a heading of 330 and a speed of 101. Hold that heading, and shut down the left engine with the fuel selector. Go to full power and full-forward prop on the right engine. Use right rudder and a slight (2–3°) right bank to hold your heading.

Now pitch up slowly to get below V_{mc} of 85 knots. You'll need nearly full right rudder to keep flying straight if you don't put in too much bank. This would be the limit of directional control in a real-world test.

Now go further. The FSX Baron will let you get to about 75 knots before it stalls. At this point, you'll see that you can't keep going straight without a significant right bank. That's V_{mc}.

Pull up further if you want and stall to see what happens. The FSX Baron will be forgiving in that you actually can recover by reducing the power and pitching down the nose. The real Baron might start a spin to the left, which is a position you never want to see in a real multiengine airplane.

DRAG DEMO

Reset the flight with Ctrl+;. This time you'll fully feather one engine and look at how various speeds and drag items affect your rate of descent.

Shut down the left engine with the fuel selector, and feather the prop. Now open the cowl flaps on the right engine in, and adjust the power so you're maintaining a constant altitude. It should require about 22 inches of MP with full rpm. This is your baseline, and you won't touch the power for the rest of the demo.

Figure 23-20: Expect to see quite a rate of descent and a low pitch attitude with both full flaps and gear extended.

Any change to your speed or extension of flaps or gear should create a rate of descent. Try flying at V_{yse} –10 knots, or 91 knots. You'll see an initial climb, but as you hold 91 knots and don't adjust the power, you'll start coming back down about –300 fpm. Now try V_{yse} +10 knots, or 111 knots. You'll see a big drop at first, but then you'll settle down to a steady rate of descent at about –400 fpm.

Return to 101 knots, and you'll get back to level flight. Drop the gear, and note your descent. Now add approach flaps. Now add full flaps (see Figure 23-20). Now try gear up but full flaps…you get the idea. Feel free to fill out the following chart as you go.

When you're done, get ready to fly faster and higher than ever before. It's time for your King Air checkout, which is Bonus Chapter 1 on this book's website at www.wiley.com. After you finish that chapter, return here to begin multiplayer flying.

Speed	Flaps	Gear	Rate of Descent
101	Up	Up	0
91	Up	Up	
111	Up	Up	
101	Up	Down	
101	Approach	Down	
101	Full	Down	
101	Full	Up	
101	Approach	Up	

640

PART I
PREFLIGHT

PART II
SPORT PILOT

PART III
PRIVATE PILOT

PART IV
INSTRUMENT RATING

PART V
COMMERCIAL LICENSE

PART VI
ATP AND BEYOND

ACCIDENT CHAIN

KNOW YOUR PRIORITIES

Location: Roosevelt, Utah

Aircraft: Beech Baron

Injuries: 1 minor

"According to the pilot, the left engine began to run rough shortly after departing Runway 07. He noticed a loss in indicated fuel pressure, and within a few moments, the left engine lost power and then quit. The pilot made several unsuccessful attempts to restart the engine. The pilot attempted an immediate left turn to return to the airport. The 270° left turn resulted in a loss of altitude and improper line-up with Runway 25.

"The pilot completed a 90° right turn as the airplane crossed the airport's access road. The airplane continued to descend as it struck several trees and impacted terrain southwest of the airport. The impact separated both engines and the nose and main landing gear assemblies from the fuselage. Approximately 3 feet of the outboard section of each wing was crushed upwards and aft. According to an FAA inspector, the mixture was in the full rich position and the fuel boost pumps were off. Although the airplane's right wing was compromised, there was visible fuel in the left wing."

We can't help but wonder about those "several unsuccessful attempts to restart the engine." Had the pilot accepted the engine failure and secured the engine, there may have been enough altitude and time to return to the airport and land. Troubleshooting an engine on a parked airplane is far preferable to troubleshooting an engine on a crashed airplane.

KEY POINTS FOR REAL FLYING AND FSX BUILT-INS

The following are some key points from this chapter:

- Understand the aerodynamics of single-engine flying in a light twin.

- Learn engine-out procedures.

- Practice engine-out in various scenarios.

- Practice the multiengine checkride demo.

Here are the lessons and missions to study after reading this chapter:

- *Lessons*: None apply to this chapter.

- *Missions*: Losing an engine might be a factor in several missions, but if we told you which ones, we'd spoil the surprise.

ATP AND BEYOND

CONTENTS

"I HAVE FLOWN IN JUST ABOUT EVERYTHING, WITH ALL KINDS OF PILOTS IN ALL PARTS OF THE WORLD—BRITISH, FRENCH, PAKISTANI, IRANIAN, JAPANESE, CHINESE—AND THERE WASN'T A DIME'S WORTH OF DIFFERENCE BETWEEN ANY OF THEM EXCEPT FOR ONE UNCHANGING, CERTAIN FACT: THE BEST, MOST SKILLFUL PILOT HAD THE MOST EXPERIENCE."

—CHUCK YEAGER

646

| PART I | PART II | PART III | PART IV | PART V | PART VI |
| FLIGHT | SPORT PILOT | PRIVATE PILOT | INSTRUMENT RATING | COMMERCIAL LICENSE | ATP AND BEYOND |

Sharing the Virtual Skies

Flight simulation on the home computer can be an engaging, full-sensory experience. It can also get kind of lonely after a while. The ability to fly in real time with other virtual pilots in the same virtual world has been with Flight Simulator for several years now. (In fact, in Combat Flight Simulator versions you can even shoot other players down.)

Multiplayer is also the jumping-off point into the world of Internet-based flight simulator play. This is a huge and vibrant community, and it's probably worth a book unto itself.

To keep things simple, we've broken up the exploration of multiplayer across three chapters. This chapter is strictly about the multiplayer function built into FSX. Chapters 25 and 26 are devoted to two of the biggest communal uses of Flight Simulator, virtual airlines and virtual air traffic control. In addition, Bonus Chapter 2 on the website at www.wiley.com is all about learning to fly jets, which are the most common aircraft flown in virtual airlines and controlled by virtual air traffic control.

How Multiplayer Works

Getting the most out of your multiplayer requires understanding a bit about how multiplayer works in FSX. In many ways, it's *less* sophisticated than people commonly think.

It seems like you're flying in a single virtual world when you're part of a multiplayer session. It's as if you're all flying on one big computer somewhere. But that's not what's happening. Each player's own computer is simulating each player's virtual world, so if five pilots are flying together, at least five separate computers are running five copies of Flight Simulator, all running at once.

Each computer is creating the virtual world for its user, and each of those worlds could look a bit different. If one user is running a top-of-the-line gaming system with all the visual effects cranked up, her virtual world and aircraft might look photorealistic. Another player flying in formation with her might have a basic system running at the lowest settings practical. His view of the world will be quite different. There might even be objects such as trees, vehicles, or even computer-generated airplanes in one gamer's virtual world that don't exist in another's.

What all the gamers will see in common, though, is the presence, position, and flight of other players' aircraft. This information is part of what is being exchanged between the five computers all playing together. It's being exchanged through one computer that is acting as the *host*. The host computer is the one that created that particular multiplayer session and determined the ground rules for play (you'll learn more about this in a bit).

So if player A takes off from an airport and enters a left traffic pattern to return for landing, each other player in that part of the world will see that airplane take off and turn left. If player A continues around the pattern, comes back to the runway, and bounces on landing, everyone who happens to be looking will see the mistake.

But they have to be looking. Unlike a game that directs all players into one area, each player could be anywhere in the virtual world on Flight Simulator. (They could be anywhere in the real world, too, but that's not the point here.) If you crash and burn in Borneo, the folks flying in Auckland won't know about it.

Clouds, winds, barometric pressure, and so on, are the same for all players in one area, so you can't have one person flying in clear skies while someone next to them is in the clouds. Exactly how those clouds appear onscreen, though, is local to each computer and could vary widely.

GETTING INTO MULTIPLAYER

You start multiplayer mode from the FSX home screen. On the left, click Multiplayer. You now have two options for multiplayer, playing with others on your local network or playing over the Internet using a service called GameSpy.

Local networking is for playing with other folks in the office (after-hours we hope) or when you have multiple computers at home. This is the simplest way to host a session. You'll need to enter a player name so other people on the network can identify you. Then you click Sign In. If there's a game running already, you can join it. If not, you can host your own. These steps are the same as when you use the Internet to find other gamers, so before we get into details, let's look at GameSpy (see Figure 24-1).

Using GameSpy is free, but you'll need to create an account first. You can do this with the Create New Account button on the bottom left of the screen. The player name you select will be seen by other players. You must decide whether you want to use your real name or some secret identity. Other information won't be revealed. After you create the account, you can enter your password and log in.

GameSpy for FSX is divided into *lobbies*. These are just virtual divisions to help organize sessions with different purposes. By far, the busiest lobby is Free Flight, and it's where you'll be when you first log in. There are separate lobbies for airliner flying, flight training, and so on. To switch to a different lobby, use the pull-down menu on the right of the screen. There's no hard rule about what has to happen in what lobby.

In general, if you're hosting a session and you want strangers to join in, use the Free Flight lobby because that's where most people are. If you want to host a session just for friends, tell them which other lobby you're heading for and have them meet you there. It'll be easier to find your session in the list.

Figure 24-1: If you don't already have a GameSpy account, click Create New Account below the password page, and follow the steps to make one.

648

PART I	PART II	PART III	PART IV	PART V	PART VI
PREFLIGHT	SPORT PILOT	PRIVATE PILOT	INSTRUMENT RATING	COMMERCIAL LICENSE	ATP AND BEYOND

The list, shown in Figure 24-2, has the name of each session, how many players are currently flying out of how many total can fly, the quality and speed of the connection of the host computer, the nearest airport so you have some clue where in the world you'll be flying, and whether the session supports voice communication within FSX. You can sort the list by any of these criteria by clicking the header at the top of that column.

To leave GameSpy, click the Leave Lobby button at the bottom of the screen.

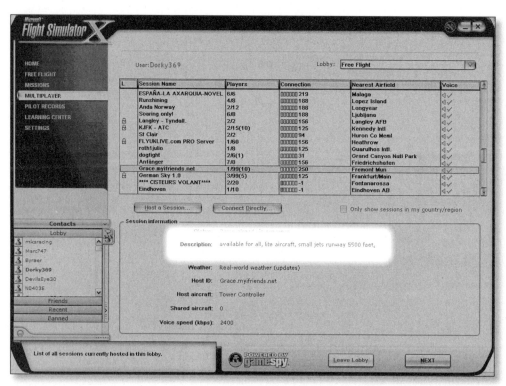

Figure 24-2: Each session has detailed information that appears below it. Be sure to read this before you try to join, and make sure to include this information for others to see if you're the host.

 FLY THE EUROPEAN NIGHT

The busiest time for most flight-simulation multiplayer gatherings is evening—in Europe. Remember you're often flying with people all over the world. U.S. pilots enjoy some of the lowest real-world flying costs in the world. Pilots looking for a cheaper flying fix will be online after work in their own time zone. There is another peak of traffic as night reaches the Far East.

 CONNECTION SPEED

If you see a really poor connection speed—all red and a number 1—it might not be a bad connection. If GameSpy can't determine the speed, it shows it as super-poor.

CONTACTS AND FRIENDS

In the lobby, you can see all the people logged in to that lobby. You can also chat, but it's an open chat with everyone in the lobby at that moment. You can also assign any of these people to a list of "friends." The purpose of friends is partly to let you find people you know (and trust) quickly among all the people who are logged in. You can also restrict certain activities, such as joining your session, to your list of friends. Friends can also be invited to private multiplayer sessions and can be engaged in a private chat.

To add someone as a friend, right-click their name, and select Add to Friends List. If someone is ever pestering you and you want to block their chats, you can ban them.

When you join a session, this list changes to show only the people logged in to that specific session. That's the same list you'll see in the game chat window after you start playing.

HOSTING A MULTIPLAYER SESSION

It might seem backwards to talk about hosting a multiplayer session before talking about joining one. You'll probably join one before you host, but it's helpful to know what's going on behind the scenes before you start to play.

650

| PART I | PART II | PART III | PART IV | PART V | PART VI |
| PREFLIGHT | SPORT PILOT | PRIVATE PILOT | INSTRUMENT RATING | COMMERCIAL LICENSE | ATP AND BEYOND |

To host your own session, click the Host a Session button. You'll see the screen shown in Figure 24-3 where you can give the session a name, description, and optional password. If you put in a password, a lock icon appears on your session's listing in the lobby, indicating that players must know that password to join. This is handy if you're flying with friends and don't want strangers in the game.

You'll also have options as to whether the session is visible on GameSpy, your local network, both, or not visible at all. That last option is really just for surreptitious play on local networks. Click Next when you're ready to select an aircraft, location, and weather.

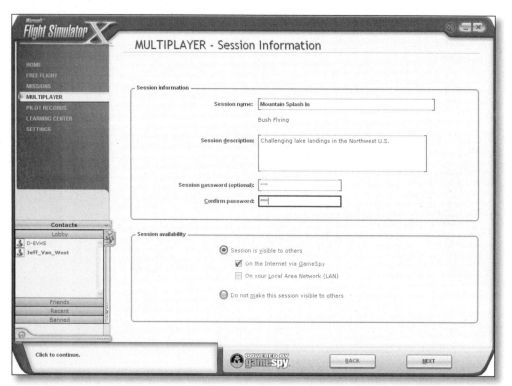

Figure 24-3: Unless you are planning to have others connect directly to your computer, don't select an invisible session. You'll get mighty lonely.

The Session Conditions screen (Figure 24-4) is a lot like the Free Flight screen you've seen before. The only new features are that you can select your role as pilot or controller, and you can choose whether you want the chat window open or not at start-up. You can open or close the chat window at any time during play (see "Let's Chat" later in this chapter), but when you start playing as pilot or controller, you're stuck doing that until you leave the session. You can also set options for a shared aircraft. Click Next to set the last round of options.

As the host, you have a few extra options to set. These include the maximum number of players in the session (up to 99) and how many slots are reserved for your friends (see the sidebar "Contacts and Friends"). You'll also set whether the session will allow voice transmissions.

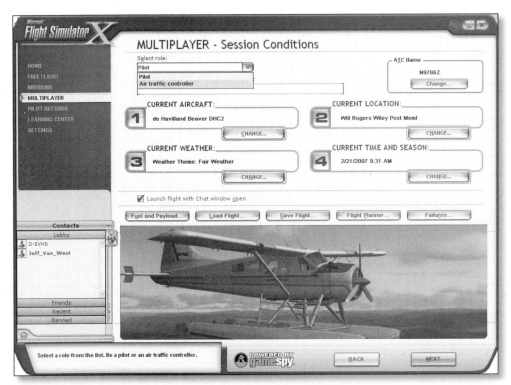

Figure 24-4: When you select an airplane, it's only the airplane you're flying. Other people could join flying anything they want.

This is a great feature—if you have a fast Internet connection. The sound quality is decent, but it's not as good as you'd get using something like Skype to talk while you play. The benefits of having voice in the games are that it's a common platform that all participants can use and that you can select the option that sound is active using the aircraft radios only. If you choose that feature, you'll have to be on the same radio frequency as another player to talk with them. As we've mentioned elsewhere in this book, having two sound cards—one for voice and one for all other sounds—in your computer greatly improves the voice quality.

652

PART I	PART II	PART III	PART IV	PART V	PART VI
PREFLIGHT	SPORT PILOT	PRIVATE PILOT	INSTRUMENT RATING	COMMERCIAL LICENSE	ATP AND BEYOND

You can use the advanced settings (Figure 24-5) to change how much freedom and control the joining players have.

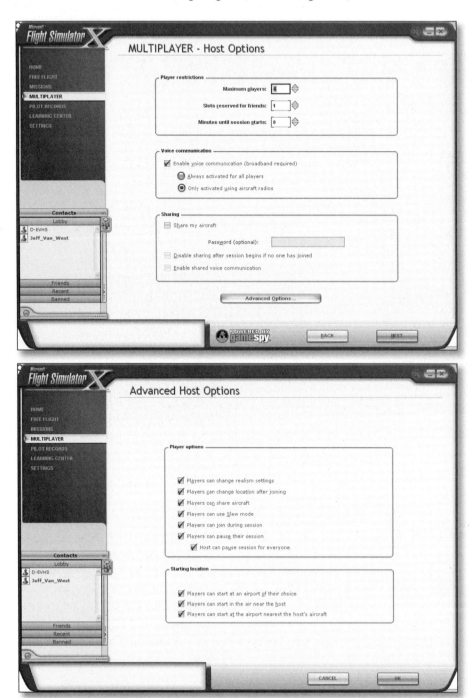

Figure 24-5: The advanced settings are all on by default, giving other players maximum freedom of control.

Click Next to start hosting the session. You'll see a briefing room screen (Figure 24-6) that displays how many players have joined. You also have one last chance to change your role or location. When all, or enough, players have joined, you can start the session.

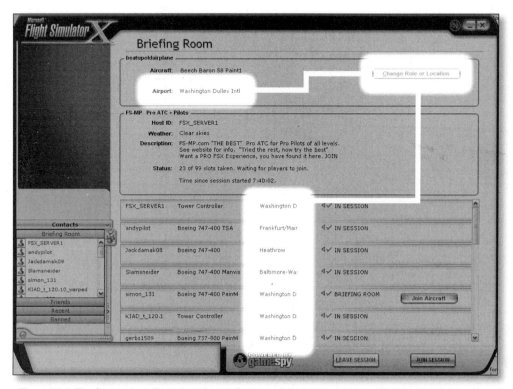

Figure 24-6: The Change Location tab at the briefing room is handy to put yourself at an airport near other players currently in the game.

SETTING UP SHARED AIRCRAFT

The option to share a cockpit is new to FSX and has great potential. For the first time, two players can share control of one aircraft. We discuss how this works during play in "Flying with Another Pilot" later in this chapter, but to even have the option, you must enable it. You do this on the same screen where you named your session (see Figure 24-7). You can set a password here that applies only to someone else trying to join your aircraft, rather than the entire session.

When you join a session that someone else hosts, you have a similar option to make your aircraft shared.

654

PART I	PART II	PART III	PART IV	PART V	PART VI
PREFLIGHT	SPORT PILOT	PRIVATE PILOT	INSTRUMENT RATING	COMMERCIAL LICENSE	ATP AND BEYOND

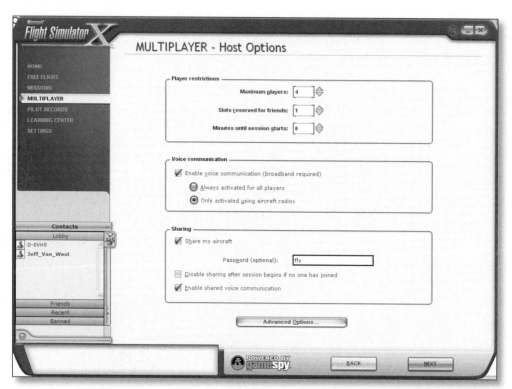

Figure 24-7: Note that you have the option to disable sharing after the session begins and you start flying. This way, no one can "take over" your flying aircraft.

Joining a Multiplayer Session

Joining a session is a simpler version of what you do to host a session. Find the session you want in the list for your current lobby, select the session in the list, and click Next. You'll see a screen similar to Figure 24-4 where you select your aircraft and location. There aren't as many options because you're not the host.

No Inappropriate Spawning

One big problem on virtual flying networks is caused by the default action that Flight Simulator uses when you move to a new airport: unless you select the start-up point to be a parking spot on the ramp or at a gate, Flight Simulator will put you on the end of the "active" runway. If you connect to the online network while you're still on the runway, you will suddenly appear there to everyone else already on the network (called *spawning on the runway*). If another plane was landing or taking off from that runway, you could cause a collision or, at the least, force them to evade you.

The solution is either to select a parking spot when you join a game and set your default airport or to set the game to join in the air, as shown in Figure 24-8. If you select the ground, you'll need to set your location to an airport of your choosing and then choose one of the parking areas. Then you can click OK.

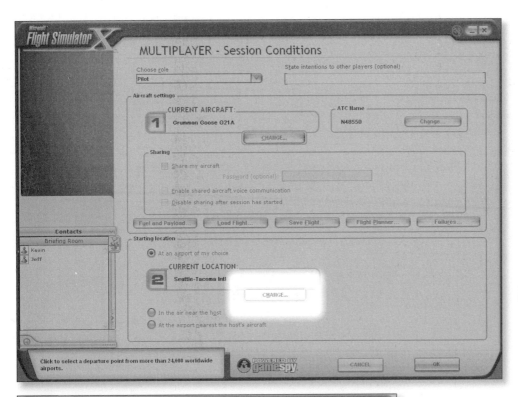

Figure 24-8: Although this guarantees you won't materialize on the active runway, it might take you a few moments to figure out where you actually are.

656

| PART I | PART II | PART III | PART IV | PART V | PART VI |
| PREFLIGHT | SPORT PILOT | PRIVATE PILOT | INSTRUMENT RATING | COMMERCIAL LICENSE | ATP AND BEYOND |

Before you join the session, save this flight by clicking the Save Flight button. It doesn't need a memorable name—even "temporary" is just fine. That way, if you crash, you'll reset to that position off the runway rather than FSX's default of the active runway.

If you join a session that's already in progress, you'll start flying immediately. If the host hasn't started the session yet, you'll have to wait.

To get out of a shared session, just hit the Esc key on your keyboard. You won't stop the session for anyone else. If the host ends the session, however, it ends for everyone.

DIRECT CONNECT

You can connect directly to a host computer if you know its IP address. We won't go into the details here, but know that you can connect locally or over the Internet without GameSpy if you're tech savvy and want to make that happen.

INSIDE THE GAME

BONUS VIEWS

If you have the processor and video power to do it, it's helpful to have a top-down window open while you're on the ground or near busy airports. There can be a lot of airplanes in the air or on the ramp, and if you hit one, you end two people's game. This isn't essential, but you might want to consider it.

It's also handy at busy airports sometimes to taxi from a locked spot view just above and behind your aircraft to get a better big picture. This is super-handy moving around the airport at night. There are plenty of times at busy airports where we wish we could have done this with our own real-world aircraft.

JOINING A SHARED AIRCRAFT

If you want to join a shared aircraft, you actually don't do it on the aircraft selection page. You do it in the briefing page that comes next. When you get to the selection page, click Next with whatever happens to be selected—except be sure that Share My Aircraft is *not* selected. If that option is selected, FSX won't let you share some else's aircraft.

When you get to the briefing page, you'll see a list of all the people in the game. Open seats on other aircraft will appear with Join Aircraft buttons. Click the button (and enter the password if needed) to join that aircraft. When you join an aircraft, the other pilot will see you in a shared seat if they are still on the briefing page or see a message that you joined if you join in-flight.

▼ STUDENT OF THE CRAFT

NOT OPEN TO EVERYONE

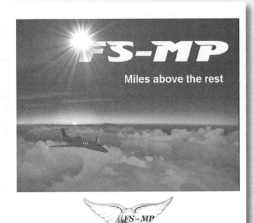

FLIGHT SIMULATOR - MULTI PLAYER
Introductory User Manual
http://www.fs-mp.com

Release 1.0 (January 24, 2007)

At the time of this writing, FSX had just been released, but there was already a need for more organization than the general chaos that could break out in unregulated multiplayer sessions. There are organizations that run password-protected games on FSX multiplayer, but there is actually a server computer behind it.

To play on these sessions, you'll have to register on the website that accompanies that community. In many cases this requires reading the site's policies and applying for membership. This might seem like a lot of work, but if you're looking for a realistic experience with other knowledgeable enthusiasts, it's probably worth it. Many of these sites organize virtual events, provide live flight training, and host forums where you can ask questions and chat with like-minded gamers. Some links to virtual communities appear in Appendix E on this book's website at **www.wiley.com**.

PLAYING WELL WITH OTHERS

You're in the shared session. Now what? It depends on the session, but the short answer is, join the fun. If you're in the air, fly around and see whether you can form up with other pilots. If you're on the ground, you can contact a ground controller for a clearance to taxi or do it on your own. No matter what you do, just remember that you're in a game with others now and have a certain responsibility to play by the group rules to ensure everyone has a good experience.

658

PART I	PART II	PART III	PART IV	PART V	PART VI
PREFLIGHT	SPORT PILOT	PRIVATE PILOT	INSTRUMENT RATING	COMMERCIAL LICENSE	ATP AND BEYOND

LET'S CHAT

Figure 24-9: The chat window is a good thing to check out when you first enter the session.

The chat window is a key tool for multiplayer. Not only does it let you communicate directly with any player in the game, but you'll often see general instructions there, such as a commonly used radio frequency or the first frequency to call when you enter the game.

To see the chat window (Figure 24-9), press Ctrl+Shift+] on your keyboard. You'll see all the players currently logged in and a history of what has been said recently. You can enter text in the bottom-right part of the chat window and click the Send button. Note that everyone with their chat window open will see what you typed.

One common frustration with the chat window is intending to type something on your keyboard to control your aircraft and typing a letter in the chat window instead. The easy way to handle this is to close the chat window when you're not using it, but then you won't see any messages that come up during the game.

The other option is to use Ctrl+Tab on your keyboard to switch to the other FSX windows. This lets you fly with the chat window inactive. You will want to make it smaller at the very least if you don't close it.

RADIO CHATTER

Back at the beginning of your training at Post Mills, Vermont, there wasn't much need for the radio. There isn't much need for the radio at the real Post Mills either. After you start flying into busier airports with more airplanes in the sky, you live and die by the radio. Having the radio work in multiplayer is essential to both realism and just having everybody get along.

Voice communications are determined by the host of the session when he or she creates it. One option is no voice. You'll see a red, no sound icon in the list of available sessions by the ones with no voice support. Voice can be on all the time to all players, which is sort of like a big conference call. Or, you can use the aircraft radios.

LISTEN IN

You can actually hear the radio traffic for many of the sessions after you log in but before you start flying.

Using the radios is the most realistic. In fact, you must tune the correct radio frequency to hear and be heard by other players. You also can't just talk. You must "key your microphone." This is just like in the real airplane where the pilot pushes a button to talk. On FSX, it's the Caps Lock key. You must hold it down while you talk and then let it go to listen, just like the real world. Although you must be on the same frequency to talk to another player using the aircraft radios, the "signal" can be heard anywhere in the virtual world.

If you ever need to broadcast something to all players, regardless of the radio frequency they are on, you can press Shift+Caps Lock. We recommend you avoid this in public games.

KEEPING IT REAL

PUSH TO TALK

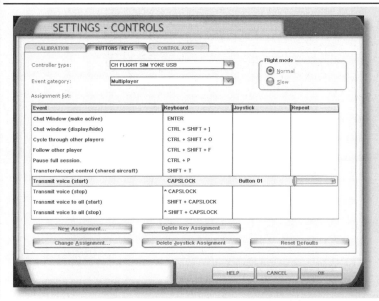

For added realism, choose Options > Settings> Controls and go to the Buttons and Keys tab to add the transmit control to your joystick or control yoke. The actual command is in the Multiplayer events and is Transmit Voice (Start).

TWO COMMUNICATION BUGS

At the time of this writing, FSX had two known bugs with voice communication. One is that if you leave the chat window open, sometimes you can hear radio chatter that's not on your frequency, and therefore other pilots can't hear you no matter what you do. Close the window to fix this. Also, COM1 can create problems in a shared cockpit. If you're using a shared cockpit, make all your radio calls on COM2.

660

| PART I | PART II | PART III | PART IV | PART V | PART VI |
| PREFLIGHT | SPORT PILOT | PRIVATE PILOT | INSTRUMENT RATING | COMMERCIAL LICENSE | ATP AND BEYOND |

LISTEN FIRST

Also like the real world is how you need to listen before you speak. Nothing muddies communication like several people trying to transmit at once. You got a taste of this with virtual ATC in FSX if you ever tried to transmit while the synthetic voice was speaking.

As far as what to say, use your experiences with virtual ATC as a guide. Many communities, particularly the organized ones, are quite willing to coach you too. The more realistic you are, the better the experience for them. Lots of real-world student pilots have fear about talking on the radio. Flying in a virtual world but with real people is a great way to get over your radio jitters, and your mistakes are part of the reality of flying out there.

INSIDE THE GAME

THAT SOUNDS BETTER

Good sound is key to happy multiplayer flying. It's worth checking your sound settings, if you're having problems or the balance of sounds isn't quite right for you. A common problem is that voice sounds are unchecked. If this is true, you'll be able to transmit on the radios in multiplayer but not receive. Another problem is that the engine noise is set too high and makes it hard to hear the radio. Granted, this can be realistic, but it's not much fun. Do the virtual equivalent of getting a noise-canceling aviation headset by just turning the engine noise down.

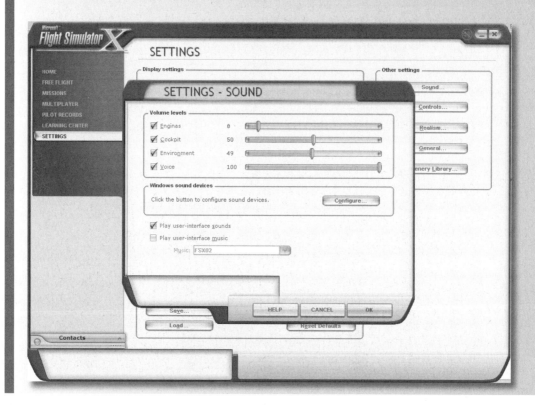

FLYING WITH OTHER AIRPLANES

Finding other aircraft is tough in either the virtual sky or the real one. To make things easier, turn on the aircraft labels so you can see other airplanes in the sky. You can turn these on and control what you see by choosing Options > Settings > Display and going to the Traffic tab. You can then toggle the labels on and off with Ctrl+Shift+L.

Even then it can be tough to spot a specific aircraft if you want to get over to it. There's a new view option in multiplayer, though, that lets FSX show you which way to look. Choose View > New View, and find the player you're looking for. The view opens as a virtual cockpit view looking directly toward that player (see Figure 24-10). Head off in that direction.

When you have that aircraft in sight, you can maneuver as near to it as you want. Formation flying is a whole new level of skill. Luckily, the consequences for messing up are not nearly as nasty in FSX as they are in real life. We aren't experts in formation flying ourselves, but the general idea is to make small changes and keep the communication between the aircraft flowing. One aircraft should be the flight leader and announce all turns, climbs, and descents. After you have things figured out, you can work with other pilots to try formation maneuvers, takeoffs, and landings.

Figure 24-10: The label can be hard to see, but if the view is looking off your left wing, turn left.

662

PART I PREFLIGHT | PART II SPORT PILOT | PART III PRIVATE PILOT | PART IV INSTRUMENT RATING | PART V COMMERCIAL LICENSE | PART VI ATP AND BEYOND

It can help quite a bit to zoom out the view a bit when you fly in formation (see Figure 24-11). It's also critical that you match your speed and altitude with the other airplane. Pressing Shift+Z to show these numbers at the top of the screen can be helpful.

Figure 24-11: You can have quite dissimilar aircraft flying in formation, such as this Extra 300 and Cessna Caravan. They just need to be able to fly at similar speeds.

INSIDE THE GAME

FLYING A SKYHAWK BY DEFAULT

One issue with multiplayer is that your computer might not have the aircraft model that some-one else is flying. In that case, FSX will substitute it with the closest aircraft of that type that it has. This means if someone is flying a Navy SNJ (a WWII advanced training airplane) and you don't have the SNJ in your list of aircraft, you might see a Cessna 172 SP instead. It will have a Cessna Skyhawk label above it; however, it will perform like the supercharged Navy combat trainer rather than a Skyhawk.

In this particular case, you might see the Skyhawk resting on its tail because the airplane it's emulating is a tailwheel.

FLYING WITH ANOTHER PILOT

FSX's new option to share cockpits is a great feature with lots of potential. Two pilots can fly together in a crew environment, which is a huge boon for virtual airlines (see Chapter 24). It also allows for virtual flight instruction where you as the student—or maybe you as the instructor—can fly along with another pilot and practice your technique.

Beware, though. The other pilot has access to all the conditions that the host allowed when he or she set up the session. This means the other pilot might be able to fail systems on you, change the weather, or even slew the aircraft to a new location.

When you're flying with another pilot or instructor in a real-world airplane, it's essential that you both know who is controlling the airplane. Although it's common to split up duties such as one pilot handling the radios and communications and another flying the airplane, only one pilot should be on the controls at a time. Real-world pilots handle this with "positive exchange of flight controls." An exchange might sound like this:

Pilot 1: "You have the flight controls."

Pilot 2: "I have the flight controls."

Pilot 1 (confirming): "You have the flight controls."

It may sound overly formal, but just imagine what could happen if the airplane was coming in to land and each pilot thought the other one would lift the nose to flare. Ouch.

In FSX, the game handles this for you. Only one pilot can control the throttle, yoke, and rudder at once. Either pilot can control nonessential items such as radios or landing gear and flap levels. To switch who has control, either pilot presses Shift+T on their keyboard. This sends a request (as shown in Figure 24-12) to the other pilot to either release or take over the controls as appropriate. The pilot accepts with Shift+T, and the exchange is complete. Sometimes you'll see a short screen flicker when control is exchanged.

Figure 24-12: If you don't want the change of controls, just don't type Shift+T, and the offer will time out.

664

PART I
PREFLIGHT

PART II
SPORT PILOT

PART III
PRIVATE PILOT

PART IV
INSTRUMENT RATING

PART V
COMMERCIAL LICENSE

PART VI
ATP AND BEYOND

When you're the Pilot-Not-Flying (PNF), you might want to tap A on your keyboard to actually put yourself in the right seat of the airplane. Note that since the PNF can change your autopilot settings, you can control the aircraft while it is flying on autopilot even when you don't have control.

INSIDE THE GAME

MULTIPLAYER IN FLIGHT SIM 2004

Multiplayer in FS 2004 (FS9) is a bit different from FSX. In FS9, you start flying and then choose Flights > Multiplayer. You can then connect to a hosted session by IP address or host a session. (You used to be able to connect to a shared session view the MS Gaming Zone, similar to GameSpy, but that is no longer supported.)

Our experience is that FSX and FS9 don't work well directly over a network to create a multiplayer session. Also, FSX doesn't connect correctly to some multiplayer sessions hosted on the Internet outside of GameSpy.

Many of the Internet sessions use a free hosting application called FS host (www.chocolatesoftware.com/fshost). The FS host website also has a free client that lets FSX connect to FSHost servers. If you're trying to get FS9 and FSX to connect to each other, either locally or over the Internet, you can use the FSHost software as a bridge.

Climbing into the Tower

The option for taking a role as a tower controller is available in the Deluxe version of FSX. This is a cool new feature and offers some of the functions that were available previously only by using add-on programs to Flight Simulator. The ATC functions are still more limited than what you'll find in some of those programs, but they're built in and convenient.

Chapter 26 is devoted entirely to virtual ATC, so right now we'll just cover how to join a multiplayer session as a controller and what you'll see when you get there.

Getting the Controller Job

Joining as a controller starts the same as any multiplayer session, but on the first Session Conditions screen you'll select Air Traffic Controller from the Choose Role pull-down menu.

All the options will become unavailable except the one to start at an airport of your choice (see Figure 24-13). Make sure this is the airport you want, and click Next. You'll come to the Briefing room page. Click Next again to take the elevator up to the tower cab.

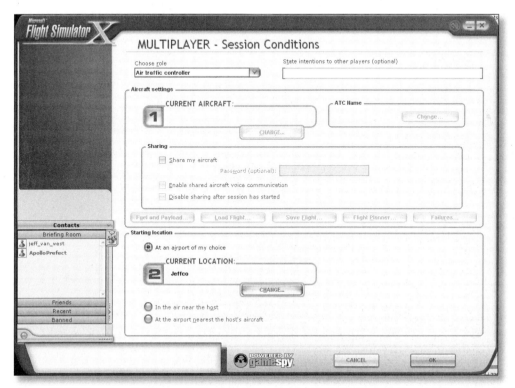

Figure 24-13: The only option for a controller is to choose the airport. Just make sure it's one where some virtual pilots are flying.

666

PART I
PREFLIGHT

PART II
SPORT PILOT

PART III
PRIVATE PILOT

PART IV
INSTRUMENT RATING

PART V
COMMERCIAL LICENSE

PART VI
ATP AND BEYOND

Figure 24-14: The control screens in the tower cab really do work, but it's much easier to open these items as floating windows.

When you appear in the tower, you'll be in the ATC equivalent of the virtual cockpit. Using the hat switch on your yoke should let you pan around and see the entire airport. Note that buildings may block your view of some aircraft, just like in the real world. This view is cool but not that practical (see Figure 24-14). Press F10 on your keyboard to go to the tower version of the 2D cockpit.

You'll see a small control palette in the upper left of the screen. Click all the buttons except Fade In and Fade Out and Next Station to see all that ATC has to offer. The palettes will arrange generally as shown in Figure 24-15. You might want to resize the radar screen smaller or larger depending on how you plan to use it.

Figure 24-15: You can overlay these floating windows over the virtual tower cab and pan around. Press F9 for the panning view, and then choose View > Instrument Panel > Panel Options. This can be cumbersome, though.

Local Info

Here you see the local time and two critical pieces of information tower controllers often give pilots, the winds, and the current altimeter.

Communication Radios

The ATC communication radios are similar to the audio panel you're used to from the aircraft. You can dial any frequency you want by putting your mouse over the numbers and using the mouse scroll wheel, but the key frequencies for that airport are listed below and can simply be clicked to use. The frequency you click will become active in whichever radio you have set to transmit (TX). This is the frequency you will speak on if you key your microphone. Click the TX box by either frequency to select it for use. The one in use shows up with a blue background. The one not in use has a black background.

You can receive (RX) on either or both frequencies at once. Click the appropriate RX to listen in. Note that if you want to change the frequency that you aren't transmitting on using the listed frequencies, you'll need to quickly turn on TX for that radio, click the frequency you want to make it active, and then click the other TX to switch your transmitter back.

Radar Settings and Screen

The radar settings and radar screen work together as the settings change what you see on the screen. Zoom and pan (the four-way triangles) are straightforward. Most of the other buttons toggle the visibility of items on and off on the radar screen. Some of these items, such as a compass rose, just toggle on and off. Others, like the airport symbols, have three modes. They can be off, on just as icons, or on as icons with labels. The corresponding buttons are black for off, blue with 1 for on, and purple with 2 for on and labeled.

Labels are great as you're learning your way around the airspace or when a pilot references a fix or airport you don't know.

Session Info

Session Info gives you details of different aircraft in your airspace. Click any aircraft in the list to see more information.

A Better View

The Fade In and Fade Out buttons apply transparency to the radar station controls so you can see through them better. Often this kind of visual effect requires high-end computers, but with the static ATC view, you can often get descent results even on low-end computers. The next station button switches your view to the next chair in the tower but bumps you back to the virtual cockpit view.

You can use the hat switch while you're in the F10 tower cab view to look in different parts of the sky, but it's much better to be able to pan around.

668

PART I	PART II	PART III	PART IV	PART V	PART VI
PREFLIGHT	SPORT PILOT	PRIVATE PILOT	INSTRUMENT RATING	COMMERCIAL LICENSE	ATP AND BEYOND

Figure 24-16: It's easier to see everything standing on the roof and with the controls set to fade out a bit.

We found the most flexible option was choosing View > Outside View > Locked Spot. This is actually the view from above and behind the tower, but it lets you pan around to see everything (see Figure 24-16). Combine that with the ATC floating palettes, and you have the best seat in the house. The only catch is that the panning control is backwards on the hat switch of what you might think, but you can get used to that quickly.

You can have two controllers in the tower, but it's not like a shared cockpit. Those two people have their own controls and can see what the other one is doing. They must coordinate who does what between them. Some organized sessions will assign an intratower frequency for just this purpose.

 INSIDE THE GAME

FOLLOW THAT AIRCRAFT

Finding an aircraft from the tower can be just as hard as finding it in the air. You can use the same view trick to have your view automatically find and follow a specific aircraft. You can also zoom in close to see the airplane.

Choose View Mode and then the aircraft you want to see to switch your whole view to that aircraft (or just right-click the screen, and choose the aircraft from the list). If you want to view the aircraft only in a pop-up window, choose View Mode > New View instead.

YOUR WORLD, THEIR WORLD

As we said, how much control you have over the virtual world depends on the host's initial settings for the session. If you're hosting a session, think carefully about what you want to be able to do or not do. A flight instruction session would benefit greatly from the host/instructor being able to do a global pause for the session and from the option of slewing the aircraft to different places and altitudes quickly. A super-realistic session at LAX should have these features turned off, as shown in Figure 24-17.

Note as well that you always have control over your own aircraft and views. Even in a shared cockpit, one pilot could be flying the airplane with high realism, and the other could use the easy flight model and autorudder.

The built-in multiplayer within FSX isn't the only way to fly with other pilots and controllers. There are other host programs out there and other communities. In the next two chapters, you'll look at signing up with a virtual airline or working with a virtual ATC. Most of these communities will be flying transport-category jets. If you'd like to pause for a moment and learn about flying jets, read Bonus Chapter 2 on the website to do your 737 checkout.

Figure 24-17: Don't go trying to change the world in multiplayer. You'll just have to fly what you're faced with…just like in the real world.

670

PART I	PART II	PART III	PART IV	PART V	PART VI
PREFLIGHT	SHORT PILOT	PRIVATE PILOT	INSTRUMENT RATING	COMMERCIAL LICENSE	ATP AND BEYOND

KEY POINTS FOR REAL FLYING AND FSX BUILT-INS

The following are some key points from this chapter:

- Understand how to find and fly with other pilots.

- Know how to do a positive exchange of controls.

- Use the radios to talk with other real humans.

- Understand how to work the tower controls.

Here are the lessons and missions to study after reading this chapter:

- *Lessons*: None apply to this chapter, but there is extensive information about multiplayer in the Learning Center.

- *Missions*: None.

VIRTUAL AIRLINES AND ONLINE FLYING

"WE BANNED EMERGENCIES. IT WAS RIDICULOUS. O'HARE WAS HAVING FOUR EMERGENCIES A NIGHT, AND THEY DON'T GET FOUR A MONTH IN THE REAL WORLD. THEY'D CALL THE TOWER AND SAY, 'EMERGENCY! ENGINES OUT.' I KNOW WHAT PEOPLE ARE DOING: MAYBE THEY NEED TO GO EAT DINNER, SO THEY CALL IN AN EMERGENCY SO THEY DON'T HAVE TO WAIT IN A HOLDING PATTERN TO LAND."

—HARV STEIN, FOUNDER OF VATSIM
(VIRTUAL AIR TRAFFIC SIMULATION NETWORK),
IN AN INTERVIEW FOR WIRED MAGAZINE, MARCH 2003

672

PART I	PART II	PART III	PART IV	PART V	PART VI
PREFLIGHT	SPORT PILOT	PRIVATE PILOT	INSTRUMENT RATING	COMMERCIAL LICENSE	ATP AND BEYOND

VIRTUAL AIRLINES

You've made it! You've worked your way up from a student pilot in the Piper J-3 Cub to become an ATP in the Boeing 737, flying all your missions and taking the checkrides for each certificate and rating. Now what?

This is the same question real-world pilots ask, although they usually ask the question right after they get their Private Pilot Certificate. Sure, there will be the obligatory flights with family and friends to show off their new skills, but unless real-world pilots are on the track to have a career in aviation or they use their plane for business, there isn't much incentive to fly on a regular basis.

To fill this need, flight clubs have formed, offering organized activities, usually a variety of aircraft, and, at the very least, camaraderie with other like-minded people. Even on days the weather (or airplanes in maintenance) prevents flying, you can find pilots together at the airport having a "hangar-flying" session, telling tales both large and small of their flying adventures. Even nonpilots join flight clubs, just for the chance to fly along on these adventures.

Figure 25-1: A virtual airline *is a group of sim pilots who fly aircraft painted in liveries of a real or imaginary airline.* (Courtesy WestWind Virtual Airlines)

Virtual pilots don't necessarily have that built-in community, because the flying is usually done solo on your own computer. But the need for a connection with others still exists. Although the multiplayer aspects of FSX are one of the most powerful tools for collaborating with other sim pilots, simmers have been joining together since the early editions of flight simulators, long before multiplayer was a possibility. One form of collaboration is the virtual airline (see Figure 25-1).

The idea is this: sim pilots who are part of a virtual airline fly airline-like routes (with appropriate planes) on their own, and then use a website (or online bulletin board system in the early days) to report their flights. Some more sophisticated virtual airlines create specific (or even real-world) routes and timetables for added realism. And once flight simulators began allowing users to create their own aircraft—and paint aircraft in different colors and liveries (logos, and so on)—virtual airlines made customized aircraft that could be downloaded and flown.

Some virtual airlines are designed to replicate real-world airlines; in fact, the idea of virtual airlines probably started with sim pilots wanting to fly for their favorite airline. There is a United Virtual Airlines, British Airways Virtual, Qantas Virtual Airways, and many more. Some real-world airlines are uncomfortable with their virtual facsimiles, and some virtual airlines have had to shut down because of lawsuits and other hassles from the real-world airline, even though the virtual representation was really just a "club" and money was not involved. Other real-world airlines, such as United Airlines, are supportive of their virtual counterpart and might even host the virtual-airline website on their own computers.

But many other virtual airlines have no real-world counterpart; they are completely made up, including the logos and paint jobs on the airplanes. Still, these virtual airlines can be as sophisticated as those replicating real-world airlines.

KEEPING IT REAL

VIRTUAL REALITY SUES REALITY

Several years ago, the virtual airline Jetstar International Airlines started legal action against the real-world Qantas, claiming copyright and trademark infringement by Qantas' new Jetstar Airways subsidiary. Apparently the virtual airline existed for several years before Qantas created its low-cost airline.

The virtual Jetstar claimed the real-world Jetstar Airways logos and color scheme were so similar to the virtual livery that it constituted an infringement. And, according to the CEO of the virtual Jetstar, when the real-world Jetstar Airways started offering cheap tickets for a promotion, the virtual airline's web servers were overwhelmed with emails and requests for tickets, plus solicitations for employment by real-world pilots.

As part of an agreement, the virtual Jetstar rebranded to become Trans International Airlines (a long-defunct real-world airline) and is now an active virtual airline. Meanwhile, a new virtual airline was created by a different group of people with the intent to replicate Jetstar Airways' routes and aircraft, so now there is Jetstar Virtual Airways.

FINDING A VIRTUAL AIRLINE

Figure 25-2: Many virtual airlines have aircraft painted just like a real-world airline. (Courtesy United Virtual Airlines)

Hundreds, if not thousands, of virtual airlines exist today. Finding one that you'd like to join can be a tedious process. One way to start is the same way the original ones were created: find the virtual equivalent of your favorite real-world airline (see Figure 25-2). Or just find the virtual airline that flies the airplanes and liveries you like to view. (You'll be spending lots of time looking at your own airplane, after all.)

There are also certain unique virtual airlines that are not run in the passenger "airline" sense but, for simplicity, are grouped among virtual airline, such as virtual military forces, virtual cargo airlines, virtual business jet organizations, and so on. These organizations fly appropriate aircraft and have their own paint schemes, just like regular virtual airlines.

674

| PART I | PART II | PART III | PART IV | PART V | PART VI |
| PREFLIGHT | SPORT PILOT | PRIVATE PILOT | INSTRUMENT RATING | COMMERCIAL LICENSE | ATP AND BEYOND |

But once you begin flying for a virtual airline, you'll discover other attributes of a good virtual airline are just as important as the types of airplanes and liveries. If you like the idea of true simulation—a realistic representation of a real-world airline—then you'll want to find one that has prescribed routes to fly on specified schedules with promotions based on seniority and more. On the other hand, if you just want some camaraderie and the chance to fly specially painted aircraft on your own time and to places only you want to go, then a more casual airline is for you.

As with all hobby groups, the personalities of the members are what make the virtual airline right for you. Many airlines have a web-based message forum (bulletin board) for communication, and some forums are open to the public. Spending time looking through a virtual airline's forum can give you a good sense of the kind of people the airline attracts.

HUBS AND PILOT BASES

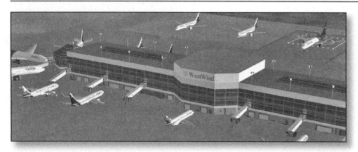

Figure 25-3: Virtual airline hubs give a sim pilot a home base from which to fly. (Courtesy WestWind Virtual Airlines)

When a virtual airline is big enough that keeping track of all the pilots is a chore for the volunteer managers, the airline might subdivide into hubs (see Figure 25-3). The concept is similar to pilot bases in real-world airlines: pilots are grouped together at a major airport (an airline's hub) to start and end a series of flights, and a hub manager (a volunteer, of course) is responsible for the pilots at that hub.

Just like real-world pilots, virtual airline pilots don't need to live in the city where their hub is located. However, virtual airlines don't require you to start every flight at your hub airport; usually you can choose any flight in the airline's schedule, even if it is on the opposite side of the world. (After all, this is supposed to be *fun*, not a *job*!)

In other words, the only real reason to divide into hubs is administrative: the pilots are grouped into manageable chunks so that hub managers don't have too many pilots to keep track of.

MOVING UP THE RANKS

Most virtual airlines have a specific ranking system for their pilots (see Figure 25-4). Just as real-world airlines start pilots as first officers in the right seat for some period of time before advancing to the captain spot in the left seat, virtual airlines have a promotion scale based on your flight time with the airline.

The most common system involves restricting which airplanes you're allowed to fly. New virtual pilots are typically allowed to fly only the small turboprop airplanes (such as the Beech 1900, which is based on the King Air) on short routes from local hubs. After every flight, or every few days or weeks, the pilot reports the number of flight hours accrued on some kind of web-based form or by email to the hub manager or the virtual airline's chief pilot. (It's totally based on the honor system, because there is no way to prove you really flew all the time you said you did.)

Pilots and Management Rank Insignia Page

Rank Insignia	Category	Title	Required Hours	Available Equipment
	CAT III	Captain	0-149.9 Hours	Saab 340B (SF3) ATR72 (AT7) ERJ-135 (ER3) ERJ-140 (ERD) ERJ-145 (ER4) CRJ-700 (CR7) Boeing 737-800 (B738) Boeing MD-80/83 (M80/M83)
	CAT IV	Senior Captain	150-399.9 Hours	CAT III plus Boeing 757-200 (B757) Boeing 767-200 (B762) Boeing 767-300 (B763)
	CAT V	Command Captain	400-899.9 Hours	CAT IV plus Boeing 777-200 (B777) Airbus A300-600 (AB3)
	CAT VI	Fleet Captain	900+ Hours	Entire Fleet

Figure 25-4: Virtual ranks with virtual stripes in a virtual airline—but real pride. (Courtesy American Virtual Airlines)

Once a pilot has enough flight time—maybe 10 hours, maybe 50, depending on the airline—the pilot can apply for a promotion. Once promoted, the pilot can then fly more advanced aircraft—perhaps a regional jet or small business jet—and longer routes. A promotion to the third level, perhaps after 100 hours of flight, allows larger aircraft like a Boeing 737, and so on, until the pilot is flying Boeing 747s and Airbus A340s on long, international routes.

Some virtual airlines have created "checkrides" for each promotion, which are predefined missions or routes the pilot must fly, and then the pilot must report certain aspects of the flight (such as the radio frequency the flight simulator ATC switched you to when crossing the XYZ VOR).

Once a pilot has worked in the virtual airline for a while and gotten to know people through the online forums or multiplayer flying (see the "Multiplayer" section), there may be opportunity to become "management" at the airline. Like all volunteer organizations, this really means an opportunity to provide time and talent for little recognition and no reward, but some people enjoy the chance to help other virtual pilots and to provide a fun environment. And like all volunteer organizations, the more you put into it, the more you get out of it.

MULTIPLAYER

Figure 25-5: Fly-ins online bring many pilots in a virtual airline together at one airport. (Courtesy American Virtual Airlines)

A virtual airline is a great place to meet other pilots who can use the multiplayer system built into FSX and previous versions of Flight Simulator (see Figure 25-5). By setting up a multiplayer server—or using one of several virtual air traffic servers—virtual airlines have created opportunities to fly with other pilots in the same virtual world, such as the following:

- *Fly-ins*: You depart from or fly to the same airport, at coordinated times, so that you can see the other planes and pilots.

- *Air shows*: While all the aircraft are parked at an airport, one or more pilots fly aerobatics or other challenging demonstration maneuvers.

- *Formation flying*: Pilots practice traditional formation (close or far, depending on the speed of your Internet connection and the server you're using).

676

PART I	PART II	PART III	PART IV	PART V	PART VI
PREFLIGHT	SPORT PILOT	PRIVATE PILOT	INSTRUMENT RATING	COMMERCIAL LICENSE	ATP AND BEYOND

- *Races*: Air races could be flown over a distance course or around a track at someplace like the real-world air races in Reno, Nevada.

A virtual airline could also make great use of the "same-cockpit" multiplayer feature of FSX:

- *Training*: New pilots could learn the procedures of airline flying with an experienced training pilot.

- *Checkrides*: When ready to become a "line" pilot for a virtual airline—or when moving up to more sophisticated aircraft as part of a promotion—a pilot would fly with an airline check pilot in the virtual cockpit, ensuring the pilot follows the procedures created by the airline

- *Two-pilot crew*: Virtual airlines could set up specific two-pilot procedures for the most realistic airline flights possible in the computer-simulation world.

As we're writing this book, however, not many virtual airline pilots have FSX, so not many virtual airlines are using the same-cockpit feature yet. But this seems to be a great opportunity for virtual airlines to become even more realistic.

ONLINE FLYING

Although FSX does include integrated multiplayer functionality through GameSpy or through direct connection to another virtual pilot's computer, for more than 10 years flight simmers have had other online, multiplayer networks available for flying with other virtual pilots (see Figure 25-6). Those networks also have created virtual ATC, with people who learn how to be air traffic controllers. (You can find instructions for becoming a virtual controller in the next chapter.)

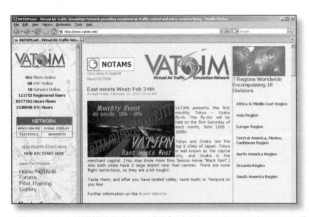

Figure 25-6: VATSIM (left) and IVAO (right) are the two largest online, multiplayer flight sim networks. (Courtesy VATSIM and IVAO)

Most of these networks are free (even the special connection software, other than FSX, is free) and are supported by donations of money, server time, and volunteer time. The big ones that have been in existence for quite a while are the Virtual Air Traffic Simulation (VATSIM) network and the International Virtual Aviation Organization (IVAO). VATSIM is the largest network, with more than 110,000 registered members, including one of the authors of this book. Therefore, we'll use VATSIM in the following examples; IVAO and other such systems operate similarly.

⬇ STUDENT OF THE CRAFT

MULTIPLE VIRTUAL REALITIES

It seems odd that there would be more than one virtual flight simulation network available; after all, if the reason to fly on such a network is to be able to see other airplanes and interact with virtual air traffic control, why would you want to spread out the available pilots and controllers over multiple networks?

The answer seems to be the same one that causes problems with many real-world volunteer organizations: conflict between personalities. The first major virtual flying network was SATCO, formed in 1997. In 1998, disagreements among some in management caused a group to split off and form IVAO. A few years later, SATCO morphed into VATSIM. And in late 2005, a management conflict at IVAO caused another split there; confusingly, both of those organizations continue to use the name IVAO, and their websites look identical.

However, there are big differences in the number of pilots and controllers available on each of these three systems, depending on where you're flying. On a recent weekday, VATSIM (www .vatsim.net) had 600 pilots and controllers online at the same time during the evening in European time zones and 500 during the North American evening. IVAO (www.ivao.aero) had slightly higher numbers during the European weekday evening but less than 200 during the North American evening. Both VATSIM and IVAO can have up to 1,000 people—including hundreds of virtual controllers—online during busy weekends. The "second" IVAO (www .ivao.org), however, had only one pilot and no ATC during a recent weekday evening in the European time zones.

STARTING OUT

Virtual pilot networks use proprietary software that runs alongside the flight simulator (usually MSFS, but some software can work with other flight simulators). The original software was Squawkbox, and it's still used on VATSIM by pilots flying earlier versions of MSFS; as of this writing, though, it is still being optimized to work with FSX. Until that product (Squawkbox v.4) is released, FSX pilots are encouraged to use another free product called FSInn (see Figure 25-7). A discussion for how to use the software is beyond the scope of this book (and is well-documented by FSInn's authors anyway), but we will give you some basic information about what it does.

678

PART I PREFLIGHT | PART II SPORT PILOT | PART III PRIVATE PILOT | PART IV INSTRUMENT RATING | PART V COMMERCIAL LICENSE | PART VI ATP AND BEYOND

Figure 25-7: FSInn runs as an add-on to FSX to provide a connection to VATSIM.

The website of each organization has instructions for downloading and using the particular software. In each case the software is free and is thoroughly checked to ensure it won't corrupt most computer systems or allow hackers to gain access to your computer.

The job of connection software such as FSInn is twofold: to send to a server (for example, VATSIM) information about your FSX airplane and to get from that server information about every other airplane nearby so that FSX can display those aircraft using its multiplayer technology. The information it sends and receives is at least geographic coordinates (latitude and longitude), altitude, heading, and attitude.

At some point, usually during login, FSInn will also tell the server what kind of plane you're flying and what livery it has been "painted" with. With the right added software, then, other virtual pilots connected to the same server and located near you will see you in the right kind of plane, with your virtual airline logo, and so on.

Of course, when you send and receive information from a server rather than directly to another person's computer running FSX, there is more of a delay. And with enough airplanes in the same area, the amount of information coming in on your Internet connection can get overwhelming. Therefore, the server updates your position and that of other airplanes only once a second or so. This can make the movement of other airplanes appear quite jerky, like they jump from place to place. Formation flying, for instance, can be quite difficult. But when you want the added realism of more airplanes around your virtual world, with real humans controlling them instead of the FSX virtual ATC, it is worth the minor hassle.

To add realism, the server maintains the current weather reports for every real-world airport that creates a weather report. When you are connected to the server, FSInn gets the current weather report for your location and tells FSX the report; FSX then creates the appropriate weather for you to see. Usually this ends up being the same as if you'd selected Real World Weather on the World > Weather menu, but for technical reasons it is better to use the server's weather report for your location—that way, all the other pilots (and ATC) will have the same weather, and for instance, you'll all use the runway facing into the wind.

COMMUNICATION

When you get ready to fly a particular flight on a virtual air traffic network, you have to choose a call sign. This could be your virtual airline ID number, the flight number of the route (like real-world airlines), or just the tail number

Figure 25-8: FSInn text (chat) communication with controllers and pilots

of your airplane. For some people, this is a chance to make up a tail number with meaning for yourself, such as your initials and birthday, or those of your sweetie. Or just pick something humorous. (Did you notice the call sign we used for the Beech Baron in the figures for the "Commercial Pilot" chapters? N44EE—say it out loud, remembering to use the phonetic pronunciation for the letters. We also like "B4RJ" and "1234FT.")

All virtual flying systems are set up to allow text communications ("chat") between pilots and controllers (see Figure 25-8). The good ones are even set up so your flight simulator COM radios work correctly; if you're on the wrong frequency, no one will see your typing.

However, virtual pilots quickly grew frustrated with typing their requests to ATC. (At least with the FSX ATC window you have to type only a number or two to tell ATC what you want.) When Voice over IP (VoIP) technology became widely available, online pilots and controllers immediately gravitated to it. Each network chooses which of the various VoIP systems it uses, such as TeamSpeak or Ventrilo. Big networks such as VATSIM, however, actually incorporate voice capability into the ATC and pilot software, so you don't have to do a separate installation.

If you don't have a microphone/headset setup, you can at least have the other people's voices come out your speakers, and then you type your replies in the text chat system. But headsets with integrated microphones are now so cheap (less than $20 for a basic set) that most online pilots and controllers use them. However, we hope these networks will never *require* voice, because many people, for physiological or personal reasons, do not use voice communication. Unlike the real world, online flying and controlling can be done entirely through text chat, and that is a great opportunity for such people.

Sometimes you'll want to talk to one particular person, either another pilot or a controller, and you won't want everyone to be able to hear it. In the real world, that's not an option; even selecting an unused radio frequency doesn't assure that it'll be a private conversation. Online networks, however, usually have some kind of private chat capability. This might be used for a conversation among pilots of a virtual airline so they can keep their main radio frequency on the local ATC channel, or it could be between a controller and a pilot to discuss topics (such as training a new pilot) that don't belong on the open radio frequency.

TRAINING AND EXPERIENCE

Speaking of training pilots, most online networks don't actually require it before connecting. Big networks such as VATSIM have extensive resources for learning how to be a virtual pilot and how to fly and communicate on the virtual flying network (see Figure 25-9), but there is no requirement for the new pilot to actually do the training.

680

PART I
PREFLIGHT

PART II
SPORT PILOT

PART III
PRIVATE PILOT

PART IV
INSTRUMENT RATING

PART V
COMMERCIAL LICENSE

PART VI
ATP AND BEYOND

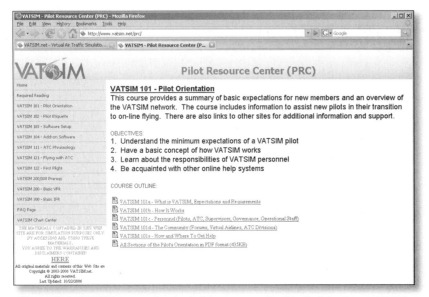

Figure 25-9: VATSIM has an extensive training program for virtual pilots. (Courtesy VATSIM)

This can lead to challenging situations, where a "newbie" doesn't behave in realistic or helpful ways. Like all such hobby situations, you have to cultivate a relaxed attitude toward others. Open a private chat with the pilot to help them figure things out without clogging up the radio. Be patient and sympathetic—you were a new pilot once, too. Conversely, when you're the new pilot, feel free to ask for help from anyone. The more pilots and controllers that are on (and know what they're doing), the more fun it is for everyone.

One surprise that many new virtual pilots discover when connecting to an online system is the wide range in age and experience of other pilots and controllers. There is usually no age restriction, because no money is involved, and there are no "adult-only" activities happening; therefore, it is not unusual for planes and even controller positions to be staffed by teenagers or even preteens. Of course, you don't know it, because there is nothing in the system to tell you how old the person is. If you have voice communication capability, then you might guess some are young because of the way they talk, but that can be misleading, too. But this is not just a video game for many: a surprising number of young virtual pilots and controllers go on to become real-world pilots and controllers.

At the other end of the age spectrum is a group of people who have plenty of time for a hobby like this: those who are retired from full-time work. Virtual airlines and virtual ATC groups are a great place for someone who "always wanted to be a pilot" or controller and now has the time and inclination to learn the basics and to enjoy it without making a real career out of it.

REAL (VIRTUAL) CONTROLLERS

Compared to earlier flight simulators, the ATC system in FSX is powerful and realistic. But compared to reality, there is a lot to be desired.

As we've mentioned throughout this book, it is really hard to get the FSX ATC to do the whole range of activities we do in real-world flying, especially when IFR or in IMC. For instance, real-world controllers will give us a block of airspace to work in, and traffic permitting, we can do all kinds of training maneuvers—IMC or VMC—and then ask ATC for vectors back home. FSX ATC is meant for point-to-point flights, from one airport to another.

And, of course, only the most recent versions of MSFS have built-in ATC. Before MSFS 2002, there wasn't any ATC at all in the game. So when Squawkbox and the original online networks such as SATCO were created in 1997, the idea of virtual controllers came quickly. After all, the servers had all the information a controller would need about every flight in the virtual world: their geographic position, altitude, speed and direction, type of airplane, and aircraft call sign. All you needed was software that could display the aircraft on a window that looked like a controller's radar screen. Volunteers again came to the rescue and created ProController, supplanted now (on VATSIM, anyway) by the Advanced Simulated Radar Client (ASRC). Current software even lets the controller see your entire flight plan as you created it in FSX.

We'll discuss how to become a virtual air traffic controller in the next chapter, but the following sections cover some issues about working with online ATC that are different from FSX ATC.

ORGANIZATIONS

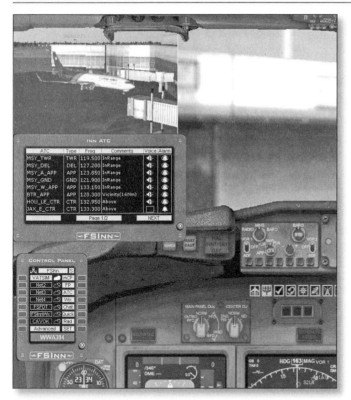

Figure 25-10: Controllers in your vicinity show up in the ATC window in FSInn.

Just as in the real world, the virtual ATC world is divided into regions both by countries and by *flight information regions* (FIRs, also known as *centers* or ARTCCs in the United States). When virtual controllers get started, they usually join a particular FIR/ARTCC and learn the procedures there.

If a controller is performing as a tower controller and that airport doesn't have a ground controller, then the tower controller will also do the duties of the ground controller (such as giving you an IFR clearance or instructions to taxi to the active runway). A radar controller at an airport, likewise, can act as the tower controller (and ground controller) of any airport within the boundaries of the approach/departure airspace (see "BTR_APP" in Figure 25-10). And a FIR/ARTCC controller can, if he is the only one available, act as approach/departure, tower, ground, and clearance.

TRAINING

Unlike being an online pilot, where there are no training requirements, air traffic controllers in the virtual flying networks are trained in their work before they're allowed to control. Virtual controllers usually start by learning to be ground controllers and clearance delivery specialists. (Some organizations allow a beginning controller to be in

682

| PART I | PART II | PART III | PART IV | PART V | PART VI |
| PREFLIGHT | SPORT PILOT | PRIVATE PILOT | INSTRUMENT RATING | COMMERCIAL LICENSE | ATP AND BEYOND |

the tower position, too.) After studying, they take online tests and have to pass with good scores just to be able to connect as a controller. The network restricts which position a new controller can connect as, and once the controller is promoted (by being observed controlling traffic), they can move up to the tower position, then radar approach/departure, and finally en route (center).

This means you can almost always expect the virtual controller to be able to give you at least the minimum service a real-world controller could do. They can give you a clearance to your destination (although they might not know whether the route is any good…that's up to you). They can guide you to the runway, clear you for takeoff when there is no one else landing or taking off, vector you to your first waypoints, and bring you in the same way for approach and landing. So, even new controllers are just as good as the FSX ATC controllers, at least for the level of their position.

Experienced controllers can do more, of course. If you want your vectors to the ILS to be longer than usual, or shorter, they can adapt. If you want to try an unusual procedure, they probably can get the charts for it and can help you fly it. If you and the controller both use voice communication, an experienced controller probably can say the full name of your destination airport, rather than saying, "Cleared to Echo-Golf-Lima-Lima…" If you're new at being an online pilot, you'll see they're probably good at explaining the steps to help you. (Most virtual controllers start out as online pilots and continue to fly sometimes, too.) And unlike the computer-generated ATC, human controllers can use other runways besides the "primary" one if you want to practice crosswind landings, for instance, or to take off in between a long line of fly-in arrivals.

THEY'RE ONLY HUMAN

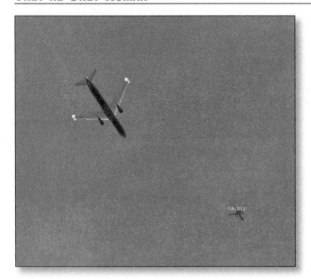

Figure 25-11: When you're being vectored by ATC, you're still required to see and avoid other traffic and obstacles— whether you're flying in the real world or on an online, multiplayer network. (Courtesy United Virtual Airlines)

Most virtual controllers are not (and never were) real-world controllers. (However, some are active real-world controllers…and do this for a hobby!) In fact, like virtual pilots, most virtual controllers are not even real-world pilots. This means they learned about flying from flight simulators or from their own studies. So, the level of realism and skill varies a lot from controller to controller.

Although they are good, virtual controllers are more likely to make mistakes than FSX ATC. They might vector you into a hill or building; they might put you too close to another aircraft (see Figure 25-11); they might send you toward Manhattan, New York, when you meant to go to Manhattan, Kansas; and they may forget to hand you off to the next controller as you leave their airspace. These are not common mistakes, especially for experienced virtual controllers, but they happen more often than in the real world and more often than FSX ATC.

We tell you this not to make you fear using virtual air traffic controllers but to remind you to be both forgiving and proactive with them. Be as realistic as possible in your communication, share your knowledge politely and privately (if you know the real-world way to do something), and make sure you keep good situational awareness so you can double-check the controller's instructions before you hit that hill. Talking to a real human, even if imperfect, is still better than having the ATC window pop up and wait for you to select a numbered response.

NOBODY HOME

If there are only 30 virtual controllers in the whole world when you sign on (not uncommon for a quiet morning), they are not likely to be controlling the airspace you want to fly in, even if they are close (see Figure 25-12). For instance, if you're departing from London's Heathrow airport and there is a tower controller at Gatwick airport, just 22 miles away, she isn't allowed to give you ATC service. If, however, the London FIR controller is online (the call sign is something like EGTT_CTR), then you can talk to that controller for ground, tower, and departure services from Heathrow.

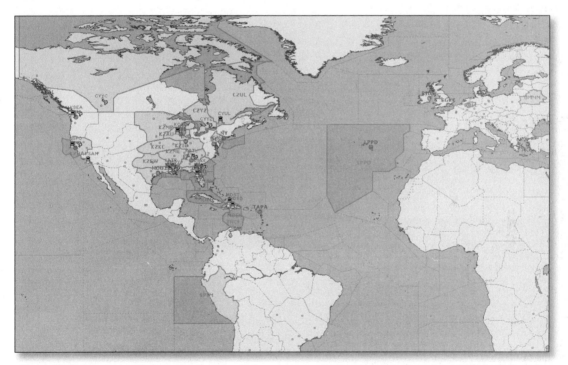

Figure 25-12: There are websites as well as stand-alone programs (such as ServInfo shown here) that show where in the world virtual controllers are active. (Courtesy Michael Frantzeskakis)

Even at the busiest time, with hundreds of controllers online, you will probably have ATC for little or none of the trip if you're in a quiet corner of the world. People tend to learn ATC near where they live in the real world, so they are concentrated in high-population countries where lots of people own computers and have Internet connections.

That leaves you with two options. The first is to behave the same way you would in the real world at an airport without a controller: announce your intentions to the other nearby aircraft on a common traffic frequency.

684

PART I	PART II	PART III	PART IV	PART V	PART VI
PREFLIGHT	SPORT PILOT	PRIVATE PILOT	INSTRUMENT RATING	COMMERCIAL LICENSE	ATP AND BEYOND

A better solution, though, is to do something you can't do in the real world: relocate. If there aren't controllers at the airports you want to use, fly instead wherever the controllers are. Systems such as VATSIM have maps on their websites that show where controllers are currently active, so you can take a quick glance, relocate your aircraft in FSX, and then log in at an airport with a controller. It's a good idea to ask those controllers how long they'll be on; you'd hate to get all your flight planning done and taxi to the runway only to hear, "Closing for the night; report your intentions to other traffic on the CTAF. Good night." (We're told there are even some real-world controllers who shut down for the night with no warning at all.)

EVENTS

Figure 25-13: At a virtual fly-in, you might see dozens of planes on and near an airport, such as this event in New Orleans.

Because there aren't enough controllers and pilots to make realistic ATC and busy traffic anywhere you'd like to fly and any *time* you'd like to fly, pilots and controllers have begun setting up special events that concentrate people into one area (see Figure 25-13).

Groups of pilots, such as virtual airlines or ad hoc groups with common interests, will announce in advance a planned flight, hoping pilots will free up their schedule for that particular flight. Pilot groups will usually choose a particular route, from one airport to the next, trying to depart and arrive about the same time. (One organization, called Group Flight, is currently running a monthly flight from one national capital to another.) The group will also arrange with the controller organizations at each end of their flight so they can at least have ATC for takeoff and landing.

Virtual controllers also create prearranged events. Usually this is a commitment to pilots that a particular airport will have more controllers than usual (for instance, with every position staffed, from clearance delivery through center). But the largest events occur when a whole FIR/ARTCC staffs every position they can; one of the largest occurs in Los Angeles and Oakland ARTCCs, "California Screamin'," which has more than 50 controllers in just those two centers and hundreds of flights occurring within California over five hours.

Although the realism of lots of air traffic controllers and dozens of planes flying in and out is exciting and challenging (you do remember how to hold, don't you?), major events such as this can cause problems for the virtual pilot. First, not everyone is as skilled at either controlling or flying, so mistakes are made, and they compound with the speed and complexity of so many airplanes and controllers. Second, with so many airplanes visible nearby, your flight simulator will start to slow down its frame rate. More than once we've experienced breaking out of the clouds on an instrument approach into an event airport only to find our flight sim frame drop so low that we could not control the airplane and we crashed. Because flight sim usually puts your airplane back where you started after a crash, this can be quite annoying; it's usually better to put your display settings on a lower level than usual and turn off the realism option about detecting crashes so that you bounce on the ground rather than crashing.

For all the challenges, though, the most realism we've ever seen in online flying has been during the big events with dozens of well-trained virtual controllers and hundreds of experienced virtual pilots flying realistically and professionally.

KEY POINTS FOR REAL FLYING AND *FSX* BUILT-INS

The following are some key points from this chapter:

- Some virtual airlines are run like real-world airlines, and you can get a taste for being a professional pilot by joining one of these organizations.

- Flying online with many other pilots at one airport is more realistic than using FSX computer-generated air traffic.

- When flying with a good virtual controller, you can get training (especially on instrument procedures) that is almost as good as real-life training.

FSX has no built-in lessons or missions about virtual airlines and online flying.

VIRTUAL AIR TRAFFIC CONTROL

"WHEN THE ART OF RADIO COMMUNICATION BETWEEN PI-
LOTS AND ATC IS IMPROVED, THE RESULT WILL BE VASTLY IN-
CREASED AREAS OF SIGNIFICANT MISUNDERSTANDINGS."

—ROBERT LIVINGSTON, *FLYING THE AERONCA*

"THE SIMILARITY BETWEEN AIR TRAFFIC CONTROLLERS AND
PILOTS? IF A PILOT SCREWS UP, THE PILOT DIES. IF ATC SCREWS
UP, THE PILOT DIES."

—CLICHÉ

688

PART I	PART II	PART III	PART IV	PART V	PART VI
PREFLIGHT	SPORT PILOT	PRIVATE PILOT	INSTRUMENT RATING	COMMERCIAL LICENSE	ATP AND BEYOND

PUSHING TIN

It may seem odd for this book to have a chapter that seems to have nothing to do with being a pilot. But, in fact, there are some excellent reasons to become a virtual air traffic controller (ATC). People who are (or will become) real-world pilots gain a much better understanding of the system (mostly for instrument and professional flying) when they know what ATC can and cannot do and how ATC works.

Both sim and real-world pilots can gain a lot by becoming virtual controllers. In addition to just the added understanding of how things work, virtual controlling can bring a new challenge to your flying and keep you from stagnating and becoming bored or complacent. Being a controller forces more realism, because you find you have to use standard procedures and terminology or the variety of pilots you'll encounter won't understand your instructions.

Being a virtual controller is more demanding than being a virtual pilot in the multiplayer environment, because pilots' expectations are higher. The virtual controller can have a big effect on the pilots' enjoyment of the game. If a virtual pilot screws up (such as pulling on to the runway when another plane is on short final approach), it isn't likely to affect anyone else's enjoyment of the game, except perhaps the pilot landing; and he might even enjoy the challenge of a go-around. But if the virtual controller tells the first plane to taxi onto the runway and causes the second to go around (or worse, a collision that forces both pilots' FSX to reset to their starting points), then the controller has had a big effect on both of the two pilot's game play. One poor controller can make a bunch of pilots angry enough to log out and find other session.

Whether you use the FSX tower-controller simulator in multiplayer mode (Figure 26-1) or you join an online network as a controller, you'll need to understand the general ways the software works, and that's what the first half of this chapter is about. In the second half, we'll teach you the responsibilities of each controller position, from clearance delivery and ground control up through the en route (usually called *center*) controller position. We can't cover everything you'll need to know—after all, whole books have been written about that—but you'll get a taste so you can see whether you'd like to take on the challenge of becoming a virtual controller.

Figure 26-1: You've learned how to be a virtual pilot; now are you ready to go behind the scope and be a virtual air traffic controller?

SOFTWARE REQUIREMENTS

You don't need FSX to become a virtual controller. In fact, you don't need a flight simulation program at all. The built-in ATC function of FSX (Deluxe version only) is only one of several ways to be a controller.

FSX ATC

The FSX multiplayer system that allows you to be an air traffic controller is really just a control tower simulator (Figure 26-2); you're looking out the windows of a tower, visually sequencing other multiplayer pilots to and from the runways.

The simulator's basic radar screen is OK for use as a radar controller (such as approach control), although in that function it isn't nearly as good as a stand-alone program on an online network. But it certainly is easier to get started, because you already have all the software you need. It even has built-in voice communication.

Figure 26-2: The FSX tower controller position has a basic radar screen, but mostly you're looking out the tower cab windows.

ONLINE NETWORK ATC

Most people getting started controlling with an online network such as VATSIM already have done virtual flying on the network (as described in Chapter 25), so they are familiar with the pilot side of working with a human controller. But for VATSIM controllers, the interface is completely different; they use the Advanced Simulated Radar Client (ASRC; shown in Figure 26-3) rather than Flight Simulator.

ASRC is a Windows-based program that was created by two VATSIM controllers, one of whom was training to become a real-world controller at the time. It is intended to replicate the radar screen that real controllers use for approach/departure control or, by changing a setting, the radar screen used by en route (FIR/ARTCC) controllers. (In some ways, however, the software has more functionality than real-world radar screens.)

690

PART I
PREFLIGHT

PART II
SPORT PILOT

PART III
PRIVATE PILOT

PART IV
INSTRUMENT RATING

PART V
COMMERCIAL LICENSE

PART VI
ATP AND BEYOND

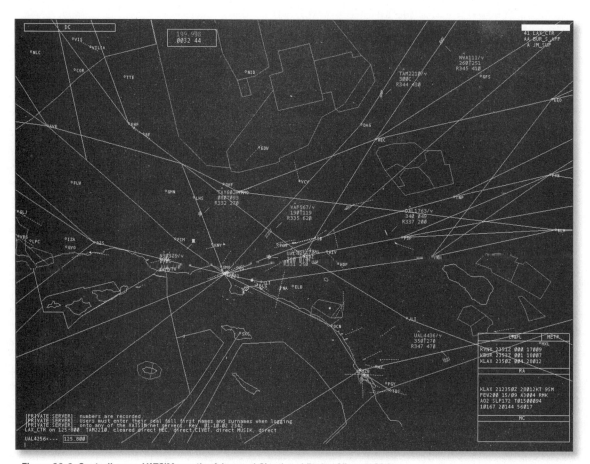

Figure 26-3: Controllers on VATSIM use the Advanced Simulated Radar Client (ASRC).

Tower controllers and ground/clearance delivery positions on VATSIM also use ASRC, although the aircraft are still displayed on a radar screen, so it isn't realistic. Perhaps someday there will be a reliable method for a tower controller to connect to VATSIM using the FSX tower simulator, but as of this writing, there are technical problems with that.

ASRC is free to download and free to use on VATSIM. Extensive documentation is also available to teach student controllers how to set up and use ASRC. Once you have the software, you can begin training to become a controller.

BECOMING A CONTROLLER

If you use the FSX tower controller position in a multiplayer setup with other pilots, you'll need to study the built-in training information to understand how to use the radar unit and other controls. However, nothing is stopping you from going on to GameSpy and joining an unregulated multiplayer session as a controller, even if you don't know what you're doing.

For more organized GameSpy sessions and the online networks such as VATSIM and IVAO, however, extensive training programs are available, and you'll be required to go through them before you start controlling on the network. We'll use examples from VATSIM because we're familiar with it, but IVAO has similar procedures and is especially designed for European ATC.

If you're already a pilot on a virtual network, you have all the permission you need to be an observing controller on the network. You can't control any traffic—in fact, you can't talk to any aircraft at all—but you can use the radar screen and watch traffic moving around. This is a good way to get used to the software and to follow along in your studies.

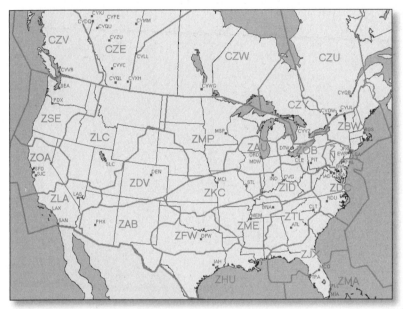

Figure 26-4: Countries are divided into FIRs (ARTCCs in the United States), and you need to choose one to begin your ATC training.

Once you're ready to learn to be an online controller, you have to choose a region and division to control in. (A *region* is usually a continent, and a *division* is a small group of countries.) You can change later, but the first division's trainers will direct your initial training program. Usually there will be some generic training to get comfortable with the software, and then you'll choose a FIR/ARTCC to join (see Figure 26-4). (FIR is *flight information region*, and ARTCC is *air route traffic control center*, which is the FIR equivalent in the United States. Both are often called *center*.) The trainers in your FIR/ARTCC will guide the rest of your training. Again, you can change FIR/ARTCCs later, but most people choose the FIR/ARTCC where they live in real-life, because they're familiar with the airports, landmarks, and geography in that area.

THE RADAR SCREEN

The main interface of air traffic control is the radar screen, where aircraft are represented with their position over the ground. Before you can get started at all, you need to load into the software (such as ASRC) a sector file that represents the area (FIR/ARTCC) you're going to control (see Figure 26-5). This sector file will allow ASRC to display the location of VORs, NDBs, fixes, airports, and runways, as well as low- and high-altitude airways. Sophisticated sector files might also include geographic items such as lakes and mountain peaks, airport taxiways and terminal buildings, airspace boundaries, and so on.

Figure 26-5: The basic ASRC radar screen without any aircraft. You can turn each item (such as fixes, VORs, airports, and airways) on and off, and you can change their color to your own preferences. (You can even make the background any color, although most people keep that a realistic black.)

When you use the controller software to connect to the online network, the network will send you information about any aircraft within the vicinity of your controlling area. Aircraft are displayed in one of several ways, depending on what the pilot is doing and whether you're controlling (technically called *tracking*) that aircraft. (These examples are based on VATSIM, and you can see them when the radar is in DSR mode—see "Radar Modes for Different ATC Positions"—for working as a center controller.)

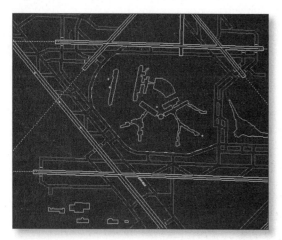

Figure 26-6: The + symbols are primary targets (transponders off).

When a virtual pilot first connects to an online network, the pilot will first appear as a primary target (see Figure 26-6). This just means the (simulated) radar has detected an aircraft, but there isn't a transponder reply coming back because the pilot's transponder is off or on standby. (As in the real world, pilots are usually asked to keep their transponder set to standby until cleared for takeoff, when they turn it on, and then turn it back to standby after landing.)

▼ INSIDE THE GAME

RADAR MODES FOR DIFFERENT ATC POSITIONS

Real-world controllers use completely different computer systems depending on whether they are approach controllers or en route (center) controllers. ASRC, the software used by controllers on VATSIM, is designed to replicate both of those two types of radar screens, called DSR for center controllers and ARTS for approach controllers. The virtual controller can select from a radar-type menu whether they want they want to use the DSR or ARTS display.

In addition, because online networks don't yet have an option for tower and ground controller positions where the controller can actually watch the aircraft out the windows—as you can using FSX ATC—they have to use the same radar screen software. This isn't realistic, of course, but the solution is that the tower/ground controller can select their radar type from that same menu. If they select Tower mode, the controllers can see the aircraft call sign, altitude, and speed, even if the pilot has their transponder off. Setting the radar on Ground mode allows the ground controller to see just the call sign of the airplanes, again even if the pilot has not turned on the transponder. This allows the ground controller to know where a particular airplane is located on the airport, without forcing the unrealistic situation of turning on transponders while still on the ground.

Once a pilot turns the transponder on (usually to the ALT—altitude—position), the controller will see two things happen. First, the airplane icon on the screen will change to indicate the secondary reply has been received (Figure 26-7). Second, you will see two numbers near the icon: the aircraft's altitude and the transponder code.

With a few keystrokes, the controller can see more information about an aircraft; this is called a *datatag* (see Figure 26-8). Datatag information includes the aircraft type, ground speed, destination, whether the plane is climbing, descending or level, and an altitude assigned by a controller if the plane has not yet reached that altitude. The ground speed data comes from the radar computer itself: like a GPS, it checks where the aircraft was last time the radar got an updated position and where it is now, checks how much time elapsed, and makes a simple calculation of ground speed. The aircraft type comes from what the pilot selected when he logged into the system. The destination comes from the pilot's flight plan (once he files one). And only the controller who is tracking an aircraft can assign a temporary altitude.

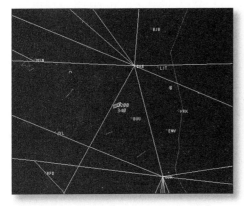

Figure 26-7: A secondary target (transponder on) showing squawk code (2200) and altitude (FL340 - 34,000 feet)

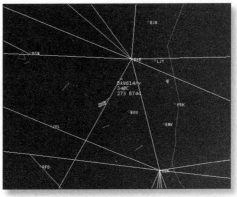

Figure 26-8: Full datatag for an aircraft. On the last line, the right group cycles among the aircraft type, destination, and current ground speed.

694

PART I	PART II	PART III	PART IV	PART V	PART VI
PREFLIGHT	SPORT PILOT	PRIVATE PILOT	INSTRUMENT RATING	COMMERCIAL LICENSE	ATP AND BEYOND

As aircraft fly along, the radar displays a glowing history trail where they have been in the past few seconds. When you're actually tracking an aircraft, a *vector* line stretches out in front of the aircraft a few miles to show which way it is going.

It's often necessary to see the flight plan filed by the pilot, and the software has that function (see Figure 26-9). And if you're the controller tracking a flight, you can change the flight plan (such as adding a departure or arrival procedure, amending the altitude, or even changing the whole route if there is some reason the original one is no good). However, just like the real world, the pilot can't see the changes you make to their flight plan, so you'll have to tell the pilot, "I have a change to your flight plan; advise when ready to copy." You can even create a new flight plan if a pilot doesn't know how to file one.

Finally, there is also a function to check the weather at any airport (Figure 26-10); the software retrieves the METAR weather from the game server, not real-world weather—they're usually similar but not always.

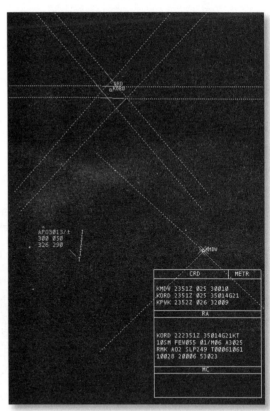

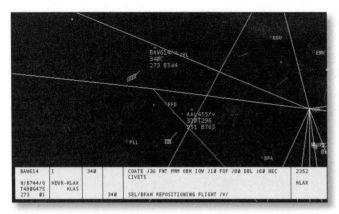

Figure 26-9: If there is a flight plan on the server for that flight, you can call it up on your screen.

Figure 26-10: Winds and altimeter settings, as well as a full METAR report for an airport, are available as well.

⬇ KEEPING IT REAL

GETTING THE FLICK

As you learn to become an air traffic controller—real or virtual—the biggest challenge comes as you increase the number of aircraft you're tracking. Rarely are you just sitting there, waiting for a pilot to call you. Instead, you have to keep track of when to give the pilot instructions, and the more planes you're tracking, the more things you have to remember. If you concentrate too long on one plane, others may miss turns, head toward a mountain, or collide with other planes.

Controllers call it *getting the flick*—you're able to remember each plane's next action and how long you have until you need to give the instruction. You jump from one plane to another, putting a lower priority on those that don't require immediate attention. It takes knowledge, experience, and concentration. It's multitasking that is both a science and an art.

COMMUNICATION

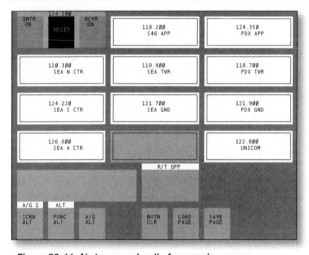

Figure 26-11: Air-to-ground radio frequencies are programmed here.

In the early days of virtual ATC, the only way to communicate with virtual pilots was with text. People got pretty good at typing abbreviations, and software for both the pilot and the controller came with shortcuts and hotkeys that would allow just a few keystrokes to expand to big mouthfuls. (There's nothing quite as annoying as intercepting the glideslope on an ILS during bumpy weather and having to move your hands from the control yoke to the keyboard in order to type, "Berlin Tower, Lufthansa 547 heavy, inbound on ILS.")

Fortunately, Voice over Internet (VoIP) technology now allows controllers and pilots to use headsets with microphones to communicate realistically. It's much faster and (virtually) safer too.

ASRC has a pop-up window with programmable buttons (Figure 26-11) so you can preset different frequencies (and different voice servers) for the different controller positions you usually work. There is also a screen for direct ground-to-ground connections with other controllers (see Figure 26-12).

Virtual controllers using voice communication have one a big advantage over real-world controllers, though: they can use text communication as a backup. For instance, when a controller needs to change a pilot's route and the route includes some unusual fixes or VORs the pilot might not know, the controller just has to send the revised route in a text message, rather than phonetically spelling out each fix. Text communication also allows people who can't use voice (for instance, those who are deaf or mute) to participate in aviation in ways they just can't do in the real world.

696

PART I
PREFLIGHT

PART II
SPORT PILOT

PART III
PRIVATE PILOT

PART IV
INSTRUMENT RATING

PART V
COMMERCIAL LICENSE

PART VI
ATP AND BEYOND

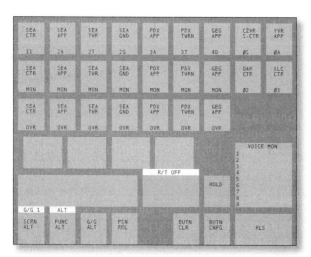

Figure 26-12: Ground-to-ground radio frequencies (for talking to other controllers) are programmed here.

The radios on the online networks work just like multiplayer between two pilots: pilots and controller have to be on the same radio frequency to communicate. Just as in FSX airplanes, the controller can talk and listen on one radio frequency while monitoring (just listening) another frequency. For instance, a controller could play the role of both ground controller and tower controller. When a pilot calls on the ground control frequency, the controller would switch the transmitter to that channel but leave the tower frequency on listen only; when switching back to the tower frequency, the ground frequency would stay on listen mode so the controller could hear anyone calling there again.

Online networks also allow for voice or text communication between controllers to work out handing off aircraft (see the next section) or other arrangements or to conduct training.

Finally, online networks have still one more communication method: private text chat between two people, either controllers or pilots. This is handy as a controller when you are working with a pilot who is clueless how to operate in the system. Instead of clogging up the main radio frequency (voice or text) with instructions to the pilot (which would not be realistic at all; a real-world controller would just say, "Go get a flight instructor, and then call me back"), you can tutor the pilot on a private text chat message while you go about your regular controlling with the other pilots.

WORKING WITH OTHER CONTROLLERS

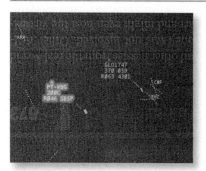

Figure 26-13: A flashing datatag means another controller is trying to hand off that aircraft to you.

One of the most important skills you will learn as a beginning controller on an online network is how to work with other controllers. The most common activity between controllers is the *handoff*, the process of transferring control of an aircraft from one controller to the next. In real life, and on VATSIM, the central computer ensures that only one controller can have *control* of an aircraft at a time. But planes are meant to travel, so inevitably they will move into another controller's area; before that happens, the new controller must be ready for the flight.

A few minutes before a flight enters the new airspace, the controller who has responsibility for the flight will send an automated signal to the next controller; on that second controller's radar screen, the flight datatag will appear, flashing on and off, and a tone will sound (see Figure 26-13). The second controller checks the vicinity to make sure there aren't any traffic conflicts and then accepts the handoff with an automatic reply. Without any chat or voice interaction, then, the two controllers transfer control.

If for some reason the second controller doesn't accept the handoff (too busy or away from the keyboard—AFK in game slang), the first controller cannot allow the flight to get into the second controller's airspace. That usually means the controller has to put the flight into a hold right at that spot until the handoff is accepted. (Several years ago when real-world French controllers went on strike, they didn't tell their U.K. counterparts about it. There were lots of unexpected holds that day!)

Once the handoff *is* accepted, the first controller tells the pilot to contact the second controller on whatever radio frequency that controller is using.

When everything is running smoothly, controllers don't need to talk to each other at all. But because most virtual pilots aren't real-world pilots and most virtual controllers aren't real-world controllers, things don't always go so smoothly. So ASRC has a communication system between controllers. This could be a text chat box, or it could be voice chat on a separate, ground-to-ground channel. Controllers will coordinate, for instance, if a pilot is asking to fly an unusual route or the pilot is inexperienced and needs some extra help. When a controller is getting busy and needs the preceding controllers to slow down the number of handoffs, that too will be coordinated with ground-to-ground communication.

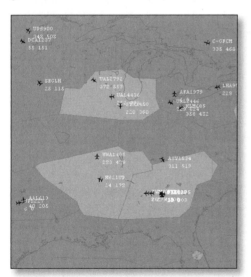

In the real world, there will always be a controller to accept a flight when they get close to the next airspace. During quiet periods (like the middle of the night), the controller might be working a huge chunk of airspace, but nonetheless there is always someone in the next airspace. That's not at all true for an online network. As we mentioned in Chapter 25, it's common to have large areas without a controller (see Figure 26-14). So what happens when you're controlling a certain airspace and a flight is going into an area where there isn't a controller? You treat it just like they're leaving the ATC system entirely: have them switch to the UNICOM frequency (122.8 for all of VATSIM, for example) to report their position to other pilots, and tell them squawk 2200 (a generic IFR transponder code). The pilot will have to regularly check their network information to see when they get close to another virtual controller who is online.

Figure 26-14: On this display of active ARTCCs and aircraft, only the lighter shaded areas have controllers available. Pilots flying in the darker areas communicate only with each other.

▼ STUDENT OF THE CRAFT

ATC TODAY AND TOMORROW

The equipment on board aircraft and on the ground is getting smarter and smarter. Take the transponder as an example. The latest transponders—Mode S transponders in the United States—have the ability to exchange data with ground-based computers. This data can include the call sign, GPS position, and speed of the aircraft. The transponder could also get information about other aircraft, too.

Continued

698

| PART I | PART II | PART III | PART IV | PART V | PART VI |
| PREFLIGHT | SPORT PILOT | PRIVATE PILOT | INSTRUMENT RATING | COMMERCIAL LICENSE | ATP AND BEYOND |

Take this concept a bit further and beef it up with a more robust transceiver, and you get a system called Automatic Dependent Surveillance—Broadcast (ADS-B). This is a complex system, but one of its components is traffic control for pilots. Pilots in ADS-B aircraft have a display in the cockpit that shows them other ADS-B aircraft, including the aircraft's call sign, position, and speed, as well as all the nearby targets seen by ATC radar. ADS-B is available in many places around the world today, although it's far from standardized and uses different equipment in different aircraft and countries.

The next step has been tested experimentally as part of the NASA Small Aircraft Transportation System (SATS). SATS aircraft can be their own ATC. They communicate with other aircraft and with automated ground stations to keep a safe zone around the aircraft at all times. They can even sequence themselves for instrument approaches without any human help.

Is the controller's job in danger? Not for a while. But in the coming decades we expect the role of ATC will shift to leverage much of the cockpit power of both computers and pilots, including text communication, just as in FSX.

ATC POSITIONS FROM THE GROUND UP

As mentioned earlier, if you play the role of the control tower in FSX's multiplayer system, there is no training requirement and no limitations on what position you hold in the tower. However, the equipment isn't well designed for playing the role of a radar controller at approach/departure or en route positions. The duties of each position discussed next apply somewhat to the FSX controller position, but we'll mostly deal with roles on online networks such as VATSIM.

CLEARANCE DELIVERY

The job of the clearance delivery controller is—surprise!—to deliver a clearance to the pilot. Flight-sim pilots are already used to this position, when the ATC voice says, "Beech N350KA is cleared to Aspen airport…" But delivering ATC's clearance to the pilot is the last in a series of steps the clearance delivery person had to do.

When a pilot files a flight plan with an online network, the flight plan is available for all virtual controllers to look at (see Figure 26-15). The flight plan contains the aircraft call sign, type of aircraft, and takeoff/landing airports, of course, and the controller usually doesn't need to change those. But the pilot usually also files a route and altitude, and the controller might change those.

Altitude is the easiest to discover a need for a change: if the route goes eastbound, the pilot should be flying at odd thousand altitudes; westbound it is even thousand altitudes. (This assumes the pilot is flying IFR; rarely does a virtual pilot file a flight plan if they're flying VFR on an online system.) The clearance delivery controller checks the route—which is not an easy thing to do if the controller is new and not familiar with the area—and then checks the altitude requested. If there is an error, the controller usually asks, "16,000 feet is not available for that direction of flight; would you prefer 15,000 or 17,000?"

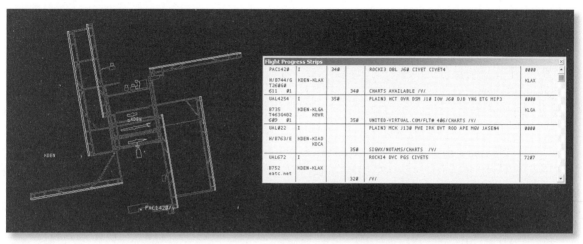

Figure 26-15: The clearance delivery controller works with a flight strip bay filled with flight plans of aircraft departing from that airport.

If the airspace is complicated or several radar controllers are available, the controllers might want the flights to climb only to a certain altitude after takeoff and then level off. The clearance delivery controller will then add that to the clearance: "Climb and maintain 9,000; expect FL230 10 minutes after departure."

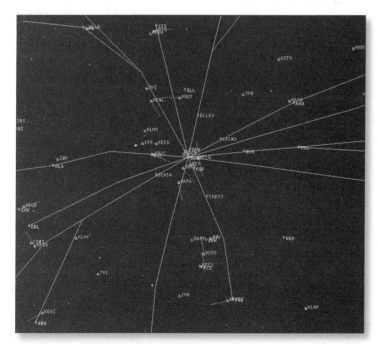

Figure 26-16: These standard departure routes from Denver ensure outbound traffic stays away from inbound traffic.

Nine times out of ten, the route the pilot chose is irrelevant; unlike the real world, there is so little traffic in virtual online networks that controllers don't care where you go. However, if it is busy at the departure airport, the radar controllers might tell the clearance delivery controller to force pilots on certain routes; usually, controllers prefer the official departure procedures published for real-world pilots (see Figure 26-16). However, most online pilots don't have copies of the departure procedures, so the clearance delivery controller will either direct the pilot to websites to get the procedures or read off the procedure (or a shorthand version).

A route change may also be necessary if there is some kind of agreement between FIRs/ARTCCs for routing between two airports. These preferred routes are common in the real world, and sometimes are used in virtual networks as well, especially during busy times.

700

| PART I | PART II | PART III | PART IV | PART V | PART VI |
| PREFLIGHT | SPORT PILOT | PRIVATE PILOT | INSTRUMENT RATING | COMMERCIAL LICENSE | ATP AND BEYOND |

Regardless, if the route is different from the pilot originally filed on a flight plan, the clearance delivery controller has to put that revised route in the clearance when it is read off (and read back by the pilot).

Because virtual controllers are not as numerous as real-world controllers, it can be hard for a pilot to know who he is supposed to talk to next. The clearance delivery controller, when reading off the whole clearance, will mention the name and frequency of the first radar controller that the pilot will call after takeoff. That way the pilot can program his aircraft radios with the next controller's frequency so that when he is busy right after takeoff, he doesn't have to mess with the mouse dialing in a new frequency.

The transponder system is also used in online networks, and the clearance delivery controller will, by tapping some keys, get a unique transponder number for that aircraft.

After all this, then the clearance delivery controller is ready to give the pilot the clearance. Let's hope the controller will have looked at (and changed) the flight plan as soon as the pilot filed it, rather than waiting until the pilot asked for the clearance.

Remember the CRAFT acronym from the chapters about IFR? Now, as the controller, you have to say it yourself, rather than just reading back what the controller said:

- *C*: Clearance limit (almost always the destination in online virtual networks)

- *R*: Route

- *A*: Altitude

- *F*: Frequency

- *T*: Transponder

⬇ BY THE BOOK

THE CONTROLLER'S BIBLE

Real-world air traffic controllers in the United States have quite a few resources for training and reference, but the most important is FAA Order 7110.65: Air Traffic Control. Like the FAR/AIM for pilots, the 7110 is the bible of rules and procedures controllers use every day. Serious virtual controllers (and those who want to become real-world controllers) study this book so they can make virtual controlling as real as possible. It's available online at `http://www.faa.gov/atpubs/ATC/INDEX.HTM`.

GROUND CONTROL

The ground controller has a relatively simple job: get the planes to and from the runways (see Figure 26-17). Of course, the ground controller will need to know the current weather (especially winds) at the airport so they can send the pilots to the runway that is closest to a headwind. In fact, the ground controller should be prepared to read each pilot the entire local weather, because the automated ATIS system that real-world airports (and nonmultiplayer FSX) has is limited in functionality on online networks.

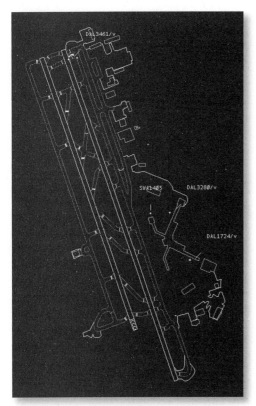

Figure 26-17: Ground controllers use the same radar screen as other controllers, but they usually have taxiways depicted, and the aircraft datatags contain just the call sign.

If a lot of pilots are getting ready to depart, the departure controller (see "Approach (and Departure) Control" later in this chapter) might prefer not to send two aircraft in a row along the same route, because there could be conflicts if the second plane was faster and started to catch up with the first. Thus, the departure controller might ask the ground controller to sequence the planes along the taxiway (getting ready to take off) so that routes alternate.

Ground controllers also help guide pilots who've just landed to get to their gate, especially because in virtual flying the pilots are more likely not to have an airport diagram. Real-world pilots always have these diagrams for the airports they fly to, and virtual controllers need them too, so they can give *progressive taxi* instructions to wayward virtual pilots. However, these diagrams don't show exactly where each gate is, so the virtual controller isn't likely to be able to direct the pilot to the gate. Then again, virtual pilots mostly don't care about getting to exactly the right gate, because virtual passengers aren't picky about where they get off.

If no one is available to be the clearance delivery controller, the ground controller will do that work, too; therefore, a ground controller learns both roles right from the start. New controllers on online networks such as VATSIM usually are allowed to do only clearance delivery and ground control until they can prove they know these roles well enough to move up to tower controller.

TOWER (LOCAL) CONTROL

There are not many things a controller can say that are more fun than "Cleared for takeoff" and then watch a pilot launch from their runway (see Figure 26-18). The tower controller is the one who gets to say it. Officially called the *local controller*, this person is in charge of the runways, and the rule the tower controller executes is relatively simple: only one airplane at a time can be on a runway. There are a few exceptions, such as when the runway is very long and the two airplanes are small and slow or when one plane has just landed and the controller lets a second plane taxi onto the runway to get ready for takeoff.

But making sure that rule doesn't get broken isn't as easy as you might think. For instance, when one plane is landing, how far back should the next plane be on final approach? (It depends on their speed, of course.) Is there enough room between those two landing airplanes to slip a departure onto the runway and take off in time? (This depends not only on the arrival's speed and distance but also on how good the pilot is that is taking off. Can he accept an immediate departure, or is he a new pilot and might not move quickly?)

702

PART I	PART II	PART III	PART IV	PART V	PART VI
PREFLIGHT	SPORT PILOT	PRIVATE PILOT	INSTRUMENT RATING	COMMERCIAL LICENSE	ATP AND BEYOND

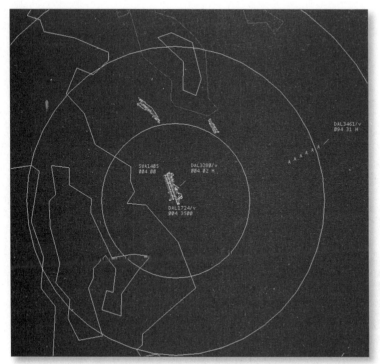

Figure 26-18: Tower controllers need to see the entire vicinity of an airport, out to about 10 miles away.

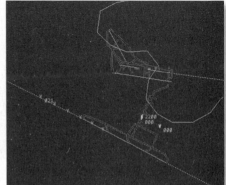

Figure 26-19: VFR planes show up as a "V" symbol, with just their altitude indicated.

Most of the pilots flying online are flying IFR flights, even if it is good weather, because they want to fly using ATC and VFR flights don't need ATC's help very much. IFR flights usually get vectors to the runway from the radar (approach) controller, either to an ILS or to a visual approach, so they're usually already spaced out and easy to get onto the runway safely. But more and more pilots are flying VFR on online networks (see Figure 26-19) and expecting the service real-world pilots get VFR at a tower-controlled airport…such as instructions for entering the traffic pattern, when to turn from downwind to the base leg, and so on. This introduces a good challenge for the virtual controller, especially when the planes in the pattern are small, slow planes and there is a line of jumbo jets coming and going at the airport.

NOTE!

⬇ WATCH OUT FOR WAKE

Even though FSX and other flight simulators don't model wake turbulence that appears behind bigger airplanes, virtual controllers try to follow the same rules of spacing and timing to protect smaller planes. It makes for good habits if you become either a real-world pilot or a controller.

We discussed earlier in this chapter the concept of *handoffs* between controllers and that only one controller at a time can control (track) a flight. Tower controllers do not actually track a flight, because tracking can be done only with a radar system. Real-world tower controllers' primary tool is their high-tech Mark I eyeballs. (However, many control towers do have a screen showing the local radar picture for added situational awareness.) It gets confusing for virtual tower controllers because they have to use the same software that the radar controllers use, and it might seem like they're controlling the flight. But the important difference is they don't hand off the departing flight to the next controller (the departure controller), wait for the controller to accept the flight, and then tell the pilot to switch frequencies. Instead, the departure controller usually agrees to just track every plane the tower controller launches. The tower doesn't even ask; she just tells the pilot to contact the departure controller on the new frequency.

And tower controllers are there at the end of the flight, too, welcoming the pilot with a hearty "Cleared to land." Again, there is no handoff from the last radar controller; if the tower needs more room between arrivals (for instance, to get a departure out), she'll tell the radar controller directly, either in text chat or in ground-to-ground voice chat.

Again, if no ground controller is available at an airport, the tower controller will do the job of ground control and clearance delivery. Because it can be tricky to do all those jobs unless there are only one or two airplanes in the area, tower controllers need to be quite experienced at ground control at that airport.

⬇ KEEPING IT REAL

REAL-WORLD CONTROLLER SHORTAGE

In 1981, the controllers union in the United States declared a strike seeking better working conditions, and so on, even though it is illegal for government workers to strike. After more than 11,000 controllers were fired by President Reagan and replaced with supervisors, staff personnel, and military controllers, the FAA went on a hiring and training spree to replace the controllers.

Those controllers are now old enough (and have enough time working for the government) to retire. This means over the next few years, thousands of controllers will be retiring. Air traffic has returned to levels not seen since September 11, 2001, and yet there are fewer controllers every year.

This would seem to be the perfect time for a career as an air traffic controller. However, the FAA doesn't really have the budget to hire or train enough controllers to replace those who are leaving, especially since it takes several years to go from initial hire to full, professional controller (even though the new hires have already taken a college-level program in ATC). Recent changes to the union contract also have lowered the compensation for controllers, making this stressful job less worthwhile. And the FAA is counting on some new technologies that will be here soon to replace some parts of ATC, so they hope they don't have to employ as many controllers in the future.

So, it is hard to say, at this point, whether a career as a controller would be a good one for someone interested in aviation.

704

PART I	PART II	PART III	PART IV	PART V	PART VI
PREFLIGHT	SPORT PILOT	PRIVATE PILOT	INSTRUMENT RATING	COMMERCIAL LICENSE	ATP AND BEYOND

APPROACH (AND DEPARTURE) CONTROL

The first controller position that actually uses radar realistically is the approach controller, and it's usually the position a new virtual controller graduates to after getting good as a tower controller. (Departure control is essentially the same thing, so most virtual radar controllers just use the approach call sign.)

STUDENT OF THE CRAFT

ARE YOU DEPARTURE OR APPROACH?

One confusion pilots have (both in the real world and in the virtual world) is the difference between an approach controller and a departure controller. Actually, there isn't any difference; controllers are trained on the same procedures and can do all the roles. In fact, the only difference is what the pilots say, and that isn't even required. If you just took off and said, "Seattle Approach, WestWind 638 is off Sea-Tac 2,000 climbing to 8,000," the controller might not even correct you, because she's probably talking to other planes that are arriving and calling her "Seattle Approach."

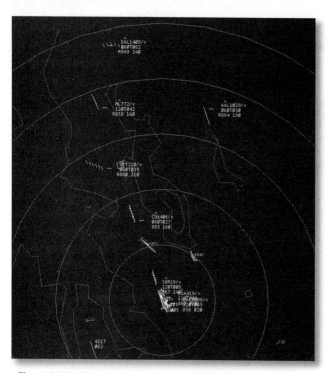

Figure 26-20: This virtual approach controller has nicely spaced out the arrivals from the north. This is sometimes called a string of pearls because, to people watching from the airport at night, the aircraft landing lights are all in a row. (If you look closely, you'll see the controller is slipping OPT220 between COA406 and ML772—now that's pushing tin!) (Screenshot by Ross Carlson; amazing vectoring by Dan Everette)

Approach control is the place new virtual controllers learn about vectoring—giving headings and altitudes for arriving and departing aircraft (see Figure 26-20). With an experienced pilot, this can be relatively simple.

Departing aircraft are "tracked" as soon as they report taking off. The controller gives a heading to get the plane to the first waypoint on the pilot's flight plan and assigns a new altitude if traffic allows it. When the plane nears the edge of the controller's airspace (if there is a controller in the next sector), the departure controller initiates handoff, and when the flight is accepted by the next controller, the departure controller tells the pilot to switch radio frequencies. Unless the flight needs to be vectored around terrain or other traffic, it can be as simple as that. It's even simpler when the pilot knows (and is flying) an official departure procedure. No vectors, maybe even no altitude changes.

Arriving aircraft usually want vectors to an ILS approach or, if the weather is good and they're confident, they'll ask for (and get) a visual approach. Arrival vectors are a little bit trickier for new controllers to learn, because you have to give pilots enough room to turn, and that's all based on their speed. Added to this is that most virtual pilots aren't real-world pilots, and the virtual controller can't expect the same level of skill from a virtual 747 captain as she can from a real-world captain. It's not uncommon for a virtual approach controller to ask a pilot whether he wants a short- or long-final approach.

As with other controlling positions, things are rarely simple for an approach controller. As mentioned, she must contend with pilots who have radically different experience levels, and most virtual pilots don't even carry charts; that means the controller has to be able to read off the ILS frequency and final approach course in addition to everything else she's doing. And although most virtual pilots go to airports with ILS approaches, once in a while a pilot will come along who wants an obscure localizer back-course approach and a hold beforehand and the full missed approach procedure after. Needless to say, the best virtual radar controllers are real-world instrument pilots or controllers, because they are able to understand all the possibilities.

FULL CONFUSION

We have a favorite pilot trick to play on virtual controllers who we know aren't real-world pilots or controllers: we ask for an unusual approach into a small airport within the controller's airspace, and then tell them we want "the full procedure." Such controllers usually panic because they don't have the charts for it and have no idea how to get us there, minimum altitudes, and so on. They don't realize that the full procedure means we, the pilots, do all the navigating, and they don't have to do anything except keep other traffic away.

The other problem virtual controllers need to learn about is lag—the delay between the time an instruction is given and when the pilot carries it out. In the real world, radio communication is instantaneous, and pilots comply relatively quickly. But in the virtual world you're at the mercy of the Internet and possibly a new pilot who doesn't respond quickly. A virtual approach controller judges the lag that is occurring (both technological and human) when she gives the first few vectors to a pilot and then remembers that when she chooses when to turn the flight to intercept final approach. (In fact, since most virtual pilots fly with the same call sign on every flight no matter what kind of plane they're in—using their virtual airline call sign or a personal tail number they like—it is easy to remember from day to day and week to week what kind of performance you can expect from a pilot.)

Virtual approach control areas are set up where there are real-world approach control airspaces (see Figure 26-21). Many such areas have more than one airport with an instrument approach, and the approach controller needs to be able to give vectors for any approach in their airspace. As you can see, the complexity begins to rise exponentially as a controller learns to work larger and larger airspace.

As with other controllers, if an airport does not have a tower or ground controller but there is an approach controller whose airspace contains that airport, the approach controller has to perform all the duties of the tower and ground controllers (and clearance delivery, for that matter). This is challenging, because it's possible to have dozens of airports within one approach-control airspace, and the skills (and keystrokes) to run each position can be quite different. True, few virtual pilots even know about those small airports, but even if everyone is flying to and from the major airport, it can still be a challenge to give vectors while working on a route clearance, changing a flight plan, and clearing an airplane to land.

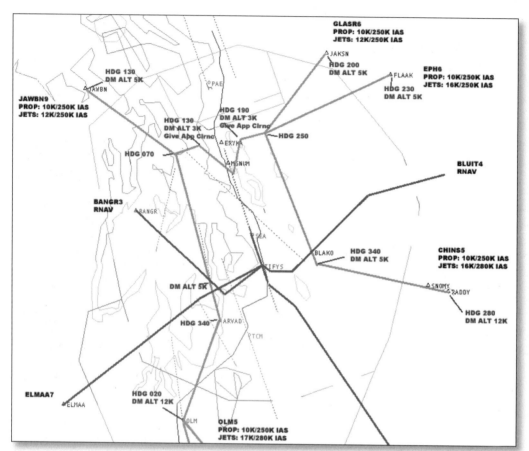

Figure 26-21: Some virtual ATC instructors created this diagram to help new controllers visualize arrivals and departures at Seattle, Washington.

En Route (Center) Control

From a pilot's point of view, the en route portion of the flight is the boring part: you put on the autopilot, it follows your waypoints, and all you have to do is change frequencies as you pass into new airspace until it's time to descend. And if virtual controllers working the center position had to track only en route flights, they would have it easy, too. But that isn't all they do.

⬇ KEEPING IT REAL

IS THIS REAL?

Just as with virtual flying, we often get asked the question about whether being a virtual air traffic controller helps if you want to become a real-world controller. There are so few who have done it that the record is incomplete at best.

But is it very realistic? Neither of the authors has ever done real-world air traffic controlling (although one of us was the air traffic manager at the virtual Seattle ARTCC on VATSIM several years ago), but we've talked to people who have done both. Like virtual flying, virtual controlling is a simplified subset of what a real-world controller does. For instance, one of the tests for being a real-world controller for a particular airspace is that you have to draw on a blank piece of paper the entire airspace: all the airports, navigation beacons, airways, fixes, approach and departure gates, and name all of them. Completely from memory. No virtual controller is ever expected to do that—partly because the software is in some ways better than what real controllers have (for example, ASRC can turn on the name of any individual fix as needed) but mostly because the traffic is so much lighter and the consequences so much less severe (it's a game, after all) for the virtual controller.

As with flying, the big issue we have is if habits are created that are contrary to real-world procedures; relearning habits is much harder than starting fresh the right way. The best way to avoid this is to train with real-world controllers, and online networks such as VATSIM have a few controllers who are active or retired real-world controllers and help train virtual controllers.

Center controllers do, indeed, work with pilots who are in the en route segment of their flight. There's usually very little to say—maybe an altitude change here or there to avoid another flight or perhaps a weather report at the pilot's destination. At some point the pilot will be ready to descend, and usually the center controller will be the one to authorize it, perhaps using a standard terminal arrival route (STAR) if the pilot knows how to fly those.

During busy times, especially fly-ins with lots of planes going in and out of a single airport, center controllers are usually the ones spacing out the planes to make sure they don't overwhelm the approach and tower controllers. The technical term is *in trail*; for instance, the approach controller may say, "Send planes to me no less than 20 miles in trail"—meaning she wants them 20 miles apart. To maintain spacing, the center controller uses tactics like requiring a pilot to fly a particular speed (faster if they're the first plane, slower if they're getting too close to the previous plane). To create a space, the controller might hold an airplane at a fix or vector it off course for a few minutes. It can be challenging, but it's not nearly as tough as it is on the approach controller who is busy at that point with vectors for a dozen planes at a time.

But you've heard us say this for the other positions in this chapter, and it applies to center as well: when an airport doesn't have an approach controller online (or tower or ground or clearance delivery controller) but the airport is within a center controller's airspace, the center controller has to do *all* the roles (see Figure 26-22) for every single airport in their airspace. A center (ARTCC or FIR) can be thousands of square miles and have hundreds of airports, dozens with instrument approaches. It is quite common for a center controller to be the only controller online in the entire virtual ARTCC/FIR. Fortunately, there are likely to be less than a half dozen airplanes in the entire area,

708

PART I	PART II	PART III	PART IV	PART V	PART VI
PILOT	SPORT PILOT	PRIVATE PILOT	INSTRUMENT RATING	COMMERCIAL LICENSE	ATP AND BEYOND

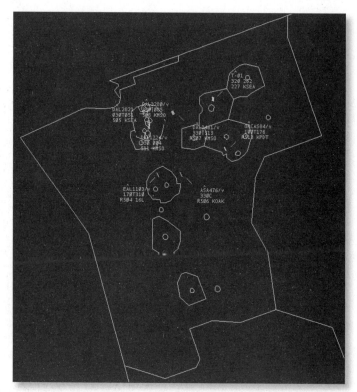

Figure 26-22: If no other virtual controllers are online in the ARTCC, the center controller has to work every plane in the entire airspace, which could be as large as a small country or several states/provinces.

so the workload is tolerable for a well-trained controller. But imagine a situation where a special event, such as a fly-in, is happening at a big airport. The approach control and tower for that airport have staffing, and the center controller is busy spacing out arrivals, handling departures, getting handoffs from other center controllers, and more. Suddenly a pilot logs into the network at a quiet airport in the center controller's airspace far from the event, and he needs his route clearance from Podunk to Nowheresville. Oh, and he doesn't have a clue about flying a "full procedure" approach at Nowheresville—he needs vectors for the approach, and he doesn't even have charts—and there are low clouds and hills around Nowheresville. That'll put a crimp in your flick!

This is why the training regimen for center controllers is strict, and most ARTCCs/FIRs require you to have spent many hours controlling at all the approach control areas in the airspace before they give you a promotion to let you control at center. But once you have the skills to handle any aircraft anywhere in the entire airspace, you can proudly state that you can push tin with the best of them, and have fun too!

KEY POINTS FOR REAL FLYING AND FSX BUILT-INS

The following are some key points from this chapter:

- Virtual ATC helps you understand a real-world controller's point of view, so you can be more safe and clear in your communication.

- As a virtual controller, you experience a wide variety of procedures in a concentrated amount of time.

- Virtual controlling is one more way to keep active and interested in flying when you can't actually get out to fly in the real world.

FSX has no built-in lessons or missions about virtual air traffic controlling.

"LEARNING SHOULD BE FUN. IF YOU DON'T HAVE FUN IN AVIA-
TION, THEN YOU DON'T LEARN, AND WHEN THE LEARNING
STOPS, YOU DIE."

—PETE CAMPBELL

710

PART I	PART II	PART III	PART IV	PART V	PART VI
PREFLIGHT	SPORT PILOT	PRIVATE PILOT	INSTRUMENT RATING	COMMERCIAL LICENSE	ATP AND BEYOND

PELICAN'S PERSPECTIVE

Congratulations, Captain! You made it all the way from being a student pilot through an ATP and even on to ATC. That's a lot of work, and you deserve high praise for a job well done. As we've said all along, this book was intended to be useful whether you're going to go on and get real-world flight training or just build up your virtual ratings, so we hope *you* have found it useful.

Old and wizened pilots are sometimes termed *pelicans*. We're not sure where this comes from, but it was probably made widespread by Ernest Gann describing advice from "a very old pelican of an aviator" in *The Black Watch*. You're not a pelican yet. Neither are we. But for each of us who hope to earn that noble title, there is only one path to get there—fly, fly, fly.

This book is just the beginning of flying, be it real-world, virtual, or a combination of both. There is more information related to this book on the website, including FSX flights, charts, several appendixes (with a command reference, online resources, troubleshooting, and more) and chapters on flying the Beechcraft King Air and the Boeing 737. The website is also the way to email the authors with questions or comments on the book. To find the website, go to `www.wiley.com` and search for *Flight Simulator X for Pilots*. You can also get to the authors via the website www `.vanwestco.com/aviation`.

Good luck with your flying wherever it takes you. And, if we ever cross paths around the real or virtual patch, please say, "Hello." We're always up for a chance to chat about things that fly.

INDEX

712

PART I
PREFLIGHT

PART II
SPORT PILOT

PART III
PRIVATE PILOT

PART IV
INSTRUMENT RATING

PART V
COMMERCIAL LICENSE

PART VI
ATP AND BEYOND

714

PART I
PREFLIGHT

PART II
SPORT PILOT

PART III
PRIVATE PILOT

PART IV
INSTRUMENT RATING

PART V
COMMERCIAL LICENSE

PART VI
ATP AND BEYOND

716

PART I PREFLIGHT   PART II SPORT PILOT   PART III PRIVATE PILOT   PART IV INSTRUMENT RATING   PART V COMMERCIAL LICENSE   **PART VI** ATP AND BEYOND

718

PART I PREFLIGHT | PART II SPORT PILOT | PART III PRIVATE PILOT | PART IV INSTRUMENT RATING | PART V COMMERCIAL LICENSE | PART VI ATP AND BEYOND

720

PART I PREFLIGHT PART II SPORT PILOT PART III PRIVATE PILOT PART IV INSTRUMENT RATING PART V COMMERCIAL LICENSE **PART VI** ATP AND BEYOND

724

PART I
PREFLIGHT

PART II
SPORT PILOT

PART III
PRIVATE PILOT

PART IV
INSTRUMENT RATING

PART V
COMMERCIAL LICENSE

PART VI
ATP AND BEYOND